MEASUREMENTS OF
HUMAN BEHAVIOR

MEASUREMENTS

of

HUMAN BEHAVIOR

REVISED EDITION

EDWARD B. GREENE

THE ODYSSEY PRESS ⚬⚬ NEW YORK

PREFACE

Since the first edition of this book was published it appears that no entirely new measuring techniques have been developed, but much progress has been made in refining test items, in analyzing the skills being tested, and in applying tests to many groups for many purposes. The one outstanding application was, of course, in the military establishments during World War II.

The only completely new chapters are Chapter XI, which deals with military contributions, and Chapter XV, in which personality theories are discussed. The other chapters have, however, been thoroughly revised by including more recent material, better explanations, and more comprehensive discussion of applications. But the primary purpose of the text is still to serve as an analytical introduction to measuring instruments, not as a final appraisal of their value. The real value of a test usually appears several years after its publication.

The arrangement of the book is somewhat altered to allow the instructor or student to specialize to meet his needs. Part I is devoted to measures of ability, and may be used alone for courses principally concerned with abilities. It contains a discussion of basic considerations in measurement, of measures of achievements and aptitudes, and of the use of elementary statistical procedures. Part II contains three chapters dealing with elementary statistics. For those who have previously survived a course in statistics, these chapters will be a short friendly refresher course. For those without previous statistical training, it is hoped that these chapters will provide an interesting new experience. Part III comprises the last ten chapters which give an introduction to theories of personality, and present in detail vari-

v

ous evaluations of appreciation, interests, attitudes, and personal integration.

The complete reproduction of tests has been avoided because of space limitations, and also to keep them from being invalidated by too broad an acquaintance with them. It is expected that the instructor will use a battery of illustrative material during the course, while observing the ethical principles discussed in Chapter I.

Acknowledgements are made with pleasure to the following who have read one or more chapters and made many constructive suggestions: Roger M. Bellows, Gerald S. Blum, Edward E. Bordin, Frances Estep, Katharine B. Greene, Max L. Hutt, Arthur E. Johnson, E. Lowell Kelly, Doris Klein, Daniel R. Miller, Carl Rush, George A. Satter, Charles E. Scholl, Jr., V. M. Tye, W. L. Wallace, and Gertha Williams.

I am indebted to the outstanding leaders in the development of mental measurements who have, usually under protest, allowed their photographs to be reproduced here. Several persons were too modest, and certainly others were inadvertently omitted.

Lastly, I wish to express my sincere thanks to the many authors and editors who have given permission to reproduce drawings, tables, and charts which represent many hundreds of hours of painstaking research.

Edward B. Greene

Ann Arbor, Michigan
March, 1952

CONTENTS

~~~~~~

PART ONE—ACHIEVEMENT AND APTITUDE

vii

ILLUSTRATIONS

Some Leaders
in
Tests and Measurements

SAMUEL J. BECK, head of the Psychological Laboratory, Michael Reese Hospital, Chicago, has contributed to the development of Rorschach techniques and to their careful application.

Affiliated Photo—Conway

GEORGE K. BENNETT, President of the Psychological Corporation, has directed the production of differential aptitude, mechanical comprehension, and clerical aptitude tests; has contributed to their interpretation and effective use in industry; and has stimulated further research.

ALFRED BINET (1857–1911), founder of the Psychological Laboratory at the Sorbonne University in Paris, France. He pioneered in collecting and formulating careful measurement techniques, and with Simon published the first widely used test of general intelligence.

CHARLOTTE BUHLER, a clinical psychologist at the University of Southern California, has made many contributions to test development and use, including performance tests from birth to six years, a valuable development of the *World Test,* and Rorschach Standardization Studies (1951).

RAYMOND B. CATTELL, Research Professor of Psychology, University of Illinois, is a student of personality organization using statistical, clinical, and psychometric approaches. He has designed intelligence and projective tests and interpreted their application in England and America.

ORLO L. CRISSEY, Industrial Psychologist, General Motors Institute, Flint, Michigan, has developed very effective programs for the selection of both workers and supervisors, making use of measures of achievement and aptitude, and of ratings.

JOHN C. FLANAGAN, Professor of Psychology and President of the American Institute for Research, University of Pittsburgh, directed research for the Cooperative Test Service, and later was in charge of the Army Air Forces Aviation Psychology Program.

ARTHUR I. GATES, Professor of Education and Head, Department of Psychological Measurement and Methods of Research, Teachers College, Columbia University, has directed the development of diagnostic tests of reading and other school subjects.

Blackstone Studios

Gene Garrett

FLORENCE L. GOODENOUGH, for nearly twenty-five years associated with the Minnesota Child Guidance Clinic, first president of the National Council of Women Psychologists, has been active in the development of mental tests and projective techniques and their careful use.

HARRY A. GREENE, Professor of Education and Director of the Bureau of Educational Research and Service, University of Iowa, has contributed very significantly to the development of measures of language and number skills.

J. P. GUILFORD, Professor of Psychology, University of Southern California, has developed carefully planned tests of interest, aptitude, and temperament, and has directed studies of these in the Army Air Forces.

MARGUERITE R. HERTZ, a lecturer at Western Reserve University and a consultant in clinical psychology, has contributed to the understanding of Rorschach results by very skillful analysis and the establishment of normative standards.

GERTRUDE HOWELL HILDRETH, Professor of Education at Brooklyn College, and long associated with Lincoln School and Teachers College of Columbia University, is one of the most persistent and significant contributors to development and application of evaluations of school children.

E. A. White

HAROLD E. JONES, Professor of Psychology and Director, Institute of Child Welfare, University of California, has, for more than twenty years, been very active in developing and using measures of ability, interest, and personalit· in longitudinal studies.

TRUMAN LEE KELLEY, Emeritus Professor of Education, Harvard University, made many important contributions to both theory and practice of test construction and to the statistical methods of interpreting results. He is known to many as a great teacher.

GEORGE FREDERICK KUDER, Professor of Psychology at Duke University, editor of *Educational and Psychological Measurement,* and of *Personnel Psychology,* has contributed to both theory and practice of measuring preferences and personality variables.

RENSIS LIKERT, Director, Survey Research Center, and Professor of Psychology, University of Michigan, has contributed to statistical methods of scaling items, and has directed the development of adequate sampling by interviews of attitudes of social and industrial significance.

EVERET F. LINDQUIST, Professor of Education, University of Iowa; Director of Iowa Every-Pupil Testing program; Director of nation-wide testing program of the Cooperative Test Service; in charge of construction and standardization of tests of general education for the U.S. Armed Forces Institute.

MAUD A. MERRILL, Professor of Psychology, Stanford University, has made notable contributions to the measurement of intelligence and personal traits, and has applied these in psychotherapy with delinquents and children.

Kee Coleman

HENRY A. MURRAY, M.D., as director of an important series of personality studies at Harvard University, has developed the Thematic Apperception Test, but has gone much further in synthesizing psychiatry, psychology physiology, and anthropology in these studies.

ARTHUR S. OTIS was a pioneer in the development of group mental tests. He generously gave all of his materials and talents to the U.S. Army during World War I, and later developed the most widely used group of intelligence tests for school and industrial use.

Matar Studio

MARION W. RICHARDSON, Director of Research, Richardson, Bellows, Henry and Co., was chief of test development and principal examiner U.S. Civil Service Commission (1940–42), and chief of Personnel Research of the Adjutant General's Office (1942–46). He has contributed much to psychometric theory, aptitude testing, and morale studies.

EDWARD KELLOGG STRONG, JR., Professor of Psychology at the Graduate School of Business, Stanford University, and Director of the Vocational Interest Research Center, developed a unique method for appraising vocational interests and made many contributions to the application of psychology to business and personnel management.

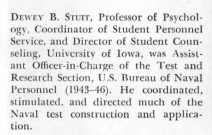

DEWEY B. STUIT, Professor of Psychology, Coordinator of Student Personnel Service, and Director of Student Counseling, University of Iowa, was Assistant Officer-in-Charge of the Test and Research Section, U.S. Bureau of Naval Personnel (1943–46). He coordinated, stimulated, and directed much of the Naval test construction and application.

Raleigh Ferran Stoops, Jr., Profe... ...ve Personnel at the Graduate Scho... of Business Administration... Director of the Bureau of... Research examin... iected by appli... trends and... in the applicat... business and per...

LEWIS MADISON TERMAN, at Stanford University since 1910, was among the first in this country to develop careful individual mental tests. His later work included studies of children's reading, personality of adults, longitudinal studies of Genius and collaboration with many others in the development of tests of achievement and mental ability to be used in group testing.

EDWARD LEE THORNDIKE, from 1899 to 1941 a prominent member of the staff of Teacher's College, Columbia University, pioneered in both educational psychology and mental and social measurement. His work has been definitive and inspirational. To persons struggling with difficult measurement problems he would say, "Anything that exists can be measured."

LOUIS LEON THURSTONE, with Chicago University since 1924, devised trade tests, interest questionnaires, and measures of personality early in his career. He then subjected each of these to more critical statistical analysis than anyone else. His method of factorial analysis is widely used to discover hypotheses concerning behavior.

Olan Mills

JOSEPH TIFFIN, Professor of Psychology, Purdue University, has prepared and directed the development of significant measures of dexterity, vision, and vocational aptitude and knowledge, and has pioneered many practical applications of these in industry.

Affiliated Photo—Conway

ARTHUR E. TRAXLER, Associate Director of the Educational Records Bureau, has been very effective in preparing cumulative records and interpreting results of testing programs in schools and colleges. He has developed a number of adequate tests of grade and high school achievement and reading.

RALPH W. TYLER, Dean of the Division
of Social Sciences, Chicago University,
has been one of the outstanding leaders
in defining and evaluating educational
objectives.

Fabian Bachrach

DAVID WECHSLER, Chief Psychologist,
Bellevue Psychiatric Hospital, and Clinical Professor of Medical Psychology,
College of Medicine, New York University, has developed measures of
adult intelligence and personality.

PART ONE

ACHIEVEMENT AND APTITUDE

CHAPTER I

INTRODUCTION

~~~~~~

This chapter answers concisely seven important questions about the measurement of human behavior:

What is behavior?
What is measurement?
What agencies provide tests?
What agencies use tests?
What ethical standards are important?
What are the requirements of a good examiner?
What are the limitations of measurement?

Other chapters in this book present in greater detail the answers to these questions.

Definitions. The words *test, item, measuring instrument, scale,* and *inventory* are used somewhat interchangeably, but they have distinct meanings of their own. The word *test* may refer either to an examining procedure or to printed questions which are used in an examination of skill. An *item* is a prescribed stimulus which usually yields a unit score. A *measuring instrument* is a set of items which have been given a standard set of values called a scale. A *scale* is a numerical scheme of reference consisting of points or steps that are usually equivalent in some respect. An *inventory* is a list of personal characteristics used in rating or judging oneself or others. When cast in the form of questions the inventory becomes a *questionnaire.*

WHAT IS BEHAVIOR?

The term *behavior* refers to any series of acts of an individual which occur in a particular place during a particular time. The indi-

3

vidual may be an object, a person, or a hypothetical entity, for example, an electron. The acts may be thought of as purely physical or as involving mental phenomena. No attempt will be made here to lay down rigid distinctions between physical and mental phenomena. In general phenomena refer to forces, movements, and qualities of chemical elements, or to combinations of elements, either animate or inanimate. Under mental phenomena are grouped acts of living organisms which are difficult to describe entirely in physical terms. These acts include wishes, memories of experiences, and beliefs, most of which involve symbols, and all of which seem to be dependent upon the activity of nervous tissue. Mental acts at present must be studied indirectly, for brain elements are too small and too easily destroyed to be observed and measured directly. Many investigators believe that mental and physical acts can be explained by the same natural laws. Certainly there is no sharp line separating them. The nature of mental acts and mental organization is discussed throughout the book, particularly in Chapters II, V, VII, and VIII.

WHAT IS MEASUREMENT?

Broadly speaking, *measurement* is any kind of comparison reported in numerical fashion. All measurements involve two somewhat independent processes: a comparison and a mathematical procedure, called scaling, which gives a number, called a score, to the results of the comparison. Two types of comparisons are in general use:

Qualitative comparisons.   Here, two or more persons or objects are compared to determine whether they have the same qualities. Qualitative judgments of a rough sort would be used in the examination of two persons to find if both can hear or if both can solve arithmetic problems.

Quantitative comparisons.   After qualitative similarities have been established, comparisons of amount can be made. Judgments of this type are illustrated by estimating which of two persons has the more acute hearing, or which has more arithmetical ability.

From these two types of comparisons, convenient units of amount can sometimes be specified with great precision. Chapter IV describes the most frequently used units of comparisons for appraising human abilities.

How Are Measuring Instruments Developed?

Many of the measurement techniques used by psychologists were partly developed by persons working in physical sciences and then adapted to the appraisal of activities of persons or animals. This fact makes it possible for persons well trained in measurement techniques to understand one another's methods fairly well, even though they work in different fields. All scales of measurement have been developed along similar lines.

A good measuring scale is the result of many years of hard work. The procedure is well illustrated by the development of measures of the hearing of a boy who is suspected of being somewhat deaf. One of the crudest measures is made by observing to see whether the boy responds to ordinary sounds by turning his head or by trying to see what made the sounds. One cannot definitely establish deafness from such observation, however, since the child may, for example, be feeble-minded or uncooperative, and therefore may not respond normally.

For a more careful diagnosis the youngster may be taken into a quiet room and asked to tell whether or not he hears a watch ticking. The watch may be held at various distances from one ear while his other ear is covered. This method of ascertaining deafness is better than the first, but it is neither complete nor accurate. The youngster may be deaf to certain tones only, or he may think that he hears the watch when he does not.

A further refinement in the measurement of hearing can be made with an audiometer, a machine which speaks into one ear at a time. The child is asked to report the numbers which he hears. The best audiometers give a wide sample of vowel and consonant sounds at various intensities. A record may be obtained which shows all of the child's answers. From these answers a measure of his range of hearing for pitch, intensity, and vowels and consonants may be obtained. Because there may be some chance successes, however, the test may not be entirely accurate and complete. Also, if the child is very young or mentally retarded, or if he has a speech defect, he may not be able to report correctly the sounds he hears. Hence, this measurement of hearing is limited by the subject's ability to report sounds. A still more precise way of measuring hearing does not require the reproduction of sounds, but presents two sounds following which the child is asked to indicate by a simple movement whether they are the same or different.

There are still some unknown factors present in this situation. For instance, we can never be sure that a child has done his best. If the test situation is somewhat strange and terrifying to him, he may wish to cooperate, but fail to do so. If the boy is suffering from a head cold or fatigue he may not be able to do his best. In spite of all precautions, therefore, one must admit that the best appraisals are only approximations rather than true measures of actual conditions. This same admission must be made for all measurement in any science.

From this account of the development of measurement of hearing it appears that at first there existed only a rough concept of not being able to hear. After much experimentation this concept was discarded. In its place three more precise concepts which can be appraised numerically are now used. These are pitch discrimination, intensity discrimination, and discrimination of spoken sounds which are complex combinations of various pitches, intensities, and rhythms. The construction of instruments for measuring each kind of hearing phenomenon requires considerable mechanical skill. Refinements that insure still greater precision are still being discovered from time to time. The construction of scales is discussed in Chapters III, IV, and VIII, in greater detail.

In order to standardize a test an extensive program of preparations is necessary. Such a program includes the following steps:

1. Decide specifically what is to be measured, and how. This step should give the test a clear objective.

2. Secure a large number of sample items or defined stimulus situations in order to guarantee a good coverage of the area to be tested.

3. Try out the items on small but representative groups having known characteristics. This step furnishes a basis for validating items and the test as a whole. Validation is the process of finding out what value a test has in a particular situation.

4. Analyze the responses to each item to determine such attributes as content, relation to other items, relation to criteria of success, and difficulty. In this way the best items are selected and the others are revised.

5. Revise items to make them more significant in obtaining the objectives.

6. Cross-validate the items, that is, repeat steps 3, 4, and 5, using a new group of persons. This step is necessary to avoid chance or random errors in the first tryout.

7. Prepare final revisions. This step yields two or more equivalent forms of highly important items, with the best arrangement for administration and scoring.

8. Secure standard results by testing large groups of persons selected as representative samples.

These eight steps require careful planning, great determination, time, the cooperation of many persons in school and industry, and usually a considerable amount of ready money.

Sources of Information about Tests

Since testing is developing rapidly, you may wish to know where the most recent information about tests can be found. Publishers are usually well informed concerning the use of a test. For technical criticisms, read the journals or Buros, *Mental Measurements Yearbooks* (Rutgers University, New Brunswick, New Jersey). Two excellent periodicals containing abstracts are found in many libraries: *Psychological Abstracts,* published by the American Psychological Association (1515 Massachusetts Avenue, Washington 5, D.C.) includes the sections shown in Illus. 1, many of which refer to measures.

ILLUS. 1. CONTENTS OF PSYCHOLOGICAL ABSTRACTS

GENERAL
Theory & Systems • Methods & Apparatus • New Tests • Statistics • Reference Works • Organizations • History & Biography • Professional Problems of Psychology

PHYSIOLOGICAL PSYCHOLOGY
Nervous System

RECEPTIVE AND PERCEPTUAL PROCESSES
Vision • Audition

RESPONSE PROCESSES

COMPLEX PROCESSES AND ORGANIZATIONS
Learning & Memory • Thinking & Imagination • Intelligence • Personality • Aesthetics

DEVELOPMENTAL PSYCHOLOGY
Childhood & Adolescence • Maturity & Old Age

SOCIAL PSYCHOLOGY
Methods & Measurements • Cultures & Cultural Relations • Social Institutions • Language & Communication • Social Action

CLINICAL PSYCHOLOGY, GUIDANCE, COUNSELING
Methodology, Techniques • Diagnosis & Evaluation • Treatment Methods • Child Guidance • Vocational Guidance

BEHAVIOR DEVIATIONS
Mental Deficiency • Behavior Problems • Speech Disorders • Crime & Delinquency • Psychoses • Psychoneuroses • Psychosomatics • Clinical Neurology • Sensory Defects

EDUCATIONAL PSYCHOLOGY
School Learning • Interests, Attitudes & Habits • Special Education • Educational Guidance • Educational Measurement • Education Staff Personnel

PERSONNEL PSYCHOLOGY
Selection & Placement • Labor-Management Relations

INDUSTRIAL AND OTHER APPLICATIONS
Industry • Business & Commerce • Professions
(By permission of the Editor of *Psychological Abstracts.*)

Child Development Abstracts, published by the Society for Research in Child Development (National Research Council, 2101 Constitution Avenue, Washington 25, D.C.) contains the sections shown in Illus. 2.

ILLUS. 2. CONTENTS OF CHILD DEVELOPMENT ABSTRACTS
I. ABSTRACTS OF ARTICLES
   A. MORPHOLOGY: Anatomy; Embryology; Anthropometry; Somatic Constitution
   B. PHYSIOLOGY AND BIOCHEMISTRY: Growth; Endocrines; Hormones; Nutrition; Vitamins
   C. CLINICAL MEDICINE AND PATHOLOGY: Dentistry; Immunology; Diagnostic Tests
   D. PSYCHOLOGY: Behavior; Intelligence; Learning; Personality
   E. PSYCHIATRY AND MENTAL HYGIENE: Crime; Delinquency
   F. PUBLIC HEALTH AND HYGIENE: Epidemiology; Morbidity; Mortality
   G. HUMAN BIOLOGY AND DEMOGRAPHY: Genetics; Natality and Fertility; Population; Race and Sex Differences
   H. EDUCATION: Class Curriculum; Vocational Guidance
   I. SOCIOLOGY AND ECONOMICS: Laws; Family; Marriage and Divorce
II. BOOK NOTICES
   AUTHOR INDEX

(By permission of the Editor of *Child Development Abstracts.*)

WHAT AGENCIES PROVIDE TESTS?

In the past many standard tests have been prepared by government agencies, nonprofit organizations, and private individuals.

Government Agencies

Four types of government agencies have designed or adapted standard tests: civil service jurisdictions, military establishments, the United States Employment Service, and offices of education. The civil service groups include federal, state, and municipal agencies, all of which provide millions of aptitude or skill and knowledge tests each year as part of the qualifying examinations of job applicants. Practically every type of job is covered. The military establishments have found that aptitude and performance tests aid enormously in the most effective selection of men for training or skilled jobs. The United States Employment Service has developed specific batteries of aptitude tests for certain occupations, a General Aptitude Test Battery, and a series of short Oral Trade Tests, to detect bluffers and to recognize skilled journeymen. The state departments of education of New York, Ohio, and Indiana are among the few school systems that publish tests of academic achievement.

Nonprofit Agencies

Among nonprofit organizations that publish tests the largest is doubtless the Educational Testing Service, Princeton, New Jersey. It was granted a charter in 1947 as a nonprofit corporation in the State of New York. It has no stockholders and is under the complete control of a distinguished board of trustees who represent many areas in education. It unites in a single organization the testing activities of the following three previously independent groups: (a) the American Council on Education, which sponsors the Psychological Examination for high school graduates, the Cooperative Test Service for high school achievement tests, and the National Committee on Teacher Examination; (b) the College Entrance Examination Board, which issues annual tests covering high school subjects and also a scholastic aptitude test; (c) the Carnegie Foundation for the Advancement of Teaching, which prepares examinations of achievement and aptitude of college graduates.

The Educational Testing Service coordinates the work of these three groups and eliminates unnecessary duplications. It also undertakes basic research, and explores new areas in the field of testing, using grants from various foundations.

Private Agencies

Private agencies and individuals still account for the production of the largest variety of tests on the market. A list of publishers is given in Appendix I and a list of tests in Appendix II.[1]

In the past the most active test development has been in measuring intelligence and achievement in school subjects in grade schools and high schools. College achievement testing is fairly well developed, and recently industrial testing has made great strides. School achievement tests are now enlarging their function by measuring results of education other than subject mastery; for example, good personal adjustments vocationally, socially, and as a citizen in a democracy are being measured by this type of test. Measures of interests and personal adjustments or drives are also now being developed rapidly.

WHAT AGENCIES USE TESTS?

Four kinds of agencies—educational, industrial, clinical, and civic —frequently apply standard measures of behavior.

Educators use tests both for individual diagnosis and promotion,

[1] See pp. 731ff.

and for appraisals of a method of instruction or of an instructor. The diagnostic use of tests can be of great benefit to the student, if his failings are recognized and a remedial course is made available to him. The greatest benefits are derived when vocational and educational counseling are combined with teaching, for counseling involves a plan of individual development. In order to make such a plan the counselor needs the detailed information yielded by the most accurate tests.

The use of standard tests has in some instances led to undesirable results. Teachers have felt driven to prepare their pupils to meet certain test requirements rather than to develop in the students a mastery of skills in a reasonable sequence. Many astute educators consider that this drive to insure that pupils meet certain requirements is a serious menace to good teaching. Surveys by means of tests are of considerable value both to administrators and to teachers when the goals of instruction are not sacrificed to coaching or cramming procedures.

Industrial agencies have used tests principally in the selection or promotion of employees. Civil service departments use more tests than any other agency, and their use has on numerous occasions increased the effectiveness of an employed group. Clerical workers in private industry have also been frequently appraised by standard tests. Large industrial agencies are beginning to use tests for individual guidance in order to determine whether an applicant is well fitted for some position for which he did not apply. Tests have also been used in directing employees toward various courses of training. In the realm of production standard tests and questionnaires are sometimes used to detect the effect of fatigue, monotony, physical and social working conditions, and payment systems. In the field of merchandising standardized questionnaires are widely used to ascertain the effects of printed advertisements and radio programs on various groups. Chapters IX and XI give samples of the use of tests in industry and military services.

Clinical agencies at times deal with persons who are mentally abnormal in some degree—the feeble-minded, the psychotic, the epileptic, the emotional deviate, and the delinquent. A few special tests of moral and neurotic tendencies have been constructed, but the majority of tests applied only in the clinical field are designed to aid in determining the deeper aspects of personal integration.

Civic leaders and agencies are becoming aware of the accuracy of appraisals of public opinion on controversial issues. Rough straw votes of unrepresentative samples of a group of voters have been found to be unreliable, but when a few unambiguous questions of fact or preference are presented, the results are significant. The development of more agencies for appraising attitudes toward economic, social, and political issues is going on rapidly. These will have a marked effect on political actions in a democratic state.

It is interesting to note a marked tendency among the different types of agencies to use the same types of tests. The school is interested in vocational success, mental health, and the development of character and self-government; hence it uses all types of tests. Industrial agencies find that success in school is one of the best indicators of success in business. They therefore use many tests of educational achievement, as well as tests of character and vocational fitness. Clinical agencies are interested in restoring a person to normal life in school or the community, so they try to evaluate all aspects of a person. All of these agencies are becoming convinced that the whole person has to be considered in any adequate plan for his social development or continued employment.

ETHICAL STANDARDS FOR DISTRIBUTION OF TESTS

No one knows exactly how many mental tests are given each year in the United States, but several have estimated that approximately 20 million Americans take about 60 million tests. As in the case of any large-scale enterprise, careless and unethical practices have at times arisen. The American Psychological Association established a committee on ethical standards; and a subcommittee on tests through its chairman, Donald Super, made a report in 1949. The report contains a long list of unethical incidents, and defines ethical practices.

The following situations taken from the report illustrate the use of *unethical practices:*

1. A personnel man employed by a medium-sized steel company called for advice on a testing problem. He had given a battery of well-known tests to candidates, had scored them, and wanted to be told over the telephone what he should use as a passing score. He had made no validating studies and had no idea that they should be made.

2. An executive was greatly perturbed about a series of personality tests appearing weekly in a magazine with the name of a lecturer in psychology in a university attached to the test. The office manager cut out the tests from week to week and administered the tests to his office staff and then gave back interpretations. This procedure caused a lot of unrest in the office and the executive told his office manager that no more tests were to be given in his organization. The office manager claimed the tests were very good as they were published by a member of the psychology staff of a near-by university.

3. A scoring service issues tests and sends scores to private individuals, even though its official policy is not to do so. A number of persons have been seen who have been hurt by this practice of leaving test interpretation to untrained individuals.

4. A local firm using psychological tests in consulting work employs no psychologists. One staff member took a course with an industrial psychologist teaching in a near-by university and the firm implies that the psychologist is associated with its operations. The firm seems to have no difficulty getting tests.

5. In one large company a group of personnel workers were studying testing at a near-by university. They administered tests they were studying to employees and counseled them, sometimes even going over the scoring with them. In doing so they not only failed to make use of local validation data available in another section of the same department, but interfered with validation studies and the promotional use of these tests by that section.

6. A widely publicized test developed by the federal government was released to a commercial publisher for civilian publication. As the test was of a type outdated even when first developed, and was released because of the development of an up-to-date type of substitute, the publisher is actively marketing an inferior product under unusually good auspices.

7. A book on a projective test depicts it as entirely new and validated for screening: it is actually a revision, and the conclusions concerning validation have since been uniformly contradicted by a number of careful studies by other investigators.

8. The manual for a well-known test cites a number of studies showing its validity in practical use, but fails to cite equally good studies showing unfavorable results.

9. In another such case the manual reports validity coefficients against "ratings on vocational courses *as high as* .84" [italics added] without describing the groups tested or citing any of the other, implicitly lower, correlations found.

10. An interest inventory standardized on 12th grade students was advertised as suitable for use with high school, college, and adult populations. However, work with another interest inventory has demonstrated significant changes in certain types of interest in adolescence and early childhood.

11. A book on executive ability gives the impression that the author's test of "executive ability" is well validated. Investigation showed that the author actually had no data which could be examined, either in raw or in analyzed form, the ostensible reason being their confidential nature.

The following five *ethical practices* and the rules for applying them are summarized from material in the report by Super:

1. *Preparation.* Those who prepare tests have the responsibility of carefully describing their procedures and of securing adequate

norms and evidences of validity. The limitations of a test should be clearly stated in the manual.

2. *Publication.* A test, except for experimental purposes, should not be published before it is carefully prepared and standardized. Unjustifiable claims are an indication of lack of responsibility. The publication of parts of standardized tests in popular magazines or books may invalidate the test.

3. *Application.* No one should recommend or assume responsibility for a testing program who is not thoroughly qualified. Advertisers or representatives of publishing houses should usually not serve as consultants on testing programs, and psychologists who recommend the publications of only one company should be viewed with suspicion. Those assuming responsibility for a testing program should always have continuous firsthand supervision of the program.

4. *Teaching.* Persons teaching the administration and interpretation of tests should admit only students who have the prerequisite training. Test materials should be retained only by graduate students who will use and protect the material properly. For didactic purposes the persons to be tested should be given a reasonable satisfaction for their contribution.

5. *Release of Scores.* Individual test scores should be released only to those who can make a reasonable interpretation of them. They should not be released if they are likely to result in discouragement or social or emotional disturbances.

THE REQUIREMENTS OF A GOOD EXAMINER

The preceding description of the most frequent uses of tests leads to the question, what are the necessary qualifications of one who is competent to administer and interpret test results?

Five qualifications seem necessary. First, a good examiner must know why and how to build up a clear set of concepts. Securing this knowledge is often the most difficult part of the training, for concepts, even the simplest, are difficult to understand and to keep from becoming ambiguous. This difficulty is particularly troublesome in the measurement of behavior, for the basic concepts are intangible and still somewhat controversial. The analysis of the processes involved in a response is one of the major persistent problems of psychologists.

Second, a good examiner must be familiar with the best testing instruments. To measure the power of a gasoline engine, one must have a well-standardized device for measuring work done in a given period.

Since a person responds in many more ways than does an engine, mental measurement is considerably more difficult than measuring a gasoline engine.

Third, a good examiner must know when he has obtained a good sample of performance. Thus, in measuring the power of an engine, the tester must control his experiment. The engine must be run at a standard rate, using standard temperatures and standard fuels and lubricants. Only with such controls can its power be compared accurately with that of other engines using the same standards. In mental measurement controls are just as necessary but far more difficult to secure. If one wishes to have a good representative sample of a person's speed of reading, it is important that he have not only a good reading test, but also control of motivation, fatigue, and accuracy of performance.

ILLUS. 3. VARIABLES IN A TEST SITUATION

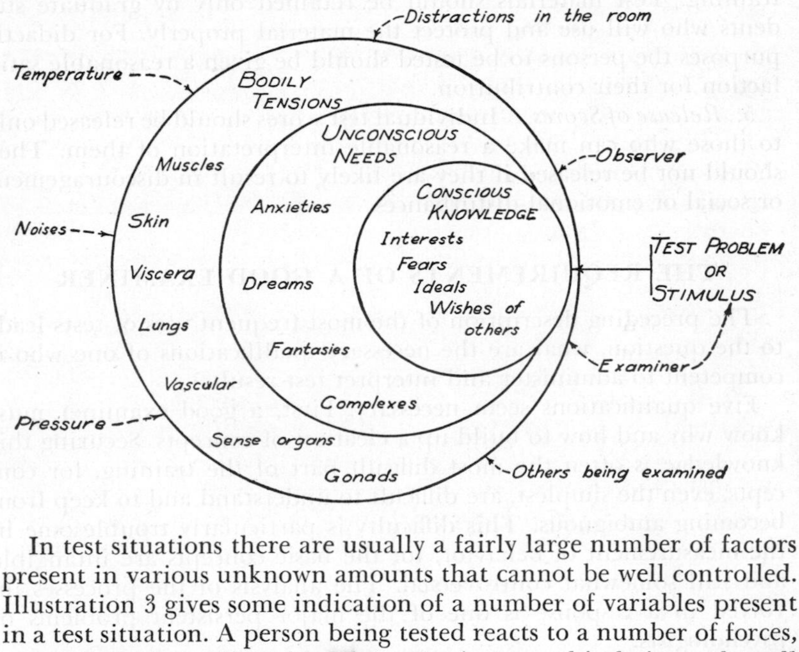

In test situations there are usually a fairly large number of factors present in various unknown amounts that cannot be well controlled. Illustration 3 gives some indication of a number of variables present in a test situation. A person being tested reacts to a number of forces, some of which conflict with others. For instance, his desire to do well on the test may be in conflict with his desire to take it easy, or to do something more entertaining. His fear of failure may be strong enough to set up disturbing thoughts and physiological reactions. He may be fatigued or suffering from a cold, or a fever, or indigestion. He may be distracted by objects in the room or by others with whom he is competing. The examiner may inspire or discourage him. He may have obsessions or delusions which make it difficult for him to keep his mind on the task. It is a prime concern of the examiner to evaluate such forces in the test situation, and in many instances this evaluation is more important in appraising behavior than are the results of the test. In tests of adjustment, interests, or attitudes, the examiner's task is to control and vary the situational stresses so that fairly typical reaction patterns will emerge. Some have taken into account the external forces which impinge on a person under the general heading of press or outside stimuli, representing them by arrows. The forces which originate within the person are grouped under the heading needs or drives. These terms should be defined more carefully, however, before they are accepted for use.

To a large extent we select the stimuli to which we pay attention. For instance, you may not notice a radio program in the next room, but I may be driven nearly mad by it. This employee or pupil cringes and withdraws from me, although I talk and act in a friendly manner. The examiner may represent an unreasonable, and possibly imagined, authority, or the examinee may have stolen something, and be fearful of being discovered. The task of a good examiner, then, is not only to ascertain and record the facts of behavior, but also to determine the causal sequence in which they occur.

Fourth, a good examiner must have the ability to judge and use available norms, which are the scores of representative groups. Unfortunately, most of the available norms are from small or specially selected groups. A person who is well trained in measurement will know the special derivation of each set of published results and be able to make allowances for it.

Fifth and finally, a good examiner must have ability to report and interpret correctly test findings. If the measurement is part of an experimental procedure, then the findings must be checked with the hypothesis; if the measurement is for individual purposes, then the limits of prediction should be known and specified. Interpretation is one of the most important and difficult parts of the work. A large number of persons who can give tests under standard conditions cannot make accurate interpretations. These persons are useful as laboratory technicians, but they should be supervised by a well-trained specialist.

The usual training for an expert in the field of mental measurement includes undergraduate emphasis in college upon mathematics, biology, sociology; and at least three years of graduate work, specializing in statistical procedures; experimental, systematic, and abnormal psychology; and the theory and application of numerical appraisals of behavior.

LIMITATIONS OF TESTING TECHNIQUES

Thus far the nature of mental measures and some of their uses have been described. It behooves us to become aware of certain of their limitations that are often overlooked. Three types of limitations are important.

First, mental measurement techniques cannot be expected to make decisions for a person. They can only present the evidence more clearly. From careful measurement it may appear that a student's chances of average success in a course in electrical engineering, or in second-year French, or in medicine, are one in one hundred. But the tests cannot decide for a person whether or not he shall attempt the course or the profession. Often a person must experience failure in order to be made to realize his limitations.

Second, the best tests available cannot, at present, predict with great accuracy what a person will do in complex learning or vocational situations. This limitation exists because people vary in motives, emotional balance, social acceptance, health, opportunities, and in many other ways which are not checked by a series of tests. Even from a very complete study of a person, predictions of success ten years later have seldom been very accurate. To be sure, most of the predictions of success in college or industry from a particular test or a battery of tests are much better than chance, but still they are of limited value for individual counseling. Chapter III discusses how accurate various predictions of behavior should be in order to be of value to individuals.

Third, mental tests ordinarily cannot show why a person made a particular score, but only that he did make the score. This is true of all measures of behavior. For instance, within certain limits, the speed of an automobile can be measured in miles per hour, but the speed record does not indicate why it goes slowly or rapidly. A large number of factors, such as engine and chassis design, road and wind friction, fuels, and oils, affect the total speed. The contributory factors in measures of human behavior are considerably more complex. Thus, a speed-of-reading test score depends upon such variables as visual acuity, fatigue, verbal information, verbal skills, and desire to succeed, about which one is often uninformed. As more careful controls are exercised in testing, the unknown variables will be reduced, and the scores will become more precise and valuable.

STUDY GUIDE QUESTIONS

1. Define succinctly: test inventory, measuring instrument, item, rating, scale, estimate, belief, behavior, validation.

2. What are the main differences between qualitative and quantitative judgments?

3. How are good measuring instruments developed?

4. What facts should be known about each item and why?

5. Why should a standardized test be cross-validated?

6. What types of agencies produce tests?

7. What advantages and disadvantages are there in having many agencies competing in the development and distribution of tests?

8. Why do most types of agencies now tend to use the same types of evaluations?

9. Summarize the ethical principles for test publication and distribution.

10. List the elements of training required for examiners.

11. Why are tests not a panacea for solving many problems of a personal nature in schools and industries?

CHAPTER II

TYPES OF APPRAISALS

∿∿∿∿∿∿∿∿∿∿∿∿∿∿∿∿∿∿∿∿∿∿∿∿∿∿∿∿∿∿∿∿∿∿∿

This chapter gives an over-all view of almost all available types of appraisals of human behavior, presents a few examples of appraisals, and refers to many which are discussed in other chapters. Also, it contains a classification of tests according to purpose and type of administration.

PERSONAL TRAITS

There are two main approaches to measurement. In one a person is considered a complex unit, and a general intelligence or general adjustment score is sought which will reflect total functioning. In the other a person is considered to be made up of many related parts, some of which may function with considerable independence. Separate measures are sought for each independent part or for its corresponding pattern of behavior. The nature and degree of relationship between parts are subjects of considerable research. The second approach, being analytical, has been on the whole more fruitful than the first, but both have made their contributions.

The word *trait* in this text is used to refer to any physical aspect of a person, such as height, size of brain, or pulse rate; or to any mental aspect, such as speed of reading, attitudes toward war, or ideals about home life. Traits usually have three important attributes: intangibility, multiple causation, and normal distribution.

Intangibility. A few traits, for example, height and weight are tangible, that is, they can be measured directly. Most others—reading ability, fears, needs, etc.—are intangible, and can only be inferred from a series of observations after the behavior which indicates the trait is carefully reported, classified, and counted. This procedure is called *indirect appraisal,* and it always involves the weighting of items to produce scores.

Multiple causation. All traits are the result of a large number of factors. Thus a person's height at any time is the result of an inherited tendency to growth of bones and connecting tissues, which is related to a goodly number of genes, and also the result of nutrition, exercise, and posture. These contribute to a complex growth curve for stature, which is not the same as the growth curve for weight, teeth, or mental ability. A person's attitude toward the Chinese will depend upon such factors as his age, experience, the color of his own skin, his economic status, the attitudes of his family and friends, and his independence of thought.

Normal distribution. Among persons selected at random from a large population the amount of a trait possessed by each will vary from a very small to a very large amount, with a large proportion of the group possessing a moderate amount of the trait. When the results are presented graphically they most often form a normal or bell-shaped curve (Illus. 121).

All traits, even those that seem to be the least complex, are apparently related to many others. It is possible, however, and also desirable, to classify traits according to their similarities and differences. A good classification will prevent conjecture and result in much more accurate measures.

It is generally agreed that there are at least five major groups or categories of traits: physical, bodily reactions, cognitive, motivational, and integrative. The names of these groups are, however, not all well agreed upon as yet, hence definitions are in order.

Physical Traits

Physical traits are those derived from the structure and materials of a person's body: the size and shape of limbs, bones, and various organs, color and texture of eyes, hair, skin, tissues, and the like. They are not described in this text except with reference to the work of Sheldon (1940) in Chapter XV.

Bodily Reactions

Bodily reactions give rise to four kinds of traits. *Physiological* traits arise from reactions of the involuntary muscles and glands—vascular changes, breathing, temperature regulation, electrical conduction, chemical changes, and tensions or pressures. These reactions determine basic energy reserves and expenditures. *Reaction times* to stimuli are different from physiological changes in that they usually involve sense organs and voluntary as well as involuntary muscles. The central nervous system is also essential.

Psychophysical sensitivity is indicated by the speed and accuracy of one's sensory acuity, by arousing specific sense organs with carefully prepared stimuli. These may involve vision, hearing, touch, pressure, taste, temperature, smell, and movement. *Motor skills,* such as dexterity, athletic skill, endurance, agility, and strength, are still

ILLUS. 4. AIMING TEST, MICHIGAN NONVERBAL SERIES

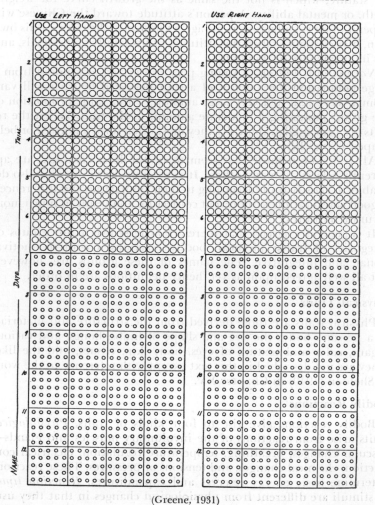

(Greene, 1931)

more complex traits, which are to a large extent physical or physiological (Chapter IX). The units of measurement in this field are usually in terms of amount of work done, such as hits or errors on a target, as in an aiming test (Illus. 4); number of contacts in a given time, as in a steadiness test (Illus. 5); number of movements completed in a given time, as in various manipulation tests (Illus. 6), or the maximum force exerted (Illus. 7). Sometimes the amount of work is held constant for all persons, and the score is in terms of the time needed to finish the work. Further descriptions of tests of this kind are given in Chapter IX.

ILLUS. 5. GURNEE TRACING APPARATUS	ILLUS. 6. THE MINNESOTA RATE OF MANIPULATING TEST

(Courtesy of the C. H. Stoelting Co., Chicago, Ill.)	Posed by Dr. Bing Chung Ling (Manufactured by the Educational Test Bureau, Minneapolis, Minn.)

Cognitive Processes

Cognition is used here to mean the process of knowing and of thinking. Tests of these processes all involve measuring the ability to answer specific questions correctly. Correctness is determined by arbitrary definitions and judgments formulated by the authors of the tests. Four large subdivisions of cognition—perception, learning, reasoning, and knowledge—are usually recognized as being independent to a large degree.

Perception. Perception tests are indicators of one's speed and

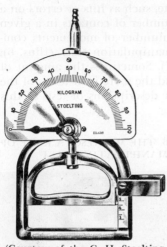

(Courtesy of the C. H. Stoelting
Co., Chicago, Ill.)

accuracy of discrimination from direct comparison of such stimuli as sound, chemical, temporal, and spatial patterns. Tests of perception are illustrated by a number and name-comparison test (Illus. 8) and by a form-comparison test (Illus. 147). The unit of measurement for these tests is usually a judgment of same or different, and the raw score is the number of correct judgments in a standard series that can be made in a given period of time, usually from 3 to 10 minutes.

Another group of tests that are usually classed as perceptual are called attention-span tests. In these, visual stimuli are exposed for a brief period, say one tenth of a second, and then the subject is asked to reproduce or to name them. These tests are not widely used because the necessary lighting and timing are difficult to control. They can best be given in a laboratory.

More widely used are the immediate-memory-span tests. These, which are also sometimes placed in this perception group, require the reproduction or recognition of stimuli just observed. In these tests stimuli are usually presented one at a time, and the subject is asked to reproduce each exactly as given. Auditory spans for digits, disconnected words, sentences, and bead chains are used in the Stanford-Binet Test, Terman and Merrill (1937). Baker and Leland (1935) developed tests of visual spans for letters and small pictures. Seashore (1919) standardized a test for immediate memory of short tonal phrases. These tests are not dependent solely upon perception of pattern; they also involve a short retention span. It seems likely, however, that good retention over short periods depends upon clear perception of the elements and their relationships. The score for each of these span tests is usually the number of elements recorded correctly during a standard testing situation. Sometimes the longest series of items that can be reproduced is taken as the score.

Learning. Although learning often takes place during a test, and many definitions of intelligence include learning as its most important element, tests designed to measure learning are not common. This lack of tests of learning is due to the slowness with which learn-

ILLUS. 8. MINNESOTA VOCATIONAL TEST FOR CLERICAL WORKERS

(Arranged by Dorothy M. Andrew under the direction of
Donald G. Paterson and Howard P. Longstaff)

Name_____Date_____

TEST 1 — Number Comparison	TEST 2 — Name Comparison
Number Right _____	Number Right _____
Number Wrong _____	Number Wrong _____
Score = R — W _____	Score = R — W _____
Percentile Rating _____	Percentile Rating _____

Instructions

On the inside pages there are two tests. One of the tests consists of pairs of names and the other of pairs of numbers. If the two names or the two numbers of a pair are *exactly the same* make a check mark ($\sqrt{}$) on the line between them; if they are *different*, make no mark on that line. When the examiner says "Stop!" draw a line under the last pair at which you have looked.

Samples done correctly of pairs of *Numbers*

79542   79524
_____

5794367 $\sqrt{}$ 5794367
_____

Samples done correctly of pairs of *Names*

John C. Linder   John C. Lender
_____

Investors Syndicate $\sqrt{}$ Investors Syndicate

Now try the samples below.

66273894   66273984
_____

527384578   527384578
_____

New York World   New York World
_____

Cargill Grain Co.   Cargil Grain Co.
_____

This is a test for Speed and Accuracy. Work as fast as you can without making mistakes.

Do not turn this page until you are told to begin.

ing usually takes place and the many serious difficulties encountered in measuring it.

Tests which are doubtless affected by speed of learning include the digit-symbol test (Illus. 9). In this test the numbers are to be translated into the symbols which are printed immediately beneath

ILLUS. 9. UNITED STATES ARMY BETA TEST 4. DIGIT SYMBOL TEST

Test 4

1	2	3	4	5	6	7	8	9
−	И	コ	L	U	0	∧	X	=

3	1	2	1	3	2	1	4	2	3	5	2	9	1	4

1.

6	3	1	5	4	2	7	6	3	8	7	2	9	5	4

2.

6	3	7	2	8	1	9	5	8	4	7	3	6	9	5

3.

1	9	2	8	3	7	4	6	5	9	4	8	5	7	6

4.

9	3	8	6	4	1	5	7	2	6	2	4	8	1	3

5.

4	9	5	1	7	5	2	6	9	3	7	8	4	1	8

6

(By permission of C. H. Stoelting Company and Henry Holt & Company.)

the members at the top of the test page. Other examples of this type of test are the indexing and classification tests shown in Illus. 10, and various tests of code writing. All of these require the learning of associations. The unit of measurement is the correct placement of a symbol according to the code. The total score depends upon the speed and accuracy with which symbols are placed. In laboratory situations speed of learning with mirror drawing, mazes, and nonsense syllables has been extensively studied. In school situations measures of the acquisition of language and mathematical skills have been given much attention. These studies result in estimates of speed of learning, but few standardized tests have resulted.

Reasoning. The outstanding characteristic of reasoning is the solution of a problem by the production of a new pattern of behavior

ILLUS. 10. O'ROURKE CLERICAL APTITUDE TEST, JUNIOR GRADE,
(CLERICAL PROBLEMS)

Form 1

O'Rourke Series of Aids in Placement and Guidance

PRINT YOUR NAME .... Date .... 19 ....
     (Last name)   (First name)   (Middle initial)   (Month) (Day) (Year)

Age now ....
                  (Years)   (Months)

Write the last school grade you COMPLETED .... Age at that time ....

You will have five minutes to study the samples on this page. The tests on the following pages are like these. Be sure you understand the samples.

Time commenced ....

SAMPLES

FILE DRAWERS

Sample I. You are to file alphabetically in the file drawers shown at the right. Each drawer contains six folders. After each of the names listed below the third file drawer, you are to write the number of the folder in which that name should be filed.

6. Bi-Bz	12. Dr-Dz	18. Ha-Hd
5. Be-Bh	11. Di-Dq	17. Gp-Gz
4. Ba-Bd	10. Da-Dh	16. Ga-Go
3. Ap-Az	9. Co-Cz	15. Fa-Fz
2. Ah-Ao	8. Ch-Cn	14. Em-Ez
1. Aa-Ag	7. Ca-Cg	13. Ea-El

The first name, "Appel," should be filed in the folder for names from Ap to Az. This folder is numbered 3, so 3 is written after the name "Appel." The second name, "Cecil," should be filed between Ca and Cg, which is folder No. 7, so 7 is written after it. "Denby" should be filed in folder "Da-Dh," so WRITE 10 AFTER "DENBY". Next write the number of the folder in which "Earl" should be filed. The number of the correct folder is 13.

Name	Folder
1. Appel	3
2. Cecil	7
3. Denby	____
4. Earl	____

Sample II. Write a C after the name of each man in the list at the right who is a teacher, is between 25 and 40 years of age, and resides in either Indiana or Illinois.

Name	Age	Occupation	Residence	
Beach, R. P.	38	Teacher	Michigan	
Mark, J. K.	33	Teacher	Indiana	C
Savoy, W. T.	23	Student	Indiana	
Bard, T. I.	31	Teacher	Illinois	

Nothing is written after Mr. Beach's name, as his residence is neither Indiana nor Illinois. C is written after Mr. Mark's name, as he is a teacher, is between 25 and 40, and resides in Indiana. You should not write anything after Mr. Savoy's name, as he is not a teacher. Write C after Mr. Bard's name as he is a teacher, is 31 years old, and is from Illinois.

Sample III. If the name, the address, and the charge are not exactly the same in the copy as in the original, X is to be written on the line at the right. If the copy is the same as the original, write S.

	Original			Copy		Check
Name	Address	Charge	Name	Address	Charge	here
Harris, E. G.	38 Oak St.,	$38.95	Harris, E. G.	26 Oak St.,	$38.95	X
Graves, L. R.	21 Rex Ave.,	$16.16	Graves, L. R.	21 Rex Ave.,	$16.16	S
Overt, P. W.	15 End St.,	$ 5.00	Overt, P. W.	15 End St.,	$10.00	

The first is marked X because the address was copied incorrectly. S is written after the second, as the name, address, and charge were all copied exactly as in the original. In the third, a mistake was made in copying the charge, so WRITE X ON THE LINE.

DO NOT TURN THIS PAGE

(By permission of the Psychological Institute, Washington, D.C.)

out of experiences which were previously arranged in other patterns. Under reasoning are included tests of inference and of problem solving.

In inference tests the subject is asked either to detect inconsistencies or to make inferences of his own. In the simplest form two objects or statements are presented, and the subject must show their

ILLUS. 11. SYLLOGISM TEST

Directions: In each section below, read the first sentence and the line marked a. If what a says follows from the first sentence, make a circle around the T in line a. If what a says is false according to the first sentence, circle the F. If the statement in a need not follow from the first sentence, circle the Q. Do the same for lines b and c. The sample below is marked correctly.

Sample: All good dancers dance frequently; the men in this house do not dance frequently; therefore, —
  a. The men in this house are not good dancers   Ⓣ F Q
  b. All frequent dancers are good dancers   T F Ⓠ
  c. Some good dancers are in this house   T Ⓕ Q

Form A.
  1. All the people living on this farm are related to the Joneses; these old men live on this farm; therefore, —
  a. These old men are related to the Joneses.   T F Q
  b. All the people related to the Joneses are these old men.   T F Q
  c. Some people related to the Joneses are not these old men. T F Q

(After Wilkins, 1928.)

relationships by comparing each with a third. This form is seen in a syllogism test (Illus. 11) in which the subject is asked to check those inferences which can be correctly deduced from preliminary statements. Other illustrations are reading tests (Illus. 67 and Illus. 68) in which the subject is asked to interpret a paragraph. A more complex form of reasoning test is shown in the interpretation of scientific data (Illus. 12). In this test the subject is asked to check the inferences which may be correctly drawn from an account of a situation in which four or five variables are involved. The unit of measurement in these tests is usually a judgment of *true, false,* or *undetermined* relationship.

Other fairly common forms of tests which involve reasoning are analogies, page 231, and disarranged sentences, Illus. 69. In both of these, isolated words or figures are to be matched or arranged according to relationships indicated in a context.

In problem-solving tests a person must become aware of a problem, select a hypothesis or plan for solution, and then apply this

ILLUS. 12. COOPERATIVE CHEMISTRY TEST

A. SELECTION OF FACTS

Directions: Following are a number of incomplete statements each of which may be completed by one or more of the words or phrases given below the statement. Place a plus sign (+) in the parentheses after those words or phrases which will make the statement true, as in the following sample.

Sample: Oxygen is an element which:

a. Acts chemically as a metal . . . .(   ) a.
b. Unites with hydrogen forming water . . . .(+) b.
c. Is a good conductor of electricity . . . .(   ) c.
d. Is rarely found in nature . . . .(   ) d.
e. Supports combustion . . . .(+) e.

B. TERMINOLOGY

Directions: Below is a numbered list of chemical terms arranged in alphabetical order. Following the list are several definitions or descriptions of terms used in Chemistry. Read each definition or description, decide what term it is, then place the number of the term in the parentheses after the definition or description.

1. Acid salt	16. Ketone
2. Aliphatic compounds	17. Kindling temperature
3. Amalgam	18. Metalloids
4. Anhydrous	19. Molar solution
5. Aromatic compounds	20. Mole
6. Atom	21. Molecule
7. Atomic number	22. Monel metal
8. Basic salt	23. Normal salt
9. Carboxyl	24. Osmosis
10. Critical temperature	25. Saturated solution
11. Esters	26. Solute
12. Heat of solution	27. Solvent
13. Hydrogenation	28. Spontaneous combustion
14. Inversion	29. Standard solution
15. Invertase	30. Zymase

a. Elements which possess in some degree the physical properties of metals and the chemical properties of nonmetals . . . .(   ) a.
b. Characterized by one or more six carbon atom rings . . . .(   ) b.
c. A compound composed of a negative ion other than hydroxyl or oxygen in combination with some positive ion other than hydrogen . . . .(   ) c.
d. Characterized by an open chain of carbon atoms . . . .(   ) d.
e. A mixture of mercury and one or more other metals . . . . . .(   ) e.
f. Process by which sucrose is changed into a mixture of equal parts of glucose and fructose . . . .(   ) f.
g. Characteristic of substances which are not combined with water . .(   ) g.
h. A group of elements which characterize the organic acids . . . .(   ) h.
i. Burning produced by slow oxidation and the accumulation of heat .(   ) i.
j. Smallest unit of a substance which takes part in ordinary chemical changes . . . .(   ) j.
k. The temperature at which a substance begins to glow or bursts into a flame . . . .(j k

ILLUS. 12. COOPERATIVE CHEMISTRY TEST (*Cont'd*)

C. APPLICATION OF PRINCIPLES

Directions: In each of the following exercises a problem is given. Below each problem are two lists of statements. The first list contains statements which can be used to answer the problem. Place a plus sign (+) in the parentheses after the statement or statements which <u>answer</u> <u>the</u> <u>problem</u>. The second list contains statements which can be used to explain the right answers. Place a plus sign (+) in the parentheses after the statement or statements which <u>give</u> <u>the</u> <u>reasons</u> <u>for</u> <u>the</u> <u>right</u> <u>answers</u>. Some of the other statements are true but do not explain the right answers; <u>do</u> <u>not</u> <u>check</u> <u>these</u>. In doing these exercises then, you are to place a plus sign (+) in the parentheses after the statements which <u>answer</u> <u>the</u> <u>problem</u> and which <u>give</u> <u>the</u> <u>reasons</u> <u>for</u> <u>the</u> <u>RIGHT</u> <u>answers</u>.

Sample: Coal gas which has not been previously mixed with air is burned at a gas jet. At another similar gas jet the coal gas is mixed with air before it is burned. Will there be any difference in the amount of light given off by the flames of the two gas jets? Why? If a cool aluminum pan is placed over each flame will there be any difference in the amount of soot deposited on the pan in the two cases? Why?

The flame at the first gas jet will give off:

a. More light than the flame at the second gas jet . . . . (+) a.
b. The same amount of light as the flame at the second gas jet . . . ( ) b.
c. Less light than the flame at the second jet . . . . ( ) c.

The soot deposited by the first gas jet will be:

d. More than that deposited by the second gas jet . . . . (+) d.
e. Less than that deposited by the second gas jet . . . . ( ) e.

Check the following statements which give the reason for the answer or answers you checked above.

f. Incomplete combustion leaves some uncombined carbon in the flame . (+) f.
g. The presence of nitrogen retards combustion . . . . ( ) g.
h. Particles of uncombined carbon glow when heated . . . . (+) h.
i. Combustion is more complete in the first flame . . . . ( ) i.
j. The amount of air mixed with the gas does not affect the amount of light produced by the burning gas . . . . ( ) j.
k. Some uncombined carbon in a flame is deposited on a cool surface placed in a flame . . . . (+) k.

In the above exercise, the statements which answer the problem are <u>a</u> and <u>d</u>. These statements are checked because they tell what would be likely to happen. Statements <u>f</u>, <u>h</u>, and <u>k</u> have also been checked because they are reasons which help to explain why <u>a</u> and <u>d</u> would happen. You will notice that statement <u>g</u> is a true statement but it does not give a reason for any of the right answers; hence it is not checked. The other statements are not true and are not checked. Do each exercise in this way.

(Samples from Hendricks *et al.*, 1934. By permission of the Cooperative Test Service, Inc.)

plan in order to find if it is the correct one. If it solves the problem, he scores a point; if it does not, he must discard it and seek another solution. Illustrations of this type of test are seen in (*a*) mathematical problems (Illus. 70 and Illus. 73), (*b*) the assembly of apparatus (Illus. 13), (*c*) pencil mazes (Illus. 54) in which a person can see the

ILLUS. 13. MINNESOTA MECHANICAL ASSEMBLY TEST MATERIALS

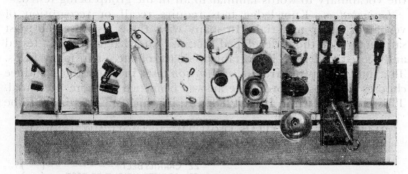

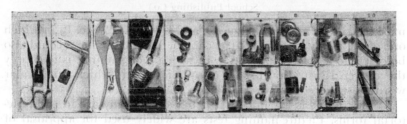

Top, Box A; Center, Box B; Bottom, Box C
(Paterson et al., 1930. By permission of the Marietta Apparatus Co.)

whole maze at once and must try to evolve a plan for finding a way through it, and (*d*) many verbal situations in which one must try out several hypotheses. The unit of measurement is a problem or a part of the problem to be solved. Sometimes the method of solution and the time used are also noted.

Reasoning is common in ordinary life, but reasoning ability is very difficult to measure on a quantitative basis, for different persons have different amounts of information to aid them in the solution of a problem. Some persons may know the solution before the problem is presented. In order to evaluate reasoning activities it is necessary to eliminate differences in relevant information. This elimination may be accomplished with fair success in verbal tests by limiting the vocabulary to words familiar to all in the group being tested.

Knowledge. Knowledge tests require recall or recognition of verbal or other materials. In many ways these tests are the most satisfactory of those developed, because knowledge is easily tested and scored and is an important predictor of success in many fields. The most structured are the *recognition* tests, in which the examinee chooses the most appropriate answer from two or more presented. This type is shown in Illus. 12, Sec. A, in which statements are to be

ILLUS. 14. LATHE ITEMS FROM THE DETROIT MECHANICAL
APTITUDES TEST FOR BOYS

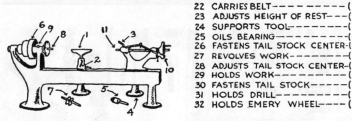

22 CARRIES BELT---- -----(   )
23 ADJUSTS HEIGHT OF REST---(   )
24 SUPPORTS TOOL--------(   )
25 OILS BEARING---------(   )
26 FASTENS TAIL STOCK CENTER-(   )
27 REVOLVES WORK--------(   )
28 ADJUSTS TAIL STOCK CENTER-(   )
29 HOLDS WORK----------(   )
30 FASTENS TAIL STOCK-----(   )
31 HOLDS DRILL---------(   )
32 HOLDS EMERY WHEEL----(   )

(Baker and Crockett, 1928. By permission of the authors and the Public
School Publishing Co.)

marked true or not marked at all, and by Illus. 12, Sec. B, in which one of the thirty answers is to be chosen. All of these items could also be cast into a *recall* type of test, in which the examinee is to supply the answer. Illustration 147 is a completion test in which a particular word must be recalled to complete a sentence.

Knowledge tests are not limited to words; many are in good pictorial forms. Picture-naming tests are widely used for appraisal of preschool and mechanical vocabularies. When knowledge of the use or the motion of parts of a machine is to be tested, picture tests are often superior to word tests. Illustration 14 presents a lathe, the parts of which are numbered. The subject is asked to indicate which parts perform certain functions. In almost all knowledge tests the unit of measurement is an item correctly answered, and the raw score is the total number of correct answers. Sometimes corrections for chance successes are applied as described in Chapter IV. Information items form the chief component of many achievement, intelligence, and aptitude tests.

Motivation (Goal Seeking)

Motivation includes all goal-seeking activities, which are usually grouped under needs, interests, and attitudes, or sentiments. No sharp lines are to be drawn between these three terms, but needs are often related to basic physiological processes, interests to specific personal goals, and attitudes or sentiments to broad generalized ideals for society. Principal needs—those essential to survival—are for food, air, light, warmth, sex, exercise, avoidance of pain, and sleep. These are always determined to some extent by inheritance, but a particular seeking activity also depends somewhat on the environment. Interest and attitudes seem to depend mainly upon cultural ideals: social, political, religious, vocational, artistic, and recreational. Strictly speaking there are no good measures of goal-seeking activities, but appraisals are made by time sampling, questionnaires, ratings, logs, interviews, case histories, and projective techniques.

For the evaluation of typical attitudes and interests, a large number of rating scales or inventories have been developed, some of which use self-ratings and some the ratings of others. Self-ratings are considered to be among the best ways of evaluating interests and attitudes of adults. Illustration 15, in which attitudes toward the church are to be appraised; and Illus. 16, in which a person expresses an artistic preference among designs, are self-rating tests. The unit of measurement is based upon a judgment of like, indifference, or dislike for a particular activity, or upon a choice between items. Raw scores show total likes or dislikes and also particular regions of interest.

Self-ratings are often considered to be invalid, owing to the fact that it is difficult for a person to evaluate his feelings accurately, and to the fact that he may purposely falsify his report in order to bring the results more into line with what is socially acceptable. Ratings are also affected by ambiguities in definitions, as when persons are asked to evaluate rather complex traits, such as tact or reasoning ability. Lastly, ratings are sometimes subject to halo effects, which occur when one general classification, such as attractive or unattractive, influences the rater's judgment on a large number of other traits of a more specific nature, for example, neatness, promptness, kindness, and intelligence. The refinement of ratings is discussed in Chapter XVI.

ILLUS. 15. ATTITUDE TOWARD THE CHURCH

Check every statement with which you fully agree:

1. I think the church is a divine institution, and it commands my highest loyalty and respect.
3. I feel the good done by the church is not worth the money and energy spent on it.
5. I believe that the church is losing ground as education advances.
7. The teaching of the church is altogether too superficial to be of interest to me.
9. I think the church has a most important influence in the development of moral habits and attitudes.
11. I regard the church as a harmful institution, breeding narrow mindedness, fanaticism, intolerance.
13. I believe in the ideals of my church, but I am tired of its denominationalism.
15. I'm not much against the church, but when I cannot agree with its leaders I stay away.
17. I believe that the church practices the Golden Rule fairly well and has a consequent good influence.
19. I feel the church is ridiculous, for it cannot give examples of what it preaches.
21. My church is the primary guiding influence in my life.
23. My attitude toward the church is one of neglect due to lack of interest.
25. I am sympathetic toward the church, but I am not active in its work.
27. I know too little about any church to express an opinion.
29. I am slightly prejudiced against the church and attend only on special occasions.
31. There is much wrong in my church, but I feel it is so important that it is my duty to help improve it.
33. I think the church is unreservedly stupid and futile.
35. I feel the church is petty, easily disturbed by matters of little importance.
37. I believe the church is non-scientific, depending for its influence upon fear of God and hell.
39. It seems absurd to me for a thinking man to be interested in the church.
41. I believe that anyone who will work in a modern church will appreciate its indispensable value.
43. My attitude toward the church is passive, with a slight tendency to disfavor it.
45. I have nothing but contempt for the church.

(Abbreviated from Thurstone and Chave, 1929, p. 23. By permission of
The University of Chicago Press.)

Integrative Traits

Integrative traits are ways in which energy is directed in working or playing, or in meeting problems or conflicts. One person may run away from a serious automobile accident; another may ignore it and continue what he is doing, no matter how foolish; another may imagine the situation is different from what it really is; another may explode into aimless screaming; while still another may take sensible steps to give first aid. All except the last of these ways of behaving, when carried to extremes, are typical of various abnormalities or insanities, and indicate poor integration.

A normal person must somehow reconcile various conflicting drives and use his skills to advance toward desirable goals. This process of controlling or channeling drives is best measured by observations and by *projective* tests. In projective tests the stimulus is purposely left vague, and the directions encourage one to indicate by word or movement whatever the stimulus suggests. One often shows his own deeper or unconscious wishes or fears, and the degree of inner conflict by associations and fantasies. Thus, in the Kent-Rosanoff Free Association Test (Illus. 17) a person is asked to respond to a stimulus word with the first word that occurs to him. His answer depends, not only on what words he knows, but also on his mood and his emotional reactions to situations represented by the words. Another test of this particular kind is the Rorschach Test (1921), in which one is asked to state all ideas that are suggested to him by ten ink blots as they are presented to him. Other tests use as stimuli objects, pictures, puppets, incomplete sentences, clay, paints, and other materials. The units of measurement are the number of various types of responses given. They are interpreted according to the degree to which they conform to patterns previously determined by tabulating results from various groups. These standards are at present complex qualitative descriptions rather than quantitative scales, but quantitative standardizations are being developed. This field of measurement is growing more rapidly than all others but is the most difficult to develop.

ILLUS. 16. SAMPLE OF THE ARTISTIC PREFERENCE TEST

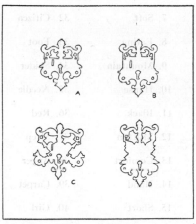

(McAdory, 1929, p. 6. By permission of the Bureau of Publications, Teachers College, Columbia University.)

There are, of course, no pure tests or ways of appraising a single aspect of behavior. Thus objective-type test scores are definitely influenced by one's attitude toward the tests and his emotional balance. Self-ratings are decidedly influenced by ability to discriminate accurately, and projective techniques always yield evidence of thinking efficiency as well as of motives and of integration. Tests are classified according to the activities which seem most often represented by the scores.

ILLUS. 17. THE KENT-ROSANOFF FREE ASSOCIATION WORDS

1. Table	26. Wish	51. Stem	76. Bitter
2. Dark	27. River	52. Lamp	77. Hammer
3. Music	28. White	53. Dream	78. Thirsty
4. Sickness	29. Beautiful	54. Yellow	79. City
5. Man	30. Window	55. Bread	80. Square
6. Deep	31. Rough	56. Justice	81. Butter
7. Soft	32. Citizen	57. Boy	82. Doctor
8. Eating	33. Foot	58. Light	83. Loud
9. Mountain	34. Spider	59. Health	84. Thief
10. House	35. Needle	60. Bible	85. Lion
11. Black	36. Red	61. Memory	86. Joy
12. Mutton	37. Sleep	62. Sheep	87. Bed
13. Comfort	38. Anger	63. Bath	88. Heavy
14. Hand	39. Carpet	64. Cottage	89. Tobacco
15. Short	40. Girl	65. Swift	90. Baby
16. Fruit	41. High	66. Blue	91. Moon
17. Butterfly	42. Working	67. Hungry	92. Scissors
18. Smooth	43. Sour	68. Priest	93. Quiet
19. Command	44. Earth	69. Ocean	94. Green
20. Chair	45. Trouble	70. Head	95. Salt
21. Sweet	46. Soldier	71. Stove	96. Street
22. Whistle	47. Cabbage	72. Long	97. King
23. Woman	48. Hard	73. Religion	98. Cheese
24. Cold	49. Eagle	74. Whiskey	99. Blossom
25. Slow	50. Stomach	75. Child	100. Afraid

(Rosanoff, 1920.   By permission of John Wiley and Sons, Inc., New York.)

INCLUSIVE TECHNIQUES

Other techniques which yield valuable estimates of many aspects of a person are time sampling, logs, interviews, and case histories.

Time Sampling

Observations of uncontrolled situations are generally made by what is known as the time-sampling method. Observers take samples of performance at regular intervals during a day or over longer periods of time. The results show the frequency with which types of behavior patterns appear in certain situations. One disadvantage of this method is the difficulty of getting observers to agree upon reports of what they have seen. Even when the observers have had considerable training, marked discrepancies sometimes appear in their reports. When the reports show that the observers do agree, it may be that in some instances they have eliminated the controversial data upon which they could not agree. Such reports are not complete and may fail to show true relationships. This same difficulty is presented in all kinds of observation, but it seems to be more serious in time sampling, with the preconceived ideas of the observer serving to direct the attention toward certain types of behavior. In spite of these difficulties, Jersild and Meigs (1939) have summarized studies where the results are consistent and fairly complete. The unit of measurement is usually the noticed type of behavior, recorded as operating at one of the regular periods of sampling. The raw score is the number and duration of the periods of the activities under consideration (Chapter XXIV).

Logs

Another method of recording behavior is by use of a log. This differs from direct observation in that the observer records pertinent outstanding events over a considerable period, for example, an hour or a whole day. In many cases outstanding events are significant of behavior, and for certain purposes logs are valuable. Teachers' and camp counselors' logs are often used to check results of tests and ratings.

One disadvantage of this method is that it is dependent upon emotional and subjective variables in the observer. If the observer is feeling particularly well and happy, he will probably not record as many annoying episodes as when he is suffering from a severe headache. Unless the log is recorded regularly and with considerable attention given to the methods of recording, it is extremely difficult to summarize. In many instances logs have proved to be so vague as to be useless for comparing persons or groups.

Interviews

Because interviewing represents an exceedingly adaptable method of securing data, it is more useful than some of the other methods. It allows the interviewer to ask questions in such a way as to secure the confidence of the person who is being interviewed. Confidence is difficult to obtain by means of written or oral tests when individuals are on guard and reluctant to show exactly what they can do or what they are thinking. With a well-defined outline for interviewing, many aspects of behavior can be systematically covered and a fair appraisal made in a short time.

Interviews, however, may in addition to appraising a person, give information and suggestions. It is often difficult to avoid suggesting, by leading questions, the answers which one wishes to get. Interviews have another disadvantage—that of being relatively unstandardized. The results are difficult to handle numerically unless a standard rating technique is used. Interviews are used for nearly all types of employment, counseling, clinical, and psychoanalytical appraisals.

Case Histories and Biographies

Case histories and biographies are among the most useful kinds of records used in evaluating development over a long period. A careful case history will include: a record of family history, physical development, health, tests of progress in intellectual pursuits, social and economic adjustments, and emotional patterns of development. It will try to show how much these aspects are dependent upon environment and how they are related to one another. It is on the basis of careful case histories and tests that the most accurate predictions can be made.

One disadvantage of the case-history method is the great difficulty of getting a true record of events which occurred several years previously. Case histories usually include rather vague memories of a person, his friends, parents, and teachers, which have been influenced by the forgetting and improvising processes. Case histories of the same person made up by two investigators sometimes differ in important respects. The best case histories are those which have been started at an early age and thereafter continued by additions at regular periods.

TYPES OF TESTS

Formal and Informal Tests

There are three main differences between an informal test and a formal or standardized test. (1) The formal test has more rigidly standardized directions for administration and scoring which come from the revision of many preliminary trials. (2) The context of a formal test has been more thoroughly scrutinized to include only important facts and skills, and to eliminate ambiguities and chance factors. (3) The formal test has usually been more widely applied, so that norms are available for many persons in various age, grade, or occupational groups.

While these differences are all in favor of the formal test, still an informal test is often preferred because it can be constructed to fit the needs of a particular situation more aptly. Such a situation occurs so frequently in industry and in Progressive schools that employment specialists and teachers in these organizations should be prepared to construct their own tests. Chapter IV deals with the construction of test items.

Achievement, Aptitude, and Psychological Tests

Mental tests may be classified into three groups according to their chief uses: (a) to measure present ability—achievement tests; (b) to predict success—aptitude tests; (c) to diagnose behavior—tests of psychological processes.

Achievement Tests. Achievement tests are designed to measure skills and information which have been learned, either in particular courses of training or from experience elsewhere. There are widely used tests for nearly all school subjects at various grade levels (Chapter VII). Test items for achievement tests are generally selected from those which have been used by teachers as indications of success in a course of instruction. For example, if a large group of competent teachers agree that the data for a test item have been taught in a course on American history, then that item is considered relevant for a test of this subject. The first criterion of exclusion or inclusion then is the agreement of competent judges on its relevancy.

A group of Progressive educators has set up ideals which are much more inclusive than the mastery of certain subject matter. A typical list of these ideals is given by Raths (1938, p. 90) who summarized the work of the evaluation staff of the Commission on the Relation of School and College, of the Progressive Education Association, as follows:

1. Improved habits and abilities with relation to reflective thinking
2. Wider and richer interests
3. An increasing consistency in important attitudes
4. Increasing facilities to adjust socially
5. Developing creativeness
6. Improved study skills and work habits
7. An increasing stock of vital information
8. A wider and better appreciation of literature, the arts, and music
9. A developing sensitivity to socially significant problems
10. A functional philosophy of life

The construction of precise instruments to measure progress toward these ten objectives is a gigantic task, but operational definitions have been provided for most of these ideals and marked progress is recorded in various chapters in Part III.

Aptitude Tests.   A number of tests have been called aptitude tests by their authors. Inspection of these shows that they demand similar skills and information as achievement and psychological tests. Often the same items are found in all three types. Although there is no agreement among psychologists on one technical definition of the word *aptitude,* the following three are fairly common:

Aptitude tests are any tests which happen to predict later success to some degree. It must be demonstrated that high standing on the test will indicate great success after some specialized training. This point of view is voiced by Bingham (1937) and by other authors.

According to another definition aptitude tests are those measures of achievement which will predict some future development, but which will not themselves increase or change significantly with any further development. This definition is used by Paterson and Darley (1936), who offer the Minnesota Clerical Test (Illus. 8). This type of definition generally implies that all persons tested have, through previous maturation and experience, reached fairly high levels of proficiency in the skills tested. Hence, those with high scores have demonstrated their ability to develop in work of a similar nature.

The third type of aptitude indicator is not a single score, but a series of scores arranged in a curve of individual development. This indicator is seldom used, for it is difficult to secure records for a number of persons, which are comparable in amounts of practice and motivation. For the most careful predictions, developmental curves would certainly be much better than one test score. Because of this, there is a strong emphasis in mental measurements today upon securing curves of long-time development.

When a test is to be used to predict success in an occupational or professional school, it should, according to one theory, include items which measure all the factors which contribute to success and give these items about the same weight in the test score that they have in producing success. It has, however, been found difficult to decide which factors are important in the development of occupational successes. In order to construct an aptitude test which will give good prediction, a program must be followed which will

1. Select a fairly large variety of items which seem to have some predictive value. The selection of items is usually aided by a careful analysis of the skills of those experienced in an occupation.
2. Apply these tests to a large number of persons who are just beginning training for an occupation or profession.
3. At yearly periods after training has been finished, secure ratings or other indications of occupational success.
4. Compare the ratings of success with the various test scores.
5. Combine the test scores to give the best prediction of success. Often a number of the original tests are eliminated before a final combination of tests for an aptitude scale is made.

This procedure has been followed with good results in certain industrial and school situations.

Psychological Tests. These tests are designed to appraise traits which have significance in a psychological analysis. They include tests of intelligence, tests of mental abilities, such as perception, reasoning, and learning, and tests of motivation and integration, such as interest, attitudes, and patterns of adjustment.

Altitude, Speed, and Breadth Tests

The three types of tests just described may be reclassified according to altitude, speed, and breadth.

Altitude Tests. Altitude tests, sometimes called *power* tests, allow a liberal amount of time so that all persons tested will attempt nearly all the items which they could possibly pass. The scores of an altitude test yield an indicator of the highest level which a person achieves. The best altitude tests are constructed from carefully scaled items which increase in complexity as the test progresses.

Speed Tests. Speed tests, which are also called *rate* tests, are of two kinds. One, called a time-limit test, is composed of items which are all of similar difficulty, as in the name-comparison test (Illus. 8), and the aiming test (Illus. 4). A time limit is used which is so short that none of the group can finish the test. The second, called a work-limit test, requires a standard series of operations, and the score is the time needed to complete the operations at a given level of excellence.

This is illustrated by an assembly or a form-board test where materials are to be put together to form a pattern (Illus. 45 through Illus. 50).

Breadth Tests. Breadth tests are designed to measure one's range or variety of skills or information. Great speed is not required, and complexity is fairly constant. A good illustration of this type is the Cooperative Test of Current Events, which samples a person's knowledge of recent developments in five fields: science, economics, foreign affairs, arts, and recreation.

Many tests are combinations of altitude, rate, and breadth items; but mixed tests are not desirable, for they do not allow clear interpretation of results. For instance, when an altitude test is given with rather short time limits, two persons may receive the same score for different reasons. One may be a fast yet superficial worker who makes his maximum score during the time allowed. Another person may have greater ability, but work so cautiously that he is just getting warmed up when time is called. By similar logic items which are carefully graded for complexity of thought for an altitude test should not be mixed with those which are simply rare, although rare items may be appropriate in a breadth test. Likewise, the breadth items should not be given with short time limits, since the main point of a breadth test is to enumerate the various facts which a person knows. Frequently one finds interesting temperament or motivation indices in the relative speed at which persons work, so that a record of this factor in any kind of test is often desirable.

The usual method of establishing time limits involves trying out items upon typical groups of persons. This method is employed with all well-standardized tests. Altitude tests have been found to give adequate samples of ability if enough time is given to allow approximately 90 per cent of the group to attempt every item. This is generally the case when the tests depend to a large degree upon information; when the items have been arranged in order of difficulty; and when the range of difficulty is such that at least 5 per cent of the group can succeed on the hardest items and 5 per cent will fail on the easiest items.

Individual and Group Tests

Both individual and group tests are available for many types of behavior. Individual testing situations are usually better controlled than group situations, and are more useful in the following situations:

1. When oral responses are needed, such as in reading aloud and answering questions.

2. When subjects do not readily follow directions or cooperate. (This would generally be true of persons below eight years of age, and of defective and maladjusted persons.)
3. When forms or instruments, such as form boards, puzzles, and machine assembly, are to be manipulated.
4. When it is desirable to evaluate the subject's adjustment to the test situation, such as his persistence, cautiousness, emotional episodes of anger or fear, teasing, balking, or nervous habits.
5. Whenever it is desirable and possible to evaluate the subject's methods of work, such as the use of random movements, methodical comparisons, and reasoning.

Group tests are more useful than individual tests:
1. When it is desirable to avoid close personal relations with an examiner.
2. When it is desirable to compare the effects of group stimulation with the effects of isolation.
3. When the subjects can and will cooperate well.
4. When the results of group tests have proved to be accurate enough to be useful in a particular situation. (Many group tests of written work seem to be as effective as individual tests above the 8-year level.)
5. When economy of time and effort is important.

STUDY GUIDE QUESTIONS

1. What are the relative advantages of measures which strive to evaluate one unitary trait as compared with measures of general mental ability?
2. How are the five major categories of traits distinguished from one another?
3. What are the usual units of measurement for aiming, steadiness, and dexterity tests?
4. What is essential activity in all perceptual tests?
5. How are immediate memory-span tests scored?
6. Why are direct measures of learning very rare?
7. What are the main essentials of a good reasoning test?
8. Why are knowledge tests the best developed at present?
9. What are the advantages and disadvantages of self-ratings?
10. What is the procedure in projective techniques?
11. What differences are there between achievement and aptitude tests?
12. Distinguish altitude, speed, and breadth tests.
13. What are the relative advantages of individual and group tests?

CHAPTER III

CHARACTERISTICS OF A GOOD INSTRUMENT

~~~~~~

Few persons will undertake to prepare a well-standardized test, but many wish to know the theoretical differences between satisfactory and unsatisfactory tests, and what can be considered sound evidence of these differences. This chapter [1] gives certain logical and statistical ways of defining and expressing the characteristics of a satisfactory measuring instrument. Three characteristics are commonly attributed to such tests: practical aspects, reliability, and uniqueness.

PRACTICAL ASPECTS

For practical purposes a good testing instrument requires minimum time, cost, and effort in its administration, scoring, and interpretation. It is clear that, as the testing situation varies, the relative importance of these aspects will change. Moreover a good testing instrument will allow a good sampling of the abilities of a person without disturbing or embarrassing him, unless, as is sometimes the case, the test is designed to appraise one's behavior in a stress situation. In order to avoid coaching but to provide for growth studies, two or more equivalent forms should be available. The practical requirements of a satisfactory test include the following:

    a. Optimum difficulty of items

    b. Scoring

---

[1] The last half of this chapter beginning with page 50 is difficult to understand without a fair background of elementary statistics, such as is found in Chapters XII and XIII.

    1. Objective-type tests
    2. Efficient scoring devices
  c. Adequate interpretation
    1. Adequate and easily understood norms to use in comparing a person with others of his own age, sex, and status
    2. Validity: prediction of success
  d. Ease of administration
    1. Short time-allowance
    2. Little or no supervision, except for recorded observations
    3. Simple, clear directions
    4. Minimum of materials
    5. Two or more equivalent forms
    6. Situations of interest to the examinee

Some of these requirements conflict with the others. For instance, great economy of time given to administration usually reduces the significance of the results. Since the administrative aspects are dealt with in many other places in this book, only the first five aspects will be discussed here.

Optimum Difficulty of Items

Difficulty of an item for a given group is usually determined by the percentage of persons in the group who succeed on that item. A group of items is considered to have only one level of difficulty when all of the items are passed by about the same proportion of a given group of persons. In test construction the levels of difficulty that shall be included always constitute a problem. If one desires to measure each individual in a group with great accuracy, then items from all levels of difficulty must be included in the test in sufficient numbers to avoid chance effects. However, if one desires merely to divide a group of persons into a small number of divisions, then only those items are needed which will indicate the division boundaries. The simplest situation is one in which two persons are to be placed— one in the upper and the other in the lower half. Since the items failed or passed by both persons would not serve to distinguish between them, the optimum difficulty would be represented by those items which one person passed and the other failed. A more complex situation would be one in which a large group is to be separated into an upper and a lower half. In this case the only items needed are those which most clearly differentiate among the persons of medium ability. Such items would be neither the easiest, for they would distinguish only among the least able persons, nor the hardest, for they would discriminate only among the most able. The items passed by 50 per cent of the group would most adequately separate the group into halves. Where test items have been applied to single-age groups in particular environments, it has been possible to construct scales with definite degrees of difficulty with considerable accuracy.

Scoring

A good test is so designed as to make its scoring as simple as possible. For many tests of mental ability, coordination, and preference, scoring can be made automatic. For the more variable projective techniques, however, the judgment of the scorer is very important. With the latter, scoring can be made more accurate and uniform by training the scorers in precise concepts, operational definitions, and samples.

Objective-type Tests. This term refers only to tests that can be objectively scored after they have been administered. If all persons who score a test arrive at exactly the same score, the procedure has been *objective*. Multiple-choice and completion-type items are often called objective-type tests, because the scoring is done by using a predetermined key. However, there is no guarantee that the key represents widespread agreement of competent judges. Many tests contain ambiguous and controversial items which reflect a subjective bias of the author. If the scorers must use their own judgment in determining the significance of an answer, and if they disagree because of differences in standards, then the scoring is considered somewhat subjective. Objectivity in scoring is, of course, highly desirable, for it is only by attaining high objectivity that wide standardization and careful analysis of items are possible.

Efficient Scoring Devices. The design of an item determines both speed and accuracy in scoring the answer. Ordinarily, the two processes which must be completed to obtain a test score are: checking the answers with a key and counting the correct answers to get the total. Errors and omissions must also be counted if the total score is to be corrected for chance successes.

In essay- or completion-type lists the key consists of a list of correct answers which must be compared with those the subject has written. There are no mechanical short cuts to scoring such tests, but scoring can be speeded up a little in completion-type tests by having all answers placed in a column where they can be easily compared with a key.

For true-false, multiple-choice, or matching tests three scoring devices are used: stencils, automatic devices, and machine scorers. Each results in a great saving of time and in increased accuracy, especially when large numbers of tests are to be scored. No simple rule can be laid down for effecting economies in scoring, for there are at least three variables: cost of clerical labor, cost of devising and printing automatic scoring keys, and cost of operating the machine.

Stencil scoring. In scoring true-false and multiple-choice items a printed stencil or scoring key is sometimes placed over or beside the test answers. When this has been done a clerk can quickly see which answers are correct. When a large number of tests must be scored, the examinee may be required to indicate his answers on a separate answer sheet. The marked answer sheets are then run through a machine which prints the correct answers with colored ink near the subject's answers, which can then be rapidly checked.

Automatic scoring devices. One of the most difficult steps in stencil scoring—checking answers against a key—is eliminated by automatic scoring. For example, a fairly large number of tests are printed in such a way that the subject's mark on the test will indicate the correctness of his answer on a key, which is placed where the examinee cannot see it while taking the test.

Many tests have a key composed of small squares printed on the back of the answer sheet or on a sheet just beneath the answer sheet. The key is concealed during the test, and revealed for scoring by breaking the glued edges apart. A thin coating of carbon is so placed that when the subject makes an X with an ordinary pencil to indicate his choice, the X is impressed on the key sheet. To find the number of correct answers, one simply counts the squares on the key sheet which have X's in them.

Toops (1937) used a sharp-pointed stylus or large pin for the automatic scoring of the Ohio State University College Entrance Examination. Test booklets and answer sheets are printed separately. The answer sheets contain rows of numbered squares. A key sheet, just beneath the answer sheet, has a square printed under each correct answer. The person being tested makes a pinhole in the square which corresponds to his choice, and a pinhole is simultaneously made in the key sheet. Several key sheets can be used at once when duplicate records are desired. A number of authors have adopted this method.

Although these automatic scoring devices do not furnish a total score they do allow the scores to be counted directly from the marks made on a key by the person who takes the test. Accuracy and speed of scoring are thus greatly increased.

To promote student learning by immediately revealing whether test questions have been answered correctly, Troyer and Angell (1950) published a series of answer sheets. These can be used for any tests that are composed to correspond to a prearranged key. Two sets of keys are available for (*a*) 300 2-choice items to a page, or (*b*) 150 4-

choice or 5-choice items to a page, or (*c*) 210 2-choice and multiple-choice items to a page. Since a number of studies have shown that certain kinds of rote learning take place more quickly when correct answers are provided, this type of answer sheet should receive serious consideration. It is more economical and simpler than the several mechanical devices that have been marketed to indicate immediately the correctness of an answer.

Machine scoring. The International Business Machines (IBM) Scorer (1938) uses carefully printed sheets, such as that shown in Illus. 18, upon which the person marks all his answers with a special pencil. As can be seen, the sheet is printed with small parallel lines

ILLUS. 18. MECHANICALLY SCORED ANSWER SHEET

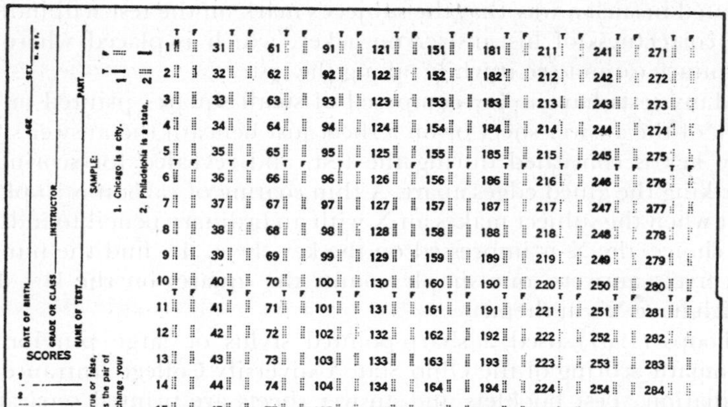

(Courtesy of the International Business Machines Corporation.)

showing where the pencil marks should be placed in indicating true items, false items, or multiple choices. To score this sheet, it is inserted in the machine, a lever is moved, and the total score is read from a dial. The scoring is accomplished by electrical contacts with the pencil marks. Each sheet can be scored for ten separate divisions, as well as for the total. Corrections for guessing can be obtained by setting a dial on the machine. By this method three hundred true-false items can be scored simultaneously. The sheets can be run through the machine as quickly as the operator can insert them and write down the scores. The operator needs little special training beyond that of a clerical worker. Another device tabulates the number of times each item is correctly answered.

The International Business Machines Corporation has also developed a method of marking answers or ratings directly on a stiff $3\frac{1}{4}$- by $7\frac{1}{4}$-inch card. The marks are punched in the card by a machine, and can be used for immediate tabulation and item analysis.

Adequate Interpretation

It is often much easier to administer and score a test than it is to interpret the results. There are three usual means of interpretations, namely, a person's stand in a group is indicated, or his probable chance of success in a particular situation is predicted, or some aspects of his personality can be inferred from the pattern of scores.

Place in a Group. One's place in a group is usually shown by a centile, which is a number from 0 to 100 which indicates the proportion of a group which a person surpasses. Other indicators are standard scores, T-scores, and variations of these, which are explained in Chapter XII. For growing persons mental age (MA), intelligence quotient (IQ), and educational age (EA) are used to show level or rate of growth (Chapter VI). One has a mental age of 10 if his score on a mental test is the same as that of the average ten-year-old. Intelligence quotient is defined in several different ways, but usually it is one's mental age divided by his chronological age, with the quotient multiplied by 100 (to avoid decimal points). Roughly it shows one's rate of growth. For instance, an IQ of 100 means that one is growing at the same rate as the average person; an IQ of 150 means that one is accelerated 50 per cent; and an IQ of 70 indicates 30 per cent below normal. Educational age and educational quotient are based on school achievement tests rather than on general mental tests. One's mental age and educational age often show differences which need to be investigated to determine why one is doing better or worse than might be expected.

Letters (usually A, B, C, D, and E) are used a great deal in schools to indicate the various places, or the steps of progress that the members of a group may take in a subject, or in industriousness, or a combination of these. Unless letters used as grades are clearly defined, however, they are difficult to interpret. In large groups where there is likely to be a wide distribution of ability, letter grades are often given arbitrary values. For instance one college has determined that the distribution of grades for freshmen and sophomores shall be: A, 15 per cent; B, 30 per cent; C, 40 per cent; D, 10 per cent; E, 5 per cent. Grades for large classes are expected to conform fairly well to these proportions.

Test norms show where one's place is in a group to which one belongs or wants to join. A *norm* is a set of figures which show the distribution of scores of a group. Age groups are essential to the study of growth or senescence. The best norms use limited age groups —1 or 2 months for small children, and 6 or more months for adolescents and adults. (See Chapters V and VI.) Sex groups are studied when the two sexes show different patterns of responses. Separate norms for the sexes are now given in many achievement and personality measures. Occupational group norms are often used for classification or employment tests, and school- or college-grade norms are used for achievement tests.

This variety of group norms is useful but somewhat confusing when the same person is given test scores and centiles for different groups. For example, one veteran's record showed that he was in the 70th centile of a large adult group on the Army General Classification Test, in the 40th centile of a group of freshmen engineers on an engineering aptitude test, and in the 90th centile of a group of high school boys on the Kuder Preference for Mechanical Work Test. Illustration 21 (page 58) shows the usual relation between groups of adults in frequency distributions of language- and number-ability tests. Scores are marked at the base of the chart, and the number of persons making each score is shown by the height of the vertical column above the score. It appears that the middle of the adult group is near the lower end of the distribution of scores of high school graduates, and the middle of the high school graduates group is near the lower end of the distribution of scores of the college graduates. Other sections of each group can be similarly related, as inspection of the chart shows. Charts of this kind are needed but are not available for many types of tests and preferences.

Validity: Prediction of Success. In order to give an indication of one's probable chances of success in a given course of study or occupation, the author of the test must furnish evidence that, in similar situations, the test scores were related to success to a certain degree.

The most common evidence is a correlation coefficient, which is some number between —1.00 and +1.00. Plus one indicates a perfect prediction, 0 a chance relationship, and —1 a perfect negative relation. Numbers less than 1.00 indicate less than perfect correlation. (Chapter XIII describes how the numbers are calculated.) Success in school subjects can usually be predicted from the most appropriate tests by correlations as high as .50 to .75. Success in skilled trades and clerical work is not quite as well predicted, but it can be predicted much better than chance. Correlations such as these are generally called *validity coefficients*. A correlation coefficient is *not* a percentage, and it does not show any causal relation between patterns of behavior. It simply indicates coincidence of position in a group when persons in the group are placed by two different appraisals. The size of a coefficient has the following rough significance when the group is large—300 or more. For smaller groups the correlations are in general less significant (Illus. 142).

.95 to 1.00   The coincidence is nearly perfect. One type of success can be predicted from the other very well. A reliable test will predict a retest to this extent.

.75 to .95   Good individual predictions can be made for most of the group, but there will be some divergence.

.50 to .75   These coefficients are not high enough to make good individual predictions, because many who are below average on one test will be above average on the other. The extremes of the group are predicted fairly well. Coefficients are useful for indicating group trends.

.25 to .50   These coefficients are too low for individual use, but they roughly indicate group trends, and can be used to supplement other kinds of predictions.

0 to .25   These coefficients are often not significantly different from zero.

It is often inferred that a test has high validity because it looks as though it should. Validity of this type is called *face validity*. On this topic Guilford (1946, p. 437) wrote:

Even sophisticated judgment often goes astray on decisions as to what a test measures. A test designed to measure common-sense judgment when factor analyzed turns out to be a test of mechanical experience. A test designed as a reasoning test is found to be one of numerical facility, when analyzed. A test of pilot interest proves to have some variance, indeed, in that factor, but it is stronger in variance for the verbal factor. A test designed to test the ability to maintain orientation in space turns out to be primarily a measure of perceptual speed. This list could be extended. The moral of it is that in test construction and in job analysis, things are not always what they seem. This is primarily because our categories of aptitudes and traits have been faulty. Empirically determined factors, on the other hand, when sufficiently well defined, seem to be stable and dependable, and they are amenable to direct observation once they have been brought to light. This discussion does not necessarily argue against the use of "face validity" in tests. Face validity makes tests more palatable to the public. But face validity may have nothing whatever to do with actual validity, and it should be remembered that the problem of actual validity is never solved just because a test has face validity.

RELIABILITY

The characteristic which makes a test yield the same results when applied a number of times is called *reliability*. Reliability is highly desirable, for prediction is impossible or very difficult if, through practice or chance, a person gets a radically different score on a repetition of the same test. For two trials of the same test on a large group, reliability is best indicated by a correlation coefficient. When the test cannot be repeated, there are a number of other methods that can be used fairly successfully as substitutes. Four coefficients are commonly used: retest reliability, split-half reliability, equivalent-form reliability, and Kuder-Richardson estimates (Chapter X). Since these procedures sometimes give different results, they should not be confused. In all cases a high coefficient is considered an indication of small random variations, and a low coefficient indicates either random or systematic variations or both.

Retest reliability is secured by giving a group the same test twice within a few days. When it is difficult to secure two tests of the same group, a split-half reliability may be secured by correlating scores on one half of a test with scores on the other half. Often the scores for odd-numbered items are correlated with the scores for even-numbered items. Correlations from the halves of a test, given on the same day, are frequently from .05 to .10 points higher than correlations from the same halves given a few days apart. The differences are due in part to changes in attitudes or conditions of the persons tested.

The correlation between halves of a test indicates only the variations between the halves. Since the test is to be used as a whole, it is desirable to know the probable reliability of the test as a whole. This can be calculated from the Brown-Spearman (Spearman, 1910) formula for prophesying the probable effect of lengthening a test. The self-correlation of two tests which are made n times as long as they were originally, where r_{11} is the known correlation of the two originals, would be:

$$r_{nn} = \frac{nr_{11}}{1 + (n - 1)r_{11}}$$

For example, if the two halves of a test correlate .60 with each other, the whole test would probably correlate .75 with another test of similar length and design, that is:

$$r_{nn} = \frac{2 \times .60}{1 + (1 \times .60)} = \frac{1.20}{1.60} = .75$$

This formula may be used to find how long a test must be made to achieve a particular self-correlation. Of course, the formula would not apply if, by lengthening a test, one introduced new factors, such as fatigue, loss of interest, new sorts of items, or practice on the part of individuals.

The equivalent-form reliability coefficient is secured by correlating two forms of a test that are intended to sample the same ability. Equivalent-form reliabilities are usually from .05 to .10 points smaller than retest reliabilities, for equivalent forms have different specific items, while a retest uses the items of the original test. Since retest reliabilities are also sometimes inflated when previous performances are specifically remembered, equivalent-form reliabilities are preferred for test appraisal.

Reliabilities are also indicated by the Standard Error of Estimate of a score based on equivalent-form correlations. Some authors prefer this indicator because it gives immediate knowledge of the probable range of a score (Chapter XIII).

UNIQUENESS

The most difficult requirement for satisfactory interpretation is that characteristic of a test which makes a given score always represent the same pattern of behavior. Many tests include items which sample different kinds of behavior. For instance, if a test includes number, language, and spatial items, two persons may earn the same score, but for different reasons. One may do well in language but poorly in mathematics, and the other may have just the opposite skill.

Factorial Analysis

As tests have become more widely used and scrutinized, the demands for unequivocal scores have become more numerous. In addition to subjective analyses to determine the elements of a test, the statistical technique called factorial analysis has gained considerable usage. The several types of factorial analysis have given somewhat different results, but there is also much agreement among them. Each seeks to analyze the factors, usually the smallest number of factors, which explain the variations of scores of a group of persons on a battery of tests. From factorial analyses the amount of variation due to each factor may be estimated for each test. This is called *factor loading* of a test. The factorial composition of a test is indicated by its pattern of factor loadings. Certain tests show large loadings of several factors. These are called *impure* or *heterogeneous* tests, for they do not allow a clear interpretation of results. Other tests show large loadings of only one factor and small or zero loadings of all other factors. These are called *pure* or *homogeneous* tests, and are considered to have high factorial validity. They are more desirable because they yield clear interpretations and lend themselves to careful analyses better than the less pure test. Chapter XIV illustrates the use of factorial analysis in the selection of test items.

Sampling

A considerable number of technical studies of homogeneity of tests are in progress (Chapter XIV), but a simple check of the validity of a test may be applied when one wishes to find out how well two samples represent a large block of test items. This check is important since mental tests must usually of necessity be short. Modern tests are often made by selecting about forty items from among several hundred. To check the validity of two short tests which have been made up of items chosen from a large number, one must apply both to a fairly large group of persons who are thought to differ widely in their knowledge of the information tested. Next, the scores from the two forms must be correlated. When correlations are low, one must conclude that some factors influence the scores on one test, but do not influence the scores on the other in the same way. This correlation procedure is necessary to eliminate poor samples, but it still does not guarantee that good samples of the master list have been secured, for factors within the master list may correlate highly with other factors not included in it. Such extraneous items or factors may creep in during the construction or administration of various test forms. It is further necessary to prove that nothing but the factor one desires to measure is represented by each test score. It is impossible to prove this with a simple correlation technique, *for a correlation coefficient never shows mental processes but simply coincidence in relative position*. For more adequate proof, one must use direct observation to appraise the behavior represented by the test scores.

As stated on page 50 reliability is the characteristic which makes a test yield the same results when applied a number of times. This identity of results is important because a test cannot be quantitatively valid unless it is reliable. Its validity coefficient cannot be greater than its reliability coefficient. Several methods of computing reliability are described below.

Item Analysis

One characteristic of a test which is evidence of reliability is *internal consistency*. A test is considered to have high internal consistency when each item or subtest of a battery is found to arrange a tested group of persons in the same order of excellence as that indicated by the total score. This characteristic is always a valuable one for tests that are constructed to appraise *one* independent factor. Of the various methods of evaluating internal consistency, two that are widely used will be described—the *split-group* method and the *correlation* method.

The *split-group method* first divides a large group of persons into subgroups, usually thirds or fourths, on the basis of their total scores on a test made up of many items. Then the percentages of persons in the highest and the lowest thirds who pass each item are found (Illus. 19). If on an item the lowest third does as well as or better

ILLUS. 19. EVALUATION OF TRUE-FALSE ITEMS

Per Cents Passing, and Correlations

	ITEM						
	A	B	C	D	E	F	G
Highest third	95%	57%	96%	65%	33%	95%	85%
Middle third	65	54	94	67	54	92	54
Lowest third	50	59	97	63	68	64	56
Correlation with total score	.74	.14	.07	− .06	− .32	.30	.32

than the highest third, one must infer that the item and the total test do not measure the same processes. If all of the highest in the group pass the item, and all of the lowest fail it, then the item divides the group into classes much as the whole test divides the group.

This split-group method is illustrated by Anderson's (1935) report on an analysis of a 222-item examination in educational psychology. On the basis of discrimination between the lowest, middle, and highest thirds, 86 items were classified as good, 83 as poor, and 53 as intermediate. The scores of each student on good and poor items were calculated. The means of the good and the poor items were nearly the same—50.3 and 55.3—but the scores on the total 222 items correlated with the scores on the 86 good items .95, and with the 83 poor items .45. The correlations of final grade in the course with the good items was .90, with the poor .22, and with the total score .89. The split-half reliability for the total examination was .864, for the good items .832, and for the poor items .06.

These figures show that the split-group evaluation allowed a selection of approximately one third of the total items, which gave as good discrimination as the whole examination, and which predicted final grades in the course a trifle better than did the whole examination. It was further shown that the total items do not correlate quite so well with high school rank and scores on the Iowa English Examination as do the good items alone. The study might well be followed up by further work to show the smallest number of good items which would be needed to allow satisfactory discrimination of this group of students and of other similar groups.

Another illustration of the use of this method is seen in the work of Terman, et al. (1917), (Illus. 38). Here the percentages of high, low, and medium IQ groups who passed each item are indicated. Since the chronological age (CA) was nearly constant for each group, the IQ in this case represents the total score of the test. Nearly all the items show large differences between the lowest and the middle group. The differences between the middle and the highest groups are usually smaller, owing to the fact that the items were chosen so that the middle group would have more than 50 per cent correct. Items which did not show as large discriminations were omitted from the Stanford Revisions of the Binet Test.

The *correlation method,* which is preferred since it seems to involve less work, correlates the scores made on each item with the scores from the whole test, or with some other desired criteria. If such a correlation is high and positive, it is likely that the item differentiates between persons in the same manner that the whole test does. If the correlation is low or negative, success on the item is likely to be determined either by chance or by other factors than those which affect the test as a whole. Illustration 19 shows the results of applying both split-group and correlation methods.

Item A is passed by 95 per cent of the highest third, 65 per cent of the middle third, and 50 per cent of the lowest third, and its correlation with the total is .74. This item is considered good in the sense that it results in nearly the same classification of persons as the whole test. A test composed only of such items is said to have high *internal consistency.*

Item B, a true-false item, which is usually passed with approximately chance success by all thirds, with a correlation so low that it indicates a nearly random relationship, is shown by these figures to be too difficult for this group of persons.

Item C is usually passed by almost all of each third and its correlation is nearly zero. Clearly it is too easy to affect the relative standing of persons in this group.

Items D and E both indicate ambiguity. The figures for Item D show that all thirds of the group had the same success and that their scores are considerably above chance. There is a small negative correlation with the total. Item E is passed with less than chance success by the highest third. The middle and lowest thirds succeed much better on this item. The correlation with the total is —.32. The most probable explanation of the results on Items D and E is either (1) that the persons in the highest and lowest thirds interpreted the items differently, or (2) that the item measures a skill which is negatively related to the skills measured by the total scores. Both Items D and E are of doubtful value in this test.

Items F and G exhibit partial success in classifying the persons tested. Item F distinguishes between the lowest and the middle third, but not between the middle and the highest third. The opposite is true of Item G. Both items have a positive but low correlation with the criterion. Although they may be used in the test, they are not so effective as is Item A. Such statistical analysis of the effectiveness of items is so easily made that it should frequently be employed. It shows conclusively where chance successes and ambiguities affect the scores.

Literally thousands of items were analyzed by AAF technicians using for the most part a *phi coefficient* (ϕ) (Chapter XIV). This procedure computes an index between passing or failing an item and belonging to either the highest or the lowest part of a large group according to total test scores or by some other criterion. The result is similar to a correlation coefficient. This procedure saves time since the papers can be grouped into high and low criterion groups at the start, and thereafter the frequency of correct answers can be rapidly counted visually or by machine. The phi coefficient is somewhat higher for items with 50 per cent difficulty than for either more difficult or easier items, therefore when the latter are desired they must be found by an additional inspection for difficulties.

A test may have a high degree of internal consistency but a low correlation with any criteria of success. A test may also be constructed to have high internal consistency by selecting each item to predict some criterion of success. Such a test will be the most valid predictor of some practical success. For example, Uhrbrock and Richardson (1933) divided a group of supervisors into thirds on the basis of estimates of efficiency. The proportion of persons in each third who passed each of 820 items was found. The eighty-five items which best differentiated the thirds were found to correlate .71 with supervisory ability, whereas a test of four hundred unselected items predicted supervisory success with a correlation of only .49. This study shows that by this method the best items for predicting success can be selected rather quickly. Tests constructed by this method must always be checked, however, by a tryout on an entirely new group. Such a tryout is called *cross validation*.

The inclusion in a test of items which have low correlations with any criterion produces a measuring instrument which has low internal consistency, and prevents any careful analysis of mental processes. One cannot safely conclude from such a test that there is any clear pattern of behavior or skill present; the opposite is more likely. Fairly high internal consistency, however, still does not guarantee the appraisal of one independent factor. Several factors may be represented by the various items or by any one item. Only by a detailed psychological analysis (Chapter XIV) can the factor pattern become known.

This discussion of test validity and reliability is intended to be merely introductory. It points to the need for better methods of appraising the worth of a test—methods that will clearly distinguish both qualitative and quantitative aspects. No simple method is likely to appear, but interested students will find the more extensive practical and theoretical discussions well summarized by Brown and Thomson (1925), Thurstone (1946), Guilford (1942), Garrett (1947), and R. L. Thorndike (1947).

SCORE SHEET FOR APPRAISING A TEST

Very few tests are rated above 90 by a good examiner. Illustration 20 is a score sheet for appraising a published test. Procure a test and its manual of directions; then evaluate it on this score sheet.

ILLUS. 20. SCORE SHEET FOR APPRAISING A TEST

Title
Author   Publisher
Range   No. of Forms   Time Required
Publisher   Cost
References

Directions: Rate each item, using the following numbers:
   4 for excellent, unusually well done
   3 for satisfactory
   2 for adequate for most situations
   1 for serious omissions or difficulties
   0 for omitted or misleading

MANUAL
   1. How adequate is the manual (completeness, arrangement, ease of
      reading)?   1

PURPOSE AND PREPARATION OF ITEMS

2. How clearly does the author explain what traits are to be evaluated? What precautions are taken to eliminate extraneous factors? Are speed, power, or breadth tests clearly distinguished? 2
3. How well did the author evaluate each item? 3
4. To what extent is a good sampling of the trait guaranteed by selection of topics or control of situations? Are enough items included for a reliable measure? 4
5. To what extent are items ambiguous or stated with too difficult vocabulary levels? Are pictures well drawn? 5
6. How well are items scaled to give equal units and the needed range of difficulty? 6

ADMINISTRATION AND SCORING

7. How well is the purpose of the test explained, and students motivated to cooperate? 7
8. How adequate are directions and practice periods? 8
9. How hard is it to find the right place to put the answer? Separate answer sheets often make this a source of error. 9
10. How hard is it to find and follow directions for administration? 10
11. Are time limits well set? 11
12. Is the test scored automatically (4), by machine (3), by hand (2), subjectively (1)? 12
13. Are adequate spaces provided for recording results? 13
14. Are corrections for chance success adequate? 14
15. Are scoring weights used appropriately? 15

NORMS FOR INDIVIDUAL PREDICTIONS

16. Are the shapes of distributions clearly given? How do they compare with a normal distribution? What deviations should be expected? 16
17. Are the norms given for large representative samples? 17
18. Are norms given for sex, age, grade, occupation, or other needed groups? 18
19. Are norms well presented by centiles, age equivalents, standard scores, I.G.'s, etc.? 19

RELIABILITY

20. How adequate are the indications of reliability? (Method used, groups sampled.) Are standard errors of estimate reported? Are some parts of the test more reliable than others? 20
21. Is reliability enough for individual predictions? 21

VALIDITY. How well is validity established by:

22. Cross validation? 22
23. Difference between criteria groups? 23
24. Judgments of experts? 24
25. Correlations with other measures? 25
26. Factorial analyses? 26

RATER .... Total Score _____

ILLUS. 21. COMPARISON OF GROUP DISTRIBUTIONS

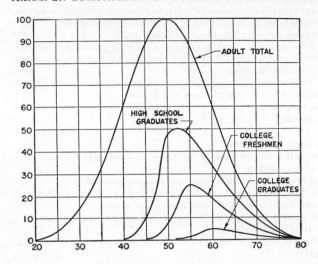

STUDY GUIDE QUESTIONS

1. What determines ease of administration?

2. How is the optimum difficulty of items related to the group to be tested?

3. What are objective tests? What are their limitations?

4. Describe the use of stencils, machines, and automatic scoring devices.

5. How is one's place in a group indicated?

6. Show why the group must be fairly adequately described in order to yield a true interpretation.

7. What are validity coefficients?

8. What is face validity? How much can it be relied upon?

9. What is test reliability?

10. How is test uniqueness or purity defined?

11. What do the factor loadings for each test show?

12. How can two equivalent samples of a large group of items be prepared?

13. How may the Brown-Spearman formula be used to indicate the number of items a test should have to reach a desired reliability coefficient?

14. What is meant by internal consistency? How may it be used to improve a test?

15. Define: mean, median, centile, norm, coefficients of correlation.

CHAPTER IV

CONSTRUCTION OF TEST ITEMS

~~~~~~

In Chapter III the standards for judging the worth of a test were described. This chapter outlines the relative advantages of using the various types of items; gives certain rules for their construction; and discusses chance success, guessing, and corrections for guessing.

WHEN SHOULD NEW ITEMS BE CONSTRUCTED?

Widely standardized tests have the advantage of being, for the most part, well constructed, reliable, and accompanied by useful norms, but they often contain elements that are not wanted and omit material that is wanted. For classroom examinations of a particular course, standard achievement tests can seldom be used, because courses vary considerably from school to school, and even within the same school. Likewise for industrial or military training or selection, the job requirements often need to be fairly specific. To meet these special needs, usually local ones, good examinations should be prepared. Essays or recitations have been used for a long time, and are still the only satisfactory means of appraising composition and speech. However, items having from two to five choices not only result in great economy in scoring, but allow the author of the test, if he is diligent, to get precise indications of the degrees of mastery of the knowledge or skill which he wishes to measure.

At first acquaintance, tests using short items seem to be the answer to the overworked instructor's need for valid and easily constructed tests of information or skill. This belief is sadly dispelled by a few attempts to construct items. Even items which have been worked over by several persons often prove of little value. Thus, Wood (1927) found that almost 30 per cent of the items used in an examination of law students were ineffective in discriminating the poorer from the better students. Anderson (1935) found that one third of the items used in an educational psychology test were more adequate for appraisal of the work of the course than was the whole test. Some of the items were merely useless for distinguishing the bright from the dull students, and some introduced errors of measurement through ambiguities.

TYPES OF TEST ITEMS

Items may be classified into types according to the number and arrangement of their elements. The type determines to a large extent the economy of administration and scoring, and the presence of factors causing chance errors. Type of question also determines the processes needed for success, but to a smaller extent.

It should be stated before proceeding with this discussion that, regardless of the type of question, the best test for a particular appraisal is that which has the largest proportion of valid items in it. Validity, discussed in Chapter III, cannot be known very definitely before the test has been tried out on a fairly large sample of persons. Suppose, however, that a number of different types of items which cover the same material have been tried out on a group and that the various types all show significant correlations with the criteria. It is then reasonable to ask which type of test question is the best to use in a particular situation. Five types of commonly found items are presented in Illus. 22.

MERITS OF VARIOUS TYPES OF ITEMS

If the purposes and time limits of a testing program are definitely fixed, then the question, which is the best type of item? can be answered. Some of the answers are summarized by ratings in Illus. 23. These ratings represent this writer's opinion, based on numerous observations as well as on a number of studies by other investigators. Since ratings depend to a marked degree upon personal experience, they might vary considerably if made by another judge. Thus, the ease of composition of a particular type of item is dependent, at least in part, on one's experience. To a lesser degree judgments of ease of administration and scoring are reflections of personal experience in these activities. For many test situations, however, the advantages and disadvantages of various forms are fairly clear.

ILLUS. 22. TYPES OF TEST ITEMS

1. TRUE-FALSE ITEMS. These require a judgment that a given statement is true or false as:
   The sum of 6 and 7 is 13.   T   F
2. COMPLETION-TYPE ITEMS. These direct the subject to complete a picture or a statement by supplying an appropriate element as:
   The sum of 6 and 7 is ———
3. MULTIPLE-CHOICE ITEMS. These call for a choice of a correct answer to a question from several incorrect answers as:
   The sum of 6 and 7 is 12, 13, 14, 15, 17.
4. MATCHING ITEMS. These demand that each of a list of elements, usually about 10, be matched for significant relationships with elements chosen from another list as:
   Write the number of the book in front of its author's name:

AUTHOR	BOOK
...... Poe	1. Faerie Queene
...... DeFoe	2. Plain Tales from the Hills
...... Dickens	3. Pickwick Papers
...... Spenser	4. The Gold Bug
...... Tennyson	5. The Taming of the Shrew
...... Byron	6. Don Juan
...... Kavanagh	7. The Four Hundred
...... Kipling	8. The Idylls of the King
...... Conrad	9. Lord Jim
...... Shakespeare	10. The Odyssey
	11. Robinson Crusoe
	12. The Pearl Fountain

5. ESSAY ITEMS. *Describe briefly the mental process involved in multiplying a four-place number by a two-place number.*

Illustration 23 shows the true-false test item ranked first in three aspects: administration, ease of scoring,[1] and short time per item. It is given the second rank for economy of printed space, ease of composition, and clarity; and the third, for freedom from chance success, dependence on recall rather than recognition, and analysis of results. Complexity of thinking on true-false items is usually small, though it can be made great; hence no definite rating is given. This aspect is assigned a question mark. True-false test items are probably the best to use:

1. If one is faced with a situation in which time is short for composing, administering, and scoring a test.
2. If the test will have to be scored by clerical helpers who are ignorant of the subject.

[1] Another aspect, accuracy of hand scoring, was investigated by Dunlap (1938). From a rescoring of 398 Terman Group Tests of Mental Ability it was found that true-false and 2-choice items had nearly twice as many errors as completion or multiple-choice items. Nearly 10 per cent of items were mis-scored on the true-false tests—a serious error.

3. If complexity of thinking and recall of information are not considered as important as a wide range of information.
4. If occasional chance successes and failures are not too serious.

ILLUS. 23. MERITS OF TYPES OF ITEMS

(1 is the highest rank; 2, next highest; and 3, lowest)

	TYPE OF ITEM					
	1	2	3	4	5	6
	True-False	Completion	Multiple-Choice	Matching	Rearrange	Essay
1. Easy to compose	2	2	3	2	2	1
2. Easy to understand directions	1	1	1	2	2	1
3. Short time per item	1	3	1	1	1	?
4. Little printed space per item	2	2	2	1	3	1
5. Easy to score; no partial credits	1	2	1	1	1	3
6. Free from chance success	3	1	1	1	1	3
7. Complexity of thinking	?	?	?	1	1	1
8. Question clear, not a puzzle	2	3	1	1	1	2
9. Dependence on recall, not recognition	3	2	3	2	2	1
10. Analysis of results *	3	2	1	2	2	1

* Evidence showing why the examinee failed; types of errors or omissions.

In Illus. 23 the completion type of test item is rated high in ease of administration and freedom from chance successes, and second in ease of composition, amount of printed space, ease of scoring, dependence on recall rather than on recognition, and analysis of results. It is third in the length of time needed and in the clarity of the questions, but complexity of thinking is not rated for this type. Some, who prefer the completion to the true-false type, believe that completion items are less likely to suggest wrong answers and to encourage superficial thinking.

A type of test item which combines some of the good points of both the true-false and the completion types is the multiple-choice type. It is administered and scored about as fast as the true-false type, and is almost as free from chance errors as the completion type. A multiple-choice item is particularly well suited to mathematics, spelling, and vocabulary tests. It is much more widely used in standardized test forms than any other type of item.

Matching-test items are particularly well suited to the classification of facts, such as are found in Chemistry (Illus. 12), and Mechanical

Appliances (Illus. 14). They allow some analysis of results and eliminate chance successes fairly well. In Illus. 23 they are given the highest rank with regard to six aspects, and the second rank with regard to the other four.

A rearrangement-test item has approximately the same good points as a matching-test item, and may allow slightly more precision in scoring. Directions for matching and for rearrangement of items are not as easy to understand as the directions for some of the other types, but they can be readily grasped by the average sixth grade pupil, or an adult who is above the lowest 8 per cent of the population in academic status.

An essay-type item calls for an oral or a written explanation or exposition of facts. It is one of the easiest types of item to compose, yet the hardest to score, since innumerable variations appear in the answers. It usually demands more recall and organization of ideas than any of the other types. For this reason the essay-type item is widely used in appraising problem-solving abilities of advanced students. It is also the most usual way of appraising verbal compositions. It is the only type of test in which the examinee has an opportunity to give expression to his individual style and poetic fancy. In the field of literature it can never be replaced by short-answer items. Since long essays are more difficult to score than short ones, a common practice in educational tests is to limit the essay to 150 words, or to a definite space. This limitation has the advantage of making the examinee think out his answer clearly before he writes it.

Another approach to the relative value of various forms of items is the effect which they may have upon students' methods of study. Meyer's (1936) report is typical of several others. He told equated groups of students to prepare for one of the following types of examinations: true-false, multiple-choice, completion, and essay. At the end of regulated study periods all groups were given all four types of examinations. He found that the students who had prepared for the essay tests showed better average scores on all forms of tests than the other students. Those who had prepared for the completion-type tests came next, while those who had prepared for the true-false and multiple-choice tests had almost the same average scores.

A number of persons have tried out tests which combine two of the forms just mentioned. A true-false form was combined with a completion form by McClusky (1934), who asked students to correct the items which they had marked false by writing additional facts on the test form. This procedure makes the administration and scoring of this test much longer than is true of a true-false test, but it may give a clearer picture of a student's knowledge of the subject. To a limited extent it is thought to avoid the retention of false information from false items.

Other tests combine the multiple-choice and completion forms. Curtis (1928) gave his students four choices for each item and also a blank in which a still more appropriate answer might be written. This combination increases the time needed for administering and scoring the tests by a considerable amount, depending upon the particular questions and students. It has the advantage of making the students think harder to give a good answer than does the multiple-choice form. It is also of use to those who wish to revise multiple-choice test items, for students often write somewhat plausible but wrong answers which, if included as given choices, would make the test item more discriminating than before. This source of alternate choices is important since it is usually difficult to find three wrong choices which are sufficiently like the right choice to make the discrimination as difficult as it needs to be, and which are not so close to the right answer as to be considered synonymous by some authorities.

Another interesting combination is made by directing examinees to read a statement, and then to answer short questions about it. The questions may be true-false or multiple-choice items, such as:

Place a plus sign (+) in front of each item that supports the first statement, and a zero (0) in front of each item which does not.

RELATIVE TIME ALLOWANCES

Ratings similar to those in Illus. 23 on time per item have been determined somewhat more precisely for special cases by the study of the periods actually needed by various persons. When various types of items are so constructed as to have nearly the same content, as reported by Ruch and Stoddard (1927), then the relative time per item can be determined with considerable accuracy. Completion items and items which had seven choices were both answered at the rate of about 4 per minute; 5- and 3-choice items at the rate of 5 per minute, and 2-choice items at 6 per minute. These figures apply to particular historical information tests given in high school.

The writer has found that, in general, easy information items show small differences in time between completion and true-false forms. Difficult information items are answered much more quickly in the true-false than in the completion form, sometimes five times as rapidly. When complexity of reasoning is an important factor in success, then the time needed per item increases greatly. When the various forms of items are not constructed so as to be nearly equiva-

ILLUS. 24. KNOWLEDGE AND SKILL REQUIREMENTS—CLERICAL CLASSES

(From the Author's File)

TOPIC	1 Clerk V (Chief)	2 Clerk IV (Prin.)	3 Clerk III (Sr.)	4 Clerk II (Interm.)	5 Clerk I (Jr.)	6 Typist II (Sr.)	7 Typist I (Jr.)	8 Minute Clerk or Secretary	9 Stenographer III (Sr.)	10 Stenographer II (Interm.)	11 Stenographer I (Jr.)	12 Telephone Oper.	13 Duplicating Mach. Oper.	14 Addressograph Oper.	15 Calculating Mach. Oper.
Grammar, Punctuation	3	2	1			2	1	3	3	2	2				
Spelling	3	2	1			2	2	3	3	3	3				
Vocabulary	3	3	2	2	1	2	2	3	3	3	2	1	1	1	1
Reading skill	3	3	2	2	1	2	2	3	3	2	2	1	1	1	1
Correspondence	3	2	1			2	1	3	3	2	1				
Composition, editorial reports	3 *	1	1			1		3	2	2	1				
Calculation	3	3	2	2	1	2		2	2	2	1	1	1	1	1
Communication	2 *	3	2	1		1			2	2	1	1	1		
Reception	3 *	2 *	1 *	1		1			3	3	1				
Forms	3 *	2	2	1		1			2	2	1	1			
Files	3 *	2 *	2 *	1		1			2	2	1	1			
Library	2 *	2 *	1 *						2	2	1				
Calcul. machine operation and use	2 *	2 *	1												1
Addressograph operation and use	2 *	2	1 *						2	2	1			1	
Duplicating machines	2 *	2 *	1 *	1		1			2	2	1		1		
Typewriting						2	1	2	2	2	1				
Purchasing	2 *	2 *	1 *												
Receiving	2 *	2 *	1 *												
Stores	2 *	2 *	1 *												
Required Skill															
Typing (words per minute)						55	45	55	55	45	45				
Stenography								100	100	80	80				
Transcribe own notes									45	45	35	25			
Supervision	3	2	1	1		1		2	1	1					
Management	2	1													
Personnel	2	1													

LEGEND: Advanced Level = 3; Intermediate Level = 2; Elementary Level = 1.

* May be selected as an optional special skill for supervisory positions and tested at the advanced level in very large organizations.

lent in content, it is not possible to predict any typical time requirements.

The fact that 2-choice or true-false items are answered more rapidly than the other forms of items makes it possible to use a greater number of 2-choice items in a given period. Thus the true-false tests may make up for their chance errors of measurement by including a larger number of items (Illus. 25, columns 1 and 8).

DETERMINATION OF SPECIFIC GOALS

Before starting to construct test items the first task is to set specific goals for your examination. If information learned in a particular course is to be measured, then the syllabus of the course should be followed in detail. If knowledge required for an occupation is to be tested, then a master list of important facts is needed. For determining the knowledge requirements of a job, Guilford and Lacey (1947) and others have pointed out that job analyses are important. When making a job analysis the basic measurable primary traits should be kept in mind as well as the specific knowledge required. A job analysis should also show the most difficult elements of the job, and from a study of successful and unsuccessful workers discover the trait differences among them.

Civil service examiners usually construct tables in great detail to help them prepare thorough examinations, as shown in Illus. 24. Here the topic, amount, and level of difficulty of each requirement are indicated for various clerical classes. When a large file of items, classified by topic and difficulty for a known group, is available, a test can be quickly compiled. Many civil service testing units now have more than fifty thousand items on hand. Over a period of a few years an individual teacher or a group can develop and list on separate cards several hundred tested items. Each item should show the dates when it was used, the degree of difficulty, and the validities for each group.

RULES FOR TEST CONSTRUCTION

The following rules apply to the construction of almost all test items, but they are particularly applicable to objective-type tests. First general rules are given, then more specific ones.

General Rules

1. *Use positive statements.*   This rule may be broken occasionally, but negative statements often lead to confusion, particularly in true-false statements. Thus the item,

T F   An IQ of 70 is usually not exceeded by the lowest 1 per cent of a large random population

is true, but it is less likely to be misread if it is revised thus:

T F   An IQ of 70 is usually exceeded by the highest 99 per cent of a large random population.

2. *Avoid the unqualified use of words which have two or more meanings.* This rule is hard to follow because one's own mental set usually gives only one interpretation to a statement at a time. Thus the essay item,

Describe the principal factors in mental-test success

permits at least two interpretations. Some persons interpret it to mean: describe the main factors which allow an individual to succeed on a battery of tests. To others the question seems to be concerned with the factors which make a test successful on the market or in a particular survey. Therefore the item should be revised to establish the correct interpretation.

3. *Avoid using unnecessarily long or rare words except when they are to be defined.*   Otherwise you may have a test of vocabulary rather than one testing what you are trying to measure.

4. *Incorporate only one independent idea in a question.*   This rule is particularly important in short-answer items. Thus the item,

T F   A correlation coefficient may show the amount of coincidence of ranks on two tests and the reliability of the tests,

has a first clause which is true, and a second clause which is false or incomplete as it stands. It should be made into two items, one including the first clause, and the other somewhat as follows:

T F   The reliability of a test may be shown by a correlation coefficient based on two trials of the test on the same group of persons given on the same day.

5. *Avoid broad generalizations of time or place.*   Violations of this rule are fairly common and very serious because the better informed students will usually know of more exceptions to a generalization than the other students. Thus the item,

T F   The best test for selecting women machine operators was found by Miss Hayes to be a simple measure of dexterity on a peg board,

was supposed to be true according to one interpretation of the article, but according to other interpretations it was false. It should be revised to be less inclusive, thus,

T F The best test in point of administrative costs for selecting women machine operators was found by Hayes to be a simple measure of dexterity on a peg board,

Another example of too broad a generalization is:

T F The usual correction for chance success or failure in true-false tests is justified when students are told not to guess.

This item is theoretically true, but there are many situations in which it would not be true practically. It should be revised to cover a more specific situation, such as:

T F The usual correction for chance success or failure on a 50-item true-false test is desirable when some students have omitted a considerable proportion of the items.

6. *Avoid telegraphic brevity which leaves one in doubt as to the meaning.* Thus the completion item,

The meanings of words depend upon _____,

is too brief for a simple interpretation—one that can be made by a single phrase. Also, the fourth grade history item,

Lincoln's policy toward the slaves was one of _____,

has too many possible answers.

7. *Read the test item aloud.* By doing this one can often discover how a statement can be made more simple.

Specific Rules

Multiple-Choice Items. Each multiple-choice item consists of a statement which is followed by the several choices. The statement, which may be a long paragraph or a short phrase, should be devised according to the rules given above, and be devoid of unnecessary padding or irrelevant material. It should not be a test of ability to read complex material unless that is the purpose of the test. Even when a good statement has been found it may be far from being a satisfactory item because its alternatives may be hard to find and arrange. The following suggestions are useful for the construction of multiple-choice items:

a. Make use of completion-test responses. One of the best ways of securing good alternate but wrong responses for a multiple-choice test which has been used many times with good results, is to try out the same items first as completion tests. Some of the wrong answers are likely to be more diagnostic than alternates which a group of examiners or experts might think up.

b. The position of the right answer should not always be the same.

However, numbered answers should be placed in numerical order so that they can be found easily.

    c. Avoid suggesting the right or wrong answer, thus:

        1) Choices which are not grammatically in line with the beginning of the item are usually the result of patch work, and hence are wrong answers.

        2) An unusually long, detailed choice is often the right answer.

        3) Choices which contain *always* or *never* are likely to be false.

Matching Items. With questions accompanied by two lists of items to be matched, one list should contain one or two more items than the other, so that the process of eliminating known answers will not lead to correct choices of unknowns.

DETECTING AMBIGUITIES

Two methods of procedure have proved effective in detecting ambiguous items: (*a*) observation of behavior and (*b*) statistical analyses. Observational methods are of great value in both performance and verbal-testing evaluation. Ambiguity of scores can be detected in a performance test by watching several persons work. Thus, in assembly or manipulation tests, the observation may show that one person interpreted the task quite differently from another, and solved it differently. Scores in such cases represent different skills and are therefore not comparable. The most valuable results from such situations are often not numerical scores, but descriptions of how different persons went about the work. Thus one person may assemble a lock slowly and without necessary movements and achieve the same time score as another person who moves fast and tries out a number of more or less random combinations before hitting upon the right one. The time score alone cannot be given an unambiguous interpretation. For the most adequate measurement of skills it is necessary to arrange the test situation or the directions so that both persons will use nearly the same processes.

In verbal tests ambiguities of interpretation may often be directly observed either by taking the test and recording your own puzzling experiences, or by asking others to tell you how they interpret each item. Subjective analyses of this sort are practical. In the evaluation of a local objective test, one should, if possible, allow a period of a week or more between its construction and its inspection, in which partly to forget the original mental set or bias which determined the form and the selection of certain test items, and to take another point of view. Sometimes, after such an evaluation, the results are startling. After a subjective analysis has been made and the test has been applied to a group, a statistical analysis should be made as described in Chapter III.

CHANCE SUCCESS

Theoretical Considerations

In tests that require the examinee to choose one of two or more answers that are presented to him, there is an opportunity for success without knowledge. Thus, in desperation many a student faced by an unknown item has taken out his lucky penny and given his answer according to its performance.

If all students answer all items in true-false or multiple-choice tests, no statistical correction for chance success will change their relative rank order. For this reason and because guesses are usually more often right than wrong, some examiners ask all persons to guess when they are not sure, but if some persons are cautious and omit the doubtful items, then corrections for chance successes usually change the rank order of the examinees. In many standardized tests persons are urged not to guess. Whatever directions are used, however, it has usually been found that some persons will guess to a considerable extent and some will not.

When there are but two choices, as in true-false items, and there are equal numbers of true and of false items, then half of the items would be guessed right on a chance basis alone. If we assume that a person's wrong items are doubtful items at which he guesses, and that he got as many doubtful ones wrong as right, his chance successes can be removed from his score by subtracting the number wrong from the number right ($R - W$).

When three choices are presented for each item, the mean chance success on a number of items is one in three, and the corrected score is the number right minus one half the number wrong, $R - \dfrac{W}{2}$; when there are four choices, the corrected score is $R - \dfrac{W}{3}$, and for five choices, $R - \dfrac{W}{4}$, and for n choices, $R - \dfrac{W}{n-1}$.

These corrections are probably not so effective as is often supposed, for the assumption that all wrong answers are pure guesses is doubtless unwarranted in a large proportion of the cases. Moreover, in multiple-choice items the discriminations between alternatives are seldom of equal difficulty—an assumption made in applying the formula for correction. Furthermore, the person who is lucky exceeds the mean chance success and gets credit for some of his guesses even when the correction is applied, and the person who is unlucky gets less credit than he should. This latter case is probably rare, because a person's hunches, and sometimes even his sheer guesses, are usually a little better than chance. Often one has some information which can be used in selecting an answer, but which is not judged to be complete.

Practically, one may decide whether or not to correct for possible chance successes and failures from empirical evidence and the intended use of the results. Let us see what happened when actual test results were corrected for chance effects.

The Results of Correcting for Chance

A very good evaluation of the results of correcting for chance is seen in the work of Ruch and Stoddard (1925), who compared the following five types of tests in American history:

1. Recall: The American Revolution began in the year ....
2. Five choices: The American Revolution began in 1762 1775
   1783 1789 1812 ....
3. Three choices: The American Revolution began in 1762
   1775 1789 ....
4. Two choices: The American Revolution began in 1762 1775 ....
5. True-False: The American Revolution began in 1775 ......T F

Two forms of each type were constructed, each containing one hundred items. These were then given to large groups of high school students. The recall type was always given first, followed by one of the other types. Some of the results are shown in Illus. 25. The first column indicates that on the average more than twice as many items were chosen correctly as were recalled. When the theoretical correction for chance success was made (column 2) the true-false type showed approximately the same mean score as the recall type, but the other tests had considerably higher means. Columns 3, 4, and 5 contrast the theoretical chance success with the actual chance success. Column 5 shows that the 5-choice type had the greatest excess of actual over theoretical success. The excesses were probably due to a small but important additional context furnished by each choice that was added.

The reliabilities, as shown by correlating two equivalent forms, are given in columns 6, 7, and 8. The scores which had been corrected for chance have nearly the same reliabilities as the uncorrected scores. Column 8 indicates that all the forms would have had nearly the same self-correlations if they had been constructed to fill the same period of time. Another important finding, not shown in the illustration, is that all of the choice tests showed larger standard devia-

ILLUS. 25. EFFECTS OF CORRECTING FOR CHANCE

Each Test Consisted of 100 Item Tests

	(1) MEANS	(2)	(3) CHANCE SUCCESSES	(4)	(5)	(6) RELIABILITY: EQUIVALENT FORMS	(7)	(8)
	Uncorrected	Corrected	Theoretical	Actual	Excess of Actual	Uncorrected	Corrected	18.7 Min. Each Uncorrected[3]
Recall	23.0	23.0	00.0	00.0	00.0	.896	.896	.896
5-Choice	50.0	40.8	15.4[1]	27.0[2]	11.6	.886	.873	.901
3-Choice	57.0	40.6	25.7	34.0	8.3	.748	.806	.806
2-Choice	67.6	40.1	38.5	44.0	6.1	.849	.811	.902
True-False	57.7	24.8	38.5	34.7	− 3.8	.714	.578	.820

[1] Since 23 items were recalled, it is assumed that 77 items were "guessed." In a five-choice test one fifth of these, or 15.4, would theoretically be guessed correctly on a pure chance basis.

[2] Found by subtracting the recall-test mean from the means of the other tests.

[3] Theoretical self-correlations when the choice tests are lengthened to fill a period equal to that needed for the recall-type test.

(Adapted from Ruch and Stoddard, 1925, Table 65. By permission of the Journal of Educational Psychology.)

tions when corrected for chance. This increase is due to the fact that students with lower uncorrected scores lost more by the correction than those with higher scores.

The Results of Telling Students Not to Guess

In a similar investigation Ruch and Stoddard (1927) directed half of a large group of students to guess, when in doubt, and others not to guess. The results are shown in part in Illus. 26 for 2,453 pupils in the seventh, eighth, eleventh, and twelfth grades. The raw-score correlations of any two equivalent forms were slightly higher among students who were told not to guess than among students who were told to guess. Self-reliabilities were thus improved (compare columns 1 and 4), and corrections for chance successes were then of little value (compare columns 4 and 5). This result indicates a slight advantage in telling students not to guess. The illustration also shows that some students did not guess when asked to do so, for if all students had answered every item, the correction for guessing would not have changed anyone's position in the group, and the correlations for corrected and uncorrected scores would have been the same in columns 1 and 2.

The correlations of the scores on choice tests with the recall-test scores were nearly the same for both groups of students. The corrected scores corresponded little better than the uncorrected to recall-test scores. If one assumes that the recall type of test is the most valid form of measurement, then he must conclude that directions to guess or not to guess had little effect upon the validity of the choice-types of tests.

Similar results were secured by Toops (1921) using Trade Tests on college students, and by Andrew and Bird (1938) using questions in psychology courses. These studies lead to the conclusions that

1. The five types of test items measure different information and skills only to a small extent.

2. All types have high and similar reliabilities when work periods are the same.

3. Theoretical corrections for chance reduced total scores, increased standard deviations, and usually did not change reliability or validity.

4. Directions not to guess reduced mean raw scores from 10 to 20 per cent, reduced the mean corrected scores between 2 and 3 per cent, and increased the reliability and validity slightly.

5. The true-false and 2-choice tests showed more chance results than the other tests, and hence larger corrections for chance.

Theoretical corrections for chance are not applied widely on

ILLUS. 26. EFFECTS OF GUESS VERSUS DO-NOT-GUESS DIRECTIONS

| TEST | RELIABILITY: 2 Equivalent Forms | | | | | | VALIDITY: Correlation with Recall Type | | | | | | MEANS | | | |
| | "Guess" | | | "Do Not Guess" | | | "Guess" | | | "Do Not Guess" | | | "Guess" | | "Not Guess" | |
	(1) Unc.	(2) Corr.	(3) Diff. (2-1)	(4) Unc.	(5) Corr.	(6) Diff. (5-4)	(7) Unc.	(8) Corr.	(9) Diff. (8-7)	(10) Unc.	(11) Corr.	(12) Corr. (11-10)	(13) Unc.	(14) Corr.	(15) Unc.	(16) Corr.
Recall	.950												27		27	
7-Response	.80	.84	.04	.89	.91	.02	.87	.87	.00	.93	.93	.00	50	41	45	40
5-Response	.86	.90	.04	.86	.88	.02	.91	.91	.00	.89	.92	.03	54	43	48	42
3-Response	.84	.86	.02	.89	.89	.00	.84	.85	.01	.85	.92	.07	62	43	54	41
2-Response	.75	.86	.11	.86	.84	−.01	.86	.86	.00	.74	.77	.03	72	43	65	45
True-False	.64	.78	.14	.89	.84	−.05	.80	.84	.04	.75	.86	.11	66	32	51	31
Mean	.78	.85	.08	.88	.87	−.01	.85	.87	.02							

NOTE: The italicized values show all differences which are 3.0 or more times their probable errors, and hence are probably "significant differences." Nearest whole numbers are used.

(Adapted from Ruch and Stoddard, 1927, pp. 289–290. By permission of the World Book Co.)

multiple-choice items, but are usually applied to true-false or 2-choice items, because

1. Corrections for chance reduce total scores, and so may give a more accurate picture of one's actual ability.

2. Corrections usually increase individual differences in raw scores.

3. The validity of a test, it is believed, may be improved by corrections for chance. (On this, however, no clear evidence is available.)

4. Corrections for chance will be a protection against criticism.

Avoidance of Chance Results

The discussion of chance errors and successes leads to the conclusion that in many forms of tests they may be small enough to be ignored, but that there are no sure ways of entirely correcting for chance errors in individual scores. The three ways of avoiding chance successes through methods used in construction of items and tests are:

a. The test may include a large number of items. This allows the *law of averages* to reduce the chance errors in the score. If one hundred or more true-false items are given, the errors in scores due to chance are usually relatively smaller than when only ten are given. A person's luck is more likely to change during a long test than during a short one.

b. The items may have four or more choices; or completion items, where the possible wrong items are numerous, may be used.[2] A multiple-choice test item with four choices allows on the average only one third as many to be guessed right as guessed wrong. In tests composed of such items the correction for chance is usually a small proportion of a total score.

c. Persons may be asked to indicate whether they are sure or doubtful of their answers, and then more credit may be given for sure answers. The proportions of sure answers which are correct are also indices of caution in the test situation. This index of caution has not been widely studied, but it seems to offer an interesting indication of a personality trait. West (1923), Trow (1923), and Greene (1929, 1938) found tendencies for persons to vary in cautiousness according to the type of material, their familiarity with it, and their temperaments and training in exactness. In general the more abstract material showed lower percentages of sure items correct than did the concrete material, and persons with high scores had much higher

---

[2] A completion item may, however, involve a choice between two easily recalled alternatives, such as:

Plato was born _____ Aristotle.
The Amazon River is _____ in length than the Nile.

percentages of sure items correct than did the poorly informed. There was a marked tendency for the less able students to mark nearly as many items "sure" as did the more able students.

STUDY GUIDE QUESTIONS

1. Why should teachers and employment examiners be alert to prepare needed items?

2. What are the relative advantages of essay-type and multiple-choice-type items?

3. How can the merits of various types of items be determined?

4. Even though chance successes are more common in the true-false type, why are true-false tests and 5-choice tests usually of about equal reliability when given the same time allowances?

5. What are the advantages of having a file of tested items? What facts should be given for each item?

6. How may the specific goals of a test of information be established? Of a test of problem solving? Of a test of attitudes? Of a test for job requirements?

7. Prepare five multiple-choice items on the contents of this chapter, following the rules for item construction.

8. Review the material on item difficulty and validity in Chapter III.

9. To what extent did Ruch and Stoddard find that varying the type of item changed the reliability of the tests?

10. To what extent did directions *to guess* or *not to guess* affect the validity of the test?

11. When all persons answer every item, what statistical corrections for chance success are desirable on a true-false test?

12. What can be done to reduce or avoid chance answers?

CHAPTER V

TESTS OF
EARLY CHILDHOOD

~~~~~~

This chapter reviews some of the standard scales which have been designed to measure growth in bodily control, social relations, perception, language use, and problem-solving ability. Also, reading readiness tests are described, and several examples of individual and group predictions are shown.

INTRODUCTION

Interest in early stages of human development has a fairly long history which has been well reviewed by Baldwin and Stecher (1924). Among the more important early contributions to this subject are *The School of Infancy* by Comenius (1628), and Rousseau's *Émile* (1762), a discussion of individual freedom. These were followed by Basedow (1770), Herbart (1898), and Froebel (1826), who described and applied liberal methods of education, and led the way for a number of treatises on infants, biographies of babies, and schools for early training. Four developments have given new impetus to studies of young children in the United States:

1. The psychoanalytic movement, which has stressed the importance of early emotional maladjustments, as discussed by Anna Freud (1925), Kanner (1935), and Thom (1922)
2. The establishment of day nurseries, partly from philanthropic motives
3. The theories of a group called behaviorists—Krasnagorski (1907), Watson (1913), and Weiss (1925)—who emphasized direct observation of behavior

4. John Dewey's emphasis since 1899 on the experimental and social aspects of early education

These developments have led to the gradual growth of experimental training centers. One was started at the University of Chicago in 1906, and others soon after at the University of Iowa, the Merrill-Palmer School in Detroit, Yale University, the University of Minnesota, and the University of California. Now a fairly large number of colleges and universities have well-planned centers for the study of early childhood.

The three main problems for research which these centers have attacked are much the same as those dealt with in studies of older persons, namely:

1. What is the mean curve of development for a particular function and what deviations are found in a normal group?

2. Which sequences of development are usually found; which, only occasionally?

3. To what extent are developments in various activities independent of each other? To what extent may they be explained as due to general factors? Do some inhibit others?

To answer such questions requires accurate observations over long periods of time and the collection of significant data on growth of the same individuals. To render more accurate observations, a number of tests have been designed.

Binet included fourteen tests for children from three to six years of age in his 1905 Scale. Goddard (1910) and Terman (1916) translated these and added other tests for the same age groups. Kuhlmann (1922) developed a scale which included five items each at the 3-, 6-, 12-, 18-, and 24-month levels, and eight tests each at the 3-, 4-, and 5-year levels. During the last quarter of a century a score or more tentative scales have been published which include observations of motor development, perceptual activities, and complex verbal adjustments. This book will not attempt to review the voluminous literature on prenatal and neonatal development. Tests for infants generally include age groups of three to eighteen months, and tests of preschool children those of eighteen to sixty months. There is no sharp line between these two, but standardized tests for preschool children are more numerous.

DESCRIPTION OF SCALES

There is a marked trend toward analytical procedures in the construction of preschool tests, but as yet conclusive analyses of factors are lacking. A list of important preschool scales is given in Appendix II; seven of these are described in this section.

Gesell and Amatruda (1947) Developmental Diagnosis

The work of Gesell and his associates at the Yale Institute of Human Relations, which has been carried on since 1923, has been the most detailed and extensive in the field of infant and child development. Their 1947 book is a revision of several earlier volumes. From 1927 to 1931, 107 infants were given monthly examinations and elaborate appraisals of their social and physical environments were made. The infants were selected from homes of middle socio-economic status. Their parents were of North European extraction. Birth history, gestation period, and physical status were held within specified limits to give the group further homogeneity, which was considered desirable in that it results in less variability of norms for a group.

The materials used included a standard crib with a movable platform, a cup, spoon, saucer, set of cubes, rattle, bell, ring on a string, crayon and paper, pictures, a box, and a ball. These articles were of minute specifications of size and shape, color, weight, and texture to insure standard testing conditions.

The reactions of the 107 infants to standard presentations of these articles were recorded on printed sheets, and also on twelve thousand feet of film, and in a large atlas. Printed norms show the percentages of each age group that responded in a particular manner to a particular situation. There were, for example, 84 items listed under behavior in response to the bell, 125 items refer to responses to one or more cubes, and 48 to the presentation with a cup. Illustrations 27 and 28 give the norms for cup behavior.

Three kinds of items appear in this illustration: increasing, decreasing, and focal items. The increasing items are those which show larger percentages with increasing age, as in 1, 6, 7, and 16. The decreasing items show smaller percentages with age, as in 2 and 8. The focal items at first show larger percentages with increasing age, but later show smaller percentages, as in 3, 25, and 30. From tables such as these, the "critical age" for each item was determined. For increasing items the critical age is the first age at which an item is passed by 50 per cent of the group; for focal items the critical age is the age of the maximum percentage.

The examination of an infant results in a record of observed responses. Items were placed in each schedule according to their critical ages. For convenience a schedule is given for each of the following

ILLUS. 27. CUP BEHAVIOR

12 weeks to 36 weeks

Cp.	Behavior Items	12	16	20	24	28	32	36
1.	Regards immediately	81	89	97	100	100	100	100
2.	Regards momentarily	37	22	9	3	—	—	—
3.	Regards recurrently	44	68	28	21	4	18	15
4.	Regards prolongedly (n.m.p.) *	56	69					
5.	Regards prolongedly	37	57	47	3	—	—	—
6.	Regards predominantly	73	93	94	100	100	100	100
7.	Regards consistently	0	5	38	66	100	100	100
8.	Shifts regard	80	73	31	23	10	25	23
9.	Shifts regard to surroundings	40	33	6	3	—	4	15
10.	Shifts regard to hand	47	45	13	7	—	—	—
11.	Shifts regard from cup to hand	20	28	15	3			
12.	Arm increases activity (s.p. or n.m.p.) *	75	79	78	93	100	100	100
13.	Brings hand to mouth (s.p. or n.m.p.)	50	21					
14.	Hands active on table top (s.p. or n.m.p.)	36	67					
15.	Approaches (n.m.p.)	44	79					
16.	Approaches	6	25	72	91	100	100	100
17.	Approaches promptly (n.m.p.)	25	55					
18.	Approaches promptly	6	13	44	81	96	100	100
19.	Approaches after delay (n.m.p.)	25	23					
20.	Approaches with both hands	6	11	34	41	69	50	50
21.	Approaches handle first	0	5	25	38	56	64	58
22.	Contacts (n.m.p.)	44	62					
23.	Contacts	6	15	69	91	100	100	100
24.	Dislodges on contact (n.m.p.)	25	52					
25.	Dislodges on contact		9	53	50	38	29	8
26.	Grasps			13	52	85	100	100
27.	Grasps with both hands (n.m.p. or s.p.)		5	22	53	52	36	42
28.	Grasps with both hands			3	28	33	32	31
29.	Grasps with one hand			9	35	52	75	69
30.	Manipulates with hands encircling cup			6	24	56	50	42
31.	Manipulates grasping by rim			0	0	45	64	62
32.	Manipulates grasping by handle			6	31	59	92	81
33.	Pushes or hits		14	31	30	41	3	4
34.	Pushes or drags cup			19	24	33	50	31
35.	Bangs on table top			3	6	37	36	58
36.	Turns cup over on table top			6	26	14	17	8
37.	Lifts cup			6	45	82	100	100
38.	Lifts by handle			6	35	59	79	81
39.	Brings to mouth			3	24	63	60	66
40.	Manipulates above table top			0	21	67	86	89
41.	Manipulates initially above table top			3	3	26	18	35
42.	Holds with both hands			3	35	63	46	46
43.	Transfers		—	—	—	19	43	42
44.	Turns cup right side up			6	3	56	71	62
45.	Rotates			3	—	3	21	31
46.	Drops			6	38	63	61	42
47.	Drops and resecures			—	7	15	39	19
48.	Fusses	6	7	12	27	7	18	11

* n.m.p. = near median position.　s.p. = standard position.

(By permission of Gesell and Thompson (1938, p. 109) and the Macmillan Co.)

ILLUS. 28. GROWTH OF CUP BEHAVIOR

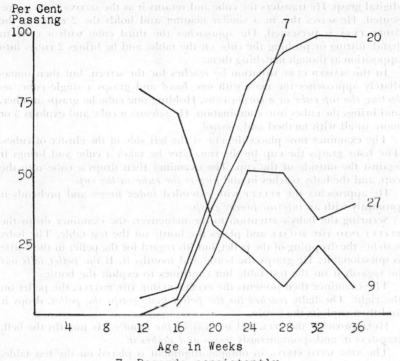

Age in Weeks

7 Regards consistently

9 Shifts regard to surroundings

23 Approaches with both hands

27 Grasps with both hands

(Drawn from Gesell and Thompson, 1938.)

key ages: 4, 16, 28, and 40 weeks and 12, 18, 24, and 36 months. Each schedule also includes typical behavior for ages a few weeks or months above and below the key age. Illustration 29 shows the schedule for 40 weeks. Each schedule includes items designed to reveal four areas of development: motor, adaptive, language, and personal-social. The text contains more than a hundred line drawings, as well as descriptive statements to help the examiner decide accurately the level of performance which he has observed. Thus according to Gesell and Amatruda (1947) the typical behavior at 40 weeks is:

The forty-week infant sits with good postural control and without support before the test table.

He gives immediate heed to the FIRST CUBE and seizes it with a radial digital grasp. He transfers the cube and retains it as the SECOND CUBE is presented. He seizes this in a similar manner and holds the 2 cubes as the THIRD CUBE is presented. He approaches the third cube with a cube in hand, hitting or pushing the cube on the table, and he brings 2 cubes into apposition as though matching them.

In the MASSED CUBE situation he reaches for the screen, but then immediately approaches the mass with *one hand* and grasps a single cube, *selecting the top cube or a corner cube.* Holding one cube he grasps another, and brings the cubes into combination. He *releases* a cube and exploits 3 or more in all with method and *control.*

The examiner now places the CUP at the left side of the cluster of cubes. The baby grasps the cup by the rim, later he takes a cube and brings it against the outside of the cup. The examiner then drops a cube into the cup, and the baby reaches in and *fingers the cube in the cup.*

He approaches the PELLET with extended *index finger* and prehends it promptly with an *inferior pincer grasp.*

Securing the baby's attention to the maneuver, the examiner drops the PELLET INTO THE BOTTLE and places the bottle on the test table. The baby watches the dropping of the pellet, but his regard for the pellet in the bottle is questionable. He grasps the bottle and mouths it. If the *pellet falls out* he *regards* it on the test table but continues to exploit the bottle.

The examiner then presents the PELLET BESIDE THE BOTTLE, the pellet on the right. The baby *reaches for the pellet first, grasps the pellet,* drops it and then exploits the bottle.

He approaches the BELL and *seizes it by the handle.* He mouths the bell, transfers it, and spontaneously *waves and shakes it.*

The RING WITH STRING in oblique alignment is placed on the test table. He reaches directly toward the ring first, then *plucks the string* easily, pulls in the ring, transfers the ring and manipulates the string.

The FORMBOARD is placed with the round hole at the baby's right, and the baby is offered the round block. He pulls at the formboard (the examiner holds it firm), accepts the round block, transfers and releases it. The examiner inserts the block in the round hole, and the baby pulls and pries at it and removes it with considerable difficulty. He again transfers and releases the block.

The test table is now removed and the baby is offered the BALL. He mouths the ball and releases it but cannot be induced to respond to the examiner's demonstrations and invitations to roll or toss the ball back and forth in cooperative ball play.

He is then confronted by a MIRROR. He regards his image, *leans forward* and smiles and vocalizes as he pats the glass. He is offered the ball which he accepts and retains; he disregards the mirrored ball.

POSTURAL BEHAVIOR is now observed. He has already displayed his ability to *sit with good control.* Enticed by a lure, he *goes from the sitting to the prone position.* In prone he gets up on his hands and knees and *creeps* forward. Holding a railing he *pulls himself to his feet,* stands holding on, and *lowers himself* again. When his *hands are held, he stands supporting his full weight.*

He VOCALIZES *mama* and *dada*, and has *one other "word."* He imitates sounds (cough, click, razz) and responds to "no-no" and his name.

He is REPORTED to hold his bottle and to feed himself a cracker. He *pata-cakes* and waves *bye-bye.*[1]

The examiner enters a plus sign whenever the child demonstrates the behavior pattern, or the mother reliably reports its presence, or when more mature similar patterns have been displayed. He enters a minus sign whenever a child's behavior fails to demonstrate a pattern. The child's maturity level or age in any field is at the point where the "aggregate of plus signs changes to an aggregate of minus signs." If the plus and minus signs are both found over a wide range, the range is indicated by giving the high and low limits, for example, *"adaptive behavior,* twenty to thirty-two weeks." Four developmental quotients (DQ's) may be secured by dividing the maturity age by the chronological age in each area, and a general developmental quotient may be found by averaging the four, if they are close together.

Gesell has long stressed the need for appraising the whole personality. More than two hundred pages are given to detailed descriptions of children who show amentias, endocrine disorders, convulsive disorders, abnormal neuro-motor signs, cerebral injury, blindness, deafness, prematurity, precocity, and environmental retardation. Growth-trend charts, showing both temporary patterns and the patterns which normally replace them, are given in detail along with an excellent glossary. The examiner is urged to take into account all factors which influence behavior—illness, fatigue, apprehension, insecurity, personality deviations, and language usage in the home, etc. The appraisal must be penetrating and must sum up "personal characteristics, integrity of organization, and latent and realized possibilities." Two typical reports of examinations taken from Gesell and Amatruda (*Developmental Diagnosis,* 1947, pp. 151, 313) are given here:

1. [He] had always been a very "good baby," content to be left alone for hours. Development had always been slow. He was first examined at $3\frac{1}{2}$ years of age. Left to his own devices he wandered about the room aimlessly climbing, screaming, whistling, and fingering objects idly. He did respond in some measure to loud, stern, insistent commands and could thus be induced to conform to the requirements of the examination. His general maturity level was approximately 12 to 21 months, DQ 45–50. He built a tower of cubes, dumped the pellet from the bottle, turned the pages of a book and placed all the forms in the formboard; he had no words.

[1] Arnold Gesell and Catherine S. Amatruda, *Developmental Diagnosis, Normal and Abnormal Child Development,* Harper & Bros.

ILLUS. 29. DEVELOPMENTAL SCHEDULES

KEY AGE: 40 Weeks

36 Weeks	40 Weeks	44 Weeks
Motor	**Motor**	**Motor**
Sit: 10 min. +, steady	Sit: indefinitely, steady	St: (at rail) lifts, replaces, foot (*48w)
Sit: leans forward, re-erects	Sit: goes over to prone	Bell: grasps by top of handle
St: holds rail, full weight	St: holds rail, re-erects	
Cube: radial digital grasp	St: pulls to feet at rail (*15m)	
Pellet: prehends, scissors grasp (*40w)	Pr: creeps (*15m)	
	Cube: crude release (*15m)	
	Pellet: grasps promptly	
	Pellet: inferior pincer grasp (*48w)	
	Ring-str: plucks string easily	
Adaptive	**Adaptive**	Cup-cu: removes cube from cup
Cube: grasps 3rd cube (*40w)	Cube: matches 2 cubes (*15m)	Cup-cu: (Dem.) cube into cup without release (*52w)
Cube: hits, pushes cube with cube (*15m)	Cup-cu: touches cube in cup	Pellet in bo: points at P thru glass (*18m)
Cup-cu: cube against cup (*44w)	Pellet: index finger approach	Bell: regards & pokes clapper
Pellet & bo: approaches bottle first (*40w)	Pellet in bo: regards P if drops out	Ring-str: approaches string first
Ring-str: manipulates string	Pellet & bo: approaches P first	
	Pellet & bo: grasps P	
	Bell: grasps by handle	
	Bell: spontaneously waves or shakes	
Language	**Language**	**Personal-Social**
Vo: dada (or equivalent)	Vo: dada & mama	So: ext. toy to person, no release (*52w)
Vo: imitates sounds	Vo: 1 "word"	Feeding: drinks from cup (in part)
Comp: responds to name, no-no	Comp: bye & patacake	Mirror: reaches image ball in hand (*52w)
	Personal-Social	
Feeding: holds bottle (*15m)	So: waves bye and patacakes (*...)	
Feeding: feeds self cracker		

(Gesell and Amatruda, *op. cit.*, p. 55. These schedules are among the eight which are discussed in Chapter III.)

At 5½ *years,* after two years in a special school, he is controlled, obedient and "trustworthy," having stabilized his activities and advanced in social adaptability. Developmentally, however, he has made essentially no progress. DQ 25–30.

The decelerating developmental trend has reduced this boy from a high-grade imbecile level to a high-grade idiot level. In a suitable environment and with skillful training much of his disturbing erratic behavior has disappeared. He is another example of simple primary deficiency.

2. [She] was taken off the maternity ward for adoption. She was known to be the offspring of well-educated parents. This fact has added support to the high opinion which we soon gained of her developmental potentialities. At *8 weeks* she gave no evidence of advanced status; but at *20 weeks* her performance proved to be definitely above the average. Her drive was strong, tense, almost excited; her manipulation so active that it resulted in a two-stage transfer of the ring. At *40 weeks* her adaptive behavior almost attained a one-year level. She made a determined effort to place the pellet into the bottle. She took huge delight in the whole examination and displayed a mature kind of amiability in her cooperativeness. At *2 years* there was the same excellent rapport with the examiner. Her responses were immediate, decisive and of excellent quality. Her performance was above the 30-months level in the motor and language fields. In a nursery-school group at 2½ *years* she is credited with superior postural control, versatility in jungle-gym play activity, adeptness in solving mechanical problems, a delightful sense of humor, and a capacity to protect her own status without aggressiveness in the social group. She is an attractive child with indubitably superior growth potentialities.

The validity of the testing schedule is thought to be high by its authors because of the way the schedule was developed. The method of selecting the infants, the allocation of the items to four fields of behavior, and the determination of a critical age for each item, on the basis of the percentage of infants who demonstrated the item— all these were arrived at through study. Neither systematic errors in applying or summarizing the scale, nor random errors in scoring have as yet been reported. The training of the examiner is very important in securing comparable results.

Along with these measures of behavior Gesell and Thompson (1938) listed the following fourteen direct measurements which are included in nearly all careful anthropometric studies:

1. Length from soles of feet to vertex (total length)
2. Length from soles of feet to suprasternal notch
3. Length from soles of feet to pubes
4. Biacromial diameter
5. Thorax diameter
6. Biscristal diameter

7. Head circumference
8. Thorax circumference
9. Weight
10. Number of erupted teeth
11. Head-neck length
12. Body length
13. Eye color
14. Hair color

From these direct measurements fifteen indices were found by dividing various measures by other measures. These specifications for measurement, described by Dawson (1936), were agreed upon at the 14th International Congress of Prehistoric Anthropology and Archaeology. Measures of infants were taken in the recumbent position, using a measuring board. Older children and adults were measured in the erect position.

Gesell's Development Schedules, 18 to 60 Months

To measure older children, Gesell and others (1940) issued a detailed test manual and described their theoretical approach in their book, *The First Five Years of Life* (Harper & Bros.). This book describes normal behavior under four headings which may be roughly outlined as follows:

1. *Motor Development:* the organization of movements, upright posture, walking and running, prehension and manipulation, and laterality and directionality.
2. *Adaptive Behavior:* block building, form adaptation, form discrimination, drawing, number concepts, immediate memory, comparative judgments, and problem solving.
3. *Language Development:* (1) developmental stages: jargon, vocabularies, phrases, sentences, understanding, articulation, (2) behavior situations: picture books, use of language, parts of body, naming objects, following directions, picture cards, analysis of pictures, action-agent, comprehension, "What must you do? When?" prepositions, humor.
4. *Personal-Social:* eating, sleeping, elimination, dressing, communication, play activities, aesthetic behavior, and developmental detachment.

For examination purposes printed test schedules are available for the following months: 15, 18, 21, 24, 30, 36, 42, 48, 54, 60, and 72.

A complete examination usually requires several sessions on various days in addition to interviews with parents. The results are given in descriptive maturity-level ratings in each field, together with reports on marked deviations from these levels and a summary of the child's reaction to the whole test. Further characterizations are given which go beyond the psychometric findings. Thus, for adaptive behavior, evidences of unusual inquisitiveness, originality, or decisiveness are recorded, but no attempt is made to rate their magnitude. These characterizations, which are typical of the results of projective techniques (Chapter XXIII), are supported by specific manifestations which may in time yield quantitative results. Among the fifteen traits to be observed (p. 307) are:

1. *Energy output:* general amount and intensity of activity
2. *Motor demeanor:* posture, general muscular control and poise, motor coordination, and facility of motor adjustment
3. *Self-dependence:* self-reliance and self-sufficiency
4. *Social responsiveness:* reaction to other persons and to the attitudes of adults and of other children
5. *Family attachment:* closeness of affection; degree of identification with the family group
6. *Communicativeness:* expressive reference to others by means of gesture and vocalization
7. *Adaptivity:* capacity to adjust to new situations
8. *Exploitation of environment:* utilization and elaboration of environment and circumstances in order to gain new experience
9. *Sense of humor:* sensitiveness and playful reactiveness to surprise, novelty, and incongruity in social situations
10. *Emotional adjustment:* balance and stability of emotional response in provocative situations
11. *Emotional expressiveness:* liveliness and subtlety of expressive behavior in emotional situations
12. *Reaction to success:* expression of satisfaction in successful endeavor
13. *Reaction to restriction:* expressiveness of behavior in reaction to failure, discomfort, disappointment, frustration
14. *Readiness of smiling:* facility and frequency of smiling
15. *Readiness of crying:* promptness and facility of frowning and tears

A sample of part of a record from Gesell's *The First Five Years of Life* (1940, p. 307) is given below:

As early as the ages of 8 and 12 weeks the highly dynamic personality of Boy D made a strong impression even when observed only through the medium of the cinema. The following adjectives were used to characterize his individuality: quick, active, happy, friendly, well-adjusted, vigorous, forceful, alert, inquisitive. Although he was definitely extrovertive he showed at the early age of 24 weeks a surprising discriminativeness in reading the facial expressions of his mother. By the age of 28 weeks he had developed a moderate temper technique for influencing domestic situations which did not altogether please him. He was able to shift quickly in his emotional response from smiling to crying and from crying to smiling to achieve a desired end. At the age of 5 years, likewise, his emotional reactions are labile and versatile. He is facile in changing his emotional responses. He is highly perceptive of emotional expressions in others, and correspondingly, highly adaptive in social situations. With this emotional alertness, he shows a relatively vigorous detachment from his mother as well as affection for her. He is not given to persisting moods. We do not get the impression that his emotional characteristics have been primarily determined by his life experiences. The underlying nature of his "emotivity" at 12 weeks, at 52 weeks, and at 260 weeks seems rather constant. With altered outward configurations a certain characteristicness in emotional reactions is quite likely to persist in his later life.

Another important book by Gesell and his colleagues, *Biographies of Child Development* (1939), gives follow-through reports on thirty-one children for a period of more than 10 years and growth studies of fifty-one other children for shorter periods. The difficulties of appraising the same traits over various periods are shown, but certain marked consistencies are noted.

Minnesota Preschool Tests, 1½ to 6 Years (Goodenough, 1932)

This test is divided into verbal and nonverbal parts which may be given separately or together. To make it possible to retest the child without having the results of the second test affected by specific memories of tasks of the first test, two forms have been provided.

Both the verbal and the nonverbal series are given to the subject with verbal instructions, but the comprehension of instructions is easy in those tests that have been classed as nonverbal. Since the author used few nonverbal tests for children under three years, the distinction between verbal and nonverbal tests is not considered to be useful at ages below three years.

A preliminary selection of tests to be used was made from a survey of previous work and from original materials. This preliminary series was applied to one hundred children in each of nine half-year chronological periods. Their parents represented a cross-section of occupational levels. An analysis of the children's responses was the basis for the final selection of items. Items without intrinsic interest for the children, or causing a pronounced emotional reaction, or otherwise inappropriate were eliminated. The twenty-six subtests given in Illus. 30 were retained and arranged in a somewhat random order for a standard presentation. It was thought that this order sustained interest by variety of task and by having easy items mixed with harder items. The items were assigned various points of credit according to their difficulty. In scoring a test the points of credit are totaled, and then changed to MA's or standard scores. The test items are arranged for convenience in administration in a large book of envelopes with instructions and materials for each test placed together.

Correlations are high between scores achieved on an equivalent form of the test given within a period ranging from one to seven days when computations are made for various chronological age groups of

ILLUS. 30. MINNESOTA PRESCHOOL TEST

Form A

1. Part of body : ears ___ chin ___ **2**
2. Objects in pictures : chair ___ apple ___ house ___ flower ___ **4**
3. Naming objects : ball ___ watch ___ pencil ___ scissors ___ **4**
4. Copying drawings : circle ___ triangle ___ diamond ___ . . **3**
5. Imitative drawing : Horiz. stroke ___ vertical cross ___ . . **2**
6. Block building : three cube pyramid ___ six cube pyramid ___. **2**
7. Response to pictures : a. nouns ___   b. nouns ___
       prep or verbs ___   prep or verbs **18**
8. Cube imitation : 1234 ___ 12342 ___ 1324 ___ 1423 ___ 14324
___ **5**
9. Command : drink ___ **1**
10. Comprehension : hungry ___ sleepy ___ house on fire ___ . . **3**
11. Discrimination of forms : number correct ___ number wrong
___ **10**
12. Naming from memory : doll ___ pencil ___ penny ___ horse
___ shoe ___ fork ___ **6**
13. Recognition of forms : a. ___ b. ___ c. ___ . . **3**
14. Colors : red ___ blue ___ pink ___ white ___ brown ___ . . **5**
15. Tracing forms : circle ___ square ___ irregular forms ___ **6**
16. Picture puzzles : horse ___ goat ___ apple ___ camel ___ . **9**
17. Incomplete pictures : bird ___ girl ___ watch ___ **14**
18. Digit span : 2 digits ___ 3 digits ___ 4 digits ___ **3**
19. Picture puzzles : bird ___ flower ___ giraffe ___ **8**
20. Paper folding **1**
21. Absurdities : a. ___ b. ___ c. ___ d. ___ e. ___ **5**
22. Mutilated pictures foot ___ finger ___ **2**
23. Vocabulary : a. ___ b. ___ c. ___ d. ___ e. ___ f. ___ g. ___ **7**
24. Opposites : a. ___ b. ___ c. ___ d. ___ e. ___ f. ___ . . **6**
25. Clock : 8 : 10 ___ 1 : 50 ___ 12 : 00 ___ 1 : 10 ___ **4**
26. Speech during examination **2**

Scores added by _____ Total verbal **80**

Checked by _____ Total Nonverbal **55**

(Arranged from Goodenough, 1932. By permission of the Educational Test Bureau, Minneapolis, Minn.)

6-month intervals. The correlations range from .68 to .94 for the verbal series, with a mean of .86. For the nonverbal series the correlations range from .67 to .92, with a mean of .89. This mean indicates that prediction from scores on one test for scores on a second test within a short interval will be fairly accurate. Correction for practice effect is made by subtracting 2 C-score points from the second test, if the second test is given within the week. Goodenough (1932) states that the tests are about equally reliable at all ages within the scope of the test—from eighteen months up to six years.

Goodenough Measurement of Intelligence by Drawing, 3½ to 13½ Years

Goodenough (1926) concluded, from her own observations and from a thorough study of others' research, that children's drawings could be used as an indication of intellectual development. She devised a test in which children draw a man from memory. The examiner gives the following directions to a group of children:

> On these papers I want you to make a picture of a man. Make the very best picture that you can. Take your time and work very carefully. I want to see whether the boys and girls in —— School can do as well as those in other schools. Try very hard and see what good pictures you can make.

Judicious praise in general terms is advised as, for example, "These drawings are fine; you boys and girls are doing very well." Suggestions by the children are not allowed. The test usually takes no more than 10 minutes.

Goodenough chose a man as the standard subject for the drawings because it is one with which all children are familiar, it has universal interest and appeal, and a man's clothing is more uniform than that of a woman or a child.

The children on whom the test was standardized were selected at random except for age-grade classification. They were within the normal range for in-grade-at-age.

The points used for scoring were chosen because they showed:
1. A regular increase in the percentage of children succeeding at successive ages
2. A rapid increase in this percentage
3. A clear differentiation between the performances of children who were of the same age, but of different school grades

Point credits were given for the presence of a line representing part of a man and also for correct proportion and perspective. The points are all described in detail and illustrated by specimen drawings with scores attached, as in Illus. 31. It is possible to secure scores up to

51 points, which can be turned into mental age scores. Two points is the score for the average child of three and one half years; 6 points is the score for a child of four and one half years; and 10 points is the score for a child of five and one half years, on up to a score of 42 for a child of thirteen and one half years. Material for more complex psychological analysis of the products is given in the book, but the test is chiefly used as a tentative classification of intelligence.

The use of a single sample of drawing is defended by Goodenough, who found a correlation of .937 ⊥ .006 between two tests on successive days for 194 children in the first grade. In another instance, by computing the score by the split-half method, and by using the Spearman-Brown formula, a mean reliability of .77 was found for ages from five to ten taken separately. "The probable error of estimate of a true IQ earned on the drawing test is approximately 5.4 points at all ages from five to ten years." Other investigators have reported that drawings are very much influenced by a child's emotional conflicts and that the Goodenough scores are often affected by emotional blocking.

ILLUS. 31. DRAWING OF A MAN

(Goodenough, 1928. By permission of the World Book Co.)

Cattell Infant Intelligence Scale

Psyche Cattell (1940) issued an Infant Intelligence Scale which was composed of items similar to those of the Gesell Development Schedules, the Merrill-Palmer Preschool Test, the Minnesota Preschool Test, and Charlotte Buhler's First-Year-of-Life Scales. Items from 1,346 examinations of 274 children were analyzed and placed in a scale on the following bases:

1. Items for which successful responses showed significant increases over several 3-month periods and for which the responses finally approached 100-per-cent success.
2. Items which were easy to administer and score, and required little subjective judgment. Cumbersome apparatus was avoided.
3. Items which were interesting to most children at the ages where the items were used.
4. Items which tested mental abilities rather than socially developed skills or control of the large muscles.

5. Items which tested similar abilities at other ages.

The final arrangement included five regular and two alternate tests at each of nineteen age levels ranging from two to thirty months.

These tests were finally so placed as to yield Development Quotients similar to those secured by the same children in the Stanford-Binet Test Form L, at three or three and one-half or four years of age. At no age did the median IQ differ from the Stanford-Binet IQ by more than two points.

The median changes between two successive IQ's were much larger (about 11 points) before twelve months of age than after, when they were about 7 points. The test at three months of age had a split-half reliability of .56 with the Spearman-Brown estimate. It correlated only .10 with the Stanford-Binet, Form L, given at thirty-six months. The predictive value of high ratings at three months was considerably better than that of low ratings. In other words poor scores could result from many factors, but high scores actually represented high ability.

The tests at six, nine, and twelve months of age all had reliabilities of about .88, and at thirty-six months their correlations with the III-6 Stanford-Binet scores were .34, .18, and .56 respectively. Reliabilities and correlations with the Stanford-Binet were higher (.70 to .83) for ages above eighteen months.

The variations in IQ are thought to be due to individual changes in growth curves or tempo of development rather than to inadequacy of the tests. The causes of some of these changes seem to be innate and some seem to stem from serious illness. A great deal of work is needed to determine the probable rate-of-growth trends in individuals and in homogeneous groups.

The scoring is in terms of months of growth and, since each age level contains five items, the credit in terms of time for each item passed is one fifth of the period covered. The tests at each level cover the preceding period; for instance, the test in the fourth month covers the period between the third and fourth months.

Cattell emphasizes that great care must be used in interpreting results. If an important decision is to be made, a second examination should be given after several weeks, and a third examination 6 months later. This procedure is especially important when illness or lack of cooperation is evident. She believes that parents should seldom be told what the IQ of the child is.

The California Preschool Schedule

A scale known as the California Preschool Schedule, Macfarlane (1938), has been compiled of tests from Stutsman, Kuhlmann, Binet,

Terman, and local authors. It is important because it is probably the most analytical of the preschool scales and because it has been used in a thorough growth study. It covers ages from 15 to 84 months and has two equivalent forms. The record sheets classify the items into ten groups, as follows:

1. *Motor skills:* pegs, buttons, pins, bow knot
2. *Block building:* tower, door, design, stair
3. *Drawings:* scribbling, vertical and horizontal lines, circle, triangle, diamond
4. *Discrimination of form:* cards, form boards
5. *Discrimination of spatial relation:* cover on box, in, or under
6. *Discrimination of number and size:* large and small blocks, count objects to 10, ½ of 6, and 8
7. *Language comprehension:* points to picture, action agent, opposites
8. *Language facility:* expressiveness, use of language, preposition, pronouns, past, plurals
9. *Memory span:* finds object, memory for 9 objects
10. *Completion, nonverbal:* mends doll, watch, pictures

This classification is descriptive of the materials and symbols rather than of the mental processes used. The scale probably does not have enough items in each class to make a reliable profile, but it does allow one to compare 3 types of motor skills, 3 types of discrimination, 2 of language use, and 2 of memory functions. Such comparisons will lead to a knowledge of the interrelation of these skills and eventually to more analytical scales.

Primary Mental Abilities Test, Ages 5 and 6

The most thorough statistical approach to measurements in early childhood is probably that of Thelma Gwinn Thurstone and L. L. Thurstone, who defined intelligence as a composite of abilities for acquiring knowledge of various types. After extensive studies of intellectual abilities over a period of 20 years, the authors found eight components of intellectual ability which they proved to be stable and independent characteristics of a person. After tests for adults had been developed, they turned their attention to five-year-olds. Seventy tests were constructed including all the known types of preschool and readiness tests, and certain new varieties. Factor analyses were carried out for groups of two hundred children in kindergarten and first grade, and five primary factors were found which could be readily identified. The purest measures of each factor were incorporated into the Primary Mental Abilities Test for Ages 5 and 6. All the tests require a child to cross out or underline or draw lines in a booklet in response to oral directions by the examiner. In order to help children keep their attention centered at the right place on the page, a white cardboard marker is placed by the child just under the item being considered. Approximately seven practice and thirty-five test problems are given for each primary ability. The five tests are described as follows: [2]

1. *Verbal Meaning.* The ability to understand words is tested in five ways:

    a. Vocabulary. In a row of four pictures the child is asked to cross out the one named.

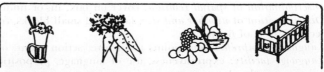

Put your marker under the first row of pictures. Mark the fruit.

    b. Sentence Comprehension. In a row of four pictures the youngster marks one which is the answer to a question.

Slide your marker down. Which one is used to wake soldiers in camp? Mark it.

    c. Sentence Completion. The child is requested to mark one of four pictures to show which fits into the blank in a sentence.

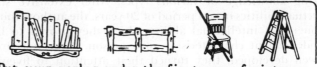

Put your marker under the first row of pictures. Mark the picture that finishes this story: If you want to reach a book on a shelf and you have no ladder you may use a .... Mark it.

[2] These items are taken from the examiner's manual giving directions and correct answers, by permission of T. G. Thurstone, L. L. Thurstone, and The Science Research Associates. In the test booklet each picture is approximately one inch square.

d. Paragraph Comprehension. The central meaning of a short statement must be illustrated.

Put your marker under the first row of pictures. Mark the picture that goes with this story: After he had washed his face and eaten his breakfast Jack carried his book to school. Mark it.

e. Auditory Discrimination. Two words that sound nearly alike are to be distinguished.

Slide your marker down. Bear and pear. Mark PEAR.

2. *Perceptual Speed.* The ability to locate details quickly is measured by

   a. Pictures

In every row of pictures you are to do two things. First mark the picture all by itself in the little box. Then find the picture in the big box which is exactly like the picture in the little box and mark it too. Work fast. Do as many as you can on these two pages before I tell you to stop. Are you ready? BEGIN.

(Allow exactly ONE AND ONE-HALF MINUTES from the time you say "BEGIN.")

 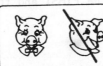

b. Forms

In every row of pictures you are to do two
things. First mark the picture all by itself
in the ring. Then find the picture which is
exactly like the picture in the ring and mark it
too. Work fast. Do as many as you can on these
two pages before I tell you to stop. Are you
ready? BEGIN.

(Allow exactly TWO MINUTES from the time you say.
"BEGIN".)

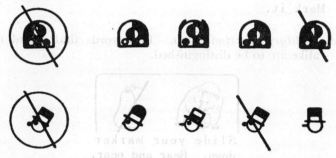

3. *Quantitative Ability.*   This is the ability required for counting.
It is measured by three subtests:

   a. Counting

Put your marker under the first row of pictures
- the airplanes. Mark THREE airplanes. THREE.

   b. Comprehension of quantitative concepts

Put your marker under the first row of pictures
- the fish. Mark the FIRST and the LAST fish.

c. Story problem

**Put your marker under the first row of pictures
- the shovels. Billy and George want to dig in
the yard. How many shovels do they need? Mark
them.**

4. *Motor.* This is a line-drawing test.

**Put your marker under the first two rows of
dots in the box. They look like this. (Point
on blackboard.) Someone has made some of the
lines for us. We're going to finish the row.
We draw lines from the top dots to the bottom
dots like this. (Illustrate on blackboard.)
Now you do it in your book. Draw lines from
the top dots to the bottom dots. Finish the
row. (Give individual help where needed.)**

**Move your marker down to the next two rows of
dots in the box. See how FAST you can do this
row but be careful. Draw lines from the top
dots to the bottom dots. Be sure to hit both
dots.**

5. *Space.* There are two tests for this ability.
   a. Squares. The child is requested to mark one of four drawings which would fit into the drawing at the left.

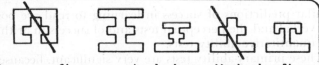

**Put your finger on the locket. Mark the first
picture in the row. That is PART of a square.
Find the REST of the square and mark it.**

b. Copying.   The child is to complete the picture on the right so that it looks like the picture on the left.

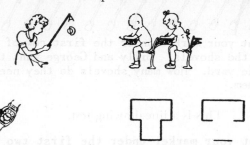

Put your finger on the wrist-watch. Make the children's drawing look just like the teacher's drawing.

The test is administered during two half-hour periods according to instructions given in a 24-page booklet. Groups of from five to ten pupils can be tested at once if they are cooperative. Large tables or desks close together are not satisfactory, because children are too used to looking at each other's work. Only tests for perceptual speed and motor factors are timed. The exact words to be used for each item are printed in the instructor's manual. The scores, which are the total numbers of items correctly marked, are recorded on a profile sheet which yields age scores ranging from three to seven years, in steps of two months for each subtest, and also for the total of four tests (the motor test is omitted in the total of mental tests). The ability-age scores may be divided by chronological-age scores to give quotients of development. For over-all success in the first grade the prognosis from these tests is:

Over 6 yrs. 6 mos.	definitely ready
6 years to 6–5	probably ready
5–6 to 5–11	probably not ready
5–0 to 5–5	definitely not ready

Similar predictions of success in learning to read are possible from the verbal and the perceptual tests and of success in arithmetic from the quantitative ability tests.

These primary-ability tests are very significant, because they yield scores which are unequivocal and which cover five important and relatively independent abilities. They give a research tool for important studies of growth and the effects of training. They pilot the way toward more careful analytical approaches to evaluation at lower and higher age levels.

Measures of Reading Readiness

A number of tests designed to indicate the development which is needed by those who are starting to learn to read have appeared. Such tests are usually called reading readiness tests. Observations have shown that such indicators may be found:

1. By measuring the child's ability in tasks which normally are formed progressively better during the first year of school.
2. By securing his intelligence test score.
3. By securing teacher ratings of interest in reading.
4. By measuring language ability, motor coordination, hearing, and visual discrimination.
5. By finding how well informed the child is about his own environment.
6. By learning the type of emotional adjustment or interest which he shows toward other children, adults, materials in the school situation, and toward himself.

The greater number of the tests for reading readiness are not comprehensive enough to take in all these factors. Usually the limitations of space, time, and money reduce them to paper-and-pencil tests sampling a few indicators. The Metropolitan Readiness Test, the Monroe Reading Aptitude Tests, and the Betts Ready-to-Read Tests are typical.

Metropolitan Readiness Test. Although the Metropolitan Readiness Test has been designed as a group test, it is suggested that the group be small, preferably with fewer than ten children. It may be given individually if necessary, though, of course, the same standardized directions are to be followed. Hildreth, Griffiths, and Orleans (1933) described their test as follows:

The test consists of six parts. The first is a test of perception, involving recognition of similarities. It consists of 23 items ranged in order of difficulty and including both pictorial material and symbols (Illus. 32).

Test 2 is a second perception test, involving the copying of 11 figures. This type of test has proved to be highly diagnostic of mental maturity in young children, and several of the items are comparable with those contained in the Binet series. The factor of reversals, which enters into a number of the items, has been found to be correlated with lack of experience and with immaturity of perceptual abilities in young children.

Tests 3 and 4 are designed as measures of vocabulary. They consist respectively of 19 and 15 sets of rows of four pictures each. In Test 3 the child is to select the picture that illustrates the word the examiner names. This is a test of understanding or comprehension of language—not a test of the child's language usage. Test 4 is similar in organization, but requires the child to comprehend phrases and sentences instead of individual words.

The extra conversation, which is really not absolutely necessary for the location of the right picture by the child, is added to make the test one of more sustained attention comparable to the attention span required to listen to stories and the like, in the beginning work in reading.

Test 5 measures number knowledge. By means of 40 items it measures achievement in number vocabulary, counting ordinal numbers, recognition of written numbers, writing numbers, interpreting number symbols, the meaning of number terms, the meaning of fractional parts, recognition of forms, telling time, the use of numbers in simple problems. By using the picture form of material and certain checking devices, the varied aspects of number knowledge can be very satisfactorily explored.

Test 6 appraises common knowledge by means of a multiple-choice picture test of 16 items. The child is required to select from a row of four pictures the one that satisfies the examiner's description. The test is short, but gives good evidence of variability within a group at first-grade entrance.

ILLUS. 32. SAMPLES FROM THE
METROPOLITAN READINESS TEST

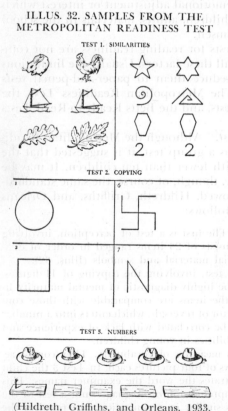

TEST 1. SIMILARITIES

TEST 2. COPYING

TEST 5. NUMBERS

(Hildreth, Griffiths, and Orleans, 1933. By permission of the World Book Co.)

Centile norms for each half-year from five and one-half to eight years are furnished for total scores. These show slightly larger improvements on the part of the advanced rather than of the retarded children during this period. The average child improves from a total 64 at five years, nine months, to 78 at seven years, nine months.

Monroe (1935) Reading Aptitude Tests. The Monroe Reading Aptitude Tests include items similar to those in the Metropolitan Readiness Test and also measures of immediate memory spans, articulation, auditory discrimination, speed and accuracy of hand and eye coordination, and lateral dominance. Seventeen tests are grouped into six sections, each of which has a separate score. A profile of six ability patterns is therefore available:

A. Visual Tests
1. *Memory of orientation of forms.* The child must observe a diagram which the teacher exposes and then draw a line around the one, of two smaller pictures in his booklet, which is like it. The two small pictures are lateral or vertical opposites of each other. The test was designed to detect perceptual reversals. Twelve pairs of pictures are used.
2. *Ocular-motor control and attention.* This test requires one to indicate the path from a picture of a boy to one of three small pictures of houses. Nine diagrams of increasing complexity are used.
3. *Memory of forms.* This test asks a child to draw a set of four small pictures immediately after they have been exposed for 10 seconds. Four sets of pictures are used.

B. Motor Tests
1. *Speed.* The child is asked to place dots in ¼ inch printed circles for 60 seconds.
2. *Steadiness.* The task is to draw a pencil line on a row of dots and dashes, without time limits.
3. *Writing name.* The child is asked to write his name with each hand.

C. Auditory Tests
1. *Word-discrimination.* A small picture is presented and three words are pronounced. Thus, for the picture of a small sailboat, the words *beet, boat,* and *boot* are spoken. The task is to indicate which of the three words is the name of the picture. In all, nine pictures are presented.
2. *Sound-blending.* Three small pictures are presented at a time, and the examiner pronounces the name of one of them, separating vowel and consonant sounds. The task is to blend the sounds into a word and to circle the picture which was named.
3. *Auditory memory.* A short story is read aloud by the examiner, and the child is asked to "tell what the story was about." Twenty-two ideas may be given separate credits.

D. Articulation Tests
1. *Reproduction.* The child is asked to pronounce a series of twenty-four words or phrases, ranging in difficulty from *baby* to *transcontinental.*
2. *Speed.* For this test the directions are, "I want to see how quickly you can talk. When I say go, say *banana, banana, banana, banana,* as quickly as you can. Keep on saying it till I say stop. Ready, Go!" Fifteen seconds are allowed. Similar trials are given, using *long ago* and *take a bite.*

E. Language Tests
1. *Vocabulary.* Twelve rows of three small pictures each are presented. The task is to draw a circle around the object named by examiner.
2. *Classification.* "Name all the animals you can think of as quickly as you can." Thirty seconds are allowed. The same procedure is used for things to eat and for toys.

   3. *Sentence length.* A picture of a farmer and two boys is shown while
      the examiner says, "Here is a pretty picture. What is the picture
      about?" The score is the number of words in the longest sentence or
      phrase used.
F.   Laterality Tests
      Score equal number of right-side preferences.
   1. *Hand preference.* Writing, throwing a ball, pretending to comb hair,
      holding a bat (shoulder), threading a needle, winding thread on a
      spool, folding hands (uppermost thumb), and folding arms (outer-
      most arm).
   2. *Eye preference.* The child holds the large end of the paper cone to
      his face and is asked to look at three objects about the room. The
      eye used for sighting is noted. The eye used to peep through a small
      hole in a piece of cardboard which the child holds before his face
      is also noted.
   3. *Foot preference.* Hopping, kicking an imaginary football, and climb-
      ing upon a low chair.

   Ten of the items may be administered to small groups, and seven
must be given to individuals. Norms for 434 children from five and
one-half to eight and one-half years are given in smoothed percentile
curves. The odd-even reliability of the entire test was found to be
.87, but that of the separate sections was not given. The correlation
between total Monroe scores and reading achievement one year
later, as shown by a combined score on Gray's Oral Paragraphs and
the Iota Word Test, was .75 among eighty-five first grade children.
The separate sections of the Monroe test all correlated between .50
and .60 with the combined score, with the exception of .18 for right-
side dominance. Monroe suggested remedial procedures for aiding
children with special difficulties.
   Betts (1936) Ready-to-Read Tests. All of the Betts Ready-to-Read
Tests are given individually and require more complicated apparatus
than those mentioned above. They do not include special measures
of comprehension but do include the following four types of measures:

1. *Visual Perception*
      a. Discrimination of letter forms
      b. Discrimination of word forms and vocabulary
2. *Auditory and Articulation*
      a. Phonetic perception of letter groups
      b. Auditory span for sentences
      c. Auditory fusion of vowel and consonant sounds into words
      d. Repetition of sounds
      e. Acuity of hearing: Number read in a low voice at 20 feet
3. *Visual Mechanism:* tested by a stereoscope

a. Acuity of each eye and of both
b. Binocular fusion and balance
c. Depth perception
d. Near-sightedness
4. *Lateral Dominance:* hand, foot, and eye

Measures similar to these have generally been found to show low correlations with reading success in the first grade, because motivation, information, and reasoning ability may overcome mechanical and perceptual handicaps. Auditory and visual handicaps, however, should be detected at an early age to avoid unnecessary strain.

Summary of Descriptions of Scales

These brief reviews are only enough to show that the items included in the various scales employ a wide variety of test situations. A clear understanding of test results comes only from a large number of direct observations of tests in actual progress and a thorough study of child development.

Two methods of selecting items have been illustrated here. In one stimulus situations were secured which were thought to indicate a factor of intelligence or to predict reading ability. In the other (shown in Gesell's work), there was at first a wide random selection of stimulus situations intended to give a fairly complete picture of behavior. Later, items were grouped into classes which seemed to show related forms of behavior. Selection by means of careful statistical analyses of relationship has been accomplished in the Primary Mental Abilities Test. The scaling of items in all these tests is achieved by converting raw scores into mental ages.

SOME RESULTS OF MEASUREMENT

Typical results of measurements of preschool children will be discussed under two headings: usual order of development, and correlational studies of growth.

The Usual Order of Development

A number of observations have been made to show the order of development of behavior patterns. In the sphere of motor coordination the results are fairly uniform from person to person on a number of patterns. Thus Shirley (1933) reported a definite order of emergence of motor patterns in locomotion, and Halverson (1931) reported approximate ages at which a definite series of prehension patterns developed. He described (p. 218) the stages as follows:

1) *No contact* includes all instances wherein infants for some reason fail even to touch the cube.

2) *Contact only* includes instances in which infants succeed in touching but not in securing the cube.

3) *Primitive squeeze.* The infant thrusts the hand beyond the cube and corrals it by pulling it toward him on the table with thumb, wrist, or hand until he succeeds in squeezing it against the other hand or the body. The primitive squeeze is not a true grasp for the hand does not actually grip the cube.

4) The first form of actual grasp is the *squeeze grasp.* The hand, palm-in, approaches the cube laterally on the table to envelop it. At the moment of contact the fingers close on the cube so as to press it strongly against the heel of the palm with the thumb extended on the upper face of the cube. This grasp is clumsy and usually results in failure to hold the cube, at least no infant has succeeded in raising the cube from the table with this grasp.

5) In the *hand grasp* the infant brings the pronated hand down pawlike fully upon the cube, curls the fingers down on the far face of the cube with the thumb paralleling the digits on the adjacent surface, and presses the cube firmly against the heel of the palm. The fingers appear to be of equal importance in grasping and the thumb seems to lack tonicity.

6) The *palm grasp* is accomplished by setting the pronated hand down on the cube so that the fingers curl over the top and far down on the further face with the thumb pointing down against the near face to oppose the fingers in forcing the cube against the palm. We have now for the first time active thumb-opposition. This new feature in the thumb repertoire of functions and the simultaneous budding into prominence of the forefinger are mainly responsible for the higher types of grasp which follow. Up to this point all digits function in holding the cube in the middle of the palm. From now on only the first three digits function prominently in grasping so that we find the cube no longer in the middle of the palm but shifted to the radial edge of the hand. A faulty palm grasp becomes a hand grasp. As a matter of fact, the hand grasp is often due to the failure of the thumb to orient itself properly for opposition to the other digits.

7) In the *superior-palm grasp* the infant sets only the radial side of the palm down on the cube with the thumb against the near side opposing the first two fingers, which are curled down on the far side. In closure the digits press the cube against the thumb and palm.

8) The *inferior-forefinger* grasp greatly resembles the superior-palm grasp. There is the same thumb-forefinger opposition, but the digits at the end of the approach point more medianward than downward (tendencies of this change of pointing appear in the superior-palm grasp), an angle of approach which makes thumb-opposition simple, and the cube is no longer pressed against the palm. This type of grasp represents an achievement of no small degree for the infant, for here is a clear demonstration of the fact that the digits are beginning to act independently of the palm in grasping and holding. Heretofore, the infant uses the palm in grasping to make up for the shortcomings in gripping by the digits. Now he finds that he can

make the necessary fine adjustments of the proper digits to secure his grasp and can maintain the delicately balanced pressure of the digits against the near and far faces of the cube to insure its being held. We may say that the advance in grasping from the palm type to the forefinger type marks the change from a three-surface grasp to a two-surface grasp—a tri-directional pressure gives way to a di-directional pressure. The inferior-forefinger grasp is not a true fingertip grasp, however, for the cube is still well up toward the palm so that a considerable portion of the palmar surfaces of the digits contacts with the cube.

9) The *forefinger grasp* is essentially a fingertip grasp. The cube is well out on the tips of the first three digits (sometimes four digits) with the thumb opposed to the fingers. Up to this point, all types of grasp require that the hand come to rest on the table before the cube can be raised. Thus the table serves as a base or leverage point for lifting the hand after it grasps the cube. In the forefinger type of grasp the digits are pretty well extended, distinct flexion appearing only at the metacarpophalangeal joints. In earlier forms of grasp the digits curl about the cube.

10) The *superior-finger grasp* is similar to the forefinger grasp, except that the infant in grasping does not have to place any portion of his hand on the table top to aid the placement of the digits against the cube, nor does he require the table for leverage in raising the cube. The hand alights on the cube, attains its grip, and raises the cube deftly and neatly. True, the hand may touch or brush the table as the hand settles on the cube, but the presence of the table about the cube is not essential to grasping or raising it.

Similar studies also show order of growth in language patterns. Within the first few hours after birth there is, according to Lewis (1936), a period during which the cries accompanying discomfort and the sounds accompanying comfortable situations can be distinguished by careful observers. This is followed in the second or third months by *babblings*. Babblings are repetitions of comfort sounds which seem to be produced because they give pleasure to the one making them. Lewis believes that this is a rudimentary form of aesthetic experience which may profoundly affect the adult's appreciations of music and poetry. During the first three or four months there also occur imitations of adult speech in which there is only a rough similarity between what the child hears and what he produces. According to Lewis, imitation of intonation is rare unless the child is experiencing the same emotional pattern as the adult.

At about the fourth month a stage follows which lasts from 4 to 6 months, during which time little imitation is reported by many careful observers. This marked decrease in imitation is thought to be due to the fact that during this period the child develops responses to the meaning of what he hears and that these new associations prevent responses to mere sound. There is also a development of variety in vocalization. This period is followed by one in which a large amount of definite imitation of both form and intonation occurs. For the first time *echolalia* and imitation are noted. Echolalia is a marked tendency for a child to imitate immediately what he hears in an apparently meaningless way. This is the kind of imitation that is characteristic of extremely feeble-minded children at later ages. It also gives a child important practice in speaking adult phonetic forms. Persistent echolalia may prove a hindrance to the acquisition of language as an instrument, but it is a necessary stage of development during which the child gives close attention to the perception and vocal reproduction of words.

The growth of language from this point on is a matter of rapid accumulation of phonetic forms and new concepts. A child comprehends more spoken words than he uses in his own speech, and this doubtless lasts throughout life. Also, a five- or six-year-old understands written words before writing them. These processes, however, come in fairly close succession, and are dependent upon the concepts which the individual develops. Precise concepts lead to the rapid and accurate use of words, and this accurate use of words leads in turn to the development of more complex concepts. The order of the development of concepts and modes of thought is not easy to appraise, since observations and test results usually record end-results and not the mental processes which produced them.

Challenging and much challenged discussions of concept development are found in Piaget's three volumes (1926, 1929, 1930), in Stern (1914), in Koffka (1928), and in the reports of psychoanalytical investigators, for example, Anna Freud (1925) and Kanner (1935). These investigators have not reported standardized testing methods, but they have made detailed observations which are of great value.

The results of the most careful testing of both language and non-language patterns are still far from complete, but the order of difficulty of items on standard tests is an indication of their most probable order of development in the individuals who were used to standardize the test. From Illus. 27, Cup Behavior, one could calculate the probability that any item in the list would precede any other item. The items which reach a maximum earlier will probably precede the items which reach a maximum later. The order of development will almost certainly be: regarding, approaching, contacting, grasping, and manipulating.

The development of social behavior, also shows a fairly definite order in which simpler types of perception and memory precede the more complex coordinations and judgments.

Correlational Studies of Growth

Correlation analyses of measures of small children at various ages have not yet given very clear results because the samples used were too small, and the tests were usually subject to large accidental variations. A number of correlations have already been quoted along with descriptions of the scales. The following reports are all fragmentary but they indicate certain typical relationships, and they point the way for future research.

Bayley (1933) studied forty-nine infants from birth to three years, using items from scales by Kuhlmann (1922), Gesell (1925) and Jones (1926). Each infant was given at least six examinations. The result showed such low correlations between items and between trials that Bayley states, "The behavior growth of early months of infant development has little predictive relation to the later development of intelligence—even though the later behavior may depend in large part on the previously matured, elementary neural connections or behavior patterns." Correlations between total scores on consecutive trials ranged from .71 to .89 with a mean at .82, but the correlation between age and test total during the first year was .98. These high correlations between consecutive trials were probably due to differences in age level, rather than to similarities in mental organization. If the ages of the infants were held constant, the correlations between trials would become nearly zero.

Illustration 33 shows the changes in IQ reported by Bayley (1940) from successive tests of one child over a period of 9 years. Bayley summarized a study of forty-eight children from one month to nine years of age as follows:

In an attempt to find some measure of mental ability that would rate children consistently during the first nine years, several combinations of scores were studied.

1. A Developmental Score made up of the sum of the items of the separate mental and motor tests yielded no greater consistency than did the mental test alone.

2. A selection of items from the California Preschool Mental Scale improved slightly the correlations of the two- and three-year tests with later performance, but the improvement was not great enough to produce constant scores over four or five years.

3. Tests of vocabulary given at from six to nine years of age gave scores moderately related to language tests at three and three and a half years, and were not significantly related to the age of first talking or to early mental-test scores.

4. Tests of formboard and puzzle-board performance (at five and a half to eight and a half years), although related to mental-test and vocabulary

scores at similar ages, were unrelated to tests of ability during the first year.

It was concluded that mental organization changes with growth, and that the rate of change is especially rapid before two years of age.

Bayley also reported that correlations between the educational levels of the midparent (an average of both parents) and the scores of infants between one and fifteen months of age are slightly negative. With further growth, however, the relationship changed and at three years of age reached a positive correlation of .47.

ILLUS. 33. GROWTH CURVE OF EARLY CHILDHOOD

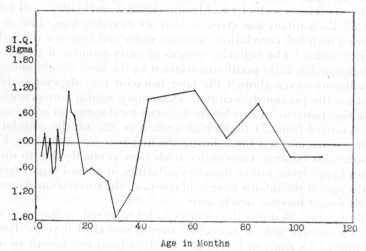

Note: This child varies from the average from +1.20 to -1.80 Standard Deviations by the age of 30 months. Variations of this degree were fairly common among preschool children.

(Bayley, 1940, p. 25. By permission of the National Society for the Study of Education.)

Furfey and Muehlenbeim (1932) used the Linfert-Hierholzer Scale (1928) with groups of infants who were six, nine, and twelve months of age. Later eighty-one of these children were tested by the Stanford-Binet (1932) scale at the age of four years, three months. The correlation between the two scales was .00±.07. This zero correlation may mean that the two scales were measuring uncorrelated patterns. It may also be due to variations in individual growth or organization at various ages. Most of the tests for infants are heavily weighted with manipulative skills, whereas the Stanford-Binet requires much use of language at the age of four years.

Macfarlane (1938) concluded from a 4-year study of 244 preschool children that mental ability, as indicated on the California Preschool Schedule, showed less predictability as the intervals between tests increased. The correlations between tests separated by 6-month intervals ranged from .68 to .72. The correlations between tests given at twenty-one and seventy-two months were approximately .30. Macfarlane also found very low correlations between the child's mental-test score and midparent's education. These ranged from .07 at twenty-one months, to .12 at thirty-six months, to .33 at seventy-two months. No simple explanation of these results is apparent. Since the test material included a wide variety of mental and motor skills, any simple interpretation is improbable. It may be that the content of the tests changed with age, or that the organization of traits in the child became more stable.

A study of the intellectual status of 226 adults who had been tested on at least one Minnesota Preschool Test before six years of age was reported by Maurer (1946), who located these adults from the records of a group of 1,091, and succeeded in getting them to take a 21-minute revision of the Alpha Test. She determined the correlations of total scores and also the predictive value of separate items in various preschool tests. On the basis of these correlations seventeen out of thirty tests were considered significantly predictive. The 30 tests were classified by Maurer [3] as follows:

Predictive Tests	*Nonpredictive Tests*
Imitative drawing *	Pointing out parts of the body
Block building (2 parts)	Pointing out objects in pictures
Response to pictures (nouns)	Naming familiar objects
Knox cube imitation *	Copying drawings (borderline) *
Discrimination of forms *	Response to pictures (verbs)
Naming colors	Obeying simple commands
Tracing a form *	Comprehension
Picture puzzles (rectangular) *	Naming objects from memory
Incomplete pictures	Aesthetic comparisons
Digit span	Recognition of forms (borderline) *
Picture puzzles (diagonal) *	Paper folding *
Definitions	Imitating position of clock hands
Absurdities	Speech
Mutilated pictures *	
Vocabulary	
Comprehension of directions	
Giving word opposites	

* Nonverbal tests

[3] Lists of tests used with the permission of Katharine G. Maurer and the University of Minnesota Press.

ILLUS. 34. GROWTH CURVE OF EARLY CHILDHOOD

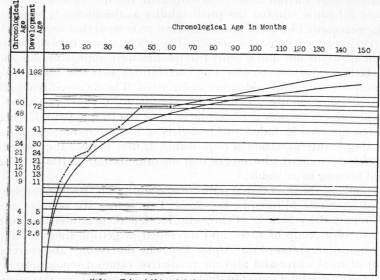

Note: This child maintains a position slightly above average with very little variation. The average is shown by a logarithmic curve used by Gesell.

(Gesell, 1940, p. 152. By permission of the National Society for the Study of Education.)

Maurer points out that in general the predictive items required adaptability to a novel situation, while the nonpredictive items were too easily affected by recent experience or were too dependent upon motor or language skills. Naming familiar objects and pointing to parts of the body were thought to be nonpredictive because naming and pointing use rote memory only. Among the best predictive tests were: memory for digits, word opposites, picture puzzles, block designs, and comprehending directions. In a validation study using forty-six cases the correlations between total preschool items and Alpha scores ranged from .0 to .80 for small age groups (4 to 23 persons) and were about .32 for the combined age groups. When preschool scores were recalculated, using only the predictive items, the correlations remained about the same, indicating that the nonpredictive items were useless.

Studies such as this are of great significance, because they show consistencies in behavior over long periods of time and illustrate an approach which can be made more diagnostic by the selection of various primary abilities as criteria.

Gesell (1929) reported that a diagnosis of mental defect might safely be made by an expert worker during the first year of the subject's life. His reports are based on clinical studies and do not utilize correlation analyses either of items or of total test scores.

Illustration 34 presents one of Gesell's typical records. Here the developmental age shows regular progress from two months to twelve years. He concludes:

The foregoing cases were selected from some 10,000 now on file at the Yale Clinic of Child Development. Numerous biographic case studies by members of the staff have strengthened the conclusion that the basic trends and tempo of behavior development, as a rule, manifest themselves in infancy. If a child has normal growth potentialities, it is almost certain that they will reveal themselves to clinical perception in the first two years of life. Temporary "irregularities" of development are more frequently encountered throughout the preschool years, because of the nascency and interdependencies of behavior patterns during this formative period. In a few extremely exceptional instances, bound up with obscure emotional and physical factors, the signs of normality may be delayed as long as three years. On the other hand, virtually every case of primary feeblemindedness can be diagnosed in the first year of life. In a wide clinical experience we have never seen a case of secondary feeblemindedness due to educational or environmental deprivation, although we have seen an occasional case in which the IQ itself had descended to an apparently defective level.

STUDY GUIDE QUESTIONS

1. What aspects of infants' growth are measured by Gesell's scales?
2. How is cup behavior indicated and scored?
3. What are the principal components of postural behavior?
4. What are "increasing," "decreasing," and "focal" items?
5. What are the advantages and disadvantages of total scores on preschool scales?
6. What is the basis for scoring Goodenough's draw-a-man test?
7. How is problem solving measured before three years?
8. What skills are measured in reading-readiness tests?
9. Compare the Minnesota, California, and Cattell preschool scales for range, analysis of content, adequacy of sampling, and administration.
10. What stages in language development are recognized?
11. What predictions from one age to another are usual on infant scales? preschool scales? reading-readiness tests?
12. What explanations of variation in individual growth are given?

CHAPTER VI

INDIVIDUAL TESTS OF ABILITY

Several important individual tests of general intelligence will be considered in this chapter. Their content will be presented, and the reasons for the selection of certain items and methods of scoring will be discussed. The principal uses of these tests are described, and a list of needed research activities is given.

CHARACTERISTICS OF BINET-TYPE TESTS

The individual tests that have been, and still are, applied most widely, both in this country and abroad, are principally of the Binet type. No accurate estimate of the number of such tests given annually is obtainable, but it can be safely said that they are used almost universally in studies of behavior difficulties and delinquency among children, and to a lesser extent in studies of adults.

Binet-type tests employ a wide variety of tasks designed to distinguish between bright and dull persons. They are administered individually, and oral directions are used. The order of their presentation may be varied somewhat at the discretion of the examiner in order to secure a good sample of the subject's ability. These tests also have a total score and sometimes a profile of separate scores. The score is usually given in terms of MA and IQ, or corresponding centiles of age groups. The test items are arranged according to mental-age levels, or simply according to relative difficulty.

112

Early Scales

Alfred Binet, born in 1857, in Nice, France, studied medicine under Charcot and Féré, and with Beaunis founded the Psychological Laboratory at the Sorbonne in Paris in 1889. He was an energetic worker, and during his professional life he conducted a very large number of technical researches. When in 1895 he became particularly interested in mental measurement, he and a student named Henri evaluated the tests which were then available. They decided that there was need for fewer tests of sensory processes and for more tests of complex thought processes. In 1898 Binet described current tests, most of which were not of his own invention, but which he thought would indicate accuracy of judgment and general mental ability. He mentioned the following tests specifically: mental calculation, drawing a square, reconstruction of disarranged sentences, comprehension of abstract passages, questions of moral or social propriety, immediate memory for numbers and for objects, and imitation of paper folding. It is interesting to note that nearly all of these tests with slight variations are used in practically all of the more recent Binet-type tests and also in many group tests of intelligence. Binet also emphasized the idea that mental measurement should result in a rating of persons with reference to one another rather than in an absolute rating of ability.

In 1900 Binet published "Attention and Adaptation," which reported a study of the differences between two groups of children: five who had been classified as bright by their teachers and principal; and six, as dull. The children of both groups averaged approximately eleven years of age. The two groups showed no large differences on tests of simple reaction time or of choice reaction time, perception of small variations in metronome speed, immediate memory for words, and speed of counting dots. He did find large differences between the groups on tests of tactile sensibility on the back of the hand; copying letters, words, and designs; cancelling letters from a printed page; and addition. He concluded that the bright showed a quicker and more accurate perception and solution of difficulties, and he defined attention as mental adaptation to a new situation. He was convinced that speed of routine acts had no relation to intelligence.

After various studies of cephalic indices and 2-point thresholds on the skin, he again turned to mental tests and reported, in 1902, a large number of tests of free association of verbal processes on his two daughters: Marguerite, age fourteen and one-half, and Armande, age thirteen. No quantitative results were given, but Marguerite was clearly shown to be precise, practical-minded, well oriented in space but not in time, and little given to reverie. Armande was more imaginative, vague, detached, delighted in fantasies, and had a tendency to verbalism.

In 1904 he worked with Simon in comparing feeble-minded and normal children and in 1905 they published a list of thirty tests which were arranged in order of difficulty. These items, shown in Illus. 35, were thought to depend more on broad cultural experiences than on specific academic training.

On the basis of testing approximately fifty normal children and a larger number of mentally retarded children, called aments, tenta-

ILLUS. 35. THE 1905 BINET SCALE

1. Visual co-ordination of head and eyes
2. Grasp a cube placed on the palm
3. Grasp a cube held in line of vision
4. Make a choice between pieces of wood and chocolate
5. Unwrap chocolate from paper
6. Obey simple orders; imitate gestures
7. Touch head, nose, ear, cap, key, and string
8. Find objects which the experimenter names in a picture
9. Name objects pointed out in a picture
10. Tell which of two lines is the longer
11. Immediate memory for three digits
12. Tell which of two weights is the heavier
13. Suggestibility:
    a. Find object which is not among those presented, as in No. 8
    b. Point to *patapoum* and *mitchevo* (nonsense words) in the picture No. 8
    c. Tell which of two equal lines is the longer
14. Give definitions of *house, horse, fork,* and *mama*
15. Immediate memory for sentences of fifteen words
16. Give differences between: paper and cardboard; fly and butterfly; wood and glass
17. Immediate memory for thirteen pictures of familiar objects
18. Immediate memory for two designs, exposed ten seconds
19. Immediate memory for list of digits, three, four, or five in the series
20. Give similarities between: blood and wild poppy; fly, butterfly, and flea; newspaper, label, and picture
21. Just noticeable differences in length of lines
22. Arrange three, six, nine, twelve, and fifteen gram weights in order
23. Find which weight has been removed from No. 22
24. Find rhymes
25. Complete simple sentence by adding one word (after Ebbinghaus)
26. Construct sentence containing *Paris, gutter, fortune*
27. Knowledge of what is the best thing to do in twenty-five situations of graded difficulty
28. Reverse clock hands at 3 : 57, at 5 : 40, and tell the time it would be
29. Draw results of folding a piece of paper into quarters and cutting the once folded edge
30. Distinguish between liking and respecting, between being sad and bored

(Peterson, 1925, p. 172.   By permission of the World Book Co.)

tive norms were given. The first five tests were found to be passed by idiots and two-year-olds. The ninth test was the upper limit for normal three-year-olds, the fourteenth test for five-year-olds, and the fifteenth for adult imbeciles. The sixteenth item separated five- from seven-year-olds effectively. Morons fell below the twelve-year level in the test, and were more clearly distinguished from normal children by verbal than by nonverbal tests. The discrimination between higher age groups was made on the basis of type of answer. The authors realized keenly the need of more precise standards and more cases.

Working independently in Worcester, Massachusetts, Terman (1906) published a comparison of seven superior and seven dull boys on tests of ingenuity, logical processes, mathematics, mastery of language, interpretation of fables, learning to play chess, immediate memory for numbers, for forms, and for stories, puzzle solution, and motor ability. A number of these tests had been described in earlier works, but most of them were originated by Terman. He found that the dull boys, who were older and stronger, excelled the bright on motor tests, but fell behind them on the mental tests. Many of these tests were standardized later.

At the University of Rome, also working somewhat independently, Sante de Sanctis (1906) designed six tests to be used for classification of the feeble-minded. His battery emphasized what are now known as performance tests, in which one had to select and manipulate various colored balls and cubes and plane figures.

At the Vineland Training School in New Jersey, Goddard (1909) collected and devised twenty-five tests to be used in the diagnosis of feeble-mindedness before he saw Binet's work.

In 1908 Binet incorporated the mental-level concept into a new scale of fifty-nine items. Three to eight items were selected to represent each age level from three to thirteen years. Each test was assigned a certain number of months' credit, and a person's score was the total years and months of mental age which he had earned. The scale was arranged so that the average child of a particular chronological age would have a corresponding mental age.

This work was eagerly read. Translations of the 1908 scale were applied in Italy by Ferrari (1908), and by Treves and Soffiotti (1909); in Switzerland by Descœudres (1911); in Germany by Bobertag (1912); in America by Goddard (1911), Kuhlmann (1911), Terman and Childs (1912); and in England by Johnson (1911). All of these investigators reported that Binet's tests resulted in too large a percentage of children rated as superior below the age of ten years, and too small a percentage in the higher age levels.

Stern (1914), however, considered that this agreement of findings

from six different countries using different languages and testing
children from different environments was strong evidence that the
tests measured the "general developmental conditions of intelligence
—and not mere fragments of knowledge and attainments acquired by
chance."

In Germany Stern (1900) published a book on differential psychology and Meumann (1905) made an extensive review of test literature
which indicated notable advances in Germany before Binet's first
scale became widely used. Meumann pointed out the need of an
indication of rate of development, because the older feeble-minded
children were more retarded in mental age than the younger. To
meet this need, Kuhlmann (1912), Stern (1914), and Yerkes, Bridges,
and Hardwick (1915), apparently working independently, suggested
indices to be found by dividing an individual's achievement by the
age-group average. Terman (1916) divided the MA by the CA and
called the resulting index an IQ.

Terman became so much interested in the 1908 Binet scale that he
applied a translation of it to four hundred nonselected children. He
was then convinced that the scale was practical in spite of imperfec-
tions in sampling and scaling techniques. He set about to correct
some of these defects. The idea, which Binet and others had often
repeated, that an adequate measure of intelligence can only be secured from a variety of tests was accepted because the pooled results
seemed to distinguish between bright and dull better than any one
single type of test.

Binet's last scale appeared in 1911, the year in which he died. Several reading and writing tests which he believed depended too much
on special training were omitted. He relocated many of the items,
particularly in the higher age groups. These changes resulted in a
scale which had five items at each age from three years to adult,
omitting the eleven-, the thirteen-, and the fifteen-year levels.

Terman's Revisions

In 1916 Terman published a revision of the 1911 Binet scale upon
which he and his associates had been at work four years. The original
items were restated to remove ambiguities in administration and
scoring. The scale included tests for children of three years to adults
of superior ability. It was rapidly adopted as the standard individual test of intelligence by most of the schools and clinics in America.

Terman's 1916 scale was replaced after 20 years of wide application
by a revision published in 1937 by Terman and Merrill. Most of the
items of the 1916 scale were retained and the scale was extended
down to the two-year level, and up to the twenty-two-year level. The

1937 revision provides two equivalent forms, called Forms L and M (see Illus. 36). Both forms contain tests for each 6-month level from two to five years, and for each 12-month level from five to fourteen years, and for four higher levels. The four highest levels are called the Average Adult, Superior Adult I, Superior Adult II, and Superior Adult III. An inspection of Illus. 36 gives a rough idea of the types of processes used in these scales. At the earlier ages, objects, pictures, and parts of the body are more often included in the test situation than at later age levels. Tests of immediate memory spans for words and numbers are found throughout the scale. At the higher levels are found more items which seem to depend upon abstract verbal and numerical reasoning. The reasoning elements at any age level seem to the writer to contribute less to the average score than recall of learned factual material. A large box of standard materials is used at age levels from two to six years. Some of these materials are shown in Illus. 37. Cards with standard pictures and other printed material are also used at later ages.

The authors discuss the tests qualitatively. Thus, on page 235 verbal absurdities at the eight-year level are evaluated as follows:

The detection of absurdities has again shown itself to be one of the most valid and serviceable of our tests. No other test in the scale, with the exception of vocabulary, yields more consistently high correlations with total score. These range from .72 to .75 for a single age group. The test appears to be little influenced by schooling or by differences in social status.

The purpose of the test is to discover whether the subject can point out the intellectually irreconcilable elements of the situation presented. The only difficulty is in judging whether the response shows that the subject has seen the incongruity. The child who has seen the point instantly often indicates that fact by repeating the critical phrase, and the dull, uncomprehending child may just try to say over what you have said. . . .

In discussing the Memory for Designs Test in the ninth year (p. 248), the authors write:

The figures are, of course, perceived as meaningful wholes; that is, the lines of the figures constitute designs and, in so far as they are recalled, are recalled as related. Whatever may be the processes involved—attention, visual memory, kinesthesis—it is very certain that they differ from one individual to another and that the dependence, for instance, on visual cues is more marked in some children than in others. It is often possible to note the utilization of kinesthetic cues as the child practices the designs with pencil in air during the ten-second exposure interval.

For *half credit* all of the elements must be present, but inaccuracies due to omission or addition of details or to irregularities in size and shape of the figures are overlooked. The samples on pages 250–51 indicate the standard for plus, half credit, and minus.

ILLUS. 36. REVISED STANFORD-BINET TESTS OF INTELLIGENCE

Partial Outline of Form L

YEAR II

(6 tests count 1 month each, or 4 *tests, 1½ months each.)

1. * Place three small blocks into similar holes in a board.
2. Point to toys when their names are given.
3. * Point to parts of a large paper doll when parts are named.
4. Build a four-cube tower after demonstration.
5. * Name common objects from separate pictures.
6. * Use a two-word sentence spontaneously; See kitty.
    Alternate: Obey simple commands to manipulate small toys.

YEAR III–6

(6 tests count 1 month each, or 4 * tests count 1½ months each.)

1. * Obey simple commands to manipulate small toys.
2. * Name common objects from separate pictures.
3. Point to the longer of two sticks.
4. Name at least three objects shown in one picture.
5. * Point to objects to indicate use: Show me which one we drink out of.
6. * Tell what to do in common situations.
    Alternate: Draw a cross with a pencil after demonstration.

YEAR VI

(6 tests count 2 months each, or 4 * tests count 3 months each.)

1. * Define five words orally by description, use, or classification.
2. * Make a simple bead-chain pattern from memory after a demonstration.
3. Tell what part is missing from four pictured objects.
4. * Select certain numbers of blocks from a pile.
5. * Point to one of five pictured objects which is different from the rest.
6. Draw a pencil line through a sample maze to make the shortest path.

YEAR X

(6 tests count 2 months each, or 4 * tests count 3 months each.)

1. * Define eleven words orally.
2. Explain why the pictured actions of a person are foolish.
3. * Read a passage of 48 words, then recall from memory a considerable portion of it.
4. * Give two reasons to support an oral statement.
5. * Name as many disconnected words as possible in one minute.
6. Repeat six digits after one oral presentation.

AVERAGE ADULT

(8 tests count 2 months each, or 4 * tests count 4 months each.)

1. * Define twenty words orally.
2. * Transcribe a short message in a code which is exposed.
3. * Give differences between two abstract words.
4. Read short arithmetical problems and give answer without using paper and pencil.
5. Tell what proverbs mean in own language.
6. * Give oral solution of a practical mechanical problem which is presented orally.
7. After one oral presentation, repeat a 24-syllable sentence without error.
8. Tell in what way verbal opposites are alike.

SUPERIOR ADULT

(6 tests count 6 months each, or 4 * tests count 9 months each.)

1. * Define 30 words orally.
2. Read aloud a problem concerning direction and distance travelled, and give answers without using paper and pencil.
3. * Give opposites of words by analogy.
4. * Watch examiner fold and cut a piece of paper, then make a pencil drawing to show how the paper would look if it were unfolded.
5. * Read silently while the examiner reads aloud a simple geometric progression problem, then give answers without using paper and pencil.
6. Repeat 9 digits after one oral presentation.

* Tests included in shorter form.

(Arranged from Terman and Merrill, 1937. By permission of the Houghton Mifflin Co.)

ILLUS. 37. STANFORD-BINET TEST MATERIAL

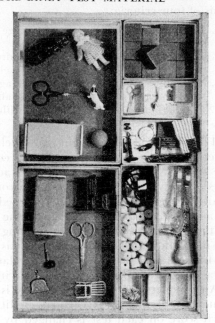

(Terman and Merrill, 1937. By permission of the Houghton Mifflin Co.)

Kuhlmann's Revisions

Kuhlmann (1922) brought out a revision of the 1911 Binet upon which he and some of his staff had been working seven years. It was a remarkably thorough piece of work, which extended the scale downward to the three-month level and up to a mental age of fifteen years. He included 129 items, counting a test once for each age group in which it is used. Of the original Binet tests thirty-seven were retained, but a number of these were modified or shifted to other age levels. The number of tests in each age group above two years was increased to eight. Credit was allowed for both speed and accuracy on many items.

Kuhlmann's (1939) *Tests of Mental Development* is the work of the staff of the Division of Examination and Classification of the Minnesota State Department of Public Instruction. About three thousand nonselected public school and preschool children were used to evaluate 121 tests which had been chosen from various sources, particularly Kuhlmann's earlier test and Gesell's (1928) studies of infancy and human growth. Eighty-nine regular tests and nineteen supplementary tests were finally included in the scale on the basis of four criteria:

1. Large increases in raw scores from age to age, in those tests which had several elements
2. Large increases in per cents of children in successive age levels who pass a test (in those tests which were either passed or failed)
3. Variability in raw scores in a single age group (a wide distribution of scores in one test was considered desirable)
4. Correlations of single test scores with total scores (high correlations were preferred)

The scores below the eight-year level, that is, on the easiest sixty-three tests, were the number of items correct. On more difficult tests the score used was speed-times-accuracy. Speed was usually calculated by dividing the right-minus-wrong elements by the time in seconds. The tests were usually limited to one or two minutes. Accuracy was calculated by dividing the number of correct elements by the number attempted. Multiplying speed by accuracy penalized the inaccurate worker. This penalty was imposed by Kuhlmann when he found fairly large negative correlations between speed and accuracy, although both were related to intelligence and age.

An innovation in this test battery is the use of a point scale designed by Heinis to give equal credits to equal units of growth. Each score on each test is changed by the use of conversion tables to mental units, called MU points. A person's total score, the sum of these points, can be changed to his mental age by another table. IQ's and Per cents of the Average (PA) [1] may be obtained from an 82-page table. The PA is preferred by Kuhlmann since it has proved to be more constant than the IQ's in retests over a period of years. He also found that age groups had more constant standard deviations for PA than for IQ scores. The standard deviation for PA's was eight points, approximately one half that of the IQ's. Kuhlmann believed that this smaller range of PA's is a better representation of actual individual differences in intellect than was the larger range of IQ's.

Point Scales

In 1915 and in 1923 Yerkes and others published a revision of Binet's work which did not assign tests to mental-age levels, but allowed credit of various points for each item. The total points could be converted into a corresponding mental age by reference to a table. Point scales are well illustrated by the work of Baker and Leland (1935), who published a battery of nineteen tests, each of

[1] The PA is an index secured by dividing a person's MU points by the average MU points for his age group.

which contained from 14 to 360 points. This battery includes the main types of items which are included in the Stanford-Binet Forms, and in addition a hand-and-eye coordination test. It needs a little more time for administration than the Stanford-Binet, but it has the advantage of including more items of each type, thus insuring a better appraisal of the individual, and of allowing a profile of results which shows a person's strong and weak points. This analysis is particularly valuable in remedial work and counseling.

In criticism of this scale it should be mentioned that the standardization is not so complete as is desirable, and that the profile does not indicate traits which are known to be independent or unitary. Profiles such as this probably represent fairly independent behavior patterns, however, and are often more useful than a single mental-age score. From analysis of such profiles knowledge of independent variables will eventually come.

The Wechsler-Bellevue Scale for Adults [2]

The Wechsler-Bellevue Scale is a widely used individual point scale for the examination of adolescents and adults. The test items have been selected to appeal to adults and to sample their abilities. Wechsler (1944) states that the purpose of the scale is twofold: to measure intelligence and to show diagnostic patterns of subtests.

He defines intelligence as "the aggregate or global capacity of the individual to act purposefully, to think rationally, and to deal effectively with his environment." He gives three reasons for thinking that intelligence is not the mere sum of abilities:

1. The ultimate products of intelligent behavior are not only a function of the number of abilities or their quality but also of the way in which they are combined, that is, of their configuration.
2. Factors other than intellectual ability, for example, those of drive and incentive, enter into intelligent behavior.
3. Finally, while different orders of intelligent behavior may require varying degrees of intellectual ability, an excess of any given ability may add relatively little effectiveness to the behavior as a whole.

The Tests. The scale consists of eleven types of tests, all of which are old in style, but new in content. Wechsler developed contents which seem more interesting and certainly more thorough than those of earlier tests. Six of the tests are termed verbal, and five performance tests. The latter may be applied advantageously to those with language or hearing handicaps, and the former to those with defective

---

[2] Wechsler has recently published a scale for children which is similar in construction.

vision. The verbal tests, all of which use oral directions and answers, are listed below. The correlations for ages twenty to thirty-four between scores on the subtest and scores on the whole scale are given in parentheses.

1. *Information:* Twenty-five questions, 7 involving geographical location and distance, 3 authorship, 3 measures, 3 hard definitions, and one each in aviation, date, inventor, name of the President, average height, population, etc. The difficulty range is large. (r = .66)
2. *General comprehension:* Twelve questions involving knowledge, judgment, and attitudes. Such as, "What would you do if you found a letter that was already sealed, stamped, and addressed?" (r = .66)
3. *Arithmetical reasoning:* Ten problems, to be done mentally, involving simple language, analysis of a problem, and computation. (r. = .63)
4. *Digits forward and backward:* The score is the longest span (list of digits) to be repeated correctly; similar to the digit spans in the Stanford-Binet Scale. (r = .51)
5. *Verbal similarities:* Twelve pairs of words, such as *egg—seed,* for which one common aspect must be mentioned, as in the Stanford-Binet Scale. (r = .73)

Alternate: A 42-word vocabulary test ranging in difficulty from *apple* to *traduce* (r = .85) is the alternate test in the above series of verbal tests. The performance tests include:

6. *Picture completion:* Fifteen cards, on which pictures of common objects are lacking essential parts. The examinee must tell which parts are missing. (r = .61)
7. *Picture arrangements:* Six series of cards similar to comic strips to be arranged in temporal order. The shortest series has three cards, and the longest six cards. (r = .51)
8. *Object assembly:* Three pictures cut apart: a manikin, a feature profile similar to those used by Pintner and Paterson (1917), and a hand. (r = .41 to .51)
9. *Block designs:* Seven designs similar to the Kohs (1927) Series. Only red and white colors are used. (r = .73)
10. *Digit-symbol:* Similar to the U.S. Army Beta Test No. 4 (Illus. 9). This is a paper-and-pencil test in which one must write in the squares symbols which correspond to the given digits as shown in the key at the top of the test page. (r = .63)

Interpretation of Tests. All of the tests have been standardized on age groups of normal persons. IQ's are given for each 3-month period from ten to fourteen years, and for fifteen- and sixteen-year groups, for a group from seventeen through nineteen years, and for eight five-year groups from twenty through fifty-nine years. In each of the original groups there were from 50 to 175 subjects.

The scoring of this scale, like that of all oral individual scales, is rather intricate. The responses for each item yield zero, half, or full credit, or varying points according to the examiner's judgment of the correctness and completeness of performance. The 22 pages of criteria for scoring leave many close decisions to the examiner's judgment. The raw scores for each of the tests are given approximately equal weight, by converting them into points on a scale for which the mean is arbitrarily set at 10, and the standard deviation (SD) at 3 points. The sum of the verbal-test scores yields a verbal MA and IQ, and the performance tests yield similar indices. A total MA and IQ are also available.

All of these indices are secured from tables which have been prepared so that the mean IQ will be 100 and the Probable Error (PE) 10. Since an SD is 1.4826 PE in a normal curve, the SD is approximately 15 for these IQ's. This is slightly smaller than the SD of 17 used by Terman and Merrill (1937). The total split-half reliability corrected for attenuation was .90, and the correlations between verbal and performance sections corrected for attenuation was .83 in a group of 355 adults. The median correlation of separate tests with total scores was approximately .65 for this group, with Vocabulary Similarities and Block Designs showing the highest correlations (from .70 to .85) and Object Assembly and Digit Span the lowest (from .41 to .50).

Intelligence Quotient Redefined. While retaining the IQ, Wechsler redefined it simply as the place of an individual in a group of individuals of approximately the same age. The average for any age will thus be 100 and the probable error, 10 points. Standard scores or centiles have therefore a constant relationship with IQ's. In defining IQ in this way, Wechsler has ceased to use the concept of mental age for calculating purposes. For practical purposes he shows scores corresponding to age-group averages so that one's absolute ability as well as the relative position in the group may be given. Illustration 42B shows the classification and distributions.

CONSTRUCTION OF BINET-TYPE TESTS

Two main procedures are necessary in the construction of any mental test: the selection of items and the scaling of items.

Selection of Items

The principal criteria used in selecting an item for Binet-type scales are described below.

Discrimination between Bright and Dull Children. In spite of the mass of data available, little has been published lately to show which items really discriminate best between normal and defective groups of the same chronological age. Burt (1922), Merrill (1924), and McNemar (1942), however, have confirmed the earlier work by showing, in scores of groups selected on the basis of school progress, large mean differences on the usual tests of facility in the use of language and number symbols, and smaller mean differences on motor and performance tests.

How items are selected is shown in Illus. 38, which compares the percentages of persons of the same chronological age in three IQ groups who passed each item listed. This shows that the first item in the sixth year (distinguishing right from left parts of the body), was passed by 43 per cent of the six-year-olds whose IQ's were below 96, by 70 per cent of the six-year-olds whose IQ's ranged from 96 to 105 inclusive, and by 89 per cent of the six-year-olds whose IQ's were above 105. A glance at this illustration shows that there are fairly large differences among these IQ groups on nearly all items. Items which did not show as large differences were eliminated by Terman. Selection of items in this fashion undoubtedly increases the internal consistency of a test.

In this illustration the indications of brightness are IQ's which were determined from the test items themselves. Hence the differences between IQ groups are doubtless somewhat larger than would be found among groups which were selected for relative brightness by some other method, for example, a teacher's ratings.

A Correlation between Item Scores and Total Scores. Terman and Merrill (1938) and McNemar (1942) published correlations between item scores and total scores. The highest are those for vocabulary which, for various age groups, range from .65 to .91, median .81. The lowest correlations reported are for block counting, .43; counting taps, .50; motor coordination, .46; and picture absurdities, .56.

Fourteen detailed factor analyses of many of the 1937 Stanford Revision items are reported by McNemar (1942). In all fourteen matrices a first common factor accounts for from 35 to 50 per cent of the variance of various items. A second factor accounts for from 5 to 11 per cent, and a third for from 4 to 7 per cent. The first factor seems to be nearly the same at various ages and to be a combination of general thinking and verbal knowledge, which is heavily emphasized. The second and third factors appear to be somewhat different at different ages. At the earlier ages there is evidence of a motor factor, and at the later ages there is evidence of a verbal, number, memory, or problem factor. These results seem to be almost the same as the results obtained by Burt (1922) in a similar study.

ILLUS. 38. RELATIVE DIFFICULTY OF ITEMS FOR NORMAL, RETARDED, AND SUPERIOR SUBJECTS

Per Cents of Single-Year Groups

		A			B		
		CA Constant IQ's			MA Constant IQ's		
		Below 96	96– 105	Above 105	Below 70	90– 110	Above 140
Year VI	1. Right and left	43	70	89	63	69	75
	2. Mutilated pictures	32	66	86	88	63	25
	3. Thirteen pennies	40	77	96	88	81	50
	4. Comprehension (2)	50	68	85	75	69	100
	5. Four coins	54	79	83	94	92	0
	6. 16–19 syllables	57	65	78	33	42	67
	Al.* A.M. and P.M.	64	82	86	—	—	—
Year VII	1. Fingers	53	68	85	91	85	50
	2. Description of picture	48	52	80	67	70	83
	3. Five digits	62	74	80	61	64	83
	4. Bow knot	43	71	78	55	71	33
	5. Differences	48	74	95	45	55	33
	6. Diamond	38	58	82	77	64	66
	Al. Days of work	33	62	85	—	—	—
	Al. Three digits reversed	39	55	75	—	—	—
Year VIII	1. Ball and Field	48	60	69	61	30	47
	2. 20–1, count backward	35	55	83	67	69	40
	3. Comprehension (3)	52	80	80	76	78	100
	4. Similarities	44	57	83	28	46	73
	5. Superior definitions	44	60	80	61	81	87
	6. Vocabulary (20)	26	57	74	45	43	40
	Al. Six coins	53	64	71	—	—	—
	Al. Dictation	65	90	100	—	—	—
Year IX	1. Date	48	68	88	71	63	26
	2. Weights	37	58	82	47	47	91
	3. Change	39	60	73	83	67	31
	4. Four digits reversed	45	62	88	58	67	54
	5. Three words	49	67	91	83	65	68
	6. Rhymes	39	67	88	59	58	91
	Al. Months	39	55	85	—	—	—
	Al. Stamps	40	76	91	—	—	—
Year X	1. Vocabulary (30)	20	60	80	39	56	35
	2. Absurdities	35	60	84	83	79	71
	3. Designs	45	57	70	71	65	38
	4. Reading and repeating	45	63	84	80	86	80
	5. Comprehension (4)	25	64	76	67	56	57
	6. Sixty words	30	70	76	61	71	81
	Al. Six digits	55	67	81	—	—	—
	Al. 20–22 syllables	45	57	79	—	—	—
	Al. Healy's form board	55	67	76	—	—	—

* Alternate.

(A. from Terman *et al.*, 1917. By permission of the Editor, *Educational Psychology Monographs;* B. from Merrill, 1924. By permission of the Editor, *Comparative Psychology Monographs.*)

Kuhlmann (1939) published correlations between total scores and separate items for age groups of approximately 150 pupils. The median was approximately .45. There was a marked tendency for the harder tasks to show smaller correlations than the easier. Thus, the tests used below the age of three years had a median correlation with the total score of approximately .91; from three to five and one half years, of .50; and above five and one half years, of .39. This finding may indicate a much greater internal consistency at the lower ages, or it may be due to other factors, such as the length of the tests and the range of scores in a group.

The results of both Kuhlmann and Terman lead one to suspect that a number of highly independent factors are sampled by these tests—a hypothesis discussed in Chapter VIII.

Discrimination among Adjacent Age Groups. Illustration 39 shows the selection of items which distinguish between adjacent chronological age groups, and the percentages of persons who passed

ILLUS. 39. PER CENTS OF AGE GROUPS PASSING ITEMS

Test	*Age*											
	3	4	5	6	7	8	9	10	11	12	13	14
AGE XI												
Absurdities	0	0	0	0	5	24	29	49	70	79	96	97
Difficult Questions . .	0	0	0	1	6	13	28	48	64	76	92	95
Sixty Words . . .	0	0	0	4	7	21	27	43	60	74	88	92
Seven Numbers . .	0	0	0	2	5	18	25	44	59	68	80	92
Sentence Building (1)	0	0	0	0	3	16	20	43	58	68	81	89

(After Burt, 1922, Table III.)

various items. From this data a growth curve for each item may be prepared (Illus. 40). The most desirable item is one which shows a rapid period of growth, both before and after the age which is to be measured. Such items will distinguish between adjacent age groups better than items which show little increase during the ages to be compared. The items shown in Illus. 39 were selected in part because they had fairly similar and regular growth curves. Other items have been found (Illus. 75, page 196) which do not show such similar and regular growth curves. The shapes of such curves depend undoubtedly upon both native and environmental factors. A special training

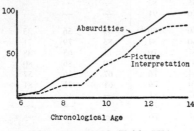

ILLUS. 40. PER CENTS OF AGE
GROUPS PASSING BINET ITEMS

Absurdities
Picture Interpretation

Chronological Age

(After Burt, 1922, Table III.)

period often results in a rapid rise in a growth curve. Training is therefore an important factor in determining both the difficulty of an item for a particular age group and the resulting MA scores for persons in that group.

Other Criteria. In the 1937 Stanford Revision, the items were selected after six successive revisions which involved shifting items from one form to another, and sometimes modifying the scoring to make an item harder or easier. The following features were considered to be desirable in the final selection of items: (1) ease of scoring, (2) short time requirements, (3) interest to subjects, (4) balancing or elimination of sex differences, and (5) equal means and standard deviation of IQ's at various age levels.

In attaining these features, thirty thousand cards were used for the mechanical tabulation of the results of the testing of the 3,184 native-born white persons in the standardization group. The authors Terman and Merrill (1937, p. 22) write:

By means of the Hollerith sorter it was then possible to plot for each test the curve showing per cent of subjects passing in successive ages throughout the range, also the curve of per cent passing by successive intervals of composite total score on the two forms. This was done for the sexes separately as a basis for eliminating tests which were relatively less fair to one sex than the other. It was possible also to compare the scores on the form given first with those on the form given second, to study the effect of practice, and to allow for it in the computation of the composite IQ's. The correlation of each test with composite total score (equivalent to correlation with mental age) was computed separately for each test, thus providing a basis for the elimination of the least valid tests. One important use of the Hollerith data was in connection with the balancing of the two scales; it was important that at each level the two scales should be as nearly alike as possible with respect to the relative difficulty of the tests located at that level and with respect to their correlation with total score.

These criteria of selecting items for a Binet-type test have often been challenged for the lack of analysis of the psychological factors involved. Brightness and age status are probably complex resultants of a number of forces which may be independent. Methods of analyzing such forces are discussed in Chapter XIV. For the present, let us assume that items which seem most appropriate have been selected, and consider the next step, which is the scaling.

Scaling of Items

Mental age is usually defined by a score on a test which represents the average of a narrow age group. For instance, the average score of a group of children just six years old is taken as the 6-year standard; persons who make this score are said to have a mental age of 6. There are two methods of changing test scores into mental age scores. One, called *point scaling*, assigns points of credit to all the items in a test, sums the individual credits, and then finds the average scores of various age groups. Point scaling is easy to apply since it only requires that the items be roughly placed in order of difficulty so that the subject is presented with all the tasks on which he is likely to succeed. This method has been used by Yerkes et al. (1915), Baker and Leland (1935), and Kuhlmann (1939). The other method, called age-level scaling, assigns test items to particular age levels and allows a number of months of credit for each item. This method, used by Terman, is hard to apply because it is difficult to find items which fit exactly into a particular age level.

Assignment to an Age Level. The process of assigning an item to a particular age level is rather intricate. First, the items are administered to a fairly large group of persons of various ages. Then the per cents of persons who pass the item are recorded, as in Illus. 39. An inspection of this illustration will show approximately at what age 50 per cent of a group pass the item, and how well any item discriminates between age groups. Here an item in the eleven-year level, Absurdities, shows at age nine, 29 per cent passing; at age ten, 49 per cent passing; at age eleven, 70 per cent passing; and at age twelve, 79 per cent passing. One is justified in concluding that it does discriminate fairly well among nine-, ten-, and eleven-year groups, but not between eleven- and twelve-year groups.

Illustration 39 also shows that the eleven-year group ranged from 58 to 70 per cent passing the five items for this age level. If all persons in the eleven-year group were just eleven years old, items would be needed at this level which were passed by just 50 per cent of the group in order to give the average person an MA of eleven years. This eleven-year-old group, however, included children from eleven years to eleven years, eleven months, with an average of eleven years, six months. Hence, if the item is to represent an eleven-year level only, the per cent passing must be higher than 50 per cent.

In the 1916 Terman scale, the items assigned to each age level had various mean per cents passing, as shown in Illus. 41. The smaller per cents passing shown in the higher age levels are due to the fact that growth increments become smaller with age. This fact is also shown in Illus. 39, where the differences between per cents passing in adjacent age groups are larger among the younger age groups than among the older.

The average per cents shown in Illus. 41 are central tendencies. Actually the items assigned to a particular age level are not all of the same difficulty. Illustration 38 shows that the range was considerable. In year eight the range is from 55 to 90 per cent. The more recent revision has a smaller range of difficulty at each year level. The problem of reducing this range is a persistent one because the figures for one age group will often differ from the figures for another age group which has had somewhat different training. Nearly all the more recent revisions have used for standardization groups of children who were within one month of a particular birthday. This procedure results in greater accuracy in the location of tests at a particular age level, but does not eliminate the difficulty of securing tests which were passed by a certain per cent of an age group.

When the scaling of items is at last completed, the final form of the test is ready for wider use. Its correct application and scoring require a great deal of preliminary training. Persons wishing to become proficient examiners should have, in addition to a college major in psychology, at least a year of special work in observing and administering tests under careful supervision. Thorough interpretation of scores requires even wider experience, including a knowledge of social factors which may affect the results, and a knowledge of probable sources of error.

ILLUS. 41. AVERAGE PER CENTS OF AN AGE GROUP PASSING THE 1916 STANFORD-BINET TESTS FOR THAT AGE

Age	Per Cent
3	77.0
4	77.0
5	71.3
6	70.8
7	68.0
8	63.2
9	62.3
10	64.5
12	62.4
14	55.6
Average Adult	59.8
Superior Adult	*37.4

* Per cent of Average Adult sample.

(After Terman *et al.*, 1917, p. 158. By permission of the Editor, *Educational Psychology Monographs*.)

INTERPRETATION OF MENTAL AGES

Mental age scores from Binet-type scales have the advantages of being widely referred to, fairly easily calculated, and in some respects easily understood. Since one often gets useful information from these scales, he should be aware of their main limitations. Some of the sources of error in the use of mental ages are discussed here.

Inequality of Steps

Nearly all studies of mental growth show that increments of growth decrease from year to year. For most of the available scales the observed differences between mental ages two and three years are much more noticeable than the differences between mental ages nine and ten years. Many of the mental age scales ignore this important fact, and their use leads to conclusions that a mental age of eight years represents twice the ability of a mental age of four, or that the year's growth from one to two years is equal to that from eleven to twelve years. Such statements, although common, are of doubtful value since they require special interpretations.

Changes in Meaning of Mental Ages above Adult Level

It is altogether impossible to measure persons in the upper half of the adult population on ordinary mental age scales, for they surpass the average adult's score, and a mental age was originally defined as the average score made by an age group. In order to overcome this difficulty, Terman (1916) and later several others have arbitrarily extended mental age scales above the average adult level. Thus, a mental age of 20 is not the score of an average twenty-year-old, but of a person who is generally in the highest 5 per cent of the twenty-year-olds. Mental age in this case loses its original meaning of representing the average of a particular age group, and becomes an arbitrary point fixed above the average in such a way that the IQ's of adults will be distributed according to some hypothesis.

In assigning arbitrary MA's above the average adult, Terman and Merrill (1937) assumed that adults should have the same distribution of IQ's as the children who can be measured by using true MA scores, that is, children from approximately five to ten years of age. These age groups were found to have fairly normal distributions of IQ's with the mean near 100 and the standard deviation approximately 17. The scaling method used for adults was as follows: tests which were passed by less than half of the adults tested were arranged in order of difficulty as shown by the percentage passing. They were then assigned places in various adult levels, and given a certain number of months-of-growth credit so that the adult sample would have an average IQ near 100 and a standard deviation of 17. This process resulted in a Superior Adult Level I, which corresponds to a mental age of seventeen years, four months, with six tests (Illus. 36), each of which is assigned a mental age credit of 4 months. The Superior Adult Level II contains six tests, the successful completion of each of which is given credit of 5 months. The Superior Adult Level III, which corresponds to a mental age of twenty-two years, ten months, has six harder tests in it, each of which is assigned credit of 6 months.

These changes in the meaning of mental age above the average adult level are not as widely understood as they should be, and this misunderstanding has led to many errors in interpreting results.

Moreover, the methods of assigning arbitrary mental age values are not well agreed upon, so that various authors have devised different standards which are not interchangeable.

Processes Measured at Different Ages

An inspection of all the Binet-type scales shows a distinct tendency away from the use of pictures or objects and toward more abstract verbal skills with increasing MA levels. In order to allow correct interpretation, more research is needed to show the amount of similarity or dissimilarity of processes sampled at various age levels.

Components of Equal Mental Ages

The question has often been raised whether a mental age of 10 in a ten-year-old represents the same abilities as a mental age of 10 in a fifteen-year-old. The answer has been given by elaborate studies comparing the scores of retarded and normal children of the same MA's (Illus. 38B). This illustration shows that Items VI–1 and VI–6 are more difficult for retarded than for normal or superior children, whereas VI–2, VI–3, and VI–5 are much easier for the retarded than for the superior. Burt (1922) and Merrill (1924), summarizing the work of others as well as their own, state that there is a marked tendency for older persons in an MA group to succeed better than the younger on items which depend to some extent on muscular maturation or rote memory. Verbal discriminations, unusual interpretations, and number relations are, however, relatively easier for the bright than for the dull. These results indicate that there may be several fairly independent variables in the test situation, such as rote memory for familiar facts, observation and comparison activities, and number combinations.

Thompson and Magaret (1947) compared responses of 441 defectives on the Stanford-Binet Form L with the percentages of responses of the standardizing group. Thirty items were found which showed significant differences between groups of similar mental ages. The defectives were superior on 11 items and inferior on 19. The results support the following three hypotheses:

1. Items dependent upon practical experience are about as difficult for normals as for the defectives.

2. Items where "rigidity" is a handicap are equally difficult for normals and defectives.

3. Items which were more heavily loaded with McNemar's general factor for the Stanford-Binet are easier for the normals than for the retarded.

This evidence is confirmed by other observers. A mental age of ten in the case of the retarded person usually represents a slow rote performance, whereas a mental age of ten in the case of a superior person represents success in quick observations and inferences. The speed factor, which seems important to many in evaluating superior mental ability, does not count much on the Stanford-Binet or Bellevue scales, but it is stressed in the higher levels of Kuhlmann's Revision. Since MA's and IQ's are not designed for analytical work, they do not demonstrate these qualitative differences between bright and dull children. Variations in the meaning of MA's can be overcome only by designing tests in which a certain score will always represent a particular pattern of skill.

INTERPRETATION OF INTELLIGENCE QUOTIENTS

Because the IQ is so widely used, its main limitations need to be examined closely. These may be considered under the following five headings.

Similarity of Average IQ's

One criterion of comparability is seen in the average scores of various age groups. If average scores are all 100 or nearly 100, then one can be sure that persons with IQ's of 100 all stand at the middle or 50th centile of their age groups. On the 1937 revision of the Stanford-Binet Scale, the average IQ's of various age groups used for standardization actually ranged from 100 to 109. This means that an IQ of 100 represents the 50th centile in one group and approximately the 30th centile in another, since the standard deviations of these groups were all approximately 17 points. The authors found, however, that smoothed curves of average IQ's showed less variation, and it is usually the case that larger populations give more constant average scores. Hence these variations in mean IQ's are only considered to be a serious source of error in careful studies of growth.

Similarity of Standard Deviations of IQ's

Frequency distribution of IQ's of various age groups have usually given curves which appear to be nearly normal in shape, with the mean at approximately 100 and the standard deviation about 17. Illustration 42 (A and B) contains distributions of IQ's and two commonly used classifications of brightness.

There may be, however, differences in the dispersions of IQ's for various age groups. Kuhlmann (1939) reported larger SD's in preschool groups than among the older groups. Terman and Merrill

ILLUS. 42A. DISTRIBUTIONS OF COMPOSITE L-M IQ'S OF THE
STANDARDIZATION GROUP

IQ	Classifications	Per Cent
160–169		0.03
150–159	very superior	0.2
140–149		1.1
130–139	superior	3.1
120–129		8.2
110–119	high average	18.1
100–109	normal or average	23.5
90–99		23.0
80–89	low average	14.5
70–79	borderline defective	5.6
60–69		2.0
50–59	mentally defective	0.4
40–49		0.2
30–39		0.03

NOTE: The normal group in A is more inclusive than in B. Merrill pointed out
that the distribution of scores in B was somewhat skewed toward the higher end
of the scale.

(Merrill, 1938. By permission of the Editor, *Journal of Educational
Psychology*.)

ILLUS. 42B. WECHSLER'S STATISTICAL BASIS OF INTELLIGENCE
CLASSIFICATIONS (THEORETICAL) *

Classification	Limits in Terms of PE	IQ Limits	Per Cent Included	Centile
Defective	—3 and below	65 and below	2.15	0.00
Borderline	—2 to —3	66–79	6.72	2.16
Dull Normal	—1 to —2	80–90	16.13	8.87
Average	—1 to +1	91–110	50.00	25.
Bright Normal	+1 to +2	111–119	16.13	75.
Superior	+2 to +3	120–127	6.72	91.14
Very Superior	+3 and over	128 and over	2.15	97.86

(After Wechsler 1944, p. 40. By permission of the author and
Williams & Wilkins Company.)

(1937) attempted to keep dispersions constant at approximately 17
points by selection of items, but variations still appear. They point
out (p. 40):

Attention, however, should be drawn to ages six and twelve, where the
relatively low and high values respectively are deviations too extreme to
be explained as purely chance fluctuations. The high variability at age
twelve might conceivably be ascribed to the differential age of the onset
of pubescence, although it has yet to be demonstrated that pubescence
is significantly related to the rate of menal growth. Whether the atypical
IQ variability at age six resides in the character of the sampling at that

age, or whether it is perhaps an artifact of the nature of the scale at that level cannot be determined from the available data. In the lack of positive proof to the contrary, we are probably justified in assuming that the true variability is approximately constant from age to age. Repeated tests of the same subjects from early childhood to maturity will be necessary to determine whether this assumption is in accord with the facts.

McNemar (1942) has emphatically pointed out, however, that the normal shape of the usually found IQ distributions does not mean that intelligence is normally distributed in the groups tested. The shape of the distribution is dependent partly upon the units of measurement, and upon the accuracy with which a trait is sampled, neither of which can be directly observed.

Calculation for Adults

When an attempt is made to calculate IQ's for adults, a serious difficulty is met, because mental age gradually stops increasing during adolescence, while chronological age, of course, increases continuously. The difficulty is illustrated by the case of a person who had an MA of 16 when he was sixteen years old, and hence an IQ of 100. The same person might still have an MA of 16 at the age of twenty-four, which, if IQ's were calculated as before, would result in an IQ of sixty-seven. Such a change in IQ is undesirable and with the usual interpretation of IQ's it would be ridiculous. In order to have adults' IQ's remain constant, Terman decided to let chronological age remain constant from the time when mental age seemed to cease increasing in normal individuals.

A good deal of work has been done to find the average age of reaching maturity of intelligence or general ability, but no definite point has been found because growth ceases gradually, and it is difficult to secure good samples of the whole adult population. Moreover, scores in some skill and information tests continue to increase after others have ceased. For these reasons various authors differ in fixing the age of maximum mental growth. The results of measuring white soldiers in the United States Army showed that the average recruit made approximately the same Stanford-Binet score as a school youngster of thirteen years and nine months of age. Terman (1916) placed mental maturity at sixteen years, Pintner (1931) at fourteen years, Baker (1935) at fifteen years and eight months, Kuhlmann (1922) at eighteen years, Terman and Merrill at sixteen years, Kuhlmann (1939) at sixteen years, and Wechsler (1944) at twenty years. These discrepancies may be overlooked in rough comparisons, but they often make it inadvisable to compare scores from one scale with those of another without adjustment. It seems probable that there will always be discrepancies in estimation of the average age of reaching maturity until independent components of the skills which are to be tested are defined more accurately and measured separately.

Older Persons Given Higher IQ's

Wechsler has found, as was previously demonstrated by several others, that mean test scores declined for age groups after twenty years. However, he believes that the IQ should not decline, even though a person's absolute ability or speed has decreased. Therefore, he has published tables in which the same score yields a higher IQ as age increases. For instance, a total score of 98 will give an IQ of 100 at twenty years of age, of 102 at twenty-five years, 104 at thirty years, 106 at thirty-five years, and reaches 114 at fifty-five years. Wechsler's IQ's are consistent with his definition of an IQ—that it corresponds to a definite centile of a group. He also gives an efficiency quotient, which is simply the IQ taken from his "Table for Adults, 20 to 24 years." This age group is regarded as the most efficient on the scale. Once more we are made aware that good test interpretation requires considerable study of test norms.

Constancy of the IQ

Great importance has been attached to constancy of the IQ of a person who is tested at various ages for two reasons. One is found in the hypothesis that an IQ represents a constant native ability to develop. None of the leaders in the field of measurement subscribes to this hypothesis without reservations, but it has often been assumed to be true by others. The constancy of obtained IQ's is mistaken for evidence that the IQ's indicate native capacity. This conclusion is justified only if the environment has been held rigidly constant. In normal society enormous differences in motivation or opportunity to develop are sometimes apparent even in the same family. Thus a constantly low IQ in a child may sometimes mean a continuously poor environment.

The other reason for attaching great importance to the finding of fairly constant IQ's is the need for accurate predictions. In order to allow accurate predictions, an individual's IQ must either be nearly the same from year to year or vary in regular fashion. For example, if a girl's IQ were 140 at the age of eight, 96 at the age of ten, and 115 at the age of twelve, one could not predict from any test what she would rate on the next test.

Although a large number of studies have been made to determine how constant IQ's actually are in various groups of persons over various time intervals, these studies are as yet inconclusive, because of the difficulties of accurate measurement which have been discussed and because of the difficulties of studying the same children over long periods of time in a constant environment. A good deal of interesting work in determining the constancy of the IQ has been done, however, the results of which will be discussed under changes in the size of individual IQ's, and under correlations between tests. Changes in IQ's are of practical significance because they show what estimates are actually available for individual predictions. Correlations between tests are theoretically more significant, however, because they are not affected by certain types of scaling errors. For instance, a very high correlation between two tests may be found when the IQ's of a group have all gone up or down or when they have a greater or smaller dispersion on the second test.

Changes in Size of IQ. A number of studies have been made of changes in IQ's over periods of less than 3 months. When the environment was not markedly changed, most of these studies show an average improvement of about 5 points in IQ from the first to the second test. One of the most complete and interesting studies is that of Terman and Merrill (1937), who reported that all their correlations between IQ's on the two forms, L and M, were distinctly fan-shaped, with the larger variations occurring among the higher IQ's. From combined results of ages from three to eighteen years, the average differences between IQ's on the two forms ranged from 2.49 for persons below 70 IQ, to 5.92 for persons above 130 IQ. The 1,291 persons whose IQ's were from 90 to 109 showed an average difference of 5.09 points, which means that approximately one half of the sample group varied by more than 5 points and the other half by less than 5 points on a retest given a few days later. The mean variation of the superior groups was slightly more, and of the inferior somewhat less than 5 points.

Another interesting report is that of Psyche Cattell (1931), who obtained retests on the 1916 Stanford-Binet test at intervals of from zero to seventy-two months. Illustration 43 summarizes her findings in part. The striking thing is the loss of IQ in the children who were below average and the gain in those above average. This tendency is very marked in the longer intervals. No simple explanation of this was given. It may be that the retarded reach their maturity earlier than the accelerated, or the results may be due, in part at least, to difficulties in scaling items, particularly at the upper end of the scale.

Similar findings are summarized by Conrad, Freeman, and Jones (1944), who reviewed research done over a period of 20 years.

ILLUS. 43. MEDIAN IQ CHANGES OVER VARIOUS PERIODS
AFTER CATTELL, 1931

	MONTHS BETWEEN TESTS 0 to 24		MONTHS BETWEEN TESTS 36 to 72	
IQ	N	POINTS CHANGED	N	POINTS CHANGED
below 70	11	+ 4.0	15	− 7.0
70–79	41	− 0.8	38	− 3.5
80–89	75	+ 0.8	110	− 3.3
90–99	116	− 0.6	193	− 2.2
100–109	127	+ 1.1	166	+ 1.7
110–119	138	+ 1.1	101	+ 1.4
120–129	66	+ 0.8	35	+ 4.8
130–139	26	+ 1.5	13	+ 16.0
140 +	18	+ 8.5	0	—

(After Cattell, 1931, p. 547, Stanford-Binet Test. By permission of the Editor, *Journal of Educational Psychology*.)

Correlations between Tests. Numerous studies have been made of correlations between tests and retests. In general, the correlations over longer periods are smaller than the correlations over shorter periods.

Terman and Merrill (1937) reported that correlations between Forms L and M, administered within a few days, have a median of .88 for ages two to six years, and of .93 for ages above six years. The members of the twenty-one age groups were all within 4 weeks of a birthday or half-birthday. The spread of scores and the consequent correlations are therefore smaller than would be found in age groups with ranges larger than 8 weeks. The authors also calculated correlations (p. 46) for IQ's from Forms L and M for five IQ groups in single age groups:

130 and over	.898
111–129	.912
90–109	.924
70–89	.945
Below 70	.982

The lower IQ's appear to be more stable than the higher, but all are highly predictable. Correlations usually drop to about .70 when the first test is given to a subject who is more than five years of age and the retest is given after an interval of 3 years. For earlier ages or greater periods between tests the correlations are lower.

Follow-up studies of a group of a thousand gifted children were reported by Terman and Oden (1947). At the time of the original tests in the early 1920s the group had Stanford-Binet IQ's of 135 or more. The average IQ was about 150. About 20 years later 950 individuals, who averaged 152 in IQ on the original test, were re-tested using a difficult synonym-antonym and analogies test called the Concept Mastery Test. The average age at the time of retest was about thirty years. The results were not easy to interpret since no large random sample of adults had been tested with the Concept Mastery Test. From results of testing college students with both the Concept Mastery Test and the ACE Psychological Test or the Thorn-dike CAVD Tests, it seemed probable, however, that the gifted adult group scores in the Concept Mastery Test were about 2.1 standard deviations above an estimate mean for adults in general, or an average IQ of 134. This apparent regression from an average IQ of 152 to 134 (18 points) may be accounted for in part by the unreliability of the two tests, and the fact that the two tests probably do not measure the same types of skills. The authors estimate that about 9 points or one half the amount of regression is due to test unreliability, about 4 points to differences in functions measured, and about 5 points to maturational and environmental changes. About 6.8 per cent of the group earned Concept Mastery scores below the average of college students. There was evidence that some of these scores were not representative of true ability because they were made by persons who had graduated with honors from leading universities and were outstanding lawyers, physicians, or engineers.

R. L. Thorndike (1948) reported a similar study based on a steeply graded power test of vocabulary, used on a large adult voting sample, and the Concept Mastery Test. He estimated the average score of those retested by Terman to be about 1.73 standard deviations above the voting adult average. If the original childhood average IQ is taken to be 3.00 standard deviations above the mean, the gifted group had regressed about 40 per cent of their original position. The adults who were so outstanding as children now spread out over the highest quarter of adult voters, but about half of them fall in the highest 5 per cent. In childhood they all fall in the highest 1 per cent.

PERFORMANCE TESTS

Most of the tests described thus far in this chapter purport to measure general intelligence by evaluating oral or motor responses to a variety of oral requests. Inspections and analyses of results have shown that such tests tend to be measures of verbal comprehension and expression to a large degree. The difficulty of applying language tests of intelligence to various groups was apparent at an early date. Differences in language training, speech ability, hearing, and spoken language were so commonly found that nonlanguage tests of intelligence were among the earliest to be designed and standardized. Seguin (1846) devised a form board which was essentially the same as that now used in several scales (Illus. 44). In 1911 Witmer described

ILLUS. 44. MATERIALS FOR THE PINTNER-PATERSON SCALE

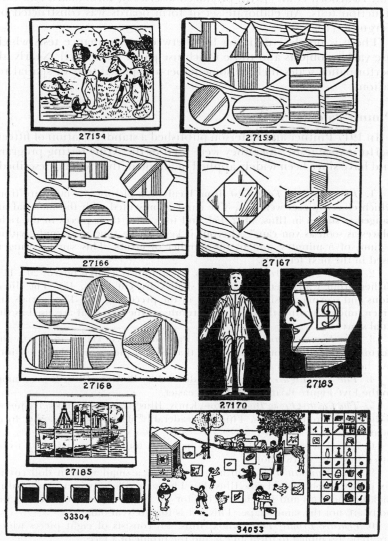

(Courtesy of the C. H. Stoelting Co., Chicago, Ill.)

a cylinder test and a revision of the Seguin Form Board. Knox (1914) designed a series of tests for estimating mental defects among immigrants at Ellis Island. Healy and Fernald (1911) produced a series of performance tests, and Pintner and Paterson (1915) adapted a Binet Scale to the deaf. Kelley (1916) devised a construction test, and Dearborn et al. (1916) produced a series of form-board and construction tests. An elaborate set of form boards was constructed by Ferguson (1920).

There is no clear dividing line between performance tests which use various objects and those which use paper and pencil. Nearly all performance scales include some paper-and-pencil tests of spatial relations.

Pintner-Paterson Scale

In 1917 Pintner and Paterson published a standardization of fifteen performance tests. Since they were used in the Army testing program and have since been widely applied or adapted, they will be described:

1. *The Mare and Foal Test* (from Healy) is a picture of a farmyard from which eleven pieces were cut. The child is presented with the material arranged as shown in Illus. 44, 27154, and told, "Put these pieces in the right places as soon as you can." A record is kept of the time in seconds, within a limit of 5 minutes, and of the number of errors. This same scoring is used in the next ten tests.

2. *The Seguin Form Board* (Illus. 44, 27159) is a large board, 20 x 14⅜ inches, from which ten geometrical shapes are cut (Illus. 45). The directions and scoring are similar to those in the preceding test. Three trials are given, one right after the other, and results of the best trial are used as the final scores.

3. *Five-Figure Board* (devised by Paterson, Illus. 44) is similar to the Seguin Board, but more complex in that eleven pieces must be fitted into five holes. One trial is allowed.

4. *The Two-Figure Form Board* (devised by Pintner, Illus. 46) is similar to the Five-Figure Board, but slightly easier.

5. *The Casuist Form Board* (from Knox, Illus. 47) consists of twelve pieces to be fitted into four holes. This is considerably harder than the other form boards.

6, 7, 8. These are smaller boards in which four or five pieces are to be fitted into one or two holes.

9. *The Manikin Test* (Pintner) consists of a small wooden doll cut in six pieces which are laid out (Illus. 48). The main difficulty is encountered in making the arms and legs fit exactly, for the places where they fit into the body are not the same shape. This test is for five-year-olds.

10. *Feature Profile Test* (Knox, Illus. 49) consists of eight pieces which are to be assembled to form an ear and the profile of a face.

ILLUS. 45. SEGUIN FORM BOARD   ILLUS. 46. TWO-FIGURE FORM
BOARD

Posed by Frank P. Greene

Posed by Mungo Miller

(Manufactured by the C. H. Stoelting Co., Chicago, Ill.)

ILLUS. 47. CASUIST FORM BOARD   ILLUS. 48. THE MANIKIN
TEST

(Manufactured by the C. H. Stoelting Co., Chicago, Ill.)

ILLUS. 49. THE FEATURE
PROFILE TEST

ILLUS. 50. THE HEALY PICTURE
COMPLETION TEST, FORM I

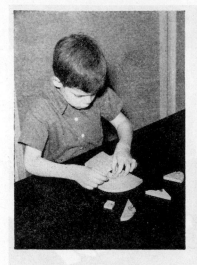

Posed by Donald Johnson

(Manufactured by the C. H. Stoelting Co., Chicago, Ill.)

11. *The Ship Test* (after Glueck, Illus. 44) is a picture of a steamship cut into ten rectangular pieces of equal size.

12. *The Picture Completion Test* (Healy) consists of a large picture of a rural scene, or of several rural scenes put together. Ten small squares are cut out, as shown in Illus. 50. These are to be filled by selecting the most suitable pictures from among forty-eight squares. The score is the number of blanks correctly filled in 10 minutes. Actually, 5 minutes is usually ample time, so the test has been standardized with a 5-minute time limit.

13. *The Substitution Test* (Woodworth and Wells) is a paper-and-pencil test in which rows of five sorts of geometric figures are to be marked with numbers according to the key at the top of the page. The score is the time needed to finish fifty figures (Illus. 51).

14. *The Adaptation Board* (Goddard) consists of a board with four round holes, three of them 6.8 cm. in diameter and the fourth 7 cm. The child is shown how one block fits exactly into the large hole, and then he is asked to "Put it into the right hole" when the board is placed in four different positions. The score is the number of correct trials (see Illus. 52).

15. *The Cube Imitation Test* (Illus. 53) consists of five black, one-inch cubes. Four cubes are placed about 2 inches apart in a row on the table in front of the examinee. With the fifth cube, the examiner taps the other four in a particular order at the rate of one tap a second. Then the examinee is told, "Now you do what I did." The order is simple at first but later becomes more complex. The score is the number of correct trials, which, of course, reflects the difficult task completed.

ILLUS. 51. SUBSTITUTION TEST

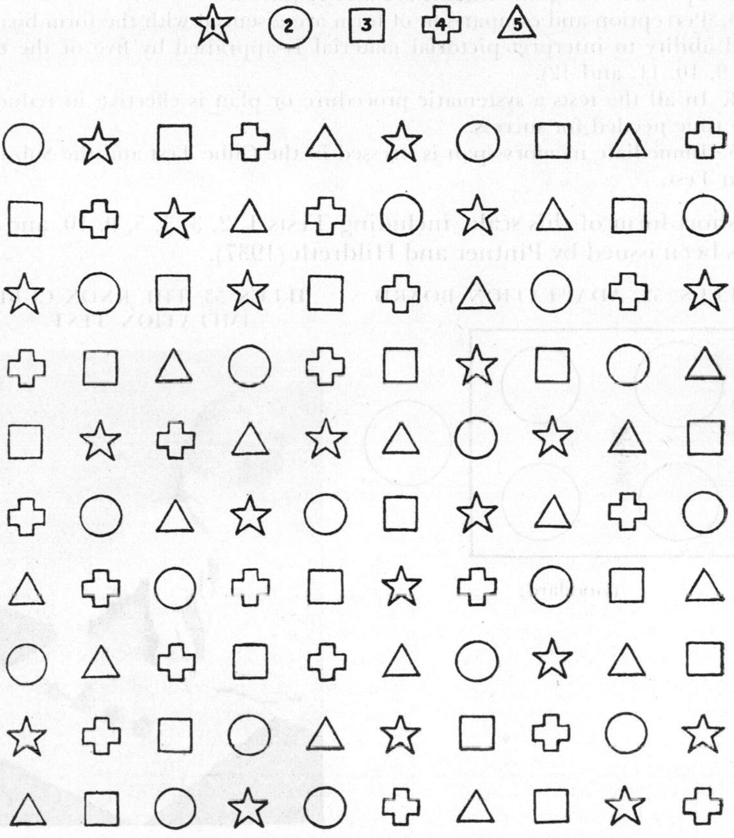

(Woodworth and Wells, 1911. By permission of the Editor,
Psychological Monographs.)

The authors prepared a modified age scale and a point scale from their results, including time, errors, and total accomplishment. They also published percentiles for each test for each age group and mental-age tables for each test. To secure a single representative mental age, they suggested using a person's median mental age, and this practice has been widely followed. The authors did not offer a systematic analysis of the processes needed for success in these tests, but some aspects seem obvious:

1. Twelve of the tests are speed tests where a few seconds represent the difference between successive age levels.

2. In all tests, manipulation of materials is required, and in the form board precise fitting movements are also required.

3. Perception and comparison of form are essential with the form boards, and ability to interpret pictorial material is appraised by five of the tests (1, 9, 10, 11, and 12).

4. In all the tests a systematic procedure or plan is effective in reducing the time needed for success.

5. Immediate memory span is stressed in the Cube Test and the Substitution Test.

A short form of this scale, including Tests 1, 2, 3, 4, 5, 9, 10, and 11, has been issued by Pintner and Hildreth (1937).

ILLUS. 52. ADAPTATION BOARD   ILLUS. 53. THE KNOX CUBE
                                              IMITATION TEST

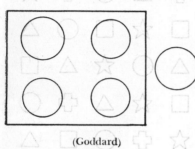

(Goddard)

(Manufactured by the **C.** H. Stoelting
Co., Chicago, Ill.)

Arthur Performance Scale

In 1930 Arthur published a restandardization of ten of the tests in the Pintner-Paterson scale (1, 2, 3, 5, 7, 9, 10, 11, 12, and 15) which were based on scores of approximately 1,100 school children from six to sixteen years of age. She also restandardized the Porteus Maze Tests and the Kohs Block Design Scale.

The Porteus Maze Test (1924) requires one to draw with a pencil through printed mazes (Illus. 54, A and B). Eleven mazes have been prepared for age levels from five years to superior adult. The mazes are called roadways, and one's pencil line must not cross any printed lines or go into any closed roads. Failure to observe these instructions leads to the immediate removal of the printed maze and a second trial with a duplicate form. Only two trials are allowed on nine of the mazes, but on the twelve- and fourteen-year levels four trials are given. Success on the later trials counts less than success on the first. The total credit is given in years and months of mental age. No time limits are set. Speed is not a factor in this score, but caution is probably a large factor.

ILLUS. 54A. PORTEUS MAZES   ILLUS. 54B. PORTEUS
MAZE TEST

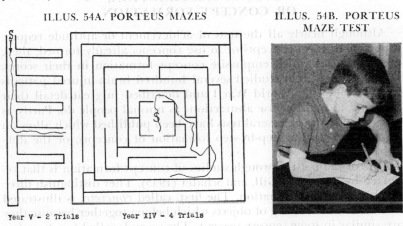

Year V - 2 Trials   Year XIV - 4 Trials

(Manufactured by the C. H. Stoelting Co., Chicago, Ill.)

The Kohs Block Design Scale (1927) requires the examinee to duplicate with colored cubes the designs on seventeen printed cards. All the cubes are the same, each having four sides colored red, white, blue, and yellow respectively; and the other two sides being divided diagonally between blue and yellow, and red and white respectively. After a simple demonstration, the cards are presented with the required number of blocks. The simplest designs use only four blocks and the most complex, sixteen. Time is limited to short working periods for each design, and the scores are points assigned on the basis of speed of completing a design.

Arthur's scoring ignored errors or number of moves, but allowed credit for either speed of performance or, in the untimed tests, achievement. Weighting the scores for errors was not found to have much effect upon one's position in a group of persons. Arthur published age equivalents for the scores of each test. She also furnished point scales which assigned credit on the basis of the power of a test to discriminate between adjacent age groups. By this procedure the relative weight allowed for a particular test may vary from year to year. She advised the summation of points to give a total score for the test. This total may be converted to a performance age (PA) by reference to a table.

A number of other nonverbal scales designed to measure general ability are described in Chapter VIII, "Group Tests of Ability."

TESTS OF ABSTRACTION, OR CONCEPT FORMATION

Although nearly all the tests of achievement or aptitude require a person to form concepts or to use concepts already formed, there are some tests which emphasize concept formation in their scores. Dr. Kurt Goldstein studied several hundred brain-injured patients for 10 years after World War I and described in great detail their inability to make or use abstractions as normal people do. Partly as a result of his work several tests have been published which allow an observer to see the step-by-step formation of concepts, or the difficulties encountered.

One of the most thorough studies of concept formation is that reported by Rapaport, Gill, and Schafer (1945). They distinguish three levels of concept formation. The first, called *concrete*, is illustrated by a nonverbal sorting of objects which belong together because they are similar in some sensory percept. The second, called *functional*, is shown by a verbal or nonverbal sorting of objects which are used together. The third, called *abstract-conceptual*, is illustrated by verbal statements indicating active induction and deduction. These authors point out that the answers for the Similarities Test of the Bellevue Scale are results of abstract-conceptual thinking, but that the test often fails to show the degree of deterioration because the patient may retain stereotypes of speech in spite of severe deterioration in concept formation. The Sorting Test of Goldstein and Scheerer (1941), which consists of objects common in everyday experience, is a better test because it reveals all three types of concept formation, and shows impairment at a stage much earlier than the Bellevue Similarities Test. The Hanfmann-Kasanin Test uses geometrical forms and colors which are not commonly used in everyday experiences. The test makes a greater demand on ability to examine and group objects according to new concepts than either of the two just mentioned.

The Sorting Test uses thirty-three objects which are common to most households: a knife, fork and spoon; a miniature knife, fork and spoon; a screwdriver and pliers, and a miniature screwdriver, pliers, hammer and hatchet; two nails and a block of wood with a nail in the center of it; two corks, two sugar cubes, a pipe, a real cigar, and cigarette; an imitation cigar and cigarette, a matchbook, a rubber ball, a rubber eraser, a rubber sink stopper, a white filing card; a green cardboard square, a red paper circle, a lock and a bicycle bell.

Part I of the test consists of seven instances when a different object is selected from the group and the subject is told to find all the remaining objects which belong with it. After each grouping the subject is asked, "Why do all these belong together?" After each complete inquiry, the objects are all grouped together again before the next trial. Part II of the test consists of twelve situations when the examiner places a group of objects before the subject and says, "Why do all these belong together?" The scoring includes three variables:

a. Adequacy of sorting is the degree to which all relevant objects are grouped together by some common or clearly defined similarity. Adequacy of verbalization is the degree to which explanations are given for grouping. The sorting and the verbalization may not be in close agreement.

b. Conceptual level. Here concrete, functional, and abstract levels, or pathological variations of these, are described. Thus the concrete level is illustrated by the explanation that the knife, fork, and spoon are grouped together because "You find them on the table." To say, "You eat with them," shows a functional level, and "They are silverware," represents the abstract level. Some pathological groupings are called by Rapaport syncretistic, fabulated, symbolic, and chain. Syncretistic definitions are so broad as to allow inclusion of nearly everything: "They all belong to men." Fabulated definitions make one object the starting point of a story which brings in other objects. Symbolic definitions radically reinterpret the meaning of objects; a piece of paper is a room, or the large and small forks are mother and daughter. Chain definitions are a series suggested by different aspects of different objects. Thus a red paper circle is placed with a red object, then the bicycle bell is added because it is round, then the pliers because they are metal. There is little retention of the conceptual frame of reference from one moment to the next.

c. Concept Span. This variable refers to the looseness or on the other hand the narrowness of grouping. Loose grouping is seen when the lump of sugar is placed with the eating utensils. Very loose grouping is seen in the case of a person who put all objects together that had the slightest roundness. The narrow grouping is seen in compulsive or overmeticulous persons who stick very rigidly to several aspects of the sample and find reasons for grouping none or only one or two objects with it. Other types of narrow grouping are due to inertia or to the use of symbolic meanings.

The Hanfmann-Kasanin Concept Formation Test and the Weigl Goldstein-Scheerer Color-Form Sorting Test each present about twenty blocks of different colors and shapes, and ask the patient to sort them into similar piles. Various procedures give clues when errors in grouping are made to help the subject find the "correct" grouping. The number and types of groupings indicate the methods of thinking. Degrees of flexibility, fluidity, persistence, and rigidity can be observed and recorded. In general those with severe brain injury of the frontal lobes can only group the blocks by one aspect at a time, such as color or tallness. When two or more aspects are required in grouping, such as tall and wide or tall and narrow, the abstraction involved is too difficult for many brain injured, even though many successive trials are allowed. A good deal of research by clinicians is now going on using material of this kind.

PRINCIPAL USES AND NEEDED RESEARCH

Individual intelligence scales are frequently used in schools and clinics. In schools they aid in the adjustment of pupils by analyzing the reasons for unusual success or failure. Among slow or fast pupils determining the MA will often help to decide how much acceleration or retardation is desirable. In clinics an MA can aid in detecting the effects of serious handicaps. Special adaptations of the Binet and of performance tests have been made for the blind by S. B. Hayes (1930, 1941) and for the deaf by Pintner (1931, 1945) and Hiskey (1941). Thus, for children who have poor hearing or vision, or who have speech, reading, or emotional difficulties, an MA and an IQ will often aid by indicating the most reasonable course of action.

When making individual applications of any test it is necessary that all important aspects of the situation be considered. For instance, John F. who is eleven years, three months of age was brought to a community clinic as a candidate for a special opportunity class. He was consistently failing in reading and arithmetic in the fourth grade in a large public school. He had missed four school days recently and admitted wandering about the city with another boy most of the time. A medical report showed negative results. He was a little overweight but normally active. On the Stanford-Binet he earned an MA of ten years, two months, and an IQ of .90, and on the Wechsler-Bellevue Test he earned a Verbal IQ of .81, a Performance IQ of .91, and a Total IQ of .86. His poorest scores were on the Arithmetical Reasoning, Digit-Span, and Digit-Symbol tests. On the latter there was some question of fatigue, but on most of the tests he seemed well motivated. He asked several times how well he was doing. On a Metropolitan Achievement Test he earned an average Educational Age of 9-3, or the equivalent of grade 3.3 ($3\frac{3}{10}$ grades). This yields an Educational Quotient of 84 (9-3/11-3). These results showed that he was a little more retarded in school achievement than in his general development. In such cases additional evaluations of social and emotional adjustments are, of course, necessary before a remedial program is advised.

Individual tests are also used to predict later successes. A recent study by R. L. Thorndike (1947) reports the prediction, from earlier Stanford-Binet scores, of scores on a difficult Verbal-Comprehension test given during the last year of high school. Illustration 55 shows

ILLUS. 55. PREDICTION OF SCHOLASTIC APTITUDE VERBAL TEST SCORES, FROM EARLIER STANFORD-BINET SCORES

Interval, in Years	N	r	σSAT *	σEST †
2	32	.71	91.0	64.1
3	52	.57	81.9	67.3
4	81	.44	98.5	88.4
5	80	.56	101.5	84.1
6	96	.55	91.3	76.3
7	95	.59	94.3	76.1
8	120	.67	92.6	68.7
9	64	.30	88.8	84.7
10	127	.49	104.0	90.7
11	173	.39	87.2	80.3
12	107	.39	87.9	81.0

* Standard deviation of Scholastic Aptitude Test.
† Standard error of estimate. $\sigma EST = \sigma_x \sqrt{1 - r^2}$

(From Thorndike, 1947. By permission of the author and the editor of the *Journal of Educational Psychology*.)

these predictions. They are large enough to be significant for groups but not for individual counseling. The correlations decrease from .71 for Binet Tests given in the tenth grade to .39 for Binet Tests given in the first grade. These correlations would be much higher if the group were not so highly selected.

Wechsler-Bellevue Scale

The uses of this scale have been reviewed by Wechsler, who found that certain mental disorders, race, age, and experience are associated with patterns or diagnostic profiles. He specifically warns against misuse of these patterns, but indicates that a careful consideration of them, together with other facts, will provide a more accurate diagnosis and prognosis. The following are samples of four patterns which seem to have been found fairly frequently:

Racial groups. There are some racial differences which are in need of further study. In general, among those tested, Jews did better on verbal than on performance tests, and Italians did better on performance than on verbal tests.

Occupations. Among adults a person's occupation may be related in some way to his scores. Carpenters generally scored higher on performance tests, and lawyers and teachers on verbal tests.

Age. Information, Comprehension, Vocabulary, Object Assembly, and Picture Completion tests hold up with advancing age better than the others do. The others decline more rapidly with age. In general the tests which *decline* with age require rapid accurate calculations, observations, or problem solving, while those which hold up with age are based principally on remote memory in contrast to immediate memory. The relative decline in normal adults (from fifty-five to fifty-nine years) is indicated by the ratio of .84 when the scores of DON'T-HOLD tests are *divided* by the total score of HOLD tests. The tests that hold up well with age are also the tests which usually hold up best among those with mental disorders.

Mental disorders. Wechsler points out that psychoses of every type, organic brain disease, and to a lesser extent most psychoneuroses show a much better performance in the verbal than in the nonverbal tests. A difference of from 8 to 10 points between verbal and nonverbal test totals is within normal range, but the amount varies with the intelligence level of the individual. Adolescent psychopaths and high-grade mental defectives, however, usually do better on the performance tests than on the verbal tests. Their failures are due to lack of the required ability rather than to disorganization of the ability.

Another clinical application is the measure of the spread of scores. Each subtest is equated to the others by means of a point scale, so that they all have a mean of 10 and a standard deviation of 3. Hence, if a subject's total score is 95, the expectancy for each subtest is 9.5, since there are ten subtests. To be significant, the amount by which the tests must differ from the mean is roughly one fourth of the mean subtest scores. Wechsler has adopted a practical method of summarizing deviations for persons with IQ's between 80 and 110, by using a plus for deviations from 1.5 to 2.5 above the mean and a minus for a similar deviation below the mean. Two pluses show a deviation of 3 or more above the mean, and two minuses show the same deviation below the mean. Illustration 56 shows a typical pattern for organic brain diseases. Wechsler also gives typical profiles for schizophrenics, neurotics, adolescent psychopaths, and mental defectives.

ILLUS. 56. ORGANIC BRAIN DISEASE PATTERN

Information	. . .	14	+
Comprehension	. .	12	+
Arithmetic .	. . .	9	
Digits .	. . .	13	+
Similarities	. .	11	
Verbal Total	. .	59	
Picture Arrangement	.	9	
Picture Composition	.	8	—
Block Design	. .	4	— —
Object Assembly	. .	1	— —
Digit-Symbol	. .	3	— —
Performance Total	.	25	
Total IQ	. . . .	95	
Verbal IQ	. .	115	
Performance IQ	.	74	

Case O = 1. Male, age thirty-four, showing definite neurological signs including marked hydrocephalus, facial weakness, slight tremor, absent abdominals. Also suggested Babinsky on left side with mild postural deviations on same side. Diagnosis: post-meningoencephalitic syndrome. At age six months patient had an injury with sequelae lasting six months, which was diagnosed as meningitis. This case shows the four most conspicuous signs of organic brain disease: large discrepancy between Verbal and Performance in favor of the former, very low Blocks combined with even lower Object Assembly and very low Digit-Symbol. While all of the test scores on the verbal part of the examination are average or above, the two lowest are Similarities and Arithmetic, which are in line with the organic picture. The only exception is the Digit Span which is good, both forward (8) and backward (6).

(After Wechsler, 1944, p. 161. By permission of the author and Williams & Wilkins Company.)

The clinical use of the Bellevue Scale has been reported on extensively by Rapaport (1945). Rabin (1945) and Watson (1946) have reviewed in fifty-one technical articles the clinical and other uses that have been reported. Rabin concludes that the Bellevue verbal scale correlates more highly than the full scale or the performance scale with most other intelligence tests. The verbal scale compares well with other tests in predicting academic success, but the performance scale is practically useless for such prediction. Rabin also feels that the measures of scatter or intrapersonal patterns have succeeded in differentiating some groups but not individuals, and that there is still insufficient agreement among group differentiations because of failures to control or allow for differences in age, race, schooling, intellectual level, and cultural factors. Long-range retest studies are still rare and much needed.

The use of deterioration indices is still in an experimental stage. Reports by Magaret and Simpson (1948) and by Garfield (1948) both indicate that for groups of fifty and one hundred mental hospital patients the Wechsler-Bellevue index of deterioration and the Shipley-Hartford Conceptual Quotient (CQ) showed correlations that were not significantly different from zero. Likewise, neither index was significantly correlated with psychiatrist's ratings of deterioration, nor with subsequent declines in total scores over a period of 11 months. These findings do not mean that these evaluations are without merit. Rather, they mean that more research is needed to define and appraise more accurately the phenomena under consideration.

Problems for Research

The Bellevue Scale opens the way to many research activities, most of which have been pointed out by Wechsler and others. Further study seems needed to establish the optimum length of the subtests for diagnostic purposes. Also the question of what abilities are actually being measured must be answered statistically sooner or later.

Cattell (1943) in a summary of theories of intelligence has defined two different kinds of mental ability, fluid and crystallized. *Fluid ability* is a "purely general ability to discriminate and perceive relations." It increases until maturity, then declines slowly. It accounts for the intercorrelations among children's tests of intelligence and among the speeded or adaptability tests of adults. *Crystallized ability* consists of memory, skills, and discriminatory habits established in a particular field. These habits were originally established through the operation of fluid ability, but no longer require insightful perception to a high degree. At all ages intelligence tests combine both fluid and crystallized ability, but in childhood fluid ability is normally predominant, while among adults the performance is more determined by crystallized abilities. For more thorough discussions of some of the problems in defining and measuring intelligence, one should consult Stoddard's *Meaning of Intelligence* (1943).

Another important field of research lies in determining the effects of environment upon measures of ability. Several authors have produced tests which they hoped would be relatively free from cultural influences, but little evidence of the value of these tests has come to hand. Allison Davis (1948) has pointed out that some of the Stanford-Binet test items seem to have a socio-economic bias. He changed certain items to eliminate what he thought were cultural loadings of content, in such a manner that the essential problem appeared to be unchanged. His results showed much smaller differences between persons in different socio-economic groups than were found when using the standard tests. His findings point to the possible injustice of using one test for many different groups, and the need for careful research to correct this situation.

A rough inspection of Wechsler's correlation matrices indicates a rather predominant verbal factor with small and unknown amounts of number, perception of form, spatial thinking, and dexterity. Reasoning is probably significant, especially in the tests which do not hold up well with age. A thoroughgoing factorial analysis followed by the development of unique measures is desirable.

Another research problem involves the method of combining and relating subtests. Although Wechsler writes that *intelligence is not a sum of abilities,* he does sum up arbitrarily weighted test scores in such a way that an IQ may have a great variety of qualitative variations. One can only roughly guess what is included in intelligence by this procedure.

A good deal of research is also needed to show the relation between modes of adjustment and test scores, particularly among persons with mental disorders. Such factors as paranoia, fear, and low energy may affect some test scores more than others.

SUMMARY

In conclusion it should be said that all of the scales discussed in this chapter originated as rough samplings of various types of behavior. Usually the types of behavior were vaguely defined by the authors of the tests, who either chose tests which distinguished the bright from the dull in school or in other situations, or chose tests for verbal or nonverbal characteristics, or for some other psychological pattern, such as reasoning or problem solving. Practically all these tests were in approximately their present form twenty or more years ago, and few of them have yet been submitted to careful studies of sampling of components, scaling, and analysis of the emotional variables in the test situation. There is great need for research in the development of individual verbal and individual performance scales, which will clearly evaluate some well-defined patterns of behavior. In order to be most useful a score must always represent the same qualitative and quantitative behavior pattern. Chapters VIII and XIV go much further into the problem of defining and measuring unique ability.

STUDY GUIDE QUESTIONS

1. What guided Binet in his selection of items?

2. What evidence is there that Binet's 1908 scale was not adequately standardized?

3. What evidence is there that bright and dull pupils were better selected by tests calling for only one skill than by tests calling for various skills? How is this evidence explained?

4. What use of speed, number, verbal comprehension, and reasoning was made in the 1937 Stanford-Binet tests?

5. In what respects does the Kuhlmann-Binet test differ most from the Stanford-Binet?

6. What age ranges are covered by the Stanford-Binet, Kuhlmann-Binet, and Wechsler-Bellevue tests?

7. How does the Wechsler-Bellevue test differ in content, arrangement, and scoring from the Stanford-Binet?

8. How does Terman define and determine the MA and the IQ of an adult?

9. How does Wechsler define and determine the MA and the IQ of an adult?

10. Indicate the relative merits of the Terman and the Wechsler methods.

11. How did Terman and Merrill select items to be included?

12. What evidence is there that a mental age of 8 represents different skills in retarded, normal, and superior children?

13. What are the usual per cents of mentally defective, average, and superior?

14. What variations are expected in retests on the Stanford-Binet within a few days? Within a year?

15. What evidence is there that Stanford-Binet scores at six years predict verbal intelligence at eighteen years?

16. What trends have been found among dull and bright children's IQs when measured from childhood through adolescence?

17. What analyses of Wechsler-Bellevue results are of value in clinical diagnoses?

18. What types of tests are included in the Pintner-Paterson Performance Scale?

19. What are the usual reliabilities of verbal and nonverbal intelligence tests, and what are the intercorrelations of these tests?

CHAPTER VII

MEASURES
OF EDUCATIONAL
ACHIEVEMENT

~~~~~~

This chapter deals with the types of instruments available for measuring the results of formal instruction, including language, number skills, and special studies. Nation-wide testing programs are also described and practical applications and correlations between tests are summarized.

CARDINAL OBJECTIVES OF EDUCATION

During the last thirty years public and private schools have undergone important changes. In many places the age of entering school has been lowered by the establishment of nursery schools, and the age of leaving school has been advanced two years—from sixteen to eighteen years. The value of practical applications of study has been demonstrated in the design of texts and in the changes in many courses. In order to bring about the best social development, the practice of promoting almost all pupils regularly has become widespread.

Objectives and methods of instruction have been scrutinized and redefined by educational leaders and classroom teachers. The ideals of the Progressive Education Association have been recorded by Smith and Tyler in *Appraising and Recording Student Progress* (1942). The National Society for the Study of Education has recently issued several yearbooks bearing on the appraisal of objectives. Especially noteworthy is the Forty-Fifth Yearbook, Brownell, *The Measurement of Understanding* (1946). The philosophy of The National Vocational Guidance Association has been voiced by Layton (1948). The National Education Association has published a number of volumes on objectives, among which are Lorge, *Methods of Research* and *Appraisal in Education* (1945); Conrad, *Psychological Tests and Their Uses* (1947); and Margaret E. Bennett, *Counseling, Guidance, and Personnel Work* (1945).

The following seven goals are found in almost all of the recent publications:

1. *Basic information.* This includes language, form, and number knowledge at all grades. These are discussed in this chapter.

2. *Skill in thinking.* Selection of evidence, drawing inferences, making practical applications. (See Chapters VII through XI.)

3. *Discovery and development of an individual's highest aptitudes.* Basic aptitudes are discussed in Chapter VIII, and artistic aptitudes in Chapter X. Special knowledge and skill tests in social sciences, physical sciences, foreign languages, and business studies are described below.

4. *Discovery and remedial treatment of poor social and emotional adjustments.* (See Chapter XXII, "Personality," Chapter XXIII, "Rorschach Methods," and Chapter XXIV, "Observations of Behavior.")

5. *Development of a sensible vocational goal.* (See Chapter XX, "Interests.")

6. *Development of interest in good civic, social, and artistic activities.* (See Chapter XXI, "Appraisals of Attitudes.")

7. *Good physical health*

The above goals show that education now, as ever, includes much more than the traditional reading, writing, and arithmetic. Those chosen for discussion have been selected on the basis of wide usage, reliability, and interesting diagnostic possibilities.

BATTERIES OF ACHIEVEMENT TESTS

Because many school systems have similar courses of study many publishers of achievement tests have developed batteries of tests (Appendix II). In order to avoid coaching or practice effects, most of these batteries are issued in more than one form. For many years the Cooperative Test Service and the College Entrance Board have issued annual forms. The other publishers issue from two to five forms at each level.

The time limits are fairly liberal in most cases, but speed of work is also a factor in certain tests. For the first, second, and third grades about 50 minutes are usually allowed, divided into two or more periods. For the fourth through the sixth grade about four 40-minute periods are generally used. For the seventh through the ninth grade six 40-minute periods are required for complete batteries.

A great deal of emphasis has been placed in recent years on the development of critical or constructive thinking. Test items to appraise the drawing of accurate inferences, however, have been common in both science and literature tests for at least twenty years (Illus. 12). Probably the presence of these items in standard batteries has helped to emphasize this important school objective.

Approximately all of the batteries are published in separate sections, and thus allow for the administration of short batteries. These usually omit some of the special subjects. Illustration 57 gives a rough comparison of topics included in achievement and reading batteries, and shows that the Traxler Reading Tests, which are typical of many, include a rate-of-reading score, which is not found in the Metropolitan Achievement Tests or the Iowa Educational Development Test. The latter includes a section on use of sources—abstracts, periodicals, indices, and library cards, etc. The Metropolitan Achievement Tests include separate scores for computation, history, and geography. The Psychological Corporation Clerical Examination includes word comparison and filing tests, which are not found in the others. More detailed descriptions are given below.

As yet only a few fragmentary studies of the relative merits of various tests are available. One should consult yearly reviews of tests, such as are found in Buros' *Mental Measurement Yearbook* and the periodic *Reviews of Educational Research*, by the American Educational Research Association, for more detailed criticism and information.

MEASUREMENT OF LANGUAGE

Language, broadly defined, is any series of oral or motor acts by which individuals communicate with one another. Language may be divided into two general classes: unlearned signals for action and symbols which refer to some experience. Animals have signal languages made up of movements and sounds which cause particular responses in other animals. These are often calls which lead to protection, flight, mating, the sharing of food, or other experiences. Such sounds seem to be developed through maturation along with the acts and without any intention on the part of the animal to give

ILLUS. 57. COMPARISON OF ACHIEVEMENT BATTERIES

Subject	Metropolitan Achievement — Primary 1-3 (60 min.)	Metropolitan Achievement — Intermediate 4-6 (220 min.)	Metropolitan Achievement — Advanced 7-12 (240 min.)	Iowa Educational Development — Grades 7-12 (290 min.)	Traxler Reading — High School 7-9 (46 min.)	Traxler Reading — High School 10-12 (46 min.)	Psychological Corporation Clerical Examination — High School (46 min.)
LANGUAGE							
Word meaning	x	x					
Paragraph meaning	x	x			x	x	
Rate of reading					x	x	
Grammar		x	x	x			
Spelling	x	x	x				
Punctuation		x	x	x			
Use of sources				x			
Comparison of words							x
COMPUTATION							
Whole numbers	x	x	x				
Fractions		x	x				
Decimals		x	x				
Per cents		x	x				
Arithmetical reason		x	x	x			
Literature			x	x			
Social studies			x	x			
History			x				
Geography		x	x				
General science			x	x			
Alphabetical filing							x

(Greene, 1951)

signals. For instance, animal psychologists usually agree that in a fight a dog barks or growls, not to scare an opponent, but because the situation sets off a series of movements which result in barking. Similarly, a mother hen does not cluck because she intends to tell the chicks that she has found food, but because the situation brings out a clucking response. Such explanations of communicative behavior among animals have been well supported by careful observations. The sounds made by small infants seem to be of this same unpremeditated variety, and among adults gestures and modes of expression often appear to be unlearned or only slightly modified by learning. Such elements of communication are important but so difficult to appraise that they are seldom recorded in test results.

A *symbol* is defined as an act or object which becomes a substitute for another. A symbol may or may not be intentionally given. Any symbol derives its meaning from the responses which it evokes. Sounds and words develop their common meanings by social agreement. Thus, the word *hot* is a symbol agreed upon by a particular group of people to refer to a common pattern of experience. Authorities usually agree that written language originated partly from pictures and partly from sound symbols. Certain spoken words probably began as imitations of characteristic sounds and as unintentional signals.

Psychologically, the most significant aspect of language is probably not the form, although that is important, but the processes of abstraction and combination. The isolation of a particular aspect of a situation is called an *abstraction*. When an abstraction is experienced in several situations and remembered, it becomes a *concept*. The simplest concepts are experiences of contrast or similarity of size, shape, length, and loudness. Concepts may also be very intricate patterns which depend upon several senses and which combine other concepts. Illustrations of complex concepts are: the rules of tennis and the meanings of the words *federalism* or *maturation*. Not all concepts are expressed or remembered verbally, but all words refer to concepts.

A complete list of important language factors would include the following somewhat independent skills and knowledges:

1. Techniques of expression: speech, grammar, punctuation, spelling, rhetoric, and handwriting
2. Word knowledge in various fields
3. Reading: complex skills of perception, comprehension, and reasoning
4. Muscular coordination, as in speech and writing
5. Visual acuity, as in reading and writing
6. Auditory acuity, as in speaking and listening

7. Knowledge of authors, publications, literary style, and form

8. Attitudes toward language usage and literature

Since the first three items cover the principal skills of language achievement, they are described here in detail. Items 4, 5, and 6 are dealt with in Chapter X. They involve elaborate techniques for diagnosis and remedial treatment. The last two factors, which concern literary discrimination and appreciation, are discussed in Chapters X and XXI.

Appraisals of Expression

Expression, either oral or written, although one of the most important and usual aspects of a person's behavior, is difficult to evaluate. Whereas aspects of expression, such as handwriting or pronunciation, can be mechanically recorded, their evaluation is always in the mind of the reader or listener. Moreover, some of the poorest expressions from a logical or a grammatical point of view have been popular and effective politically, socially, and even artistically.

Handwriting. Three kinds of evaluations of handwriting are fairly common. (1) Experts try to determine for legal evidence whether or not two or more samples were written by the same person. The way a person's handwriting may vary under different conditions is investigated. (2) Graphologists try to deduce indications of personality traits from samples of handwriting (Chapter XVII). (3) The excellence of handwriting is rated according to scaled samples of penmanship.

Scales of penmanship were among the earliest to be developed. That of Thorndike (1910), which seems to have been the first, consisted of samples reproduced with their scale values assigned by the equal-appearing-interval technique. Ayres (1912) used a similar method to devise a scale which has been widely used because he published grade norms for both quality and rate. Illustration 58 shows samples from his scale for three scale values, 20, 50, and 80. The averages for quality were found to increase from 38 for the second grade to 62 for the eighth grade, or 4 points for each grade. The rate in average words written per minute increased from 31 for the second grade to 79 for the eighth grade for the standard selection. Koos (1918) found the average quality of handwriting of adults in twenty-five different occupations to be 49.5 on the Ayres Scale, which is about the fifth-grade level.

Several check lists for a systematic recording of aspects of penmanship have appeared. Freeman (1914) devised one which not only lists defects but also notes their most common causes. Nystrom (1930) designed scales for color or heaviness, size, slant, letter spacing, word spacing, beginning and ending of strokes, and alignment. Remedial suggestions and diagrams to aid students accompanied each of the seven scales.

ILLUS. 58. AYRES HANDWRITING SCALE

	20	50	80
A	*(handwriting sample)*	*(handwriting sample)*	*(handwriting sample)*
B	*(handwriting sample)*	*(handwriting sample)*	*(handwriting sample)*
C	*(handwriting sample)*	*(handwriting sample)*	*(handwriting sample)*

About One-Third Actual Size
(Ayres, 1912. By permission of the Russell Sage Foundation.)

Scales of English Composition. In order to provide a more reliable means of grading English composition than the judgment of a single teacher, Hillegas (1912) constructed a scale for use in the fourth through the twelfth grade. It consisted of a series of short essays arranged in order of excellence by a group of judges and numbered to show standard deviation scale values and grade norms. About a dozen similar scales have appeared, among the most analytical of which is undoubtedly that of Van Wagenen (1923), who provided different scales for the following:

Exposition: Sixteen short essays on the topic "How I Earned Some Money"

Narration: Fifteen essays on "When Mother Was Away"

Description: Sixteen essays on "It Was a Sight Worth Seeing When the Troops Marched Away"

Each essay is rated for three qualities, thought content, structure, and mechanics, and the average rating is taken as an indication of general merit. In order to aid the rater, his attention is called (p. 2) to particular aspects of a composition, thus:

In rating for thought content in description, take into consideration:
  Maintenance of point of view (both physical and mental)
  Vividness of picture

Emotional reaction

Vigor and originality of diction

In rating for sentence and paragraph structure, take into consideration:

Unity

Coherence

Emphasis

Variety and complexity of sentences

The writer who uses many complex sentences shows a greater maturity of mind than the one who uses very simple or unnecessarily compound sentences, even though, from the very fact of the greater complexity, he may make more actual mistakes in structure.

In rating for mechanical errors, take into consideration:

Spelling

Punctuation (only cases of actual error, not cases where punctuation is optional)

Capital letters

Paragraphing (only cases of actual error, not matters of preference)

Here, too, one must take into consideration the range of vocabulary and complexity of expression. For instance, it is a more fundamental error to misspell "receive" than to misspell "psychological." Punctuation of very simple sentences would give less opportunity for error than that of complicated sentences or conversation.

Samples from the Description Scale, which runs from 0 to 100, are shown in Illus. 59. The scale values used by Van Wagenen were established by submitting the compositions to 119 experienced teachers who arranged them in order of excellence three times; once for thought content, once for structure, and once for mechanics. A scale value of 10 was arbitrarily assigned to a difference between two items which caused 75 per cent of judges to rate one item better than the other. The whole scale extends over ten such differences. These samples have been chosen to show nearly the same scale values for thought content, structure, and mechanics, but in school situations a composition is often found to be high in one aspect and low in the others. This diagnosis allows a teacher to aid a pupil in the most effective manner.

Since letter writing constitutes the major part of the written expression of perhaps nine tenths of adults, the scales for grading the general excellence of correspondence prepared by Lewis (1923) are of considerable interest. Five separate scales of nine items each have been assembled for (a) letters ordering material, (b) applications for a position, (c) narrative social letters, (d) expository social letters, and (e) simple narrations. Lewis suggests that pupils be allowed to compare their own compositions with those of the scale, so that they may note the good points and correct their errors. Another special

ILLUS. 59. ENGLISH COMPOSITION SCALES: DESCRIPTION
SCALE ITEMS

GENERAL MERIT 7.3

Thought Content 8   *Structure 9*   *Mechanics 6*

It was a Sight worth seeing when the Troops marched past.
Went thet marched past is was fun to watch then. And a puch of solirden narched
past.
And a puch of trump with flag and peolle with there flag.
And then cant a puch of boy and girls with cines of flag.
And there were twelte elenfeet.

GENERAL MERIT 49

Thought Content 50   *Structure 49*   *Mechanics 49*

It was a Sight Worth Seeing When the Troops Marched by.
It would send a thrill right through your body to see the troops march by. With
the drums beating and the band playing it would make any body wish to join in
with the kaki clothed men. All the soldiers looked like bunch of boys going to a
sunday school picnic instead of going to the gloomy trenches. It is wonderful to
see the soldiers keep time. The soldiers look as if they can't wait until they get
over there.

GENERAL MERIT 76

Thought Content 76   *Structure 79*   *Mechanics 73*

It Was a Sight Worth Seeing When The Boys Marched By.
The boys were going. It was hard to believe. It was hard to realize ninety
two boys from our own high school were marching before us for the last time before
they went to France. Line after line, and rank after rank passed us as we stood
looking in amazement.
The day was wonderful. There was not a cloud to be seen in the light blue sky.
There was a soft breeze from the south. The prime of our Indian summer was
here and, the boys were marching past.
Mothers, sweethearts, sisters, fathers, and brothers stood watching them as they
went by. It was a sorrowful day for many of the onlookers, because probly some
of them said good-bye for the last time and never to be welcomed home again.
Still in the heart of each mother there was a little pride which lifted their heads a
trifle higher.
An aged woman stood next to me and she said to me, "My but I hate to see Jimmy
go. He's the only one I have left, but — but I'm sort of glad he is going, because
its — its a wonderful thing hes going to fight for." Amidst her sobs she could say
no more.
Many others stood crying. A flag waved from every rank, from everyery window, and from nearly every little child.
As dusk came on everything became quiite. The boys boarded the train, the
people went home, everything was quite, the boys were gone.

(Arranged from Van Wagenen, 1923. By permission of the Educational Test
Bureau, Minneapolis, Minn., and the World Book Co.)

scale of considerable interest is that of Stewart (1934), who published graded samples of news stories from high school journalism classes.

Netzer (1938) began the standardization of an oral-composition scale for the fourth, fifth and sixth grades, after recording a large number of children's responses to pictures, incomplete stories, and objects. The children responded "best" to the objects, "next best" to the stories, and "least" to the pictures. Much more work along this line is needed.

The task of grading answers to essay-type examination questions is similar to that of appraising English compositions. Since this type of examination is probably the most common of all types, methods of grading it have been widely studied. A good many reports have appeared showing that one examiner usually differs considerably in assigning grades to essay-examination answers on two different occasions. Common self-reliability correlations, given by Stalnaker (1936), range from .40 to .60 in high school and college classes. Correlations between separate examiners have often been found to be less than these figures, owing to different standards of grading for facts, inferences, and grammar. Single readers of the Regents' and of the College Entrance Board Examinations have, however, usually shown self-reliabilities of .90 or more, and similar correlations between different readers are the rule. Stalnaker (1936) and Wrightstone (1938) have given detailed instructions for consistent grading. These include:

1. The question should require only one very definite and restricted answer, such as a statement of fact, or of an attitude, or an interpretation.

2. If several purposes or skills are to be graded, these should be graded one at a time.

3. The ideal answer should be carefully formulated and credits for partial answers agreed upon by all the judges.

Traxler and Anderson (1935) found that, when grading was carefully done, reliability of English essays of high school students was high, but that the retest-reliability of the pupils was relatively low over a short period of time. Much research is needed to show the usual relationships among such language skills as vocabulary, grammar, reasoning, and style.

Appraisals of Comprehension

The task of measuring comprehension is usually much easier and less controversial than that of measuring expression, because a comprehension test can use a multiple-choice technique and because experts can usually agree upon the scoring. Literally hundreds of tests of English Comprehension have been developed which can be scored by a clerk without knowledge of the subject, or even by a machine. Those tests which are widely used will be described under the headings: Measurement of Word Knowledge, Written Symbols, and Measures of Reading Ability.

Measurement of Word Knowledge. Knowledge of the meanings of single words is basic to all language skills; hence tests of vocabulary have become an essential part of all achievement tests. The only sure way to measure a person's vocabulary is to ask him to define all possible words. Since the unabridged dictionaries include more than half a million English words, this would take a long time. It has been found, however, that a fair estimate of a person's vocabulary can be secured in a short time by the use of well selected tests.

General word counts. In order to select important samples of words, a number of counts have been made of the words used most commonly in various communications. Thorndike (1927) and his staff produced an alphabetical list of 10,000 most commonly used words. These were found by the tabulation of about 4,000,000 words from newspapers, magazines, classics, novels, correspondence, and textbooks on common subjects. Each word was given an index number indicating its relative frequency. The *Thorndike Century Junior Dictionary* (1935), which lists and defines the 23,000 most common words, is an extension of this work to include a much larger sample of publications. A similar list of 10,000 words was produced by Horn (1926) based on the analysis of personal and business correspondence of adults, most of whom had received more than average education. Buckingham and Dolch (1936) have compiled a list of 19,000 words selected from eleven other lists and marked to indicate grade difficulty. Although the general agreement among various word counts is marked, different studies have yielded somewhat different relative frequencies of words. One of the reasons for discrepancies is the variation in words listed. Thorndike listed verbs and nouns from the same stem, as contain and container, but not the modifiers, contained and containing. He included as distinct units words which had the same root but somewhat different meanings and different frequencies, such as constituency, constituent, constitute, constitutional, constitution, and constitutionality. Persons who know one of such a series may be able to infer a correct meaning for most of the others. No thorough study has come to hand revealing the relationship between knowledge of roots and knowledge of words containing the roots. Likewise, since there is no standard and widely accepted method of counting words, it is not possible to speak of the size of a person's vocabulary in standard terms. The number of basic ideas needed for usual communication is much less than the number of words in Thorndike's list.

Special word counts. In order to examine vocabularies in special fields, word counts have been made of textbooks and other publications in both physical and social sciences. An excellent summary of master lists of terms used in the social sciences was reported by Kelley and Krey (1934) and their associates. A list of 5,200 words is given, which includes terms used in government, law, civics, political science, economics, religion, and sociology.

Minimum vocabularies. Several interesting attempts to select basic vocabularies have been made in connection with the teaching of foreign languages and the writing of dictionaries. West (1935) found that an excellent English dictionary could be written using only 1,923 words, and that 1,106 words were enough for an adequate speaking vocabulary. In a comparison with seven other minimum vocabularies, West found that all eight lists included 2,219 different words. Some of the words which seemed important to West did not appear with great frequency in Thorndike's list, but in general there was a marked relationship between frequency and usefulness of words.

Minimum vocabularies have also been devised for special fields of information. Pressey's (1934) description of the selection of items essential for the understanding of history is typical of the best work. She first made frequency counts of words in six widely used history tests. These combined with the published results of others resulted in a master list of 1,444 words. This master list was then presented to sixty-nine teachers of history in secondary schools and colleges with instructions to mark each word *essential, accessory,* or *unimportant.* The entire list was next rated by seven individuals especially trained in social studies who indicated their judgment of the values of each word outside of the history classroom. Finally, a list of 415 words was selected all of which were frequently used and highly rated for both historical and sociological usage. Illustration 60 contains the words which were finally selected.

In an earlier work Pressey (1924) prepared lists of basic concepts in fourteen fields. The fields, which are not mutually exclusive, are:

1. Grammar and Composition: English, French, Latin, and German
2. Literature
3. Arithmetic
4. Algebra and Geometry
5. History
6. General Science
7. Biology
8. Chemistry
9. Physics
10. Physiology
11. Home Economics
12. Manual Training
13. Art
14. Music

The selection of essential terms at the high school and college level for many different fields has now been completed by groups of interested teachers.

Selection of words for tests. A fairly large number of tests have been constructed to measure either general or special vocabularies, using the following procedure. A random sample of about one hundred words is selected from a word list, and test items are constructed about these words. The items are tried out on various age groups, and the order of difficulty is determined by noting the percentage of persons who succeed in each item. A final selection is made to secure a wide range of items and enough items at each level of difficulty to give a fairly precise and consistent discrimination between all persons tested. One of the first widely used tests was made by Terman (1916), who began by selecting a word on every tenth page of an 18,000-word dictionary. After preliminary trials he selected two lists of fifty words each, to measure general vocabulary for those with mental ages of eight to nineteen years. Terman and Merrill (1937) selected from these two lists forty-five words which seemed adequate to appraise general vocabulary for those with mental ages of from six to twenty-two years. This fact seems the more remarkable since a minimum of thirty words is needed to distinguish between all of these age levels. Usually only two words are needed to indicate one year's growth in mental age. The reliability of such vocabulary tests is generally high (.90 or more). Vocabulary tests are typically the most consistent of all tests since they are not affected much by speed, practice, or adjustment to the test situation.

Thorndike (1926) used his word-frequency lists in devising a test of 110 items divided into eleven levels of ten items each. The levels were scaled to represent equivalent steps, and the items in each level were chosen to be of practically the same difficulty.

Although the vocabulary tests of Terman and Thorndike were intended for use in appraising general intelligence, they are in effect achievement tests, and tests similar to these have been included in nearly every appraisal of educational achievement. More than forty of these have been standardized on a national scale. As a rule the general vocabulary tests have been found to correlate as high as .70 or more with total scores on achievement tests and intelligence tests.

If one examines the words included in many general vocabulary tests, he usually finds few terms from scientific or artistic fields. At the easier levels a large number of terms describing common objects and personal relations are found, and at the more difficult adult levels, literary, social, and business terms. This selection doubtless reflects the frequency of word usage in common communications and

ILLUS. 60. WORDS SELECTED AS THE ESSENTIAL CORE OF VOCABULARY IN HISTORY

A. GOVERNMENTAL TERMS:

ambassador	democracy	bill	appropriation
authorities	empire	declaration	appointment
consul	federal	decree	budget
governor	government	document	coinage
king	imperialism	law	currency
minister	monarchy	legislation	customs
official	republic	measure	debt
prime-minister	self-government	petition	duty
premier	tyranny	proclamation	expenditures
police	union	proposal	greenback
president		provision	mint
representative	city	report	protective
secretary	colony	resolution	revenue
senator	country	restriction	tariff
sovereign	county	statute	tax
statesman	dominion		treasury
vice-president	nation	abolish	
	province	abdicate	doctrine
assembly	state	adjourn	issue
bureau	territory	annex	policy
board	town	appoint	reservation
cabinet		authorize	
commission	alliance	compromise	centralization
committee	arbitration	concede	civil
conference	diplomacy	conciliate	civil service
congress	foreign	confiscate	domestic
council	international	enact	internal
department	negotiation	enforce	interstate
House of Rep-	neutrality	grant	local
resentatives	pact	impeach	municipal
league	peace	inaugurate	states rights
legislature	powers	nullify	
parliament	reciprocity	ratify	administration
senate	treaty	repeal	regime
session		repudiate	
	amendment	sanction	capitol
anarchy	article	veto	patriotism
commonwealth	charter		
communism	constitution	executive	prohibition
confederacy	act	legislative	reconstruction
despotism		judiciary	referendum

B. POLITICAL TERMS:

campaign	anti-slavery	majority	ballot
candidate	abolitionist	minority	election
caucus	democrat	unanimous	polls
convention	federalist		primary
deadlock	political party	conservative	suffrage
delegate	progressive	partisan	vote
nominate	republican	radical	
opponent	socialist		
plank	whig	lobbying	
platform		patronage	
politics		spoils system	
ticket			

C. ECONOMIC TERMS:

business	manufacture	employee	inflation
commerce	merchandise	employer	investment
commodity	production	labor	market
company	property	strike	panic
competition	raw material	union	speculation
consumer	rebate		stocks
exploit	shipping	bank	
export	trade	bankrupt	communication
factory		bond	public utilities
goods	corporation	capital	transportation
import	monopoly	credit	
industry	trust	crisis	prosperity
		depreciation	wealth
		finance	

ILLUS. 60. WORDS SELECTED AS THE ESSENTIAL CORE OF VOCABULARY IN HISTORY *(Cont'd)*

D. SOCIOLOGICAL TERMS:

aristocrat	rural	emigration	education
peasant	urban	expansion	institution
slave		immigration	invention
society	census	migration	reform
	inhabitants		
community	population	emancipation	people
homestead		freedom	private
pioneer	negro	independence	public
plantation	race	liberty	public opinion
settlement		oppression	standard of living
	mob		
	riot		

E. LEGAL TERMS:

arbitrary	nationality		fraud
illegal	native	jury	graft
invalid	naturalization	testimony	
justice		verdict	conspiracy
legal	appeal	violation	insurrection
rights	case	witness	rebellion
unconstitutional	convict		revolt
	crime	court	revolution
alien	decision	jurisdiction	secession
citizen	execution	supreme court	sedition
exile	injunction		smuggling
	judge	bribery	treason
		corruption	

F. MILITARY TERMS:

allies	navy	draft	invasion
belligerents	officer	mobilization	massacre
enemy	reinforcements		military
hostile	service	aggression	munitions
pirate	troops	attack	occupation
	submarine	battle	offensive
army		blockade	siege
commander	marine	bombardment	strategic
confederate	militia	campaign	surrender
cruiser	recruit	contraband	victory
general	soldier	defensive	war
fleet	veteran	embargo	
forces	volunteer	evacuation	armistice
naval		fortification	disarmament
			indemnity
			reparations

G. GEOGRAPHICAL TERMS:

boundary	district	exploration	agriculture
continent	region	navigation	irrigation
continental	section	voyage	reclamation
coast			
frontier	discover	conservation	Pan-American
prairie	expedition	natural resources	

H. RELIGIOUS TERMS:

clergy	denomination	catholicism	papacy
missionary	heresy	protestantism	pope
	intolerance		
creed	persecution	crusade	
	tolerance		

I. TERMS REFERRING TO CHRONOLOGY AND RECORDS:

ancient		history	civilized
century	era	records	primitive
current	event		
decade	modern	propaganda	movement
medieval	period	publicity	precedent
			tradition

(Pressey, 1934, p. 186. By permission of Charles Scribner's Sons.)

also the occurrence of words in dictionaries. Many examiners have, however, believed that tests of general vocabulary were more favorable to those with academic interests than to those with mechanical, agricultural, artistic or scientific interests. This belief has doubtless been a force in the creation of a number of tests of special vocabulary. Teachers in special fields have also desired such tests.

The procedure for constructing tests in special fields is similar to that used for designing general-vocabulary tests. A special master list is first obtained. Then the selection of words is made in such a way that an adequate sample of each level of frequency is thought to be included. The adequacy of the sample depends upon the use to be made of the test. After a test has been applied, the adequacy of the whole test, or of each separate item, in discriminating between individuals may be ascertained by the methods outlined in Chapters III and IV.

The Iowa Silent Reading Test, by Greene and Jorgensen (1943), includes four separate vocabulary tests: social science (20 items), physical science (15 items), mathematics (15 items), and English literature and grammar (20 items).

The Progressive Achievement Tests, Intermediate and Advanced, by Tiegs and Clark, include separate vocabularies for the same four fields, each of which consists of twenty-five items. Total vocabulary scores are secured by adding the four subtest scores (Illus. 65A).

The Michigan Vocabulary Profile Tests, Greene (1949), include eight divisions of terms:

1. *Human relations:* mental and social processes and situations
2. *Commerce:* business, manufacture, sales, economics
3. *Government:* legislative, executive, judicial
4. *Physical sciences:* physics, chemistry, mechanics
5. *Biological sciences:* zoology, anatomy, pathology
6. *Mathematics:* arithmetic, algebra, geometry, trigonometry
7. *Fine arts:* plastic, graphic, architecture
8. *Sports:* ten most common sports which adults play

Each division of the battery consists of thirty different items arranged on ten levels of difficulty. The items range in difficulty from those passed by at least 98 per cent of a group of college sophomores to those passed by 2 per cent or less of the same group. The gradation in difficulty of the items is such as to yield a test of high discriminative capacity at the senior high school and college level.

Each item consists of a definition and four words or phrases, only one of which is completely and accurately defined or described. The subject is asked to select the one which he thinks is correct. Items which correlated less than .30 with total scores in their division were eliminated.

An attempt was made to eliminate all items in which the right answer could be found solely by reasoning from knowledge of roots and prefixes or by eliminating wrong answers. This attempt was not entirely successful, but the number of items of this sort has been reduced by using the same prefixes and roots more than once in an item and by selecting wrong answers which were nearly, but not quite, synonymous with the right answer. It was desired to make an information test which would be affected as little as possible by reasoning.

Reliabilities as indicated by correlations between two equivalent forms of 30-item tests given one week apart are shown in italics in Illus. 61. These range from .78 to .94, with a median of .80. These figures show that longer tests are not necessary for fairly accurate individual predictions. If more accurate predictions are needed for a specific purpose, both forms might be used.

Illustration 61 also shows the intercorrelations among the various divisions of the Vocabulary Profile Test for a group of liberal arts college sophomores. Results for other grade groups were substantially the same. These correlations are all below .55, with a median correlation of .27. The divisions thus show a large degree of independence and would appear even more independent in a large unselected population. Practically zero correlations are found between scores in fine arts and scores in commerce, government, and physical sciences. Scores in physical sciences correlated approximately .50 with scores in biological sciences and mathematics. These figures indicate the presence of a number of fairly well-isolated factors. Psychologically there is little evidence for any functional relationship between the information in any two of these divisions, with the exception of mathematics, which is needed as a tool subject in many fields of human thinking.

Illustration 62 presents graphically the score of Henry Brown on the Michigan Vocabulary Profile Test. It appears that he was above the second-year college average in all except two fields: fine arts and sports. His highest scores were in physical sciences, where he exceeded the scores made by the lowest 98 per cent of the group. He was also in the high 10 per cent of the group in biological sciences, mathematics, and total test scores. Such profiles are valuable for appraising the technical information which a person has, and also predict fairly well his reading and composition skills in various fields.

Total Michigan Vocabulary Scores correlated .56 with the vocabulary section of the cooperative English Test and .61 with the vocabulary section of the American Council on Education Psychological Ex-

which correlated less than .30 with total scores in their division were eliminated.

An attempt was made to eliminate all items in which the right answer could be found solely by reasoning from knowledge of roots and prefixes or by eliminating wrong answers. This attempt was not entirely successful, but the proportion of such items was reduced by using the same prefixes and roots more than in an item and by including wrong answers which were nearly, but not quite, synonymous with the right answer. It is hoped to make a translation test which would be affected as little as possible by reasoning.

Reliabilities indicated by correlations between two equivalent forms of about thirty items given one week apart are shown in italics in Illustration 61. Thus, .61 is the average intercorrelation of ... These figures suggest that longer tests are not necessary for individual predictions. If more accurate predictions are needed for a specified purpose such forms ...

Illustration 61 also shows the intercorrelations among the divisions of the Michigan Vocabulary Profile Test for a group of liberal arts college sophomores. Results for other grade groups are similar; the sizes of these correlations, all of which show only a medium correlation, ... These divisions thus show a large degree of independence and indicate that even more independent indices could be selected. ... probabilities were relatively low correlations ... highest between scores in commerce, government, and physical sciences. Scores in physical science correlated approximately .50 with scores in biological sciences and mathematics. These figures indicate the presence of a number of factors, such as general factors. Incidentally, there is little evidence for any functional relationship between the information in any two of these divisions, with the exception of mathematics, which is needed as a tool in so many kinds of mathematizing.

Illustration 62 presents graphically the score of Henry Jones on the Michigan Vocabulary Profile Test. It appears that he is above the average college average in all except two fields: fine arts and sports. His highest scores were in physical science, where he exceeded the score made by the lowest 98 per cent of the group. He was also in the top fifth per cent of the group. He thought it a loss in mathematics, and that his scores have intrinsic value for forecasting the vocational education and that these values are also predictable with his reading and comprehension in various fields.

Total Michigan Profile scores correlated .30 with the vocabulary section of the Cooperative examination and .61 with the vocabulary section of the American Council Psychological Examination.

ILLUS. 61. INTERCORRELATIONS OF DIVISIONS OF MICHIGAN VOCABULARY PROFILE

Division	Form A Tests Designated by Number								Average With Total†	
(1)	1 (2)	2 (3)	3 (4)	4 (5)	5 (6)	6 (7)	7 (8)	8 (9)	Average (10)	With Total† (11)
1. Human Relations	.78*	.24	.32	.16	.25	.35	.17	.14	.23	.61
2. Commerce		.79	.40	.51	.40	.42	.07	.27	.33	.57
3. Government			.82	.31	.37	.24	.05	.24	.27	.48
4. Physical Sciences				.94	.54	.50	.00	.49	.34	.76
5. Biological Sciences					.91	.10	.36	.18	.31	.68
6. Mathematics						.86	.23	.21	.28	.55
7. Fine Arts							.79	.10	.15	.44
8. Sports								.80	.23	.48

* Numbers in italic refer to correlations between tests of thirty items each, which were intended to be equivalent samples of a Division.

† Correlations of each Division with the total are a little too high because the totals contain all Divisions.

(Greene, 1949. By permission of the World Book Co.)

amination for College Freshmen. Since all these tests have high self-correlations, the conclusion must be reached that they are measuring different and somewhat unrelated fields of information.

Written Symbols. In this division many well-prepared tests of spelling, grammar, punctuation, and sentence structure are to be found. Nearly all of these are composed of items which contain errors. The student is asked to detect the errors and in some instances to correct them.

ILLUS. 62. MICHIGAN VOCABULARY PROFILE SCORES OF
HENRY BROWN

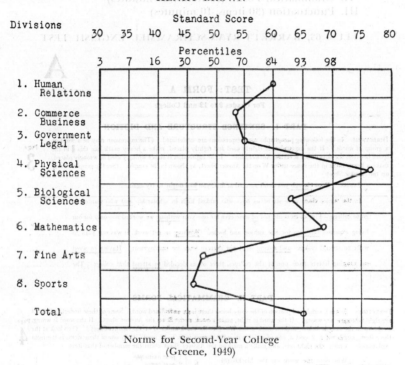

Norms for Second-Year College
(Greene, 1949)

English usage. The selection of items for tests of English usage has usually followed an investigation to reveal prevalent errors. The pioneer work of Charters (1920) shifted the emphasis from the rough scoring of papers to systematic diagnosis and remedial work. His studies showed that the misuse of fourteen common verbs gave rise to nearly 60 per cent of all oral errors. These errors were made by only 45 per cent of the students, hence individual rather than group treatment was suggested.

O'Rourke (1934), from a nation-wide study of English usage in the seventh through the twelfth grades, found that good sentence structure was the most difficult problem at all levels, that careless omissions or repetitions came second, and that ambiguous meaning came third. Errors in verb forms were uncommon, contrary to the reports of errors in the lower grades.

Illustration 63 presents parts of a typical test of language usage by Barrett et al. (1938) which yields scores for the three parts:

> I. Sentence Structure and Diction (30 items, 10 minutes)
> II. Grammatical Forms (35 items, 20 minutes)
> III. Punctuation (30 items, 10 minutes)

ILLUS. 63. BARRETT-RYAN-SCHRAMMEL ENGLISH TEST

TEST: FORM A

For Grades 9 to 12 and College

PART I. SENTENCE STRUCTURE AND DICTION

DIRECTIONS. In the following paragraphs some expressions are underlined. (The expression may be a word or a group of words.) If the expression is rightly used and rightly placed, make a heavy mark like this ▮ in the space between the dots under R on the Answer Sheet. If the expression is either wrongly used or wrongly placed, make a heavy mark in the space under W on the Answer Sheet, as shown in the sample. (See the sample answer on the Answer Sheet.)

Page
3

SAMPLE. Even though you don't succeed at first, you had ought to try again. .

In the senior class were six of us boys who ranked high in scholarship and who wanted to

go to college. Five of us could not of gone even for one year without we worked not only for our

living expenses but also for our tuition and books. Wishing to get work, it was our plan to

write to several colleges and asking what our chances were for employment. Having received

encouraging letters from one of the colleges, three of us decided to attend that college. The

PART II. GRAMMATICAL FORMS

DIRECTIONS. In each numbered portion of the story below there is an underlined word. Some of these underlined words are right and some are wrong. If the word is right, make a mark under R on the Answer Sheet. If the word is wrong, make a mark under W. (See the mark under W on the Answer Sheet.) Then look at the three items numbered 1, 2, and 3, one of which names the correct form to be used. Only one of these items is the right explanation. Choose the right one, and make a mark on the Answer Sheet under the number of that item

Page
4

SAMPLE a.	Who done the work on the blackboard yesterday?	b.	1 past participle 2 past tense ✓ 3 present tense	a, b.
1.	Before school closed in June us girls were making plans to spend part of our vacation camp-	2.	1 possessive case, to modify *girls* 2 nominative case, subject of *were making* 3 objective case, in apposition with *girls*	1, 2
3.	ing out. It was left to Jane and I to get a chaperon, for we must have one. After much	4.	1 nominative case, subject of *get* 2 objective case, object of *was left* 3 objective case, object of *to*	3, 4
5.	deliberation as to whom of our teachers would like to spend two weeks in camp, Jane suggested	6.	1 objective case, to agree with *teachers* 2 nominative case, subject of *would like* 3 objective case, object of *to*	5, 6

(Prepared by E. R. Barrett, Teresa M. Ryan, and H. E. Schrammel, Kansas State Teachers College, Emporia, Kansas. Copyright, 1938. By permission of the World Book Co.)

Scoring is simplified by having the student place all his marks on an answer sheet, which may be checked quickly. In this test some expressions in the printed text are underlined. The task is to determine whether or not the underlined expressions are rightly used. In Part II the student is asked to describe the correct form when a wrong grammatical form has been used. The test allows fairly liberal periods of work. Centile ranks are furnished which show means of 88, 96, 103, 106, and 109 for the ninth, tenth, eleventh, and twelfth grades and college freshmen respectively. Overlapping between the ninth grade and college freshmen, which is very marked, is typical of reports of this sort.

Illustration 64 is of a proofreading type of test by Wilson (1923)

ILLUS. 64. WILSON LANGUAGE ERROR TEST

Directions: This is a test to see if you can correct the mistakes that a pupil has made in writing a short story. (A short sample is then given and corrected.) That is the way you are to do in this test. There are three stories in this folder, but you are to take only the first one unless your teacher tells you differently. You are to correct all the mistakes in that story just as it has been done in the sample. Draw a line through each wrong word and write the correct word above it. Be very careful to correct every mistake. Work at your usual rate. You will be given time enough to finish unless you are very slow. Be a good sport; do your best and play fair.

STORY A

Errors   *Corrections*

Saturday Morning

Saturday morning is a busy time *at* ~~to~~ are house. A ~~feller~~ has a good chance to work.

Dorothy and I ~~Me and Dorothy~~ divide the tasks between us. Then we race to see who will finish

first. Last Saturday I *took* ~~taken~~ the breakfast dishes as one of my tasks. I am ~~especial~~

fond of washing dishes. You should have ~~saw~~ me work. I wanted to get through

so ~~as~~ I could play.

John ~~he~~ called up at eleven o'clock to see if I might play with him. I had *two* ~~too~~

rooms to dust before I could go. John saw that I ~~couldn't hardly~~ leave my work

until I had *done* ~~did~~ all of it. He brought over some doughnuts and gave them to me.

I ~~sure~~ appreciated the doughnuts. Then John helped me. It was ~~real~~ good of

him. When we had finished, I suggested playing marbles until time for dinner.

"I *haven't* ~~ain't~~ got no marbles," said John. "They *come* ~~comes~~ very handy," I replied. Then

I *gave* ~~give~~ him some of mine. I had ~~to~~ many for my bag. John and I enjoy marbles.

When dinner was ready, mother invited John to stay. "If I ~~was~~ sure my mother

wouldn't care, I should like to stay," he replied. John *saw* ~~seen~~ that he was really wanted

so he telephoned to his mother. He enjoyed the dinner and *ate* ~~et~~ heartily. When

the ~~them~~ apples ~~was~~ passed, John wanted one, but he couldn't eat ~~no~~ more. After dinner

we had another game of marbles. I ~~hopes~~ John may come over again.

16   *12*

in which twenty-eight grammatical errors are to be corrected. Median grade scores rise from 7 for grade three, to 22 at grade eight, and to 26 at grade twelve.

The question is often asked: do tests of the proofreading variety measure one's skill as well as scores taken from an actual composition? Willing (1926) made a comparison between a proofreading test containing 180 errors and an original composition. The composition revealed 12 errors per pupil, and the test, 59 errors. Although there were certain errors in the composition not represented in the test, it seems clear that the test was a more comprehensive instrument. Both kinds of appraisals should be used for remedial work, and considerable research is needed to find usual relationships between them.

A few diagnostic tests have been prepared from which a detailed check of the specific types of errors made by a student can be secured. Tiegs and Clark (1934) published the Progressive Achievement Tests Series, which contains the analysis of language errors shown in Illus. 65B (lower part of the illustration). Seven situations in which errors in Capitalization may occur are listed for remedial action; five in Punctuation; five in Words and Sentences; and 11 in Grammar. Although there are not enough items in each one of these subdivisions to yield reliable indications of special types of errors, the technique of diagnosis is probably sufficient for a great many situations. In Illus. 65A total scores for Capitalization, Punctuation, Words and Sentences, Grammar, Spelling, and Handwriting and a total language score are given in profile form for this same test. It appears that James Brown was considerably above average in Punctuation and Grammar, near the average in Capitalization and Words and Sentences, and far below average in Spelling and Handwriting.

Measures of spelling. Investigations of spelling difficulties, which are fairly numerous, are typified by the reports of Gates (1922) and Wheat (1932). Both studies agree that carelessness is a major source of error and that great improvements come from well-motivated drills. The six most common types of errors are:

Phonetic—*Wensday* for *Wednesday, hite* for *height*
Use of the vowels—*acheive* for *achieve*
Double letters—*leter* for *letter*
Omissions of silent letters and central syllables
Substitution—*goiny* for *going*
Mispronunciations—*chimley* for *chimney*

Probably all except the last of these types of errors are due to faulty visual memory.

For testing purposes the standard scales are nearly all of the survey variety in which items of increasing difficulty are presented. A typical example is the Ayres (1915) scale, which was made from a list of one thousand common words. After the words had been presented for spelling to large grade groups, the results were tabulated to show the per cent of each grade which succeeded in spelling each word. Words of approximately equal difficulty were grouped together as

ILLUS. 65A. PROGRESSIVE ACHIEVEMENT TESTS—ADVANCED
BATTERY FORM A, HIGH SCHOOL AND COLLEGE

(Diagnostic Tests keyed to the Curriculum)

Devised by Ernest W. Tiegs, Dean, University College, University of Southern California,
and Willis W. Clark, Director of Administrative Research, Los Angeles County Schools.

Name...... *James Brown* ...... Grade ... *10*

School ...... *U. High* ...... Age *15–4* Birthday ......

Teacher...... *Miss J.* ...... Date *12-12-38* Sex M/F

DIAGNOSTIC PROFILE

TEST	SUBJECT	Possible Score	Pupil's Score	Percentile Rank for Grade
1.	Reading Vocabulary	100	46	50
	A. Mathematics	25	12	40
	B. Science	25	10	25
	C. Social Science	25	14	60
	D. Literature	25	10	55
2.	Reading Comprehension	55	32	40
	E. Following Directions	10	5	40
	F. Organization	15	6	10
	G. Interpretations	30	21	50
3.	Mathematical Reasoning	60	38	80
	A. Number Concept	20	12	70
	B. Symbols and Rules	15	9	60
	C. Numbers and Equations	10	8	70
	D. Problems	15	9	85
4.	Math. Fundamentals	80	48	40
	E. Addition	20	15	55
	F. Subtraction	20	14	40
	G. Multiplication	20	9	35
	H. Division	20	10	45
5.	Language	125	74	30
	A. Capitalization	15	12	40
	B. Punctuation	10	6	70
	C. Words and Sentences	25	21	45
	D. Grammar	30	24	90
	E. Spelling	30	5	5
	F. Handwriting	15	6	20
	TOTAL	420	238	45

ILLUS. 65B. DIAGNOSTIC ANALYSIS OF LEARNING DIFFICULTIES

If the diagnostic profile on the first page of this test indicates that the pupil is making normal progress in all fields, the teacher will have no use for the following diagnostic analysis. However, where the diagnostic profile shows achievement below a desirable standard in one or more major fields, the following device will assist in isolating and analyzing the specific causes of difficulty as a basis for remedial instruction.

The numerals and capital letters in the diagnostic analysis correspond to the sections of the test similarly marked. For example, if the diagnostic profile shows unsatisfactory achievement in Test 4, Sec. E (addition in arithmetic fundamentals) an inspection of the unsatisfactory responses in this section of the test (by number) will reveal whether or not remedial instruction is needed in carrying, use of zeros, reducing to common denominators, and the like. These topics are then checked by the teacher as the basis for remedial work.

Once an adequate diagnosis has been made, remedial instruction is frequently a simple matter. However, teachers have in the past found the clerical work incident to following each individual pupil a heavy burden. Such extra work is almost completely eliminated if this diagnostic analysis is torn from the test booklet and kept on the teacher's desk, where the various items may be checked off as the pupil masters them.

READING

1. Reading Vocabulary

A. MATHEMATICS:
_____ Basic vocabulary ____ (2) __1-25

B. SCIENCE:
_____ Basic vocabulary ____ (0) __1-25

C. SOCIAL SCIENCE:
_____ Basic vocabulary ____ (14) __1-25

D. LITERATURE:
_____ Basic vocabulary ____ (0) __1-25

2. Reading Comprehension

E. FOLLOWING SPECIFIC DIRECTIONS:
_____ Directions in mathematical situations ..1, 2, 5, 9, 10
_____ Reading definitions and following directions..3, 4, 6, 7, 8

F. ORGANIZATION:
_____ Vocabulary _____1-6
_____ Use of index _____7-9
_____ Selecting references ____10-13
_____ Report outline _____14-15

G. INTERPRETATION OF MEANINGS:

_____ Selecting topic or central idea _____1, 10
_____ Understanding directly stated facts.....4, 5, 7, 8, 11, 12, 13, 14, 18, 22, 26, 28, 29
_____ Making inferences....2, 3, 6, 9, 15, 16, 17, 19, 20, 21, 23, 24, 25, 27, 30.

MATHEMATICS

3. Mathematical Reasoning

A. NUMBER CONCEPT:
_____ Writing integers _____1-3
_____ Writing money _____4
_____ Writing fractions _____5-7
_____ Roman numbers _____8-10
_____ Fractions and decimals.....11-13
_____ Exponents and roots........14-16
_____ Negative numbers _____17
_____ Abstract numbers _____18-20

B. SYMBOLS AND RULES:
_____ Symbols _____1-3, 8-10
_____ Vocabulary _____4-7
_____ Rules _____11-15

C. NUMBERS AND EQUATIONS.
_____ Negative numbers _____1-4
_____ Solving equations_____5-10

D. PROBLEMS:
_____ Simple problems _____1-2
_____ Sharing and averaging____3-4
_____ Square and cubic measure _____5-6
_____ Insurance and discount....13-15
_____ Ratio and percentage....7-11
_____ Budgeting _____12

4. Mathematical Fundamentals

E. ADDITION:
_____ Simple combinations _____1
_____ Carrying _____2-4
_____ Zeros _____1, 6
_____ Column addition _____3, 4
_____ Adding money _____4, 6
_____ Denominate numbers _____4-6
_____ Reducing fractions to common denom. ___8, 10-13
_____ Adding mixed nos. _____10-13
_____ Adding fractions and decimals _____14-15
_____ Writing decimals in column _____16-17
_____ Adding percentages _____18
_____ Adding abstract nos.____19-20

F. SUBTRACTION:
_____ Simple combinations _____1
_____ Borrowing _____2-5
_____ Zeros _____1, 3, 5
_____ Subtracting money _____4, 5
_____ Denominate numbers _____4-6
_____ Subtracting numerators.....7-8
_____ Reducing fractions to common denominators ___9-10
_____ Borrowing with mixed numbers _____12, 13

_____ Subtracting fractions from decimals _____14, 15
_____ Writing decimals in column _____16, 17
_____ Subt. abstract nos.____19, 20

G. MULTIPLICATION:
_____ Tables _____1-5
_____ Zeros in multiplicand ___2, 5
_____ Zeros in multiplier ____4, 5
_____ Two-place multipliers ___3-5
_____ Cancellation of fractions _____7, 9, 10, 11, 13
_____ Fractions and mixed numbers _____12
_____ Fractions and decimals.____16
_____ Pointing off decimals..16, 17
_____ Mult. abstract nos.____19, 20

H. DIVISION:
_____ Tables _____1-5
_____ Zeros in quotient _____1-4
_____ Remainders _____5
_____ Inverting divisor in fractions _____6-13
_____ Mixed numbers _____11-13
_____ Reducing fractions to decimals _____14
_____ Pointing off decimals....15-17
_____ Div. abstract nos._____19-20

LANGUAGE

5. Language

A. CAPITALIZATION:
_____ First word of sentence..........1
_____ Names of persons........2, 7, 9
_____ Names of places........2, 3, 8, 9
_____ Days of week and months.4, 6
_____ Titles _____5, 7
_____ First word of quotation.....6
_____ Over capitalization _____X

B. PUNCTUATION:
_____ Commas _____X
_____ Question marks _____
_____ Quotation marks _____

_____ Quotation within quotation......
_____ Over punctuation _____X

C. WORDS AND SENTENCES:
_____ Singulars and plurals....1, 8, 11
_____ Case _____5, 6, 9, 12
_____ Tense _____2, 4, 7, 8, 9, 13-15
_____ Good usage _____3
_____ Recognizing sentences.....16-25

D. GRAMMAR:
_____ Vocabulary _____1-7
_____ Parts of sentences......8-10
_____ Kind of sentences.......11-13
_____ Parts of speech.........14-30

_____ Nouns _____
_____ Pronouns _____
_____ Verbs _____
_____ Adjectives _____
_____ Adverbs _____
_____ Conjunctions _____
_____ Prepositions _____

E. SPELLING: _very poor_

F. HANDWRITING: _poor_ Quality and legibility _poor_

—2—

(This and the material reproduced on the preceding page, copyright, 1934, by E. W. Tiegs and W. W. Clark. By permission of the Southern California School Book Depository, Los Angeles, California, and the authors.)

shown in Illus. 66, where levels G, O, and Y are presented along with the per cents of words spelled correctly by each grade.

ILLUS. 66. BUCKINGHAM EXTENSION OF AYRES SPELLING SCALE

LEVELS

Grade	G	O	Y
II.	84	27	0
III.	94	50	2
IV.	99	73	8
V.		84	16
VI.		92	27
VII.		96	42
VIII.		99	58
IX.			73

G		O		Y
by	eight	remain	lemon	decision
have	afraid	direct	laughter	principle
are	uncle	appear	lying	accommodate
had	rather	liberty	mountains	accuracy
over	comfort	enough	nails	counterfeit
must	elect	fact	needle	dessert
make	aboard	board	nobody	digestible
school	jail	September	oar	immense
street	shed	station	palace	leopard
say	retire	attend	penny	marmalade
come	refuse	between	pitcher	millionaire
hand	district	public	regular	mucilage
ring	restrain	friend	repeats	orchestra
live	royal	during	reprove	parliament
kill	objection	through	sailor	perceived
late	pleasure	police	sentence	possess
let	navy	until	shining	precipice
big	fourth	madam	surface	recommended
mother	population	truly	sweeping	resemblance
three	proper	whole	sweeps	restaurant
land	judge	address	thief	seized
cold	weather	request	waist	superintendent
hot	worth	raise	waiting	surgeon
hat	contain	August	weary	thoroughly
child	figure	Tuesday	writing	
ice	sudden	struck		
play	forty	getting		
sea	instead	don't		
bread	throw	Thursday		
come	personal	canoe		
eats	everything	captain		
food	rate	cellar		
	chief	clothes		
	perfect	covered		
	second	creature		
	slide	curtain		
	farther	declared		
	duty	distance		
	intend	double		
	company	explain		
	quite	fields		
	none	floated		
	knew	holiday		

(Buckingham, 1927. By permission of the Public School Publishing Co.)

Methods of examining one's spelling ability include both recall and recognition. Dictation is one of the commonest methods and one of the most searching, since one has greater difficulty in recalling than in recognizing facts. The Stanford Achievement Test attempts to measure usual spelling habits by not telling the students that the dictation passage is a spelling test.

Another method of examination presents a printed series of words and asks the student to correct those that are misspelled. The Iowa Placement Examinations, Series E. T. I. (1925), present fifty words, of which twenty-five misspelled words are to be correctly written. The first ten of these are:

....	acceptance	....	disagreeable
....	appreciate	....	experiance
....	begining	....	evidantly
....	confirming	....	niece
....	crocheting	....	genuine

A third method of examination is illustrated by the Columbia Research Bureau English Test (1926). A word is printed four times, once correctly spelled and three times incorrectly, thus:

1. fifty	2. fivety	3. fifety	4. fivty
1. wissdom	2. wisedom	3. wisdom	4. wisdome
1. vanety	2. vanity	3. vinety	4. vanaty

The task is to select the correctly spelled form.

A fourth method of examination attempts to parallel dictation by presenting words written in a phonetic style, and then asking the examinee to give the approved English spelling; thus, *espeshally* for especially and *biznes* for business.

Research is needed to evaluate the relative advantages of these methods of examination. If enough items of a carefully graded sort are given, the results of one type of examination usually correlate highly with those of others.

Measures of Reading Ability. Since the variety of reading activities is large, many types of reading tests have been constructed. Nearly all reading tests, however, involve four language factors which seem to be somewhat independent. Two of these have just been discussed—knowledge of vocabulary and of techniques of usage and spelling. The other two factors are often called perceptual span and inference. The most common tests of reading, called general tests, demand all of these four factors in unknown amounts, but in diagnostic testing it is possible to control three factors and then to measure the fourth in fairly pure form. The analytical approach is important when a person is deficient in only one or two aspects, since it is desirable to provide a special remedy. Both general and diagnostic tests will be described. (See Appendix II.)

Reading-test situations are complicated by the fact that both speed and accuracy, which are often incompatible, are frequently desirable aspects of achievement. Since it is difficult to hold either accuracy or speed constant, the evaluation of these two aspects is a persistent problem.

General reading tests. Silent-reading tests have usually taken the form of a series of sentences or paragraphs, each of which is followed by one or more questions. As the test progresses the items become longer and more involved, the vocabulary harder, and the questions more complex.

Diagnostic tests. Diagnostic tests will be considered under three headings: (*a*) tests of simple comprehension, (*b*) tests which emphasize verbal reasoning and organization of ideas, and (*c*) tests which emphasize perceptual speed and span. The first two of these are shown in Illus. 65B (p. 178) with subheadings which yield a detailed analysis of James Brown's record. It appears from the underlined numbers, which indicate errors, that he did fairly well on simple comprehension items, but very poorly on organization and interpretation items. Illustrative items will be given from various tests.

1) *Simple Comprehension.* Here the task is to answer questions about facts stated in the context. Thus, the Sangren-Woody (1927) Reading Test, Part III, consists of Fact Materials and Part VI, of Following Directions. Portions of these are printed in Illus. 67.

2) *Verbal Reasoning and Organization.* Some of the tests in this group ask one to draw inferences from a paragraph. These are illustrated by the Gates Silent Reading Tests (1926) which yield scores for: (*a*) appreciating general significance, (*b*) predicting the outcome of given events, (*c*) understanding precise directions, and (*d*) noting details. The last two of these seem to emphasize comprehension of stated facts, but the first two (Illus. 68) require inferences as well. These cannot be considered to be pure reasoning tests because the vocabulary becomes more difficult as the test progresses.

The purest form of a verbal-reasoning test is thought to be syllogistic (Illus. 11). Although such forms are rarely found in achievement-test batteries, they have the advantage of being relatively free from vocabulary variations. A difficult syllogistic test can be made in which only a third grade vocabulary is used.

Tests of reorganization use material which has been disarranged with instructions that it be properly arranged. Disarranged sentences are shown in Illus. 69A and disarranged paragraphs in Illus. 69B. Analysis of factors leading to success in these tests is very difficult when the vocabulary load becomes greater as the reorganization becomes harder. One person may fail the test because of a poor vocabulary, another because of poor inferences.

ILLUS. 67. SAMPLES FROM THE SANGREN-WOODY READING TEST

PART III. FACT MATERIAL

Directions: Write the answer to each question on the dotted line. Use one word if possible.

The "lead" in your pencil is not made of lead. Long ago people had lead in their pencils; that is probably why the pencils we use are called lead pencils. Another mineral called "graphite" is now used. This mineral is taken from mines in the same way as coal or iron ore.

1. What did people use in their pencils long ago?......................
2. What mineral is used in the pencils now?..........................
3. From what is the mineral taken?....

....

PART VI. FOLLOWING DIRECTIONS

Directions: Do what each paragraph tells you to do.

1. At the right are two squares of different sizes. The larger square is a playground for children, and the smaller one is a garden into which children must not go. There should be a fence between the playground and the garden. Make this fence by drawing a line to separate the squares.

2. At the right are six circles. They stand for one-half dozen eggs. The second egg in the row is not a good one and cannot be used for cooking. In order that Mother will not make a mistake and use it, you must take your pencil and mark it with a cross.

(Sangren and Woody, 1927. By permission of the World Book Co.)

Tests of organization of material are shown in Illus. 69. A paragraph is printed with its phrases numbered consecutively. The student is asked to select the most important items in the paragraph and arrange them in an outline. The same type of test without numbered phrases is much more difficult to score and probably requires more organizing ability than the numbered form. Much research is needed to determine and appraise varieties of organizing ability.

3) *Perceptual Speed and Span.* The amount of written material which a person comprehends at a glance is considered to be an important aspect of reading. One rough technique for measuring perceptual speed is the flash card which is used in the earlier grades. At

ILLUS. 68. SAMPLES FROM THE GATES SILENT READING TEST

TYPE A.   TO APPRECIATE THE GENERAL SIGNIFICANCE

This is to be a reading test.   You are to read a number of paragraphs.   Below each paragraph are five words.   One of the words tells how some one described in the paragraph felt — whether sad or happy, etc.   You should draw a line under that one — and only one — word to show that you understand just how the person described in the paragraph did feel.   Now let us try a sample before we begin the real test.   Read the following paragraph and then draw a line under the word which you think tells best how the person felt.

Once upon a time a young fairy went down to the river to swim.   She jumped in with a splash.   She put out her hands and tried hard to swim.   Something seemed to be dragging her down.   Oh, it was her wings!   She had forgotten to take them off.   Fairy wings become heavy when they are wet.   She cried for help as loudly as she could.

Draw a line under the word which tells how the fairy felt.

cross   angry   weary   afraid   joyful

TYPE B.   TO PREDICT THE OUTCOME OF GIVEN EVENTS

This is to be a reading test.   You are to read a number of paragraphs.   Below each paragraph are four sentences.   Each sentence tells what is most likely to follow after the happenings that are described in the paragraph.   You should draw a line under one   and only one — of these sentences to show that you can tell what will probably happen next.   Now, let us try a sample before we begin the real test.   Read this paragraph and then draw a line under the one sentence which you think tells what will happen next.

The grocery man had a black cat.   He loved his cat very much.   One day a lady brought a big bulldog into the store.   The grocer's cat raised his back and said "Meow!   Psst!" to the bulldog.   Of course, the dog did not like that, so he growled loudly.   Before the grocery man or the lady knew what was happening, the bulldog had sprung upon the cat.

They let the fight go on
The cat slept on
The lady took her bird away
The grocery man saved his cat

(Gates, 1926.   By permission of the Bureau of Publications, Teachers College, Columbia University.)

later ages two standard tests are common: (*a*) word-and-number-comparison tests and (*b*) speed-of-reading tests.

Word-and-number-comparison tests are well illustrated by the Minnesota Test for Clerical Workers (1933), which is shown in part in Illus. 8.   The score, which is the number of items compared, depends upon perceptual speed and familiarity with words and numbers.

In speed-of-reading tests one is asked either to detect errors in a passage, or simply to read for a given time and to note the number of words which seem to have been comprehended. The first is illustrated by the Chapman-Cook Speed-of-Reading, which consists of easy paragraphs of thirty words each. Near the end of each paragraph, one word spoils the meaning by its incongruity. The task is to cross out this word. For example, Chapman (1924) uses this sentence:

It was such a cold, boisterous, and wintry day that every person who was walking wore the thinnest clothes that he could find in his clothes closet.

This type of test has been produced by several authors, and Eurich (1931) followed the general idea when he composed a speed-of-reading test at the college level, using longer paragraphs and harder words. Criticism has been directed against this type of test since it does not resemble usual reading activities, but consists of disconnected passages which do not allow usual rhythms, requires specific search for a single word rather than a comprehension of phrases, and requires the crossing out of a word.

The other type of speed-of-reading test presents a passage for continuous normal reading during a few minutes but usually fails to control comprehension in such a fashion that the scores are comparable with one another. Although directions commonly say to read slowly enough to understand what one reads, still some students interpret this to mean skimming and some, a detailed analysis. Tests of comprehension usually follow the reading of a passage, but these introduce factors of recall and possible distraction, and no satisfactory way of combining speed and comprehension scores has appeared.

ILLUS. 69. SAMPLES FROM THE IOWA SILENT READING TEST

Advanced Examination, Grades 7–12

A.

TEST 4.   SENTENCE ORGANIZATION

(Time Allowance: 4 minutes)

Directions to the Pupil: This test is given to see how well you are able to arrange groups of words into sentences.   Work all the exercises as shown in the sample.

Samples: (1) a wagon, (2) a boy, (3) had   .....*2, 3, 1*.....

(1) how small, (2) see, (3) he is   .....*2, 1, 3*.....

1 (1) wanted, (2) to go home, (3) the boy   ....

2 (1) always, (2) be rewarded, (3) good deeds, (4) should   ....

3 (1) as children, (2) they, (3) get stronger, (4) grow older   ....

B.

TEST 5. PARAGRAPH ORGANIZATION

PART C.

(Time allowance: 3 minutes)

Directions to the Pupil: The following exercises are given to test your ability to arrange the sentences of an unorganized paragraph in their proper order. Work all the exercises as shown in the sample.

Sample: (1) One man found that until he put toads in his greenhouse he could not keep insects from eating some of his flowers.

(2) Sometimes men keep toads in their greenhouses. .....*2, 1*.....

The Cattle Tick

1 (1) Once a territory has been made tick free, it is kept so by a strict quarantine against the introduction of infested animals. (2) The cotton states and the Federal government have made great progress in fighting this pest through the system of dipping cattle to rid them of the ticks. (3) Chief among the parasites of cattle is the Texas fever tick, which has caused enormous losses in the South. ......

Early French Explorers in America

2 (1) From this highly strategic post scores of explorers departed to become the pioneers of France in the new world before Boston and Philadelphia had been founded in the English settlements. (2) Quebec, founded by Champlain a year after Jamestown, is located on the St. Lawrence, eight hundred miles from the edge of the continent. (3) The early history of the Great Lakes region is the record of these French explorers. ......

C.

TEST 5. PARAGRAPH ORGANIZATION

PART B. OUTLINING

(Time Allowance: 3 minutes)

Directions to the Pupil: The following are exercises to test your ability to organize an outline giving the most important items of a paragraph. Read the following paragraphs carefully. At the right of the paragraphs are outlines partially filled in. Fill in the blank spaces in the outline from your reading of the paragraphs by placing in the outline the numbers corresponding to the brackets and be sure to select the group of words in the different brackets which will result in a well organized outline. Be sure not to include more items in the outline than have been provided for.

1. In the United States, which is the leading agricultural ⌞———1———⌟ ⌞———2———⌟ country in the world, several causes have combined to encour- ⌞——3——⌟ ⌞————4————⌟ age this industry. Of these factors, the more important are ⌞——5——⌟ ⌞——6——⌟ ⌞——7——⌟ the fertility of the soil, the variety of climate and other condi- ⌞—8—⌟ ⌞———9———⌟ tions of environment, the energy of the people, the encourage- ⌞————10————⌟ ment lent by the government to scientific agriculture, and the ⌞————11————⌟ unrivaled transportation system for marketing crops. Land ⌞——12——⌟ ⌞——13——⌟ has been very cheap. High wages in other industries have led ⌞——14——⌟ ⌞——15——⌟ ⌞——16——⌟ to the invention of machinery by which one man can do the ⌞——17——⌟ ⌞——18——⌟ work of many. There is no country in the world where ⌞———19———⌟ machinery is used so extensively in agriculture as in the United ⌞————20————⌟ States.	*Paragraph 1.* I. Factors encouraging American agriculture. A. ..... B. ..... C. ..... D. ..... E. ..... F. ..... G. .....

(Jorgensen and Greene, 1927. By permission of the Bureau of Educational Research and Service, University of Iowa and the World Book Co.)

Two elaborate and expensive techniques for measuring perceptual span of words should be mentioned. One technique, which uses a Metronoscope, presents words or phrases to a student at a given rate and asks him to record or tell what he has seen. The other technique photographs eye movement while one is reading. The first method does not resemble normal reading in certain respects, but it does give accurate records under the test conditions. It has been proposed as a means of training slow readers. The second method usually fails to evaluate comprehension, but it does show precise records of number, duration, and order of fixations on a line.

A less expensive technique for training readers has been described by Dearborn and Anderson (1938). Printed material was photographed on motion-picture film in such a way that when the film is projected, successive phrases and lines are exposed as they have been grouped by skilled readers. The exposure times are limited to approximately one fifth of a second, thus preventing more than an optimum number of fixations per phrase. The suddenness with which the units appear and disappear controls the duration of fixation time. At the beginning of training the material is simple, the phrases short, and the exposure rate slow. As training progresses, the material increases in complexity and the projection rate is more rapid. Training of this sort has resulted in considerable improvement, as shown by the Minnesota Speed of Reading Tests and the Gates Silent Reading Tests on small samples of both college students and elementary school pupils.

Various groups have called attention during the last ten years to the fact that many publications intended for popular consumption were not widely read or understood, because they were difficult to read. Edgar Dale and Jeanne S. Chall (1948) have compared their own indices of readability with those proposed by Irving Lorge (1944) and Rudolf Flesch (1946), in an attempt to determine what factors contribute to reading ease or difficulty. Lorge published one of the first simple formulas: (*a*) number of different uncommon words; (*b*) average sentence length, and (*c*) relative number of prepositional phrases. Dale's list of 769 easy words were Lorge's common words.

Flesch used three criteria: average sentence length, proportion of affixed morphemes (prefixes, suffixes, and inflectional endings), and proportion of personal pronouns. He believed the count of affixes was a better indicator of abstraction and vocabulary load than Lorge's uncommon words because the latter failed to discriminate relative difficulty above the eighth grade.

Dale and Chall found the counting of affixed morphemes to

be laborious even after some training, and marked variations between counts by different persons appeared. They also found a number of hard-to-read texts and articles in which the incidence of personal pronouns was very high. Dale's list of approximately three thousand easy words, made by trying out approximately ten thousand words on fourth-grade pupils, was applied in making counts of easy words in the same series of 376 standard reading passages, the McCall-Crabbs Standard Lessons in Reading, that were used for criteria of difficulty by Lorge and Flesch. Intercorrelations of these authors' results showed that the easy words, using Dale's 3,000-word list, correlated .683 with the McCall-Crabbs criteria, and .615 with Flesch's "affixes count." The affixes correlated .793 with easy words. The easy-word scores plus the average sentence length yielded a multiple correlation with the criteria of .70. Using these two measures, Dale and Chall have set up tentative grade levels which can be easily applied to samples from various fields.

MEASUREMENT OF MATHEMATICAL ABILITY

Tests in this group range from the simplest counting operations to highly complex problem solving. There are three types of skills involved which appear to be highly independent, at least among adults: (1) calculation from rote memory and rule, (2) abstract reasoning with numbers or letters, and (3) geometric reasoning with spatial data.

Arithmetic Tests

A popular type of general arithmetic test is called arithmetical reasoning or problem solving (Illus. 70). Tests of this sort require the three factors mentioned above in unknown combinations as well as some language ability. Nearly all of the elementary tests contain many interesting practical applications from business, architecture, surveying, and house management. Tests of this general sort are of little value for a diagnosis of basic skills, but they show the results of complex thinking about common objects.

A diagnostic test of mathematical ability is given in Illus. 65A. Here eight subdivisions are listed, and it appears that James Brown is above average in Problems, Number Concepts, Symbols and Rules, and Numbers and Equations, and near or slightly below average in Addition, Subtraction, Multiplication, and Division. Illustration 65B shows, with its detailed analysis, that his most difficult items in all eight divisions demanded skill in using fractions and decimals. He was able to handle simple and abstract numbers fairly well.

The Progressive Achievement Test and a number of similar tests

ILLUS. 70. UNITED STATES ARMY ALPHA TEST 2

TEST 2

Get the answers to these examples as quickly as you **can**.
Use the side of this page to figure on if you need to

SAMPLES
{
1 How many are 5 men and 10 men?........Answer (**15**   )
2 If you walk 4 miles an hour for 3 hours, how far
   do you walk?..........................Answer (**12**   )
}

1   How many are 40 guns and 6 guns?.................Answer (   )
2   If you save $6 a month for 5 months, how much will you
    save?...Answer (   )
3   If 32 men are divided into squads of 8, how many squads will
    there be?.......................................Answer (   )
4   Mike had 11 cigars. He bought 3 more and then smoked 6.
    How many cigars did he have left?.................Answer (   )
5   A company advanced 6 miles and retreated 3 miles. How far
    was it then from its first position?....................Answer (   )
6   How many hours will it take a truck to go 48 miles at the rate
    of 4 miles an hour?.............................Answer (   )
7   How many pencils can you buy for 40 cents at the rate of 2
    for 5 cents?....................................Answer (   )
8   A regiment marched 40 miles in five days. The first day they
    marched 9 miles, the second day 6 miles, the third 10 miles, the
    fourth 9 miles. How many miles did they march the last
    day?...Answer (   )
9   If you buy 2 packages of tobacco at 8 cents each and a pipe for
    55 cents, how much change should you get from a two-dollar
    bill?...Answer (   )
10 If it takes 8 men 2 days to dig a 160-foot drain, how many men
    are needed to dig it in half a day?...................Answer (   )
11 A dealer bought some mules for $900. He sold them for $1,000,
    making $25 on each mule. How many mules were there?..Answer (   )
12 A rectangular bin holds 600 cubic feet of lime. If the bin is 10
    feet wide and 5 feet deep, how long is it?..............Answer (   )
13 A recruit spent one-eighth of his spare change for post cards
    and four times as much for a box of letter paper, and then had
    60 cents left. How much money did he have at first?..Answer (   )
14 If 2½ tons of hay cost $20, what will 4½ tons cost?....Answer (   )
15 A ship has provisions to last her crew of 600 men 6 months.
    How long would it last 800 men?....................Answer (   )
16 If a train goes 200 yards in 10 seconds, how many feet does it
    go in a fifth of a second?..........................Answer (   )
17 A U-boat makes 10 miles an hour under water and 20 miles on
    the surface. How long will it take to cross a 100-mile channel,
    if it has to go three-fifths of the way under water?.....Answer (   )
18 If 214 squads of men are to dig 4,066 yards of trench, how
    many yards must be dug by each squad?............Answer (   )
19 A certain division contains 2,000 artillery, 15,000 infantry, and
    1,000 cavalry. If each branch is expanded proportionately
    until there are in all 19,800 men, how many will be added to the
    artillery?.......................................Answer (   )
20 A commission house which had already supplied 1,897 barrels
    of apples to a cantonment delivered the remainder of its stock
    to 28 mess halls. Of this remainder each mess hall received 47
    barrels. What was the total number of barrels supplied?.Answer (   )

(By permission of the C. H. Stoelting Co., and Henry Holt & Company)

are particularly useful for a rapid survey. The subdivisions are probably too short for reliable testing, such as is needed for appraising experimental education. Very elaborate instruments are to be found in the Compass Diagnostic Tests, by Ruch et al. (1925). Approximately 90 distinct acts were listed, and a large number of separate tests were printed. One of these, Addition of Fractions, is shown in Illus. 71. Furthermore, a Standard Arithmetic Work Book was designed to furnish both original learning situations and remedial drills. Such work books are now numerous and widely used in both traditional and progressive schools.

ILLUS. 71. SAMPLES FROM THE COMPASS DIAGNOSTIC TESTS IN ARITHMETIC

Test V: Addition of Fractions and Mixed Numbers — Form A

PART 1 — CHANGING FRACTIONS TO EQUIVALENT FORMS

Directions: Change the form of each fraction below to use the denominator given. Study the samples carefully to see how this is to be done.

$$\text{Samples:} \quad \frac{1}{8} = \frac{2}{16} \quad \frac{2}{3} = \frac{8}{12} \quad \frac{1}{3} = \frac{}{9}$$

$$\frac{1}{2} = \frac{}{12} \quad \frac{1}{2} = \frac{}{10} \quad \frac{2}{5} = \frac{}{10} \quad \frac{1}{2} = \frac{}{4} \quad \frac{4}{9} = \frac{}{36} \quad \frac{1}{12} = \frac{}{36} \quad \frac{4}{9} = \frac{}{18}$$

$$\frac{5}{6} = \frac{}{18} \quad \frac{1}{2} = \frac{}{6} \quad \frac{2}{3} = \frac{}{6} \quad \frac{3}{4} = \frac{}{44} \quad \frac{3}{5} = \frac{}{20} \quad \frac{1}{2} = \frac{}{20} \quad \frac{1}{8} = \frac{}{24}$$

PART 4 — FUNDAMENTALS OF ADDITION OF FRACTIONS

Directions: Find the sum for each example below. Do your figuring on a piece of scratch paper.

$$\frac{5}{8} + \frac{0}{8} = \qquad\qquad \frac{n}{20} + \frac{9}{5} = \qquad 9 + \frac{2}{5} + 11\frac{3}{35} + 16\frac{9}{7} =$$

$$5\frac{7}{12} + \frac{1}{2} = \qquad\qquad\quad 4\frac{2}{5} = \qquad \frac{1}{8} + 8\frac{5}{6} + 2\frac{1}{3} =$$

$$9$$

Three-tenths plus one-half = $\qquad 16^{\frac{1}{2}}_{\frac{2}{4}}$ $\qquad$ Add $\frac{1}{7}$ and $\frac{1}{11} =$

(Ruch, Knight, Greene, and Studebaker, 1925. By permission of Scott, Foresman and Co.)

Another type of analysis is illustrated by the use of the Buswell-John (1925) Diagnostic Chart. A trained observer watches a pupil work through a standard 8-page test and notes the types of errors as they are made. Illustration 72 is of a check list of errors in addition. Similar lists are available for multiplication, division, and subtraction. Direct observation gives more insight into the sources of error than unobserved test scores, particularly if the student talks as he works.

Algebra, Geometry, and Trigonometry Tests

For both high school and college, general tests of algebra, geometry, and trigonometry have been well standardized, and methodical work books are available for the elementary courses. Thorndike et al.

ILLUS. 72. TEACHER'S DIAGNOSTIC CHART FOR
INDIVIDUAL DIFFICULTIES

Fundamental Processes in Arithmetic

Teacher's Diagnosis
for pupil _____

Name_____ School_____ Grade___ Age___ IQ___

Date of Diagnosis :_____ Add.___ ; Subt.___ ; Mult.___ ; Div.___

Teacher's preliminary diagnosis _____

ADDITION : (Place a check before each habit observed in the pupil's work)

_____	a1	Errors in combinations
_____	a2	Counting
_____	a3	Added carried number last
_____	a4	Forgot to add carried number
_____	a5	Repeated work after partly done
_____	a6	Added carried number irregularly
_____	a7	Wrote number to be carried
_____	a8	Irregular procedure in column
_____	a9	Carried wrong number
_____	a10	Grouped two or more numbers
_____	a11	Splits numbers into parts
_____	a12	Used wrong fundamental operation
_____	a13	Lost place in column
_____	a14	Depended on visualization
_____	a15	Disregarded column position
_____	a16	Omitted one or more digits
_____	a17	Errors in reading numbers
_____	a18	Dropped back one or more tens
_____	a19	Derived unknown combination from familiar one
_____	a20	Disregarded one column
_____	a21	Error in writing answer
_____	a22	Skipped one or more decades
_____	a23	Carrying when there was nothing to carry
_____	a24	Used scratch paper
_____	a25	Added in pairs, giving last sum as answer
_____	a26	Added same digit in two columns
_____	a27	Wrote carried number in answer
_____	a28	Added same number twice

Habits not listed above _____

_____

(G. T. Buswell and Lenore John, 1925. By permission of the Public School
Publishing Co., Bloomington, Ill.)

(1923) wrote an elaborate *Psychology of Algebra* which listed fourteen algebraic abilities, suggested ways of eliminating unnecessary habits, and also provided or suggested drill on neglected skills.

Out of a large number of available algebra tests two will be mentioned. Lee (1930) designed a test to indicate ability to succeed in algebra. Its four parts are:

a. Arithmetic problems where algebra might be helpful
b. Number analogies, such as: $3 - 9::5 -$ 30, 15, 20, 23
c. Number series: 4, 8, 10, 20, 22, 44_____
d. Easy formulas: $A = \dfrac{ab}{2}$. Given $a = 10$, $b = 8$, to find A

Lee reported correlations of .71 among 318 high school pupils between this Algebraic Ability Test and an achievement test after one semester of algebra. This correlation is nearly the same as that between achievement tests at 9 and 18 weeks. The Algebraic Ability Test correlated .631 with algebra grades. These figures are considered to be about as high as the reliability of grades will permit.

The commonest type of algebra achievement test is illustrated by the Columbia Research Bureau Algebra Test, which has two parts. In Part I skill is required in solving equations, such as:

> 1. $X + 15 = 23$
> 14. $4X^2 - 16X - 9 = 0$
> 18. square root of $X - 2 = 6$

In Part II problems such as the following are to be solved:

2. How long must I make a garden that is 8 feet wide so that it will have as large an area as my neighbor's, which is 16 feet long and 6 feet wide?

24. The distance (S) a body falls in T seconds is expressed by the formula $S - 16T^2 + VT$, in which V is the initial velocity downward. How many seconds will it take a body to fall 640 feet if thrown downward with a velocity of 48 feet a second? (Use T for the unknown.)

The scores in Part II involve specific information outside of the field of algebra, and some of the problems can be solved without algebra. Work is now under way to prepare algebra tests which will place greater emphasis on utility and cultural aspects by the use of more challenging problems and the simplest techniques. Yielding to continuous agitation for curricula based on immediate needs and interests of students, many high schools have in recent years transformed the teaching of algebra from the techniques of solving polynomials to approaches to analytical thinking about practical situations, as tested in Part II.

A good elementary geometry achievement test is that of Schorling and Sanford (1926), part of which is shown in Illus. 73. Part I is a

ILLUS. 73. SAMPLES FROM THE SCHORLING-SANFORD
ACHIEVEMENT TEST IN PLANE GEOMETRY

Form B

Directions for Part II

DRAWING CONCLUSIONS FROM GIVEN DATA

In Part II of this test, you will be given geometric figures and certain facts
relating to each. Think what fact you could prove about each figure on the basis
of the given information and write a statement of this in the space beside the words
"We can prove that."

Be sure to use each piece of information that is given to you. You will be
allowed 12 minutes for Part II.

Example:

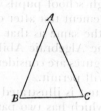

Given △*ABC* with *AB* = *AC*.

We can prove that.....................

[Since *ABC* is given as an isosceles triangle, we
can prove that ∠*B* = ∠*C*, so

　　　　　∠*B* = ∠*C*

should be written on the dotted line.]

Directions for Part V

COMPUTATION

In Part V of this test, you will be given diagrams about which certain facts
are known. You are to use these facts in computing such things as the length of
a line, the size of an angle, etc., according to the questions that are asked. Read
each question, study the figure upon which the question is based, and write the
answer in the space beside the question.

You will be allowed 12 minutes for Part V.

Example:

In the rectangle *ABCD*, *AB* is 12 in., *BC* is 8
in.

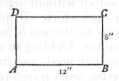

What is the area of the
rectangle? Ans. ....
[*96 sq. in.* should be written on the dotted
line.]

Now try this:

What is its perimeter? Ans. ....

Be sure to express your results in *numerical
form.*

(Schorling and Sanford, 1926. By permission of the Bureau of Publications,
Teachers College, Columbia University.)

vocabulary test. Part II requires a statement of what can be proved from given data. Part III asks that the correctness of certain conclusions be judged. Part IV requires an analysis of constructions. Part V demands the computation of distances or areas.

Total scores on tests of this kind usually correlate approximately .75 with the midyear grade for a beginning course. They also show equivalent-form reliability of about .85. The subdivisions, which are doubtless less reliable, furnish valuable evidence of a pupil's weak and strong points. The intercorrelations of the subdivisions are low enough—usually about .50—to suggest a number of independent skills, but no careful factor analysis of such skills has come to hand. A subjective analysis indicates that probably four independent factors are at work: verbal information, reasoning, spatial imagery, and number relations.

Tests of advanced work in algebra and in plane and solid geometry are found in the Cooperative Test Series. These include items to appraise calculations and reasoning as emphasized in standard textbooks.

A good standard trigonometry test is the American Council on Education Trigonometry Test (1930), following five parts of which are to be completed in 72 minutes:

I. Technical knowledge, as:
Sec O is positive and tan O is negative, the quadrant of O is: first, second, third, fourth.
II. Completion of equations:
$X = 1$, $Y = 3$; tan $O = \underline{\hspace{2cm}}$
III. Indicate method of solving verbal problem:
From the top of a cliff 350 feet high the angle of depression of a buoy is 16° 38'. Find the distance from the buoy to the top of the cliff.
IV. Indicate method of solving diagrammed problems similar to Part III.
V. This is like Part IV, but more difficult.

SPECIAL STUDIES

Achievements in special studies have been appraised with local tests more often than with standardized instruments. This practice is probably due to the variation in objectives in different localities and the lack of well-standardized, acceptable tests. Most of the published tests cover only elementary aspects, since advanced activities are extremely complex and are carried on by only a few persons. Special tests of physical sciences, social studies, foreign languages, and business will be briefly discussed.

Physical Sciences

Appraisals of the results of any science course have traditionally taken the form of questions about facts and natural laws. A good illustration is the Iowa High School Content Examination, part of which appears in Illus. 74. It consists of fifty multiple-choice questions on a variety of subjects. A more diagnostic procedure is shown by tests of the Cooperative Test Service. This nonprofit organization, established by the American Council on Education in 1930, has produced, through a large number of contributors, annual forms of reliable tests of English, foreign languages, mathematics, natural sciences, and social studies for high school and college levels. The Cooperative Chemistry Test (1934), shown in Illus. 12, is interesting because it attempts an analytical approach by the use of three parts. Part 1 requires knowledge of facts and natural laws, Part 2 requires knowledge of terminology, and Part 3 requires statements of probable outcomes and also explanations for these statements. Part 3 is probably much more dependent upon reasoning activities than Parts 1 and 2. Tests of the type of Part 3 are being more extensively used now than formerly because they are thought to appraise an important objective of the course, namely, insight into causal relationships. Buckingham and Lee (1936) found marked differences between tests of science facts and tests of ability to point out relations between laws and phenomena. Some of their freshman group made good scores on the factual tests and very low scores on the tests which demanded careful inferences. Their results, which are typical of several other reports, point to the need of measuring knowledge of facts separately from reasoning when careful analyses are desired. (Similar biology and physics tests at both high school and college levels are found in the Cooperative Test Series, the American Council on Education Series, and a number of others.) Other objectives of a science course, such as skill in the laboratory, known scientific theories, and practical applications, are difficult to appraise. Wrightstone (1936) has published an initial study of such appraisals in high school science courses.

Social Sciences

History, civics, and geography are the main social studies in high school, and nearly all the standard tests deal with these topics. Social studies broaden into the humanities in college, including economics, sociology, philosophy, psychology, and political science. A comprehensive volume by Kelley and Krey (1934) discusses tests of knowledge and attitudes in social studies. In this volume the report of Pres-

ILLUS. 74. SAMPLES FROM THE IOWA HIGH SCHOOL CONTENT
EXAMINATION

Section 3

SCIENCE

(Time allowed: 10 minutes)

1. Combustion is another name for   (1) freezing   (2) drying   (3) boiling
   (4) burning   (5) melting   . . . . .

2. A gas which supports combustion is   (1) hydrogen   (2) nitrogen
   (3) carbon dioxide   (4) oxygen   (5) carbon monoxide   . . . . .

3. $H_2SO_4 + BaCl_2 = 2 HCl$ and   (1) H_2O (2) $Ba(OH)_2$ (3) SO_3
   (4) $BaSO_4$ (5) H_2ClO_3 . . . . .

4. The freezing point on the Centigrade thermometer is $(1) - 273°$
   (2) 0°   (3) 32°   (4) 100°   (5) 212°   . . . . .

5. Substances which hasten a chemical action without themselves under-
   going any chemical change are called   (1) catalysts   (2) electro-
   lytes   (3) ionogens   (4) allotrops   (5) anhydrides   . . . . .

6. The formula for hydrochloric acid is   (1) NaOH   (2) HCl
   (3) HNO_3 (4) $MgSO_4$ (5) H_2SO_4 . . . . .

7. Hydrogen may be made by the action of hydrochloric acid on   (1) zinc
   (2) sodium chloride   (3) copper sulphate   (4) sodium
   hydroxide   (5) potassium chlorate   . . . . .

8. The length of a meter in inches is about   (1) 12   (2) 27
   (3) 39   (4) 72   (5) 144   . . . . .

9. An example of a chemical change is the   (1) desiccation of spores
   (2) oxidation of sugar   (3) dissolving of salt   (4) osmosis of
   glucose   (5) exchange of gases in the lungs   . . . . .

10. Barometers are used to measure   (1) humidity   (2) rainfall
    (3) air-pressure   (4) gravity   (5) electricity   . . . . .

11. The center of our universe is the   (1) earth   (2) moon   (3) sun
    (4) Jupiter   (5) Mars   . . . . .

12. An instrument depending on atmospheric pressure for its operation is
    the   (1) siphon   (2) hydraulic press   (3) thermometer
    (4) telephone   (5) voltaic cell   . . . . .

13. The force needed to raise a weight of 1200 pounds on a hydraulic press
    whose piston areas stand in the ratio of 1 : 6 is   (1) 100 lbs.
    (2) 200 lbs.   (3) 300 lbs.   (4) 600 lbs.   (5) 2400 lbs.   . . . . .

14. One organism which possesses antennae is the   (1) earthworm
    (2) starfish   (3) hydra   (4) amoeba   (5) grasshopper   . . . . .

15. Electric charges can be detected by means of   (1) condenser
    (2) electroscope   (3) dynamo   (4) voltaic cell   (5) spectro-
    scope   . . . . .

(Ruch, Cleeton, and Stoddard, 1925.   By permission of the Bureau of
Publications, University of Iowa.)

sey is of particular interest. She first established the master list of terms used in history, shown in Illus. 60, and then constructed multiple-choice items for 346 words and applied these items to more than 11,000 pupils in the fourth, sixth, eighth, tenth, and twelfth grades. The proportions of students in each grade who passed seven of the items are shown in Illus. 75. This figure shows that mastery of three of the items was fairly complete in the eighth grade and that

ILLUS. 75. GROWTH OF SOCIAL VOCABULARY

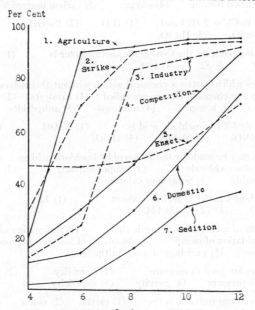

Per cents of students in grades IV to XII who succeeded on certain vocabulary items.

(After Pressey, 1934. By permission of Charles Scribner's Sons.)

the item for the word *enact* was answered about as well by the fourth as by the tenth grade. The items for the words *competition* and *domestic* showed fairly regular increases, and the item for *sedition* proved to be difficult before the tenth grade.

The seven items are shown in Illus. 76. An inspection of these items will show that some words are defined more completely than others. Certain items require difficult discriminations in word usage. The difficulty of an item is here determined partly by difficulty of defining the key word, and partly by the context of the item. In order to

ILLUS. 76. TEST OF CONCEPTS USED IN THE SOCIAL STUDIES

1. To what does agriculture refer?   (*a*) fishing   (*b*) mining   (*c*) farming   (*d*) manufacturing
2. How do laborers most often attempt to force an employer to raise their wages?   (*a*) by going to war   (*b*) by going to another factory   (*c*) by going to a foreign country   (*d*) by going on strike
3. Which phrase refers to the entire business of making woolen clothing?   (*a*) the woolen shops   (*b*) the woolen industry   (*c*) the wool-growers   (*d*) the sheep ranchers
4. Which of the following words applies to the practice of lowering of prices by one company so as to get business away from another?   (*a*) rebellion   (*b*) emigration   (*c*) output   (*d*) competition
5. Which are enacted?   (*a*) verdicts   (*b*) debts   (*c*) laws   (*d*) dispatches
6. Which word refers to the affairs relating to one's own country?   (*a*) foreign   (*b*) international   (*c*) domestic   (*d*) diplomatic
7. Which is a form of conspiracy against one's country?   (*a*) sedition   (*b*) opposition   (*c*) criticism   (*d*) immigration

(Pressey, 1934, p. 189. By permission of Charles Scribner's Sons.)

discover whether such multiple-choice items are indicative of one's ability to write a correct definition, Pressey made a comparison of scores on two vocabulary tests, using the same words. In one test the children checked multiple-choice items, such as those given in Illus. 76, and in the other, they wrote definitions for the key words. She found that approximately 70 per cent of the words correctly defined were also used correctly in the multiple-choice forms and that the correlation between total scores on the two tests was high. The form in which an item is cast undoubtedly affected the task to some degree, but the results from the two types of tests were similar. The relative advantages and the intercorrelations of various forms of test items have been discussed in Chapter IV.

From studies such as this the effectiveness of various learning situations may be compared for each item. Pressey concluded from her study (p. 174) that "not enough special vocabulary is acquired for the reading of the average textbooks used in these grades." From such studies it is also possible to compose tests of items which have known levels of difficulty for particular populations. Kelley and Krey (1934) suggested that the best items for careful scale construction were those which, like 4 and 7 in Illus. 76 and Illus. 75, show regular growth increments.

Standard high school tests of this sort are the Kelty-Moore (1934) Tests of Concepts in Social Studies, the annual American Council on Education Civics and Government Test, and the annual Cooperative Tests of American, Ancient, Modern European, English, and Medieval History, of Economics, and of Contemporary Affairs. Terminology, descriptive information, and careful inferences are measured separately, and also added to give a general score. An important contribution to measurement in American history is a handbook on selected test items by Anderson and Lindquist (1949).

A number of geography tests have been prepared by state testing bureaus. Typical of a general test is that of Torgensen (1933), which is a 64-item multiple-choice test for the sixth through the eighth grades, that requires knowledge of the earth's surface, tides, natural resources, populations, climates, and map reading.

A test of general skills basic to effective work in social sciences was published by Wrightstone (1936). The four parts, each of which consists of about twenty-five items are as follows:

1. *Obtaining facts.* This part measures a pupil's ability to read charts, graphs, and maps and to use an index.

2. *Organizing facts.* This is a test of outlining materials and judging their value.

3. *Interpreting facts.* This is a reading test in which statements are to be marked true or false according to a given paragraph.

4. *Applying generalizations.* In this part multiple choices are used, as in Illus. 12, to explain events and support the explanation.

A test similar in design and content was also published for natural sciences by the same author. General skills tests undoubtedly tap the same skills that have been described under language and mathematics, but the combination of skills is probably original.

Two interesting tests for adults in the field of social adjustment have recently been published. Horrocks and Troyer (1946) have brought out a test of diagnosis and treatment of social, emotional, physical, economic, intellectual, and academic problems of high school students, called Tests of Human Growth and Development. Three case histories are used and each history is divided into three parts of about three hundred words in length. After reading each part of a case history, the person being tested answers about twenty-five multiple-choice questions on diagnosis, and about twenty on remedial measures. Five choices ranging from true through possibly true, no evidence, possibly false, and false are to be used in answering diagnostic questions, such as "For a girl of her age, Connie is more than usually self-conscious and sensitive."

Five choices—strongly agree, agree but with reservations, undecided, disagree but with reservations, and strongly disagree—are to be used in answering such questions as "Connie needs to increase her social participation."

From 50 to 90 minutes are needed for each case. There are no time limits. Scores are secured by comparing one's answers with a key which represents the opinions of ten experts. Since there are few right and wrong answers, a weighted scoring system is used, giving less credit for the less adequate answers. The reliability correlations are about .70, and the correlations between cases were .39, .55, and .62. These tests, although far from perfect, show that a standard test in diagnosis and treatment is possible, and that the results will help to clarify language and concepts in this field, as well as to appraise ability more accurately than is usually done.

The same authors have produced an 80-item test—Test of Knowledge of Fact and Principle in Human Growth and Development—which includes a wide variety of topics, for example, the function of endocrine glands, sex differences, parent-child relationships, mental and physical growth and standards, philosophies of life, personality structures and defense mechanisms, and remedial practices. The reliability is reported to be .91 among college students. The correlations with the case-study scores range from .24 to .49 (median about .30). Centile norms are given for samples of from three hundred to eight hundred college students.

Another worth-while test in this field is reported by Helen Nahm (1948), who lists forty-three mental-hygiene principles, then sixty-six items in a Mental Hygiene Test for Nurses. The principles are illustrated by the following:

Maladjustment is usually of multiple causation rather than of one cause alone.

When individuals are frustrated in their attempts to satisfy basic personality needs, they may compensate by substituting other attainable goals, which may or may not be desirable ones. Certain types of behavior may be tension-reducing for the individual, but not acceptable to society.

An item from the Mental Hygiene Test is:

Betty L. has average ability but is failing in most of her courses. She seems restless and nervous and appears to be uninterested in anything except having a good time. Which of the following methods would probably be most effective in helping her to improve?

a. Advising her to spend more time in study.
b. Restricting her social activities until her grades improve.
c. Trying to help her to find a solution for some of her unsolved problems.

Nahm also presented an 80-item test on autocratic-democratic practices. This is an attitude test in which one is asked to indicate degree of agreement with such statements as: "Instructors and supervisors should encourage students to intelligently criticize accepted hospital routines and procedures." Centile norms for twelve schools of nursing show wide variations.

An appraisal of Activities in Social Studies, shown by the check list in Illus. 77, was used by Wrightstone (1936). It divides activities into three groups: self-initiated, cooperative, and recitational. In his comparison of traditional and progressive schools Wrightstone found that pupils in the latter showed much more self-initiated activity than those in the traditional schools. This check list is a significant instrument because it draws the attention of instructor and pupil to activities which are probably of much greater social importance than the acquisition of information in a limited field.

ILLUS. 77. CHECK LIST OF ACTIVITIES IN SOCIAL STUDIES

A. SELF-INITIATED ACTIVITIES

1. Bringing voluntarily contributions (clippings, exhibits, books, charts, etc.) for school activities
2. Submitting voluntarily and orally data, or information, gained outside school (observation, trips to buildings, places, travel, museum, radio, lectures, movies, independent reading, etc.)
3. Presenting an organized written report showing research or investigation by pupil
4. Volunteering as leader or special worker on project or task
5. Suggesting methods, materials, activities, etc., for developing a project or problem
6. Defending a point of view in which the pupil believes

B. CO-OPERATIVE ACTIVITIES

1. Criticizing (praising or challenging) a contribution
2. Asking chairman or teacher pertinent subject matter questions which relate to the theme or topic of the group discussion, excluding routine class management questions
3. Offering objects (books, chairs, pencils, etc.) to teacher, pupil, or visitors
4. Responding quickly to requests for quiet, material, etc.

C. RECITATIONAL ACTIVITIES

1. Responding to questions on assigned textbook or subject matter

(Wrightstone, 1936, p. 134. By permission of the Bureau of Publications, Teachers College, Columbia University.)

Foreign Languages

Carefully standardized tests are available for some of the skills taught in beginning courses in foreign languages. The Cooperative French Test (1934) which is in three parts, is a good illustration of such a test:

I. Consists of 80 multiple-choice items where a short statement in French is to be read and completed sensibly thus:

1. Le mari de ma grand'mère est mon—grand-père, cousin, père, oncle.

II. Here are 100 vocabulary items where a key word is to be matched with its closest synonym.

    1. retourner; 1. rentrer, 2. finir, 3. toucher, 4. recevoir, 5. tomber.

III. Here 100 grammar items appear in which the correct form is to be supplied from five choices.

Sample:

1. le	I have a pen. J'ai —— plume.	(3)
2. la		
3. une	Here is the book. Voici —— livre.	(1)
4. un		
5. no additional word	She is in France. Elle est en — France.	(5)

French teachers often criticize this sort of test. They believe that

    1. The material is too fragmentary.

    2. The material is uninteresting.

    3. Some vocabulary items can be correctly answered by noting similarities in word forms, without knowledge of French.

    4. The student is not asked to compose any French.

    5. The test situation is very different from normal reading situations.

    6. The grammar section emphasizes proofreading ability which shows little relationship to skill in correct reading or speaking in real life situations.

    7. There is no check on spelling or use of accents.

For survey purposes, however, these tests are usually recognized as valid measures of general vocabulary, proficiency in comprehension of short passages, and the commonest French syntax. The Cooperative Test Service has developed similar tests for achievement in German and Spanish. Elaborate tests of the same sort are to be found in the College Entrance Board Examinations and in the several state examination programs.

Business Achievement

Tests in this field may be conveniently placed in two groups: clerical skills and business information. The former are fairly well developed, whereas the latter are in a more experimental stage.

Clerical Tests. In 1922 Thurstone published an examination in typing in three parts. The first part presents a typewritten page upon which numerous corrections had been made with pen and ink and asks that a correct copy be made. The second part requires 40 hand written items to be typed in columns on a blank. The third contains 48 words among which misspellings are to be detected. Separate scores for errors and speed are to be recorded and also combined by the addition of total scores. The skillful typists made the lowest scores.

Blackstone (1923) standardized tests of typing in which business letters in correct typewritten form were presented to be copied during a 3-minute period. Norms for speed and accuracy of typing were given separately and also combined into a score thus:

$$\text{score} = \frac{\text{strokes-per-minute} \times 10}{\text{errors} + 10}$$

The scores were found to have a repeat reliability of .93 for a group of pupils with 20 months of instruction. The average pupil with 5 months of instruction secured 88 points, those with 20 months, 206 points, and with 30 months, 236 points.

Shorthand tests have been standardized in connection with courses of instruction. Bisbee (1933) prepared a test series which is typical. Test 1 measures skill in outlining approximately 122 different Gregg principles, 60 phrases, and 70 brief forms. In Test 2 two letters are dictated at different speeds. From this material errors in outlining were scored. Test 3 requires correct English spelling of 42 hard words. Transcription of Tests 1 and 2 is also required after their outlines have been scored. The typewritten sheets are scored for errors in transcription, spelling, and punctuation.

A number of tests have recently been standardized and issued, which illustrate a combination of achievement and closely related aptitude measures. Typical of these is the Psychological Corporation General Clerical Test (1944), which gives an over-all score to represent general clerical aptitude; three section scores (for comparison and filing, for mathematics, and for verbal skills); and nine separate test scores. The marked resemblance between this test and a standard achievement test is shown in Illus. 57. The same basic language and number skills are tested. The achievement tests give more emphasis to special subjects taught in school, while the clerical tests give more emphasis to speed in comparison of words and numbers, and filing or sorting. Other clerical tests are given in Appendix II.

One of the most complete and well-standardized series of clerical tests is issued, usually in annual form, by the Joint Committee on Tests of the United Business Education Association and the National Office Management Association. These cover the following subjects:

Test	Time, in Minutes
Bookkeeping	120
Business Fundamentals	35
Business Information	25
Filing	120
Stenography:	
Dictation	30
Transcription	120
Typing	120
Machine Calculation	120

Another complete series, the United States Armed Forces Institute examinations, which is issued by the Cooperative Test Service and the Science Research Associates, includes:

Test	Time, in Minutes
Bookkeeping and Accounting: first and second years	180
Business Arithmetic	135
Business English	120
Commercial Correspondence	120
Gregg Shorthand: Phonograph record	120
Typewriting: first and second years	60

One of the best recorded tests for stenography is that of Seashore and Bennett, which consists of standard phonograph records containing five letters dictated at different rates. Two are short and slowly given; two are of medium length and are given at average speed; and one is long and given rapidly. Alternative forms are provided. About 15 minutes are needed for dictation and 30 minutes for transcription.

A different type of stenography test is that of Blackstone and McLaughlin (1932), which has seven parts. The first six parts are short examinations of English techniques and information about business practices; the seventh, a transcription test:

1. Grammar, spelling, and punctuation errors were to be detected (30 items, 8 min.).

2. Correct syllabification was to be recognized from 4 choices (20 items, 4 min.).

3. Office practices: This is an information test with a few items concerning the right thing to do (20 items, 5 min.). Thus:

   a. Biographical sketches of men who have been successful in the arts and sciences may be found in:

      1. *The World Almanac,*   2. *The Statesman's Yearbook,*

      3. *R. G. Dun's Reports,*   4. *Who's Who.*   (——)

   b. On the first day on a new job, a girl is called by her first name by one of the men working with her. She does not like this. She should:

      1. Tell him that she prefers to be called by her last name, 2. Show her disapproval by a cold manner, 3. Call him by his first name, 4. Report him to her chief.   (——)

4. The alphabetical filing of 20 names among 28 already listed alphabetically (6 min.).

5. Abbreviations of 20 terms are to be written, such as, Certified Public Accountant (C.P.A.), and the unabbreviated expressions are to be supplied for 20 abbreviations, such as, cr. (credit), mgr. (manager) (5 min.).

6. Business organization: In this test, twenty types of information are listed, and twelve department names. The task is to indicate the department which should be consulted for each type of information (5 min.),

7. Transcription: Here short letters are read by the examiner and 12 minutes are allowed for typing. The manual provides seven letters arranged in order of difficulty or complexity, and prints the standard speed of reading the short passages in each letter. The more complex letters are to be read faster, ranging to 120 words per minute. The hardest transcriptions are allowed five times as much credit as the easier. The examiner is told to choose the letters which she thinks the class as a whole can transcribe "completely and correctly."

Norms for these seven tests are available for a thousand pupils distributed among four semesters of high school work, and for a large sample of stenographers. The stenographers and the fourth-semester pupils had the same total scores. The latter were 12 points ahead of the former in transcription, but the stenographers showed more skill in tests 2, 3, and 5. The equivalent-form reliability for the total score was reported to be .88 and correlations between scores and efficiency ratings were .62 and .79 for small groups in service.

This test is interesting because it appraises more than transcription ability. Tests 1, 2, and 5 are typical of English usage in general, Tests 3 and 6 deal with office background, and Test 4 requires filing activity, all of which can be done by persons without any stenographic training. Such items have been included in tests of general clerical work. One of the first of these was developed by Thurstone (1922). It consists of eight parts:

1. Checking addition and subtraction of numbers
2. Detecting misspelled words in a long passage
3. Drawing a line through X, Z, U, and C, but no other letters, in pied type
4. Associating letters with numbers
5. Classifying men's names according to location in cities and also alphabetically
6. Classifying insurance items according to amount and date simultaneously
7. Easy arithmetic problems
8. Matching proverbs

Since many of the skills needed in this test may be well developed before one starts formal clerical training or employment, the Thurstone Clerical Test has often been used as an aptitude test to predict success. Information concerning the use and validity of tests of this type should be sought in technical works on industrial psychology.

Bookkeeping Tests. An elaborate set of four bookkeeping tests at high school level was prepared by Breidenbaugh (1940). A Work Sheet, Balance Sheet, Profit and Loss Statement, and Closing Entries are to be filled in correctly from figures that are furnished. Knowledge of terms and business practices is also appraised by separate tests, which were constructed to cover the basic practices given in several textbooks. Their reliabilities are not given, nor is there any indication of prediction of success in bookkeeping work. The tests are designed as achievement examinations in a course of instruction.

A more general test of bookkeeping is that by Elwell-Fowlkes (1928). Without making actual calculations, one is required to give information about general theory, journalizing, classification, adjusting entries, closing the ledger, and statements. Fifty minutes are allowed to complete ninety items. Two forms are available which correlated .82 among 258 students in half-year classes.

Business Information. A general test of business information was published by Thurstone (1921) and a similar but more detailed test by Thompson (1937). In the latter, 220 items, which are to be completed in 80 minutes, are classified as follows:

arithmetic	17	organization and ownership	30
communication	26	economics	17
money and banking	30	selling and advertising	19
purchasing	11	investment and insurance	41
record filing	16	travel	13

Norms for 790 high school students are given for two equated forms. Total scores on the two forms were found to correlate approximately .94 for three groups of about one hundred students. The subtests are probably too short to be used for diagnoses of separate skills, although they do furnish a rough basis for quantitative analyses.

Tests for Professional Aptitudes

A fairly large number of tests of professional and technical aptitudes have been developed during the last few years, most of which are closely associated with the results of prerequisite courses. Some of these are given in Appendix II. They may be roughly grouped into two classes: those that are principally subject matter examinations and those that include general thinking, reading, and problem solving. Among the first class are the Graduate Record Examinations of the Carnegie Endowment for Advancement of Teaching. These do not follow the curriculum of any school, but are designed to cover broadly eight principal areas of liberal education: mathematics, physics, chemistry, biology, social studies (history, government, and economics), literature, fine arts, and general vocabulary.

Norms published each year are similar to those shown in Illus. 78, which shows the scores for 1946. There the mean scores for groups specializing in fifteen different fields of graduate study are given.

ILLUS. 78. AVERAGE SCORES ON PROFILE TESTS BY MAJOR FIELD GROUPS

First-Year Graduate Students at Eastern Universities

MEN

Major Field	Math.	Phys.	Chem.	Biol.	Hist. Govt. Econ.	Lit.	Fine Arts	Verbal
Biological Science	496	532	547	637	412	429	451	462
Chemistry	588	607	655	564	453	452	466	492
Economics	496	465	445	475	556	485	480	524
Fine Arts	397	418	407	431	472	527	656	499
Geology	505	541	525	518	434	420	457	458
Government	448	447	427	438	550	476	478	492
History	443	427	432	454	593	537	544	526
Literature	445	436	433	472	511	601	565	565
Mathematics	640	566	532	515	482	473	496	525
Mod. Languages	436	415	421	443	482	552	536	519
Music	454	448	413	452	476	533	612	536
Philosophy	483	499	458	507	520	566	553	582
Physics	631	656	580	526	455	433	462	498
Psychology	477	494	484	563	471	473	486	499
Sociology	445	445	447	489	534	505	496	504
Total	*494*	*492*	*486*	*500*	*498*	*502*	*509*	*514*

WOMEN

Major Field	Math.	Phys.	Chem.	Biol.	Hist. Govt. Econ.	Lit.	Fine Arts	Verbal
Biological Science	452	468	513	623	398	481	508	497
Economics	460	403	425	475	527	515	553	552
Education	414	344	385	426	420	502	525	461
Fine Arts	366	362	371	422	449	546	663	517
Government	414	376	393	458	525	518	547	530
History	390	353	391	447	532	519	536	518
Literature	391	359	389	452	458	577	545	544
Mathematics	587	441	409	431	410	440	442	441
Mod. Languages	389	346	383	423	419	529	536	488
Music	416	400	397	432	432	517	613	512
Psychology	434	394	395	473	427	488	496	514
Sociology	389	353	394	455	438	496	474	494
Total	*423*	*383*	*408*	*461*	*454*	*522*	*531*	*513*

First-Year Graduate Students at Midwestern Universities

MEN

Major Field	Math.	Phys.	Chem.	Biol.	Hist. Govt. Econ.	Lit.	Fine Arts	Verbal
Agriculture	465	503	529	579	358	333	347	365
Biological Science	449	507	519	587	360	374	384	382
Chemistry	546	580	620	526	388	381	404	413
Economics	444	440	428	439	473	405	410	402
Education	437	464	450	479	422	400	391	385
Engineering	569	575	563	439	360	338	366	380
Geology	495	541	525	501	395	376	379	405
Government	421	440	419	428	526	440	437	474
History	397	414	407	426	521	452	441	423
Literature	408	443	433	474	480	560	515	512
Mathematics	622	567	514	472	411	398	401	439
Mod. Languages	412	433	413	462	476	530	522	511
Physics	595	646	561	500	418	404	422	462
Psychology	481	510	499	549	445	440	441	438
Speech	397	429	409	467	424	479	445	444
Total	*481*	*509*	*505*	*492*	*407*	*397*	*407*	*412*

WOMEN

Major Field	Math.	Phys.	Chem.	Biol.	Hist. Govt. Econ.	Lit.	Fine Arts	Verbal
Biological Science	452	459	513	593	377	416	440	425
Education	385	376	389	442	367	419	423	401
Fine Arts	341	359	361	423	355	413	531	390
History	374	340	370	429	482	457	455	415
Library Science	328	358	376	451	419	494	492	445
Literature	357	349	364	440	428	540	540	481
Mod. Languages	369	339	337	437	415	526	533	482
Psychology	414	382	417	507	420	462	482	479
Social Work	338	330	366	456	385	425	427	413
Speech	336	334	350	417	363	466	440	398
Total	*381*	*373*	*396*	*461*	*388*	*449*	*457*	*427*

(By permission of the Graduate Record Examination, Educational Testing Service.)

The expected mean profiles appear. For instance, those studying biological science have high scores in fields where those studying fine arts have low scores, and vice versa. The fact that the literature and arts majors excel on the general vocabulary test indicates that it emphasizes literary, art, and musical terms.

Other tests of this same sort are the Cooperative Tests, and the College Entrance Board tests in physics, chemistry, and general science, at both the college and the high school level. They are useful for selecting technicians of less than college graduate level. A group of well-planned tests in the field of engineering is issued by the United States Armed Forces Institute, which includes at the college junior or senior level: electronics, drawing, mechanics, machine design, strength of materials, surveying, and radio and Diesel engineering.

Tests which evaluate both technical subject matter and general aptitudes are well illustrated by teaching and nursing aptitude tests, which sometimes also appraise interest or attitude. Recently the Educational Testing Service (ETS) has developed and tried out a battery of tests for law school and medical college admission. The latter is an 8-hour test which consists of the following:

General Ability
  1. Verbal ability (vocabulary and comprehension)
     Scientific materials ⎤
     Social materials   ⎬   105 min.
     Humanistic materials ⎦
  2. Quantitative ability   60 min.
Achievement
  1. Understanding of modern society   90 min.
  2. Premedical science   90 min.
                               —————
                               345 min.

In Illus. 79 there are some well-developed sample test questions from this battery.

ANALYSES OF RESULTS

Since the raw scores of achievement tests do not show the significance of the finding, several methods of interpreting scores have been devised. One group of investigators have used mean scores of age or grade groups to construct scales. Illustration 133, shows a profile which gives both educational-age (EA) and chronological-age equivalents and mean scores for each tenth of a grade from grades 2.6 to 10.0.

From this figure it appears that Eleanor Brown's highest score

ILLUS. 79. MEDICAL COLLEGE ADMISSION TEST

SAMPLE TEST QUESTIONS

The following sample test questions are intended to familiarize you with the main types of questions used in the Medical College Admission Test and with the manner in which the answers are to be recorded on the special answer sheets. When you have tried these questions, check your answers against the list of correct answers on page 14.

VOCABULARY

Sample Directions:

In answering the questions in this test, decide which of the five suggested answers has *most nearly* the *same* meaning as the capitalized word. Then, on the answer sheet, blacken the space beneath the number corresponding to that of the word you have selected.

Sample Questions:

1. CARCINOMA	2. MORES	3. AUDACIOUS
1—carcass	1—knowledge	1—splendid
2—cancer	2—laws	2—loquacious
3—calcification	3—thoughts	3—cautious
4—infection	4—customs	4—auspicious
5—excretion	5—superstitions	5—presumptuous

(In Question 1, suggested answer 2 is the "best" answer. Therefore, space 2 on the sample answer sheet has been blackened.)

COMPREHENSION

Sample Directions:

This test includes reading passages, each of which is followed by several questions based upon its content. Read each passage carefully and then answer the questions following it by selecting the best choice for each question and blackening the space beneath the corresponding number on the answer sheet.

Sample Passage:

The term *albedo* is used to indicate the reflecting power of an object. Technically defined, *albedo* is the ratio of the radiation reflected from an object to the total amount incident upon it. For example, the *albedo* of the moon is 0.073, which means that the moon reflects that fraction of the sunlight which is incident upon it.

The value of the *albedo* of a planet is a measure of the quantity of atmosphere which surrounds the object. The higher the *albedo* the thicker the atmospheric layer. In the case of objects without atmosphere, as in the case of the moon, the *albedo* combined with the color of the reflected light may be used to make estimates of the character of the material making up the surface of the object.

Sample Questions on Passage:

4. Judging from this passage, what may we infer regarding the *albedo* of the Earth?

   1—That it is greater than 0.073
   2—That it is smaller than 0.073
   3—That it is approximately the same as that of other planets

ILLUS. 79. MEDICAL COLLEGE ADMISSION TEST *(Cont'd)*

4—That it is greater than the *albedos* of other planets which are farther from
the sun
5—We cannot infer anything about the Earth's *albedo.*

5. When the *albedo* is calculated, to which of the following is the value of 1 assigned?

1—The amount of light reflected from the object
2—The amount of light the object receives
3—The total amount of light given off by the sun
4—The total amount of light received by the Earth
5—The average amount of light received by the planets

QUANTITATIVE ABILITY

Sample Directions:

In this test solve each problem and then indicate the *one* correct answer for each
in the proper space on the answer sheet.

Sample Questions:

6. It is known that every circle has an equation of the form
$$Ax^2 + Ay^2 + Bx + Cy + D = O.$$
Which of the following is the equation of a circle?

(A) $2x - 3y = 6$ (B) $x^2 - y^2 + 4x - 2y + 3 = O$
(C) $3x^2 + 3y^2 - 2x + 6y + 1 = O$ (D) $2x^2 + 3y^2 + 6x + 4y + 1 = O$
(E) None of the above

Questions 7-8

The tabulation below shows the frequency with which 600 employees of a certain
industrial plant met with accidents during a single year.

Number of Accidents per Worker	Number of Workers
0	490
1	76
2	23
3	6
4	3
5	1
6	0
7	1

7. What percentage of the workers had 4 or more accidents during the year?

(A) 0.10   (B) 0.25   (C) 0.50   (D) 0.83   (E) 5.00

8. What is the probability that one of the workers picked at random from the
group will have had more than one accident during the year?

(A) 0.023   (B) 0.034   (C) 0.046   (D) 0.057   (E) 0.200

ILLUS. 79. MEDICAL COLLEGE ADMISSION TEST (*Cont'd*)

UNDERSTANDING OF MODERN SOCIETY

Sample Directions:

Each incomplete statement in this test is followed by five words, phrases, or clauses, *one* of which will complete the statement correctly. Select the correct completion and blacken the space beneath the corresponding number on the appropriate line on the answer sheet.

Sample Questions:

9. The term "world power" refers to a nation

    1—whose products are commonly used throughout the world
    2—which maintains diplomatic agents in all the recognized sovereign nations
    3—which has a large population
    4—which has sufficient wealth and organization to exert a strong influence in world politics
    5—so strong in a military and an economic sense that it can demand representation at a general international assembly

10. Japan today presents no immediate threat to peace in the Far East principally because

    1—so much of the country has been devastated
    2—she has been stripped of her colonies and conquests
    3—the present Japanese constitution outlaws war
    4—the new Japanese government is much opposed to the military party
    5—there is now unity of purpose among the various interests in the Far East

PREMEDICAL SCIENCE

Sample Directions:

Each of the questions in this test is followed by five suggested answers. You are to select the *best* answer for each question and mark the corresponding space on the answer sheet.

Sample Questions:

11. When both the pressure and the absolute temperature of a sample of "perfect" gas are doubled, the volume of the gas is multiplied by

    1—1
    2—2
    3—4
    4—8
    5—16

12. Which one of the following is 75 per cent carbon, by weight, and 25 per cent hydrogen, by weight?

    1—C_3H
    2—CH
    3—CH_3
    4—C_2H_3
    5—CH_4

(By permission of the Educational Testing Service.)

(100 in Reading: Word Meaning) is equivalent to an EA of fifteen years, eight months, and to the mean of grade 9.7. Her lowest score (76 in dictation—in this case a spelling test) is equivalent to an EA of twelve years, and to a grade standing of 6.2. The educational ages above fifteen years and below seven years were not based upon actual measurement but upon the extrapolation [1] of a growth curve which was found to fit the scores for the intermediate ages.

Educational ages and grade equivalents are valuable for placing or promoting a pupil in schools where promotions are based upon achievement. They do not, however, furnish an indication of where a person is in his own age and grade groups, with whose members he must compete. This information is furnished by centile scores (Illus. 65A). Here the proportion of pupils that exceed a given pupil can be quickly read. A chart which combines both centile and grade norms for a single test is shown in Illus. 123. From this table it appears that about 13 per cent of students in the grades below college were retarded one grade; 10 per cent, two grades; and 8 per cent, three grades. Similarly, approximately 14 per cent were advanced one grade; 10 per cent, two grades; and 8 per cent, three grades. Figures of this sort vary according to the method of grouping students which happens to be in effect in a particular school. The spreads of age and grade scores in two city schools are contrasted in Illus. 80. Although the data refer to intelligence test scores, similar results are found when general educational achievement tests are used. The medians and the dispersions are found to be nearly the same for similar age groups, but in the grade groups, City B has higher means and greater dispersions than City A. Pressey (1933) commented on this situation as follows:

The two school systems have, therefore, created a situation educationally different out of almost identical intellectual material. Further study showed the grade differences to be due primarily to different promotion policies in the two towns. School System B retarded its children to such an extent that the average chronological age per grade was about five months above that for System A. This excessive retardation so discouraged a great many of the children that they dropped out of school as soon as possible and therefore never reached the upper grades. School System A, on the other hand, pursued a liberal promotion policy and tended to promote every child every year. As a result, the average age per grade was less than in School System B, and the children were so encouraged that more of the duller ones continued into the upper grades; even those who dropped out of school at the legal age were in a higher grade than the similar class of

---

[1] *Extrapolation* is the continuation of a curve into an unknown area by a formula computed from the curve in a known area.

children in System B. These contrasting promotion policies caused System B to require a higher standard of ability for entrance to each of the grades than did System A. The higher standard in the former may appear desirable until one remembers the large number of unhappy, retarded children who never continued beyond the middle grades of elementary school. A heavy retardation will undoubtedly raise the grade averages, not only in intelligence but also in achievement, but at the expense of the best possible individual development of the children.

In making comparisons of communities and schools, one must always be alert to the differences that are caused, not by the innate ability of the pupils but by the artificial grade grouping resulting from the particular promotion policies adopted by school officials. Unless one knows the chronological age of children in the same grades in different schools or school systems, he is quite unable to make any valid comparisons as to the meaning of the test scores.

ILLUS. 80. INTELLIGENCE OF SCHOOL CHILDREN IN
TWO SCHOOL SYSTEMS

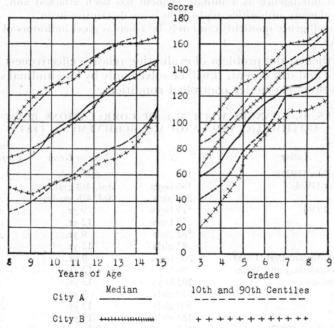

(By permission of Pressey, 1933, and Harper & Bros.)

Accomplishment Quotients

One of the cardinal objectives listed by nearly all authorities is the development of effectiveness in learning. Since one's effectiveness depends upon both his native ability and acquired skills, it was thought that relative effectiveness would be indicated by comparing them. One method of comparison used the ratio of two test scores: a general intelligence test, and an educational achievement test. Franzen (1922) divided the educational age by the mental age and secured an accomplishment quotient (AQ). Such quotients have practically gone out of use, however, for the following reasons:

1. It was shown by Rand (1925) that mental ages usually have larger dispersions than educational ages for the same group of persons.

2. Logically, the correlation between AQ's and IQ's would always be zero unless the correlation between IQ and EQ (Educational Quotient) is 1.00. This correlation is rarely or never found because the two types of tests emphasize different skills.

3. Marked difficulties have been experienced in standardizing both educational and mental ages, particularly above the average adult level.

4. The usefulness of the ratio has been questioned, for the concept of general intelligence as a unitary element has been attacked and, in the minds of many authorities, replaced by more descriptive items.

5. Intelligence quotients can rarely be taken as good indicators of native abilities.

Nevertheless, the problem of evaluating relative effectiveness is still present and still urgent. It will be solved only by longitudinal studies of development under controlled conditions.

ILLUS. 81. CHANGES WITH AGE OF CORRELATIONS BETWEEN ARITHMETIC AND LANGUAGE ACHIEVEMENT TESTS

Author	N	Year or Grade	Average Correlation
Thorndike (1926)	126	5th grade	.52
Schiller (1934)	186 boys	3rd, 4th grades	.63
	206 girls	3rd, 4th grades	.60
Asch (1936)	*79 boys	9 yr.	.68
	79 boys	12 yr.	.43
	*82 girls	9 yr.	.63
	82 girls	12 yr.	.30
Garett, Bryan, Perl (1935)	306 boys	9 yr.	.52
Vocabulary and Arith-	96 boys	12 yr.	.61
metic	102 boys	15 yr.	.37
	340 girls	9 yr.	.40
	100 girls	12 yr.	.55
	123 girls	15 yr.	.55
Buckingham (1937)	105 pupils	9th grade	.38
Co-operative Algebra, and Gates Reading			
Garett (1928)	338 men	1st yr. college	.21
Schneck (1929)	210 men	2nd yr. college	.14

* The same children retested 3 years later with the same tests.

Correlations between English and Arithmetic

Because English and arithmetic have long been considered basic subjects, their relationships have been studied by a number of authors. Some of their studies, which are summarized in Illus. 81, show a marked tendency for lower correlations in older groups. These correlations are not strictly comparable, because the types of patterns measured at various ages are only roughly alike. For instance, the Arithmetic Reasoning Test requires a larger vocabulary and more complex types of calculation at the twelfth year than at the ninth year. The skills leading to success at the ninth year may be inadequate or even detrimental at the twelfth year.

These correlations are also not strictly comparable because it is not known how much they are affected by a narrow selection of students. College groups are often selected from the highest third of the population—a process which reduces correlations considerably below what they would have been if the total adult population had been sampled.

APPLICATIONS OF TESTS

Educational achievement tests have three main uses: individual diagnoses, predictions of individual success, and evaluations of the effects of instruction. There is a wide use of tests for diagnoses of individual differences among normal, retarded and genius groups, delinquents, and those with special defects or behavior problems. Illustrations 62, 65A, 132, 133, show diagnostic profiles. From such profiles it is possible to point out a person's strong and weak points and to suggest remedial plans. This is the work of educational and clinical psychologists, about which one should consult special texts.

Scholastic Predictions

Prediction of school success is especially important for selecting and counseling students. Among the causes of variations in making predictions, the two major ones are inconsistencies in methods of assigning school grades and large changes in the interests of pupils. With these limitations, prediction correlations of .70 are usually as high as may be expected. A few typical results are:

1. Correlations between achievement-test scores in a particular subject and class grades in that subject usually range from .42 to .70 (Kohn, 1938; Gates, 1922). Dyer (1948), however, found correlations from .64 to .94 between College Entrance Board language test scores and final marks in the corresponding elementary language courses.

2. The prediction of class grades in a particular course from grades in an earlier course in the same field ranges from approximately

.40 to .70 in the usual school or college group. Greene and Jorgensen (1936) and Williamson (1937) noted a tendency for the accuracy of scholastic predictions to decrease in the higher grades.

3. The prediction of algebra and geometry grades from arithmetic tests is usually in the neighborhood of .50, from special aptitude tests, .55, and from special aptitude and English comprehension tests combined, .60. (Ayres, 1934; Richardson, 1935; Orleans, 1934; Baier, 1948; Riegel, 1949.)

4. Prediction of general scholastic average from one year to the next is usually about .60 in large groups taking different courses. (Finch and Nemzek, 1934.) When all persons take approximately the same courses in the same order, correlations approximate .75.

5. Prediction of general scholastic average from a group verbal intelligence test is usually near .70 for elementary school groups, but considerably lower for high school and college groups. (Crawford and Burnham, 1946.)

Since the actual correlations are too low for much individual use, a large number of studies have been made which show that the combined scores of several tests often yield slightly better predictions than a single score.

Optimum Age for Instruction

Typical of studies which aim to determine the most appropriate age for teaching a particular skill is that of the Committee of Seven of the Northern Illinois Conference on Supervision, reported by Washburne (1939). In 1926 this committee began investigations which have involved 30,744 children in 255 cities. Their procedure was as follows:

1. To define units of arithmetic very precisely and to devise tests to measure these units. Usually the Compass Arithmetic Test or similar tests have been used.

2. To determine the usual grade placement of a unit by a rough survey.

3. To secure cooperation of school and teachers in the teaching of a unit at one grade lower, and at one or two grades higher than the usual grade. Standard teaching procedures have been carefully described.

4. To administer five tests: a Verbal Intelligence Test, a Pretest in Arithmetic, a Teaching Test, a Final Test, and a Retention Test, 6 weeks after the final test. All of these tests except the first were practically equivalent forms.

5. To discover the relationships between these tests and to suggest optimal age and grade placements. The Committee has usually felt that a unit should be taught when three fourths of the children succeed in solving 75 per cent of the items of a retention test.

The results of one such procedure are shown in Illus. 82, where the mental ages of children are plotted against per cents of success on the total test. From this figure it appears that 33-per-cent success was reached by the average child at a mental age of five years, one month; 75 per cent at seven years, two months; and 100 per cent at nine years, ten months. If a teacher desires any particular degree of mastery, the unit can be placed accordingly; or, vice versa, if a particular degree of mastery is found among a given group, the success of the instruction may be appraised.

The use of verbal intelligence tests in this connection might be challenged on the ground that readiness for a particular arithmetic unit is a special ability which may not depend very much upon the skills needed for success on the intelligence tests. Much research is still needed to show the relationship between various predictions of arithmetical success. The Committee has, however, published fairly detailed and useful statements of the skills which have been mastered by particular mental age groups, one of which is given below:

ILLUS. 82. GROWTH OF SUCCESS ON HARD ADDITION

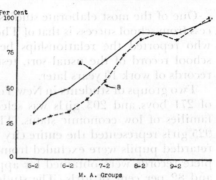

A. Per Cent of Items Passed by MA Group

B. Per Cent of Group Retaining 75 Per Cent or More Items

(After Washburne, 1939, Figure 1. By permission of the National Society for the Study of Education.)

MENTAL AGE 7–8

The addition facts with sums of 10 and under are well learned at this level, and there is little gain in further postponement. The harder addition facts and the easy subtraction facts can be successfully learned at this age, but there is a definite gain in postponing them to the next level. The desirability of systematic drill in these facts at this level is open to question, in spite of the fact that it produces satisfactory results. Many persons feel, and there is some evidence to justify the feeling, that the informal experiences and activities of mental level 6–7 should be continued and extended at this level and that systematic drill of all sorts should be postponed to the next one.

Simple comparisons of length, height, thickness, width, and the like, including the recognition that one object is two, three, or four times as high, wide, long, thick, or deep as another, are well learned. Children can also readily learn to measure lines in even inches, and, with more difficulty, to draw lines an even number of inches long. They can learn how many inches there are in a foot and in two feet.

Children can learn to read the clock on the even hour, to distinguish between morning and afternoon, to understand the symbols A.M. and P.M.

Vocational Predictions

One of the most elaborate studies of prediction of vocational success from school success is that of Thorndike (1934) and his associates, who reported the relationships between three sets of appraisals: school record of the usual sort, tests during the eighth grade, and records of work 10 years later.

Two groups of students in New York City were studied. One group of 271 boys and 203 girls was selected from schools which served families of low economic status. The other group of 826 boys and 925 girls represented the entire city population fairly well (the most retarded pupils were excluded from school). By diligent work, complete records were obtained for approximately 78 per cent of boys and 82 per cent of girls. The students whose records were incomplete because they moved away were not significantly different from the others at age fourteen. Students who could not be located or who refused to cooperate were slightly inferior to the others at age fourteen in school progress, intelligence test scores, and scholarship.

The school records which were secured, together with their retest reliabilities, are shown below:

1. Age in eighth grade, third month (.99)
2. Progress during school attendance (.92)
3. Conduct (.99)
4. Scholarship (.96)
5. Attendance (.99)
6. Age at leaving school (.97)
7. Grade at leaving school (.99)

The tests used in the eighth grade and approximate reliabilities for an age group were:

8. Clerical intelligence, Toops (.85)
9. Clerical activities (.80)
10. Stenquist Assembly Test (.40)
11. IER Assembly Test for girls (.70)
12. Arithmetic problems (above .80)
13. Language tests (above .80)
14. A combination of tests 12 and 13 called intelligence (.85)
15. Average annual earnings at ages 20 to 22 (.90)

16. Average level of jobs (.70)
17. Average liking for jobs (reliabilities not calculated, thought to be about .70)
18. Per cent of times employed (.90)
19. Number of changes of employer (thought to be near .99)

These retest reliabilities of school records and vocational records are very high. The variations were largely due to clerical errors and slight shifts in standards. The reliabilities of the tests and estimates used are considerably lower, although they are as high as is generally found for material of this sort. The test reliabilities are not high enough for good individual prediction, but they are high enough to show group trends.

All of these items were intercorrelated in order to show their predictive value. The results may be summarized as follows:

1. The age of leaving the eighth grade, scholarship, and intelligence-test scores predict fairly well the grade which will be reached at later ages. Indirectly, this finding is of vocational significance because the grade which can be completed indicated the level of college or professional work that may be attempted.

2. Among the 223 men and 247 women who did clerical work for at least nine tenths of the time at ages 20 to 22, it was found that clerical earnings correlated with the earlier tests of clerical intelligence, .26, with clerical activities, .22, and with scholarship, intelligence, and mechanical assembly to smaller degrees. Conduct and attendance showed zero relationships with clerical earnings. The highest correlation obtainable was approximately .30 for boys and .40 for girls. The correlations between level of jobs and interest in work and the school records and test were all nearly zero.

3. In the case of the 210 men and 155 women who worked nine tenths of the time at mechanical work from ages 18 to 20, none of the school records or tests showed significant correlations with earnings, liking for work, and interest. This situation was also typical of the 299 men and 76 women who had combinations of mechanical and clerical work of other varieties.

4. The higher a pupil's score in clerical and intelligence tests and in scholarship, the more likely was he to do better at clerical than at mechanical work and vice versa, but the likelihood was not large.

5. Of the eighth grade boys, 20 per cent attended college for at least one semester; and of the girls, 12 per cent.

6. About 2 per cent in the group became criminals. These were inferior to the group average at age fourteen in all respects.

7. The frequency of change of employer had slight and probably insignificant relationships to earnings, level of occupation, and interest.

8. The annual earning in white-collar jobs was greater than in mechanical jobs among women, but not among men.

9. There was much evidence that employers did not select employees on

the basis of ability alone. Had this been the case, the prediction from eighth grade records would have been materially higher.

10. The prediction of later success, if the study is carried on further, will probably be greater because many persons had not yet shown what they could do vocationally.

This study points to the need of more careful instruments for appraising abilities at early ages and factors in success at later ages. It indicates that when more precise measurements are available and when allowances are made for such disconcerting factors as health and racial prejudice, prediction of vocational success will be of considerable accuracy.

NEEDED RESEARCH

In this chapter tests have been described, but because of lack of space, have seldom been criticized or even analyzed to show their fine points. A good deal of criticism, however, has been directed from time to time at most of the tests listed here. Perhaps the most serious is that the tests often emphasize isolated bits of information which are of little value and are soon forgotten. Instead, they should emphasize a few important tools and develop problem-solving skills and attitudes. Thus it has been urged that it is of little importance to know the name of a hero in a novel, but it is important to know that he had certain ideals and that he used particular methods to solve his problems with particular results. Also, it seems of little use to memorize a formula by rote learning or to acquire a great number of data which will seldom be used or remembered. The critics feel that this undesirable emphasis is strengthened by the use of many of the current achievement tests. This is doubtless true to some extent. Few analyses of achievement tests have as yet come to hand to show what specific knowledge, reasoning, or other factors they measure. A great deal more research is needed to determine more carefully the goals of specific courses and to prepare proficiency tests in skills as well as in the usual factual items. It is now possible, however, to select a test which apparently emphasizes the particular type of knowledge and skill that is desired. And in spite of their defects, many present-day achievement tests are much more economical, reliable, and valid than those that were available a few years ago.

STUDY GUIDE QUESTIONS

1. Which of the cardinal objectives of education are not specifically concerned with measures of ability or school achievement?

2. How can composition be accurately appraised?

3. How can adequate word-knowledge tests be developed for a given field of knowledge?

4. What are the best ways of measuring grammar and punctuation?

5. Discuss the advantages of oral and written spelling tests?

6. How does the Progressive Achievement Test diagnose difficulties?

7. Prepare a paragraph-organization test. What does it measure?

8. What advantages are there in using a teacher's diagnostic chart for arithmetic difficulties?

9. What are the main components of physical-science tests?

10. What are the main components of social-science tests?

11. How can significant social science activities be appraised?

12. What elements are found in clerical tests which are not usually found in scholastic achievement tests?

13. How can the range of abilities in a given grade be compared with the range in another grade?

14. What may accomplishment quotients be used for?

15. Why are the correlations between language and arithmetic smaller in the higher grades than in the lower grades?

16. What are the usual predictions from achievement tests to success in a course of study?

17. Why do group intelligence tests predict course success about as well as specific achievement tests in elementary grades, but not in high school?

18. How can tests be used to aid in determining the optimum ages for instruction?

19. What factors have in the past seriously limited the possibility of predicting vocational success very accurately?

CHAPTER VIII

GROUP TESTS OF ABILITY

Applications of analytical methods to the measurement of abilities are discussed in this chapter. Also, current analytical batteries are described and compared for content, factorial purity, and practical use.

Primary abilities are not defined as innate traits, but as traits which are primary in the sense that they are (a) statistically independent of each other; (b) psychologically basic to many types of academic and vocational success, and (c) stable over fairly long periods of time and not influenced greatly by practice or by recent formal training.

EARLY TESTS

During the period when individual tests of the Binet type were being developed there was also an active growth in the design of mental tests for use with groups. All types of tests now widely used seem to have been fairly well developed in form before 1910. For instance, careful methods for measuring memory span were described by Jacobs (1887) and refined by Ebert and Neumann (1905). In 1889 Cattell and Bryant tried out a number of tests of both controlled and uncontrolled association, which were later developed by Jastrow (1891). The use of standard arithmetic tests in the study of association processes was begun in 1895 by Oehrn and also by Kraeplin. During 1897 Ebbinghaus published an enthusiastic account of a sentence-completion test as a real test of intelligence. In 1891 Kirkpatrick described a rather difficult vocabulary test.

In 1903 Swift published his work on interpretation of fables or proverbs. Whipple (1908) published fairly elaborate vocabulary and anagram tests and in 1909 a range-of-information tests. Cyril Burt reported elaborate experimental tests of higher mental processes in 1909. In the United States Woodworth and Wells (1911) reported their famous association tests, which included verbal analogies, opposites, part-whole, agent-action, species-genus, and hard directions. In 1913 Pyle reported an elaborate set of examinations of school children that resulted in age norms.

In 1914 Whipple published a 2-volume manual of mental and physical tests which included fifty-one tests with directions and norms, and about five hundred references to technical reports. Since that time the production of technical reports and test revisions has been voluminous, and many refinements have been made in administration, scoring, and scaling procedures.

Most of the early examiners followed the hypothesis that persons are possessed of a general faculty called intelligence, which can be measured by a variety of mental tests. They usually wished to appraise intelligence in order to make practical predictions of some sort. For an intelligence test they wished to select only those items which showed fairly high correlations with some criterion of intelligence and low correlations with one other. An important application of this method of selection was the development of the United States Army mental tests in 1917. The more recent developments of military tests are discussed in Chapter XI.

Approximately one and three-fourths of a million soldiers were tested during 1917 and 1918 by one or both of the forms developed at that time. These tests, which have since been widely applied to industrial, prison, and school groups, have also been widely copied in both form and idea. As criteria for defining intelligence, the psychologists in charge of the work of testing the soldiers decided to use combined scores of (a) formal school accomplishment, (b) scores on the Stanford-Binet test, and (c) ratings by officers. Groups of soldiers for whom these criteria were available were given batteries of thirteen preliminary verbal tests. Four of the preliminary tests were taken from the work of Otis, who generously placed them at the disposal of the committee. Several tests show great similarities to those in the Woodworth Wells series. Binet's and Thurstone's tests were also used or adapted in making up these Army tests.

The correlations of total preliminary test scores with officers' ratings of intelligence ranged from approximately .50 to .70; with Stanford-Binet Test score, .80 to .90; with Trabue Language Completion Scales, .72; with schooling, .75; and the Beta Test, .80. The lowest correlations of the separate subtests with total weighted scores (Yerkes, 1921, p. 541) were approximately .65 for tests of oral directions, memory span, disarranged sentences, and practical judgment.

The highest correlations were approximately .85 for tests of arithmetic problems, verbal opposites, information, verbal analogies, and number comparisons. The mean of the correlations between subtests for a sample of 895 soldiers was approximately .61, and the subtests which correlated most highly with the total scores also showed the highest correlations with the other subtests. These results led empirically to the conclusion, which is also mathematically obtainable, that it is impossible to secure subtests which will correlate highly with a criterion and nearly zero with each other. Subtests which had degrees of correlation with each other and with total scores similar to those shown above were finally selected and combined into a test called the United States Army Alpha Test. In constructing the test forms, several practical factors were considered. The test should

1. Be adapted for use with large groups of persons who had wide differences in ability. (The final test items ranged from those which were answered by nearly 99 per cent of a group of adults to those answered correctly by about 1 per cent.)

2. Have a number of equivalent forms to prevent cheating, or coaching, or marked practice effects. (Five forms of the Alpha tests which were found to give very similar results were prepared.)

3. Be arranged for ease and accuracy of scoring by clerical workers. (This called for a minimum of writing. The answers were usually a single number or a check mark indicating a particular choice.)

4. Render clues of malingering during an examination. (The tests did not succeed in giving accurate answers to this problem.)

5. Be interesting.

6. Be short. (The total working time of the Alpha test was limited to 24 minutes.)

The Alpha and Beta Tests

The Alpha Test is a paper-and-pencil battery with eight subtests, each placed on a separate page of a booklet and allotted a special time limit. The first is a test of span of auditory attention. The examiner reads directions which the soldiers follow by making lines or numbers on the prepared items. The directions become more complicated toward the end of the test. Thus, the directions for the second item are:

Attention! Look at 2 where the circles have numbers in them. When I say "Go" draw a line from circle 1 to circle 4 that will pass *above* circle 2 and *below* circle 3.—GO! (Allow not over 5 seconds.)

and for the eleventh item:

Attention! Look at 11. When I say "Go" draw a line through every even number that is not in a square, and also through every odd number that is in a square with a letter.—GO! (Allow not over 25 seconds.)

The second test is a 5-minute test of twenty arithmetic problems. The third test involves common sense or practical judgment, 1½ minutes being allowed for the sixteen items. The fourth test allows 1½ minutes to check forty pairs of words to show whether they are the same or opposite. The fifth test allows 2 minutes to rearrange twenty-four sentences that had been disarranged in a random fashion. The sixth test requires the completion of twenty number series, allowing 3 minutes. The seventh test consists of forty verbal analogies, with a working time of 3 minutes. The eighth test allows 4 minutes to check forty multiple-choice items of miscellaneous information. A short time is allowed to consider samples of the next test.

In order to provide a test for men who could not read English, a selection and standardizing procedure similar to that of the Alpha Test was followed, beginning with fifteen nonverbal tests. The result is called the United States Army Beta Test.

This is also a paper-and-pencil test with seven subtests. It was designed so that it could be demonstrated largely by pantomime and without many words. Before each test the examiner and a demonstrator showed on a large blackboard how the work was to be done.

The first test consists of five mazes, of which the first two were traced on the blackboard by the demonstrator. Then, when the soldiers understood what was wanted, they were told, "All right, go ahead. Do it. Hurry up." The idea of working fast was impressed on those who were working slowly, because only 2 minutes were allowed. The second test requires that sixteen pictures of piles of cubes be viewed, and the number of cubes in each be written down, 2½ minutes. The third test is a nonverbal series completion in which the pattern of x's and o's is to be completed in each line according to the way it is printed at the start of the line with a time allowance of 1¾ minutes. In the fourth test the examinee is required to associate symbols with numbers on a sheet according to a code placed at the top of the page. Two minutes are allowed. The fifth test allows 3 minutes for comparing pairs of numbers and marking with an x those pairs that are different. The sixth test allows 3 minutes for drawing in missing parts of twenty printed pictures. In the seventh test ten rather easy paper form-board problems are allowed 2½ minutes. The task is to draw lines to show how the small pieces would fit into the large figure.

CURRENT GENERAL ABILITY TESTS

The period since 1918 has witnessed the production of many group tests of mental abilities, some ostensibly to appraise intelligence and others to evaluate observing, reasoning, and learning in special situations. Most of these tests extended the scope of the Army tests by adapting them for use in the lower grades. Tests by Otis and Pressey appeared in 1918. Haggerty (1920) and Whipple (1919) published standardized tests. A group of affiliated psychologists produced the National Intelligence Test in 1920, and Terman published a group test in 1926.

Group tests are usually presented in printed form. Oral group tests that consist of verbal and number multiple-choice items and problems were standardized by Stump (1935) and by Langmuir (1946). The advantages of these tests are that they (*a*) allow all students the same amount of time for each item, (*b*) allow each student to attempt every item, and (*c*) obviate the expense of printed forms. Two alternative sets of questions have been prepared for grades 4 to 8 by Stump, and for a wide range of adults by Langmuir.

Snedden (1927) experimented with a vocabulary test that was disguised in a questionnaire on traits that may have some hereditary significance. The subject was asked which of his two parents possessed the greater amount of a certain trait—being gentle, meticulous, sanguine, etc. Seventy-five words of graded difficulty were selected and standardized on several hundred persons. Correlations with Stanford-Binet MA's were found to be in the neighborhood of .70. The interview form was further developed by Maizlish (1936), who issued a like-dislike questionnaire, and asked the subject to give reasons for his answers. The reasons showed whether or not the word was understood. This test, when given to individuals, was found to correlate .77 with Kuhlmann-Anderson tests; when given to a group, the correlation dropped to .50.

A popular variety of intelligence test for adults, known as the spiral omnibus type, was designed to eliminate the need for accurate timing of short periods. A test was desired which would give about the same total scores as the United States Army Alpha Test during a 20- or 30-minute period of continuous work. Hence, materials much like those of the Alpha were mixed together by rotating or spiraling among the tests (Illus. 83).

A list of most of the tests now available is given in Appendix II. Many of these tests are short (usually from 15 to 30 minutes are required for taking them), but a few are extensive and require from 1 hour to 2 hours. They are heavily loaded with language or language analogies, but also include arithmetic and occasionally a spatial item. They all yield a single score, which is usually converted into MA, IQ, and centile.

At the college level Thurstone (1919) inaugurated a series of

ILLUS. 83. O'ROURKE GENERAL CLASSIFICATION TEST, SENIOR GRADE

Grade of difficulty: High-school senior, College freshman

Directions and Samples

The directions and samples on this sheet are to show you the kinds of items you will find in the test. Study them carefully so you will know how you are to answer each kind of item. There will be no directions nor explanations in the test.

You are to write your answers always on the line at the right of the item.

You will be allowed 10 minutes to study the samples on the front and back of this page and answer those not answered.

WRITE

Meaning. If the word in capital letters fits into the meaning of the ANSWERS
sentence, write "correct" on the line at the right. If the meaning is   HERE
not correct, write the <u>number</u> of the word which does fit. . . .

Example : The clear day was DETAILED for the picnic.   (1) OR-
DERED (2) INVENTED (3) IDEAL (4) EXCUSED (5) DIS-
COVERED *3*

"DETAILED" does not fit the meaning of the sentence, but "IDEAL," which is marked "3," does, so "3" is written on the line at the right.

Relations. The first two words in each set are related in some way.
Write a word which is related to the third word in the same way as the second is to the first. The word you write must begin with the letter before the answer line.

Example : SHOE is to FOOT as HAT is to . . . .   H   *Head*

"Head" is written on the line at the right, because it begins with "H" and a hat is worn on the head, just as a shoe is worn on the foot.

Information. Five ways of completing the statement are suggested.
Write the <u>number</u> of the one which makes the true statement.

Example : Water is heavier than (1) paint   (2) granite   (3) iron
(4) wood   (5) sand *4*

Spelling. If every word in the sentence is correctly spelled, write
"correct" on the line at the right. If you find an incorrect word, spell that word correctly on the line at the right.

Example : His education was a great advantage . . . . . .   *advantage*

Opposite. Write the <u>number</u> of the word which means the <u>opposite</u> of
the word in capital letters.

Example : The opposite of LIGHT is (1) tinted   (2) small
(3) bright   (4) dark   (5) damp *4*

"Dark," marked "4," means the opposite of "LIGHT," so "4" is written on the line at the right.

Grammar. If the sentence is <u>grammatically</u> correct, write "correct"
on the line at the right. If you find the sentence incorrect, write what would with the least changes express the meaning correctly.

Example : The books is sold at the store. . . . .   *are*

(By permission of L. J. O'Rourke, 1935 edition, and The Psychological Institute, 3506 Patterson St., N. W., Washington, D. C.)

mental tests for college entrance under the auspices of the American Council on Education. Annual editions have been given to thousands of high school graduates. This series consists of tests of such types as vocabulary, mathematics, verbal analogies, and learning an artificial language, which are administered in periods so short that few if any students complete the work. Similarly, Thorndike began a series of intelligence tests for college entrance (1920). This series includes tests of word meaning, mathematics, and special information, for which 230 minutes are allowed. A similar excellent series called the Ohio State University Psychological Test has been designed by Toops (1937), and another series by the College Entrance Examination Board.

In order to reduce the effects of training on test scores, R. B. Cattell (1940) developed his **Culture-Free Test** for a wide range of adult ability.

The Culture-Free test is a paper-and-pencil test consisting of seven parts. It is unique in that it is a power test in a field where speed is usually stressed, and it involves two or three variables in making deductions. The Psychological Corporation applied an experimental form to two groups, each of approximately one hundred boys. One group was composed of vocational high school boys, the other of academic high school boys. Items showing significant differences between the two groups were retained. Similar item-validation studies were made among groups of college students, seventh- and eighth-grade pupils, and two hundred psychology majors. As a result Cattell's maze tests were dropped and the other tests revised. The 1945 edition consists of

1. *Classifications.* Fifteen items, each accompanied by six little pictures or diagrams. The person being tested is to find and mark two in each row which do *not* belong with the others. This is a form-analogies reasoning test where size, direction, shape, and shading are varied. (10 min.)

2. *Pool reflections.* Nine rows of six small pictures are to be inspected to find which one of each six is the exact mirrored drawing of a key picture above the row. (10 min.)

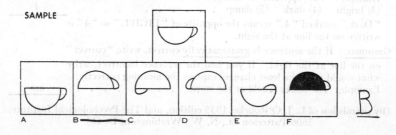

3. *Series completion.* Fifteen items, each consist of three small pictures at the left and six on the right. The task is to decide, from looking at the left series, which should come next, then to select it from the six pictures at the right. (20 min.)

4. *Matrices: 4-item relational.* Eleven items, each consist of a group of three little pictures and a blank arranged in a square on the left, and six other pictures on the right. The task is to select from the six the picture which will complete the square on the left. This is a completion test in which the pattern must be determined by making comparisons in both vertical and horizontal directions. (5 min.)

5. *Matrices: 9-item relational.* Each of the eleven items consists of eight small pictures and a blank arranged in a square. Six other pictures to choose from are below the eight. The task is to make the pattern in the square look finished, balanced, and complete. (7 min.)

SAMPLE

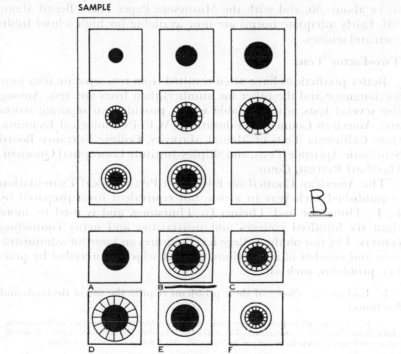

6. *Matrices: 9-item cyclical.* Each of eleven items consist of spaces for nine small pictures. The lower right-hand space is always a blank to be filled in from six other small pictures below. This test is more difficult than the fifth test, because, instead of having eight small pictures in the matrix, there are now only three or four. The rest have been torn away, and must be supplied by inferences between the matrix and the possible choices. (20 min.)

Although the tests have time limits, they are long enough to allow the pupil to finish as much as he can. The items are steeply graded. All of the tests primarily require reasoning with 2-dimension pictures, using differences of space, size, shading, and direction. Perceptual speed is not important because of the generous time limits. The fact that this is a measure of general mental ability is stressed. It may more descriptively be called a complex deduction test using *static* pictures. Motion and time sequences are not involved. Additional evidence is needed to show the effects of different cultures on this test. The split-half reliability of the whole test was .88 when it was given to 121 high school pupils. All of the parts correlate from .50 to .80 with the total score, with Test 3 showing the highest correlation. The correlation of the test with Army Alpha was found to be about .50, and with the Minnesota Paper Form Board about .60. Fairly adequate norms are now available for high school freshmen and seniors.

Two-Factor Tests

Better predictions have often resulted from two separate tests (one for language and the other for number) than from one test. Among the several tests now available which provide two separate scores are: American Council on Education (ACE) Psychological Examination, California Tests of Mental Maturity, College Entrance Board Scholastic Aptitude Tests, and Shipley Institute Conceptual Quotient, Hartford Retreat, Conn.

The American Council on Education Psychological Examination is published each year in a new but equivalent form prepared by L. L. Thurstone and Thelma G. Thurstone, and is used by more than six hundred colleges and universities and many counseling centers. The test on the college level requires an hour for administration and consists of six sections, each of which is preceded by practice problems, such as:

1. *Arithmetic.* (Some of these problems require the use of decimals and fractions.)

In this test you will be given some problems in arithmetic. After each problem there are five answers, but only one of them is the correct answer. You are to solve each problem and blacken the space on the answer sheet which corresponds to the answer you think is correct. The following problem is an example.

---

1. How many pencils can you buy for 50 cents at the rate of 2 for 5 cents?
(a) 10   (b) 20   (c) 25   (d) 100   (e) 125

Find on the answer sheet the space labeled "ARITHMETIC, Practice Problems, Page 3." The correct answer to the problem is 20, which is answer (b).

In the row numbered 1, space (b) has been blackened.

2. Completion

Look at the following definition. You are to think of the word that fits the definition.

> 1. A contest of speed.
>   B   F   M   P   R

3. Figure analogies

Look at the figures A, B, and C in Sample 1 below. Figure A is a large circle. Figure B is a small circle. By what rule is Figure A changed to make Figure B? The rule is "making it smaller." Now look at Figure C. It is a large square. What will it be if you change it by the same rule? It will be a small square of the same color as the large square. Figure 2 is a small white square. In the section of the answer sheet labeled "FIGURE ANALOGIES, Practice Problems, Page 7," the space numbered 2 in the first row has been blackened to indicate the correct answer.

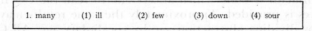

4. Same-opposite

The word at the left in the following line is "many."

>   1. many   (1) ill   (2) few   (3) down   (4) sour

One of the four words at the right means either the *same* as or the *opposite* of "many." The word "few," which is numbered 2, is the opposite of "many." In the section of the answer sheet labeled "SAME-OPPOSITE, Practice Problems, Page 9," space number 2 in the first row has been blackened.

5. Number series

The numbers in each series proceed according to some rule. For each series you are to find the *next number*.

In the first series below, each number is 2 larger than the preceding number. The *next number* in the series would be 14. Of the five answers at the right, answer (e) is, therefore, correct. In the section of the answer sheet labeled "NUMBER SERIES, Practice Problems, Page 11," space (e) in the first row has been blackened.

	Series						Next Number			
1.	2	4	6	8	10	12	10	11	12	13	14
							(a)	(b)	(c)	(d)	(e)

6. Verbal analogies

Read the following words:

>   1. foot-shoe   hand-   (1) thumb   (2) head   (3) glove   (4) finger

The first two words, *foot-shoe*, are related. The next word is *hand*. It can be combined with one of the remaining words in the row so as to make a similar pair, *hand-glove*. In the section of the answer sheet labeled "VERBAL ANALOGIES, Practice Problems, Page 13," space number 3 in the first row has been blackened.

The number of right answers in Section 1, 3, and 5 are combined to give a Q score (quantitative), and Sections 2, 4, and 6 yield an L score (language). A total score is also given. All scores for large groups are changed to centiles.

Shipley (1946) issued a short but effective scale in two parts for measuring intellectual ability, which also yields an index of intellectual impairment. The first part is a steeply graded literary vocabulary test. Ten minutes are allowed for the forty items, all of which are of the 4-choice variety. The second part is an abstraction test. Ten minutes are allowed for the twenty items, each of which requires a series completion. Numbers or letters, or both, are used. Both parts are probably little affected by the time limits, for the items use progressively rarer words or more difficult problems.

Reliability coefficients for 322 Army recruits were .87 for vocabulary, .89 for abstraction, and .90 for the total. Raw scores may be changed into vocabulary age, abstraction age, and mental age, ranging from about eight to twenty years.

The index of impairment, called the Conceptual Quotient (CQ), is based on the clinical experience that in mild degrees of mental impairment vocabulary is relatively unaffected, while capacity for conceptual thinking or abstraction declines according to the degree of impairment. A table which allows one to read the CQ from the raw scores is provided. Approximately the same results may be obtained by dividing abstraction age by vocabulary age. All CQ's below 100 are in the direction of impairment and are interpreted as follows:

CQ	Classification	Per Cent of Normal
above 90	normal	73%
85–90	slightly suspicious	10
80–84	moderately suspicious	7
75–79	quite suspicious	5
70–74	very suspicious	3
below 70	probably pathological	2

Shipley points out that for those with vocabulary scores above 32 or below 23 these conceptual quotients are not useful, because the usual relation between vocabulary and abstraction skills does not hold. Also, CQ's above 90 are commonly found with psychoneurotics and early psychotics. Chronic psychotics, however, almost always show losses in abstract thinking.

THE DEVELOPMENT OF ANALYTICAL TESTS

A few years ago many tests of ability were produced and widely distributed with the assurance of the authors that they had high reliability, and would predict a certain type of success to a moderate degree. Then it became apparent that neither reliability nor validity would indicate what was being measured, particularly when, as is usually the case, the criterion of success was complex and roughly appraised.

Later, multiple-correlation techniques were introduced to improve predictions of success. These techniques weight the tests in a battery according to the degree to which they correlate with the criteria. While they yield somewhat better predictions, these techniques also result in the selection of tests which measure unknown amounts of unknown factors, and which seem to overlap each other in content.

Since 1940 a new goal has been emphasized by certain authors of tests. The factorial purity of a test or test item has become a major consideration. *Homogeneous* or *pure tests* are defined as those whose variance is due to only one factor. They have the great advantage of yielding a definite interpretation which is relatively stable for the populations used. Pure tests also allow more economical measurement than an equal or greater number of less pure tests. Furthermore, they allow a profile of independent traits, which is more revealing than a single score.

Factorial analyses, when properly used, will provide evidence for the construction of unique tests. The advantages and limitations are given in Chapter XIV.

DESCRIPTION OF BATTERIES OF APTITUDE TESTS

In recent years the results of testing have led to general recognition of about ten large groups of factors, each of which contains from two to six fairly independent kinds of subfactors, which are sometimes called *unitary* or *primary* abilities, because they seem to exist independently in the populations studied. None of the authors of analytical tests claims that he has developed a pure measure of an ability, but much progress toward that end has been made.

The four batteries which will be reviewed in the following pages are: Chicago Tests of Primary Abilities, Guilford-Zimmerman Aptitude Survey, Differential Aptitude Test, and General Aptitude Test Battery. These batteries were chosen because they represent considerable careful research and are available. The significant batteries used recently by military authorities are described in Chapter XI.

The Chicago Tests of Primary Abilities (1943, 1946, 1948)

Thurstone and Thurstone (1943) issued the Chicago Tests of Primary Abilities, a group of eleven tests which measure six abilities, after their 20 years of extremely important pioneer work in developing and applying methods for analysis of abilities. The 1943 battery was prepared after giving preliminary tests to Chicago school children at each grade level from the fifth to the twelfth, a total of approximately twenty-five thousand pupils. The First-Grade Battery (1946) was designed for five- and six-year-olds, and the Elementary Battery (1948) for ages seven to eleven. The authors believe that the batteries furnish profiles of abilities which indicate weakness and strength in academically and vocationally important fields. In selecting the tests they considered:

1. The factorial saturation or purity of the test. Only one primary factor is conspicuously present in each test.
2. Stability of factorial saturation at age levels from eleven to seventeen years. Tests which, in this respect, tended to fluctuate considerably over the years were not retained.
3. Clear psychological interpretation.
4. Availability of parallel forms. Two forms are available.
5. Ease of administration.
6. Ease in scoring, either by hand or by machine.

The high school battery is a single booklet in which each ability, except memory, is measured by two tests. Before each test elaborate explanation and practice periods are given so that, while the total working time is 58 minutes, about 2 hours are needed for test administration. The tests are briefly described here.

N Number: The first test allows 6 minutes for seventy simple problems in addition. Each consists of four 2-place numbers which have been "added." The second test allows 5 minutes for 70 simple multiplication items, in each of which a 2-place number has been "multiplied" by a single digit. In both tests one is to determine whether the right answer has been given, then to mark a space to indicate right or wrong.

V Verbal Meaning: The first test provides 4 minutes for a 50-item vocabulary test, largely of literary terms. One of four words which has the same meaning as a key word must be underlined. The second test allows 6 minutes for forty-five completion items. In each item the one being tested reads a short definition, then marks the one of five letters which is the initial letter in the word defined, thus:

"The first meal of the day."
A——B——C——D——E——

The defined word is breakfast, so the space after B should be marked.

S Spatial Thinking: The first test allows 5 minutes for twenty items, in each of which the first figure in a row is to be compared with six other figures. The person being tested is to mark those which would be identical with the first figure if they were appropriately rotated and turned over. The second test gives 5 minutes to twenty items, in each of which the first picture of a card is to be compared with six other pictures in a row. The testee is to mark each card which, if it were slid along the table and rotated, would fit the first card. Example:

Here are more cards. Some of the cards are marked. The cards which are like the first card in this row are marked.

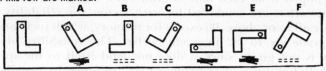

W Word Fluency: The first test allows 5 minutes to write as many words that begin with a given letter as possible. The second test provides 4 minutes to write as many words as possible that have four letters and which begin with another given letter.

R Reasoning: The first test allows 6 minutes for thirty letter-series items, in which the person tested is asked to select from five choices the letter which would come next. The second test allows 4 minutes for thirty letter-grouping items. Here the testee is to detect and mark in each item one group of four letters that does not belong with the other groups, thus:

AABC ACAD ACFH AAGG

Three of the groups have two A's.

M Memory: Twenty cards with first and last names are exposed 15 seconds each, one right after the other. Then 8 minutes are allowed for choosing and marking the right first name for the twenty last names. The choice must be made from among the seven first names for each last name.

ILLUS. 84. INTERCORRELATIONS OF COMPOSITES

	N	W	V	S	M	R
N	...					
W	.41	...				
V	.40	.54	...			
S	.28	.17	.16	...		
M	.31	.36	.35	.13	...	
R	.53	.49	.59	.29	.39	...

(By permission of L. L. Thurstone, T. G. Thurstone, and Science Research Associates.)

ILLUS. 85. VALIDITIES, PRIMARY ABILITIES

Primary Abilities

	N	W	V	S	M	R
Composite Score N	.90	.44	.39	.33	.21	.57
Composite Score W	.43	.91	.54	.20	.39	.47
Composite Score V	.41	.52	.97	.19	.38	.58
Composite Score S	.22	.15	.15	.92	.13	.34
Composite Score M	.31	.37	.36	.14	.79	.41
Composite Score R	.52	.51	.57	.34	.38	.90

(By permission of L. L. Thurstone, T. G. Thurstone, and Science Research Associates.)

Thurstone has furnished split-half reliability figures for large samples of pupils from each half of grades six, eight, ten, and twelve. When two tests are combined for each factor, the reliability coefficients are all at or above .96 except for memory, which increases from .64 in grade six to .82 in grade twelve. The reliability of Word Fluency is not given, since it does not lend itself to the split-half method. Reliabilities of individual tests are somewhat smaller, but still satisfactorily high.

Two factorial analyses are reported. First, the raw scores were correlated and their matrix (Illus. 81) resolved. Six primary factors were found, and their estimated intercorrelations formed a new matrix. The second factorial analysis was made of this matrix.

From the first analysis the loadings of each factor in each composite score were found. Each composite was found to have a high loading of one factor, and relatively low weights of the other factors (Illus. 85), which shows that each of these tests is a fairly pure measure of one factor only. The Spatial Thinking Tests are apparently the purest. While the Reasoning Tests have a loading with the reasoning primary of .90, they are the least pure, because they also have loadings above .50 with Number, Word Fluency, and Verbal Meaning.

From the second factorial analysis the loadings of a general factor on each of the estimated primary factors appeared. The results indicate that Reasoning has the heaviest loading and Memory and Spatial Thinking the smallest, and that all the intercorrelations can be well explained by one general factor, which Thurstone did not name at the time. It seems probable that it will be found to correspond to energy, motivation, and other personal factors, but more research is needed, based on the use together of all types of appraisals.

The First-Grade Battery. From the application of seventy tests to two hundred first grade pupils, Thurstone and Thurstone (1946) have shown that five factors—Verbal Meaning, Perceptual Speed, Quantitative Thinking, Motor Coordination, and Spatial Thinking —appear among five- and six-year-olds, and that these factors can be measured with sufficient accuracy to provide mental age scales for 2-month intervals for the ages of three to nine years (Chapter V). The profiles are valuable for growth studies and for prediction of success in the early grades. This is an especially interesting contribution, because it shows that reliable measures of what probably are basic aptitudes can be made before formal schooling usually begins.

Science Research Associates (SRA) Primary Mental Abilities, seven to eleven years and eleven to seventeen years. In 1947 the Thurstones issued these batteries of five tests each, in the belief that a profile of a student's learning abilities is more useful for indicating his intellectual strengths and weaknesses than a single IQ score. These five tests are identical with the first tests of the first five factors in the Chicago Tests of Primary Abilities (1943) described above. The second tests for these factors and the Memory Test (M) are omitted from the shorter SRA 1947 edition.

The more recent battery has nearly the same reliability and factorial composition as the earlier battery, but the time allowances have been cut in half (26 minutes) and the answers are to be placed on one side of an automatically carbon-scored answer sheet. Individual-profile sheets include the five primaries, and also total scores which yield IQ's. The distribution of IQ's is arbitrarily set to have a standard deviation of 16.5 points, which is very similar to that of the Stanford-Benet IQ's. (No thorough comparison of these two scales has yet come to hand.) The individual-profile sheet also gives norms for one-year age groups.

Finally, a short interpretation of scores, only part of which is given here, is directed to the persons who take the test.

People used to think that intelligence was just one ability, and that every person was born with a certain amount of it that remained about the same throughout life. Now we know that intelligence is made up of many different abilities, and that under certain conditions these abilities can be improved.

Like most people, you are undoubtedly higher in some PMA's than in others. You should concentrate on activities related to your high PMA's, because you probably have the greatest chance for success in these. *The higher you already are in a PMA, the more you probably can increase your ability to solve problems and do good work of that type through further training and practice.* But you should not neglect the PMA's in which you are low. While you may have more trouble with activities in these areas, you can probably improve yourself through training. Through training your Primary Mental Abilities, you are really *learning how to think better,* which is most important for your success in later life.

The paragraphs below tell you what each PMA score means. For easy reference you may enter your percentile ranks in the boxes located at the right of the paragraphs.

Verbal Meaning is your ability to understand ideas expressed in words. It is needed in activities where you get information by reading or listening. High ability in V is especially useful in such school courses as English, foreign languages, shorthand, history, and science. V is needed for success in such careers as secretary, teacher, editor, scientist, librarian, and executive.

Space is the ability to think about objects in two or three dimensions. Blueprint reading, for example, requires this ability. The designer, electrician, machinist, pilot, engineer, and carpenter are typical workers who need ability to visualize objects in space. S is helpful in geometry, mechanical drawing, art, manual training, radar, physics, and geography classes. . . .

The scores in these five areas give you a general picture of your present ability to deal with intellectual problems. While the results of your work on this test are important, these *PMA* scores should not be considered the *only* index of your likely success in school or in later life. There are other areas of intelligence which were not measured here. Tests for them would take too long to administer. Other factors, such as your personality, vocational interests, and how hard you work also have an important bearing upon your chances of success.

The SRA *Primary Mental Abilities* are merely a shortcut for finding out about your 'intellectual self.' They help *you to understand yourself better*—and thus to recognize your strengths and weaknesses. They can assist you in planning your school courses, career choices, and leisure activities wisely. The better you know yourself, the more successful and satisfied you can become.[1]

The Guilford-Zimmerman Aptitude Survey (1947)

Guilford and Zimmerman have issued seven tests of primary abilities which they believe will be much more effective in vocational guidance and personnel selection than the usual tests of intelligence or of clerical and mechanical ability. They also believe that a fairly complete battery would probably include twenty tests of primary abilities, and they hope to prepare all of these tests eventually. They emphasize that a comprehensive series of tests, each of which is factorially unique, has the following three advantages:

a. The one factor which dominates each test and the degree to which it determines the scores is known. Only in this situation can the meaning of a score be clearly known. Tests where two or more factors are present in unknown amounts can never be clearly interpreted.

b. A battery of *unique* tests lends itself to an enlightened selection of tests for a particular purpose, and produces a combination of weighted scores which will yield the highest possible prediction.

c. Batteries of unique tests are the most economical because they eliminate unnecessary overlapping of items and include a systematic minimum sampling of each important factor.

The seven tests which he designates by Roman numerals are as follows:

I. *Verbal Comprehension* is a wide-range, 25-minute, vocabulary test of literary, nonscientific words. There are seventy-two items, each of which requires the person taking the test to select from five choices a word "which has a meaning like the word in large type."

[1] By permission of L. L. Thurstone, T. G. Thurstone, and Science Research Associates.

II. *General Reasoning* is a test of ability to "diagnose problems" as indicated by mathematical-reasoning tests. Thirty-five minutes are allowed for twenty-seven items, each of which involves selecting the correct answer for a problem from among five choices. Algebra is helpful in this test.

III. *Numerical Operations.* Eight minutes are allowed for one hundred and eighty items of simple arithmetical computation.

IV. *Perceptual Speed.* Five minutes are allowed for seventy-two items where four black silhouettes are to be matched with four of five other silhouettes.

V. *Spatial Orientation* is designed to measure ability to see changes in direction and position. Each item consists of two small pictures of some water and land and the front end of a motorboat in which one is to imagine he is riding. He is required to check one of five choices to indicate whether in going between the first and second picture the boat has turned to the right or to the left, and is pointed higher or lower. Ten minutes are allowed for the sixty-four items. (See Illus. 86.)

VI. *Spatial Visualization* allows 30 minutes for sixty-eight items. Each item requires one to choose, from five pictures, the picture which shows how an alarm clock would look if it were turned, tilted, and rotated a given number of degrees.

VII. *Mechanical Knowledge* allows 30 minutes for fifty-five items. From five answers the one which tells how a mechanical device is used or defined is to be chosen. The first twenty items contain pictures and words, the others use words only. Items are chosen to show knowledge needed by such skilled workers as auto mechanic, plumber, carpenter, and electrician.

Tests I and II are designed to be power tests. Their items are steeply graded over a wide range of difficulty, and the time limits are long enough to allow nearly all to attempt every item. Tests III, IV, and V are speed tests with items of nearly the same difficulty and time limits so short that few finish them. Test VI is a speed and power test in that the items become progressively more difficult, but the time limit of 30 minutes is long enough for the more rapid workers to finish. Test VII is a breadth-of-information test, in which the items vary somewhat in difficulty.

Answer sheets are provided for all of the tests, except speed tests III and IV. Separate norms are given for test V when taken with and without answer sheets. The use of answer sheets for test V is not recommended, because they tend to introduce other components of perceptual speed and number.

ILLUS. 86. THE GUILFORD-ZIMMERMAN APTITUDE SURVEY

Part V Spatial Orientation

Form A

Name_____ Date_____ Score_____

Nearest age: 10   15   20   25   30   35   45   55   65   75   Sex: M   F

Years of school completed: 5   6   7   8   9   10   11   12   13   14   15   16   17   18   19

Instructions.—This is a test of your ability to see changes in direction and position. In each item you are to note how the position of the boat has changed in the second picture from its original position in the first picture.

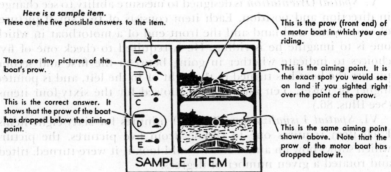

Here is a sample item. These are the five possible answers to the item.

These are tiny pictures of the boat's prow.

This is the correct answer. It shows that the prow of the boat has dropped below the aiming point.

This is the prow (front end) of a motor boat in which you are riding.

This is the aiming point. It is the exact spot you would see on land if you sighted right over the point of the prow.

This is the same aiming point shown above. Note that the prow of the motor boat has dropped below it.

SAMPLE ITEM I

(If the prow had risen, instead of dropped, the correct answer would have been C, instead of D.)

(By permission of J. P. Guilford and the Sheridan Supply Company.)

These tests were published so recently that norms are available for only male college students. Other norms are soon to be added. The reliabilities are in the .90s. The validity of each test as shown by its correlation with its dominant factor is estimated at .60 or above. Tests I, III, and VII are purest in that they have estimated validities of .80.

The tests are designed to measure independent factors. Tests II and III, both of which use numbers, show intercorrelations of only .20. The authors estimate that the true intercorrelations of factors are probably very small. The actual intercorrelations of the tests range from 0 to .55. Tests V and VI, both of which are concerned with spatial thinking, correlated .55.

A tentative list of occupations is given showing the factors which are probably important for each occupation. Thus, for airplane pilots tests IV, V, VI, and VII are indicated, and for accountants tests II and III. Critical scores for various occupations are to be prepared. In designing this battery the authors have drawn from their extensive and intensive research in the Army Air Force.

Differential Aptitude Test (DAT)

The Differential Aptitude Test is a battery of eight tests released by Bennett, Seashore, and Wesman (1947) to provide integrated measures of independent abilities for educational and vocational guidance and for employment selection. All the tests, except clerical speed and accuracy, are power tests in that they become progressively more difficult, and rather liberal time allowances are provided. Six 40-minute sessions or three 80-minute sessions are recommended. IBM answer sheets are used throughout. The tests, which are printed in separate booklets, are:

1. *Verbal Reading.* The first and the last word of each of fifty short sentences are omitted. The blanks are to be filled in with a number or a letter from four choices. (30 min.) The following is an example of a sentence:

———— is to water as eat is to ————.

1. Continue	2. Drink	3. Foot	4. Girl
A. Drive	B. Enemy	C. Food	D. Industry

The correct choices, *2* and *C,* are to be indicated on an answer sheet.

2. *Numerical Ability* is measured by forty problems which range from simple computations to simple ratio and square-root problems. Each problem is followed by four-answer choices and the statement "None of these." (30 min.)

3. *Abstract Reasoning* includes fifty nonlanguage items, each of which shows a series of four figures which is to be extended by choosing one from among five answer figures. (25 min.)

PROBLEM FIGURES   ANSWER FIGURES

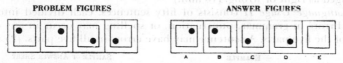

4. *Space Relations.* In this test each item consists of a 2-dimensional pattern which could be folded into one of the five 3-dimensional objects pictured. The forty patterns are complicated by the use of gray or shaded surfaces. (30 min.)

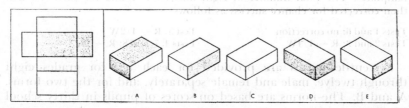

5. *Mechanical Reasoning* is measured by sixty-eight pictures showing various applications of mechanical principles—the balancing or lifting of weights, propellers, gears, pulleys, and condensation. Following each picture are 3-choice questions asking which is the heavier part; or in which direction would a part turn; or which part turns more slowly; or which is colder; etc. (30 min.) The pictures are unusually well produced.

Example:

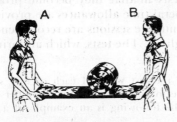

X

Which man has the heavier load?
(If equal, mark C.)

6. *Clerical Speed and Accuracy* are appraised by comparing one hundred combinations of letters and numbers. Only two letters, two digits, or one digit and one letter are grouped. Each item consists of a row of five groups, one of which is underlined. The task is to underline the same group on the answer sheet, for example:

TEST ITEMS						SAMPLE OF ANSWER SHEET				
V.	AB	AC	AD	AE	AF	AC	AE	AF	AB	AD
W.	aA	aB	BA	Ba	Bb	BA	Ba	Bb	aA	aB
X.	A7	7A	B7	7B	AB	7B	B7	AB	7A	A7
Y.	Aa	Ba	bA	BA	bB	Aa	bA	bB	Ba	BA
Z.	3A	3B	33	B3	BB	BB	3B	B3	3A	33

7. *Language Usage I* is a 100-item spelling test in which each word is to be judged as right or wrong. (10 min.)

8. *Language Usage II* consists of fifty sentences, each divided into five parts. Errors in grammar, punctuation, or spelling may occur in any or in none of the five parts. A sentence may have errors in all five parts. (25 min.)

EXAMPLE   SAMPLE OF ANSWER SHEET

Ain't we / going to the / office / next week / at all.
A   B   C   D   E

The scoring for all these tests may be done by hand or by machine from templates. The total number of right answers is found for each test and then corrected for chance success as follows:

Tests 1 and 6: no correction   Test 5: R — 1/2W
Tests 2 and 3: R — 1/4W   Tests 4, 7, and 8: R — W

Percentile norms are provided for each test for grades eight through twelve, male and female separately, and for the two forms, A and B. The norms are based on scores of pupils in thirty school systems, mostly located in the Northeastern or North Central states. In all of these grades the boys' averages surpass the girls' on Space Relations, Numerical Ability and Mechanical Reasoning, and the differences are larger in the higher grades. The girls' averages exceed the boys' on Clerical Speed and Accuracy and Language Usage. The boys and girls average nearly the same on Verbal Reasoning and Abstract Reasoning. Total scores on the whole battery are not given. All of the tests may be used separately.

The average reliability coefficients for each test based on split-half computations from samples of from one hundred to two hundred pupils, are all .87 or higher with the exception of those for Mechanical Reasoning, which are .85 for boys and .71 for girls. There is a slight tendency for the grades of the older pupils to show higher reliabilities.

In order to discover the independence of the scores, correlations for form, grade, and sex were computed between each test and all the others. The results showed correlations of from .50 to .60 between the Verbal Reasoning and all the other tests except Clerical Speed and Accuracy. Numerical Ability correlated .50 with Verbal Reasoning, .54 with Abstract Reasoning, and .50 with Language Usage: Sentences. Abstract Reasoning correlated .56 with Space Relations, .52 with Verbal Reasoning, and .51 with Mechanical Reasoning. The two Language Usage tests correlated .62. Clerical Speed and Accuracy showed correlations below .37 with all the other tests. With large adult groups these correlations would undoubtedly be smaller, but there was an unexpected tendency for the intercorrelations to increase slightly in the twelfth grade.

General Aptitude Test Battery (GATB; 1947)

The General Aptitude Test Battery was developed by the United States Employment Service, Washington, D.C., and was made available in 1947 to the various state employment service offices. According to Dvorak (1947) it is intended for the use of employment counselors in appraising the aptitudes of individuals. Eleven of the tests use paper and pencil, and written and oral directions. Their range of difficulty makes them applicable to all adults who can read and understand directions in English and handle paper-and-pencil situations. While no age or grade equivalents have been issued, it seems probable that the tests would not be applicable to individuals with less than fifth-grade accomplishments. Four of the tests require manipulation of pegs or small washers and rivets, so that for them language is a small factor in understanding the test directions. No attempt was made to have these tests look like work samples, but they are designed to indicate the aptitudes likely to be required in successful performance on a large variety of jobs. All the tests are timed and speed is an important factor, since the tests are so made that very few in a group are able to finish in the time allowed.

In order to prepare this test battery, factor-analysis studies were conducted on several experimental batteries, including in all fifty-nine tests which had been administered to 2,156 adults. These were divided into nine experimental groups. The largest group was composed of 1,079 subjects, ages from seventeen to thirty-nine years, mean age twenty-three, and all had completed at least the sixth grade. The average subject had completed the eleventh grade, and 99 per cent had completed from 8 to 16 grades. Factorial analyses of the results, using Thurstone's centroid method, were applied. These showed eleven fairly independent factors which are thought to be occupationally significant, namely, Verbal, Numerical, Spatial Thinking (2 types), Perception (2 types), Dexterity (4 types), and Intelligence. The fifteen tests with the heaviest factor loadings and the maximum internal consistency were then selected. The aptitudes are measured thus:

V Verbal is measured by a 5-minute test with sixty multiple-choice items in which one must identify relationships of same or opposite among four words. Scientific or technical terms are excluded.

N Numerical is measured by a 6-minute test of twenty-five arithmetic problems and a 5-minute test of fifty computational problems which do not include fractions or decimals.

S Spatial Thinking is measured by two tests. One of these is a 7-minute test of forty-nine multiple-choice 2-dimensional problems of rearrangement of elements. It is similar to the Minnesota Paper Form Board. The other test allows 6 minutes for forty problems of 3-dimensional surface development.

P Form Perception is measured by a 4-minute test of forty items in which pictures of objects are to be exactly matched with one of four choices. The second test allows 5 minutes for 60 items of matching paper figures. It is similar to the Minnesota Spatial Relations Test (Illus. 100).

Q Clerical Perception is measured by a 6-minute, 150-item, name-comparison test, the subject must indicate whether the names are the same or different, as in the Minnesota Clerical Test.

A Aiming is measured by a 30-second test of one hundred items which requires a pencil line to be placed on the crossbar of an H, ¼ inch high and ⅜ inch across. Aiming is also measured by a 60-second test in which three lines are to be made in each of two hundred ¼-inch squares.

T Motor Speed is measured by the last test described under Aiming and also by a 30-second test of placing three dots in each of seventy printed boxes. The boxes measure $^{10}\!/_{16}$ by $^{15}\!/_{16}$ inch and are printed in rows of seven.

F Finger Dexterity is measured by two tests: assembling and disassembling fifty rivets and washers, using a standard board for holding them. The score is the number assembled in 90 seconds and disassembled in 60 seconds.

M Manual Dexterity is measured by two tests. One requires the transference of forty-eight round 2½-inch pegs from one part of a board to another. The other requires moving the same pegs but also turning them end to end. The score is the number of pegs moved in three periods of 15 seconds each, and the number of pegs moved and turned in three periods of 30 seconds each.

G Intelligence. The authors found that a fairly heavy loading of a factor was found in all verbal and number, and in most of the spatial tests. This factor appears to have some of the properties of Spearman's G, but it has a wider significance than Thurstone's reasoning or induction factors. It has therefore been given the symbol G. It is indicated by a combination of three of the tests included above which showed significant loadings, namely, the verbal, the numerical, and the spatial thinking in three dimensions. The use of an Index of Intelligence in an analytical profile is controversial, for the three tests also appear elsewhere in the profile, and the G score may be fairly high, even when a person does poorly on one of the three tests.

During the administration of the tests, the applicant's adjustment to the situation is to be recorded to show nervousness, disabilities, copying answers or attempting to copy answers from a neighbor, lack of reading ability, writing letters instead of making check marks, and other similar acts which might affect the scores. If the examiner feels that the tests are a good sample of the worker's ability, they are scored. Hand stencils are used. The raw scores of all tests are converted to a point scale which has the mean at 100 and the standard deviation at 20 for the large general population group.

Each individual's scores are placed on a profile card which allows a quick comparison with the Occupational Aptitude Patterns (OAP). These patterns are cut-off scores of from two to four aptitudes, which have been determined by applications to groups of workers in an occupational field. Each cut-off score is the score which was made by approximately the 33rd centile of an occupational group. In other words, critical scores are given, which divide the lowest third from the upper two thirds of an occupational group. For instance, Occupational Aptitude Pattern No. 2, *Accounting and Related,* has only two cut-off scores, G-130 and N-130, which means that to have a reasonable chance of success, in this field, one must score at least 1½ standard deviations above the mean, that is, among the highest 7 per cent of the general population in both Intelligence and Number. The other tests are disregarded for this field of work.

Occupational Aptitude Pattern 4, *All-Round Metal Machining and All-Round Mechanical Repairing,* requires scores of at least 100 for four aptitudes (G, N, S, and P), which means that two thirds of the machinists and mechanics who were tested made scores on these aptitudes above the averages of the general population. A tentative list of twenty occupational aptitude patterns is given.

During the counseling interview, there is an exploration of those OAP's whose critical scores are met. Usually only the two or three OAP's which indicate one's highest skills are considered. Thus, if a client qualified on the OAP 2, 4, 11, and 16, then 11 and 16 would be disregarded because these refer to the lower skills of Routine Reporting Work and Simple Visual Inspection. It often happens that persons who have literary, accounting, mechanical, and clerical aptitudes, also meet the requirements for many kinds of routine inspection and assembly work.

This method of matching individual scores to occupational requirements avoids an over-all score, and aids in rapid interpretation. Although the GATB was standardized on adult workers, it will undoubtedly be applied also, after further standardization, to groups in high schools and colleges.

The Yale Aptitude Battery

Crawford and Burnham (1946) issued an intensive discussion of forecasting college achievement, and described a battery of seven tests, each printed in a separate booklet with a liberal time allowance —approximately 50 minutes. All except the first test were developed by the authors at Yale. Tests I, II, and III of this battery were significant in predicting success in liberal arts studies, tests III, IV, and V in pure science and mathematics, and tests V, VI, and VII in the applied sciences, for example, engineering. The battery is composed of:

1. The *verbal section* of the College Entrance Board Scholastic Aptitude Test is to a large extent a measure of literary vocabulary.

2. The *Artificial Language* test requires one to rapidly learn eight new words and a prefix, to indicate the future tense, and then to translate short statements into English.

3. The *Verbal Reasoning* test is one in which the person being tested reads a paragraph and draws conclusions or interpretations based on the paragraph. For each conclusion one marks one of five levels of probability that it is true.

4. The *Quantitative Reasoning* test uses algebra and number-series completion.

5. The *Mathematical Ingenuity* test involves skill in solving algebraic equations and making geometric statements algebraically.

6. The *Spatial Relations* test requires one to look at pictures of piles of cubes, and to determine how many cubes have one, two, three, four, or five sides painted, assuming that all sides are painted which do not touch another cube or the surface upon which they are resting.

7. The *Mechanical Ingenuity* test which directs one to look at diagrams of gears, pulleys, and forms to determine relative movements and stability.

Crawford and Burnham did not offer any figures to show the factorial purity or homogeneity of each test, but they published an intercorrelation matrix based on 856 Yale freshmen. The median of these correlations is .41, and three of them are above .60. Hence the uniqueness or independence of some of these tests is not as great as is desirable. Tests I and III, Vocabulary and Verbal Reasoning, correlated .64; tests IV and V, both of which use algebra extensively, correlated .62; and tests IV and VII, Quantitative Reasoning and Mechanical Ingenuity, correlated .61 with each other. In spite of these correlations the authors claim fairly good specificity of prediction.

California Tests of Mental Maturity

The California Tests of Mental Maturity were published by Sullivan, Clark, and Tiegs (1937) in four batteries, one for kindergarten and first grade, and the others for first to third grades, fourth to eighth, and ninth to fourteenth. In each battery sixteen subjects are distributed among five sections. The first section is designed to detect gross visual, hearing, and motor handicaps. The second section contains one immediate recall and one delayed recall test; the third, three tests involving spatial relationships; the fourth, seven tests of verbal and numerical reasoning, and the fifth, a 50-item multiple-choice vocabulary test. The test norms allow one to draw a profile (Illus. 87) showing sixteen separate scores as well as total scores for verbal and nonverbal factors and for the whole test. The reliabilities for the subtests range from .70 to .95 and for the totals from .90 to .96. The total test requires about 90 minutes. It is one of the most extensive of its kind, and the profile of scores presents a picture of skills which have been found to be somewhat independent.

PRACTICAL RESULTS

Only a few reports from among many hundreds can be cited here. Most of them show progress and promising possibilities for both academic and vocational predictions.

Age and Sex Differences

Age differences are noted by all authors of scales for school populations. The average differences between adjacent age groups shown for the SRA Primary Mental Abilities are about equal in raw-score points for each year from eleven to seventeen. Smaller-than-average differences are shown below the 25th centile, and also above the 90th

ILLUS. 87. CALIFORNIA MENTAL MATURITY TEST PROFILE

Test Advisory Committee
Ernest W. Tiegs, University of Southern California
J. Murray Lee, Director of Research, Burbank City Schools
Willis W. Clark, Los Angeles County Schools

Elementary
Grades 4-8

CALIFORNIA TEST OF MENTAL MATURITY—ELEMENTARY BATTERY
Devised by Elizabeth T. Sullivan, Willis W. Clark, and Ernest W. Tiegs

Name ...... *William Smith* ...... Grade H5 (5.7) Boy-Girl

School ...... *Lincoln* ...... Age 11 Last Birthday Dec. 14

Teacher ...... *Miss White* ...... Date *April 15, 1936*

TEST	FACTOR	Possible Score	Pupil's Score							
1.	Visual Acuity	40	38	0	28 29	Low	Average		High	40
2.	Auditory Acuity	15	15	0	9 10	Low	Average			15
3.	Motor Co-ordination	20	16	0	10 11	Low	Average	18	High	20

DIAGNOSTIC PROFILE
(Chart Pupil's Scores Here)

TEST	FACTOR	Possible Score	Pupil's Score
A.	Memory	44	36
4.	Immediate Recall*	24	18
5.	Delayed Recall	20	18
B.	Spacial Relationships	45	31
6.	Sensing Right and Left*	20	14
7.	Manipulation of Areas*	15	11
8.	Foresight in Spacial Sit'ns*	10	6
C.	Reasoning	95	57
9.	Opposites*	15	11
10.	Similarities*	15	15
11.	Analogies*	15	11
12.	Number Series*	10	2
13.	Numerical Quantity*	10	3
14.	Numerical Quantity	15	8
15.	Inference	15	7
D. 16.	Vocabulary	50	30
E.	Total Mental Factors (A+B+C+D)	234	154
F.	Language Factors (5+14+15+16)	100	63
G.	Non-Language Factors (E—F)	134	91
H.	Chronological Age		136
I.	Actual Grade Placement (Grade pupil is in)		5A

* Non-Language tests.
*Upper limits of test.

SUMMARY OF DATA

	Score	M.A. ÷	C.A.	I.Q.
E. Total Mental Factors	154	148	136	109
F. Language Factors	63	159	136	117
G. Non-Language Factors	91	134	136	99

centile. In the latter case the differences are probably due to a low ceiling for the tests. The same age patterns are seen in the Differential Aptitude Tests (DAT).

The sex differences are probably significant at all ages, but become somewhat larger among adults. The use of different norms for boys and girls is desirable when boys are competing with boys only, and girls with girls only. If both boys and girls are taking the same course or applying for the same job, however, they should be compared on the same basis. Most of the authors have not furnished norms for each sex separately, but the authors of DAT have done so. There are no significant differences in Verbal or Abstract Reasoning. The boys score higher in Number, Space Relations, and Mechanical Reasoning, and the girls score higher in Clerical Speed and Accuracy and Language Usage. Thus, a twelfth-grade boy who is at the 80th centile in spelling among boys would be only at the 58th centile among girls, and a girl at the 95th centile in Mechanical Reasoning among girls would rank at the 48th centile among boys. The reliability and validity of a test may vary a good deal when applied to different sexes, hence these differences must be carefully explored and reported.

Prediction of Academic Achievement

The criteria of academic achievement are usually the grades received in a course of study, or the average grade in a group of courses. Grades are the result of many complex interactions of ability, methods of instruction, motivation, outside distractions, various standards of grading, and other factors. Furthermore, grades are usually expressed on a 5-point scale—A, B, C, D, and E—with little or no attempt to have equal steps in this scale. Many times so few E's or A's are given that the scale is reduced, in effect, to 3 or 4 points. Such roughness in grading complex processes doubtless reduces the accuracy and hence the reliability of the grades. Analytical studies of academic grades, which show the important factors in success for particular groups in a particular course, have been outlined, and much progress has been made in defining goals of achievement in school. Two excellent summaries of this progress are found in a report by Smith and Tyler (1942) for the Committee on Evaluation of the Progressive Education Association, and in the *Forty-Fifth Yearbook of the National Society for the Study of Education* (1946). However, no reports have come to hand which clearly show the relationships between academic achievement and the more complex social and intellectual goals.

A good many writers have pointed out that unless group tests are used carefully they may lead to harmful judgments regarding both children and adults. D. A. Wooster (1947) reports a twelve-year-old boy in the fifth grade who had obtained a Henmon-Nelson Test of Mental Abilities IQ of 53. It had been assumed that his low mental-ability score was a result of poor intelligence and that this in turn had retarded his progress in learning to read. An Iowa Silent Reading Test yielded a score of 3.5 grades, but there were also successes on this test far above the sixth-grade level. An individual Stanford-Binet Test Form L gave this boy an IQ of 78 and showed that his language ability was about that of a ten-year-old boy. Later a Paterson short form showed a Performance Quotient (PQ) of 98. While these tests are not supposed to be entirely equivalent, the differences are far greater than the normal variations between tests. When the boy was asked to read portions of the Iowa Silent Reading Test it became apparent that he could scarcely read. He stumbled over the simplest words and was exceedingly slow in reading those which he did know. It appeared that he had followed instructions and put marks in certain spaces and by pure chance had attained scores which gave him a much higher rating than his true abilities warranted. The boy's social background and job experience revealed some good reasons for his poor language ability. Wooster concludes:

It is apparent that many school people have not been trained to the point of realizing that the choice of the mental-ability test appropriate for a given individual must be based upon the knowledge of the circumstances surrounding his case. The absurdity of giving a mental test involving reading to one who is deficient in reading and then concluding that his mentality is low is probably fairly common. Great harm is likely to result from such practice, but it seems that precaution must be given again and again. It should be stated categorically that no group test of any kind should be used unless there is provision for intensive individual study of those persons making those scores.

Here again the advantages of an analytical profile test become apparent.

Prediction of One-Semester Grades. One of the most careful studies of prediction of academic success from aptitude tests is that of Crawford and Burnham (1946), who used a battery of seven tests administered at the beginning of the freshman year. For example, predictions of college grades at the end of the first term for the class of 1944 are shown in Illus. 88. Each of the aptitude tests is shown to predict academic success well, that is from .42 to .57, in only the corresponding type of course. These results are highly desirable, for they will make possible more specific predictions of success than could be made from a general measure. The authors conclude that T scores

ILLUS. 88. YALE APTITUDE BATTERY PREDICTIONS FOR GRADES AT END OF FIRST-TERM COURSES

Course	Number	I Vocabulary	II Art Language	III Verbal Reason	IV Quantitative Reason	V Mathematical Ingenuity	VI Spatial Relation	VII Mechanical Ingenuity
Average of								
English and History	290	.49	.34	.40	.23	.16	.22	.17
Spanish	62	.46	.57	.40	.42	.41	—.07	.24
Physics	55	.40	.37	.52	.36	.45	.40	.24
Average of								
Mathematics and Drawing	246	.16	.23	.24	.49	.42	.46	.37
Engineering Drawing	202	.11	.07	.23	.41	.15	.55	.42

(By permission of Crawford and Burnham (1946) and the Yale University Press. Adapted from Table 9, p. 161.)

of 60 or higher indicate positive aptitudes which should be encouraged; while those under 40 are "red stop-signals" for particular fields, unless there are unusual circumstances.

Prediction of Four-Semester Grades. Goodman (1944) summarized seven reports in which Thurstone's Primary Abilities Test results had been compared with college grades for various groups. One of the most interesting was a comparison of two studies of a group of 113 women in the Home Economics Department of Pennsylvania State College, one at the end of the first semester by Virginia D. Tredick and the other at the end of the fourth semester by Elizabeth W. White. Miss White averaged the grades for all courses taken in a subject over a 2-year period and used this average as the academic criterion of success in the subject. By the end of the second year only 94 women were available for the study. Presumably this resulted in some loss in range of ability of the group.

Illustration 89 shows that the correlations between Reasoning-Ability scores and the criteria of academic success were all slightly higher after four semesters than after one. Verbal-Meaning scores correlated with English grades .55 after one semester, and .65 after four semesters. In general the changes are small and probably insignificant. For Art and English the average predictions increased as time went on; for Home Economics and Point Averages, the average predictions decreased somewhat; for Science grades, the predictions were nearly the same.

ILLUS. 89. CORRELATIONS OF PRIMARY ABILITIES WITH ACADEMIC SUCCESS AMONG HOME ECONOMICS MAJORS

Primary Ability	Art		Science		English		Home Economics		Point Average	
	1 *	4 *	1	4	1	4	1	4	1	4
Perception	.15	.13	.20	.18	.19	.20	.31	.11	.28	.19
Number	.11	.13	.46	.44	.22	.28	.20	.17	.41	.33
Verbal	.24	.29	.28	.33	.55	.65	.50	.32	.51	.49
Spatial	.25	.28	.23	.20	.10	.14	.22	.10	.28	.19
Memory	—.02	.11	.25	.28	.08	.26	.12	.02	.20	.20
Induction	.26	.25	.37	.23	.19	.18	.35	.14	.40	.24
Reasoning	.21	.30	.43	.49	.21	.30	.24	.36	.42	.45

* After one or four semesters.

(By permission of Goodman (1944) and the editors of *Educational and Psychological Measurement*.)

More research is needed to determine the reasons for these changes, which may be due to changes in grading, course content, or the students included in the study. One important finding is that as a whole the predictions of success in specific subjects were as high, or higher, after four semesters as after one semester, while the point averages, which mix all subjects together in unknown combinations, tended to go down. The point averages probably represent more heterogeneous scores after four semesters than after one.

Prediction of Success in Field of Specialization. To what extent can measures of primary abilities predict success in professional studies? No direct follow-up studies have come to hand, but Adkins (1940) reported average ability profiles of graduate students from ten universities in twelve professional fields. She noted fairly distinctive average profiles for (1) chemistry and mathematics, where the highest scores were in Number (N), Verbal Meaning (V), Spatial Thinking (S), Induction (I), and Deduction (D); (2) physics and engineering: N, S, and D; (3) accounting, business administration and pharmacy: N; and (4) medicine: very superior throughout, but slightly higher in D, V, and S. She emphasized the overlapping of distributions of scores from the various fields of specialization and the need for measures which would discriminate more effectively between these fields.

Another report by Stuit and Hudson (1942) gave profiles for groups of students in engineering, journalism, and medicine similar to those found by Adkins. These authors also compared the Primary-Ability scores with grade averages and found correlations of from —.219 to .577. The correlations in this case were lowered by the fact that only high-ranking students were included in these groups. Thus, among engineers, the Spatial ability correlated only .178 while the Verbal ability correlated .577 with grade averages. Most of the engineers made such high scores on the Spatial tests that the test probably failed to distinguish their relative abilities in this factor. This points to the need for more difficult tests of primary abilities when only the highest 8 or 10 per cent of the population is to be measured.

Other important studies of prediction of the results of military training are described in Chapter XI. Careful studies of prediction of grades in elementary or high school from academic achievement tests are discussed in Chapter VII.

Prediction of Vocational Success

Satisfactory criteria of vocational success are exceedingly hard to find and usually rather vague. Until more analytical approaches are made to both job success and workers' characteristics, predictions of success will be, as they are at present, rather sketchy. In a few situations correlations as high as .65 have been reported between production records or ratings and a weighted combination of two or three tests on small samples. However, most studies report smaller correlations of from .10 to .35, which are significant only for a rough screening of applicants. No thorough report of the application of a battery of primary-ability tests to an occupational group has yet come to hand, but Dvorak (1935) found wide variations in average scores of groups of janitors, policemen, garage mechanics, ornamental-iron workers, nurses, saleswomen, and women office clerks, when he compared four groups of tests as shown in Illus. 132. These tests seem to sample four primary abilities fairly well. The Pressey Senior Classification Test is heavily loaded with verbal meaning. The Minnesota Clerical Tests measure speed of perception with words and numbers. The dexterity tests involve speed of hand-and-eye coordination, and the mechanical-ability tests involve familiarity with small gadgets or tools, and spatial comparisons of size, shape, and position. This illustration shows that there are large differences between retail saleswomen and the groups of nurses and clerks, and that the nurses average a little higher than the clerks on the Pressey Senior Classification Test. On speed-of-perception and dexterity tests, however, the clerks are considerably ahead of the nurses, while the groups are nearly the same on the mechanical-ability tests. The saleswomen are a little above the nurses in finger dexterity but the same in tweezer dexterity. Dvorak also gave figures to show the overlapping of scores of occupational groups. Thus, on the Pressey Senior Classification Test it was found that 92.9 per cent of the clerks reached or exceeded the median score of the saleswomen. This is shown graphically in Illus. 90, where it is apparent that the upper half of the saleswomen had scores similar to those of the lower half of the clerks. One test of this type, therefore, did not distinguish

ILLUS. 90. SCORE ON PRESSEY CLASSIFICATION TEST

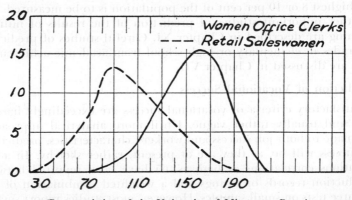

(By permission of the University of Minnesota Press.)

well between the two groups, but could be used for a rough screening. The whole profile, on the other hand, was found by Dvorak to be significant, for she took 158 individual profiles from the files at random, 90 clerks and 68 saleswomen, and mixed them together. Then, solely on the basis of the profiles and the norms shown in Illus. 132 and Illus. 90, the individuals were divided into two groups by an assistant. This resulted in the correct classification of 92.4 per cent of the workers; 5.1 per cent were doubtful, and 2.5 per cent were incorrectly classified. While it would doubtless be true that in a large random sample of employed women there would be more doubtful or incorrectly classified cases, still the typical patterns are significant.

This point brings up the question, how many of the tests in a battery are useful for the selection or promotion of particular groups? If the occupation in question makes little or no use of a particular ability, or if the less able workers do as well in it as the more able, it has been argued that the test for that ability should be omitted. Most of the present reports from industry show that only a few tests, which appeared from a job analysis to be most appropriate, have been used in any study. However, there is considerable anecdotal evidence that poor work-adjustments are often the result of lack of opportunity to use the skills or aptitudes that a person has. Thus, a woman with a marked artistic skill may have the required abilities for clerical work, but might not do well at such work. In order to avoid training and placing persons on jobs where they will not be satisfied, a fairly complete profile of abilities and knowledge would be most effective. With the analytical tests which are now available, such applications will be much more frequent.

In order to be of greatest value the tests must be applied to groups in training or without much experience, and then evaluated several months or years later from criteria of success on the job. This procedure takes time.

Prediction of Intelligence

An important study of the prediction of intelligence at college entrance from earlier tests was reported by R. L. Thorndike (1947). The verbal scores on the College Entrance Board Scholastic Aptitude Test given in the twelfth grade were taken as the terminal criteria of intelligence, because they have been issued annually in a well-standardized form since 1924. About ten thousand records of pupils from public and private secondary schools near New York City were located, and five thousand of these were selected for analysis because they seemed complete enough to be significant. Thorndike found that the prediction of the terminal-test score was about the same for all tests given at any time during the senior high school period. Thus, for the Otis S-A Higher Test the correlations were .64 when it was given in the same year as the terminal test, .65 when given the previous year, .62 after a 2-year interval, and .65 after a 3-year interval. Similar figures for the Terman Group Test were .82, .81, .77, and .69, and for the verbal score on the American Council Psychological Examination, .70, .70, .73, and .69. The results indicate that any of these tests when given in the ninth grade predicted verbal comprehension 3 years later as well as did the same test when given in the tenth, eleventh, or twelfth grade. This fact is very significant for counseling, because such data are more valuable in the earlier than in the later stages of the student's development. Tests given in the seventh and eighth grades showed somewhat poorer predictions but still significant general trends (median r about .60). Grades four, five, and six yielded predictions from Stanford-Binet Tests of approximately .59 on small samples, and the lower grades, approximately .40.

Predictions were doubtless reduced in part by the differences in functions measured at different ages and by the different tests. The Verbal Score of the C.E.B. Scholastic Aptitude (terminal test) is a fairly pure test of verbal meaning and relationship. Other tests stress this factor but also include unknown amounts of mathematical, spatial, and other types of content. The only way to avoid this difficulty is to use a battery of factorially pure tests. Predictions were also probably reduced by the limited sample of pupils available. All these figures probably come from persons in the highest quarter of the total population, and it is likely that more than half of them fall in the highest 5 per cent. A further selection was probably made in the case of the Stanford-Binet Tests, because these tests are usually given only to pupils who need special attention.

COMPARISON OF SCALES AND NEEDED RESEARCH

Purposes and Coverage

There are two different purposes for preparing analytical batteries. One, typical of Thurstone, Guilford, and the GATB and the AAF Tests (Chapter XI), is to determine and measure primary abilities as basic research tools; the other, more typical of the United States Navy Tests, the Yale Battery, and the Differential Aptitude Tests, is to predict academic or vocational success more accurately than can be done with a single index. The first purpose puts greater emphasis on mathematical analyses of correlations and the purity of test items.

The second stresses the inclusion of tests which yield the best predictions of success. The purity or independence of the tests is a secondary consideration. Both tend to avoid items indicative of purely academic achievement, interest, or personal adjustment. Both approaches have resulted in batteries which are intended to measure practically the same skills.

In order to compare the scales described above, the writer has prepared Illus. 91. Eight main groups of factors are used, which include five areas of skill: language, number, spatial thinking, mechanical principles, and dexterity. The three other main groups, perception, learning, and reasoning, are ways of thinking that may be applied to any of the five areas.

Since the eight chief groups have been subdivided and given somewhat technical definitions, they are described below. A remarkably thorough and clearly documented discussion of these is given by Guilford and Lacey (1947), from which this summary is largely drawn.

Language. This group measures the various aspects of the use of words as symbols. There appear three well-defined subgroups: (*a*) word meaning; (*b*) word fluency, which involves the rapid recall or use of previously learned words; and (*c*) written symbols or usage, which includes spelling, grammar, and punctuation. Further subdivisions of word meaning have been demonstrated by Greene (1939), who prepared eight fairly independent vocabulary scales, tentatively named: social, commercial, government, physical science, biological science, mathematics, graphic arts, and sports.

Number. This group of tests involves the use of numbers for computation, and is measured in its purest form by tests of addition, subtraction, multiplication, and division. Many authors also include arithmetical problems here, but these are always found to have high loadings of reasoning and some verbal factors. Geometrical problems also involve some spatial factors. Algebraic problems were found to have high components of general reasoning.

Spatial Thinking. This group has a core of visualizing or estimating what would happen if 2- or 3-dimensional figures were moved, rotated, or unfolded in some way. Guilford's Orientation, Test V, requires one to identify the direction of movement of oneself if one were in a pictured series. Guilford and Lacey list three spatial factors: (1) an "order of relationship between objects," (2) a right-left discrimination, and (3) a spatial factor, which as yet is difficult to name. In addition, they describe visualization as a visual-manipulative ability.

Mechanical Principles. This group of tests requires one to apply knowledge of mechanical principles or elementary physics to pictured

ILLUS. 91. COMPARISON OF APTITUDE BATTERIES

Group	Guilford-Zimmerman 1947	Chicago Primary Abilities, 1943 High School	Differential Aptitude Test, 1947	General Aptitude Test Battery, 1947	Yale Battery Crawford-Burnham, 1916
Total Time	143 min.	58 min.	173 min.	90 min.	
Language Meaning	I. Vocabulary 72-25 *	V Meaning Same 50-4 Completion 45-6	1. Verbal Reasoning Completion 50-30	V Vocabulary Same-Opposite 60-5	I. Comprehension Opposite-Synonym
Word Fluency		W Word Fluency 70-9			Wrong Word in Sentence
Usage			7. Spelling 100-10 8. Grammar 50-25		
Number	III. Arithmetical Computation 180-8	N Addition 70-6 Multiplication 70-5	2. Computation Fractions, Roots, Ratios 40-30	N Arithmetic Problems 25-6 Computation 50-5	V. Mathematical Ingenuity, Algebra
Spatial Thinking	V. Orientation 64-10 VI. Rotation 64-10 Dimensions 68-30	S Rotation 20-5 Cards 20-5	4. Fold Two to Three Dimensions 40-30	S Rotation Two Dimensions 49-7 Three Dimensions 40-6	VI. Block Counting Orthographic Views. Two-Dimensional Puzzles
Mechanical Principles	VII. Use or Definition, Pictures 55-30		5. Mechanical Reasoning, Pictures 68-30		VII. Mechanical Ingenuity, Pictures

					Approximate Grade-Range
Dexterity	Aim 1½ Speed ½ Finger Dexterity 2½ Tweezer Dexterity 2¼			II. Artificial Language	10-1¼
Perception		P Pictures 40-4 Q Names 150-6	6. Same Letters or Numbers, 5-Choice 100-3	III. Verbal Reasoning (See Number) IV. Quantitative Reasoning	5-14
Learning			3. Form-Series Completion 50-25	(See Number)	8-12
	† M Memory First-Last Names 20-14		R Letter-Series Completion 30-6 Letter Grouping 30-4		6-12
Reasoning or Problem Solving	IV. Silhouettes 72-5		II. Mathematics and Algebra 27-25		10-1¼

* Seventy-two items were allowed 25 minutes.

† Included in forms for younger children.

situations which involve weight, force, heat, and light. Two fairly different patterns are usually mixed. One pattern involves knowledge of materials and tools; and the other calls for a reasoning process when it is necessary to draw inferences and apply rules.

Dexterity. All of these tests involve hand-and-eye coordination, and four fairly independent factors appear: aiming, fine manipulation, coarser manipulation, and a simple, fast movement, such as tapping, which requires little accuracy.

Perception. Perception loading is found in all tests, but in this group of tests of perception other factors are minimized by requiring only simple judgments of *like* or *different*. Perception may, of course, depend on the keenness of a sense organ, but in these batteries only large visual patterns are used, so that unless a person has very defective vision, the test is a fairly pure measure of speed of mental comparisons. Familiarity with words or forms makes a difference, statistically and probably vocationally, but the correlations are usually fairly high between various visual-perception tests. None of these batteries includes perception of sound, but the Radio Code of the United States Navy and the Seashore Musical Tests include evaluations of this important factor.

Guilford and Lacey also describe two mental-set factors: one is the ability to keep up with rapidly changing instructions and the other the ability to grasp a wide variety of tasks requiring speed and accuracy.

Learning. All the tests in this group require one to make new associations during the test. Rote learning or immediate memory is well isolated in Thurstone's tests of associating first and last names or words and numbers. More logical learning is illustrated by the Artificial Language Test used by Crawford. Most of the scales do not include tests of learning, although learning may have considerable significance for certain vocations. Guilford and Lacey list four memory factors corresponding to immediate recall of pairs, recognition of pictorial material, recall of a picture-symbol relationship, and memory of verbal instructions.

Reasoning or Problem Solving. Under this group are considered tests of reasoning, judgment, foresight, planning—all tests which require one to formulate general rules from observed phenomena, or to apply a rule in solving a problem. All of these tests usually show significant factors in perceptual speed. Other factors, such as number, verbal, spatial relations, and mechanical experience, are found in tests where particular symbols are used.

In order to secure comparable measures of reasoning, the knowledge or information background must be kept constant. There are two possible procedures, neither one of which has yet proved practical. One procedure would be to try to prepare tests using symbols that are equally familiar to all candidates. No one has yet found such symbols, although some simple language or nonlanguage situations may be useful. The other procedure would be to get two measures—one of knowledge, the other of knowledge and reasoning—and then to remove statistically the knowledge variance from the reasoning scores. Much research is needed here. In many practical situations freedom from emotional stress is an important part of problem solution. This, too, should be measured separately by securing scores under stress and nonstress situations.

In good problem solving the following four fairly distinct activities have been observed: (*a*) grasping a whole situation so as to define the problem, not being disturbed by minor or unimportant details, (*b*) being aware of reasonable solutions or hypotheses, (*c*) trying out solutions quickly, mentally or with objects, and (*d*) selecting and applying one of the best solutions.

These four activities may occur fairly separately, but they usually seem to interact upon one another in life situations. All available factorial analyses of complex-reasoning tests have thus far yielded rather vaguely defined factors which seem to be related to combinations of mental activities and emotional adjustments. Various individuals undoubtedly use different combinations in arriving at the same score in a reasoning test. When a single score has several different meanings, vague factorial results will always follow.

No one who has worked in this field claims that these are all or even the principal abilities underlying human behavior. Nearly every factorial analysis yields statistical factors which are hard to identify, but which probably reflect variance in such aspects as energy output, speed, acquaintance with test situations, and distractions. Furthermore, there are large fields of skills involving sound, color, and physiological and structural variations which have not yet been explored by this technique.

Item Analysis: Form, Content, Number

An inspection of these scales will show that nearly all the items are in multiple-choice form, except those in the dexterity tests where the number of moves in a given time are counted. The multiple-choice form allows rapid scoring without the need of corrections for chance in most cases. The language used is made simple except where this variable is being tested.

Two arrangements of items are found. One, for power tests, places the items according to measured difficulty, the easier ones first. The other, for speed tests, as in perceptual speed, assumes that the items are of nearly equal difficulty and hence places them in random order. The content of individual items has been determined by the consensus of judges. In some instances this seems sufficient—for instance, in selecting items for simple computation, perception of form, block counting, and surface development it is not difficult to prepare very similar items. In other cases, however, the items in one test probably vary a good deal in content or processes involved. Thus vocabulary, word fluency, reading, analogies, arithmetic problems, and the various reasoning tests probably include items which are not pure measures of any one factor. Item analyses by intercorrelations are much needed here, and may well result in new types of items. The preparation of items has been channeled into types which were fairly common more than 20 years ago, while many newer types have scarcely been tried out. This sterility has probably come from laziness, tradition, and a desire to develop something which correlates highly with some well-established scale—all of which prevent progress.

The number of items used varies somewhat between authors and according to the subject matter. Thus, verbal meaning is appraised by from 50 to 70 items, number computation by 50 to 70, arithmetical problems 24 to 30 items, spatial thinking about 40 items, mechanical principles 40 to 60 items, dexterity about 100 items for each sort, perception 70 to 100 items, learning 20 to 30 items, and reasoning 27 to 50 items. Guilford-Zimmerman, the Yale Battery, and the DAT use the largest number of items, and also items which take longer to finish, so that their working time is from two to four times as long as that of the Chicago Primary Abilities or the General Aptitude Test Battery. The Yale Battery is also long, and Crawford and Burnham have emphasized that the speed requirement probably introduces a factor in the test situation which should be isolated and for some purposes avoided. In clinical practice where the patient is distractible, these tests have little value, but similar tests could and doubtless will be prepared for clinical situations.

STUDY GUIDE QUESTIONS

1. What were the principal early developments in group mental tests?
2. What criteria were used in selecting tests for the 1917 Army Alpha Test?
3. To what extent was speed a factor in the Army Alpha and Beta Tests?
4. To what extent do 2-factor and general tests differ in content?
5. What characteristics must a culture-free test have?
6. What is the design and purpose of the American Council on Education Psychological Examination?

7. How does the California Test of Mental Maturity arrive at scores for reasoning, language, and number?

8. How can deterioration in intellectual efficiency be measured?

9. Why has factorial purity of a test become a major consideration for some authors?

10. How is factorial purity demonstrated?

11. How are primary abilities defined? How are they measured?

12. To what extent are speed and power important in the Thurstone and Guilford batteries?

13. What is the significance of the general intelligence score of the General Aptitude Test Battery?

14. How are Occupational Aptitude Patterns established from the General Aptitude Test Battery?

15. What is the magnitude of age differences on most of these scales?

16. What magnitude of sex differences is usually found?

17. What evidence is there of harmful results of careless use of tests?

18. What predictions have been found for one semester? Four semesters?

19. How significantly do fields of specialization show expected profiles?

20. Why did Stuit and Hudson (1942) find such low correlations between grade averages and spatial ability among engineers?

21. How did Dvorak match individual and group profiles?

22. What are the main differences in content shown in Illus. 91?

23. What are the principal components of the language factor?

24. What is the nature of each of the eight major groups of factors?

25. What varieties of learning are tested?

26. What are the most effective measures of reasoning?

27. What types of factors are not yet well explored?

28. How may the factorial purity of individual items be discovered?

29. How can the optimum number of items needed be discovered?

CHAPTER IX

MECHANICAL AND MOTOR TESTS

~~~~~~

In this chapter certain abilities involved in motor and mechanical skills are defined, and their evaluation according to standard tests is discussed. Paper-and-pencil tests of knowledge and reasoning about tools, objects, and forces are described. Then hand-and-eye coordination, strength, reaction time, and problem solving are considered. Lastly, attempts to describe and analyze basic mechanical factors are reviewed.

PAPER-AND-PENCIL TESTS

Knowledge

Tests of knowledge are widely used in appraising achievement in apprentice and shop training, and in predicting success in future training or employment. Testing knowledge alone or knowledge coupled with mechanical reasoning has been found to be about the best single way to predict success both in training and on the job. When such tests are developed for one trade exclusively, they are called *trade tests*. Tests of the printed and oral types are described below.

Printed Tests of Mechanical Information. This type of test is illustrated by such multiple-choice items concerning woodworking as are given in Illus. 92. The items are taken from an elaborate study of mechanical ability by Paterson et al. (1930), which included appraisals of knowledge in each of the following: woodworking, print-

ILLUS. 92. MANUAL TRAINING INFORMATION TESTS

Minneapolis Public Schools

TEST A. WOODWORK

Devised by Manual Training Department Committee on Objectifying Grades on Woodwork, assisted by the Mechanical Abilities Research Staff, University of Minnesota.

Name.................................School.............................

Date of birth...Grade...............
day   month   year

Underscore shop courses you have taken: Sheet Metal, Mechanical Drawing, Electricity, Woodwork, Printing.

This is a test to see how much you know about Woodwork.

Here is a sample question already worked out. Notice how it is done.

St. Paul is the capital of 1. Ohio   2. Vermont   3. Minnesota.........(3)

The right answer is Minnesota, so Minnesota is underlined. Notice also that the word Minnesota is No. 3, so 3 is written in the parenthesis at the right hand side of the page. You are not expected to answer all the questions below. Answer just as many of them as you can.

Underline only one word in each case and be sure to put the number of that word in the parenthesis at the right-hand side of the page.

Stop. Wait for signal before beginning.
Test begins here.

1. For holding pieces of wood together while gluing, use
    1. clamps.   2. screws.   3. boards.   4. nails...............(   )
2. Holes are bored with
    1. a brace and bit.   2. an awl.   3. a planer.   4. a chisel...(   )
3. A jack plane is made of
    1. steel.   2. copper.   3. celluloid.   4. glucose...........(   )
4. A part of a brace is the
    1. chuck.   2. point.   3. break.   4. knife...............(   )
5. The marking gauge is used in
    1. laying out widths.   2. cutting small boards.   3. making joints tight.   4. boring holes...............................(   )
6. When sanding flat surfaces, the sandpaper should be backed with a
    1. flat block.   2. wooden plane.   3. cylinder.   4. piece of pumice stone...(   )

(and 132 more items)

(From Paterson *et al.*, 1930, p. 150. By permission of the
University of Minnesota Press.)

ing, mechanical drawing, sheet-metal working, and electricity. A large number and variety of examinations of this kind are prepared by teachers of mechanical subjects in high school and college and by civil service examiners. The Purdue Tests of Machine Shop Practice and of Electricity are good examples of widely standardized tests.

Pictorial tests of mechanical information resemble those shown in Illustrations 93 and 14. In Illus. 93 the subject is to choose the one of five phrases that gives the name and use of a small pictured object. In Illus. 14 the parts of a lathe are to be labeled and their functions explained.

Oral Trade Tests. In 1917 many oral tests of trade knowledge were prepared for the United States Army for a rapid, rough screening of a large number of soldiers. Each test included from fifteen to twenty-five specific questions of definition or procedure which had been found to distinguish between apprentices, journeymen, and experts in a particular trade. In 1940 the United States Employment Service developed many more oral trade questions, and brought them up to date for almost two hundred craft occupations. These tests have not been made available to private employers, in the hope of preventing their use by coaching schools. Similar written and oral tests, however, have been prepared in industry, where a large number of workers have to be screened rapidly. In general, the written tests are more extensive, more intensive, and more valid. Many employment interviewers have adapted items from both oral and written trade tests for use in particular types of interviews.

Mechanical Principles

Thurstone (1938) defined Mechanical Reasoning as one of the primary mental abilities, and measured it by printed pictorial tests, such as that shown in Illus. 147. Bennett's Test of Mechanical Comprehension (1940, 1947) includes problems of heat and light, as well as of forces of various sorts. More recently, this type of test has been greatly expanded and widely applied by the military services (Chapter XI) and has been incorporated into most of the batteries of basic abilities (Chapter VIII).

Spatial Visualization

Tests of ability to observe, compare, and visualize geometric shapes or patterns appeared in the United States Army Beta Test of Cube Counting in 1917, and have since been expanded. Illustration 94 shows a widely used paper form board for which additional norms were issued in 1948 by the Psychological Corporation. Thurstone and others have found Spatial Visualization to be an aptitude essential for

ILLUS. 93. SRA MECHANICAL APTITUDES, FORM AH

MECHANICAL KNOWLEDGE
PRACTICE EXERCISES

How much do you know about tools, machines, and other equipment used by carpenters, plumbers, electricians, gardeners, machinists, auto mechanics, housewives, and others who work with mechanical devices? *Mechanical knowledge* is important for success in mechanical activities. This first test measures your information about **mechanical devices.**

Look at the problem below:

P-1.

This is used to:
- A. chop wood ·····························
- B. scrape paint ·······················
- C. remove nails ·······················
- D. shape metal ·······················
- E. break rocks ·······················

The picture shows a **hand axe**, which is used to chop wood. An ✕ has been marked in the box after chop wood.

Now work the problems below. In each problem, put an ✕ in the box after the right answer. *Mark your answers heavily. Do NOT make any marks except your answers.*

If you wish to change an answer, draw a circle around the box like ⊗. Then mark the new answer in the usual way. DO NOT ERASE ANY MARK YOU HAVE MADE ON THE ANSWER PAD.

P-2.

This is used in:
- A. cranking gasoline engines ···········
- B. bending wood strips ···············
- C. opening cans ·······················
- D. removing spark plugs ··············
- E. boring holes in wood ··············

P-3.

This is:
- A. a machine bolt ····················
- B. a carriage bolt ···················
- C. a window bolt ·····················
- D. a stove bolt ·······················
- E. an eye bolt ·······················

You should have marked **boring holes in wood** ✕ and a **machine bolt** ✕ on the Answer Pad.

Be sure you understand how to work these problems. When the examiner gives the signal, you are to work more problems like those above.

Work quickly, but try not to make mistakes. You will have 10 minutes, but are not expected to finish in this time. *There are FIVE pages of problems.*

(By permission of Richardson, Bellows, Henry, and Co., Inc. and The Science Research Associates.)

success in all drafting work and in engineering design. The test can be made very difficult by including pictures of 3-dimensional objects and rotating them in three directions as in the Guilford-Zimmerman's Test (Illus. 86).

ILLUS. 94. THE REVISED MINNESOTA PAPER FORM BOARD

READ THE FOLLOWING DIRECTIONS VERY CAREFULLY WHILE THE EXAMINER READS THEM ALOUD

Look at the problems on the right side of this page. You will notice that there are eight of them, numbered from 1 to 8. Notice that the problems go DOWN the page.

First look at Problem 1. There are two parts in the upper left-hand corner. Now look at the five figures labelled A, B, C, D, E. You are to decide which figure shows how these parts can fit together. Let us first look at Figure A. You will notice that Figure A does **not** look like the parts in the upper left-hand would look when fitted together. Neither do Figures B, C, or D. Figure E **does** look like the parts in the upper left-hand corner would look when fitted together, so E is PRINTED in the square above ☐1 at the top of the page.

Now look at Problem 2. Decide which figure is the correct answer. As you will notice, Figure A is the correct answer, so A is printed in the square above ☐2 at the top of the page.

The answer to Problem 3 is B, so B is printed in the square above ☐3 at the top of the page.

In Problem 4, D is the correct answer, so D is printed in the square above ☐4 at the top of the page.

Now do Problems 5, 6, 7, and 8.

PRINT the letter of the correct answer in the square above the number of the example at the top of the page.

DO THESE PROBLEMS NOW.

If your answers are not the same as those which the examiner reads to you, RAISE YOUR HAND.

DO NOT OPEN THE BOOKLET UNTIL YOU ARE TOLD TO DO SO.

Some of the problems on the inside of this booklet are more difficult than those which you have already done, but the idea is exactly the same. In each problem you are to decide which figure shows the parts correctly fitted together. **Sometimes the parts have to be turned around, and sometimes they have to be turned over in order to make them fit.** In the square above ☐1 write the correct answer to Problem 1; in the square above ☐2 write the correct answer to Problem 2, and so on with the rest of the test. Start with Problem 1, and go DOWN the page. After you have finished one column, go right on with the next. Be careful not to go so fast that you make mistakes. Do not spend too much time on any one problem.

PRINT WITH CAPITAL LETTERS ONLY.

MAKE THEM SO THAT ANYONE CAN READ THEM.

DO NOT OPEN THE BOOKLET BEFORE YOU ARE TOLD TO DO SO.

YOU WILL HAVE EXACTLY 20 MINUTES TO DO THE WHOLE TEST.

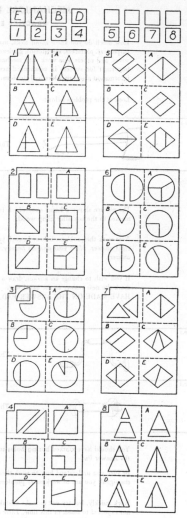

(Courtesy of Likert and Quasha, 1934.)

Computation

Nearly all mechanical work includes accurate measurement and some computation. Lawshe and Mountoux (1942) issued an Industrial Training Classification Test which revised an earlier form. This includes reading dimensions from mechanical drawings of an irregular block with four holes, of a lot with several buildings, of a bolt with two nuts, and of a fountain pen. Addition, subtraction, multiplication, and division of whole numbers, fractions, and decimals are required. More recently such tests have appeared in all batteries for mechanical prediction.

Batteries

Batteries of tests of mechanical ability are now available at college and high school levels. Moore, Lapp, and Griffin (1943) developed an Engineering and Physical Science Test with six parts:

   I. *Mathematics:* 25 problems involving algebra and square roots
  II. *Formulation:* 10 problems requiring a verbal statement is to be cast into an algebraic formula
 III. *Physical Science Comprehension:* 45 items
  IV. *Arithmetic Reasoning:* 10 items where algebra is very helpful
   V. *Verbal Comprehension:* 43 technical and literary items
  VI. *Mechanical Comprehension:* 22 items of mechanical reasoning

This test has had a wide application to candidates for admission to engineering schools.

At the high school level and for average adults the SRA Mechanical Aptitudes Test, prepared by Richardson, Bellows, Henry, and Company Inc. (1947), contains three parts. Part I consists of forty-five pictures of commonly used tools, followed by five written or printed choices (Illus. 93). Sometimes the object is simply to be named, but more often its use is to be stated. The questions cover a wide variety of tools for metal, wood, and drafting operations. Part II is a Spatial Relations test which consists of four simple key figures which remain the same and are printed on each page, and forty items, each one of which represents one of the key figures cut into two or three separate pieces. One must indicate which of the four key figures would be reconstructed if the smaller sections were properly fitted together. In some instances pieces must be rotated. This part is similar to the paper form board (Illus. 94). Part III is a Shop Arithmetic test in which most of the items are based upon drawings or tables. These require the use of language as well as computation and reasoning. Each problem has four choices and an alternative, "None of these."

The first two tests are allowed 10 minutes each and the last one 15 minutes. Separate scores are given for each part of the test because the authors feel that maximum validity or prediction of results will be found if the user develops the best weights for his particular situation. Norms for total scores are also given. The correlation between the three parts is in the neighborhood of .35, and the Kuder-Richardson Reliability is approximately .90 for a small sample of high school graduates attending trade schools. Norms are given for a wide variety of trainees and technical apprentices as well as for some journeymen.

Wrightstone and O'Toole (1946) issued the Prognostic Test of Mechanical Abilities for grades seven through twelve and adults. It includes:

1. 15 arithmetic problems featuring fractions and decimals
2. 15 problems of reading directions from simple mechanical drawings
3. 20 multiple-choice items on the identification and use of tools
4. 15 multiple-choice items of a complex paper form-board type
5. 15 multiple-choice items of measuring parts of eight drawings with a ruler

Total reliability (about .90) is somewhat higher for older students. Centile norms for 5,268 boys in seven states are furnished by grades.

MOTOR COORDINATION TESTS

The field of motor coordination has received more attention in laboratory studies than in the standard testing situations. This is probably due to the fact that thorough motor testing employs rather extensive mechanical equipment and demands individual administration. A few fairly well-standardized procedures using simple materials have been developed, which will be discussed here under five headings: reaction time, agility and strength, dexterity, steadiness, and motor rhythms.

Reaction Time

Reaction times have been extensively studied for both total and partial responses. Total reaction time is the period between the application of a stimulus, such as the sound of a bell, and some muscular response, such as the release of a telegraphic key. Partial reaction time is the period between the application of a stimulus and a change in some portion of the total reaction path.

Numerous studies of total reactions of the simplest sort have been extensively discussed by Woodworth (1938). The evidence is conclusive that for adult laboratory subjects

1. Reaction times vary with sense organ stimulated. Approximate mean reaction times in seconds, as given by moving a finger as quickly as possible after a moderate stimulus, were for

touch on the hand	.120	pain	1.000+
touch on the forehead	.130	smell	1.000+
sound	.130	salt taste	.307
light	.180	sweet taste	.496
cold	.150	acid taste	.536
warmth	.180	bitter taste	1.082

2. Reaction times vary with the intensity of the stimulus; in general, the more intense the stimulus, the quicker the response.

3. Reaction times vary with the nervous connections. Thus, the response of the right hand to stimulation of the right hand is faster than to the stimulation of the left hand or of either foot.

4. The reaction time varies with the reacting movement. A well-practiced movement is quicker than an unfamiliar movement. The force used to close a switch is much greater than necessary at first, but later in practice a smaller well-directed movement is used.

5. Ready signals are very important. Regular signals about one-half second before the stimulus result in shorter reaction times than longer, irregular, or shorter signals.

6. Discrimination reactions, such as pressing a key if a sound comes from the left but not if it comes from the right, are much slower than simple reactions.

7. Associated reaction times, such as calling out the first word that is suggested by a stimulus, vary greatly. The more familiar associations are nearly as fast as simple response time to visual stimuli, but the less familiar or the emotionally toned responses are much longer.

Van Essen (1935) reported a number of interesting observations in connection with studies of auto drivers. Manual reaction times to auditory and visual stimuli varied with the type of stimulation, thus:

1. A short stimulation gave slightly shorter reaction times than the disappearance of a continuous stimulus, and a much shorter reaction time than the appearance of a continuous stimulus.

2. The reaction times became shorter when subjects' reactions affected the stimulus, as, for instance, when lifting one's foot from a pedal extinguished a light, than when the reaction did not affect the stimulus.

3. Reactions to a more distant red light (24 meters) were faster than to nearer lights (12 meters or 2 meters) when intensity and size of retinal stimulation were held constant.

4. Repeated reaction times did not fall into a normal curve of distribution for each individual, but into several patterns which depended upon qualitative differences in reaction patterns.

Another study, showing growth and practice norms, is that of Jones (1937), who instructed his subjects as follows:

This is a test to see how fast you can move your hand. You place your hand on this board and hold it down: in a moment a light will appear in the red bulb. This is a signal that in 1, 2, or 3 seconds a buzzer in the clock will sound. When you hear that buzzer, you must lift your fingers off just as fast as you can (demonstrating). At the sound of the buzzer, a little electric clock starts; the clock stops when you lift your fingers, and by reading the dial we can tell how quick you are.

After preliminary trials, fifteen trials were taken with each hand. Some of the results were:

1. Odd-even reliability correlations for fifteen trials were approximately .87 for boys and .89 for girls.

2. No marked differences were found between mean scores for right and left hands. Correlations between right and left hand responses ranged from .80 to .86.

3. Retest correlations on groups of ninety children after a year's interval were from .60 to .72 and after 3 years, from .55 to .57.

4. Small practice effects occurred in eleven-year-old children on the second day but not thereafter during 4 days of practice.

5. Males were slightly superior to females, particularly for the left hand and at the earlier ages.

6. A marked warming-up effect was noticed during the first five trials with the right hand and during all fifteen trials of the left hand.

7. Age norms for right-hand reaction times were:

Year	No. of Cases	Mean
4.5	37	398.3
7.3	34	250.8
10.9	76	186.7
14.7	50	162.5
19.5	40 college students	156.7

8. There was some evidence that adaptation was present in groups where the test was repeated four times at yearly intervals. These groups surpassed their controls.

9. Motivation was found to be very important. The subjects were allowed to see their own reaction times on the face of a chronoscope and were urged to break their own records.

Studies of total reaction times have convinced investigators that a response is a complicated affair which should be analyzed into its constituent parts. An early analysis was made by Exner (1868), who described the following seven segments of a reaction:

1. Time needed for excitation of sense organ
2. Conduction through a sensory nerve
3. Conduction from lower spinal cord to lower brain centers
4. Conduction from sensory to motor brain centers
5. Conduction from motor center to lower cord
6. Conduction through motor nerve
7. Muscular movement

These or similar segments have been studied by means of small electrical conductors placed in or near various parts of the nervous pathway. One variety of this technique measures the time between a particular stimulus and the changes in the resistance of the skin on some part of the body. This reaction is often called a psychogalvanic reflex. An excellent review of research dealing with the galvanic skin responses is given by Woodworth (1938). Another variation of the technique records small changes in electrical resistance which occur in brain tissue or in the scalp. Photographic records of such changes are called electroencephalographs. This fascinating field, which is being rapidly developed, is reviewed periodically in *Child Development Abstracts.*

Agility and Strength

The tests for infants described in Chapter V were found to contain large sections devoted to appraisals of posture, hand and eye co-ordination, and locomotion. Tests of similar patterns of behavior have been developed for older children and adults, and the norms in some cases are fairly adequate.

A series of motor tests for children from two to six years of age were tentatively standardized on ninety-eight children by McCaskill and Wellman (1938), who describe the tests as follows (p. 141):

It was the idea from the beginning to keep each activity in the test situation as simple as possible so that it could be reproduced easily. For the ball throwing and ball bouncing a "location field" was devised for determining the distance and direction of the child's throw or bounce. This field was made of heavy brown paper 8 feet wide and 17 feet long, with a 4 inch strip of wall board at each end to anchor it. The width was marked off into zones. Zone 1 was 2 feet in width and extended down the center of the field, with zones 2, 3, and 4, each 1 foot wide, to the right and left of zone 1. The length was marked off into distances; distance 1 was 3 feet in length and distances 2, 3, 4, 5, 6, 7, and 8 each 2 feet in length. For the throw or bounce the child stood at the edge of and on the center line of the field and threw or bounced the ball to the experimenter at the opposite end of the field. The results were recorded according to zone and distance and the child's use of one or both hands.

In the catching series the ball was thrown to the child at a level with his chest each time, as nearly as was possible. The method used in the attempt to catch the ball, the successes, and whether or not the child used defense movements when the ball was tossed to him were all recorded. Two balls were used throughout, one 16¼ inches in circumference, the other 9½ inches. Three trials were given for each performance with each ball.

To determine the child's ability to maintain equilibrium and balance, a walking path and a circle were used. A demonstration was given in each case. If the child failed to respond, he was asked to follow the experimenter as she walked on the path or circle. The path, 10 feet long and 1 inch wide, was drawn on a large piece of brown paper and colored red. The circle was cut from wall board and was 4 feet in diameter. A strip (1 inch wide) was drawn around its outer border and colored red like the path. The number of times the child stepped off the path and circle on each trial was recorded. Three trials were given on each. If the child set one foot off the line for balance but did not take a step, he was not penalized.

Four heights were used for the jumping—boxes 8, 12, 18, and 28 inches in height. The child was given three trials at each height and was checked according to the method he employed in the jump.

The child was asked to hop on one and on both feet and a demonstration of each was given him. He was given three trials at each. The stages were recorded in number of steps. Four items were listed under skipping: walking, shuffle, skipping on one foot, and skipping on alternate feet. The experimenter skipped and asked the child to follow her. The shuffle has a rhythmic quality—the same foot is always forward at each advance. It is definitely in advance of walking and is not the same high step the children employ in galloping.

Both ascending and descending steps were tested on short and long flights. The short flight had 4 steps 7 inches in height with an 11 inch tread. The long flight had 11 steps of the same height and tread. The rail on both flights was 29 inches in height. The steps on which the kindergarten children were tested were slightly different. The short flight had 4 steps 7 inches in height with a tread of 10 inches and the long flight 12 steps 6¼ inches in height with a tread of 11¾ inches. The hand rail was 34 inches above the steps. The child had three trials on ascending and descending both flights of steps.

For ladder climbing two ladders were used. One had twelve rungs 6 inches apart, the other six rungs 12 inches apart. The ladders were placed at approximately a 45 degree angle each time. This placement was kept constant by placing the same ladder rung against the support each time.

In scaling these tests, months of motor age were assigned to each observed stage of development, or item, from the results of testing the standardization group. Age equivalents were calculated using Thurstone's (1925) method, which shows the age at which 50 per cent of the group passed the item, and 50 per cent failed to pass. Illustration 95 shows the motor ages for each item, which, incidentally, correspond closely to values found by Bayley (1935) for hopping, walking, and stair climbing among two- and three-year-olds. Illustration 95 also shows a point scale used for individual scores. Separate scores were provided for four kinds of activities by summing the points made on groups of items called (1) Steps and Ladders, (2) Ball Activities, (3) Jumping, and (4) Hopping, Skipping, and Walking. Norms for total scores were also published. The mean correlations between these types of motor skills for all ages combined were

ILLUS. 95. MOTOR ACHIEVEMENTS SCALE

Months	Score	Item
71	4	bouncing large ball, one hand, distance 1
68	6	catching large ball, elbows at side of body, success on 2 or three trials
65	3	bouncing large ball, both hands, distance 3
65	7	throwing small ball, both hands or one hand, distance 7
63	5	throwing large ball, both hands or one hand, distance 5
62	4	descending large ladder, alternate feet, with facility
60	4	hopping on one foot, 10 or more steps
60	3	skipping, alternate feet
57	6	throwing small ball, both hands or one hand, distance 6
56	3	descending large ladder, alternate feet, with caution
55	5	catching small ball, elbows at side of body, no success on one trial
55	4	descending long steps, alternate feet, unsupported
55	3	hopping one foot, 7 to 9 steps
53	4	throwing large ball, both hands or one hand, distance 4
53	4	descending small ladder, alternate feet, with facility
52	5	throwing small ball, both hands or one hand, distance 5
51	3	descending small ladder, alternate feet, with caution
51	5	catching large ball, elbows at side of body, no success or success on one trial
50	4	catching small ball, elbows in front of body, success on 2 or 3 trials
49	4	descending short steps, alternate feet, unsupported
48	3	descending long steps, alternate feet, with support
48	3	descending short steps, alternate feet, with support
47	4	ascending large ladder, alternate feet, with facility
46	2	bouncing large ball, both hands, distance 2
46	3	jumping 28 inches, alone, feet together
46	2	hopping one foot, 4 to 6 steps
45	3	ascending large ladder, alternate feet, with caution
45	3	walking circle, no steps off
44	4	throwing small ball, one hand or both, distance 4
44	4	catching large ball, elbows in front of body, success on 2 or 3 trials
43	1	hopping one foot, 1 to 3 steps
43	2	jumping 28 inches, alone, one foot ahead
43	3	throwing large ball, both hands or one hand, distance 3
43	2	skipping on one foot
42	4	hopping both feet, 10 or more steps
41	4	ascending long steps, alternate feet, unsupported
41	3	hopping two feet, 7 to 9 steps
40	2	hopping two feet, 4 to 6 steps
40	5	bouncing small ball, one hand, distance 2
38	2	descending large ladder, mark time, with facility
38	4	ascending small ladder, alternate feet, with facility
38	3	catching small ball, elbows in front of body, no success or successes on one trial
38	1	skipping and shuffle
38	1	hopping both feet, 1 to 3 steps
37	2	catching small ball, arms straight, success on 2 or 3 trials
37	3	jumping 18 inches, feet together, alone
37	3	walking path, no steps off
36	1	jumping 28 inches, with help
35	3	catching large ball, elbows in front of body, no success or success on one trial
35	2	walking circle, 1 to 3 steps off
34	2	catching large ball, arms straight, success on 2 or 3 trials
34	2	descending long steps, mark time, unsupported
34	3	jumping 12 inches, alone, feet together
34	3	ascending small ladder, alternate feet, with caution
33	2	ascending large ladder, mark time, with facility
33	3	throwing small ball, both hands or one hand, distance 3
33	3	jumping 8 inches, alone, feet together
31	3	ascending long steps, alternate feet, with support
31	4	ascending short steps, alternate feet, unsupported
31	2	jumping 18 inches, alone, one foot ahead
31	2	walking path, 1 to 3 steps off
30	2	throwing large ball, one hand or both hands, distance 2
29	2	throwing small ball, one hand or both hands, distance 2
29	3	ascending short steps, alternate feet, with support
29	2	ascending long steps, mark time, unsupported
28	2	ascending short steps, mark time, unsupported
28	1	walking circle, 4 to 6 steps off
28	1	walking path, 4 to 6 steps off
24	4	bouncing small ball, one hand, distance 1
24	2	ascending short steps, mark time, unsupported
24	1	jumping 18 inches, with help
24	2	jumping 12 inches, alone, one foot ahead
24	1	descending large ladder, mark time, with caution

(McCaskill and Wellman, 1938, p. 148. By permission of *Society for Research in Child Development*.)

approximately .69 for boys and .75 for girls. The true correlations between these skills would doubtless be much lower if age were held constant. The lowest correlations were between Ball Activities and Steps and Ladders, and the highest between Steps and Ladders and Hopping.

Forty-six youngsters were retested within one week. The total-score retest reliability was .98. Among the subtests the lowest reliabilities were in Ball Activities and Walking Around a Circle. The authors believe that the lower reliabilities of the Ball Activities scores were due to the fact that scoring in this instance was more minute and detailed than in some of the other tests. The boys appeared to be slightly superior to the girls on Steps and Ladders and Ball Activities, and the girls were a little ahead in Hopping and Skipping. The scores discriminated well between two- and five-year-old groups but not between five- and six-year-old groups, because the items are not difficult enough to discriminate among the six-year-olds who were above average.

An excellent summary of tests of agility and strength is given by Bovard and Cozens (1938). They include norms for anthropometric, cardiac, strength, athletic information, and physical efficiency measures among elementary school, high school, and college groups. Jones and Seashore (1944) reported a careful developmental study of fine motor and mechanical abilities during adolescence.

Dexterity

Tests which are classified as measures of dexterity characteristically appraise routine or serial perceptions and movements in terms of speed, accuracy, endurance, and force. In certain dexterity tests, such as simple tapping, perceptual discrimination is probably a minor element, and the score is largely determined by muscle and nerve functions. In more complex tests, such as serial aiming or pursuit tests, the perceptual elements may be more important in success than motor coordination. Moreover, there seem to be at least two nearly unrelated types of motor coordination: (1) ballistic movement, in which an extremity is thrown or moved rapidly in some highly automatized pattern, illustrated by simple tapping with a stylus, and (2) precision movement, in which voluntary control is continuous, as in serial aiming or tweezer dexterity.

Among the simpler ballistic tests is the tapping test described by Whipple (1914) and used in many studies since that time. The apparatus for the tapping test consists of a metal plate 2 inches square, a metal stylus, and an electric counting device. The number of taps recorded in five 5-second trials, allowing 30 seconds of rest between trials, was used as a score by Paterson *et al.* (1930). Others have used various time limits of from 5 to 60 seconds. Maximum retest correlations of about .91 were found by Muscio (1922), Gates (1928), and Greene (1931) under optimum conditions. Greene reported that 10 seconds was the optimum time limit for single trials of college students. Shorter periods seemed to introduce random variations, and longer periods were influenced by individual differences in fatigue. He also found that speed of tapping for 10 seconds with paper and pencil, a group test, correlated .77 with a 10-second trial on the Whipple apparatus.

Another tapping test which seems to measure about the same sort of coordination is pressing and releasing a telegraphic key as rapidly as possible. A fairly large number of researches have used tapping keys and automatic counters.

Tapping tests among adults have been reported to show nearly zero correlations with other motor tests and with mental test scores.

One of the earlier batteries of tests which emphasized precision of movement was that of Whitman (1925), whose series included the following activities:

1. Putting one brass pin in each hole drilled in a large board (each hand, 1 min.)
2. Putting three brass pins in each hole (using both hands, 2 mins.)
3. Assembling nuts and bolts (30 secs.)
4. Disassembling nuts and bolts (30 secs.)
5. Sorting different colored pegs (30 secs.)
6. Placing pegs of a particular color in order on a peg board (1 min.)

Whitman furnished age norms for groups from seven to fifteen years of age. O'Connor (1928) used a test similar to No. 2 and also described a test called Tweezer Dexterity, which requires a person to place metal pins, one at a time, in one hundred holes drilled in a metal plate, using a small pair of tweezers. These tests have good reliability and have predicted success fairly well in jobs which require delicate assembly of small apparatus.

There are now available about twenty dexterity tests which have been partly standardized (Appendix II). One of the best is the Purdue Dexterity Test (Illus. 96), which has two parts. In one, short metal rods are to be placed in rows of holes in a board, with each hand separately and with both hands together. In the other part, skilled finger dexterity is required when both hands are used to assemble pins and washers and place them in holes. The two tests can be given to ten workers at once and require only 2½ minutes of testing time, following directions and practice periods.

ILLUS. 96. PURDUE DEXTERITY TEST

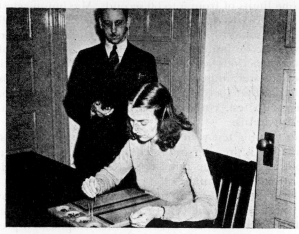

(By permission of Dr. Joseph Tiffin.)

Another dexterity test which involves timing is the Purdue Hand Precision Test (Illus. 97). Here three half-inch holes are uncovered by the rotation of a disc at the rate of 126 holes per minute. The holes are located at the corners of a triangle 3.5 inches to a side. One is asked to put a stylus into each hole as it is uncovered, without touching the sides or being caught by the shutter. After a 30-second practice period, a 2-minute test is given, during which a clock records the error time, that is, the seconds of contact between the stylus and the sides of the hole or the shutter.

A somewhat similar test is the Bennett Hand-Tool Dexterity Test (Illus. 98), in which the subject is presented with a U-shaped wooden frame, on the left-hand upright, of which there are mounted twelve bolts (three sizes of four each). The task is to remove the twelve bolts, nuts, and washers from the left side and to assemble them in a proscribed sequence on the right side. The time required is the score. For a large group of adults the range of scores was from 4 to 12 minutes, average $6\frac{1}{2}$ minutes. Test-retest correlations were approximately .91, and correlations with foremen's ratings on mechanical work was reported in the neighborhood of .45.

Steadiness

In this group are found measures of both large- and small-muscle groups. Paterson *et al.* (1930) has described a test of steadiness of large-muscle groups, called the Body-Balancing Test. The test is used to discover how long a person can balance himself on a 3-inch

ILLUS. 97. PURDUE HAND-PRECISION TEST

(By permission of Dr. Joseph Tiffin.)

ILLUS. 98. BENNETT HAND-TOOL DEXTERITY TEST

(By permission of The Psychological Corporation.)

cube of wood on the floor, using only the ball of one foot for support. A simple machine for recording postural steadiness, called an *ataxiameter*, has been described by Miles (1922). It consists of a square, balanced board upon which a person stands erect on both feet and with eyes closed. Each corner of the board is connected with an instrument which records its vertical movements. Great steadiness is indicated by little total movement. A similar device, called a *wabblemeter*, has been designed by Moss (1931).

A steadiness test of hand-and-eye coordination has been described by Whipple (1914). A brass plate with nine holes of various diameters, a metal stylus, and an automatic counter are used. The subject is required to hold the stylus in each hole 15 seconds while trying not to let it touch the edge. The hand and arm are extended and free from support. The score is the number of contacts that are electrically recorded. The median retest correlation reported by Paterson *et al.* (1930) was .62 for scores on single holes and .76 for total scores among 217 boys. Whipple also standardized a thrusting or aiming test with this apparatus.

The existence of a steadiness factor has been suggested by Seashore and Adams (1933), who applied five tests of steadiness to fifty students. The tests were Miles' ataxiameter, Beall and Hall's ataxiagraph, Seashore's modification of Whipple's steadiness test for both "position" and "thrusting," and a rifle steadiness test. The intercorrelations of these tests ranged from .44 to .59, median .48. These correlations are probably indicative of a general factor of steadiness in large-muscle coordinations.

Motor Rhythms

Ability to perform acts at a particular rate is considered to be highly important in many sorts of musical, dancing, and mechanical skills. It is difficult, however, to find a precise definition of rhythm, and a brief inspection of tests of rhythm will convince one that the patterns vary considerably. Subjective analyses usually limit the phenomena to temporal patterns and distinguish between perception of rhythmic patterns and their performance. Perception of simple rhythmic patterns can be tested by asking persons to tell whether two temporal patterns are the same, or whether one of two intervals is longer than another, as in the Seashore (1919) tests of musical talent. (See Chapter X.)

The performance of rhythmic patterns doubtless requires good perception, but it also involves to a large extent muscle and central nervous system elements. An illustration of a standardized test of simple motor rhythm is the Seashore (1928), which requires one to listen to a sequence of four notes that are played over and over again by a phonograph record for a short time. Then at a signal, one is required to keep time with the sequence by pressing a telegraph key. The score, which is automatically recorded electrically, is the number of taps in one minute which fall within .05 seconds of the exact time of the sound.

Van Alstyne and Osborne (1937) adapted this test for small children and also devised a rhythm memory test. They found boys to be slightly inferior to girls. Small practice effects were noted. Liebold (1936) found that four-year-olds could not keep time to a metronome at the rate of either once or twice per second, but that half of the five-year-olds and nearly all of the six-year-old group succeeded well. A complex test of motor rhythms is illustrated by some intricate dance steps used by Garfiel (1923). She also required persons to attempt nonsynchronized movements of the two hands. Jersild and Bienstock (1935) devised an accurate measure of stepping and clapping to music. The test scores were secured from motion-picture films, by counting the number of frames, taken at intervals of $\frac{1}{24}$ second, in which the child was in time with the music. Movements of beating time with the hand and walking were counted as in time if they fell within $\frac{1}{24}$ second of the actual beat. The relative correlations between two tests of four hundred beats each were approximately .70, and of two hundred beats, .60. Among the older children the figures were somewhat higher. Instructors' ratings were found to be highly untrustworthy when age was held constant. Correlations between hand and foot rhythms were near .82, and between hand rhythms and singing ability, .30.

Rhythms in serial mental work have been studied by Bills (1937). Mental performance was characteristically found to be discontinuous. He reported pauses which became longer and more frequent as the task became more difficult and as fatigue increased. Elaborate studies of rhythmic performance on musical instruments have been reported in the University of Iowa *Studies of the Psychology of Music*. (Chapter X.)

Batteries of Motor Tests

Several batteries of motor tests have been described which seem to have been assembled, like a general mental test, to sample a fairly wide variety of skills without attempting a careful analysis. Success on such batteries seems to depend, in various and unknown proportions, upon strength, endurance, precision, steadiness, rhythm, perceptual skill, information, and in some cases upon reasoning and planning. Most of the batteries seek to furnish separate norms for their component tests, thereby providing tools for subsequent analyses and refinements.

Two tests which seem to require principally precision, rhythm, ballistic movements, and planning, come from the Minnesota University Laboratory. The Minnesota Rate of Manipulation Test, Ziegler (1934), Illus. 6, shows the speed at which a person can turn over 120 circular blocks which fit loosely in holes in a board. Paterson *et al.* (1930) described a Packing Blocks test which measures the time needed to place 147 one-inch cubes in a wooden box. Scores for one trial of these tests were found to yield low reliabilities, but the sums of three or four trials usually show retest reliabilities of approximately .90.

Another widely used battery is the Stanford Motor Skills Tests, described by Robert Seashore (1928). Six serial dexterity tests were chosen from among more than twenty tests, so that

1. They were well adapted for use in schools and factories.
2. They took only a small amount of time (less than 2 hours).
3. The material occupied little space.
4. They were scored automatically.
5. Each test had high retest reliability (.75 to .86).
6. Each test had a low correlation with the Thorndike College Entrance Examination.
7. Each test had a low correlation with amounts of training in typing, practice on a musical instrument, and training in athletics.
8. The intercorrelations were low (mean .25).

The six parts of the Stanford Motor Skills battery test the following:

1. *The Koerth Pursuit Test* requires a person to hold the point of metal stylus on a metal disc, ½ inch in diameter, mounted on a phonograph record. The phonograph is set to revolve once per second, making the metal disc follow a circular path about 8 inches in diameter. The score is the distance during which the contact is maintained, during 20 seconds (10 trials).

2. *Motor Rhythm* (described on p. 281).

3. *Tapping Key* is a test of the speed of pressing and releasing a telegraphic key during 5-second periods (3 trials).

4. *Serial Discrimination* is a test of the speed of reaction to the four numbers, 1, 2, 3, and 4, exposed visually in random order. The reaction is made by pressing the correct one of four keys which correspond to the numbers. Each key is to be pressed and released by a different finger. The score is the number of correct reactions in 2 minutes.

5. *Brown Spool-Packer* is a test of the speed of packing spools in a small box, using both hands. Score is the number of spools packed in 3 minutes.

6. *Miles' Drill Test* is a test of the speed of rotating the handle of a small hand drill for 10 seconds (3 trials).

PUZZLE TYPE TESTS

One group of mechanical tests involves assembly or stripping of devices and requires reasoning or random manipulation. Perceptual comparisons of shape, size, and relationships are basically important, but may not be highly represented in the scores.

One of the earliest tests of mechanical assembly is the Puzzle Box of Healy and Fernald (1911). The glass-framed lid of a small wooden box may be opened by releasing, with a buttonhook, strings that have been made secure over pegs. The order in which the strings must be released can be determined by visual examination of the box, inside and out. Freeman (1916) designed a similar puzzle box, in which eleven levers had to be moved in a particular sequence in order to open the box (Illus. 99). The scores of both of these tests revealed

ILLUS. 99. FREEMAN'S PUZZLE BOX

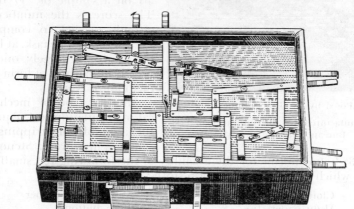

(Courtesy of the C. H. Stoelting Co., Chicago, Ill.)

large differences between sexes, and 5-minute periods were found to be too short for average adults.

Another test of this type is O'Connor's (1928) Wiggly-Block Test. Nine similar pieces of wood, with some edges cut wavy, are to be fitted together to form a solid block $9 \times 9 \times 12$ inches. The score is the time needed to finish the task.

None of these three tests has shown high enough reliability to be considered a good measuring technique. The low retest reliabilities probably reflect the fact that some persons take a long time to solve the puzzle on the first trial, but have a good memory of the solution on second trial, and that others may enjoy some chance successes on the first trial but fail to remember the solution later.

Posed by Dr. Bing Chung Ling

(Manufactured by the Educational Test Bureau, Minneapolis, Minn.)

The Minnesota Spatial Relations Test (Illus. 100) uses an elaborate set of four form boards, each of which has about sixty pieces varying in size or shape. This is an extension of a similar test devised by Link (1919). Paterson *et al.* (1930), finding Link's test was too short to give suitable reliabilities, made it about eight times as long and achieved a retest reliability of .84 on a sample of 217 boys. The score is the number of seconds needed to complete the assembly. The task, at least for adults, is largely one of visual comparison of form and methodical work.

Another type of mechanical manipulation test requires the assembly or stripping of common hardware. Stenquist (1923) found norms for the assembly of the following ten small objects which he purchased at local stores:

Clothes pin with wire spring	Wire bottle stopper
Hunt paper clip	Push button
Rubber hose shutoff	Small door lock
Chain with split links	Cupboard latch
Bicycle bell	Mouse trap

The objects, taken apart, are presented to the examinee one at a time in order of difficulty. A small screw driver is available to the examinee. The score is the number of correct assembly operations completed in 30 minutes.

Paterson *et al.* (1930) believed that the odd-even reliability of the Stenquist Assembly Test, which was found to be .72 among 217 seventh and eighth grade boys, was not high enough to be considered careful appraisal. Therefore they modified and enlarged the material to include thirty-six items in the Minnesota Mechanical Assembly Tests (Illus. 13). Success in each of these, which was scored on a

10-point scale, was found to correlate .28 or better with total scores. The highest correlations with totals were found to be in the assembly of the bicycle bell, .75; the clothes pin, .68; spark plug, .66; and chain, .64. The odd-even correlation of the total test (using the Spearman-Brown prediction formula) was .94.

The Purdue Mechanical Assembly Test (Illus. 101) consists of

ILLUS. 101. PURDUE MECHANICAL ASSEMBLY TEST

(By permission of Dr. Joseph Tiffin and the Purdue Research Foundation.)

eight similar boxes, each of which contains parts to be assembled—levels, gears, racks, pinions, and worms. One is shown the nature of the task by using one box to illustrate the task, then a certain time is allowed for assembling each of the other seven boxes. No familiar objects are included, and all principles of mechanical operation are used. A reliability of .88 is reported, and correlations of from .35 to .55 with supervisor ratings of machinists and machinist apprentices.

CORRELATION ANALYSES

A number of correlational analyses, which include performance and motor tests, have been cited in Chapter VIII. Several typical analyses, planned to evaluate factors in mechanical and motor ability, are described here. Many persons have questioned whether there is a general motor ability which underlies success in all kinds of muscular skills. The almost universal conclusion is that, although certain motor skills show high positive intercorrelations, there is no general or elemental motor factor. Perrin (1921) and Muscio (1922) came to this conclusion after applying balancing, tapping, reaction time, strength, and dexterity tests to small groups of adults.

Garfiel (1923) attempted to find an answer to this question by intercorrelating the results of sixteen tests and ratings of fifty college sophomore girls. Using the appraisals listed in Illus. 102, she found that the correlations with Alpha scores were nearly zero, and that the median of all the sixty-six intercorrelations of motor tests

ILLUS. 102. TESTS USED IN A STUDY OF MOTOR ABILITY

Test	Retest Reliability	Correlation with Criteria
1. MENTAL: United States Army Alpha Score	.92 .	. . .02
2. MOTOR SPEED:		
a. Tapping speed: Hand metal stylus, 60 seconds . . .	.69 .	. . .22
b. Foot speed: Stationary running, 30 seconds	.76 .	. . .23
c. Running: 100 yards indoor track	.85 .	. . .63
3. MOTOR CO-ORDINATION:		
a. Steadiness: Brass plate and stylus, 10/64-inch hole, contents in 60 seconds	.61 .	. . .19
b. Three-hole test: Insert stylus, 100 times	.60	
c. Target throw: Tennis ball, 12 feet, five throws . .	.07 .	. . .20
d. Picking up paper with teeth: Stand holding right toe in left hand, crossing right foot behind the body, then leaning over and grasping a piece of writing paper made to stand on the floor by folding once the long way. Passed if accomplished in 60 seconds with less than three falls		. . .44
e. Tricks: Difficult hand and foot co-ordination		. . .29
4. PREFERENCES: A check list of 12 things to do on a June afternoon, 6 of which were athletic games		. . .31
5. ANATOMICAL:		
a. Height		. . .02
b. Weight		. . .23
6. STRENGTH:		
a. Hand dynamometer	.70 .	. . .25
b. Back dynamometer	.81 .	. . .40
c. Leg dynamometer	.71 .	. . .20
d. Chest strength		. . .22
e. Lung capacity		. . .28
7. CRITERION: Ratings of 6 judges on motor ability as shown by strong accurate quick movements. Retest reliability of mean ratings, after 16 weeks was	.92 .	. . .92

(Garfiel, 1923. Arranged from Tables VI and VII. By permission of the *Archives of Psychology.*)

was .15. Eleven of these were negative; twenty-five correlations lay between zero and .20, and only four were above .40. However, a battery of tests was selected by a multiple-correlation technique which agreed with the criterion with a correlation of .79. The battery included the eight tests shown in Illus. 103. The first test, Running 100 Yards, was allotted by this technique a weight equal to approximately twice the weight of all the other tests together. The fourth test, Tricks, was allotted one third of the weight of the running test. In order to raise the prediction of the criteria, scores of two of the tests, Steadiness and Leg Dynamometer, were subtracted from the total. Garfiel concluded that there was as much evidence for the existence of a general motor factor here, as for the existence of a general mental factor among mental tests. Small and zero correlations in any battery of reliable tests, however, are probably more indicative of the presence of several unrelated factors.

ILLUS. 103. PREDICTION OF GENERAL MOTOR ABILITY

	Multiple Correlation
1. Running 100 yards	.63 *
2. Picking up paper with teeth	.70
3. Back dynamometer	.74
4. Tricks: Complex condition	.75
5. Steadiness	.77
6. Leg dynamometer	.78
7. Tapping	.77
8. Hand dynamometer	.79

* Numbers below this one show increases due to adding each test to the previous total.

(Garfiel, 1923, Table IX. By permission of *Archives of Psychology*.)

Seashore (1930) selected eight tests of serial motor skills and applied them to fifty college men. He concluded that the marked independence of highly reliable tests argued against the existence of a general motor ability.

A thorough study of mechanical abilities of high school boys was made by Paterson *et al.* (1930), who measured more than 150 boys on seven reliable tests:

1. Minnesota Assembly Boxes A, B, and C
2. Minnesota Spatial Relations Tests A, B, C, and D
3. Minnesota Paper Form Boards A and B
4. Card Sorting
5. Packing Blocks
6. Nine Hole Steadiness
7. Stenquist Mechanical Aptitude Picture Tests

The authors also evaluated interest, home activities, technical information, and the quality and quantity of articles made in the shop, and concluded that the low intercorrelations among different measures of mechanical ability suggest a high degree of specificity. Mechanical ability as measured by the tests and shop ratings had no relation to test scores of intelligence or agility, and little correspondence with ratings of environment. With tests requiring no mechanical information, they found no mean differences between academic and mechanical or engineering students on either the high school or the college level.

A factorial analysis of motor abilities among seventy-six high school boys was made by Buxton (1938), using Thurstone's method. He selected tests which

1. Included both simple and complex behavior
2. Avoided the influence of fatigue
3. Had high interest value
4. Allowed simple directions
5. Included only serial, repetitive action, where no choices were to be made

The tests used by Buxton were:

1. *Steadiness* (thrusting). Student (S) thrusts a stylus into holes on a brass plate. The score is the number of thrusts which do not touch the plate, made from a standard distance at a constant rate. Ten trials were made at each hole. The holes were smaller as the test progressed.

2. *Steadiness* (stationary). Student (S) holds the stylus in each hole for 10 seconds. The score is the number of contacts with the plate.

3. *Tapping* (three discs). Student (S) taps three metal discs in succession as fast as he can. The discs, 2 inches in diameter, are placed at the corners of a 6½-inch equilateral triangle.

4. *Tapping* (two bars). Student (S) taps as fast as possible between two vertical metal bars, 2 inches apart, with a stylus mounted on a frame strapped to the forearm to prevent wrist motion.

5. *Tapping* (wrist turn). Student (S) turns an aluminum handle as frequently as possible through an arc of 135 degrees.

6. *Packing* (cubes). Student (S) fills a low box with 64 1¾₁₆-inch cubes as quickly as possible.

7. *Packing* (spool). Student (S) fills a tray with spools as frequently as possible in a short time interval.

8. *Rotor* (mobility). Student (S) turns the handle of a small hand drill as fast as possible.

9. *Rotor* (pursuit). Student (S) tries to keep a stylus on a dime-sized disc which is rotating on a phonograph-like turntable.

The tests were repeated six or eight times, and gains on the four tests which showed the greatest average gain were included with the test scores in the statistical analysis. The analysis resulted in six factors, of which two were tentatively named by the author. One factor was called steadiness, because it was found to be significant only in the two steadiness tests and in them it was large. The second factor was labeled manipulation. It was found to be large in the two packing tests. It therefore might be described as hand-and-eye coordination in prehension, short-carry, and placing operations. None of the other four factors showed large loadings in any tests. One factor was found in tests which involved the larger muscles of the forearm, upper arm, and shoulder. Another factor was found only in the 2-bar tapping, where no visual control was needed, and where the arm movements were ballistic, that is, without precise control after being initiated. Another factor was fairly large in wrist-turning tests and another in packing-test gains. The author concludes that no general motor factor was demonstrated here, and that a larger battery of tests would be needed in order to show the patterns which may exist.

A factorial analysis was reported by Morris (1939) of results of applying the Pintner-Paterson Series, the Sylvester Form Board, the Lincoln Hollow Square, the Witner Cylinder Test, the Dearborn Form Board 3, the Porteus Maze, the Minnesota Paper Form Board, the Henmon-Nelson Intelligence Test, and the Brown Personality Test. From thirty-three scores for each of fifty-six boys nine years of age, he found three common factors. One factor was identified as Spatial Thinking, a second as Perceptual Discrimination, and a third as an Ability to Discover or to Use a Rule of Procedure. Few of the factor loadings were large, and the variances of many of the tests were not well accounted for by the loadings from these factors.

A report by Harrell (1939) showed the relationships between thirty-four tests which were applied to ninety-one cotton mill machine-fixers in Georgia. The entire battery, which required about 7 hours of work, included three of the Minnesota tests: the spatial relations boards, the assembly boxes, and the paper form boards. Among the seven tests from Whitman's Manual Dexterity Series were the nut and bolt assembly, peg boards, and pin boards. Three of Crockett's Manual Dexterity tests were used: screwing nuts on bolts, packing blocks, and laying blocks along a strip. The seven MacQuarrie tests and four of Thurstone's spatial tests were included to represent paper-and-pencil techniques. Additional information included age, school grade completed, experience on mechanical jobs, foremen's ratings of competence and mechanical ability, self-ratings of interest, and three of Thurstone's tests of verbal relations.

From an analysis five factors appeared and were tentatively named Perception of Detail, Verbal Relations, Spatial Visualization, Youth or Inexperience, and Manual Dexterity. These factors were identified from the tests which had the highest loadings in one factor and small loadings in other factors. The first three of these factors are similar to those described by Thurstone, and reported in Chapter

VIII. The Youth or Inexperience factor resulted from classifications by age and foremen's ratings.

Some of Harrell's findings about commonly used tests are contrary to usual beliefs. Thus, the Minnesota Mechanical Assembly Test did not appear to depend upon either manual dexterity or experience on mechanical jobs. On the second trial this test lost most of the Visualization factor and became more dependent upon the Perception of Detail factor. Furthermore, the Minnesota Assembly Test, the Minnesota Spatial Relations, and the Wiggly-Block Assembly, all of which involve the handling of blocks, had practically the same factor patterns as the Thurstone Spatial Relations Tests and Stenquist Mechanical Tests, *both of which are limited to paper-and-pencil situations.* These results support the hypothesis that performance tests which do not require great precision or speed of movement may usually be interpreted as tests of perception (comparison of details) or spatial imagery and reasoning. These two factors were again clearly shown to be independent. One demands rapid comparison of objects which are directly perceived, and the other requires that one imagine how things would look if they were put together or rotated.

The AAF made extensive studies of tests of visualization, mechanical comprehension, and motor coordination. The results, reported by Guilford and Lacey (1946), show that there appears only one visualization factor which accounts for 2-dimensional, 3-dimensional, and moving-parts visualization. If the forms are familiar, a visual memory factor is important. From a factorial analysis of seventeen tests studied, the following seven factors appear: (1) mechanical experience, shown by information, (2) perceptual speed, (3) verbal reading, (4) length estimation, (5) visualization, (6) spatial relations, as shown in complex motor-coordination tests and paper-and-pencil mechanical-movement tests, and (7) general or mathematical reasoning.

Jones and Seashore (1944) have summarized their own and others' work in measuring the growth and interrelation of motor and mechanical abilities. They point out that there is no evidence of a general factor in fine motor skills, but a great deal of evidence of group factors or specific factors. Low intercorrelations are the rule for all ages above two years. It also appears that although motor tests are subject to large practice effects, the practiced subjects show the same independence of motor test results as the unpracticed.

They further point out that group factors are dependent upon similar musculature, similar extent of movement, similar sensory components, and similar time and space patterns. The least variable pattern is usually more important in determining correlations than the others.

This specificity of factors in fine motor skills makes it unlikely that specific job performance will be well predicted even from a highly reliable motor test. Thus it was found that Seashore's battery of six motor tests had no predictive value for typing performance or for a typical factory machine operation. Among the best predictions are those of rifle marksmanship from steadiness tests, and of fighter pilots' work from complex coordination tests, but in neither case was the motor test an adequate basis for selection.

Guilford and Lacey conclude that while there are numerous batteries labeled mechanical ability or manual dexterity, there is little evidence that such broad unitary abilities exist or that they predict rate or final level of learning of complex practical skills. They point out that careful training in attitude as well as in skill will often yield curves of development which radically change one's position in a group.

These results indicate clearly that there is no single test of mechanical aptitude or ability, but that mechanical work of various kinds requires various combinations of about seven fairly independent mental abilities, and several more sensory and motor abilities. The best predictions will eventually come from comparing individual and job profiles.

APPLICATIONS

Reviews of the many hundreds of applications of mechanical tests to groups of apprentices and workers appear in periodicals, particularly *The Psychological Bulletin* and *The Journal of Applied Psychology*. The AAF volume by Melton (1948) gives a valuable summary. Lawshe (1948), who has discussed and presented charts of more than a hundred such studies, stresses the idea that better prediction will come when batteries of tests of independent abilities are evaluated by comparisons with ratings of success in the independent kinds of skills needed in a particular occupation. He also believed that batteries of primary-ability or aptitude tests will probably not distinguish well between candidates for various skilled trades, but that tests of specific knowledge will do this effectively and also correlate fairly well with success in apprentice training. For instance, the Purdue Test of Electrical Information is as effective as any other single test in predicting success among electrician trainees. Similarly, the Michigan Vocabulary Profile Test, which gives separate scores for eight independent fields of knowledge, was shown by Swartz and Schwab (1941) to correspond significantly to ratings of ability among thirty-seven research engineers. Three tests from this profile, those for physical science, biological science, and mathematics, yielded a critical score that included all of the two groups of engineers who were rated highest, and none of the two groups who were rated lowest, while somewhat less than half of the two middle groups reached this critical score. Means and quartile ranges of scores on the Michigan Vocabulary Profile Test were issued by Greene (1949) for twenty-four occupational groups, showing very significant differences between groups. The size of his samples, however, makes it necessary to repeat this work and to secure more valid criteria and samples from different parts of the country. Simply demonstrating that a particular average profile is typical of many successful workers in an occupation does *not* indicate that the profile has much significance for individual prediction. It is necessary to show direct relationships between profile scores and success or failure on the job.

Bennett and Fear (1943) reported that operators of lathes, grinders, milling machines, and Bullard Automatics took Bennett's Test of Mechanical Comprehension and a hand-tool dexterity test. All of those scoring in the upper 20 per cent on both tests were rated as average or above average on the job, while only 14 per cent of those who were in the lowest 30 per cent according to their test scores were so rated.

Crissey (1944) reported similar results when he applied the Minnesota Spatial Relations Test and two peg boards to a group of tool-setters. Sixty-nine per cent of those in the highest third of the composite test scores were rated as above average, while only 30 per cent of the middle third and none of the lowest third were so rated.

Jurgensen (1943) reported that the Minnesota Rate of Manipulation Test (Illus. 6), as revised by Ziegler, showed a correlation of .60 with the combined ratings of three supervisors on the speed of work of sixty operators of converting machines in a paper mill.

Tiffin and Lawshe (1944) report that employees of a hosiery mill with the poorest finger dexterity, as measured by the Purdue Peg Board, cost a company $59 each in minimum make-up before they "made the rate," while employees in the best dexterity group cost only $36.40. The authors believe that tests can indicate who should be trained, where training should start, and how adequate the training has been.

Knowles (1945) reported that a battery containing one written test of ability to learn, a carefulness test of sorting metal pieces, and one assembling-of-bolts test was effective in selecting general airplane mechanics. Of the highest half of those tested by this battery, 39 per cent were later rated as good, 58 per cent as fair, and only 4 per cent as poor.

Accident proneness was detected by Williams (1943) by a series of manipulation tests which included dotting of small circles on a revolving disk, reaction to visual or auditory stimuli by pressing the correct button, and hand-arm steadiness and strength. Those with scores in the lowest quarter had approximately twice the accident rate of the average of those in the other three quarters.

Although these studies yield practical results, most of them exhibit two rather serious shortcomings: they are based on rather small samples and use only one or two tests, so that comparisons to show which are the best tests are seldom possible. A large amount of research is now going on, which will eventually yield unique and more valuable measures.

STUDY GUIDE QUESTIONS

1. What sorts of independent mechanical skills, or factors, can be measured by paper-and-pencil tests?
2. How do tests of mechanical principles differ from those of mechanical knowledge?
3. What evidence is there that pictorial tests are superior to verbal tests in measuring mechanical principles?
4. What are the principal skills needed in a pure test of visualization?
5. Distinguish between tests of mechanical knowledge and tests of mechanical principles.
6. What is the principal characteristic of visualization tests?
7. What are the main types of motor-coordination tests?
8. How is reaction time related to the sensory organs and to age?
9. What is included in developmental tests of agility?
10. How do ballistic movements differ from precision movements?
11. What tests are available to measure motor rhythm?
12. What factors have usually appeared from analyses of batteries of mechanical and motor tests?
13. What are the usual components of batteries of mechanical-ability tests?
14. What are the principal visual functions and how are they measured?
15. What are the usual methods of measuring agility and strength?
16. What are the main varieties of dexterity tests?
17. How are motor rhythms best measured?
18. What are the usual components of batteries of motor tests?
19. To what extent are mental and motor tests usually correlated?
20. Are the various measures of steadiness highly related?
21. What practice effects are commonly found in motor tests?
22. What factors appear most frequently in tests of mechanical abilities?
23. How well do batteries of tests predict success in mechanical and engineering work?

CHAPTER X

TESTS OF SPECIAL APTITUDES

In the four preceding chapters measures of general aptitude and of primary abilities or aptitudes, measures of achievement, and measures of mechanical and motor skills were presented. Clerical and professional aptitudes were included in Chapter VII because they seem closely related to academic achievements. Measures specifically designed to appraise aptitudes for particular kinds of work or avocations remain to be illustrated. Measures related to vision, hearing, music, and graphic arts will be discussed here.

CHARACTERISTICS OF TESTS

Measures of special aptitudes are generally designed to give evidence in a narrow area of skills that are thought to be basic to a particular type of work. Most of them, therefore, seek to exclude factors of learning, intelligence, reasoning, and perceptual speed, which are fairly general and apply to many situations. Measures of aptitude are often confused with evaluations, or preference, or appreciation. While appreciation seems to be somewhat related to ability to recognize or to produce artistic or other works, certainly many are able to define and recognize different forms of art and music who cannot produce them and have no particular preference for one form. There are at least four little-related aptitudes here:

  a. To define or recognize differences; perceptual and conceptual.
  b. To construct original work.
  c. To perform as in music, dance, drama.
  d. To appreciate or prefer.

The last of these, appreciation, is a dynamic factor. (See Chapters XX and XXI.) The first three are dealt with here. The measurements of two sensory functions, vision and hearing, are reported, then appraisals of ability to recognize differences, to compose original work and to perform in music and graphic art.

VISION

The most widely used sense modality in everyday living is vision, and consequently any impairment of it is likely to cause serious need for remedy or adjustment. While various surveys show only about five-hundredths of one per cent blind persons in the United States, approximately $\frac{2}{10}$ per cent have part sight ($\frac{20}{70}$ to $\frac{20}{200}$), and about 30 per cent whose vision is seriously reduced, so that they need glasses or some other correction.

Although blind persons can succeed in many fields of study and in many occupations, a large number of industrial and business jobs require constant use and much skill of some visual function. These functions include the following:

a. Acuity. Acuity is the ability to see a pattern distinctly at a certain distance, with each eye separately and with both eyes together. This depends upon the shape of the eyeball, lens, and cornea, and obstructions in the path of light after it enters the eye, as well as the nerve connections to the brain.

b. Phoria. The muscular balance of the external muscles of each eye is called phoria. Imbalance may turn one eye vertically or laterally more than the other. Many people have some imbalance which may cause eye strain in close work. In extreme cases, known as cross eye, only one eye is used at a time.

c. Binocular depth perception. Careful laboratory tests show that binocular depth perception is usually nearly eight times as good with two good eyes as with one eye. It is accomplished in the brain by the fusion or blending of different images from two good eyes.

d. Color vision. The ability to distinguish fine differences in shade and hue is called color vision. It is dependent upon photosensitive cells in the retina of the eye. The best color-vision tests involve matching samples for both brightness and saturation, as well as reporting afterimages of colors.

e. Eye dominance. Many persons have a strong preference for sighting with one eye rather than with the other. The preference is due to the relative acuity, phoria, lateral brain dominance, and possibly to other factors.

The medical profession has developed simple charts as well as elaborate devices for measuring acuity, phoria, and other visual functions. There are a number of tools for nonclinical use by a layman.

One of the best single instruments now available for school, industrial, or business use is called the Orthorater. It yields scores on all five functions in from 3 to 6 minutes of minimum testing time. The Orthorater, shown in Illus. 104, consists of a stereoscope, lenses

ILLUS. 104. THE ORTHORATER

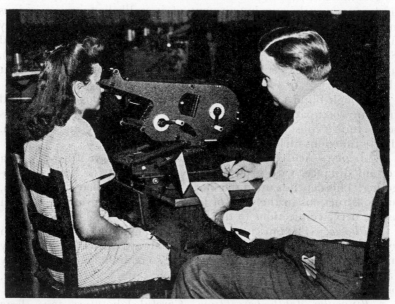

(By permission of Bausch and Lomb Optical Co., Rochester, N.Y.)

for near and far adjustments, and a set of stimulus cards with standard illumination. It is composed of twelve separate tests: seven for far vision, the optical equivalent of 26 feet, and five for near vision, 13 inches (Illus. 105). Each of these tests has been proved to be related to successful performance on various types of occupations. Individual profile sheets are quickly compared with a job profile sheet which shows shaded areas for the unacceptable scores. Thus in Illus. 105 the individual's scores meet the visual requirements of the job in all respects except for acuity of the right eye and for vertical phoria.

Tiffin (1947) and his colleagues have reported many careful applications of tests of vision in school and industry and show good results from more careful selection of workers for situations where good

ILLUS. 105. ORTHORATER SCORE CARD

VISUAL PERFORMANCE PROFILE

FAR **ELECTRIC SOLDERERS   1948**

PHORIA	VERTICAL	1	X	1			3	4	5	6	7	8		8
	LATERAL	2	X	1	2	3	4	5	6	7	8	9	10	11	12	13	14	15

ACUITY	BOTH	3	0	1	2	3	4	5	6	7	8	9	10	11	12	13	14	15
	RIGHT	4	0	1	2	3	4	5	6	7	8	9	10	11	12	13	14	15
	LEFT	5	0	1	2	3	4	5	6	7	8	9	10	11	12	13	14	15

UNAIDED

DEPTH	6	0	.1	2	3	4	5	6	7	8	9	10	11	12
COLOR	7	0	1	2	3	4	5	6	7	8	9	10	11	12	13	14	15

NEAR

ACUITY	BOTH	1	0	1	2	3	4	5	6	7	8	9	10	11	12	13	14	15
	RIGHT	2	0	1	2	3	4	5	6	7	8	9	10	11	12	13	14	15
	LEFT	3	0	1	2	3	4	5	6	7	8	9	10	11	12	13	14	15

UNAIDED

PHORIA	VERTICAL	4	X			2	3	4	5	6	7	8	9
	LATERAL	5	X	1	2	3	4	5	6	7	8	9	10	11	12	13	14	15

(By permission of Bausch and Lomb Optical Co., Rochester, N.Y.)

vision is required. The Orthorater can be operated by a careful layman with little training.

Davis (1946) reported correlations between clinical tests of acuity and phoria and the corresponding Orthorater scores for 32 women and 63 men, ranging from sixteen to sixty-five years. The correlations (p. 598) were as follows:

	Far	Near
acuity, both eyes	.82	.71
acuity, right eye	.76	.64
acuity, left eye	.82	.70
lateral phoria	.53	.64

These figures show correlations between the two procedures which are about as high as the reliabilities for each procedure will allow. In general the acuity scores show close relationships. The lateral phoria scores are too low to permit predictions, which in this instance was due in part to the rough measurement of phorias by the clinical method.

Another somewhat similar instrument, the Betts Telebinocular, is a stereoscope mounted on a stand with a movable rack for holding cards. It requires more technical competence than the Orthorater, but this can be acquired by a layman. It yields reliable scores for near and far vision, muscular balance, binocular fusion, and eye dominance.

A still more simple apparatus is the Eames' Eye Tester, which provides a series of cards and a hand stereoscope which can be used by a teacher, after a little training, to detect eye defects that need professional care. It yields fairly reliable results for near and far vision, astigmatism, binocular fusion, and eye dominance.

Good color vision is needed by artists and by certain technical workers, for example, cable splicers and chemical technicians. In the most common type of color blindness which is present in about 4 per cent of males and less than 1 per cent of females, there is a reduction in ability to distinguish red, purple, and green from a gray of similar brightness. Only a few people are unable to distinguish blues from yellows. Exact measurement of color blindness is difficult because the brightness and texture of the colored objects often give clues which allow persons to pass the test even though they may not have good color vision.

Ishihara (1939) published a booklet of colored spots printed on a good grade of cardboard, in which numbers and figures are delineated by dots of different color but of the same or nearly the same brightness as the background. While this test is good for rough, quick screening, it is not very satisfactory for diagnostic work. Some color-blind people can pass it. Another widely used test, the Holingren Yarn Test, employs colored skeins of wool, which the subject is asked to sort by colors. The Farnsworth Dichotomous Test for Color Blindness (1947) and the Farnsworth-Munsell 100-Hue Test for Anomalous Color Vision (1947) are made of colored plastic and printed on mat paper. All of these tests have colors that are likely to fade in time.

The best tests of color vision are made with pure spectral lights thrown on a white surface which has no observable texture. Such tests, however, are only made in specially constructed laboratories.

HEARING

Next to vision, hearing is probably the most important means of contact with environment. The two main dimensions of hearing are intensity and tone or pitch. Many people are deaf to certain tones, particularly high tones, and to certain intensities, usually the extreme intensities. Most deafness is caused by infections or injuries to the middle ear, which reduce the sound vibrations reaching the inner ear. The best instruments for measuring loss of hearing are called audiometers, and several good models are now available from the Western Electric Company of New York and the Maico Company of Minneapolis. When using the most common type, a group of listeners put on headphones, then write the numbers which they hear spoken. A phonograph record furnishes the stimuli to the headphones. One Western Electric Company model requires the individual being tested, when he no longer hears a tone in his headphones, to push a button and thus make a small electric light shine. The examiner regulates the intensity and frequency of vibrations by dials and records the results. This model has the advantage of being adapted for testing small children and also of including the extremely high frequencies (Illus. 106).

ILLUS. 106. AUDIOMETER

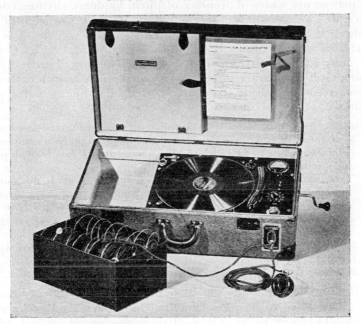

(By permission of the Western Electric Co.)

The results may then be charted showing the range of tones which can be heard with various degrees of loudness. Audible tones range through about ten octaves on the piano, from 30 double vibrations (d.v.) a second to 20,000 double vibrations. Most conversation does not range below 100 d.v. or above 7,000 d.v. Intensities in decibels are generally measured downward from an arbitrary zero placed at normal hearing. Inability to hear intensities of about 60 decibels below normal is considered *deafness*. A loss of from 20 to 60 decibels would be considered *hard of hearing*.

MUSICAL APTITUDE

There are three kinds of musical-aptitude tests: discrimination and information, rendition, and composition. The well-standardized tests in the field are for discrimination and information, but some tests of rendition will also be described.

Discrimination

Probably the most widely used tests of musical discrimination are those of Seashore (1919). By means of standard phonograph records one may secure scores of accuracy of pitch, loudness, rhythm, consonance, and tonal-sequence discrimination. The 1939 revision of the Seashore tests has three levels of difficulty or series. Series A is for unselected groups, Series B for musical groups, and Series C is a still more refined instrument for individual testing. Three 12-inch phonograph records are provided with a complete test on each side of each record. Separate scores are secured by standard testing procedures for:

1. *Pitch:* discrimination of small differences between the frequencies of vibration of two tones with intensities and duration held constant
2. *Intensity:* ability to judge which of two tones are the louder, with pitch and duration constant
3. *Time:* ability to indicate which of two short periods is the longer. The limits of the periods are marked by a pure tone of short duration
4. *Timbre:* discrimination between two complex tones which have the same total energy, but which differ in the application of the energy
5. *Tonal Memory:* ability to indicate which note in a short melody has been changed in its repetition. One note only is changed by a whole tone
6. *Rhythm:* the ability to discriminate short rhythmic patterns

The scores of fifth-grade, eighth-grade, and college students (nearly one thousand of each) were tabulated by Seashore, and then converted into centile ranks. The median scores showed marked differences although the groups overlapped almost 100 per cent. For instance, in Pitch the median fifth-grade pupil had about 67 per cent of items correct; the eighth-grade pupil, 78 per cent; and the college student, 81 per cent. The eighth-grade scores were thought to be typical of average adults. The reasons for differences among these groups are not clear. It may be that the younger groups make poorer scores because of inability to understand the directions or unwillingness to pay attention. On the other hand, it may be that acuity of discrimination improves by maturation during adolescence.

The effect of repetition of the Seashore Measures of Musical Talent was reported by Farnsworth (1931) to be small under the standard test conditions. C. E. Seashore (1919) and Brennan (1926) also reported that special musical training has little effect upon test scores. Whipple (1903) and R. H. Seashore (1926), however, reported marked improvements through training in pitch discrimination and rhythm respectively. More research is needed to show the limits of individual improvement, particularly among those who at present make low scores because of poor interest and lack of opportunity to hear music which has been accurately reproduced.

A number of similar tests have been prepared. Kwalwasser and Dykema (1930) published ten phonographic tests, the first seven of which are much like the Seashore tests. The last three involve judgments of pleasantness and association of images with tonal and rhythmic sequences. Ortmann (1929) devised tests of discrimination of pitch, intensity, and fusion, and of memory for pitch, rhythm, melody, and harmony. Tests of absolute pitch have been described, but not yet standardized. Bachern (1937) tested 103 persons for absolute pitch by asking them to identify notes struck on a piano. Seven of them were correct for every piano note, and for other musical instruments as well. Forty-four made only small errors, or errors of exactly one octave. He proposed a theory which makes absolute pitch dependent in part upon "tone chroma" within the octave.

Information

Several information tests have been standardized. Those of Kwalwasser are typical of the best. The Kwalwasser-Ruch (1924) Test of Musical Accomplishment was designed to measure ability to read musical notation from the fourth to the twelfth grade. Ten separate tests were provided to indicate:

1. Recognition of names of musical symbols
2. Recognition of names of notes in a scale
3. Detection of pitch errors in a familiar melody
4. Detection of time errors in a familiar melody
5. Recognition of pitch names
6. Knowledge of key signatures
7. Knowledge of time signatures
8. Knowledge of note values
9. Knowledge of rest values
10. Recognition of familiar melodies from notation

The items were arranged within each test according to order of difficulty, and the mean scores for four thousand children were reported. Most of the tests showed steady progress throughout the grades, but Kwalwasser found some evidence that the last two tests showed little improvement beyond the seventh grade. Girls did slightly better than boys, but the average child was found to be seriously lacking in most of the simplest fundamentals.

Another test by Kwalwasser (1927) measures verbal information about composers, compositions, and instruments. About two hundred true-false and completion items, such as those shown in Illus. 107, were designed for adults who had taken courses in musical appreciation.

ILLUS. 107. MUSICAL VOCABULARY TEST

TEST 9

Directions: The statements found below are either true or false. Read each statement carefully and then underline *true*, if the statement is correct, or *false*, if it is incorrect. The sample is marked as it should be:

Sample: Allemañde is a German dance . . . . True False

---

 1. The fantasia is a composition of strict form . . . . True False
 2. The polonaise is a Polish dance . . . . True False
 3. The oratorio is a scriptural or epic story set to music . . . . True False
 4. The coda is found in the middle section of musical compositions True False
 5. Beethoven substituted the rondo for the scherzo form in the sonata . . . . True False
 6. An etude is a study or lesson . . . . True False
 7. A waltz is written in 2–4 time . . . . True False
 8. A minuet is written in 3–4 time . . . . True False
 9. A scherzo is written in 2–4 time . . . . True False
10. A note represents a time value as well as pitch . . . . . . True False
11. A phrase is longer than a period . . . . True False
12. Polyphonic means literally "many voiced" . . . . True False

(Kwalwasser, 1927, p. 97. By permission of the Bureau of Educational Research, University of Iowa.)

Rendition

Ability to play or sing artistically has been the subject of a number of analytical studies. Seventy-four reports of appraisals of the sound of spoken prose or poetry were reviewed by Metcalf (1938). Early in the century Scripture (1902) used a vibrating membrane to transfer the vibration of the voice to a kymograph record. Shepard (1913) enlarged this apparatus to include separate records for nose and mouth of vibration and the passage of air. Seashore (1927) described an instrument which recorded photographically the pitch and intensity of vocalization over long periods of time. These instruments have been used both for the analysis of the time and intensity pattern of a passage and for the comparison of individual renditions. No simple methods of appraising either a passage or its rendition have appeared as yet. Birkhoff (1933) proposed an elaborate formula for comparing the aesthetic value of passages, in which Orderliness is divided by Complexity. Orderliness referred to alteration, assonance, rhyme, and musical vowels, and Complexity was the total number of speech sounds plus the number of word junctures which did not admit of liaison. Beebe-Canter and Pratt (1937) reported a correlation of .75 between Birkhoff's aesthetic measure and students' preferences for nonsense passages. When meaningful passages were used, the correlation dropped to .08.

Studies of the artistic rendition of a passage are illustrated by Schramm (1935). He reported that short rhythmical intervals in poetry may deviate from equality by as much as 24 per cent without impairing rhythmical effectiveness, and listed a large number of factors which contribute to rhythms, among them repetitive character of melodies, pitch of related or rhymed syllables, and precision and slurring of enunciation, of syllables, and of phrases. The best artists were considered to be those who knew the exact metrical rhythms but who deviated from them in a characteristic manner which usually defied any simple formulation.

Standard tests of sight-singing ability have been devised by Gaw (1928), Salisbury and Smith (1929), and others. The scores are a summation of errors in pitch and time, as well as omissions, hesitations, repetitions, and extra notes. Experienced judges are needed for careful examining, but the method yields fairly reliable scores.

Rendition of piano and violin music has been extensively studied and reported in a series of monographs from the State University of Iowa and also in Seashore's (1938) *Psychology of Music*. Photographic records of pitch, intensity, and timing have been made with great accuracy, and have led to minute comparisons of the performances of great artists as well as others.

Correlational Analyses

The reliabilities of tests of musical discrimination and preference have been extensively reported by Farnsworth (1931), who summarized eighty-eight published studies. He concluded that Seashore's test of pitch and total memory appeared to have sufficient reliability for diagnostic purposes. The Kwalwasser tests and the remainder of the 1919 Seashore tests "should be employed with extreme caution." The following retest reliabilities were reported for the Seashore tests:

pitch, .75; intensity, .66; time, .51; consonance, .65; rhythm, .47; and memory, .83. The Kwalwasser tests of melody and harmonic preferences had reliabilities of approximately .42 and .21 respectively. The entire Seashore battery had a retest reliability of approximately .88 for large single-age groups.

The intercorrelation of the various tests showed similar results for groups of elementary school and high school pupils and adults in several studies. The median intercorrelations of the Seashore tests were approximately .48 for college groups and .25 for lower grades. Tests of Tonal Memory and Pitch showed somewhat higher correlations, as did tests of Rhythm and Time, and Rhythm and Tonal Memory. Nearly zero correlations were reported between tests of Intensity and Consonance. These correlations are, of course, affected by the different reliabilities of the separate tests, and they would be higher if the tests were more reliable.

The Kwalwasser tests of preferences for Melody and Harmony correlated with each other .40 in an eighth-grade group and .29 in a fifth-grade group. The Seashore Tonal Memory Test correlated with the Kwalwasser tests a little better than the other Seashore tests, but all the intercorrelations were rather low; the median was .16 for the eighth grade and .17 for the fifth grade. The fact that adult and college groups usually show higher reliabilities and intercorrelations than younger groups is thought to be best explained by their better ability to pay attention and to follow directions.

The Ortmann Musical Discrimination Tests are reported by Petran (1937) to have reliabilities similar to the Seashore tests. Among a sample of 500 students, the total scores had a retest reliability of .80. The highest retest reliability of a single test was .86 for Pitch Memory and the lowest was .30 for Melody Memory. The intercorrelations of the separate tests ranged from .11 to .47.

The correlations between tests of intelligence and of musical discrimination have usually been found to be low and positive. Farnsworth (1931), summarizing sixteen such studies, reported coefficients between the separate Seashore tests and group mental tests ranging from .45 to —.08 among high school and college groups. The median, which seems to be approximately .10, would doubtless be higher if feeble-minded and brilliant students were included.

Applications

In Seashore's pioneer work (1919) an elaborate series of thirty tests and ratings were combined into profiles such as that shown in Illus. 108. The first five tests were measures of fine discrimination; the next three involved self-estimates of clearness of memories of sensations.

ILLUS. 108. MUSICAL TALENT CHART OF THEODORA

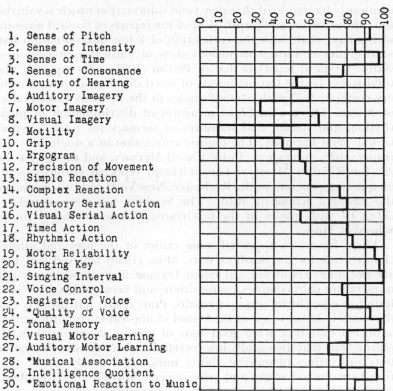

1. Sense of Pitch
2. Sense of Intensity
3. Sense of Time
4. Sense of Consonance
5. Acuity of Hearing
6. Auditory Imagery
7. Motor Imagery
8. Visual Imagery
9. Motility
10. Grip
11. Ergogram
12. Precision of Movement
13. Simple Reaction
14. Complex Reaction
15. Auditory Serial Action
16. Visual Serial Action
17. Timed Action
18. Rhythmic Action
19. Motor Reliability
20. Singing Key
21. Singing Interval
22. Voice Control
23. Register of Voice
24. *Quality of Voice
25. Tonal Memory
26. Visual Motor Learning
27. Auditory Motor Learning
28. *Musical Association
29. Intelligence Quotient
30. *Emotional Reaction to Music

* The items marked with an asterisk represent
estimates in the absence of norms.

(Seashore, 1919, p. 19. By permission of Silver, Burdett and Co.).

Tests 9 to 19 inclusive were measures of motor reactions. Items 20 to 24 appraised vocal rendition. Items 25 to 28 were measures of simple and complex learning of note associations, and Test 29, a standard IQ from a Binet test. Item 30 was a rating of emotional reaction to music. The chart is scaled in deciles of an age group, and the profile was made from records of a ten-year-old girl with remarkable musical talent. Since 1919 nearly all the tests have been made more accurate and some attention has been given to improving ratings. In addition, tests have been devised for preferences among musical compositions.

Elaborate profiles have not been used widely because of the difficulty of constructing them, but nearly everyone who has used them cautiously has reported that they yield information which is valuable to both instructor and pupil. Most of the reports of musical measurements have dealt with the correlation of a few discrimination tests with grades or ratings in various sorts of musical appreciation or skills. A typical report is that of Petran (1937), who reported that total scores on the Ortmann tests of tonal discrimination and memory correlated .57 with average grades in the Peabody Conservatory of Music. The test included measures of discrimination of pitch, rhythm, and fusion; and measures of memory for pitch, rhythm, melody, and harmony. The highest correlation of a single test with conservatory grades was .45 for Chord Memory, and the lowest was .25 for Rhythm Memory. Larson (1938) reported enthusiastically on a testing program in the Rochester, New York, public schools and the Eastman School of Music. The Seashore test scores correlated .59 ± .04 with grades in the first course of musical theory in the School of Music.

There have also appeared some critics of the uses and alleged claims made for the Seashore tests. Moos (1930) believed that they are not measures of musical talent because they stress sensory patterns rather than complex compositions and because they have been found to give chiefly negative results. Pratt (1931) felt strongly that they utterly failed to get at the kernel of musical talent, although he admitted that they were good tests of sensory discrimination. He pointed out that the usually low correlations between discrimination tests and ratings of musical ability indicated a nearly chance relation between test scores and achievement. Mursell (1937) quoted a number of studies which showed low correlations between Seashore tests and appraisal of musical ability, and concluded that the tests had been shown to be invalid.

The writer feels that although some exaggerated statements have undoubtedly been made about the usefulness of the tests of musical discrimination, still they are of value in appraising skills which may be of importance in predicting some aspects of musical success. It seems probable that particular tests of musical discrimination will predict success in particular types of musical skill better than in musical ability of all types. Analytical appraisals of musical memory and complex skills are needed as well as careful studies of their growth.

Although musical discrimination and verbal intelligence tests show small correlations, both have been found to correlate significantly with success in schools of music. Highsmith (1929) found that grades in a college of music correlated .423 with scores in the Terman

Group Intelligence Test, but only .312 with the Seashore tests. Stanton (1929) found it advisable to add a college intelligence test to the Seashore Tests of Musical Talent for purposes of selecting students for the Eastman School of Music.

Two reports which deal with scores of various racial and age groups are included here. The results were obtained from such small groups that they are in need of supplementation. Scores of Southern Negroes on the Seashore Tests of Musical Talent were discussed by Bean (1936). He reported that the Negroes in high school and college were found to be equal to the whites only in tests of rhythm. In all other tests they were definitely inferior. Lenoire (1925), however, reported that two hundred Negro children in the fifth grade had mean scores on the Seashore tests, which were definitely superior to those of a similar group of white children in rhythm and tonal memory, and not inferior in any of the other tests.

GRAPHIC ARTS

Types of Tests

Preference for Pictures or Design. The inclusion of preference tests under the heading of aptitudes may be questioned by some on the ground that preferences are essentially dynamic and not very closely related to ability or aptitude. These tests are included, however, because in many tests marked perceptual and analytical skills are used as a basis for preferences by many persons, particularly by those who do well on the tests.

In the field of appreciation of graphic art, two tests have been developed and widely used: the McAdory Art Test (1929) and the Meier-Seashore Art-Judgment Test (1930, 1940). Both of these require that a choice be made between samples which are presented.

The McAdory Art Test consists of seventy-two plates each of which contains four small variations of one picture (Illus. 16). The original drawings were taken from current art and trade magazines, and the variations involve changes in proportions, intensity, and color, which are described on the record sheet. The subject records his order of preference for each plate. One point is given for each picture ranked according to a key which represents the judgments of 100 experts. The experts included artists, architects, art teachers and critics, art buyers, and lay critics. All the keys used were agreed upon by at least 64 per cent of the experts. Separate scores can be had for the total test and also for six subdivisions: (1) furniture and utensils, (2) textiles and clothing, (3) architecture and related arts, (4) shape and line arrangements, (5) massing of dark and light, (6) color schemes.

The Meier-Seashore Test (1940) consists of 100 small uncolored pairs of pictures (Illus. 109) and a record sheet. One member of each pair of pictures is a reproduction of a recognized masterpiece chosen from landscapes, pottery, portraits, oriental drawings, woodcuts, murals, and medallions. The other member of each pair is a repro-

ILLUS. 109. ART JUDGMENT TEST

San Juan Bridge. The relative proportions of the bridge and the city have been altered.

(Meier-Seashore, 1930, No. 78. By permission of the Bureau of Educational Research and Service, University of Iowa.)

duction of the masterpiece altered in some respect. As these alterations are noted on the record sheet, the examinee's attention is called to them. They include changes of position of an outstanding object, of background, of distribution of light and shade, of horizon line, of perspective, of quality of line, and of the use of curves. Although there are no time limits for the administration of this test, it usually takes from 40 to 60 minutes. The score is the number of choices which correspond to a key. The key was made from the consensus of various artists, sculptors, directors of art training, and art teachers. The items are arranged roughly in order of difficulty of discrimination by experts.

From the application of the McAdory and Meier-Seashore Tests by various investigators to fairly large numbers of persons, it has been found that

1. Retest correlations ranged from .71 to .93, and odd-even correlations of .59 and .65 were found (McAdory, 1929, and Meier, 1939).

2. The Meier-Seashore and McAdory Tests correlated with each other

.37 in small groups of college or art students (Carroll and Eurich, 1932, and Wallis, 1930).

3. Age and grade norms show improvement in the Meier-Seashore Tests from nearly chance mean success in the eighth grade to the 87 out of 125 items for art teachers. Norms for the McAdory Test have been secured from the third grade up.

4. Women exceed men in mean scores on both tests by small but fairly significant amounts (Carroll and Eurich, 1932).

5. Artists and students with artistic training have average scores which are significantly higher than similar college students without such training.

6. Studies of Mexican children (Stolz and Manuel, 1931) showed them to have about the same scores as non-Mexican children of the same general environments and age, both groups having very low mean scores. Steggerda (1936) found 300 Navajo Indian children, ages 11 to 16, to be far below the McAdory norms of New York City whites, and concluded that the test does not reveal the artistic ability of these Indians.

7. Correlations between scores on intelligence tests and art appreciation tests are usually between .07 and .26 (Tiebout and Meier, 1936).

8. Correlations between art and appreciation tests and Bernreuter's introversion, submissiveness, and emotional stability tests were all nearly zero, among 218 students (Carroll, 1932).

Other tests which illustrate interesting approaches will be briefly described. Maitland Graves (1948) published a 90-item test of appreciation of nonrepresentative graphic art, called the Design-Judgment Test. Nonrepresentative art was used in order to avoid specific personal reactions to specific objects. The test was devised to indicate the degree to which a subject perceives or at least naively responds to figures which have different degrees of goodness according to the "basic principles of aesthetic order—unity, dominance, variety, balance, continuity, symmetry, proportion, and rhythm." These principles were explained in an earlier book by Graves (1941), *The Art of Color and Design*.

The examinee is asked to look at each page in a 5- by 9-inch booklet and indicate on a separate answer sheet the design which is preferred. Eight of the pages have three designs each and the other 82 pages two designs each, so one can theoretically get about 44 correct by chance.

The test booklet is a beautiful printing job; the backgrounds and figures are done in contrasting flat white, black, and gray. The designs show some texture, and fifteen are drawn or photographed to represent three dimensions. Basic themes and identical designs appear a number of times on several pages, always changed, however, by achromatic pattern or rotation and shown in combination with different forms (Illus. 110).

The test was constructed by trying out 150 items on groups of art teachers, art students, and others in both related and unrelated fields. Items which showed (1) agreement among art teachers, (2) significant differences between art and nonart students, and (3) the higher correlations with total test scores (internal consistency) were retained.

ILLUS. 110. GRAVES DESIGN JUDGMENT TEST, ITEMS 51 AND 74

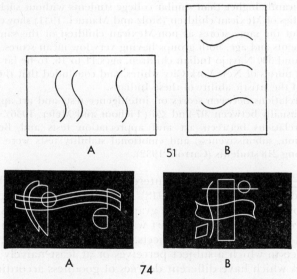

(By permission of Maitland Graves and The Psychological Corporation.)

The scoring is simply the number of correct preferences. Among fourteen groups of students reliability computed from split-half scores ranged from .81 to .86, median .83. The validity of the test is shown by its application to various groups of students *not* included in the original validation. Groups of college students of art, architecture, and illustration all showed means in the neighborhood of .75, while other college students averaged about .46. High school art students had a mean of .56 and nonart .38. These figures lead to the conclusion that much more than half of the high school populations studied prefer the poorer art.

The Whitford Test included fourteen preferences to be made in 15 minutes. Appropriateness of form, line, proportion, rhythm, color, and perspective were to be judged. Tests of one thousand Chicago school children showed that the average fourth grade pupils in "superior" schools exceeded the scores of average eighth grade pupils in "medium" schools.

The University of Wisconsin Test features three aspects of art: unity, proportion, and fitness. Nine plates were prepared, each with five small pictures: a "perfect" picture and four variations. Tests of high school and elementary grades showed progress from preferences of incongruous pictures in the early grades toward preferences for "good art" at the later ages.

Christensen's Test included 105 plates with four colorless pictures to a plate. Separate scores were given for five parts: (1) paintings of groups of persons, (2) pictures of an individual, (3) architecture and sculpture, (4) industrial arts, and (5) designs intended to illustrate abstract art.

Bird (1932) believed that these tests indicate conformity to conventional or commonly experienced products rather than true appreciation of an aesthetic sort. Pintner (1918) and Berliner (1918) found that conformity to conventional pictorial representation was well developed at the age of seven and was almost completely developed at ten, since the ranking of pictures by ten-year-olds was similar to that of average adults.

Voss (1936) found that children in the second, third, fourth, and fifth grades could be taught abstract principles of art composition by having differences between a poor and a good composition pointed out to them. As aesthetic judgment improved, pictures were comprehended less often as substitutes for objects and more often as representations of ideals or moods.

Korpeth-Tippel (1935), working in Vienna, reported that below the age of three years the predominant attitude toward pictures is nonaesthetic. Between the fourth and tenth years aesthetic preferences develop gradually, and the eleventh year shows a marked transition. Nearly all the fourteen-year-olds select the more artistic pictures of the pairs presented.

There is no way of indicating from most of these tests what the nature of aesthetic experience is. All one can say is that under the test conditions certain preferences were indicated. Whether or not a particular person responds to one or several aspects of a picture cannot be known unless we go further and try to find the reasons for his preferences.

Responses to Lines

Closely allied to the evaluations of a whole design is the aesthetic evaluation of small fragments of a design. Three studies, using both matching and reproduction techniques, illustrate this approach.

Poffenberger and Barrows (1924) asked five hundred adults to look at eighteen printed lines, and then to choose, from a list of words, one which described the way each line made them feel (Illus. 111). A marked tendency was found for a slow descending curve to be indicative of sad, lazy, and weak; slow horizontal curves, gentle and

ILLUS. 111. FEELING VALUE OF LINES

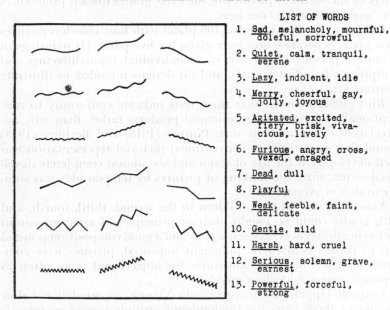

LIST OF WORDS

1. <u>Sad</u>, melancholy, mournful, doleful, sorrowful

2. <u>Quiet</u>, calm, tranquil, serene

3. <u>Lazy</u>, indolent, idle

4. <u>Merry</u>, cheerful, gay, jolly, joyous

5. <u>Agitated</u>, excited, fiery, brisk, vivacious, lively

6. <u>Furious</u>, angry, cross, vexed, enraged

7. <u>Dead</u>, dull

8. <u>Playful</u>

9. <u>Weak</u>, feeble, faint, delicate

10. <u>Gentle</u>, mild

11. <u>Harsh</u>, hard, cruel

12. <u>Serious</u>, solemn, grave, earnest

13. <u>Powerful</u>, forceful, strong

Note: One word is to be chosen from the list to indicate how each line makes you feel.

(Poffenberger and Barrows, 1924. By permission of the *Journal of Applied Psychology*.)

quiet; medium rising curves, merry and playful; rapid rising angles, agitated, furious, and powerful. A conclusion was reached that "direction of line was generally most important, rhythm next, and form least in this particular study."

In the Guilford's (1931) study, twenty-four adjectives were selected and then printed with a blank space. The instructions were:

In the space below you will find a list of adjectives. Take each in turn. You are to think of its meaning and then draw a single line which best expresses the meaning that it conveys to you. Your lines will be graded in their general form, direction, and heaviness. You will have ten minutes in which to complete this test.

The adjectives were: sad, forceful, dead, earnest, playful, tranquil, lively, cruel, joyous, quiet, grave, gentle, lazy, fiery, furious, jolly, hard, agitated, angry, faint, delicate, idle, sorrowful, and strong. The results were scored to show the conformity of an individual to the tendencies of a group of 144 students, 55 of whom were studying design. For instance, the word *idle* was represented as follows:

Form		Direction		Line	
angular	9	horizontal	110	heavy	4
curve	57	upward	9	medium	56
wave	28	down	25	light	84
straight	50				

This tabulation shows that most students drew a light horizontal, curved or straight line for the meaning of the word *idle*. Students who made such lines were given more credit than others. Wider deviations were given less credit than smaller deviations.

The scores of two groups, each containing fifty students in design, showed split-half reliabilities of approximately .65. The tests scores showed correlations of .84 and .83 with teachers' estimates of orig-inality and fertility in design, when both the tests and estimates were corrected for attenuations, but only .58 and .65, when uncorrected. The correction for attenuation theoretically removes chance errors of measurement (Chapter XIII). The actual predictive value of the test, however, is shown by uncorrected correlations. The uncorrected correlations between test scores and art grades were .18 and .58, which are fairly high for this sort of test. The art test scores correlated .18 with the United States Army Alpha for sixty-nine liberal-arts students, and .08 with the American Council on Education College Psychological Examination for freshmen among forty-eight women students. Apparently the line-drawing test involves abilities not called for in verbal mental tests.

Walton (1936) used both the Guilford and the Poffenberger and Barrows techniques. Tests of matching lines with words correlated with giving words to represent lines in the neighborhood of .51. Self-correlations between two trials of either test ranged between .26 and .70 for small groups of children. The correlations between the test of drawing-lines to represent meanings of words and other art tests were all approximately .31. Grades in school, intelligence-test scores, tests of discrimination of color harmony, and sex appeared to be unrelated to tests of matching lines and word meanings.

Responses to Color

Aesthetic responses to single colors have been studied with the hope of finding basic or marked tendencies of feeling or association.

The evidence seems to show that when texture and brightness are eliminated, the response to color is largely a learned one.

Early experiments are well illustrated by Stefanescu-Goanga (1911), who asked six subjects to give introspective reports of the effect of each of a series of colors. The number of times each color was found to be exciting, soothing, pleasing, and displeasing was reported. In general, red, orange, and yellow were stirring, warm and cheerful; green was quieting; blue, indigo, and violet were depressing, serious, cold, and sad; purple was exciting and dignified. The feelings were thought to be aroused because of associations of specific sorts.

Bullough (1910) classified responses to colors into four groups:

1. *Objective:* such as judgments of hue, saturation, and luminosity
2. *Physiological responses:* one's awareness of bodily feelings, such as excitement, weight, and warmth
3. *Associations of specific sorts:* moon, water, fire, and medicine
4. *Character:* i.e., imputing to a color a particular character or set of personal traits

He reported that in most of his observers one class of response predominated and that each type of response was usually incompatible with the others. The objective responses seemed typically intellectual; the physiological, merely adjustive; and the associative, variable or intellectual. The "character" responses were considered to be the most aesthetic because they "objectified emotion."

The findings of Bullough were not supported by the monumental work of Van Allesh (1925), which reported 20 years of observations. He found that tints and shades of all colors, when background and suggestion were avoided, evoked no typical responses, and that all observers were inconsistent in some manner. He found so little consistency in introspective responses to short exposures (7 seconds) that he avoided general conclusions. The most frequent effects reported were activity and passivity, cheerfulness, sadness, earnestness, loudness, softness, friendliness, hostility, warmth, and coolness. He also described the appearance of color as a film, a surface, or a space. He sought to have his observers see only film colors, because the other aspects seemed to arouse additional associations.

He also found disagreements and self-contradictions in preferences for pairs of colors. The responses to color pairs added ideas of harmony, based somewhat on associations with single colors. Thus, a dull brown and a bright orange seemed to represent to one observer severity and pride which did not belong together. Verbal suggestions of solemnity, grief, friendliness, joy, poverty, gave color associations which were not otherwise made. Every color and color pair could be made, by suggestions, to seem commonplace, and nearly all colors could be associated with both the tragic and comic. Color pairs were as susceptible to suggestions as single colors.

Children's responses to color have been studied by about twenty investigators using various materials and techniques. The materials were usually colored papers which were not, of course, pure and which had a definite texture as well as a color. Generalizations from such materials should not be made freely, but the following conclusions are fairly well agreed upon:

1. Infants seventy days of age discriminate between red, orange, green, and blue green when brightness differences are eliminated (Chase, 1937).

2. Four colors are clearly differentiated by the age of fifteen months (Staples, 1932).

3. Children between eight and twenty-four months are most effectively stimulated by red, next yellow, blue and green in order (Holden and Bosse, 1900).

4. Groups of four- and five-year-olds stated that orange was the favorite color; pink, second; and red, third.

Williams (1933) and Walton (1933) found that high scores in sensitivity to color harmony, as shown by the selection of a colored scarf to go with a colored dress on a doll, were found as early as the fourth year of age, but that age-group averages did not exceed chance until the eighth year. The color test scores indicated the amounts of agreement with judgments of experts. There was a gradual increase in scores to the twelfth year. College students did much better than twelve-year-olds. Intelligence-test scores, teachers' ratings of artistic ability, and scores from art tests based on form discrimination were not closely related to scores on this test of color-harmony sensitivity.

Discussion of Tests

From the descriptions of tests of artistic appreciation just given, it appears that

1. Total scores on group tests of 100 items or more give fairly stable group means.

2. Total scores are usually not reliable enough for appraisal of individuals, except when mature students of art have been tested on discrimination of patterns.

3. Low correlations between various subtests in art-appreciation batteries indicate the probable existence of several independent patterns of response. This situation results in ambiguity of interpretation of scores, for a given score can seldom be said to refer to a particular pattern of response.

These conclusions point to the need of more analytical appraisals which would show a person his profile of independent skills. A very fascinating field of research lies in this direction. From a survey of existing work, it seems probable that the following will eventually appear to be among the independent aspects of picture appreciation:

1. Discrimination of moods of isolated lines
2. Discrimination of coherence of (1) lines, (2) areas, and (3) 3-dimensional spaces
3. Discrimination of moods of colors
4. Discrimination of minute variations of theme
5. Other specific associations of personal memories, desires, prejudices or fears, as shown in part by the Rorschach technique (Chapter XXIII).
6. Feelings of satisfaction associated with the activities listed immediately above

With this tentative analysis of aspects of appreciation, let us turn to the consideration of activities involved in artistic composition.

THE NATURE OF ARTISTIC COMPOSITION

The psychological processes actually used in the creation of a design have generally been reported only in fragmentary anecdotal fashion. However, three studies which attempted a systematic observation of artists or others at work have appeared. Grippen (1933) found that creative artistic imagination was rarely demonstrated below the age of five, as shown by spontaneous drawings. By watching artistically talented six-year-olds, he discerned the following seven types of imaginative development:

1. Revision of a single memory image
2. Organization on the nature of a composite from several images, usually related
3. Improvisation of a theme, resembling the source or sources, from a number of images
4. Selection of various elements of aesthetic interest, to which other elements may be added, all based upon a single memorial or sensory experience
5. Compositional expressions arising as a reaction from a single memory touching upon some more or less strong emotional experience
6. Effective expressions appearing in appropriate compositional setting from a single vivid aspect of a larger experience residing in the child as a memorial experience
7. Fusion of compositional elements or aspects into a composition of high character, from a continuing experience over a limited time interval

A comparison of sixty-seven drawings of talented with seventy-nine drawings of nontalented children by Grippen (arranged from p. 80) showed large differences as follows:

Proportion of Drawings	Talented	Nontalented
Exhibiting composition skill	90 per cent	5 per cent
Number of verbal self-criticisms	77	4
Mean number of relevant verbal comments	64.3	72
Mean time per drawing	15 min.	3 min.
Mean number of colors used	3 plus	1 plus

These figures indicate much greater interest and activity, both mental and physical, and greater perseverance on the part of the talented children. The relative importance of motivation and ability cannot be evaluated from this study.

Patrick (1937) recorded the verbal expressions of 50 artists and 50 unpracticed sketchers who agreed to talk about their work as they worked. He concluded that both groups revealed the same four stages, which were also found in poetic creation: preparation, incubation, illumination, and verification.

Lark-Horovitz (1936) studied the drawings of untrained adults, seventy-four men and ninety-six women, whose average age was about twenty-five. The following objects were drawn from memory: violin, chair, church, duck, horse, man, woman, child, flower, automobile, and a country road. She followed Kerschensteiner's (1905) analysis of three general stages of development: schematic representation typical of children, presentation true to appearance in two dimensions, and perspective drawing.

These untrained adults made drawings much like children from six to ten years of age; most of them were of the schematic type. A questionnaire showed that most of them had tried to reconstruct the picture from memory on some logical basis but were unable to disentangle various schemata. Manual ability was thought to be of small importance, but failure to grow in graphic presentation seemed due to lack of training in visual discrimination and synthesis.

To some extent the processes in artistic composition are also indicated by studies of development of drawing ability.

Development of Drawing Ability

An examination of the extensive literature on children's drawing [1] shows a widespread belief in the existence of several stages of development. There is fairly general agreement that the preliminary stage

[1] Ayer (1916), Goodenough (1928), Tomlinson (1934), Meier (1935), and Anastasi and Foley (1936).

is one in which scribbling marks are made with no attempt at representation. Occasional similarities between objects and drawings may be noticed by the child. In the next stage important details of a person or house may be drawn as they are remembered, with only slight success in putting them together. Thus, Illustration 31 shows a man whose hands and legs are attached to his head in the absence of any body. This stage is usually one where motion or use is depicted. In a later stage the idea of the whole tends to dominate, so that the details have their proper relative size and position. Correct perspective is a still later technique. In older children more attention is given to style and fineness of detail and composition. A few specific studies state the ages of development for certain types of discrimination and compositions.

Daniels (1933) found that preschool children, ages two to five years, showed marked preferences for balanced block designs, but that preference for balanced designs was not correlated either with ability to reproduce the design with blocks or with Stanford-Binet scores. Whorley (1933) found that unified compositions of toy trees and of furniture on standard backgrounds were rarely made before the age of four. Such unity increased gradually to the age of ten. The test scores involving outdoor arrangements correlated with scores of indoor arrangements between .29 and .45 for various small groups. The investigator felt that "fitness" may have been a more important factor in the indoor model than in the outdoor model.

Saunders (1936) found that two years of intensive training showed radical changes in art ability among children in the first four grades. The improvement bore a direct relation to amount of instruction and to initial degree of artistic inferiority. Unfavorable home conditions, use of improper materials, lack of motivation, and lack of sensitivity to elements of artistic quality were found to be important deterrents to the development of drawing ability.

These reports all agree that artistic composition in the field of design is very much improved by familiarity with types of composition and their fine points. Interest, amount of mental activity, perseverance, and length of special training were very effective in improving artistic compositions.

Tests of Composition and Representation

The ability to compose an artistic work is not easy to distinguish from the ability to draw mere representations of objects.

Since there are no sharp lines between an artistic picture and one not so artistic, scales of values have been established on the basis of agreement of judges by Thorndike (1916), McCarty (1924), Kline and

Carey (1922 and 1923), and Tiebout (1933). The Thorndike scale is a series of thirty-four drawings, each of different subjects, arranged in order of excellence by sixty artists and sixty art teachers. McCarty's scale consists of three series of thirty-four drawings each, one of persons, one of horses, and one of landscapes. Each series is divided into nine steps in a scale based on ratings of sixty judges. The drawings were collected from children, ages four to eight years. The two Kline-Carey scales are intended to measure two different aspects of composition: representation and design. The first consists of fourteen graded samples of each of the following: house, tree, rabbit, and a figure in action drawn to illustrate a short story. The second includes ten or eleven graded samples of each of the following: illustration, poster, border, and structural design. Each sample is given a numerical value based on order-of-merit selections of 152 judges who were persons with considerable art training. Tiebout (1936) introduced color, and followed the plan of having children illustrate short stories or parts thereof. Paintings were made independently by each child using tempera paints under standard conditions. One hundred children in each grade from the first to the seventh inclusive contributed three drawings each. Four judges made preliminary selections of thirty paintings for each grade and ranked these in five piles according to artistic quality. Fourteen experts then arranged these selected paintings. They were advised to give consideration to "attainment of rhythm, balance, unity, and other aesthetic qualities, rather than to technique or realistic representation." In the establishment of artistic value the opinion of a few well-qualified judges was considered to be more valuable than that of a larger number of less experienced judges. In its final form the scale has from eleven to sixteen paintings for each grade. The judges' agreement upon the relative value of the scaled pictures was high; the correlations were .94 and .93 between average ratings of half of the judges with the other half. Two trained workers using these scales for classifying original drawings showed correlations of approximately .79 and .73, with the average of two other trained workers judging one hundred paintings in each grade. No figures were given for consistency of individual judges.

A novel method of appraising compositional ability, which was designed to be free from technical skill, was described by McCloy (1939). The materials used were a control board which varied the intensity and color of a screen on a small stage, a number of small clay statues and objects, and twenty-five landscapes which could be used as backgrounds. After becoming familiar with the materials, subjects were asked to arrange sets of objects "until you get the effect you like best." Colored photographs of the preferred arrangements were appraised by three selected judges according to a uniform scheme in which each of the following items was rated on a ten-point scale:

1. Arrangement and use of light and shade
2. Arrangement of figures
3. Background selection
4. Originality
   a. Compositional arrangement
   b. Emotional interpretation
5. Color
   a. Harmony
   b. Appropriateness in background

After testing twenty subjects of various ages and with various amounts of training, McCloy reached the conclusion that creative ability under these conditions bore no relationship to age after twelve years, to amount of time used, or to previous artistic training. At one extreme the various subjects exhibited arrangements which seemed entirely accidental, and at the other, arrangements which followed definite ideals formed after first seeing the clay forms.

A scale of drawing was constructed by Goodenough (1928) for the purpose of indicating intelligence rather than artistic merit (see Chapter V). An attempt was made entirely to disregard artistic merit. Nearly four thousand drawings of a man by children of various age groups were inspected to find what changes took place between successive ages in accuracy of representation. She distinguished eight steps of psychological growth, which are much like those listed by Grippen (1933) for imaginative development:

1. Seeing a resemblance between pictures and objects
2. Noting the parts to be drawn
3. Selecting the most essential parts
4. Noting relative position
5. Noting relative proportions
6. Representing parts with simplified outlines
7. Coordination of hand and eye in drawing
8. The addition of new features as the concept develops

Goodenough's scale consists of verbal descriptions of fifty-two attributes of a drawing of man, each of which is given one point. Forty illustrative drawings are also printed (see Illus. 29). Total points may be changed into a mental age. The points include the presence of parts, their attachment, proportion, and details. Motor coordination of the child is scored by the absence of unintentional irregularities. Perspective and figures drawn in profile receive extra credit. This method of scoring drawings undoubtedly gives credit to some unartistic details, but qualities of correct proportion, unity, and fitness, stressed by nearly all the analyses of art, are also given credit. This work shows a fairly clear overlapping of factors in scales of artistic and representative ability in drawing. It would be interesting to have the same drawings ranked for both values, in order to see their closest relationship. No study of this sort has come to hand.

Horn Art Aptitude Test. Horn and Smith (1945) report an Art Aptitude Inventory developed by the staff of the School of Applied Art of the Rochester Institute of Technology over a period of 8 years. The student is required to make drawings to illustrate his quality of line or shading, compositional sense, fertility of imagination, and use of abstract or natural forms. The test consists of the following three parts:

1. *Scribble Exercise.* The student is asked to draw twenty different items, for example, a book and a fork, in limited times varying from 2 to 6 seconds. The whole exercise takes about 5 minutes. This part is designed to give the student confidence and to show clarity of thought and presentation, and orderly arrangement on the entire page.

2. *Doodle Exercise.* The student is asked to draw various lines and shapes within prescribed areas. This part shows abstract-composition ability and originality.

3. *Imagery.* The student is asked to construct sketches which are suggested by key lines which are already drawn in twelve rectangles, each $2\frac{3}{4}$ by $3\frac{1}{2}$ inches. This section shows fertility of imagination, scope of interests, shading, and style.

The scoring is accomplished by comparing a completed test with samples given in the manual of directions and with samples of work by students. A person without any training can score the extremes with great accuracy, but the middle ranges can be distinguished only by fairly well-trained examiners. All parts of the test are scored for

a. *Clarity of thought.* Are sketches clean and recognizable or were there fumbling, erasures, and meaningless detail?

b. *Quality of line.* Are lines smooth, graceful, and accurate, or broken, cramped, bumpy, and fuzzy?

c. *Color.* Is there even intensity or spotty uneven pressure; is there good use of shading?

The correlation between scores assigned to the same paper by different scorers was about .85 for small highly selected groups. This agreement is considered to be very satisfactory in the light of the fact that the group was restricted.

The validity of the test is indicated by a correlation of .53 between the Art Aptitude Test given in the freshman year and grades or over-all ratings of success at the end of a 3-year art course among fifty-two seniors. The ACE Psychological Test correlated only .28 with success in the 3-year course. These correlations would be somewhat higher if the scores of those who failed to finish the course were considered. The Art Aptitude Test correlated .15 with the ACE Psychological Examination.

Intelligence and Art Tests

The relationship between intelligence and artistic ability is not clearly defined or measured by published studies.[2] Definitions of both types of ability are characterized by vagueness and lack of wide acceptance. Tests designed to measure these abilities are fairly reliable, but as yet have failed to give careful analyses of the patterns themselves. Tests of artistic composition usually fail to distinguish between creative and copying processes, and tests of intellect fail to distinguish among such abilities as rote memory, perception, and reasoning. Furthermore, in research to determine the relationship of artistic and intellectual abilities the groups of persons studied have usually been small and rather narrowly selected. The correlations quoted, therefore, are not readily comparable, and differences which are reported do not necessarily indicate differences in essential facts but perhaps merely insufficient samplings. A few typical results are given.

Goodenough (1931) reported a correlation of .74 between her drawing scale of intelligence and the Stanford-Binet IQ scores, using 334 children between the ages of three and eleven years. Slightly lower correlations were found for these same children when smaller single-age groups were used. Bird (1932) and Tiebout and Meier (1936) found correlations of approximately .43 between IQ's from the Goodenough Draw-a-Man Test and IQ's from two group tests, the Kuhlmann-Anderson and the Dearborn, using one hundred or more pupils per grade.

These same investigators found that correlations between the Draw-a-Man Test IQ's and Tiebout's score for artistic drawing were in the neighborhood of .35 for three groups of one hundred children each, in the first three grades. In the fourth grade the correlation dropped to .18. Bird's (1932) score for drawing correlated .49 with Goodenough IQ's in a group of 248, six to nine years old. Manuel and Hughes (1932) report correlations still higher (.63 to .86) be-

2 Summarized by Bird (1930) and Tiebout and Meier (1936).

tween Goodenough IQ's and their ratings of quality of drawings in 836 Mexican children in grades one to six.

Tiebout and Meier (1936) found that correlation between measures of artistic composition and verbal tests of intellect are usually higher in the first grade than in later grades. The Kuhlman-Anderson IQ's and Tiebout scores showed correlations of .35 or .40 in grades one, two, and three, and nearly zero correlations in the higher grades. No significant correlations of this sort have appeared for adult groups. High school pupils considered to be artistically superior were only slightly above the average Kuhlman-Anderson IQ's. Fifty artists selected as the most outstanding among 5,500 names listed in the *Biography of American Artists* made an average IQ of 118 on the Otis Self-Administering Test, and showed their largest numbers of errors in handling number concepts. Intelligence test scores and rating as an artist showed a zero correlation in this group.

These figures show that persons who produce artistic works are slightly superior in verbal intelligence test scores but that artistic ability is not dependent upon such intellectual capacity.

ANALYTICAL STUDIES OF ARTISTIC ABILITY

Four studies should be mentioned because they attempt to appraise skills which are thought to be component elements of artistic composition. Knauber and Pressey (1927) included separate measures of skills, which were taken from drawings or completions of drawings. Their study embraced the following eight abilities: memory for designs (long and short time), observation, accuracy, imagination, creative imagination, analyzing ability, ability to visualize, and design sensitivity.

Lewerenz (1927) prepared nine tests designed to measure basic art abilities. In these tests, which made frequent use of multiple-choice and completion items, he included the following procedures:

1. Preferences for design: Choose between four variations of one theme (14 items of increasing complexity).

2. Originality of line drawing: Draw lines between printed dots to make a picture (10 items).

3. Indicate omission of shadows in ten drawings.

4. Vocabulary of materials, processes, drawing terms, and pictures (50 pairs of words).

5. Immediate memory span: Reproduce part of a picture of a vase from memory.

6, 7, and 8. Indicate errors in pictures of cylindrical, parallel, and angular perspectives.

9. Color-matching test: Six key colors are to be matched with 46 variations in hue and shade.

Both of these batteries stress accuracy of observation and memory for details of proportion, shading, and perspective, as well as preferences for designs and pictures. This sort of battery affords a means of comparing the relationship between the various subtests and eventually showing by a factorial analysis the basic patterns in artistic drawing. Both of these batteries have subtests which are probably too short for the analysis of factors or the construction of individual profiles. The method is sound, however, and a fascinating field of research is open. A correlation between total scores of these two batteries of .64 was found in a group of sixty-four art students. Correlation between the total Lewerenz test scores and scores on the McAdory and the Meier-Seashore tests were approximately .53. Simple correlations of this sort give no clear basis of analysis, but they suggest that the tests are measuring either the same processes or related processes to a marked extent.

Tiebout (1933) and Dreps (1933) compared scores on various tests of motor coordination, observation, discrimination, and memory with ratings of artistic ability. They found that the average scores of small groups of children and adults who were rated as artistically superior exceeded significantly the average scores of similar groups rated as inferior in the following tests:

1. Completeness and accuracy of visual observation (Heilbronner and Lewerenz tests)
2. Recall of observed material after ten days or six-month intervals (Fernald)
3. Uniqueness of interpretation of ink blots (Knox)
4. Originality of line drawing (Lewerenz)
5. Form discrimination
6. Feature discrimination (Greene)
7. IQ's
8. Aesthetic judgment

Small differences of doubtful significance were found on tests of:

1. Recognition memory, immediate
2. Completion of a drawing from memory
3. Visual imagery (Griffitts)
4. Neurotic tendencies (Pressey X-O)

No significant differences were found in tests of:

1. Hand-and-eye coordination (Greene, Whipple)
2. Steadiness of movement (Wellman, Whipple)
3. Color matching (Lewerenz)

Carroll (1932) found small and unreliable correlations between ability to appreciate or create art and introversion and emotional instability. Artists as a group showed no more instability than a group of students of statistics.

Meier (1939) directed an elaborate 10-year study of artistic ability which included research by twenty coworkers as well as himself. He described six patterns which he believed to be important in graphic arts:

1. *Manual skill:* This ability is regarded as fine hand-and-eye coordination which can be noted at early ages.

2. *Energy output:* This is shown by unusual concentration on a task for long periods.

3. *Intelligence:* The usual IQ-test scores are above average, with more success, however, in parts of the test which have to do with visualizing and speed of perceiving than in the parts that have to do with number and technical vocabularies.

4. *Perceptual facility:* By this is meant the ability to observe and recall sensory experiences.

5. *Creative imagination:* This is defined as an ability to organize vivid sense impressions into a "work having some degree of aesthetic character."

6. *Aesthetic judgment:* This is considered to be the most important factor of artistic competence. It is defined as ability to recognize unity of composition, and it is measured by the Meier Seashore Art Judgment Test.

These six items were not considered to be mutually exclusive but were general terms descriptive of complex and interrelated patterns. Meier believed that the first three factors are primarily inherited through a line of ancestors, and that the last three are definitely limited by inheritance. He pointed out that future analyses of artistic ability will probably indicate that elemental functions similar to those described by Thurstone (1938) underlie these six patterns. To the writer, the first four patterns seem to be important in any sort of craft or occupation where spatial factors are important. The last two factors seem to be found principally in artists, and hence to distinguish them from other people.

Any discussion of artistic ability would be incomplete without mention of the analyses of motives which drive artists to their work. Such analysis has been attempted by psychoanalysts, and their work is fruitful and challenging (Chapter XXI).

STUDY GUIDE QUESTIONS

1. What are the characteristics of measures of special aptitudes?
2. What visual functions are usually measured and how are they measured?

3. What are the principal variations in hearing? How are they measured?

4. What aspects of musical discrimination are measured by the Seashore Measures of Musical Talent?

5. What additional aspects are measured by Kwalwasser and by Bachern?

6. What are the usual relationships between various measures of musical talent?

7. What correlations are usually found between tests of intelligence and of musical abilities?

8. How are tests of preferences for pictures related to art aptitude?

9. What aspects of drawings are altered in the Meier-Seashore Test? The Graves Design-Judgment Test? The Horn Art Aptitude Test?

10. How can tests of composition be made more reliable?

11. What are the usual correlations between artistic skills?

12. To what extent are intelligence-test scores related to artistic ability?

CHAPTER XI

MILITARY DEVELOPMENT
OF TESTS AND RATINGS

∧∧

In this chapter some of the important tests and recently developed ratings used by the military authorities will be described briefly. The Army, Navy, and Air Corps each use screening tests for all new recruits, and the more analytical tests in selecting men and women for special training and duties. Personality and interest inventories are also used by the military authorities on significant samples. The criterion of success usually available is completion of a particular course of training, and unusually good predictions are shown in many situations. A few studies give fragmentary reports on the relations between various tests and performance of military duties. The Army Alpha and Beta Tests of World War I have been described in Chapter VIII.

SCOPE OF MILITARY TESTS

During World War II the military authorities in the United States called upon the biological and social scientists to help solve many of the urgent problems of selecting, training, leading, and, when necessary, of healing members of the Armed Forces. Scientific activities in developing and using measures of behavior were usually adjusted to specific military requirements. While these requirements were similar in many respects to those of civilian schools, industries, and clinics, still they differed in that they (*a*) were often concerned with large screening operations, (*b*) had as criteria success in occupations not found in civilian life, for example, fighter piloting, and combat-troop activities of all kinds, and (c) were accomplished under ter-rific time-pressure. Also, there were (d) large reserves of available man power and (e) authority to enforce service by severe penalties.

In 1941 all the large military branches decided to set up coordi-nated selection and research programs in various locations on various problems, rather than a single strongly centralized program. This decision was made because of (1) the initial and continued difficulties with communication between widely separated units; (2) the need to have a very close practical association between particular opera-tions and selection, training, and research; and (3) the great urgency for the immediate selection of great numbers of men by the best method locally available. As the war progressed the common prob-lems of the various services were sifted through the Committee on Service Personnel, Applied Psychology Panel, and there was con-siderable exchange of specific forms and information. Several proj-ects were planned for the use of both Army and Navy, Bray (1948).

Three types of measures were used in the selection of military per-sonnel, namely, ability, interest, and adjustment. The ability tests were more adequately developed, and were relied upon much more than the measures of interest and of adjustment. In mental clinics and hospitals, however, measures of adjustment were widely used to aid in remedial procedures.

MILITARY TEST BATTERIES

The United States Army Tests

The United States Army Classification System provided standard mental tests for nearly every important problem of personnel selec-tion. The steps taken were about as follows:

1. At the induction center before a man was accepted for military service he was briefly interviewed for gross defects and literacy. If his literacy was in doubt he was given a simple test to deter-mine whether or not he could read at about the level of the fourth grade. If this test was failed, often a Visual Classifica-tion Test was given to discover if he had the ability to under-stand and follow directions.
2. The enlisted man was then sent to one of thirty reception cen-ters, where all literates were given the Army General Classifica-tion Test (AGCT), a general mechanical test, and the Radio Telegraph Operator's Aptitude Test. The last two tests were included because the Army could not expect to recruit enough trained men in these fields. A Qualification Card containing such items as education, languages, highest vocational skills,

job history, hobbies, leadership, experiences, and previous military training, was also completed by interview. Test scores were recorded on this card. If a man possessed skills that were needed at once, he was sent directly to the unit involved. Other men (about 50 per cent) were sent to Replacement Training Centers.

3. At the Replacement Training Centers individual general mental tests were given to those whose group-test scores seemed to yield insufficient data. The processes of screening men for all specialist and officer schools, for special training units, and for treatment when they were emotionally and mentally inadequate involved the use of tests such as the following:

Classification Tests
General Classification Test
Nonlanguage Test
Visual Classification Test
Higher Examination
Officer Candidate Test
Women's Classification Test (mental alertness test)
Army Information Sheet (minimum literacy test)

Aptitude Tests
Mechanical Aptitude Test
Clerical Aptitude Test
Radio Telegraph Operator's Aptitude Test
Code Learning Test
Battery of Tests for Combat Intelligence
Identification of Aerial Photographs
Map Identification
Route Tracing
Battle Maps
Perception of Detail
Map Reading
Map Orientation

Educational Achievement Examination, Army Specialized Training Program (ASTP)
Algebra
Arithmetic
English Grammar and Composition
French
General History
German
Inorganic Chemistry
Physics
Plane and Solid Geometry

Spanish
Trigonometry
United States History
Combined Algebra, Trigonometry, and Geometry

Trade Knowledge Tests
General Automotive Information Test
General Electricity and Radio Information Test
General Electrical Information Test
General Radio Information Test
Driver and Automotive Information Test

Warrant Officer Examinations
About thirty technical examinations in various fields.

The Army General Classification Test (AGCT), in four equivalent forms, was administered to more than 9 million persons during World War II. It was designed to be a test of learning ability for literate adults. The first form of the AGCT (Form 1a) was released October 1940, and the last (Form 1d) in October 1941. Forms 1a and 1b each contained 150 items and were preceded by a separate practice booklet. Forms 1c and 1d each included 10 practice items, and 140 test items. All forms rotated three types of items in this order of presentation: vocabulary, arithmetic, and block counting. The time limit was 40 minutes, and the score was the number right minus one third the number wrong, because all items had four choices. In selecting items the Committee on Classification of Military Personnel agreed to emphasize the following points of view (Personnel Research Section, 1945):

1. The tests should include both verbal and nonverbal items.

2. Assuming that modern warfare is rapidly becoming more technical, emphasis was to be placed upon items calling for spatial thinking and for quantitative reasoning.

3. It was planned to keep at a minimum items greatly influenced by amount of schooling and by cultural inequalities generally. To this end the use of information items was not planned.

4. Insofar as possible, the time or speed element was to be minimized. (This aspect was ignored in later practical situations.)

5. The General Classification Test was not to serve the purpose of trade tests.

6. It was specifically recognized that the test was not to measure personality traits. (However, it was recognized that emotional stress might seriously affect one's score.)

7. The test should appeal to the average officer and soldier as sensible.

About five thousand items were tried out on samples of enlisted men to determine difficulty as well as to find if they met the considerations listed above. Tentative norms were later set for total scores, and for easy interpretation of all forms of the test the mean T score was set at 100 and the standard deviation at 20. Table 5 shows the Roman numerals used for army grades and the corresponding distribution figures.

The reliabilities, which have been computed many times on various samples, were approximately .84 for retests at various intervals of months, .90 for alternate forms, .96 for odd-even or Kuder-Richardson methods. There were slightly negative correlations with age, —.20 to —.33 for a group of officers whose mean age was about thirty-two years. This was partly due to the fact that the AGCT was closely timed (40 minutes) and that speed was an important factor. In a group of 4,330 enlisted men correlation with age was .02.

ILLUS. 112. GRADE DISTRIBUTION OF MEN PROCESSED THROUGH RECEPTION CENTERS, 1940–44. AGCT

Army Grade	Score Limits	Percentage of Total Group
I	130 and above *	6.0
II	110–129	26.5
III	90–109	30.5
IV	60–89	27.7
V	59 and below	9.3
	Total number of cases 8,293,879	

* Mean = 100   SD = 20

The correlation between highest grade completed in school and the AGCT was approximately .70. The correlations between the AGCT and other tests of mental ability were found to be in the neighborhood of .80, but ranged from .65 for the ACE Psychological Examination to .90 for the Army Alpha, Wells' Revision, long form.

The major usefulness of the AGCT was its value in selecting men for specialist training courses. Illustration 113 shows a few of the several hundred validity coefficients that were available. These correlations are not directly comparable because the groups were preselected by education or experience, or by the AGCT itself. For instance, a prerequisite for officer candidate schools was an AGCT score of 110 and for the Army Specialized Training (AST) Program a score of 115. The correlations would, of course, have been much higher for unselected groups. In general, grades in clerical subjects, English and mathematics were predicted by the AGCT a little more accurately (.40) than grades for mechanics, radio, and motor transport, engineering, and foreign languages (.20 to .30). None of these correlations are concerned with evaluations of actual success on the job.

In April 1945, the AGCT, Form 3a was issued. It has a total score similar to that of the earlier forms but allows for a profile of subtest scores in four areas: reading and vocabulary, arithmetic computation, arithmetic reasoning, and pattern analysis.

ILLUS. 113. EXAMPLES OF VALIDITY COEFFICIENTS. AGCT

Population	Criterion	N	Mean	SD	r
Administrative Clerical Trainees, AAF	Grades	2,947	121.7	11.1	.40
Clerical Trainees, WAAC	Grades	199	116.8	12.0	.62
Airplane-Mechanic Trainees	Grades	99	104.8	10.6	.32
Aircraft Armorer Trainees	Grades	1,907	117.3	10.9	.40
Radio Operator & Mechanic Trainees, AAF	Grades	1,055	122.4	11.1	.32
Gunnery Trainees, Armored	Grades	66	120.0	12.1	.50
Motor Transport Trainees, WAAC	Grades	269	111.4	13.6	.31
Truckdriver Trainees	Road-Test Ratings	421	95.5	20.1	.13
Weather-Observer Trainees, AAF	Grades	1,042	130.2	12.5	.43
Officer Candidates, Infantry	Grades, Academic	103	123.0	10.8	.30
Officer Candidates, Infantry	Leadership Ratings	201	122.6	10.8	.12
AST Trainees, Basic Engineering	Grades, Inorganic Chemistry	222	126.6	7.8	.21
AST Trainees, Personnel Psychology	Ranks in Tests and Measurements	130	134.0	10.3	.29
West Point Cadets, 4th Class	Grades, English *	932	131.3	10.9	.40
West Point Cadets, 4th Class	Grades, Mathematics *	932	131.3	10.9	.43
West Point Cadets, 4th Class	Grades, Military Topography	932	131.3	10.9	.40
West Point Cadets, 4th Class	Grades, Tactics	932	131.3	10.9	.29
West Point Cadets, 4th Class	Grades, Spanish *	932	131.3	10.9	.19

* First term.

(By permission of the editor of the *Psychological Bulletin*.)

Occupational Norms. The widespread interest in the occupational norms from World War I Alpha and Beta Tests led two authors, Harrell (1946) and Stewart (1947), to prepare norms for various civilian occupations from the World War II tests. These studies were not of officers; the subjects are enlisted men who claimed experience in various civilian occupations.

Harrell (1946) reported norms for 774,383 men who were classified into 209 occupations in the continental Army Air Force in 1943. Only those occupational groups with at least one hundred men were included. Stewart (1947) listed 220 occupational groups including technicians and skilled and semi-skilled workers. The sample was selected from a survey made in September 1944, of approximately

150,000 soldiers or 2 per cent of all United States Army personnel. Those whose serial numbers ended in 19 or in 75 were selected for a smaller random sample of 103,998. The number was finally reduced to 68,325 men whose records were complete and who belonged to occupations which included at least twenty-five men each.

Illustration 114 gives a sample of the results in commonly found occupations. These are typical both of recent reports and also of World War I results. This table and other data that have been reported show that the spread of scores (variability) for the occupations with the highest mean scores was only about half the variability for the occupations with the lowest mean scores. For various reasons many above-average persons were found in relatively unskilled occupations, but those below average were seldom found in the more skilled occupations. This means that the test would show cut-off or critical scores for the jobs on the higher levels only. One of the most significant findings, however, is that there is *great overlapping* between occupations. This test can therefore be used only for the roughest kind of screening. Since no validity correlations are available, it should be used cautiously for individual counseling. In the selection of workers, more analytical tests, experience, interest, and special training would be more indicative of success than the AGCT scores.

The Army Individual Test of General Ability was prepared (1) to aid in deciding whether or not to discharge a man for general inaptitude and (2) to aid in clinical diagnosis. To meet these needs a battery of tests was developed which (*a*) covered the same abilities and range of abilities as the AGCT, (*b*) contained both verbal and nonverbal material, (*c*) could be given to any racial group, (*d*) could be administered by one not trained in psychometry, and (*e*) would require about an hour's time and few materials.

Seventeen tests were tried out on 250 white and 215 colored soldiers—approximately one hundred from each of the five grades of the AGCT. From correlations between these tests (the AGCT and schooling) and from the specifications above, six tests were selected:

1. *Story Memory:* A short paragraph is read to the examinee who is asked to repeat it and answer questions.
2. *Similarities-Differences:* The examinee is asked to tell how pairs of words are alike and different.
3. *Digit-Span:* Three to ten digits are to be repeated in the order given and three to nine in reverse order.
4. *Shoulder Patches:* The examinee is asked to duplicate a colored design by selecting and placing pieces from among nineteen colored cut-out designs.

5. *Trail Making:* The examinee is asked to draw a line from number to number in sequence, or from letter to letter. The score is the time used and the number of errors.

6. *Cube Assembly:* The examinee is asked to duplicate the arrangement of cubes shown in three pictures, by using twenty-four actual cubes on the table. Score is time needed.

The whole test takes about 40 minutes and showed a reliability of .93 for one thousand white soldiers. The subtest median intercorrelation was .43, with the highest correlation, .61, between the first two tests, which emphasize verbal comprehension. The lowest correlation was .32 (between Digit-Span and Cube Assembly).

In order to have the first three tests, which are verbal, contribute the same amount to the variance of the total score as the last three tests, which are nonverbal, the scores of three of the tests were

ILLUS. 114. CIVILIAN OCCUPATIONS AND AGCT SCORES

Mean = 100   SD = 20

Occupations	Number	P_{10}	P_{25}	P_{50}	P_{75}	P_{90}	Q
Professional							
Accountant	216	114	121	129	136	143	7.5
Student, mechanical engineering	62	114	122	128	135	140	6.5
Student, medicine	124	116	120	127	135	140	7.5
Writer	54	114	123	126	133	140	5.0
Teacher	360	110	117	124	132	140	7.5
Lawyer	164	112	118	124	132	141	7.0
Student, business or public admin.	152	114	118	124	131	140	6.5
Clerical							
Statistical Clerk	72	114	119	125	133	141	7.0
Bookkeeper, general	302	108	114	122	129	138	7.5
Chief Clerk	297	107	114	122	131	141	8.5
Stenographer	206	109	115	122	130	139	7.5
Tabulating Machine Operator	61	102	111	120	127	134	8.0
Clerk-Typist	616	101	110	119	126	136	9.0
Clerk, general	2,063	97	108	117	125	133	8.5
File Clerk	119	96	105	114	123	129	9.0
Stock Clerk	791	85	99	110	120	127	10.5
Sales Clerk	2,362	82	95	109	119	128	12.0
Technicians							
Draftsman, mechanical	99	105	111	120	128	135	8.5
Tool Designer	54	102	110	119	128	141	9.0
Physics Laboratory Assistant	125	95	106	116	124	133	9.0
Photographer	70	88	109	114	124	129	7.5
Parts Clerk, automotive	133	90	98	110	119	127	10.5
Installer-Repairman, Telephone & Telegraph	62	98	108	115	120	133	6.0

ILLUS. 114. CIVILIAN OCCUPATIONS AND AGCT SCORES (Cont'd)

Occupations	Number	P_{10}	P_{25}	P_{50}	P_{75}	P_{90}	Q
Mechanical trades							
Airplane Engine Mechanic	115	92	102	114	123	130	10.5
Tool Maker	147	92	101	112	123	129	11.0
Foreman, machine shop	48			110			
Machinist	617	86	99	110	120	127	10.5
Engine Lathe Operator	283	89	101	110	120	128	9.5
Machinist's Helper	429	85	96	108	118	125	11.0
Electrician, automotive	57	88	100	108	115	127	7.5
Machine Operator, designated machine	3,044	77	89	103	114	123	12.5
Truck Driver, heavy	3,473	71	83	98	111	120	14.0
Truck Driver, light	3,966	69	80	95	109	119	14.5
Construction trades							
Carpenter, heavy construction	82	87	97	112	124	132	13.5
Carpenter, general	1,004	73	86	101	113	123	13.5
Electrician	435	83	96	109	118	124	11.0
Cabinetmaker	114	80	92	108	119	130	13.5
Structural Steel Worker	107	76	88	104	119	126	15.0
Foreman, construction	281	72	88	104	118	128	15.0
Plumber	222	71	87	103	114	123	13.5
Painter, general	680	70	83	99	113	121	15.0
Construction Machine Operator	145	70	79	97	107	117	14.0
Crane Operator	128	72	87	96	111	120	12.0
Miner	502	67	75	87	103	114	14.0
Students							
Mechanical Engineering	62	114	122	128	135	140	6.5
Medicine	124	116	120	127	135	140	7.5
Chemical Engineering	73	105	117	125	134	142	8.5
Business or Public Administration	152	114	118	124	131	140	6.5
Sociology, high school, academic	2,608	92	102	113	122	129	10.0
High School, commercial	275	90	99	110	118	124	9.5
Manual Arts	60	87	99	109	121	132	11.0
High School, vocational	504	85	96	108	115	124	9.5
Other							
Teamster	284	64	74	97	104	114	15.0
Barber	166	66	79	93	109	120	15.0
Farm worker	7,475	61	70	86	103	115	16.5

(Adapted by permission of Naomi Stewart and the editors of *Educational and Psychological Measurements*.)

weighted. Standard scores having a mean of 100 and SD of 20 were provided for verbal, nonverbal, and total scores.

The correlations between the AGCT and the following individual tests were:

Story Memory	.61	Shoulder Patches	.61
Similarities-Differences	.71	Trail Making	.65
Digit-Span	.56	Cube Assembly	.54
Verbal tests	.78	Nonverbal tests	.74
	Total score	.84	

A College Qualifying Test (C-1) was given for both Army and Navy at fourteen thousand educational centers in April 1943 to about three hundred thousand officer candidates. The following data are taken from the results of this testing:

Test	Number of Items	Minutes
I. Verbal Opposites	30	
Analogies	15	
Double Definitions	15	30
II. Scientific Background Information	40	30
III. Reading of Paragraphs: Economics, History, and Biology	20	25
IV. Mathematical Problems: Algebra and Geometry	30	35
Total	150	120

Army Specialized Training Program Tests. During 1943 and 1944 more than 140 subject matter achievement tests were constructed for use in the Army Specialized Training Program. Approximately one million of these tests were given to one hundred fifty thousand trainees in two hundred colleges and universities. This nation-wide training program of the Personnel Section of the Adjutant General's Office was designed to evaluate both the achievement of individual students and the content and quality of instruction. New and somewhat equivalent forms were produced every 3 months for many of the subjects, because each term of instruction lasted 3 months, and it seemed desirable not to use the same form twice in any one institution. For some subjects as many as eight forms were produced. The basic-training phase included mathematics, physics, chemistry, English, geography, and history. The advanced phases included medicine, engineering, personnel psychology, and foreign languages.

The testing program had three important results: (1) Course outlines were revised, made more definite and more uniform, and probably more effective in learning. (2) Item analysis indicated the difficulty of items and the internal consistency of tests to a degree not before attempted. (3) Instruction became more standardized as was shown by correlations between instructors' grades and achievement test scores. This was most noticeable in the less-standardized courses, for example, English and geography.

The prediction of success on these achievement tests from a college qualifying examination designed to select candidates for the AST program was as high as .74 for combined achievement scores in mathematics, physics, and chemistry. Instructors' grades for this same combination of courses correlated only from .45 to .55, showing either that the instructors' grades were less reliable or that they measured other factors. These results are similar to those reported for the Navy V-12 program by Crawford and Burnham (1945).

The Army Air Force Batteries

The AAF had two batteries: the Qualifying Examination (Davis, 1947), for all candidates; and the Air Crew Classification Battery (DuBois, 1947). The latter was used at classification centers to assign those who had passed the Qualifying Examination to the most appropriate air crew training, such as fighter pilot, bomber pilot, navigator, bombardier, radar observer, and flight engineer.

The Qualifying Examination. The Qualifying Examination was designed for use in selecting men who could become good officers and pilots. It was a power test with a liberal time allowance (3 hours) and corrections for guessing, so that there was no advantage in the examinee's marking every item.

Illustration 115 lists the parts of the AAF Qualifying Examination, 1942, 1943, and 1944. The General Vocabulary and Contemporary Affairs Subtests of the 1942 battery were replaced by information about driving an automobile, flying, and aviation, which were also considered to be indirect indications of strength of interests. The mathematics problems of the 1942 battery and the tests of 1943 on estimating distances were omitted in later batteries, since they failed to bear out the earlier predictions of success in basic pilot training. Part of this decrease may have been due to changes in standards of pilot training. The Reading Comprehension and Mechanical Comprehension Tests were retained and improved so that their validity correlations were nearly doubled. Two rather difficult visual perception tests, Planning Circuits and Hidden Figures, were introduced in 1943, and the latter was retained in 1944. Both of these seemed to give better prediction when used as speed tests, but in this examination speed was never stressed.

The correlations in Illus. 115 show that the AAF Qualifying Examination was able to save a great deal of delay and expense in pilot training. From approximately 1,200,000 men who were given

ILLUS. 115. ARMY AIR FORCE QUALIFYING EXAMINATION CORRE-
LATED WITH GRADUATION FROM BASIC PILOT TRAINING

	Number of Items	Biserial Correlation
FORM AC10A, 1942		
Section		
Vocabulary, General	45	—.04
Reading Comprehension	15	.14
Judgment, Practical	15	.36
Mathematics Problems	30	.14
Contemporary Affairs Information	30	.24
Mechanical Comprehension	15	.29
Total	150	.20
FORM AC12I, 1943		
Section		
Planning Circuits	45	.26
Hidden Figures	45	.31
Path Distance	30	.14
Point Distance	30	.17
Judgment Reasoning	25	.33
Aviation Information	35	.34
Mechanical Comprehension	60	.48
Total	270	.51
FORM AC14L, 1944		
Section		
Reading Comprehension	15	.26
Information: Drive, Fly, Aviation	50	.29
Mechanical Comprehension	60	.60
Hidden Figures	25	.36
Total	150	.62

the qualifying test, 100,000 were accepted for flight training. A passing mark was usually set so that about 35 per cent of men above the mark graduated from advanced pilot training, while only 11 per cent of those below the mark finished. Before the testing program became effective it was necessary to enroll 397 men in order to graduate one hundred, but after the qualifying examination was used only 180 men were enrolled. If in addition the Air Crew Classification Battery was used only 150 men were enrolled.

Air Crew Classification. The first battery of the Air Crew Classification Test appeared in February 1942, and there were ten revisions by June 1945. About 6 hours were needed for approximately twenty-one tests, of which from four to six required apparatus and the rest used paper and pencil. The later batteries included the same broad fields as the earlier ones, but fewer short tests of perception and more of technical information and spatial thinking were used. Biographical data were also included in the final scores.

Stanine scores were composites of the scores of these classification subtests, weighted differently to predict success in various training situations. Stanines are scores on a 9-point scale, each point representing a range of scores of one half a standard deviation. In this way the first stanine always includes the lowest 4 per cent of the group, the second stanine the next 7 per cent, etc. (Illus. 116).

ILLUS. 116. COMPARISON OF STANINES, CENTILES, AND AREAS

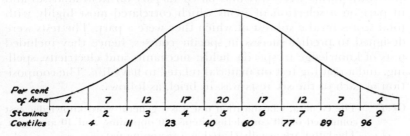

Per cent of Area	4	7	12	17	20	17	12	7	4
Stanines	1	2	3	4	5	6	7	8	9
Centiles	4	11	23	40	60	77	89	96	

The first stanines for the earlier batteries were computed from estimates of judges. As soon as validation data were obtained, stanines were computed by using multiple regression weights. Because it was desired that stanine scores should be as independent of each other as possible, different tests as well as different weights on the same tests were used to some degree. The correlations between stanines in the 1944 battery ranged from .50 between navigator and fighter pilot, to .90 between fighter and bomber pilot. The heaviest loadings for navigator were Numerical and Verbal; for bombardier, Perceptual, Numerical, and Spatial; for pilots, Psychomotor, Coordination, and Mechanical Experience; and for officer quality, Verbal and General Reasoning, Flanagan and Ritts (1944).

The AAF Air Crew Classification Test was used with approximately six hundred thousand candidates. The prediction by pilots' stanine scores of graduation or elimination from elementary pilot training (DuBois, 1947) was calculated for twenty-eight large groups of trainees over a period of 3 years. The earliest biserial correlations were .31, .33, and .44; the latest, .70, .46, and .63. Eliminations were computed for each stanine on primary, basic, and advanced pilot training among about fifty thousand cadets during a period of 2 years. Eighty per cent of the first stanine were eliminated, but only about 15 per cent of the ninth stanine. In 1944 and 1945 prediction by bombardier stanine score of graduation from the bombardier courses ranged from .27 to .36; and similar figures for navigator training ranged from .45 to .50 for large groups, but from .35 to .79 for smaller groups. None of these predictions was improved significantly by the addition of measures or estimates of interest, of temperament, or of adjustment.

Navy Batteries

The United States Navy Basic Test Battery (Stuit, 1947), first administered in 1943, had six parts, which were not selected directly from factorial analyses nor intended to be pure tests. The second and third forms were revisions based in part on item analyses and in part on a selection of items which correlated most highly with total scores on the subtest of which they were a part. The tests were designed to predict success in specific courses, hence they included tests of knowledge in specific fields: mechanics and electricity, spelling, and a reading test on material related to navy life. The composition of each of the six tests was, in brief, as follows:

GCT. The General Classification test was a general word knowledge test composed of 30 completion items, 30 opposites, and 40 analogies. The latter are usually classed as a reasoning test.

READ. The Reading test was made up of 30 5-choice items based on short paragraphs.

ARI. The Arithmetic Reasoning test had 30 verbally stated problems.

MAT. The Mechanical Aptitude test consisted of 45 Block Counting items, 44 Mechanical Comprehension, and 40 Surface-Development items.

MKM. The Mechanical Knowledge, Mechanical, contained 75 items, of which 35 were pictorial and 40 written.

MKE. The Mechanical Knowledge, Electrical test consisted of 60 items, of which 25 were pictorial and 35 written.

Three special-aptitude tests were added later to round out the battery:

CLER. The Clerical Aptitude test had 55 alphabetizing, 83 name-comparison, and 75 number-comparison items.

SPELL. The Spelling test had 50 items, in each of which one of five words was misspelled.

CODE. The Radio Code test—speed of response, which was developed for the Army and Navy by the National Research Defense Committee, consisted of a learning unit in which three characters were taught, and then a unit used to test candidates in receiving the three characters, but at four different speeds.

The Spearman-Brown reliabilities for Form 2 ranged from .88 to .95 (median .90) and the alternate form reliabilities ran about 6 or 7 points lower. The subtests correlated with age from —.09 to .19 and with highest grade completed from .39 for MKM to .65 for both CST and CLER (median .56). The intercorrelations of subtests on Form 2 ranged from .33 between MKM and SPELL, to .85 between GCT and READ (median about .66). The GCT had the highest median correlation with the seven other subtests, and MKM was a close second. CODE was least related to the others. These showed much higher intercorrelations than are considered desirable for independent tests, but the predictions of success were high enough to be useful.

The prediction of final grades in seven types of elemental training from six tests of the Basic Test Battery were reported for groups of a thousand or more. These showed that for all the schools together the Arithmetic Reasoning Test gave slightly better prediction than the others (about .50) and the Reading Test slightly lower prediction (.37). The Mechanical Knowledge Test (MKM) gave the best single prediction (.64) for aviation machinists' mates. The Mechanical Knowledge, Electrical (MKE), and Arithmetic Reasoning (ARI) Tests predicted electrical training success most highly (.57 each). For diesel training the MKE gave the best prediction (.46) and for machinists' mates the Arithmetic Reasoning (ARI) prediction (.49) was slightly ahead of the rest. In basic engineering the Arithmetic Reasoning (ARI) Test predicted success with a .60. These are all significant predictions for group success.

Of 46,500 trainees assigned to ten navy schools, eleven thousand were assigned who had scores below that recommended, usually because of quota pressure. The percentage of failure due to lack of aptitude among the eleven thousand was about $4\frac{1}{2}$ times as large as among those above the recommended cut-off score. The percentage of failure due to lack of interest showed a similar pattern (Chapter XXII).

A criterion of performance on shipboard was secured by rank, order, and rating, adjusted to eliminate amount of experience. Separate rankings were made of three characteristics: petty officer qualities, technical competence, and over-all desirability. The correlations between them were so high (.80 to .95) that only the technical competence ratings were used as criteria of success.

A sample of 1,868 men on 27 different ships—9 destroyers, 12 carriers, and 6 cruisers—was studied. Six naval ratings or occupations were reported separately. The results from the six tests of the basic battery were given in detail. For radio mates and signal mates average correlations of success with technical competence were highest for the General Classification Test and Arithmetic Reasoning (about .31). Technical competence of radar operators was predicted best by Arithmetic Reasoning, .44; of fire controlmen by Mechanical

Aptitude, .33; of machinists' mates and gunners' mates by Mechanical Knowledge, .36. There were smaller but usually significant correlations between years of civilian education and test scores, and between civilian education and criteria of success. The correlations with the other tests in the battery were all lower (from —.11 up).

The United States Navy also developed the following series of tests for officers:

1. *The Officer Qualification Test, Form 2,* was a one-hour test of one hundred items which included 50 Verbal Opposites, 30 Mechanical Comprehension, and 20 Arithmetic Reasoning items. It was used as a screening test for civilian applicants for commissions.

2. *The Officer Classification Test, Form X-1,* was an aptitude test containing 255 items. It was more difficult than the Officer Qualification Test and had relatively shorter time limits. It included:

	Number of Items	Time in Minutes
Verbal Opposites	60	60
Mechanical Comprehension	45	20
Electrical and Mechanical Information	45	10
Mathematical Problems	45	45
Block Assembly	30	15
Rotation of Solid Figures	30	20
Total	255	170

The United States Navy activities in defining goals and measuring achievement both for officers and for enlisted men (Stuit, 1947) were outstanding. For instance, among the Elementary Enlisted Schools both paper-and-pencil tests and performance tests were developed which measured the important skills and knowledge in each course. To conserve time, multiple sets of equipment were used, routine operations were omitted, and key or difficult aspects were stressed. For objective scoring proctor's sheets were made specific. This required agreement on the most acceptable procedures and often resulted in conferences at which procedures were improved.

COMPARISON OF MILITARY BATTERIES

Four batteries are compared in Illus. 117, two from the Navy and two from the Army Air Force. These were chosen because they were devised to give analytic results. Illustration 117 shows that in each of these batteries, tests were included to measure nearly all of the primary factors given in the column on the left. The time limit ranged from 130 to 229 minutes of actual working time. The AAF Air Crew

ILLUS. 117. COMPARISON OF MILITARY BATTERIES

Factors	U.S. Navy Basic Battery #2, 1942 206 Min.	U.S. Navy Officer Classification x – 1 1942 130 Min.	AAF Qualifying AC121 (1943) 180 Min.	AAF Air Crew Classification 1944 229 Min.
Language: Meaning	Sentence Completion 30-10 Opposites 30-10	Opposites 60-20	*Information	Reading Comprehension C1614A 36-30 General Information CF505F 100-36
Word Fluency Usage	Alphabetizing 55-4 Spelling 50-12	Opposites 30-10		
Number	(See Reasoning)	(See Reasoning)	(See Reasoning)	Dial and Table Reading CP 622A 146-24 Numerical Operation C1702B 180-10
Spatial	Block Counting 45-6 Surface Development 40-8	Block Assembly 30-15 Rotation Solid Figures 30-20		Instrument Comprehension C1616C 60-15
Mechanical: Principles Knowledge	Mechanical Comprehension 44-20 Mechanical Knowledge Electrical 60-18 Mechanical 75-19	Comprehension 45-20 Knowledge 45-10	Mechanical Comprehension 60- Aviation Information 35-	Principles C1903B 40-20 Information Auto 51905B 30-15
Dexterity				Rotary Pursuit CP410B Rudder Control CM120B Finger Dexterity CM 16A Complex Coordination CM710A 2-Hand Coordination CM101A Discriminate Reaction Time CP6ND
Perceptual Speed	Name Comparison 83-5 Number Comparison 75-4 Radio Code Sound 150-30		Planning Circuits 45- Hidden Figure 45- Path Distance 30- Point Distance 30-	Orientation Sp. I and II CP501-503B 99-10 Speed of Identification CP610A 48-4
Learning	Radio Code			
Reasoning	Analogies 40-15 Arithmetical Reasoning 30-30 Reading	Mathematical Reasoning 45-45 *Verbal Reasoning 75- *Revision	Judgment and Reason 25- *Reading 15- *Form AC14L, 1944	Judgment C1307C 30-30 Arithmetical Reasoning C1206C 30-35

Classification Test showed more specialization of contents than the others. No figures have as yet come in to show the correlation between the parts of different batteries which have been designed to measure somewhat similar skills. It seems probable that certain of these tests, for example, Vocabulary and Reading, will correlate highly, whereas in tests of Spatial and Mechanical Knowledge there may be large differences in content and emphasis, which will probably yield low correlations. Similarly, in the Perceptual Speed Test the type of objects and the methods of procedure will probably produce different results. A comparison of this table with Illus. 85 shows that these military batteries and the general-aptitude batteries overlap to a large extent. In the future it will be possible to combine these various batteries so as to predict success fairly accurately in a large variety of civilian and military occupations.

MILITARY PERSONALITY INVENTORIES

Ellis and Conrad (1948) reviewed seventy-six references on the application of personality inventories in military service. They compared various inventories with two types of criteria: (a) psychiatric classifications, both before and after induction, and (b) success, as shown by either graduation from a course of training or ratings of performance on the job. Approximately 40 per cent of the reports concern officers or enlisted men in the United States Army Air Force, 32 per cent Navy, 16 per cent Army, and 12 per cent selectees. A large variety of inventories was used, but most of them were short screening devices developed by the psychologists in the Armed Services. For example, approximately 40 per cent of the studies used the Personal Inventory (Shipley, 1946), and 29 per cent the Cornell Service Index (Weider, 1945), both of which consist of short lists of questions regarding one's own health, habits, worries, and adjustments. The other studies included the Bell Adjustment Inventory, the Minnesota Multiphasic Personality Inventory (MMPI), the Humm-Wadsworth Temperament Scale, and the three Guilford-Martin Inventories.

The inventories, even the short ones, proved to be fairly effective as rough screening devices among selectees. For example, the Cornell Service Index cut-off score could be set to detect from 71 to 89 per cent of the men rejected as the result of neuropsychiatric interviews, while indicating about 15 per cent of the "false positives," that is, men judged to be unstable by the inventory, but not by the interview. The cutting scores could be set to detect from 60 to 70 per cent of those disenrolled for neuropsychiatric reasons, while including from 2 to 13 per cent of the false positives. From 50 to 69 per cent of the psychiatric discharges from the Navy were identified by the Personal Inventory, including from 4 to 14 per cent of false positives. The shorter scales did not attempt to identify the type of clinical syndrome. The MMPI was reported by some authors, but not by others, to have fairly close correlations with clinical diagnoses.

Success in completing a course of training or in performance in combat was not well predicted by any of the inventories. For example, failures in schools for primary pilot training and for advanced pilot training and in schools for submarine men, parachute soldiers, marine-officer candidates, navigators, radar operators, and bombardiers were seldom predicted with a significant correlation. The highest correlations reported were .48 for a group of 1,039 officer candidates and .39 for 1,079 parachute trainees, but most of the correlations were much lower. Ratings by submarine officers of the performance of their men showed correlations not significantly different from zero with Shipley's Personal Inventory (Satter, 1945). Ratings of 185 marine officers by superior officers on combat proficiency showed a correlation of .15.

Why should these inventories detect maladjusted persons as revealed by neuropsychiatric interviews before and after enlistment, but fail to indicate success in training or in combat? Two reasons are advanced by Ellis and Conrad (1948): first, the groups in training and in combat were so highly selected that there were few, if any, seriously maladjusted persons in these groups; second, the less well-adjusted persons may have been strongly motivated to make a poor showing on the inventory so that they would be discharged or hospitalized. There is also evidence that occasionally the inventory scores were available and used informally as part of the basis for a psychiatric classification.

From such studies as these it seems safe to conclude that for screening a large unselected adult group a short personal inventory will detect about 75 per cent of the men who should be rejected from the Armed Forces for neuropsychiatric reasons. It cannot be assumed from these studies, however, that the short personal inventory will be effective in civilian personnel work. With highly selected groups or with those who are motivated to misrepresent themselves it would probably not be of value. With other groups some items after a detailed analysis might be found to have significance.

ASSESSMENT OF MEN

One of the most extensive and intensive applications of role playing to the study of personality factors was made by the Office of

Strategic Services (OSS) which was set up by the President and Congress to meet the special conditions of World War II. The functions of this office was (*a*) to collect and analyze information concerning the activities of the enemy nations; and (*b*) to conduct operations behind the enemy's lines by aiding and training the resistance groups by means of the radio and pamphlets, and in other ways. Approximately five thousand members of the Strategic Services organization were appraised intensively over a 3-day period at one station, or during one day at another. It was decided to assess each man primarily on a cluster of dispositions, abilities, and traits which were thought to be essential to the performance of almost every OSS job overseas. A list of about twenty variables was finally reduced to the following seven:

1. Motivation for assignment
2. Energy and initiative
3. Effective intelligence: ability to select strategic goals and the most efficient means of obtaining them, resourcefulness, originality, good judgment in dealing with people
4. Emotional stability, steadiness under pressure
5. Social relations: good team-play, freedom from disturbing prejudices and annoying traits
6. Leadership: social initiative, ability to evoke cooperation, acceptance of responsibility
7. Security: ability to keep secrets and to use discretion

In addition to these seven variables, three others were occasionally used as required:

8. Physical ability: ruggedness, stamina, agility
9. Observing and recording: being able to evaluate information and to record it very accurately
10. Propaganda skill: ability to see enemy vulnerability and to devise subversive techniques of some sort or other

In order to appraise the various candidates on these traits, six different methods were used:

1. Interviews, which were both formal and informal, over a period of several days
2. Observations throughout a 3-day period
3. Individual-task situations, where a single candidate had to deal with one or more persons in achieving his end
4. Group-task situations, where a team of candidates was instructed to cooperate in performing a task
5. Projective tests which revealed some of the inhibited tendencies of the candidates
6. Ratings by associates, in which the candidate's skills and his acceptance by his coworkers were noted

Each of these methods was subdivided. For instance, in the individual-task situations, each candidate had to direct two assistants in helping him to erect a wooden structure. The assistants were stooges who were instructed to be recalcitrant. Again, the candidate had to interview a person applying for a position in a secret organization; or two candidates had to deal with each other in face-to-face situations which were somewhat prescribed. In order to make the test situations as effective as possible, they were made similar to those which would be met in actual war conditions. For example, in appraising leadership a group was taken to a road where one candidate in the presence of a whole group was told to take charge of the situation: men had blown up a bridge a mile away, and he must meet a truck a mile away in another direction with only 10 minutes to spend in getting across this road. The road had been mined with a new type of sensitive mine which he would not be able to neutralize or dig up. The road was assumed to lie between two white lines, and the leader and his men were permitted to work up and down the road as far as the white lines extended. The destruction of the bridge had aroused the enemy, but they did not know in which direction the men who blew it up had gone.

Since each situation furnishes evidence for more than one of the traits under consideration, a 6-point rating scale was adopted for each variable as follows: very poor, 7 per cent; inferior, 18 per cent; low average, 25 per cent; high average, 25 per cent; superior, 18 per cent; very superior, 7 per cent. The percentages indicated the proportion of men who would fall in each category if the variable happened to be normally distributed in the population of candidates. By combining one or more of the categories, this scale was sometimes converted into a 2-point, 3-point, or 4-point scale.

A thorough statistical analysis of results shows the correlations between the variables. Correlations between motivations for assignment and other variables were as follows:

social relations	.45	security	.23
energy and initiative	.44	effective intelligence	.22
emotional stability	.43	physical ability	.22
leadership	.36	observing and recording	.18
propaganda skill	.35		

Likewise, the correlations of these assessments with appraisals of actual success in the theater of war were found for small samples. These correlations indicated roughly that effective intelligence was the best single predictor of success. All the other variables showed correlations not significantly different from zero. The samples available for this validation study were, however, usually small, and the methods of appraising workers' effectiveness were probably not as well-standardized or as reliable as the methods used in the original assessments. Effective intelligence was measured not only by test, but also by behavior in a stress interview, in discussion and debate, and by practical judgment and leadership. For practical purposes the results of these assessments were always reported to the commanding officers in simple and nontechnical terms.

CONTRIBUTIONS FROM MILITARY EXPERIENCES WITH TESTS

Flanagan (1948) has summarized some of the most important conclusions from the AAF programs under the following headings:

Relative Importance of Aptitude and Training

The comparisons of many groups in many training situations brought out great differences among instructors in the same school and even greater differences between schools. The program expanded so rapidly that civilian and military training officers were given a large amount of freedom in developing their training programs. By comparing the training in one situation with success in later situations, it became apparent that success in both basic and advanced training was determined to a much greater extent by aptitudes, as shown on the Air Crew Classification Tests, than by the instructor or by the quality of his training. This was true of both pilots and bombardiers. One should not generalize too freely from these results, however; a great deal more research on the content and effectiveness of specific training activities is needed.

Test Forms

It was found that by using sufficient ingenuity all paper-and-pencil methods could be set up in multiple-choice form suitable for machine scoring. By using photographs of instrument faces, of model airplanes, of terrain taken several thousand feet in the air, and the like, it was possible to obtain sample situations. Even some psychomotor functions and reactions to motion pictures were successfully adapted to answer sheets.

Apparatus tests were employed to a much greater degree than ever before by having timing and counting accomplished by means of electrical devices conveniently arranged on the examiner's control desk. In this way one examiner could administer complicated coordination tests to four or more persons at once.

Test Content

In order to measure unique, stable, and important traits, tests were designed to have one principal factorial loading on skills that had been learned or practiced over a long period of time and which showed considerable prediction of success of a particular kind. Sufficient practice was given preliminary to the test proper to allow for "warming up" and for the development of skill in the test situation. Both speed and power tests were found to be of value.

Statistical Procedures

Batteries of tests of independent traits were found to be more effective and more economical in predicting success than tests which had not been analyzed, and probably included a variety of unknown factors in unknown amounts. In order to provide such tests, not only the total scores but also each item of the tests had to be evaluated for factorial purity and difficulty. Great economy in the statistical procedure was accomplished by the use of parts of a group rather than the whole, and by standard forms and machine methods. It was found advisable to use a second sample in item analyses to avoid various kinds of systematic and random variations. (Using a second sample to confirm the first analysis is called *cross validation*.)

Job Requirements

A great deal of emphasis was placed on defining job requirements in terms of abilities, interests, and adjustments, and on indicating their relative importance. It was found that both workers and supervisors were inaccurate with regard to such analyses. Their judgments were usually vague stereotypes, and they confused ability with motivation. To analyze jobs, considerable training is needed in defining independent traits and giving actual examples and in practice under supervision. The value of a judgment depends to a large extent upon the judge's knowledge of individual differences in the traits under consideration.

Job analysis must determine evidence of the possession of critical requirements—those that make the difference between success and failure in important aspects of the job. These can best be determined by studying the causes of good and poor performance. Valuable evidence of this kind was given by individuals concerning their own errors and concerning the effective and ineffective acts of their supervisors, or those whom they supervised.

The best evidence of critical job requirements will come from a follow-up study in which traits are carefully measured before training and checked later against success. This kind of study is found to be extremely difficult. It is dangerous to assume that because successful and unsuccessful individuals differ with respect to a trait now, they probably showed similar differences before they were selected for training. Failure may affect the trait rather than be caused by the trait.

Criteria of Success

The important problem in all validation is the securing of good measures of success. To be effective these criteria must evaluate independent skills separately, and for actual operations rather than for training situations. The most relevant, reliable, and unbiased criteria seemed to be objective measures of combat proficiency, but these were often highly related to opportunity. Ratings based on direct and systematic operations were fairly useful, but ratings based on general impressions, reports, or incidents were the least valuable. Reliability was considerably increased by focusing the rater's attention on one well-defined trait while comparing all individuals in a group. The forced-choice technique where raters were not able to determine the scoring procedure (Chapter XVI) was effective in certain situations.

STUDY GUIDE QUESTIONS

1. In what ways did the objectives of testing programs in military establishments differ from those of testing programs in educational systems? In what ways were they alike?

2. How did the Army General Classification Test differ from the Navy Basic Test Battery?

3. What percentiles of the military population are represented by scores of from 110 to 129 on the Army General Classification Test?

4. What relations were found between AGCT scores and highest grade completed in school, the ACE Psychological Examinations, and the Army Alpha Test?

5. What relations were found between scores on the AGCT and success in various types of military training?

6. What is the significance of the AGCT occupational norms?

7. How did the AAF Qualifying Examination and the Air Crew Classification Test differ in purpose and composition?

8. How were stanine scores for the various air crew positions computed? What predictive value did they have?

9. How well did the Navy Basic Test Battery predict success in navy training and success on board ship?

10. Compare the content of military batteries with the content of achievement batteries (Illus. 57) and aptitude batteries (Illus. 86).

11. How effective was the use of short personality inventories in military selection?

12. How did the OSS appraise behavior—particularly behavior under stress?

13. What evidence is there that batteries of tests of independent traits were more economical and effective than unanalyzed tests?

PART TWO

ELEMENTARY STATISTICS

CHAPTER XII

THE INTERPRETATION
OF SCORES

∿∿∿

In the previous chapters the various ways of sampling a person's behavior by recording his responses to particular types of test items have been discussed. The total number of credited responses, called the *raw score,* represents the performance of a person in a test situation. The raw score, however, is of little use by itself. For instance, no one is much the wiser by learning that Frank's score in a vocabulary test was twenty words correctly defined. The raw score is given significance only by comparing it with other scores. One of the most important facts to know about a person is his position in a standard group, for this shows how well he is equipped to meet competition. This chapter describes several common ways of interpreting raw scores in terms of one's relative position in a group. Furthermore, it shows how groups can be measured and compared.

THE LIMITS OF A SCORE

Since a score on a test is only an approximate indicator of the results of an observation, it has variable limits. Within the limits of the precision of the measuring instrument a test score is considered to be a *midpoint* of a scale unit. For example, in measuring the height of a person many times with a ruler, one is likely to make errors and to record values above the true length as often as below it. Hence, any obtained score such as 50 is usually thought of as representing values from 49.5000 to 50.49999. The midpoint of this unit is 50.0.

FREQUENCY OR DISTRIBUTION TABLES

The immediate result of testing a group of persons is simply a pile of corrected test sheets, or a list of scores, see Illus. 118. In order to compare these scores conveniently, they are arranged in a frequency table, a table which shows the number of times each score was made. The number of persons who have made a particular score indicates the *frequency* of that score. Illustration 119 shows the steps usually followed in making a frequency table. First, one finds the *range of scores,* which is the difference between the highest and the lowest scores in a group. If the range is large, it is not advisable to count the number of times each score was made. Unnecessary work is eliminated by tabulating scores in small groups, called *class intervals.* Since it has been found that ten class intervals allow one to calculate group norms about as accurately as a larger number of class intervals, the range of scores is divided by 10 to find the size of the class interval. For instance, the range of scores in Illus. 118 is $71 - 27 = 44$, and this divided by 10 is 4.4. To simplify tabulations the next highest whole number—5—is taken as the class interval to be used. The scores are then written as in the first column of Illus. 119 showing the limits of each class interval. Following a common usage for scales of distances or time, the lower limit of each class interval is often used alone, as in the second column Illus. 119. These limits are usually selected so that they are multiples of the interval chosen. The smallest scores are put at the lower end of the column, and the highest at the upper end. The number of persons whose scores are found in a class interval is indicated by the tab marks in the third column, and by the frequencies in the fourth.

HISTOGRAMS AND FREQUENCY CURVES

It is often easier to understand distribution tables when they are pictured, and one of the best ways of picturing them is by drawing a *histogram.* A histogram is drawn on graph paper with the base line divided into class intervals, and a standard area above this line is allotted to each person. Thus, in Illus. 120 each person is represented by one small rectangle. The whole figure represents the data shown in Illus. 119. A *frequency curve* is a histogram which has been smoothed according to some method, usually by connecting the mid-points of adjoining columns, as in Illus. 120. A frequency curve is supposed to be a slightly truer picture of a distribution than a histogram, since the cases in a class interval are seldom actually distributed evenly over the whole interval, as they are in a histogram. On close

ILLUS. 118. RAW SCORES MADE BY 100 STUDENTS ON A NUMBER COMPARISON TEST

35	40	50	43	60	53	45	50	71	43
45	60	36	60	55	47	42	45	55	52
46	44	51	62	44	52	33	44	63	37
39	62	66	39	59	58	43	44	38	44
56	39	47	41	40	36	40	48	55	58
50	47	45	42	50	30	39	33	51	36
57	60	32	69	53	50	55	53	48	27
40	47	35	58	63	53	64	35	54	49
45	62	45	33	43	61	64	46	42	49
53	57	54	59	48	30	50	49	29	37

Number of Scores (N) = 100
Sum of Scores (Σ) = 4796
Mean (M) = 47.96

ILLUS. 119. FREQUENCY TABLE OF SCORES IN ILLUS. 118
Class Interval of Five

(1) Class Interval	(2) Lower Limit Score	(3) Tabs				Frequencies (4)	Frequencies Cumulative (5)
70–74	70	1				1	100
65–69	65	11				2	99
60–64	60	ᴎ̶ᴚ̶ᴧ	ᴎ̶ᴚ̶ᴧ	11		12	97
55–59	55	ᴎ̶ᴚ̶ᴧ	ᴎ̶ᴚ̶ᴧ	11		12	85
50–54	50	ᴎ̶ᴚ̶ᴧ	ᴎ̶ᴚ̶ᴧ	ᴎ̶ᴚ̶ᴧ	11	17	73
45–49	45	ᴎ̶ᴚ̶ᴧ	ᴎ̶ᴚ̶ᴧ	ᴎ̶ᴚ̶ᴧ	111	18	56
40–44	40	ᴎ̶ᴚ̶ᴧ	ᴎ̶ᴚ̶ᴧ	ᴎ̶ᴚ̶ᴧ	11	17	38
35–39	35	ᴎ̶ᴚ̶ᴧ	ᴎ̶ᴚ̶ᴧ	111		13	21
30–34	30	ᴎ̶ᴚ̶ᴧ	1			6	8
25–29	25	11				2	2

N is the sum of column (1) . . . 100

Calculation of Quartiles and Centiles

P_{75} = 75th centile = 3rd quartile = 54.5 + (2/12)5 = 55.33
P_{50} = 50th centile = median = 44.5 + (12/18)5 = 47.83
P_{25} = 25th centile = 1st quartile = 39.5 + (4/17)5 = 40.67

$$Q = \frac{P_{75} - P_{25}}{2} = \frac{55.33 - 40.67}{2} = 7.33$$

P_{90} = 90th centile = 59.5 + (5/12)5 = 61.58
P_{10} = 10th centile = 34.5 + (2/13)5 = 35.27

$$Sk = \text{Skewness} = \left(\frac{P_{90} - P_{10}}{2}\right) - P_{50} = \frac{96.85}{2} - 47.83 = .60$$

inspection they are found to be distributed unevenly, with more cases falling at that end of the interval which is nearer the center of the whole group. When a frequency curve has a large number of class intervals, and represents a large number of cases, the surface will be smooth indeed. It can then be considered a continuous curved line, as in Illus. 121.

ILLUS. 120. HISTOGRAM AND FREQUENCY CURVE
OF SCORES IN ILLUS. 118

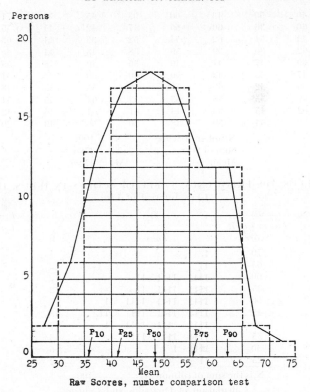

Raw Scores, number comparison test

Note: All numbers refer to the lower limit
of their class intervals.

NORMAL FREQUENCY CURVE

Frequency curves have been compiled for literally thousands of
cases in hundreds of biological, physical, and psychological studies,
and a striking similarity among these curves is the rule. A large number of them closely resemble what is known as the *normal curve of
distribution* or the *Gaussian curve*. The normal curve (Illus. 121) has
been found in many instances to be typical of large samples of

1. Mechanical variations, such as the distribution of heads and
   tails shown after tossing coins, combinations of playing cards,
   and numbers in wheels of chance
2. Mathematical combinations, such as polynomial expansions

3. Physiological phenomena: height, weight, pulse rate, and ossification
4. Social phenomena: number of books in private homes and attitudes toward various social and political institutions
5. Mental abilities: information and skills in school subjects, intelligence tests, occupational skills, and errors in observation

ILLUS. 121. NORMAL CURVE

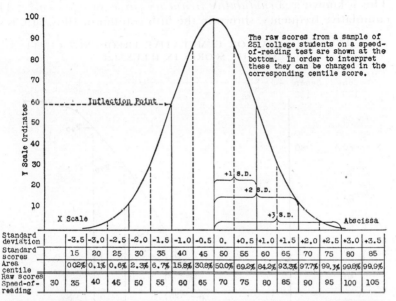

The raw scores from a sample of 251 college students on a speed-of-reading test are shown at the bottom. In order to interpret these they can be changed in the corresponding centile score.

Standard deviation	-3.5	-3.0	-2.5	-2.0	-1.5	-1.0	-0.5	0.	+0.5	+1.0	+1.5	+2.0	+2.5	+3.0	+3.5
Standard scores	15	20	25	30	35	40	45	50	55	60	65	70	75	80	85
Area centile	0.02%	0.1%	0.6%	2.3%	6.7%	15.8%	30.8%	50.0%	69.2%	84.2%	93.3%	97.7%	99.3%	99.8%	99.9%
Raw scores Speed-of-reading	30	35	40	45	50	55	60	65	70	75	80	85	90	95	100	105

This curve always has the same relation between X and Y values. Thus, if the height at the mean is 100, then the height at + or — one SD is 60. The proportion of the area which lies between the curve, the base line, and any two perpendiculars can be calculated with great accuracy.

The shape of this curve, which has been studied closely, is worth noting, for its characteristics have led to the development of an important scaling technique. First, observe that the greatest frequency of scores is at the midpoint. From the midpoint the sides slope down, slowly at first, then more rapidly until a point in the curve, called the *inflection point*, is reached, whence the curve flattens out gradually. The curve continues until it becomes almost parallel with the base line. Theoretically, the curve would never touch the base line if the cases were infinite in number, but it would continue to approach the base indefinitely. Actually, there are always highest and lowest scores in the measurement of individuals in a real group. The normal curve, whose dimensions are constant and well-known, has become a standard with which group measures may be compared.

OGIVE CURVE

Another useful picturing of a distribution of scores shows the number of persons whose scores fall above or below a score (Illus. 122). This is known as a *cumulative frequency curve,* or *ogive curve.* The cumulative frequency, shown in the fifth column of Illus. 119, is se-

ILLUS. 122. OGIVE OR CUMULATIVE FREQUENCY CURVE OF THE SCORES IN ILLUS. 121

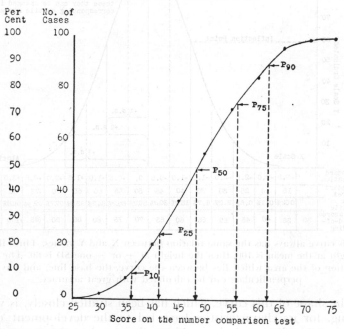

cured by adding the frequency of each class interval to the sum of the frequencies of all the intervals below it. An ogive curve is made by laying off the scores on the base line, or *abscissa,* and the total number or per cent of cases on the *ordinate,* or vertical line. The number of cases in the lowest class interval is indicated by a dot over the score which is the upper limit of the lowest class interval. The upper limit is used to indicate the number of persons who fell below this score. The number of persons in both the first and second class intervals are added together and indicated by a point over the upper limit of the second class interval. Similar procedures are used for the other intervals. Each point on the curve then represents the number of persons whose scores fall below a particular score. Of course the number falling above any score can also be quickly found from this chart.

RANKS, CENTILES, QUARTILES, DECILES, AND LETTER GRADES

One of the simplest ways of describing a person's position in a group is to indicate his *rank* when the members of the group are arranged in order of size of scores. Ranks are valuable for indicating how many persons received scores that are above that of a given person. This is all that one needs to know if he is considering test results in situations, such as assigning a definite number of scholarships or filling a definite number of positions. When knowledge of relative excellence is desirable, however, as for a wider distribution of grades or other awards, it can be secured by the use of *centiles*. The centile shows the proportion of the group which falls below a given score. Thus, a centile of 75 means that one did better than 75 per cent of the group, but not as well as the highest 25 per cent. Centiles may be read directly from an ogive curve, such as that shown in Illus. 122, or they may be calculated, as in Illus. 119. Centiles, also called *percentiles,* have as their symbol P, with a subscript to indicate the particular centile. To calculate the 75th centile score (P_{75}) the score of the 75th person [1] from the bottom must be found, for there are just one hundred persons in this group.[2]

The cumulative frequencies in the fifth column of Illus. 119 show that 73 scores fell below the class interval 55 to 59.99. Hence, two cases in this interval are needed to reach the 75th in the group. It is customary to calculate this score in all large groups by *interpolation,* which is the process of estimating a value between two given values by the use of a ratio. In this case, the given values are the limits of the class interval, and the ratio is $\frac{2}{12}$, since two of the twelve cases in this class interval are needed. Therefore P_{75} is found by adding $\frac{2}{12}$ of the size of the class interval, 5, to the lower limit of the class interval.

$$P_{75} = 54.5 + (\tfrac{2}{12})5 = 55.33$$

[1] This calculation would be more precise if the score were found which lies halfway between the 75th and 76th person. For usual work this refinement is not considered necessary.

[2] If the number were 160, the P_{75} would be the score of the 120th person, $(160 \times .75 = 120)$.

Centiles are useful indicators of a person's position in his group, since nearly everyone with as much as a sixth-grade education can understand them. They are probably the scores used most frequently for adults. Illustration 123 allows raw scores to be changed rapidly to centiles by reading the centile value from the top of the column. For

ILLUS. 123. CONVERSION TABLE FOR MICHIGAN SPEED OF READING TEST

Forms 1 and 2

Items Correct												1937 Revision (7 min.)
Detroit Sample												N = 3302
						T Score						Mean
			30	35	40	45	50	55	60	65	70	%
	Age in	Raw				Centile Rank						Cor-
Grade	School	Score	2	7	16	30	50	70	84	93	98	rect
Senior	21–0	——	41	45	49	53	57	61	65	69	73	98
Junior	20–1	——	38	42	46	50	54	58	62	66	70	97
Sophomore	19–1	——	36	40	44	48	52	58	60	64	68	95
Freshman	18–1	——	31	35	40	44	49	54	58	62	66	94
12.0	17–2	——	30	34	38	42	46	50	54	58	62	96
11.0	16–3	——	27	31	35	39	43	47	51	55	59	96
10.0	15–3	——	23	27	31	35	40	45	49	54	58	96
9.0	14–5	——	18	22	27	31	36	41	45	49	54	95
8.0	13–6	——	16	20	24	28	32	36	40	44	48	94
7.0	12–7	——	14	17	21	24	28	32	35	39	42	91
6.0	11–7	——	9	12	16	19	23	27	30	34	37	87
5.0	10–6	——	3	6	10	13	17	21	24	28	31	80
4.0	9–5	——	0	2	5	8	11	14	17	20	23	72
3.0	8–4	——	0	0	0	0	3	6	9	12	15	40
					Letter Grades							
			E		D		C		B		A	

NOTE—(All numbers refer to lower limits of class intervals)

(Greene, 1937. By permission of The Psychological Corporation.)

instance, if a boy in the sixth grade received a score of 34, his centile rank would be 93, and it further appears that his score is nearly as high as that of the average ninth grade student. This table was prepared by securing scores for fairly large groups in each grade and then finding the scores which corresponded to each of the centiles. Such tables are now available for a large number of standard tests.

Another fairly common way of indicating a person's position in a group is to say in which quarter of the group his score falls. The dividing lines between quarters are called *quartiles,* and these are the 25th, 50th, and 75th centiles.

In some classifications letter systems are used for grades. In these a definite proportion of a group is sometimes arbitrarily assigned a particular letter. Illustration 124 shows three letter gradings that are in use. From this it appears that in the United States Army examinations a person was given a grade of A if he fell in the highest 4 per cent of the examinees. On the Strong Interest Blank a rating of A is as-

ILLUS. 124. THE ASSIGNMENT OF LETTER RATINGS TO PROPORTIONS OF A GROUP

	1	2	3
A	4.09%	75%	17%
B	8.82	25	25
C+	16.69	0	
C	26.78	0	33
C—	21.86	0	
D	14.38	0	18
E	7.38	0	7

1. United States Army, June 1918. Memoir National Academy Sciences. 1921, XV, p. 421.
2. Strong's Interest Blank (1931).
3. A distribution of grades from an elementary psychology class.

signed to a person when his score falls among the highest 75 per cent of scores of an occupational group. On a distribution of grades from an elementary psychology class, a rating of A was assigned to the highest 17 per cent of the group. The usefulness of letter ratings is limited, therefore, by the variation in their meanings.

DIMENSIONS OF A GROUP OF SCORES

Frequency tables and their corresponding curves have three aspects or dimensions: central tendency, dispersion of scores, and shape. A *central tendency* is a single score near the center of a group which may be used to represent the standing of the whole group. *Dispersions* show the range of scores found in various portions of a group. The *shape of a curve* indicates its symmetry, or skewness, and its irregularities. These dimensions can be described by numerical indicators which are useful for comparing groups, and persons within groups.

Central Tendencies

The three common measures of the central tendency of a group are: the arithmetic mean, the mode, and the median, all of which are called averages.

Mean. In this book the mean refers to the arithmetic mean unless otherwise indicated. It represents a point of balance which would be found if all scores in a group were assigned the same weight and then arranged along a horizontal beam according to class intervals. The histogram in Illus. 120 is a picture of such an arrangement. If this histogram were a pile of bricks on a straight beam,[3] then it would be possible to find a point of balance at which the bricks on one side of the point would equal in weight the bricks on the other side. This concept of balance underlies many treatments of psychological material, and implies two basic assumptions: (1) that the psychological scale is comparable to a *linear* scale, such as distance in a straight line; (2) that members of a group can be considered to be a number of equal, unrelated weights, that is, their measured qualities are unaffected by their position. Both of these assumptions have been challenged with regard to special situations, but they seem to be appropriate in many test situations, and the mean is probably the most commonly used central tendency.

One way to find a mean is to add the scores of all the persons in the group and to divide this total by the number of persons in the group. By using this method the mean for the scores in Illus. 118 is found to be 47.96. If a large number of persons are to be measured, an adding machine will save a great deal of time.

A short-cut in finding a mean is first to guess at the probable mean score, and then make the necessary corrections. In Illus. 125 the guessed mean is arbitrarily taken as the midpoint of the class interval, 45–49.9, which seems from inspection to be nearest the middle of the distribution. The deviations, or number of steps, of all class intervals from this class interval are placed in the third column, and the frequency of class interval is multiplied by its respective deviation, as in the fourth column. The deviations above the guessed mean are marked plus, and those below, minus. The total minus deviations are subtracted from the plus deviations (90 − 69 = +21) to find the amount and direction of the correction for guessing. The result, +21 deviations, divided by the total number of cases, is the mean correction. This amount is multiplied by the size of the class interval to make its units of the same denomination as those of the raw score. Finally, this correction is added to the guessed mean, 47. The result is 48.05, which is taken as the mean of the distribution. Illustration 125 also gives a general equation with letters substituted for the words and phrases used here. Such equations are a great convenience, for the letters or algebraic symbols are more quickly writ-

---

[3] To make a better illustration, the beam itself should have no weight at all.

ten and read than the words they represent. Since these symbols are widely used, it is advisable to learn them.

ILLUS. 125. CALCULATION OF MEAN AND STANDARD DEVIATION OF SCORES IN ILLUS. 118

$$N = 100$$

1	2	3	4	5
SCORES	FREQUENCIES	DEVIATIONS	FREQUENCY OF DEVIATIONS	SQUARED DEVIATIONS.
X	f	x'	fx'	f(x')²
70	1	5	5	25
65	2	4	8	32
60	12	3	36	108
55	12	2	24	48
50	17	1	17	17
45	18	0	0	0
40	17	—1	—17	17
35	13	—2	—26	52
30	6	—3	—18	54
25	2	—4	— 8	32
sums (Σ)	100		90	385
			—69	
			21	

$$M = M' + \frac{(\Sigma x')i}{N}$$

$$= 47 + \frac{(21)5}{100} = 47 + 1.05$$

$$= 48.05 \text{ or } 48.1$$

$$SD = i\sqrt{\frac{\Sigma(x')^2}{N} - \left(\frac{\Sigma x'}{N}\right)^2}$$

$$= 5\sqrt{3.85 - (.21)^2} = 53.81$$

$$= 5(1.95) = 9.75 = 9.8$$

LEGEND:	M = Mean	x' = Deviation from Guessed
	M' = Guessed Mean	Mean
	Σ = Sum of	i = Class Interval Size
	N = Number of Cases	SD or σ = Standard Deviation
	X = Raw Scores	f = Frequency of Cases in
		a Class Interval

Mode. The *mode* of a group is defined as that score or class interval which has the largest frequency. It is found by making a frequency distribution and inspecting it. Illustrations 120 and 125 show one mode which is at 47, the midpoint of the class interval with the largest frequency, 18 persons.

In some cases a frequency curve shows two or more modes. Two class intervals which have large frequencies may be separated by class intervals having smaller frequencies, as in Illus. 126. Sometimes these bimodal curves result from combining data from what would otherwise form two separate unimodal curves, as is apparently the case in Illus. 126. Occasionally bimodal curves are the result of poor measurement techniques. As bimodal curves are rather rare in the measurement of human skills under normal conditions, they need to be scrutinized carefully, and the data on which they are based should be analyzed to find the cause of abnormality.

ILLUS. 126. BIMODAL CURVE, CRITICAL SCORE

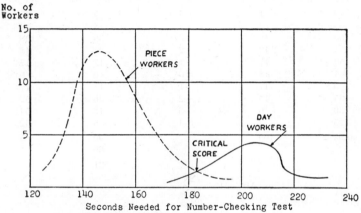

(From Link, 1918. Reproduced by permission of the Macmillan Co.)

Median. The *median* is defined as the middle score (P_{50}) in a group when the scores are arranged according to size. The median is found by an interpolation of the scores in the class interval which contains the middle score. If we take the middle score as that of the fiftieth person in a group of one hundred, or the 50th centile, then in the fifth column of Illus. 112, it appears that this centile falls in the class interval 45–49.9. Thirty-eight persons are below this class interval; therefore the twelfth person from the bottom of this class interval is the fiftieth person in the group. His approximate score can be calculated by interpolation when it is assumed that the eighteen scores in this class interval are evenly distributed over the whole interval. When the interval is small compared with the number of cases falling in this interval, this assumption does not introduce an appreciable error. From this assumption $12\frac{2}{18}$ of the size of the class interval (5) must be added to its lower limit (44.5) to secure the score of the fiftieth person. In this instance the median is 47.8. (Median = $44.5 + (12\frac{2}{18})5 = 47.8$).

The Uses of Central Tendencies. The question often arises: which central tendency is the best? The answer depends upon the distribution of the scores and their intended use. In a normal curve the three central tendencies are identical, but in an irregular or a skewed curve they will differ (Illus. 127). A curve is said to be skewed from the normal when it is not symmetrical.

Let us consider a situation in which the most representative score of a group is desirable. Of the three the mean is most affected by the extreme scores of a group, so that when the extreme scores are thought to be rather insignificant, the median or mode is used. The mean represents a true center of balance in a group, and it is generally preferred when the scores represent precise measurements. The mode indicates the most frequent score in a group, and it also shows when bimodality occurs.

ILLUS. 127. SKEWNESS

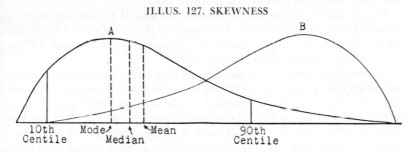

In addition to using a central tendency as the most representative score of a group, it is also used in calculating various interesting ratios which are described later in this book.

Dispersions

The amount of dispersion exhibited by a group is usually revealed by one of four indicators: the total range, the quartile deviation, the probable error, or the standard deviation.[4]

Total Range. The total range of scores is the difference between the highest and lowest scores in a group. Its use in securing class intervals has already been described. It is not, however, used commonly for comparing the dispersions of two groups of persons, because its size depends upon the two extreme scores. These two scores often

---

[4] Another indication of dispersion which is also used occasionally is called the average deviation, AD, or mean deviation, MD, or mean variation, MV. It is found by summing all deviations from the mean regardless of sign, and dividing this sum by the number of scores. In a normal curve the AD is one half the range of the middle 57.5 per cent of cases.

vary considerably in several chance samplings, particularly in small groups, so that other indications of dispersion which are less affected by chance are more useful.

Quartile Deviation and Probable Error.   Both the quartile deviation (Q) and the probable error (PE) are found by taking one half the range of the middle 50 per cent of the cases in a group. The Q is used for actual measures, and the PE is applied to hypothetical situations where the probable variation which would occur through chance is desired for purposes of prediction. Q is found by subtracting the 25th centile from the 75th centile, and dividing the remainder by 2.

$$Q = \frac{P_{75} - P_{25}}{2}$$

The calculation of Q is shown in Illus. 119.

The probable error (PE) is usually calculated by multiplying the standard deviation by .6745. The figure is the ratio of the PE to the SD of all normal curves. Both the standard deviation and PE are used only for normal distribution curves.

Standard Deviation.   If one should drop perpendiculars from the two inflection points of a normal curve of distribution to the base line, the total area thus bounded would include 68.27 per cent, or roughly two thirds of the whole area. The distance on the base line from the mean to the foot of such a perpendicular is known as a *standard deviation.* Its usual symbols are a small sigma (σ) or the initials SD. The SD, used as a unit of measurement, can be laid out along the base line a number of times, as in Illus. 121. The normal curve extends approximately $2\frac{1}{2}$ SD in each direction from the mean, and the total length of the base line needed to include 98.76 per cent of the cases is 5 SD. The percentage of the area which lies above each hundredth of an SD has been calculated to twelve decimal places. A standard deviation has therefore become a precise indicator of position in a group. The SD has another advantage: it produces a scale whose steps are equal in the sense that they represent equally often-noticed differences. Theoretically, the difference between scores of persons who are .5 and .6 SD above the mean can be noticed by a competent group of judges just as often as a difference of .1 can be noticed anywhere in the scale. This provides a method of scaling scores of psychological phenomena, which is comparable with the best physical scales, since all scales are based on the ability of competent judges to notice certain differences equally often.

The Shape of a Curve.   Before calculating the standard deviation for any group, one must be reasonably sure that his figures fit a normal distribution curve fairly well. Tests for goodness of fit include those for skewness (Sk) and kurtosis (Ku). A curve is said to have *skewness* when it is not symmetrical. *Kurtosis* is the relative flatness of a curve. A curve varies from normal kurtosis when it is relatively more peaked, *leptokurtic,* or more flattened, *platykurtic,* than the normal curve.

Skewness can be roughly measured by the formula $Sk = \dfrac{P_{90} + P_{10}}{2} - P_{50}$ (Garrett, 1937, p. 299). When Sk is zero the curve is symmetrical. When Sk is positive the curve extends farther to the right than to the left of the mean (shown as A in Illus. 127). When Sk is negative, the curve will resemble B in Illus. 127. From Illus. 119 the skewness of the distribution is found to be .60.

The kurtosis of a curve can be roughly found by the formula $Ku = \dfrac{Q}{(P_{90} - P_{10})}$ (Garrett, 1937, p. 230). This formula gives a value of .263 for the normal curve. The distribution in Illus. 119 shows a kurtosis of .275. The amount by which a curve may deviate from the normal shape in either skewness or kurtosis by chance errors of measurement can be known from formulas in Garrett or other statistical texts. Small variations from the normal curve introduce insignificant errors in practical comparisons.

Calculation of a Standard Deviation. Since the curve in Illus. 120 has shown nearly normal values for both skewness and kurtosis, the formulas which have been designed for use with a normal curve may be safely applied. The calculation of the standard deviation for the scores in Illus. 120 is shown in Illus. 125. It is found by the following steps:

1. The deviations from the guessed mean are squared and added in the fifth column.

2. The sum of the squared deviations is divided by the number of cases. This result is the mean of the squared deviations.

3. The mean of the squared deviations is corrected for the error caused by the use of the guessed mean by subtracting the square of the mean deviation. If the deviations had been measured from the true mean, this step would not have been necessary, but it is nearly always quicker to use a guessed mean and the correction than to find the correct mean and then measure deviations from it.

4. The square root of the corrected mean of the squared deviations is found and multiplied by the class interval. This is the SD.

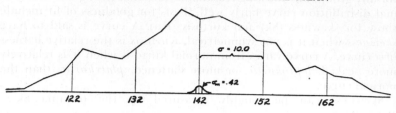

LEVEL OF SIGNIFICANCE

The discussion in the preceding sections indicates that these measures of a group of scores are likely to vary somewhat if they are repeated. Sometimes it is important to know how much they are likely to vary for a representative group. This can be determined in two ways: one is by actual repetitions of measures of the same group, and the other by mathematical estimates. Making actual trials is, of course, the best method, but, since it is extremely expensive and time consuming, the statistical method is generally used. It is assumed that the more persons in the group, the more accurate or representative will be the results. Also, it is assumed that if the group were actually measured many times, the means would fall into a normal distribution, whose standard deviation is called the *standard error* of the mean (σ_m). The formula for which is $\sigma_m = \dfrac{\sigma}{\sqrt{N\text{-}1}}$.

Thus if a group of 570 pilot candidates have a mean of 142 and a σ of 10, then $\sigma_m = \dfrac{10}{\sqrt{569}} = \dfrac{10}{23.87} = .42$. (See Illus. 128.)

We can say how much the mean is likely to vary in this group because we know the proportions of the normal curve which correspond to standard deviations. These are given in Illus. 121, and in greater detail in Illus. 129. For instance, one standard deviation below the mean corresponds to a centile of 15.87. The chances are therefore about 16 in 100 that the mean pilot score would on many repetitions fall below 141.58 (142 — .42). Since two standard deviations below the mean correspond to a centile of 2.28, the probability is only a little more than 2 in 100 that the mean will fall below 141.16, which is two standard deviations below the mean actually found (142 — .84).

The actual variation in score (.84) is called a *fiduciary limit* and corresponds to plus or minus two standard deviations. Fiduciary limits can be found for any desired level of significance. It can be said with great certainty that the mean will not fall by chance more

ILLUS. 129. CORRESPONDING VALUES OF STANDARD DEVIATIONS, T SCORES, CENTILES, AND ORDINATES OF THE NORMAL PROBABILITY CURVE

1 Standard Deviation	2 T Score	3 Centile [1]	4 Ordinate [2]	1 Standard Deviation	2 T Score	3 Centile [1]	4 Ordinate [2]
3.0	80	99.86	.0044	— .1	49	46.02	.3970
2.9	79	99.81	.0060	— .2	48	42.07	.3910
2.8	78	99.74	.0079	— .3	47	38.21	.3814
2.7	77	99.65	.0104	— .4	46	34.46	.3683
2.6	76	99.53	.0136	— .5	45	30.85	.3521
2.5	75	99.38	.0175	— .6	44	27.43	.3332
2.4	74	99.18	.0224	— .7	43	24.20	.3123
2.3	73	98.93	.0283	— .8	42	31.19	.2897
2.2	72	98.61	.0355	— .9	41	18.41	.2661
2.1	71	98.21	.0440	—1.0	40	15.87	.2420
2.0	70	97.72	.0540	—1.1	39	13.57	.2179
1.9	69	97.13	.0656	—1.2	38	11.51	.1942
1.8	68	96.41	.0790	—1.3	37	9.86	.1714
1.7	67	95.54	.0940	—1.4	36	8.08	.1497
1.6	66	94.52	.1109	—1.5	35	6.68	.1295
1.5	65	93.32	.1295	—1.6	34	5.48	.1109
1.4	64	91.92	.1497	—1.7	33	4.46	.0940
1.3	63	90.32	.1714	—1.8	32	3.59	.0790
1.2	62	88.49	.1942	—1.9	31	2.87	.0656
1.1	61	86.43	.2179	—2.0	30	2.28	.0540
1.0	60	84.13	.2420	—2.1	29	1.79	.0440
0.9	59	81.59	.2661	—2.2	28	1.39	.0355
0.8	58	78.81	.2897	—2.3	27	1.07	.0283
0.7	57	75.80	.3123	—2.4	26	.82	.0224
0.6	56	72.57	.3332	— 2.5	25	.62	.0175
0.5	55	69.15	.3521	—2.6	24	.47	.0136
0.4	54	65.54	.3684	—2.7	23	.35	.0104
0.3	53	61.79	.3814	—2.8	22	.26	.0079
0.2	52	57.93	.3910	—2.9	21	.19	.0060
0.1	51	53.98	.3970	—3.0	20	.135	.0044
0.0	50	50.00	.3989				

[1] Proportion of total area below the point indicated by the standard deviation.
[2] Relative height of curve at the point indicated by the standard deviation.

(Arranged from Pearson, 1914, by permission of the editor of *Biometrika*.)

than three standard errors below or above what was actually found.
The reliabilities of measures of dispersion are likewise calculated by assuming that the chance forces which cause them to vary are related to the size of the group. Thus the standard error of a

$$\sigma = \frac{\sigma}{\sqrt{2N}}.$$

These probabilities are often referred to as *levels of significance* or *levels of confidence*. The one-per-cent level of significance simply means that the probability is not more than 1 in 100 that a given variation above or below an obtained measure will happen by chance. A 5-per-cent level of significance means that similar chances are only 5 in 100. For large groups, for example five hundred cases, the one-per-cent level of significance of a difference between an obtained mean and a given score would be a point 2.58 standard deviations below or above the obtained mean, and the 5-per-cent level would be a point 1.97 standard deviations from the mean (Illus. 129). For small groups of from 25 to 50, these numbers are slightly larger, 2.179 and 2.06 respectively. For small samples (less than 25) the centiles in Illus. 129 are too small at the extremes. R. A. Fisher (1925) computed tables for such probabilities which he called t (Illus. 130). Thus a logical development of this consideration of levels of significance is the *null hypothesis*—a statement that the observed differences in certain situations probably do *not* represent real differences, but can be explained purely by chance, i.e., random variations in sampling.

The probability that a certain variation or difference will occur by chance is known from many careful measures of situations, such as the chance distribution of heads when coins are tossed, or of cards when random selections are made, or of many other permutations and combinations. The mathematical study of probabilities has yielded accurate formulae for predictions of chance. When applied to the difference between means (Chapter XIII), the null hypothesis states that there is probably *no* real difference between the true means of the two samples if the difference divided by its own sigma (D/σ) is less than 2.58, because such a difference would occur by pure chance about 1 in 100 times.

When applied to a mean, the null hypothesis states that there is probably no chance that the true mean varies away from the observed mean more than three times its own standard error, since 2.58 SE will include all except the one half of one per cent at each extreme.

USES OF MEASURES OF DISPERSION

Two common uses of measures of dispersion, the comparison of groups and the comparison of individuals in a group, are described below.

Group Comparisons

Often an investigator wants to indicate which of two groups has a larger dispersion of scores on a test. For instance, in employment or

ILLUS. 130. DISTRIBUTION OF T RATIOS FOR VARIOUS DEGREES OF
FREEDOM; SIGNIFICANT AT 5-PER-CENT AND 1-PER-CENT LEVELS

Degrees of Freedom *	Level of Significance		Degrees of Freedom	Level of Significance	
	5%	1%		5%	1%
1	12.706	63.657	21	2.080	2.831
2	4.303	9.925	22	2.074	2.819
3	3.182	5.841	23	2.069	2.807
4	2.776	4.604	24	2.064	2.797
5	2.571	4.032	25	2.060	2.787
6	2.447	3.707	26	2.056	2.779
7	2.365	3.499	27	2.052	2.771
8	2.306	3.355	28	2.048	2.763
9	2.262	3.250	29	2.045	2.756
10	2.228	3.169	30	2.042	2.750
11	2.201	3.106	35	2.030	2.724
12	2.179	3.055	40	2.021	2.704
13	2.160	3.012	45	2.014	2.690
14	2.145	2.977	50	2.008	2.678
15	2.131	2.947	100	1.984	2.626
16	2.120	2.921	200	1.972	2.601
17	2.110	2.898	300	1.968	2.592
18	2.101	2.878	500	1.965	2.586
19	2.093	2.861	1000	1.962	2.581
20	2.086	2.845	∞	1.960	2.576

* *Degrees of freedom* are defined as the number of persons in the group being
measured times the number of tests of variables. If only one test is used the degrees
of freedom equal N, the total number of persons.

Note: This table is read as follows: Where there is one degree of freedom the
difference between the mean and the other score under consideration must be
12.706 times the sigma in order to be significant at the 5-per-cent level, or when
there are 20 degrees of freedom a similar difference must be 2.086 times the sigma
in order to be significant at the 5-per-cent level, and 2.845 times the sigma in order
to be significant at the 1-per-cent level.

(Adapted from Fisher and Yates *Statistical Tables for Biological, Agricultural,
and Medical Research,* Oliver & Boyd, Ltd., Edinburgh, by permission of the
authors and publishers.)

educational work it is important for administrators to know the
range of abilities of the persons in various groups with whom they
are dealing. When the groups have a normal form of distribution,
either the quartile deviation or the standard deviation is a convenient
measure of dispersion. When groups of 50 or less are compared, the
Q is used because it is less affected by extreme scores than is the SD.
Illustration 131 shows two groups of service ratings which are com-

ILLUS. 131. DIFFERENCES IN DISPERSION

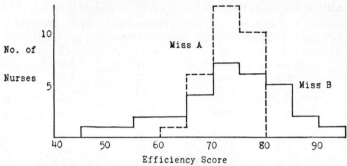

Efficiency Score

Both supervisors gave the same median score for the group, 72.6. Miss A assigned no very high or low grades, hence their quartile range (Q) is 3.1. Miss B used a much wider range of scores so that their Q is 7.7.

pared in this fashion. In order to have these ratings comparable the ranges for each supervisor must be nearly the same, or be made the same by assigning standard scores or centiles to the ratings.

Individual Comparisons

A frequent use of measures of deviation is the indication of a person's position in a known group of persons. A person's raw score may be changed to a *standard score,* sometimes indicated by z, by subtracting the mean (M) of the group from the person's score (X), and dividing the remainder by the standard deviation (σ) of the group. Thus, if John scored 39 (Illus. 118), he would have a standard score of —.92, since his score would be —.92 standard deviations below the mean.

$$z = \text{standard score} = \frac{X - M}{\sigma} = \frac{39 - 48}{9.8} = \frac{-9}{9.8} = -.918 \text{ or } -.92$$

In order to eliminate decimal points and minus signs which are somewhat troublesome, standard scores are often changed to T scores. Standard deviations and equivalent T scores are shown in Illus. 121 and Illus. 129. In T scores the mean of a group is placed arbitrarily at 50, and one standard deviation is given the value of 10. Thus, John, whose raw score is 39, would have a T score of 40.1.

$$\text{T score} = \frac{(X - M)10}{\sigma} + 50 = \frac{(39 - 48)10}{9.8} + 50 = -.92 + 50 = 40.8$$

T Scores Versus Centiles

T scores have an advantage not enjoyed by centiles in that scores may be added and subtracted without fear of introducing errors due to inequality of scaling. This statement can be understood when one looks at a normal frequency curve (Illus. 121). It is evident in this illustration that the distance between the 50th and 69th centiles on the base line is the same as the distance between the 93rd and 97th centiles. This is due to the fact that in a normal curve the frequency of scores is greater toward the center of the distribution. If a person's scores on two tests are averaged, using centiles, an error is introduced. For example, if Frank made T scores of 50 and 70 on two tests, the mean of his T scores is $60 \left(\dfrac{50 - 70}{2} \right)$. These T scores correspond to the 50th and 97.72 centiles in Illus. 129. The mean of these centiles is $73.8 \left(\dfrac{50 - 97.72}{2} \right)$ which corresponds to a T score of only 56.4 instead of the correct standard score of 60. The use of centiles has introduced an error in this case of 3.6 points. Such errors are usually ignored because the original scores are rather rough and errors seldom change one's position in a group.

Profiles

A person's ability can be portrayed by recording graphically his scores on several tests that are considered to be important and some-what independent. Such a graphic record, called a *profile,* is constructed by plotting a person's scores on a profile chart. Such a chart is made by laying off on graph paper a line which represents the mean of a group and other parallel lines which represent units of dispersion, such as standard scores. A profile is one of the most interesting and valuable ways to represent results of tests, for it gives a person a clear picture of his strong and weak subjects. For the greatest convenience the raw scores are placed at the proper intervals for each test in order that the person may find his position in a group by simply placing dots beneath the numbers which represent his scores. Lines connecting these dots help to make a quick comparison. In Illus. 132 mean-score profiles are shown for four occupational groups on eight different tests based on T scores of a large adult population.

Similar profiles may be constructed from age scales in which the scores in each test have been given chronological age equivalents. Thus, Illus. 133 shows a profile from a Stanford Achievement Test. This profile has the advantage of showing scores for average age groups and grades in school. It also has the advantage of being composed of steps which are probably as equivalent as the steps in the standard deviation scales, because age differences become smaller with advancing age.

To Combine a Person's Score on Several Tests

Occasionally one wishes to have a single score which will represent a person's ability on several different tests. The selection of the best way to combine scores depends upon what use is to be made of the combination. One way to combine test results is to average a person's T scores. Where few tests are involved the median is preferred since it is less sensitive to extreme scores than is the mean.

ILLUS. 132. OCCUPATIONAL PROFILES FROM STANDARD TESTS

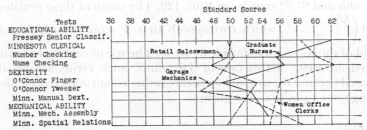

(Adapted from Dvorak, 1935. By permission of the University of Minnesota Press.)

Weighted Scores

In some instances it is considered desirable to give more weight to the scores in one test than to those in another. Methods of weighting the scores are of two kinds. One method gives more credit for a harder task or a task that is considered more important than another. Doing this is generally a rather arbitrary matter. For example, in many examinations the number of items correct on an arithmetic test is multiplied by some weight such as 4, whereas the scores on several other tests may be simply the number of items correct. Another method uses a statistical analysis which shows how well various scores predict a certain criterion. In order to make the best prediction, scores are given various weights. Methods of combining scores in a way to make the best possible prediction of a particular criterion are to be found in standard statistical texts.

An able discussion of the effects of weighting various standard scores upon their combined results is given by Guilford (1942), McNemar (1949), and Garrett (1947), who point out that the differences between various weightings depend upon (1) the number of scores which are combined, (2) the uniqueness of the various scores, (3) the shape of the distribution curve of each score, and (4) whether the weights are constant or variable.

ILLUS. 133. PROFILE, STANFORD ACHIEVEMENT TEST

EDUCATIONAL PROFILE CHART: NEW STANFORD ACHIEVEMENT TEST, ADVANCED EXAMINATION

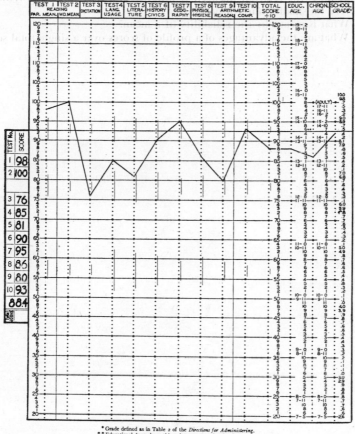

* Grade defined as in Table 2 of the *Directions for Administering*.
** Educational Ages above this point are extrapolated values.
See *Guide for Interpreting* for explanation of vertical lines.

(Kelley, Ruch, and Terman, 1941. By permission of the World Book Co.)

STUDY GUIDE QUESTIONS

1. Define concisely: scale, frequency table, range of scores, class, interval, histogram, frequency curve, normal curve, ogive curve, rank, centile, quartile.
2. Define mean, median, and mode. What advantages has each?
3. How does the use of a guessed mean save time in calculating the true mean?
4. For what do the following symbols stand: M, Md, G.M., Σ, N, X, x_1, i, SD, σ, P_{10}, σ_m, z, T score?

5. How can letter grades be given a similar meaning in various situations?

6. How can centiles or T scores be found from raw scores?

7. What is the relation between Q and SD in a normal curve? Which is preferred for small groups of persons?

8. What is meant by the reliability of a mean?

9. What are the advantages of a profile of scores over a single total score?

CHAPTER XIII

MEASURES OF RELATIONSHIP

~~~~~~

This chapter indicates the principal ways of finding and indicating the relationships between measures. Such information is useful in selecting items for tests, in predicting future success from present scores, and in theoretical analyses of elements of behavior. First, scattergrams and bar charts are discussed, then correlation coefficients are illustrated. Lastly, certain errors which make correlations too high or too low are presented.

PREDICTIONS OF PROBABLE SCORES FROM KNOWN SCORES

To a great extent psychological measurement is intended to render an accurate prediction of the probable quality and quantity of an individual's development. Predictions are based upon the assumption that an individual will develop as persons known to be similar to him have developed in the past. They may take the form of a statement of probability: that a person will have a certain score in one variable when he has a particular score in another. The technique for ascertaining such probabilities is relatively simple. Much credit for developing this technique goes to Sir Francis Galton (1886) in connection with his studies of the inheritance of genius. Starting with sheets of graph paper and some pins, he devised a method of measuring relationships among variables.

Scatter Diagrams

In finding relationships between parents and children, Galton arranged his data on graph paper, as shown in Illus. 123, so that the heights of adult children were indicated on the base line, the X scale, and the heights of midparents (average of the two parents) on a vertical line, the Y scale. For each parent-child pair a pin was placed to show the scores of both the midparent and the child. Thus, a midparent's score of 71 and a child's score of 64 would be represented by a pin in square A, which lies in the column containing the child's score and the row containing the adult's score. Such charts, called *scatter diagrams, scattergrams,* or *double entry tables,* allow one to see at a glance the main aspects of relationship. For instance, in Illus. 134 it appears that there is a marked relationship between the heights of parents and the heights of their children, but some pairs in the upper right and lower left portions show marked deviations from the general rule. There is also a marked tendency for children to be a little nearer the average height of the group than their parents, and vice versa.

ILLUS. 134. SCATTER DIAGRAM WITH PINS

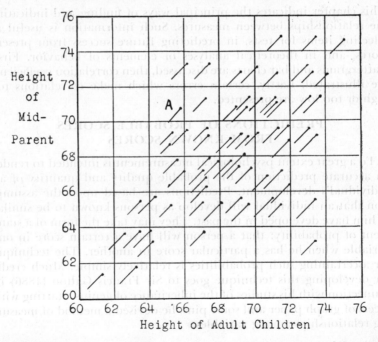

Bar Charts

For small groups, and on relatively unstandardized material, simple scattergrams or bar charts show trends effectively. Illustration

135 shows the results of comparing scores on a selection test with ratings of success in a clerical position. The following steps are to be taken in making such a chart:

a. Make a scattergram with the X scale (horizontal) showing the preliminary score and the Y scale (vertical) showing the criterion.

b. Determine the level of success which is desired in this particular situation. (This is usually the work of the supervisory or management staff.)

c. Draw a horizontal line on the chart dividing the group into two subgroups; the high group will include those who attained the desired level of success, and the low group those that did not. (In this case the line is drawn at 4.)

d. Draw a vertical line so that a large proportion of the satisfactory workers will fall to the right of it and a large proportion of the unsatisfactory to the left. This line, placed at 30, is tentatively called the *critical score.* The critical score may, of course, be shifted to the right or to the left as the needs of the organization or the caliber of applicants for work change.

e. Compute the percentage of each subgroup that falls to the right and to the left of the line. If a critical score of 31 were used, this would indicate that 75 per cent of the high group and only 20 per cent of the low group would be included, while 25 per cent of the high group and 80 per cent of the low group would be excluded.

f. Draw a bar chart which shows for each subgroup the percentage of persons to the right and to the left of the critical score.

ILLUS. 135. SCATTERGRAM AND BAR CHART

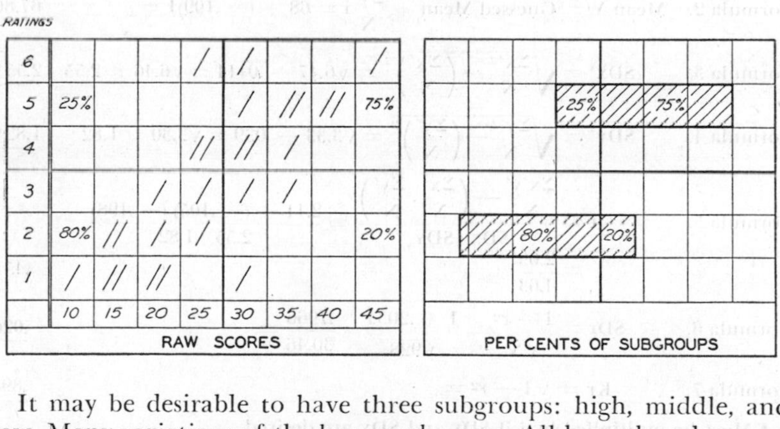

It may be desirable to have three subgroups: high, middle, and low. Many variations of the bar graph occur. All have the advantage of showing graphically what the effects of using a particular cut-off

ILLUS. 136. CORRELATION TABLE

Adult Children   i = 1 inch

Parents	61	62	63	64	65	66	67	68	69	70	71	72	73	74	y'	f	fy'	f(y')²	x'y' +	x'y' −
73												1	3		5	4	20	100	95	
72								1	2	1	2	7	2	4	4	19	76	304	258	
71				1	3	4	3	5	10	4	9	2	2		3	43	129	387	285	39
70	1		1		1	1	3	12	18	14	7	4	3	3	2	68	136	272	232	40
69			1	16	4	17	27	20	33	25	20	11	4	5	1	183	183	183	237	142
68	1			7	11	16	25	31	34	48	21	18	4	3	0	219	544			
67			3	5	14	15	36	38	28	38	19	11	4		-1	211	211	211	254	125
66			3	3	5	2	17	17	14	13	4				-2	78	156	312	220	42
65	1			9	5	7	11	11	7	7	5	2	1		-3	66	198	594	378	81
64	1	1	4	4	1	5	5	2							-4	23	92	368	268	8
63	1		2	4	1	2	2	1	1						-5	14	70	350	210	5

	61	62	63	64	65	66	67	68	69	70	71	72	73	74	summary
x'	-7	-6	-5	-4	-3	-2	-1	0	1	2	3	4	5	6	7 727
f	5	7	32	59	48	117	138	120	167	99	64	41	17	14	928 −183 3081 2467 482
fx'	35	42	160	236	144	234	138		167	198	192	164	85	84	(−989 / +890) 890 −99 Sum x'
fx'²	245	252	800	944	432	468	138		167	396	576	656	425	504	6003 Sum x'²

Right‑hand totals: Sum y', Sum y'², Sum x y = 1985

Answers

Formula 1. Mean X = Guessed Mean $+ \dfrac{\Sigma x'}{N} i = 68 + (+.105)1 =$ __68.11__

Formula 2. Mean Y = Guessed Mean $+ \dfrac{\Sigma y'}{N} i = 68 + (-.199)1 =$ __67.80__

Formula 3. $SD_{x'} = \sqrt{\dfrac{\Sigma x'^2}{N} - \left(\dfrac{\Sigma x'}{N}\right)^2} = \sqrt{6.47 - .0114} = \sqrt{6.46} = 2.55$ __2.55*__

Formula 4. $SD_{Y'} = \sqrt{\dfrac{\Sigma y'^2}{N} - \left(\dfrac{\Sigma y'}{N}\right)^2} = \sqrt{3.33 - .039} = \sqrt{3.30} = 1.82$ __1.82*__

Formula 5. $r = \dfrac{\dfrac{\Sigma x'y'}{N} - \left(\dfrac{\Sigma x'}{N} \cdot \dfrac{\Sigma y'}{N}\right)}{SD_x \cdot SD_Y} = \dfrac{2.11 - (-.105)(-.198)}{2.55 \quad 1.82}$

$= \dfrac{2.09}{4.63}$ __.451__

Formula 6. $SD_r = \dfrac{1 - r^2}{\sqrt{N}} = \dfrac{1 - .2034}{\sqrt{928}} = \dfrac{.7966}{30.46} =$ __.026__

Formula 7. $K_r = \sqrt{1 - r^2} =$ __.898__

* Must be multiplied by i if SDx and SDy are desired.

(From data in Galton, 1886.)

score would probably be. Another equally good method is to use distribution curves for the groups to be compared, as shown in Illus. 126.

Regression Lines

When larger groups or more precise measures are involved, bar charts are often very useful, but more detailed indices of relation may also be desired. For example, in order to predict the most probable height of a child from midparents of a particular height, say 69 inches, Galton assumed that the most frequent height would be the same as the median height of children in the particular row of 69-inch parents. A glance at Illus. 136 shows this median height to be a trifle less than 69 inches.

The general relationship between parents' and children's heights will be indicated by a line drawn through the medians of the vertical rows, which is called a *regression line of children* on parents. A similar line drawn through the midpoints of the horizontal columns is called the *regression line of parents* on children. When both of these lines happen to be straight, one of them alone is enough to show both relationships. Illustration 136 shows regression lines that are slightly curved and broken. Straight lines could be drawn in such a way, however, that they pass near the median points. Since this is the case, the regression lines can be treated as if they are straight.[1]

Upon inspection of Illus. 136 it will be seen that all midparents who were in the class interval labeled 70 had children whose median height was lower—69 inches. Short midparents in class interval 63 had children whose median height was higher—65 inches. From such measures Galton generalized his famous law of filial regression, namely, that children tend to be more like the central tendency of the group than do their parents.

The term regression line is now applied to all lines which indicate the relation between the class intervals on one scale and the corresponding mean or median scores on another scale. When the regression line is straight, this relation can be found and given a quantitative value for the group as a whole by measuring its slope from the base line.

[1] The line of best fit, that is, the line which has the smallest total deviation from all the dots, can be calculated. Its slope is given by the product-moment correlation coefficient described in the next section.

Slope of Regression Lines; Correlation Coefficients

The slope of a straight regression line from the base line can be indicated by the ratio between the distances from the horizontal and vertical scales or axes, and any point except zero on the regression line. Thus, in Illus. 137, Diagram 3, the point P is 3 units from the horizontal axis or base line, and 5 units from the vertical axis. The ratio between these two lines ($\frac{3}{5} = .60$) will be the same as the ratio of two similar lines measured from another point on the same regression line.

The slope (in this case .60) is known in trigonometry as the *tangent* of the angle between the regression line and the base. Since tangents have been calculated carefully for many angles, the tangent is a convenient figure to use for the slope of a line. When the horizontal and vertical scales are changed to standard deviation units, variations in raw scores are eliminated from a scatter diagram. In this case the tangent of the regression angle is the correlation coefficient. The correlation coefficient thus shows the slope of a regression line when the two tests are scaled alike. For a 45-degree angle the tangent and the correlation coefficient are 1.00. If the regression angle approaches zero, the correlation coefficient approaches zero. A zero indicates that the relationship between the variables compared is merely chance.

A *chance relationship* means that a person who makes a particular score in one test has the same probability as anyone else in the group of making any one of the scores in the other test. Illustration 137 shows regression lines and correlation coefficients for six typical situations. Diagrams 1 to 4 illustrate elliptical or circular boundaries and regular distributions which probably indicate that both variables are normally distributed. If the tally marks show large gaps, as in Diagram 5, it is clear that the variables are irregularly distributed. If the marks show a fan-shaped distribution, as in Diagram 6, the correspondence of scores between the two variables is evidently much closer at the lower end than at the higher end of the distribution.

Product-Moment Correlation Coefficients

Since the process of making scatter diagrams and drawing regression lines is laborious, shorter methods have been devised for calculating relationships. One of the best and most commonly used, the *product-moment correlation* method developed by Pearson (1904), is designed for use when both tests show fairly normal distributions, when the regression lines are approximately straight, and when large numbers of individuals are involved.

The product-moment correlation method makes use of the fact

ILLUS. 137. TYPICAL SCATTER DIAGRAMS AND REGRESSION LINES

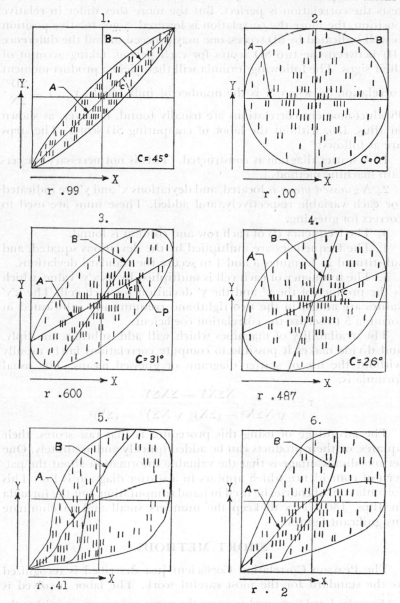

that if all persons have exactly the same relative position on two tests the correlation is perfect. But the more they differ in relative position, the more the correlation is lowered. Since relative position is well indicated by SD scores, one may proceed to find the difference (D) between the two SD scores for each person, taking account of their signs. The following formula will then yield a product-moment correlation (r) when N is the number of individuals: $r = 1 - \dfrac{\Sigma D^2}{2N}$.

Product-moment correlations are usually found, however, as shown in Illus. 136, without the labor of computing SD scores. The steps are as follows: [2]

1. A scatter diagram is constructed. (This is not necessary for certain machine methods.)

2. A *guessed mean* is located, and deviations x′ and y′ are indicated for each variable respectively, and added. These sums are used to correct for guessing.

3. The frequency (f) of each row and column is found.

4. The frequencies are multiplied by the deviations squared, and substituted in formulas 3 and 4 to secure the standard deviations.

5. The frequency of each cell is multiplied by its x′y′ value, which is the product of the x′ and the y′ deviation for each cell. The x′y′ values are added in the two righthand columns and substituted in formula 5 to secure the correlation coefficient.

The availability of machines which will add, subtract, multiply, and divide makes it possible to compute correlations fairly rapidly without the use of scatter diagrams or guessed means. The usual formula is:

$$r = \frac{N\Sigma XY - \Sigma X \Sigma Y}{\sqrt{N\Sigma X^2 - (\Sigma X)^2} \; \sqrt{N\Sigma Y^2 - (\Sigma Y)^2}}$$

The advantage of using this procedure is that raw scores, their squares, or their products can be added quickly and accurately. One serious disadvantage is that the valuable information about the pattern of coincidence which appears in a scatter diagram is lost. This formula can, of course, be used in hand computation, but the formula in Illus. 136 serves to keep the numbers small and to eliminate insignificant figures.

SHORT METHODS

The Pearson Correlation Coefficient just described is recognized as the standard for the most careful work. The labor involved is

[2] Formulas 1 and 2 are used to secure the means and are not essential to the product-moment method.

usually great, however, even when the best machines available are used. Shorter methods are sufficiently adequate: (1) when very small samples are measured, and one or two extreme scores would bear a large share in determining the coefficient, (2) when one or both variables yield only two scores, such as true or false, pass or fail, and (3) when large samples are measured, so that each part of each distribution is well represented. Three short methods—the rank order, the tetrachoric, and the biserial correlation methods—will be described.

Rank-Order Correlation Coefficients

When a group is small, correlation coefficients are often secured by the rank-order method. Illustration 138 shows how a correlation of .564 was found between clerical test scores and a supervisor's rank-

ILLUS. 138. RANK-ORDER CORRELATION METHOD

INDIVIDUAL	CLERICAL TEST		SUPERVISOR'S RANKING	D	D²
	Score	Rank			
Metcalf, C.	76	1	6	5	25
Adams, J.	75	2	3	1	1
Bushee, L.	43	3	1	2	4
Jones, F. C.	42	4	2	2	4
Coover, L.	41	5	5	0	
Cook, F.	36	6.5	8.5	2	4
Tostlebee, F.	36	6.5	8.5	2	4
Bahrman, K.	27	9	10	1	1
Hewitt, T. S.	27	9	7	2	4
Shumaker, L.	27	9	4	* 5	25
					72

$$N - 10$$

$$\text{Rho} = \rho = 1 - \frac{6 \Sigma D^2}{n(n^2 -)}$$

$$= 1 - \frac{432}{10 \times 99} = 1 - .436$$

$$= .564$$

ing of ten persons. First, the scores are changed to ranks; then the differences (D) between each person's two ranks are found and squared. Lastly, the sum of the squared differences is substituted in the formula:

$$\text{Rho} = \rho = 1 - \frac{6 \Sigma D^2}{n(n^2 - 1)}$$

Rho (ρ) will be 1.00 and thus show a perfect correlation if the D's are all zero. Rho will be .00 if the ranks have only a chance relationship, and —1.00 when there is a perfect negative relationship. Rho is nearly always a little smaller than r, a product-moment correlation for the same set of figures.

Tetrachoric Correlations

When a large number of correlations are desired, a short method, called the tetrachoric method, is sometimes used. Theoretically one has to have about twice as many cases to get the same reliability from a tetrachoric as from a Pearsonian correlation, but the labor involved is much less. The procedure is as follows:

ILLUS. 139. TETRACHORIC
CORRELATION DATA

$$r_t = .79$$

CRITERIA	TEST				TOTAL	
	LOW		HIGH			
	f	%	f	%	f	%
HIGH	3	9	14	43	17	52
	a		b		p	
LOW	12	36	4	12	16	48
	c		d		q	
TOTAL	15	45	18	55	33	100
	q		p			

a. By using convenient points, usually somewhere near the middle of each distribution, divide a scattergram into quarters (Illus. 139).

b. Determine the percentages of the whole group that lie in each quarter and in each half.

c. Insert these figures in nomographs prepared by Cheshire, Saffir, and Thurstone (1938), or by Jenkins (1950). The value of the tetrachoric r for the data in Illus. 139 is .79.

Biserial Correlations

When one of the variables yields only two categories, such as pass and fail, a biserial correlation can be computed as shown in Illus. 140.

Kuder-Richardson Formula 21

This is an indication of reliability which is widely used in preference to the split-half Spearman-Brown Formula. It is preferred because reliability coefficients can be calculated in about 2 minutes when only the mean, the SD, and the number of items are known:

$$r_{tt} = \frac{n}{n-1} \cdot \frac{\sigma^2 - n\,\overline{p}\,\overline{q}}{\sigma^2}$$

in which

r_{tt} is the correlation of a test with itself, n is the number of unweighted items in the test, σ is the standard deviation of scores, and

ILLUS. 140. BISERIAL CORRELATION

Score	Fail	Pass	Total
55		3	3
50	1	7	8
45	1	5	6
40	2	7	9
35	7	4	11
30	3	2	5
25	1	1	2
20	6		6
Total	21	29	50
Per cent	42%	58%	100%

$$\text{Biserial } r = \frac{M_p - M_f}{\sigma_t}\left(\frac{pq}{y}\right)$$

An illustration is as follows:

Where M_p is the mean of the pass column

M_f is the mean of the fail column

p is the per cent of cases in one column

q is the per cent of cases in the other column

σ_t is the standard deviation of the whole group of scores

y is the ordinate of the normal curve for values corresponding to p and q, when they are assumed to represent areas under the normal curve (Illus. 129).

Substituting values for the present problem.

$$\text{Biserial } r = \frac{46.0 - 35.4}{9.5} \times \frac{.42 \times .58}{.39}$$

$$= \frac{10.6}{9.5} \times \frac{.2436}{.39}$$

$$= 1.11 \times .624$$

$$= .692$$

$\bar{p}$ is $\dfrac{M_t}{n}$ where M_t is the mean of the scores. This is the average item difficulty. $\bar{q}$ is $(1 - \bar{p})$.

Kuder-Richardson Formula 21, which gives values that are slightly lower than the Spearman-Brown estimates, assumes that all the items in the test have the same difficulty. Although this assumption is seldom true, it usually introduces only a small error in the estimation. Another formula is provided for situations where a small number of items and large differences in their difficulty make it inadvisable to use Formula 21.

PREDICTIONS OF A SCORE

It is often desirable to determine the probable limits of a particular estimate. They can be determined by applying correlation coefficients to the respective distributions as follows:

Individual Predictions

When the score on one test is known individual predictions of the most probable score on another test can be made in two ways: from a scatter diagram, and from an equation which represents a regression line.

Prediction from a scatter diagram is made by finding the most frequent score in Y which corresponds to a particular score in X. For example, in Illus. 136 the most probable height of a child whose midparents are in the 63.0 class interval is 65.0 inches.

Prediction from a regression equation avoids the rather lengthy process of making a scatter diagram and calculating the central tendencies of each class interval. Regression equations also give a little better prediction since they are less affected by minor variations of a chance variety than are the central tendencies of class intervals. Regression lines smooth out minor chance deflections. In finding the most probable height of children (X scale) from parents who are 63.5 inches tall (Y scale) a convenient formula to use is $\overline{X} - M_X = r_{XY}\dfrac{\sigma_X}{\sigma_Y}(Y - M_Y)$. This formula looks more complicated than it is, for it is really a short statement of familiar terms, namely,

$\overline{X}$ is the score to be predicted.

M_x (called M sub X) is the mean of all X scores $= 68.4$ inches.

Y is the given score $= 63.5$ inches.

M_y (M sub Y) is the mean of all Y scores $= 68.3$ inches.

r_{XY} is the correlation coefficient found between X and Y which shows the slope of the regression line $= .451$.

σ_X and σ_Y are the standard deviations of the X and Y distributions (included to equalize the group dispersions).

The most probable height of the child is therefore:

$$\overline{X} = r_{XY}\frac{(\sigma_X)}{(\sigma_Y)}(Y - M_Y) + M_X$$

$$= [.451\,\frac{(2.55)}{(1.82)}(63.5 - 68.3)] + 68.4$$

$$= 65.37$$

Standard Error of Estimate

Since the score just found, 65.37, is the most probable score, it is of value to find out how accurate the prediction is. A particular son's height may, of course, vary considerably from the most probable height. The probable amount of this variation can be found by calculating the standard deviation of the estimated score. This is called a *standard error of estimate,* and is written $\sigma_{X \cdot Y}$ when the variation of a predicted X score for a given value of Y is desired. From a standard error of estimate the range of scores which will include any particular proportion of children in a particular row can be found.

A general standard error of estimate [3] to apply to all probable scores is given in the formula $\sigma_{X \cdot Y} = \sigma_X \sqrt{1 - r_{XY}^2}$. When applied to the data in Illus. 136, it becomes

$$\sigma_{X \cdot Y} = 2.55 \sqrt{1 - (.451)^2}$$
$$= 2.55 \, (.887)$$
$$= 2.26$$

From this it appears that the middle 68 per cent of the children who have parents of a particular height will fall within heights ranging from 2.26 inches above to 2.26 inches below the most probable score. For instance, when the most probable score of a child is 65.37, the middle 68 per cent of the children will range from 63.11 to 67.63 inches in height.

We can also predict what are the chances in 100 that a child of parents of a certain height will attain any given height, by finding the proportion of all the children of parents of this height who have reached the given height. This is done by finding the difference between the most probable height of children and the given height, and dividing this difference by the standard error of estimate. The result of this division will be the number of standard deviations from the most probable height, and this can easily be translated from Illus. 129 into percentages. Suppose we wish to know what the chances are that Frank, whose parents average 63.5 inches, will be 62 inches or less in height. We have just found that his most probable height will be 65.37 inches and the standard error of estimate is 2.26 inches. The difference, 65.37 — 62, divided by the standard error of estimate gives 1.49. Illus. 129 shows that —1.49 standard deviations is equivalent to the 6.9 centile. We may, therefore, conclude that Frank has only about 7 chances in 100 of being as short as 62 inches. These calculations may seem a bit complicated at first, but, after working out several examples, the routine becomes easy. In practice it is often desirable to make such predictions.

[3] The formula is only approximate, since it gives one standard error of estimate for all columns. From inspection of a scatter diagram one can see that this is not actually the case. The columns near the end have smaller dispersions than those in the middle. The standard error of estimate is the average standard deviation of the columns. It is commonly used for individual predictions.

Standard Error of a Score

The same logic has been applied to prediction of the probable variation of any single score on a test. It has been shown that if two tests correlate highly, the standard error of estimate of a score predicted from one test to the other will be very small. Similarly, if a test has a high self-correlation on two trials, the standard error of estimate of a score predicted from one trial to the other will be small. Since in this case the same test has been repeated, some authors conclude that the tendency for a single score to vary by chance from its true value can be shown by the formula for a standard error of a score, which is expressed thus: $\sigma_\infty = \sigma_1 \sqrt{1 - r_{12}}$. Here ∞ indicates the theoretical standard deviation of an infinite number of obtained scores from the most probable true score; σ_1 is the standard deviation of the actual scores in trial 1 of the test; and r_{12} is the correlation between trials 1 and 2.

This formula may be applied only when the means and sigmas of the two trials are nearly the same. The standard error of a score would not show the true tendency toward variation if the scores or their dispersions should become larger or smaller with repetitions.

The standard error of a score is often a more practical indication of the predictive value of a test than the correlation between trials, since it shows the amount of variation which may be expected. In a revision of the Binet Scale, Terman and Merrill (1937) reported that IQ's from 90 to 109 had standard errors of 4.51 when the estimated correlation between two forms of the test was .924. This means that the chances are 2 out of 3 that the true IQ is not higher or lower than the obtained IQ by more than 4.51 points when the obtained IQ is between 90 and 109.

Standard Error of a Difference (σ_{diff})

Often one is eager to know whether the difference between the means of two groups would be likely to occur by chance if the measures were repeated a number of times. Suppose that 570 men who succeeded in a pilot-training course had a mean score on a physical science knowledge test of 142, SD 10, and 211 men who failed the same course had a mean of 141, SD 7, what is the probability that the difference of one point between the means would happen by chance if the same groups were measured with the same test a number of times?

Because the work of retesting would be so great, estimates are generally used. We can estimate the probability if we assume that

  a. The differences will fall into a normal curve if we measured them a large number of times.

b. The size of the difference depends upon the range of scores of both groups.

c. The reliabilities of the means depend upon the number of persons measured.

d. The observed difference can be taken as the best available indication of the true or average difference.

Since these assumptions can be demonstrated to be reasonably true, the standard deviation of the hypothetical distribution of differences, also called the *standard error of a difference,* is given as:

$$\sigma_{diff} = \sqrt{\sigma_{m_1}^2 + \sigma_{m_2}^2}$$

For the pilots' scores cited above the standard error of the difference is:

$$\sigma_{diff} = \sqrt{.42^2 + .49^2} = .54$$

When the difference between means is based on two scores of the same group of persons, the correlation must be considered, for a high correlation means, among other things, that there is little random shifting of scores. The standard error of this difference is expressed thus:

$$\sigma_{diff} = \sqrt{\sigma_{m_1}^2 + \sigma_{m_2}^2 - 2r\sigma_{m_1}\sigma_{m_2}}$$

Thus, if 570 men showed a mean of 142 (SD 10) on a test before training, and 152 (SD 11) on the same test after training, and there is a correlation of .82 between tests, then

$$\sigma_{diff} = \sqrt{.42^2 + .46^2 - 2(.82)\ (.42)\ (.46)}$$
$$= \sqrt{.1764 + .2116 - .3168}$$
$$= \sqrt{.3870 - .3168}$$
$$= .0702$$

Critical Ratio

In order to determine just how significant a difference between means is, the difference is divided by its own standard error of estimate. This ratio is often called the *critical ratio* and is written: $CR = \dfrac{Diff}{\sigma_{diff}}$. The CR is a widely used index which derives its significance from the fact that the SD is a normal curve always bears a definite relation to the area or centile scores of the distribution. These are shown in Illus. 121 and Illus. 129. Several elaborate published tables give these figures in six or more decimal places. For ordinary purposes two decimals are enough. Thus, in the example of successful and unsuccessful pilots given above, the critical ratio is: $CR = \dfrac{diff}{\sigma_{diff}} = \dfrac{1}{.54} = 1.85.$

Examination of Illus. 129 shows that 1.85 standard deviations below the mean equal a centile of 3.32, which means that the difference will probably be as low as zero by chance in a little more than 3 times in 100.

If the CR is more than 3.00, the hypothetical differences would be as small as zero only 14 times in 10,000, because the normal curve has only $^{14}/_{10,000}$ths of its area as much as 3 SD's below the mean. Hence the probabilities are small that a difference which is three times its own SD will occur by chance.

APPLICATIONS OF CORRELATION TECHNIQUES

The use of correlation techniques has spread remarkably during the last 20 years. Every field of psychological investigation now makes use of them in situations where relationships are to be appraised. A complete list of such situations would be too long to present here, but the main applications of these techniques include related persons, related scores, and related items.

Related Persons

Pairs of persons who are related in some ways are measured and the score of one member of a pair is plotted against the score of the other member. This method is of prime importance in studies of inheritance where familial resemblances are being scrutinized. Studies of pairs of identical twins, of mothers and daughters, of fathers and sons, of siblings, of cousins, and of grandparents and grandchildren have shown typical relationships by correlation techniques.

Related Scores

When a group of persons have been appraised in two situations, the scores in one situation may be plotted against the scores in the other. Literally thousands of studies of this sort have been made to show relationships of tests or ratings. Correlations between test scores and later success in school or occupation are commonly used to predict success within known limits. In animal experimentation correlations of performance scores with measures of deprivation or of brain injuries have proved useful.

Related Items

When a group of items has been rated or ranked for some quality, such as difficulty, aesthetic quality, or emotional value, the ranks assigned by one judge may be correlated with those assigned by other judges. This procedure has been used to show linearity of relationships between items when judged by various groups, relationships which must be known in the accurate scaling of test items.

ERRORS IN APPLYING CORRELATION COEFFICIENTS

The widespread use of regression and prediction formulas makes it necessary to guard against spuriously high or low correlation coefficients. Spuriously high or low r's are sometimes obtained if regression lines and prediction formulas which are not applicable to the case are used. Some of these errors can be avoided rather easily, but others are hard to eliminate. Correlation techniques must be carefully interpreted in order to give a clear representation of the facts.

Errors Which Usually Lower Correlations below Their True Value

The following six types of errors tend to make correlation coefficients lower than they would be if normal groups were carefully measured:

Grouping of Results in Large Class Intervals. If, in the construction of a scatter diagram, results are grouped into too few class intervals, say two or three, some scores are treated as if they were nearer the center of the group than they are. This procedure usually results in a slightly smaller correlation coefficient than would result from using fifteen class intervals, because a high correlation generally depends upon having wide and accurately determined deviations among a group of scores. A correction for this type of error is given in standard texts on statistics. The amount of correction is generally small, hence it is used for only the most careful kind of comparisons.

A Curved Regression Line. It sometimes happens that regression lines are curved rather than straight, as in Illus. 137, Diagrams 5 and 6. Curved regression lines may be caused by skewed distributions or by unequal steps in a scale. A product-moment correlation coefficient for such situations will be too low. The true correlation coefficient may be found by using the *eta* formula. There are several ways of finding out whether a regression line is curved, without actually drawing a large scatter diagram. These procedures are given in more advanced texts on statistics.

Samples Chosen from Part of a Group. Correlation coefficients from parts of a group are usually smaller than those from the whole group. The reason for this is that in a small homogeneous group, sharp contrasts in ability are usually lacking. If all persons in a group make the same or nearly the same scores on a test, the correlation with any other test will be nearly zero. Thus it happens that a correlation of .50 among college students or among feeble-minded persons may represent about the same degree of coincidence as a correlation of .75 in an unselected population. Illus. 141 shows the result of selecting a small part of a larger group for correlation purposes. Comparable results are difficult to secure when various unrepresentative samples of population are studied. A correction for the limited range of ability in restricted samples is given by Kelley (1924, p. 223).

ILLUS. 141. SCATTER DIAGRAM SHOWING THE EFFECT OF SAMPLING NARROW PORTIONS OF A NORMAL GROUP

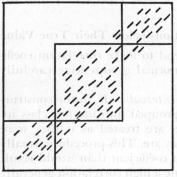

The correlation of scores for the total is approximately .81, but the scores in the smaller squares correlate nearly zero.

Random Errors. The correlation between two different measures will generally be too low because test scores or estimates are only approximations of true scores. Random errors of measurement in one test are by definition not coincident with those in another test, and therefore, they reduce coefficients of correlation. When the self-correlations of the two tests are known, there are several ways of correcting for this reduction, which is called *attenuation.* The corrections are small if the two tests have high self-correlations. In other words, when there are large chance variations in each of two tests, their measured relationships will show a large increase if corrected for attenuation.

Sampling of More Than One Process in a Test. Many tests allow the subjects to succeed by the use of different processes. Thus a high score in the Minnesota Spatial Relations Test may be due to rapid manipulation, or to methodical planning, or to specific memory of a plan of work. This situation is usually true of all puzzles and form boards, and of many verbal tests. In general, the more able persons make their scores through good planning, the less able score through rapid manipulation, and either group may use memory. The chief factor discriminating between individuals in any test will vary according to the ability of the persons taking the test. It is probable that such variations in processes lead to lower correlations between repetitions of a test than would be found if the same processes were measured in all persons in a group. A remedy for this situation is to devise tests in which success can be had by only one particular combination of processes. The construction of tests of this sort is a difficult and challenging problem.

Use of Raw Scores Instead of Ranks. It sometimes appears that the correlation between raw-score patterns on two variables is low when the relationship between ranks as shown in an individual's profile is high. This is found, for instance, in comparing interests with vocabulary. We cannot ascertain by correlating scores, whether a person's field of greatest interest corresponds to his field of greatest information, since a low score might in the case of a poorly informed person represent his field of greatest information. This problem can be solved by finding the correlation between the ranks of the test scores and the ranks of interest scores in an individual's profile. The tests may be assigned ranks by first plotting sigma scores on an individual profile, then noting their order. An illustration of the differences between correlating raw scores and correlating ranks in individual profiles was reported by Fryer (1931). The correlations between scores in academic tests and preferences for academic subjects were nearly zero. When the correlations between these same variables were based on ranks in individual profiles, they were much higher, with a median of .60. This was taken to indicate that a person's highest preference is likely to be his field of highest academic achievement.

Errors Which Raise Correlations Spuriously

There are three main types of errors which make correlations too high:

Sampling of Extremes. It is possible to choose persons from a group so that relationships appear higher than they would if the total population were included. This would happen if one omitted a number of cases from the middle of the group (Illus. 141) as the greatest variations between scores on two tests are usually found in the middle two thirds of the cases. Although such selection is not common, it occurs occasionally in samples from special clinics or employment situations.

Sampling a Third Variable. If one compares the scores of two tests for a group composed of children who range from six to twelve years of age, the correlations will be spuriously high, because of the high correlation with age which nearly all skills have during periods of rapid growth. Younger children make lower scores on all tests, because of less maturity.

A similar error is introduced when IQ's from two tests of children of various chronological ages are correlated. IQ's are secured by dividing the MA by the CA. The division of MA's by CA's results in artificially raising the correlation, for the CA's used for each child are the same in both tests.

There are two methods of avoiding these errors. The common procedure is to correlate only the scores within separate age groups. The other method is to calculate what the correlation would be if the effects of age were removed. This can be done by the partial-correlation technique shown in any good statistical manual. It is inadvisable to use partial correlations if the spurious factor can be removed directly.

A similar situation is often found in interpreting a correlation between any two tests. Thus, speed-of-reading tests and arithmetic tests both involve cooperation with the examiner. If poor cooperation and poor ability go together, as is often the case, the correlations found between scores on the two tests will be higher than correlations between pure measures of ability would be. This problem of analyzing the factors which raise or lower correlations is a complex and persistent one. It is discussed in greater detail in Chapter XIV.

Correlating a Part with the Whole.   In many situations one wishes to find out whether a part of a test is consistent with the whole test. The correlations between single items and total scores are likely to be spuriously high if the item makes up a considerable part of the total. Corrections are not large enough to be considered essential if the item to be evaluated is one of ten or more items each of which has equal weight in the total.

HOW LARGE MUST CORRELATIONS BE FOR THE PURPOSE OF PREDICTIONS?

A practical question is often asked: is this correlation high enough to be useful for predicting individual successes or failures? From the discussion above it is clear that no definite limits can be set, and that a correlation must be interpreted in its total situation. One must always take into account the factors which have just been discussed because they may introduce errors into the correlation coefficients. If errors have been eliminated as far as possible, then there are two ways of evaluating the significance of a correlation. One shows the standard error of correlation; the other gives an indication of how much the standard error of estimate is reduced by an increase in the size of the correlation.

Probable Error of a Correlation Coefficient

The standard error of a correlation (σ_r) is used to indicate the extent of errors in a random sampling. It shows how much the coefficient will probably vary on a chance basis, that is, if the same or similar groups of persons were measured in the same way many times. The σ_r shows the theoretical range of the middle 68 per cent of r's obtained by random sampling. If an r is three times its own σ_r, it is highly improbable that the r's true value will be as low as zero, since this would occur less than once in a thousand trials. Both an increase in the total number of cases in a group and an increase in the size of the correlation will result in a decrease in the size of the σ_r. The calculation of the σ_r is shown in Illus. 136 using a formula, however, which is not recommended for all correlations. For a more complete understanding one must consult an advanced text.

The σ_r tells the probability that an r will vary. Thus, if two coefficients, one of .50 and the other of .90, have the same σ_r, they are equally variable measures. This is a valuable bit of information since it tells how much the correlation coefficient may be expected to vary upon retrials. It does not, however, tell how much better the prediction for individual cases is when the r is .90 than when it is .50. The inaccuracy of a prediction is indicated by the coefficient of alienation.

Coefficient of Alienation (k)

It will be recalled that the prediction of the most probable score in one variable from a score in another, was made by means of the regression equation. The variability of the most probable score was then evaluated by means of the standard error of estimate. Since the standard error of estimate was calculated from the correlation coefficient, it is possible to show the relationship between these two indices. If the correlation between variables X and Y is zero, then the standard error of estimate ($\sigma_{X \cdot Y}$) is the same as the standard deviation for the whole Y distribution. In this case the errors in predicting scores on one variable (Y) from those on another variable (X) are maximum. The only prediction that can be made is that one's Y score will be somewhere among all the Y scores, and that one's most probable Y score will be the mean score. If the correlation is larger than zero, the standard error of estimate will be smaller than the standard deviation of Y. The proportion by which the standard deviation of Y is reduced is called the *coefficient of alienation*. This coefficient is equal to $\sqrt{1 - r^2}$ and its magnitude for various correlation coefficients is shown in Illus. 142. Reading from this table, the coefficient of alienation for the correlation coefficient for .451 in Illus. 142 is approximately .898. In other words, the standard error of estimating a child's height is .898 of the standard deviation of the entire group of children.

It also appears from Illus. 142 that the correlation must be .90 to re-

ILLUS. 142. COEFFICIENT OF ALIENATION k FOR VALUES OF r FROM .00 TO 1.00

r	k
.00	1.0000
.10	.9950
.20	.9798
.30	.9539
.40	.9165
.50	.8660
.60	.8000
.70	.7141
.80	.6000
.866	.5000
.90	.4539
.95	.3122
.98	.1990
.99	.1411
1.00	.0000

(Garrett, 1937. By permission of Longmans, Green and Co.)

duce standard error of estimate to 45 per cent of the standard deviation of the total distribution. The correlation must be .995 to reduce it to 10 per cent. This means that it is wise to be cautious in placing faith in individual predictions made when the correlations are less than .90. Since most of the correlations reported between raw scores and various criteria of success are in the neighborhood of .50, predictions for individual success on the basis of a single comparison are usually too far from accuracy to be useful. This fact does not discourage the careful worker, but makes him realize the need for much more precise measures.

STUDY GUIDE QUESTIONS

1. Define concisely: scattergram, bar chart, regression line, correlation coefficient.

2. When should bar charts be used to show relationships?

3. What is the logic of the correlation by Pearson?

4. When should the biserial r be used?

5. What are the advantages of the Kuder-Richardson Reliability Formula?

6. Define standard error of a score, standard error of a mean, standard error of a difference, critical ratio, and level of significance.

7. What kinds of situations make a correlation spuriously high? Spuriously low?

8. Of what use are standard errors of coefficients and coefficients of alienation?

CHAPTER XIV

FACTORIAL ANALYSES

~~~~~~

ASSUMPTIONS

The previous chapters have described the main categories of behavior and how particular samples of skills and information can be given numerical representation. Another persistent problem in the study of behavior is approached in this chapter, namely, how are abilities of persons related? Answers to this question are fairly numerous and usually hypothetical. Persons are so complex that patterns of personality have not as yet been well established.

There are, however, two methods widely used for the analysis of mental organization: one, biographical; the other, statistical. The biographical method records a sequence of events which are related in time and space. It has the advantage of showing apparent causal relationships and, if carefully done, it furnishes a valuable analysis of trends. However, it usually fails to provide a basis for the most adequate comparison between persons, and to give numerical analyses of what might be considered elements or forces in the patterns described. The second, or statistical method, shows the coincidence between various measures of persons. It may be used to study either simultaneous relationships or temporal sequences. Eventually, logical syntheses of such quantitative results yield a body of natural laws.

The psychologist's search for elements of behavior is much like the chemist's search for earth elements of fifty years ago. The chemists secured samples of organic and inorganic compounds and subjected them to rigid tests which showed their reactions to various forces, such as gravity, electricity, pressure, and heat. On the basis of these tests the samples were classified into groups of compounds which

401

behaved similarly. After years of research it was found that compounds which behave in similar fashion usually have common elements which can be isolated. An element is described as a unique substance which cannot be divided into other substances. Although the isolation of an element is usually an important step in its recognition, isolation is not absolutely necessary for recognition. An element may be described and measured accurately (a) if it is present in different amounts in a number of the samples which are available, (b) if it reacts to the tests differently from other elements present, and (c) if its reactions to the tests are the same in combination and in isolation. This sort of analysis depends upon having a large number of samples which are qualitatively and quantitatively different.

Similarly, persons may be taken as the samples to be analyzed, subjected to various tests, and classified according to similarities of responses. For the analysis of factors in test scores, two assumptions are usually made:

1. All the scores on a given test represent the same factors. This assumption is not representative of a large number of tests when the same scores represent different ability patterns, but it is representative of carefully controlled situations. Unless one is sure that a particular score represents the same pattern in all persons at all times, the comparisons are inconclusive. There is no absolute criterion to which one can appeal. Here, as in all other sciences, one must rely upon the agreement of observers who are considered to be competent.

2. A high correlation between two tests indicates similar processes in both tests. This assumption is also likely to be false in many test situations. A high correlation simply indicates that all persons have the same relative place in each test distribution. It does not show what factors have caused them to take these positions in the group. Only in carefully controlled situations may one make this assumption.

From these two considerations it is clear that a high or a low correlation is most significant when the test conditions are rigidly controlled. Few, if any, studies of persons have appeared that allow an uncontroversial interpretation of the factors involved in a correlation, but so much work of a preliminary nature has been accomplished that no discussion of mental measurement can ignore it. This chapter gives a brief introduction to mathematical methods that have been proposed for analyzing test relationships, a field of study in which the methods are still rapidly developing.

FACTORS

The last fifty years have witnessed a marked development in the analysis of psychological data by means of techniques which assume that the relations found between tests are due to the existence of common elements or factors. A factor is defined as some element in the test which can be distinguished from other elements. Factors may be distinguished psychologically by observation, or mathematically by showing whether persons who are high on one test are high on another. If scores on two tests have a zero correlation with each other, they do not exhibit any factors in common. One of the main problems is the reconciliation of mathematical and psychological factors.

SPEARMAN'S CONTRIBUTION

Spearman (1904) searched for the simplest explanation of the relations seen in correlation matrices. A *correlation matrix* is a table which shows the correlation of each test in the battery with each of the other tests, as in Illus. 143. He reported that the relation shown in Illus. 143 could be ascribed to one general factor which was present in all five tests in various amounts. In this case he showed that every individual score of every ability or attitude which is represented in the matrix could be divided theoretically into two independent kinds of factors: one the general factor, called *g*, and other specific factors, called *s*, which vary from test to test. A number of other explanations of the relations shown in Illus. 143 are, of course, possible, but Spear-

ILLUS. 143. CORRELATION MATRIX FOR FIVE MENTAL TESTS

		Oppo-sites	*Comple-tion*	*Memory*	*Discrimi-nation*	*Can-cella-tion*
Opposites	. . . 1		.80	.60	.30	.30
Completion .	. . 2	.80		.48	.24	.24
Memory .	. . . 3	.60	.48		.18	.18
Discrimination .	. 4	.30	.24	.18		.09
Cancellation	. . 5	.30	.24	.18	.09	

(Spearman, 1927, p. 74. By permission of the Macmillan Co.)

man preferred this one, since it was the simplest explanation of the intercorrelations, and it corresponded to his psychological analysis of the tests. For Spearman's arguments and mathematical proof one should consult his *Psychology through the Ages* (1938), or Guilford (1936).

Spearman found that a *g* factor would not account for intercorrelations in all matrices, but only in those which were limited to tests of abstract comparison, as in Illus. 143. When tests were included which depended principally on motor coordination or sensory discrimination, one general factor could not completely account for all the correlations of the matrix. It was then necessary to include *group factors* to account for the correlations. From these studies he concluded that mental organization can be most adequately described as due to three kinds of factors: a general factor, found in nearly all mental tests; group factors, found only in groups of similar tests; and specific factors, found only in one test.

The General Factor (g)

From the analyses of many batteries of tests, Spearman and his students have tentatively named some of these factors. The general, or *g*, factor is found in large amounts in tests of abstraction, whether verbal or nonverbal, and in smaller amounts in tests of perceptual discrimination. It was not found in tests of rote memory or rote learning. Speed and accuracy are interchangeable measures of *g* when complexity is held constant. The *g* factor is therefore described by Spearman as a special sort of energy which can be applied to making comparisons or drawing inferences. Some have thought this a good definition of intelligence, but Spearman has pointed out that most intelligence tests have large rote memory factors; hence they are not good measures of *g*, although some amount of *g* is usually present.

Group Factors

The group factors which have been isolated by Spearman seem to fall into two general classes: those due to independent abilities and those due to variations in *g*. The ability factors are called mechanical, arithmetical, musical, logical, and psychological. The mechanical and arithmetical factors are to be found in spatial and number tests. The logical factor is independent of the *g* factor, for from Spearman's analysis it is a technique of logical comparison which is different from a general mental energy. The psychological factors, of which there were four, are described as bases of judgments used in making decisions concerning (1) concrete objects, (2) abstract ideas, (3) moral concepts, and (4) interest and pleasures. It was found that some persons excelled in one kind of judgment and some in another, so that correlations within these fields were higher than would be expected from the presence of a *g* factor alone. A group factor of goal consistency, also called *will,* is indicated by the fact that higher correlations than can be explained by *g* alone are found in tests which demand a persistence of motive. Spearman (1927) did not find evidence of group factors for speed, attention span, sensory discrimination, motor coordination, or language. More complete research by Holzinger (1935), however, recognizes group factors for verbal ability, motor and mental speed, attention, and imagination.

The group factors attributable to variations in the *g* factor are called *perseveration* and *fatigue*. These are typically character traits. Perseveration is indicated by ease or difficulty in changing quickly from one activity to another. Fatigue is indicated when a person's scores in one test decrease after a fatiguing experience more rapidly than his scores in a different test. Groups of persons having the same fatigue patterns will show higher correlations after fatigue than other groups will.

Much difficulty has been experienced in distinguishing among the general, the group, and the specific factors. For instance, if the variety of tests in a battery is small, a *g* (general factor) may be found common to all of them. If these same tests are included among a larger variety of tests, this *g* factor might become a group factor. Likewise, in a small battery of tests it is quite likely that a factor will appear in one test only, and hence be called a *specific factor*. But when a large number and variety of tests are used, these specific factors will often become *group* factors. It seems, therefore, that the classification into general, group, and specific factors is more dependent upon the particular battery of tests used than upon the mental organization of persons tested. There is reason to believe that Spearman's *g* factor and many *s* factors will become group factors when a large enough battery of tests is used.

Other factorial analyses have been described by Hotelling (1933), Kelley (1928), Burt (1938), and several others using somewhat different assumptions and securing different results. The field is still a controversial one. All of these workers have devised methods for determining (*a*) which factors account for the relationships of a given correlation matrix, (*b*) how much of each factor is used in each test, and (*c*) how much is shown in an individual's score on a test.

THURSTONE'S METHOD

The general method of Thurstone (1946) will be discussed because it has been more widely used than the others. The mathematical explanation of a correlation analysis should be secured from Thurstone's work, but the main assumptions and procedures will be briefly presented here.

Analyses of a Score

Since test scores are basic materials, a working hypothesis is needed for their analysis. Thurstone, as well as almost all other statistical analysts, defines a test as a situation in which a person's position is determined by a number of forces.[1] The simplest possible case would be that in which only a single force is operating. This is shown in Illus. 144A, where all persons in the group may be represented by points on a straight line. The direction of the force is indicated by the arrow and the amount of the force by the distance from zero to the point representing the scores of persons, H, I, J. This is the situation diagrammed in any frequency curve, ogive, or histogram. The score of H $= 5x$, of I $= 10x$, and of J $= 15x$. Any person's score may be represented as S $=$ ax, where a is a certain amount of x.

A more complex score would be that which resulted from the operation of two independent forces. This is shown in Illus. 144B,

ILLUS. 144. GRAPHIC REPRESENTATION OF INDEPENDENT VARIABLES

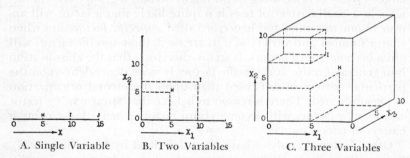

A. Single Variable   B. Two Variables   C. Three Variables

where the position of a person's score can be accurately described as the resultant forces x_1 and x_2. In this case H's score $= 5x_1 + 5x_2$, and I's score $= 10x_1 + 7x_2$, and any score would be S $= a_1x_1 + a_2x_2$.

A still more complex test might involve three independent forces as shown in Illus. 144C. Here H's score on Test A must be represented by:

$$H = 5x_1 + 4x_2 + 7x_3$$
$$I = 5x_1 + 7x_2 + 1x_3$$

and any score by:

$$S = a_1x_1 + a_2x_2 + a_3x_3$$

[1] The use of the word *force* in this chapter should not be interpreted literally as a mechanical entity in all of its applications. In some instances it simply refers to a parameter in a system of measures.

From these figures it is apparent that the plus signs do not indicate simple addition of similar elements, but a combination of particular amounts of forces working independently of each other. Such forces are called *vectors*. Their independence is shown by their different directions, since force x_1 may vary without introducing any change in x_2. When two forces operate at right angles to each other, they are called *orthogonal*. In actual space one can distinguish simultaneously only three directions at right angles to each other. In a mental test, however, it is possible to imagine more than three factors which would be unrelated. Hence the score of a person on any test may be indicated by

$$\text{Score} = S = a_1x_1 + a_2x_2 + a_3x_3 \cdots a_nx_n$$

Analyses of a Group of Scores on a Test

Since any score on a particular test may be considered as the resultant of the component forces, a group of scores may likewise be thought of as resulting from the same forces. A group of scores is best described by their variation from a central tendency. The standard deviation, which is commonly used as a measure of dispersion, is a convenient index for the analysis of variation of a group of scores. If only one force is effective in a test, then the standard deviation is a direct measure of the variation of the force among individuals. If, however, we assume that two, and only two, forces are operative, then the standard deviation is a resultant of both forces. If we further assume that the two forces are independent of each other, they can be diagrammed at right angles to each other as in Illus. 145. There the total scores on Test A are represented by the diagonal line, and the amounts of the two component forces, x and y, by the horizontal and vertical lines. The standard deviations are shown by the points under the distribution curves. The standard deviations of the forces, x and y, bear a definite relationship to the standard deviation of Test A. According to the Pythagorean theorem, the square of the standard deviation of Test A (σ_A^2) is always the sum of the squares of the standard deviations of forces x and y:

$$\sigma_A^2 = \sigma_x^2 + \sigma_y^2$$

Because the square of the sigma is convenient as a measure in these analyses, it is called the *variance* of a group of scores. The variance of a test which has only two component factors can be completely described from the variances of those factors.

When more than two factors are present, the variance of the total score still equals the sum of the variances of all the component factors.

ILLUS. 145. THE DISPERSION OF TOTAL SCORES AND OF COMPONENT FORCES

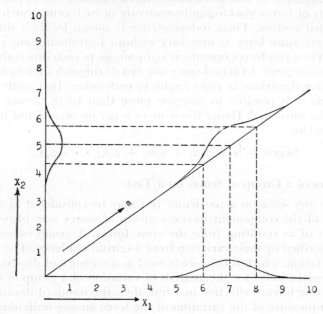

Thurstone has shown that the total variance of any test may be analyzed into three kinds of factors, called common or group factors, specific factors, and chance factors. *Common factors* are defined as those which are found in at least two tests in the battery. *Specific factors* are those found only in one test, and *chance factors* are those due to random variations. To simplify calculations, the variance of total scores is made equal to one by using standard scores instead of raw scores throughout. The total variance of a test then can be indicated by

$$\sigma_A{}^2 = \sigma_{A_x}{}^2 + \sigma_{A_y}{}^2 + \sigma_{A_z}{}^2 \cdots \cdots \sigma_{A_n}{}^2 + \sigma_{A_s}{}^2 + \sigma_{A_c}{}^2 = 1$$

where

A represents total scores on Test A.

A_x is the amount of variation in total scores due to factor x.

x, y, z, and n are factors common to A and also at least one other test.

s is a specific factor, and c is a chance factor.

$\sigma_{A_x}{}^2$ is the per cent of σ_A which is due to x, since all the factors add to 1.00. It is also defined as the square of the loading of factor x in Test A.

Common Factors

The calculation of the common factors in a test is possible from the intercorrelations between tests, because the correlation of any two tests is equal to the covariance of their common factors. Hence, a product-moment correlation can be analyzed as

$$r_{AB} = \sigma_{A_x} \sigma_{B_x} + \sigma_{A_y} \sigma_{B_y} + \sigma_{A_z} \sigma_{B_z} \cdot \cdot \cdot \cdot \cdot \cdot \sigma_{A_n} \sigma_{B_n}$$

where

A and B are total test scores.

σ_{A_x}, σ_{A_y}, σ_{A_z}, and σ_{A} are the *factor loadings* of Test A in factors x, y, z, and n. The factor loading in x shows the variation in A scores which is due to variations in the x factor. It is also a correlation of Test A with factor x. σ_{B_x}, σ_{B_y}, σ_{B_z}, and σ_{B_n} are the factor loadings of Test B in factor x, y, z, and n.

In a practical test situation one does not usually know with any mathematical certainty how many factors are common to two or more tests. Test results, however, may be made to furnish a correlation matrix which shows the relations between tests. Thurstone (1946) described a unique solution which determines the smallest number of factors needed to account for the test correlations. The matrix is treated as a determinant and solved by a method which assumes that all factor loadings should be positive within the tolerance of sampling errors, and that the number of zero loadings should be made as great as possible to give unambiguous results.

In Thurstone's centroid method a central or average value based on all correlations in the matrix is found. From this center, factor axes can be computed and drawn as in Illus. 146, showing the relations of tests and clusters of tests. On a flat surface only two unrelated axes can be drawn, but in statistical practice a fairly large number of unrelated axes appear. These may be shown as radii of a sphere or series of spheres. One of the principal problems of analysis is that of determining a center. If new tests are added to the battery or new subjects tested, the center may change.

Another feature of Thurstone's method is the rotation of factor axes to yield the smallest loadings. Thus, in Illus. 146 there are two sets of axes, X and Y, and X′ and Y′. Each test is first represented by its loadings on the X and Y axes. All the loadings are high on both axes because the tests lie at considerable distance from either axis. In order to present a simple picture, Thurstone rotates the axes to give the maximum number of zero or near-zero scores and

ILLUS. 146. ROTATION OF AXES

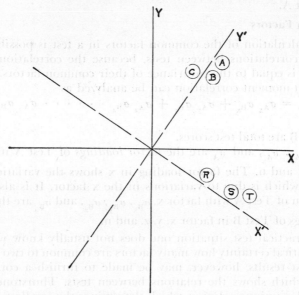

A centroid graph showing rotation of axes to reduce negative weights and to increase the number of near-zero weights. Each circle shows the position of a test as computed from the X and Y axes. The tests in the lower right quadrant have negative Y weights. With the same center a new set of X′ and Y′ axes can be drawn or computed so that one cluster of tests has near-zero scores on the Y′ axes and the other on the X′ axes, and neither cluster has significantly minus weights.

to avoid minus values. He has shown that this rotation, not only gives a simpler structure, but also yields factor loadings for a test which tend to remain the same when the test battery is changed or when new subjects are used.

This method gives a fairly complete solution of unique factors in a particular battery of tests, without, however, giving the factors names which represent particular forces or psychological processes. Names of processes are usually given to mathematical factors from an inspection of the tests which show the highest loadings.

Chance and Specific Factors

The chance variations (c) in test scores may be measured by a correlation of two trials of the test, assuming that no systematic changes have occurred between trials. The variance due to specific factors (s) which are not found in any other test can be found by subtracting all the other elements in the total variance from 1.

EXAMPLES OF FACTORIAL ANALYSES

Two examples are given here to show the results of applying a factorial analysis to the scores of a battery of tests of a group. One is Thurstone's analysis of primary mental traits; the other, Mosier's analysis of personality traits. Other examples are given in this book.

Thurstone's Test of Primary Traits

Thurstone presented a group of college students with fifty-seven carefully controlled tests requiring 15 hours of work. The tests included nearly every existing variety of verbal and nonverbal thinking, but did not include adjustments-to-persons or motor tests. The scores of each test were correlated with the scores of each of the others, and the resulting matrix yielded twelve factors, of which nine were sufficiently large to be identified. The tests which had large loadings, and hence were considered to be the best indicators of factors, are shown in Illus. 147. Using these and similar tests, a scale for superior adults has been constructed which discloses a person's relative position in these primary abilities.

Illustration 148 shows the factor loadings for the tests just described together with the percentage of the total variance, which is indicated in the h² column, and the retest reliability. From this illustration it appears that some tests have fairly heavy loadings in more than one factor. Thus, Figure Classification shows a loading of .39 in factor S, Spatial Visualization; .40 in factor I, Induction; and .40 in factor D, Deduction. Such tests are not of as great analytical value as multiplication, which is well accounted for by factor N, Number Facility. It is also clear from the h² column that some of the items are not completely accounted for by these factor loadings. Since the tests are shown to have high reliabilities, it is probable that tests with small h² values, such as Figure Classification, demand skills or adjustments not well represented by any of these factors. This condition can be remedied only by more extensive study.

Mosier's Analysis of Personality Traits

Mosier (1937), who followed a procedure reported by Guilford (1936), selected from several lists of personality traits the items which seemed most diagnostic for clinical use. These items which are shown in Illus. 149 were administered twice, with one week intervening, to five hundred male students at the University of Florida. The scores for the forty-two items and also for the American Council on Education Psychological Examination were intercorrelated. From

ILLUS. 147. TESTS OF PRIMARY ABILITIES

1. SPATIAL RELATIONS (S)

Cubes (adapted from Brigham, 1932): factor loading, .626

The drawings in this test represent cubes. There is a different design on each face of the cube. A cube has six faces.

Notice that both of the drawings below can represent the same cube. Be sure you see that the first and second drawings represent the same cube turned into two different positions. Since both drawings can represent the same cube, a plus sign (+) has been placed in the blank square at the right.

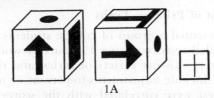

1A

Notice that the two drawings below represent two different cubes and that a minus sign (−) has been placed in the blank square at the right. Be sure that you see that it would be impossible to turn the cube shown in the first drawing so that it would look EXACTLY like the cube shown in the second drawing. Unless you see this clearly, you cannot solve the test items. There is a different design on each face of the cube.

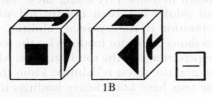

1B

2. PERCEPTUAL SPEED, VISUAL (P)

Word grouping: factor loading, .573

In the line below, notice that the four words, dog, lion, cat and giraffe, can be grouped together because they are all names of animals. The word chair does not belong with the others because it is not the name of an animal. Since chair is the second word, 2 is written in the blank at the right.

1—dog   2—chair   3—cat   4—lion   5—giraffe   2

Similarly, four of the words in the line below can be grouped together because they are alike in some way, while one of the words does not belong because it is different. Write the number of that word in the blank at the right.

1—carrot   2—radish   3—beet   4—book   5—turnip   —

3. NUMBER CALCULATIONS (N)

Addition: factor loading, .755

Addition is a simple test of ordinary addition of seven two-digit numbers.

17
64
93
21
14
17
65

Multiplication: factor loading, .812

Multiplication is a simple test involving the multiplication of six-digit numbers by a single-digit number.

7245986
4

ILLUS. 147. TESTS OF PRIMARY ABILITIES (Cont'd)

4. VERBAL RELATIONS (V)

Inventive Opposites: factor loading, .635

This is a test of ability to think of words. Think of two different words opposite in meaning to the word <u>narrow</u> below. One word should begin with <u>b</u>. The other should begin with <u>w</u>. The words are <u>broad</u> and <u>wide</u>. These words have been written in the blanks.

> narrow   b_____   w_____

Now think of two words opposite in meaning to the word <u>large</u>. The first should begin with <u>l</u>; the second with <u>s</u>.

> large   l_____   s_____

The words are <u>little</u> and <u>small</u>. Write little in the first blank. Write small in the second.

> strong   f_____   w_____
>
> wrong   r_____   c_____
>
> dark   b_____   l_____

5. WORD FORMS (W)

Anagrams: factor loading, 5.34

Make as many different words as you can, using only the letters in the word G–E–N–E–R–A–T–I–O–N–S. You may use long or short words and may include the names of persons, places, or foreign words. In any one word do not use a letter more times than it appears in G–E–N–E–R–A–T–I–O–N–S.

Sample words have been written in the first few lines. Continue writing as many words as you can, using only the letters given.

> G–E–N–E–R–A–T–I–O–N–S
> 1. ART_____
> 2. ERA_____
> 3. SNORE_____
> 4. _____

Disarranged Words: factor loading, .512

Rearrange the letters on each of the following lines to spell the name of an animal. In the first line, the letters (ebar) can be arranged to spell bear, which is written in the blank space. In the next line, the letters (odg) spell dog, which is written in the blank space. In the same way the letters (atc) spell cat.

ANIMALS

> ebar   <u>bear</u>
>
> odg   <u>dog</u>
>
> atc   <u>cat</u>

Rearrange the letters on each of the following lines to spell the name of a boy. The first two names have already been written for you. Write the third.

BOYS' NAMES

> lpau   <u>Paul</u>
>
> rcla   <u>Carl</u>
>
> honj   ____

Rearrange the letters on each of the following lines to spell the name of a bird.

BIRDS

> uckd   _____
>
> cowr   _____
>
> wahk   _____

6. IMMEDIATE MEMORY SPAN (M)

Word-number: factor loading, .529

Word-number was prepared as a test involving memorizing. The subject memorizes a set of paired associates. Each stimulus word is to be associated with a response number. In the recall the subject is given the stimulus word, and he is asked to write the corresponding response number. The test is arranged with instructions and a fore-exercise followed by a recall. A second fore-exercise, which is longer, is then given

ILLUS. 147. TESTS OF PRIMARY ABILITIES *(Cont'd)*

It is followed by a recall. The test proper with twenty words and associated numbers is then presented. This is followed by the recall. The test really consists of three sections with a presentation and recall in each section. This was done in order to make sure that the subjects understood the nature of the task.

Number-number: factor loading, .664

Number-number is a paired-associates test in the same form as the two previous tests in which the stimulus consists of a two-digit number, and the response is another two-digit number. This test is also given in two sections with two parts for each section. Together with the instructions the subject is given five paired numbers to associate. He is then asked to recall the five response numbers when the stimulus numbers are presented. He is given the opportunity to write the numbers if he wants to learn them in that manner. Then follow the memorizing of the twenty pairs of numbers and the recall in which the twenty stimulus numbers are presented in random order. The subject is asked to fill in the response numbers.

7. INDUCTION (I)

Number series: factor loading, .503

The numbers in each row of this test follow one another according to some rule. You are to find the rule and fill in the blanks to fit the rule.

In the example below each number can be obtained from the one before it by the rule add 2. The blanks have been filled in accordingly.

2 4 6 8 10 __12__ __14__

Find the rule in the series below and fill in the blanks. You may use addition, subtraction, multiplication, division, or any combination of these.

10 8 11 ___ 12 ___ 13

The above series goes by alternate steps of subtracting 2 and adding 3. You should have written 9 and 10 in the blanks.

Find the rule in each series below and write the numbers in the blanks accordingly. There is a different rule for each line. Go right ahead. Do not wait for any signal.

19 18 17 ___ 15 14 ___
8 11 14 ___ 20
27 ___ 23 23 19 19

Figure Classification: factor loading, .405 (Also called Spearman's Form Analogies Test)

In each line below, there is a rule by which the symbols in Group I differ from those in Group II. There is a new rule for each line. Your problem is to discover the rule in each line. Some sample problems are worked for you below.

In the first line below the rule is that the symbols in Group I are horizontal while those in Group II are vertical. Each of the test symbols at the right belongs either to Group I or to Group II. The test symbols that belong to Group I have been checked.

Group I	Group II	Test Symbols

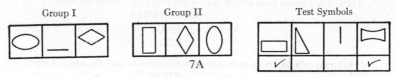

7A

The rule in the problem below is that the figures in Group I are closed while those in Group II are open. Now check the test symbols that belong to Group I.

Group I	Group II	Test Symbols

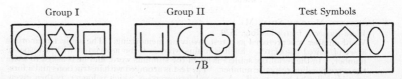

7B

ILLUS. 147. TESTS OF PRIMARY ABILITIES (Cont'd)

You should have checked the third and fourth symbols. They are closed figures.

8. REASONING (R)

Arithmetical Reasoning: factor loading, .583
Arithmetical Reasoning contains nineteen problems and is similar to current tests of this type.
Mechanical Movements: factor loading, .414
In this test you will be shown pictures of mechanical movements. You will be asked questions about them.

In each picture the part that makes the others move is called the driver. The solid black circles represent axles which can turn but cannot move from where they are shown.

Now answer the questions after each of the pictures below. Go right ahead.

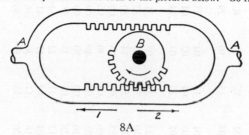

8A

1. If B starts moving in the direction shown, which way will A move, 1 or 2? . . . . _____

2. In which direction will A be moving when B has turned half way around from where it is now? . . . . _____''
Vocabulary, general: factor loading, .515
Word Knowledge is the Thorndike Vocabulary Test.

9. DEDUCTION (D)

False Premises: factor loading, .578
This is a test of your ability to tell the difference between good and bad reasoning. You must judge only the reasoning in the following arguments because every statement is false or even absurd.

The first argument below is good reasoning and is marked plus (+). The second argument appears similar but is bad reasoning and is marked minus (−).

All haystacks are catfish. All catfish are typewriters.
Therefore all haystacks are typewriters.   +

All haystacks are typewriters. All catfish are typewriters.
Therefore all haystacks are catfish.   −

Reasoning: factor loading, .525
This is a test of your ability to tell the difference between good and bad reasoning. The first argument below is good reasoning and is marked plus (+). The second argument appears similar but is bad reasoning and is marked minus (−).

All sports are dangerous, and football is a sport.
Therefore, football is dangerous. |

Some sports are dangerous, and football is a sport.
Therefore, football is dangerous.   −

Now mark the two arguments below in the same way.

All wealthy men pay taxes. Mr. White pays taxes.
Therefore, Mr. White is wealthy.   _____

All wealthy men pay taxes. Mr. White is wealthy.
Therefore, Mr. White pays taxes.   _____

The first argument above is bad and should have been marked minus (−). The second should have been marked plus (+).

(Arranged from Thurstone, 1938. By permission of the Editor, *Psychometrika Monographs.*)

ILLUS. 148. FACTORIAL LOADINGS OF MENTAL TESTS

Factor	Test	S	P	N	V	M	W	I	R	D	h²	Reliability
Spatial (S)	Cubes	.63	.21	.20	.06	.03	.15	.10	.29	.27	.75	.86
Perceptual Speed (P)	Word Group	.11	.57	.08	.46	.01	.13	.04	.23	.17	.71	.95
Number (N)	Addition	.06	.03	.75	.19	.05	.04	.02	.04	.22	.68	.85
	Multiplication	.02	.09	.81	.02	.07	.28	.07	.14	.03	.79	.73
Verbal Relations (V)	Inventive Opposites	.07	.19	.05	.63	.22	.33	.03	.31	.05	.81	.91
Word Forms (W)	Dis. Words	.06	.22	.06	.10	.10	.51	.03	.22	.22	.55	.95
	Anagrams	.04	.00	.09	.18	.13	.53	.14	.10	.20	.56	—
Memory Span (M)	Word-Numb.	.01	.07	.02	.12	.53	.06	.03	.09	.22	.42	.91
	Numb.-Numb.	.04	.08	.24	.02	.66	.03	.30	.06	.11	.62	.68
Induction (I)	Fig. Class	.39	.19	.08	.30	.05	.06	.40	.09	.40	.64	.90
	Numb. Series	.06	.35	.35	.17	.26	.00	.50	.09	.29	.68	.80
Reasoning (R)	Arith. Reas.	.08	.01	.38	.38	.28	.03	.33	.58	.08	.84	.80
	Vocab.	.03	.41	.12	.03	.12	.41	.22	.54	.16	.96	.84
	Mech. Mov.	.07	.19	.09	.42	.04	.02	.17	.41	.40	.67	.69
Deduction (T)	Reason	.05	.05	.04	.42	.18	.17	.20	.36	.52	.81	.84
	False Prem.	.02	.01	.03	.42	.26	.16	.19	.36	.58	.77	.50

(Arranged from Thurstone, 1938, from Tables 3 and 4. By permission of the Editor, *Psychometrika Monographs*.)

ILLUS. 149. QUESTIONNAIRE ITEMS ON NEUROTIC BEHAVIOR

1. Do you get stage fright?
2. Do you have difficulty in starting conversation with a stranger?
3. Do you worry too long over humiliating experiences?
4. Do you often feel lonesome, even when you are with other people?
5. Do you consider yourself a rather nervous person?
6. Are your feelings easily hurt?
7. Do you keep in the background on social occasions?
8. Do ideas run through your head so that you cannot sleep?
9. Are you frequently burdened by a sense of remorse?
10. Do you worry over possible misfortune?
11. Do your feelings alternate between happiness and sadness without apparent reason?
12. Are you troubled with shyness?
13. Do you daydream frequently?
14. Have you ever had spells of dizziness?
15. Do you get discouraged easily?
16. Do your interests change quickly?
17. Are you easily moved to tears?
18. Does it bother you to have people watch you at work, even when you do it well?
19. Can you stand criticism without feeling hurt?
20. Do you have difficulty making friends?
21. Are you troubled with the idea that people are watching you on the street?
22. Does your mind often wander badly so that you lose track of what you are doing?
23. Have you ever been depressed because of low marks in school?
24. Are you touchy on various subjects?
25. Are you often in a state of excitement?
26. Do you frequently feel grouchy?
27. Do you feel self-conscious when you recite in class?
28. Do you often feel just miserable?
29. Does some particular useless thought keep coming into your mind to bother you?
30. Do you hesitate to volunteer in a class recitation?
31. Are you frequently in low spirits?
32. Do you often experience periods of loneliness?
33. Do you often feel self-conscious in the presence of superiors?
34. Do you lack self-confidence?
35. Do you find it difficult to speak in public?
36. Do you often feel self-conscious because of your personal appearance?
37. If you see an accident, are you quick to take an active part in giving help?
38. Do you feel that you must do a thing over several times before you leave it?
39. Are you troubled with feelings of inferiority?
40. Do you often find that you cannot make up your mind until the time for action has passed?
41. Do you have ups and downs in mood without apparent cause?
42. Are you in general self-confident about your abilities?
43. (Above the median, A. C. E. Psychological Examination.)

(Mosier, 1937, p. 280. By permission of the Editor, *Psychometrika*.)

the matrix of 780 correlations, eight independent factors emerged through the use of Thurstone's Centroid method. These were reduced by graphic rotation to the simple structure shown in Illus. 150. The highest loadings in each factor are underlined. The tentative interpretation of these factors is given on the basis of those items which show the highest loadings:

1. *Cycloid:* The first trait is closely identified with the tendency to have wide mood swings.

2. *Depression:* This is shown by feelings of loneliness, sadness, depreciation, and anxiety.

3. *Hypersensitivity:* This trait is psychological rather than physiological. It is represented by hurt feelings and an inability to stand criticism.

4. *Inferiority:* This is shown by lack of self-confidence both in social situations and mechanical and thought problems.

5. *Social Introversion:* This is typical of persons who are shy and self-conscious in small, informal groups.

6. *Platform Shyness:* This is associated with stage-fright and appearance among strangers.

7. *Mental Ability,* also called cognitive defect: This is shown by poor grades in school, and on the American Council Test.

8. *Autistic Tendency:* This is shown by frequent daydreaming and wishful thinking of an emotional sort.

Illustration 150 also shows how factorial analyses may be used to construct better scales by selecting items which are completely explained by only one factor. If an item shows heavy loading in more than one factor, its interpretation will be difficult. Thus, item 11 is good in the sense that it depends upon only one factor, but item 2 is less valuable for analytical purposes because it has moderate loadings in two variables.

The per cent of variance due to all the factors is shown in column h^2. Item 41 is good because nearly all its variance is accounted for in this analysis. It has small random or specific loadings to reduce its value as an analytical tool. Specific factor loadings can probably be reduced still more by factor analyses of more elaborate scales. Item 16 is of little value for careful measurement because its h^2 shows that only 28 per cent of its variance is accounted for.

Mosier interprets his results to mean that each of the factors will probably not be found on subsequent research to contain elements found in any other factor.

Each factor may, on subsequent analysis, appear to be a composite of several other more basic and elemental factors. The existence of these eight independent factors is supported to a considerable extent by the reports of Guilford and Lacey (1947), Whisler (1934), Vernon (1938), Layman (1937), Cattell (1947), and several others.

ILLUS. 150. FACTOR LOADINGS OF PERSONALITY TRAITS

Item   *Loadings on Primary Traits (See Items in Illus. 149)*

No.	C	D	H	I	S	P	Co	Au	h^2
1.	048*	026	131	252	234	766	017	− 098	738
2.	− 079	118	075	048	572	350	− 235	− 045	532
3.	250	020	380	067	302	− 117	064	183	355
4.	073	679	006	181	026	− 032	− 032	467	719
5.	206	129	452	− 156	163	121	− 034	199	363
6.	251	115	518	077	065	032	112	119	378
7.	− 057	282	− 068	001	668	128	− 043	− 067	56²
8.	026	200	260	− 089	155	− 055	042	467	363
9.	298	271	236	− 011	− 010	− 076	050	481	451
10.	409	151	083	− 103	248	− 046	113	316	377
11.	808	141	− 011	010	− 057	013	− 012	274	757
12.	− 045	009	003	218	708	362	− 052	002	687
13.	023	018	106	221	− 054	000	075	620	447
15.	202	098	397	498	154	012	254	075	545
16.	289	− 125	240	221	000	− 106	179	168	279
18.	001	− 013	206	003	475	206	274	020	382
19.	010	097	471	307	− 057	016	244	046	386
20.	002	500	067	299	420	126	− 361	− 228	718
21.	142	131	080	170	479	139	− 013	461	531
22.	262	− 011	− 001	349	− 053	− 031	248	190	296
23.	165	066	008	− 090	104	203	549	066	386
24.	158	200	143	142	094	102	346	176	273
25.	290	001	417	− 004	− 134	174	− 006	342	419
26.	387	346	310	187	− 026	052	− 036	199	443
27.	− 026	033	− 009	180	278	720	149	037	656
28.	431	560	298	− 092	099	− 069	158	190	673
29.	252	033	047	− 002	063	− 057	507	403	494
30.	− 140	084	020	096	319	503	328	− 018	490
31.	513	591	200	085	116	016	181	142	698
32.	161	714	088	035	161	− 045	100	490	795
33.	045	− 092	080	293	459	419	− 018	223	534
34.	100	236	046	655	499	172	− 018	− 030	766
35.	005	040	− 022	282	184	799	− 036	− 036	760
36.	− 003	022	023	109	344	184	− 019	475	388
38.	147	081	067	− 032	214	− 041	267	− 038	153
39.	145	042	041	425	595	113	045	209	619
40.	317	053	256	144	306	106	196	180	364
41.	849	199	038	037	014	− 128	− 035	246	851
42.	− 033	066	− 131	585	516	049	004	− 018	635
43.	017	− 019	228	174	083	− 101	− 428	172	308

* Decimal points properly preceding each entry have been omitted.

(Mosier, 1937, p. 283.   By permission of the Editor, *Psychometrika.*)

Homogeneous Tests

At the beginning of this chapter the importance of having a single psychological function measured by a single scale was emphasized. Such a scale is not easy to prepare logically or statistically, because differences in mental processes at various levels of difficulty and in the attitudes and personality traits are hard to observe or control. Several approaches are used in addition to the logical one. Loevinger (1948) summarized these and has given an Index of Homogeneity which has the advantages of being rather simple to apply and universal in its application. Ferguson (1941) proposed a method determining homogeneity of items. Names of people were placed on a checkerboard, from left to right in order of increasing total scores at the tops of the columns, and items were placed in order of increasing difficulty in ascending rows. If the test is perfectly homogeneous the pluses for correct answers made by each person for each item will lie above a diagonal broken line on such a checkerboard. Items which do not measure the same factor will show different plus and minus patterns. Also, persons who are atypical of the group will show irregular plus and minus patterns in the columns. Guttman (1947) has described an ingenious mechanical device, called a Scalogram Board, for accomplishing the same thing that Ferguson achieved with his table, but with a smaller number of items. In these analyses it is assumed that in a perfectly homogeneous test, two persons who get the same scores will have exactly the same pattern of correct answers. These techniques are similar to the process of correlating each item with the total test score. But they go further in showing clusters of items which are related by virtue of being answered in similar fashion by certain portions of the subjects. A more analytical technique is that of correlating each item with all the rest, as was shown above in Mosier's work. This method provides a matrix upon which a factorial analysis can be made. By a careful use of factorial analysis it will be possible to show the factor loading of each item in terms of the factors that are revealed. From this analysis items that have a high loading in one factor and a small loading in other factors can be found.

LIMITATIONS AND ADVANTAGES
OF FACTORIAL ANALYSES

The procedures outlined above, as well as factorial procedures generally, place fairly clear limitations upon the usefulness of a factorial analysis, for example:

1. The method should only be applied when all scores in a particular test can be shown to represent the same combinations of factors.

2. The factors which are discovered represent patterns of behavior which are independent only in the sense that they do not

usually appear in similar or related amounts in the same persons.

3. The factors may be thought of as forces or arrangements which are found within or without the individuals. They may act against or in the same direction as other forces, not in purely additive combinations alone.

4. All factors are, like highest common factors, the most complex factors that are common to the persons who have been tested. It is quite probable that most of these factors may consist of a number of smaller independent factors.

5. The number of common factors found in any battery of tests will vary with the items which are included and the abilities of the persons tested. Hence, even though two groups of persons are appraised by the same tests, analyses of the two groups will often yield different factor loadings.

Factorial analyses have the following advantages:

1. They allow a mathematical analysis of elements or forces in tests of individuals according to specific assumptions. The assumptions can be varied to fit experimental findings.

2. They show which tests involve several factors and which involve a few factors or only one. The selection of tests or items which are pure measures of a particular factor is thus advanced. Factorial analysis is undoubtedly one of the best methods of evaluating an item, and a great boon in the construction of analytical scales.

3. They show, with statistical precision, the types of patterns which are not found together in the same individual. From such analyses individual profiles can be constructed of factors which are distinctly independent in a particular group of persons.

4. They yield analyses of all kinds of forces, intellectual, environmental, and emotional, which are operating in the test situation. Examiners often lose sight of one variable when they are closely examining another, hence a factorial analysis is a good check on subjective analyses, and leads to a discovery of new factors.

5. They can also be applied to job analysis, and job ratings, and thus yield more effective criteria of success.

STUDY GUIDE QUESTIONS

1. What are the two basic assumptions made in applying a factorial analysis? Which test situations most nearly conform to these assumptions? Which least?

2. How may common factors be defined?

3. Define correlation matrix, general factor, group factor, specific factor according to Spearman.

4. What factors did Spearman describe?

5. Define variance, vector, score, orthogonal force, factor loading.
6. How may the total variance of any test be expressed in a formula which combines common, specific, and chance factors.
7. Give examples of the tests most highly saturated by the primary factors isolated by Thurstone.
8. Which in Illus. 148 are unique?
9. Which in Illus. 150 are unique?
10. How can factorial analysis be used to develop purer or unique measures?

PART THREE

DYNAMIC PATTERNS

CHAPTER XV

PERSONALITY: DYNAMIC THEORY AND STRUCTURE

This chapter first gives an exposition of the concepts of personality common to almost all theories of personality. Then four specialized theories, which usually supplement each other, are discussed: (*a*) those having physical or physiological bases, (*b*) clinical theories based on studies of insane or poorly adjusted persons, (*c*) psychoanalytical theory which emphasizes the results of studies of sexual development, and (*d*) psychological theories emphasizing learning and social behavior.

INTRODUCTION

The evaluation of personal dynamics goes far beyond simple measurement, for it seeks to make a complete picture of various component parts of an individual and the forces which activate them.

A human being consists physically of from four to five billion cells, placed in relation to each other in complex fashion and forming several hundred somewhat independent reaction systems, which grow and decline at different rates, and serve different bodily or social functions. The cells of the body are for the most part small and easily destroyed and cannot be directly observed while functioning. In spite of some notable advances in knowledge concerning the functions of the brain areas, the physical mechanics of perceiving, thinking, or feeling are still to be well demonstrated. It seems that there is sometimes considerable elasticity and partial substitution of function and of dominance among the various reaction systems, which further complicates the study. It is small wonder, therefore, that for almost any complex physical human behavior, fairly competent judges often have a difficult time agreeing on just what has been done physically, and a much more difficult time explaining why it was done. When competent observers can agree upon identifying and measuring the complicated patterns of behavior and the causes of these patterns, there will be a well-developed science. At present we are still in the process of defining and identifying patterns.

Among the many theories of personality there are certain recurring concepts that form common ground. Psychologists Edward L. Thorndike (1935), Robert S. Woodworth (1938), and Gordon W. Allport (1937), clinical psychologists Lawrence F. Shaffer (1936) and Robert W. White (1948), psychiatrists Otto Fenichel (1945) and Sigmund Freud (1938), and social psychologists Kimball Young (1947) and Gardner Murphy (1947) agree fairly well in using the following eleven concepts.

1. *The physical continuum.* A human being's acts are closely related in a continuum of activity, which means that all of his acts are parts of a complex stream of action, and are caused by what went before, and, in turn, cause further action.

2. *Consciousness and unconscious activity.* Behavior cannot always be observed directly, but is inferred. That which can be observed by another person is called *overt activity;* the remainder is called *covert* or *inner activity.* Part of covert activity is known to oneself, for example, a person is aware of multiplying 48 by 56 mentally and can report this activity. This type of covert activity is called *conscious covert activity.* But other activities go on within us, of which we may have little or no direct evidence. They therefore cannot be observed or reported on. An activity of this kind is called *unconscious activity.* It can only be inferred from acts which are hard to explain by any conscious activity. For example, a student feels compelled to carry her gym shoes to her history class for no conscious reason. Unconscious activity is sometimes given a subdivision, called *subconscious* activity, which includes those acts that we observe rarely, or can remember only under special conditions, such as hypnotism and great fear or excitement, or under a long intense process of recall such as occurs during psychoanalysis. It is this inaccessibility of inner behavior that has given rise to demonology, astrology, and many other schemes which purport to reveal and explain what is beyond the reach of the conscious mind.

Most authorities agree that an infant is largely motivated by unconscious needs, some of which may continue throughout life. Also, unconscious wishes or fears may be acquired by severely frustrating or unpleasant experiences.

3. *Inherited and environmental factors.* An individual starts life as a single cell which results from the complex union of two other cells. The substances in the single cell grow or enlarge by assimilating animal and vegetable substances from outside the cell. Rate and type of enlargement are determined both by the substances in the cell and by the substances which it assimilates. Thus even at the start of life the influences of heredity and environment are combined.

4. *Differentiation of cells.* The original single cell soon subdivides rapidly. At first all the cells seem to have the same internal qualities, but soon it is apparent that their location in the body determines their specialization of function. Due to the pull of gravity or to other forces, one portion of the embryo develops more rapidly than the other and becomes the head. A gradient of activity is established from the head to the tail. The outer cells develop into skin, sense organs, brain and the central nervous system. The middle layers of cells develop into bones and muscles attached to the bones, and the inner cells, into the viscera. A few cells which remain isolated in the gonads or reproductive organs are the germ cells. An infant at birth acts only in complex patterns of surging movements. As nerve and muscle fibers grow more mature, small groups of muscles are able to make independent movements, and a large number of new combinations of movements are possible. By adulthood these become fine dexterity and agility.

5. *Maturation and senesence.* At birth growth is very rapid, but the process gradually slows down until in the adult there is no further increase in the number of cells. Throughout life there is a continual replacement of wornout cells until old age when the replacement process gradually declines in both quality and quantity of cells. The process of growth is regulated in part by the innate characteristics of the cells and in part by the amounts of mineral substances they retain. A number of internal glands also regulate the maintenance and growth of various parts of the body.

6. *Individual differences.* Persons differ at birth in the relative maturation of various parts of the body. The absolute differences increase until maturity is reached; the relative differences are harder to determine. At maturity the smallest individuals are from one half to one third the size of the largest ones. Many psychologists believe that relative differences in mental abilities are considerably greater.

7. *Learning.* Shortly after birth a type of learning called *condi-*

tioning is common. This is a process whereby stimuli begin to elicit reactions which were not called out at first. From time to time these stimuli were part of reaction patterns which they now recall in part. Thus the *word* book comes to represent a type of *object* book by their being experienced together under certain conditions. Numbers, symbols, and feelings of fear or anger are associated in thousands of combinations.

8. *Adjustment patterns.* In an infant four adjustment patterns appear: (*a*) seeking, when the infant is restless and apparently needs something, (*b*) satisfaction or pleasure, when his wants are met and the infant relaxes, (*c*) dissatisfaction or anger, when his wants are not satisfied promptly enough and he becomes violently and destructively active, and (*d*) fear or anxiety, when he is overwhelmed by some real injury or imaginary injury and withdraws, if possible, to a safer place. These adjustment patterns are sometimes called *emotions,* but the word emotion has so many meanings that it should not be used without qualification.

9. *Needs.* It is from these adjustment patterns that one's needs, conscious or unconscious, are known. A person is moved, or motivated to action, by his needs. In an infant needs or drives are nearly all related to his physical well being. Soon thereafter he develops great pleasure in immediate friendly activities. In adolescence satisfactions come to be related to long-term activities, such as a building project. In adults, as ideals are developed more clearly and consciously, these long-term activities become still more dominant sources of satisfaction.

10. *Conflicts.* Because of all these different needs and drives, conflicts of many sorts appear. One may have a conflict on the physiological level due to the need for a drink of water and the need for additional rest. Or a physiological need may conflict with a mental or social need. For instance, one may need exercise but also wish to finish listening to a lecture on economics. Sometimes a conscious wish may conflict with an unconscious one. Thus I may wish to be considerate of a person, but at the same time have a subconscious wish to get rid of him. Likewise conflicts frequently arise between imaginary and real satisfactions. For example, a person's day dreams and fantasies may become so pleasant, in contrast to the sordid realities of his life, that he will shut himself off from reality and become disoriented.

11. *Modes of solving conflicts.* Authorities differ considerably over theories concerning the solution of conflicts. At one extreme are the mechanists who believe that a person's activities are all the result of natural laws which govern mechanical forces. Thus when

there is a conflict, the action taken is always the resultant of the various forces present at the moment. At the other extreme are those who believe that some superhuman being can put aside natural laws and bring about results which defy mechanical principles. Somewhere in between these who hold extreme beliefs are those who believe that they operate according to natural laws but that some of these principles are not well understood, and that they can influence or direct their own actions a good deal by a process of will or choice. Most psychologists explain choice as the result of an inherited and learned readiness to respond to certain situations in a particular way. This readiness is sometimes called an ideal or attitude (Chapter XXI). Thus some persons think of themselves as perfect and important and choose immediate and selfish actions, blaming others for all their failures and dissatisfactions. Others think of themselves as weak and imperfect and blame themselves or feel guilty or anxious about many situations. Many take a middle position. They admit some weaknesses but also realize their strengths, and try to analyze the causes of their behavior and to plan constructive and cooperative behavior.

From considerations such as these a number of authors have roughly classified persons according to how well they solve their conflicts. Four levels of adjustment are described here:

Good adjustment. The well-adjusted adult has average or strong energy and physiological impulses, balanced by a well-developed set of ideals for himself and society. His energy is directed to allow adequate personal satisfactions and to contribute to the reasonable satisfactions of those about him. He is closely in touch with reality, but has a good imagination.

Fair adjustment. This person has strong impulses which occasionally break through into aggressive or foolish action, but usually his ideals, which are not very well thought through and organized, channel his behavior into actions which are socially acceptable. While he is fairly well oriented he is not objective about some superstitions and fears.

Poor adjustment. Two types appear here, both of which have many fantasies which seem quite real.

a. One type has weak impulses and strong social ideals. The combination results in anxiety and compulsive behavior.

b. The second type has such strong impulses that he reacts with violent aggression or uncontrollable fears. His ideals for himself and society are variable and poorly defined.

Disorientation. Two types of persons constitute this class:

a. One type has fairly normal impulses and thinking ability but has largely withdrawn emotionally and lost touch with reality. A person of this type lives in his own imaginary world. He may imagine himself as including a large part of the world, as in some catatonic states; or he may think of himself as most normal people do, but imagine that other people and things have his thoughts and fears, as in paranoia.

b. The other type has lost touch with reality through a deterioration of mental processes due to such causes as great fatigue, disease, excitement, drugs, and old age. These people are confused about themselves and society, and their impulses are also usually impaired.

PHYSICAL BASES

Any appraisal of human behavior must somewhere attempt an analysis and quantification of bodily form. Sheldon (1940) summarized the previous work of about thirty investigators and reported a detailed study of bodily dimensions of four thousand white adult males. He found that measures from photographs were more reliable than measures taken by calipers of the soft parts of the body. He devised a method of photographing persons with a standard 5- by 7-inch portrait camera which was placed at a standard height and distance from the subject, who was on a pedestal at a standard distance

ILLUS. 151. SOMATOTYPES FROM SHELDON

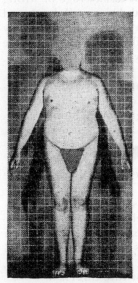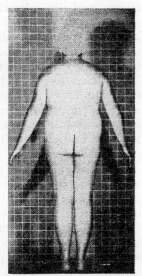

A. Extreme endomorphy
(From Sheldon, 1940. By permission of W. H. Sheldon and Harper & Bros.)

ILLUS. 151. SOMATOTYPES FROM SHELDON *(Cont'd)*

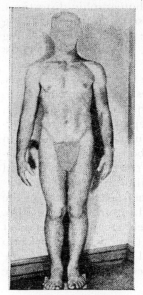 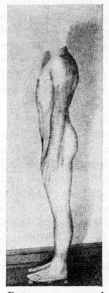 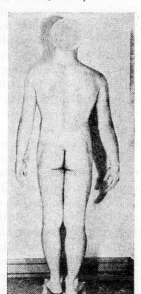

B. Extreme mesomorphy

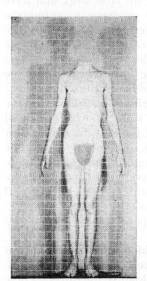 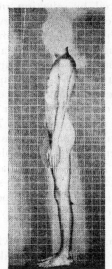 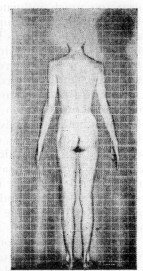

C. Extreme ectomorphy

(From Sheldon, 1940. By permission of W. H. Sheldon and Harper & Bros.)

from a lined neutral-gray background. It was thus possible to take full-length pictures sufficiently free from photographic distortions, whose measurements agreed highly with those taken from the living body. The photographic measures had the advantage of yielding indicators of typical posture and curvature. However, actual measures of height and weight were always taken.

Sheldon stated that from inspection of the four thousand subjects, three, and only three, pronounced extremes stood out, which corresponded roughly to Kretchmer's three types of pyknic, athletic, and asthenic persons. Sheldon, however, rejected Kretchmer's terminology because he wished to make certain important changes in definition, and to show a relation between body structure and relative dominance of three layers of tissue. His three body types, called *somatotypes,* are described in Illus. 151 and Illus. 152. The *endomorphic* type is related to dominance of the inner layers of cells in the embryo which by adulthood have developed into the viscera (Illus. 151A). The *mesomorphic* type shows relatively greater development of the mesial or middle layer of embryonic tissue which grows into bone and voluntary muscles (Illus. 151B) and the *ectomorphic* to the outer layer which is the basis for brain, nerves, skin, and most of the sense organs (Illus. 151C).

The main criticisms of Sheldon's work are that the three types were established by inspection and logic, and that his later work may have been too much influenced by selection of evidence to support a theory. Sheldon's basic measurements, however, are sound, and future research can modify his hypothesis if modification is needed. One of the difficulties of devising morphologic scales is caused by the fact that even in a large group few persons are found in the extreme categories, and the mixtures present complex combinations.

After use of elaborate rank-order procedures based on specific measurements, Sheldon devised a tripolar scale in which each of the three bodily types is represented on a 7-point scale, using 7 for the most extreme form, and 1 for its almost complete absence. The steps in each scale are identified by morphological indices and photographs. In this scheme a 711 type would have 7 points on the endomorphic scale, and one each on the other scales. A 444 type would represent an equal blending of all three types (Illus. 155). Of the 343 mathematically possible combinations of types, 76 have been found and described.

To aid in classification, the body was divided into five regions for which seventeen separate measures were taken (Illus. 153 and Illus. 154). Each region yielded its own morphological measures. These measures combined gave the general morphological type and also yielded evidence of the amount of disagreement, called *dysplasia,* among the five regions. The amount of dysplasia was calculated by summing the differences between the five regions. The total difference in the sample (Illus. 154) was 20, which Sheldon found to be about the 96th centile in the adult male sample, the mean of which was 10.22. The dysplasias are reported to be more important in several mental diseases than the total body type.

ILLUS. 152. DESCRIPTION OF SHELDON'S SOMATOTYPES

	Endomorphic	*Mesomorphic*	*Ectomorphic*
Body	Round, soft, no muscle due to subcutaneous fat, front-to-back and side-to-side diameters about equal in head, neck, trunk and limbs. Long trunk and large volume. Pseudo-breast in male, but abdomen larger than thorax.	Square, hard, large muscles. Some fat. Lateral diameters much greater than anteroposterior Thorax larger than abdomen, and wider at shoulders than waist. Broad hips. Trunk may be long or short.	Thin, shoulders droop and are narrow, trunk abdomen short and shallow. Thorax larger but shallow.
Neck	Short, obtuse angle with chin.	Long, large muscles on sides.	Slender, bends forward.
Face	Wide, both lower and upper; ears and nose flat.	Large eyebrows, cheekbones and jaws. Bones and muscles prominent.	Small, lean features. Chin recedes. Upper ears project. Length more than width.
Head	Large, spherical.	Cubical.	Large cranium.
Limbs	Short, tapering, weak, small hands and feet.	Massive and strong, large hands, large joints.	Long, especially in distal segments, long fingers and toes.
Vertebra	Nearly straight.	Slight S, bowing in at lumbar region.	Marked S.
Genetalia	Small.	Well-developed, compact.	Elongated.
Skin	Soft, velvety, smooth.	Thick, coarse, easily tanned, wrinkled, large pores.	Thin, dry, fine wrinkles, does not tan.
Bones	Small.	Large, thick, heavy.	Small, delicate, prominent.
Hair	Medium amount, fine texture; prematurely bald on back of head.	Variable in amount. Coarse, bald in front.	Fine or very fine, baldness rare, hard to comb.

(Adapted from Sheldon, 1940, Chap. III. By permission of W. H. Sheldon and Harper & Bros.)

ILLUS. 153. LOCATIONS FOR MEASURING SEVENTEEN DIAMETERS

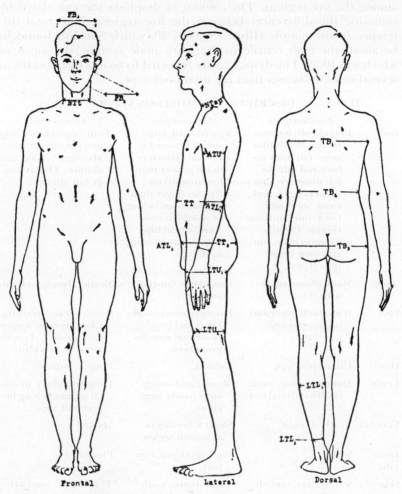

Frontal   Lateral   Dorsal

(From Sheldon, 1940. By permission of W. H. Sheldon and Harper & Bros.)

Two reports of factorial analyses of bodily measures should be considered here, one by Thurstone (1946) and the other by Burt (1947). Thurstone used on one hundred male adults, ten measurements which had been made by Hammond. The measurements included: 2 of height, standing and sitting; 3 of the hand span, length and breadth; 4 of the trunk, shoulder, chest, and hip breadth, and chest depth; and 3 of the head, breadth, length, and height. He found

ILLUS. 154. SHELDON'S REGIONS FOR MORPHOLOGICAL
MEASUREMENT

Region	Sample
I. Head, Face, and Neck	361
II. Thoracic Trunk	252
III. Arms, Shoulder, and Hands	451
IV. Abdominal Trunk	362
V. Legs and Feet	352
Medians by column	352

(By permission of W. H. Sheldon and Harper & Bros.)

four primary factors which were concerned with bone length, head size, girth, and hand size.

Burt, who began studies of this kind 40 years ago, summarized a number of studies in 1947, all of which yielded, according to Burt's "simple summation" method, a general factor of size, which can be expressed as a size quotient analogous to an IQ. This size quotient has high predictive value, and correlations between siblings of about .50 were reported among London school children. Among English, Irish, Welsh, American, and Jewish adult males, factor patterns were found which were similar to those in a sample of 528 Royal Air Force men. Using seventeen physical measurements, a general size factor appears which is about as large as all the other factors together. When this is removed two broad group factors emerge; one associated with weight, and with neck, waist, and thigh girth; the other with height and leg length. Then two pairs of narrower group factors emerge as subdivisions of each broad group factor. These are most closely related to trunk girth, limb girth, sitting height, and thigh length.

These factorial studies support Sheldon's analysis of types as far as they go, but they do not include many of the variables that Sheldon used, and the statistical treatment does not yield composite or pattern scores of any kind. It seems probable that more research in this field will show fairly stable physiological patterns related to various temperament patterns (Illus. 215).

CLINICAL SYNDROMES

Another approach to the study of behavior is that of psychiatrists who follow Kraepelin (1895) in his description of clinical syndromes. *Syndrome* means literally "a running together," and in this instance it refers to a combination of symptoms or patterns of behavior. Syndromes are not easy to describe or to agree upon. Since the same patterns of behavior may appear in several syndromes, they are not

ILLUS. 155. SHELDON'S GYNANDROMORPHY SAMPLES

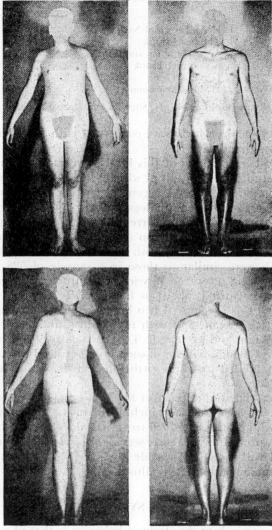

(From Sheldon, 1940. By permission of W. H. Sheldon and Harper & Bros.)

Two individuals of different somatotype showing different degrees of gynandromorphy. The individual on the left is of a somatotype, 523–524, normally high in gynandromorphy. The individual on the right is of a somatotype, 262–172, normally low in gynandromorphy.

ILLUS. 155. SHELDON'S GYNANDROMORPHY SAMPLES *(Cont'd)*

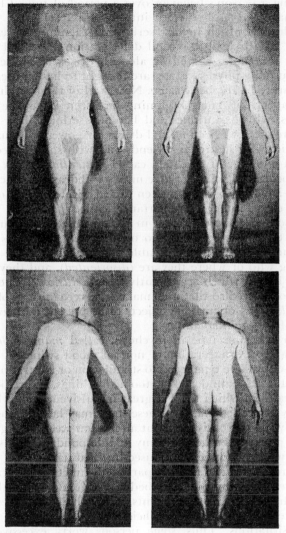

(From Sheldon, 1940. By permission of W. H. Sheldon and Harper & Bros.)

Two individuals of the same somatotype, 442, showing different degrees of gynandromorphy. These physiques are of the same somatotype in all regions of the body except the second (thoracic trunk). The individual on the left is higher and the one on the right is lower in gynandromorphy, than is the average 442.

clearly independent of one another. Syndromes can be identified only by studying a person's behavior over a period of time. Clinical syndromes may be roughly divided into two groups:

1. Syndromes which involve serious disorientation over long periods and usually lead to mental deterioration are called *psychoses*. They are sometimes caused by alcohol, drugs, and disease or injury, but usually physical causes are thought to hasten the psychosis, rather than to be the basic cause. Nearly all of these syndromes lead to hospitalization. Their beginnings are seen in failure to adjust to persons, which continues and becomes serious. Basic needs for security are met by rejection, and drives for power or sexual satisfaction conflict with desires for friends and with socially accepted behavior. In one type of psychosis, called *dementia praecox* or *schizophrenia*, people with fairly active minds withdraw from actual situations into a world of fantasy, often tinged with thoughts of persecution and exaggerated self-importance, called *paranoia*. The more these persons become engrossed in their own thoughts and wishes, the more they become unable to observe clearly what is going on around them. They become unable to give an accurate statement concerning who or where they are (*disoriented*), and they accept as true their beliefs which are patently false (*delusions*). Their perception is also affected so that they make false recognitions of common objects (*illusions*) or imagine objects to be present and accept these visions as facts (*hallucinations*).

Another common type of psychosis, called *manic-depressive insanity*, is a gross exaggeration of normal mood swings. A person of the manic-depressive type reacts to stimulation or frustration by great excitement, elation, undertaking too many things, and rapid activity. Extreme cases in which there is great impulsiveness and, later, lack of memory are called *manias*. These states may last months or years, but usually the person is worn out after a few weeks and goes into a *depressed* phase when he is gloomy and despondent, and sometimes in a *coma* when he cannot be aroused by the usual means.

2. Syndromes which involve partial disfunction are called *psychoneuroses*. These may be described as exaggerated bad habits. They are thought of as poor adjustments, which, however, often prevent further breakdown by giving sufficient protection to the person in ordinary situations. Thus, some persons worry excessively about bodily functions (*hypochondriasis*), but the worry in itself gives some satisfaction and may prevent more serious maladjustment. In others, feelings of guilt and fear of the future are converted into involuntary physical symptoms—paralysis, anesthesia, or cardiac or digestive difficulties (*conversion hysterias*). Hysterical symptoms often last for

years, since they usually gain sympathy and protection for the individual. They may be rapidly cured by strong emotional convictions, such as faith healing, but the cures are not likely to be permanent unless the sick person achieves sufficient security and insight.

Other persons develop unreasonable fears (*phobias*) about particular situations or objects as a result of shocking and embarrassing situations. While a phobia may be burdensome, it may have protective value in preventing the person from getting into the same or a similar situation. Other persons perform acts without knowing why or having good reason, called *obsessive* or *compulsive* acts (*psychasthenias*). In some persons discouragement and lack of self-confidence reach a stage of severe depression and suicidal tendencies, or, their conflicts may lead to a conscious disregard of social responsibilities, and to lying, stealing, alcoholism, and immorality. These actions characterize the *psychopathic personality*.

Each of the above types may be independent of the others, but sometimes they are combined, probably reflecting social pressures and weaknesses in several areas. All are basically types of disorganization resulting from conflicts and feelings of frustration.

Many competent psychiatrists have pointed out that while these rough classifications of syndromes are convenient, they are not easy to use accurately. They are either too vague or too elaborate to be used in understanding basic causes.

PSYCHOANALYTIC THEORY

The psychoanalytic theory of personality structure as described by Freud (1938), Healy, Bronner, and Bowers (1930), and Fenichel (1945), postulates three structural parts which are not clearly separated, but nevertheless have distinct functions (Illus. 3). None of these parts has a specific location in the body, and all depend upon brain processes which are, of course, related to sensory and motor processes. The largest part, called the *id*, is the reservoir of instinctive impulses, some of which appear at birth and some later. The id also contains memories of experiences or wishes which have been forced out of consciousness (*repressed*). The structure or content of the id can never be known directly, but is inferred from various irrational acts and from dreams. The id continually drives a person by impulses for personal pleasure called *libido*, which include sex and protection, and by impulses for death called *mortido*.

In a newborn infant the id is the only component of personality. It consists of inherited needs or drives and of instincts which unfold at later periods. The id is the source of nearly all the internal drives a person has throughout life. As perception, memory, and reasoning develop, a second component, the *ego*, or the conscious self, takes shape. The ego includes ideas and ideals of one's own physical and mental abilities, as well as attitudes and knowledge of the environment. The ego receives impulses from the attitudes of the id, and at the same time is aware of pressure from the environment. The ego is a coordinator. In maturity the various id drives are usually merged and channeled by the ego into socially acceptable activities, but in early life and also in various stress situations the ego may be ineffective with disastrous results.

At an early age a third component of personality gradually develops called the *superego*. It is defined as a strong unreasonable set of prohibitions learned in childhood, the prohibitions of parents and society. Some of these prohibitions are later seen as reasonable and become part of the ego along with the constructive ideals for society which one accepts. This part of the ego corresponds roughly to conscience.

Serious personality deviations occur when any one of the three components—the id, ego, and superego—becomes too dominant. Thus, when the superego, representing oppressive restrictions of society, real or imagined, is too strong, the person feels anxious, guilty, and fearful. When the ego becomes too dominant, the person may withdraw from society and also retreat from his own id impulses, or he may try to be a dictator. When the id is too dominating, the person is too impulsively aggressive, lustful, gluttonous, and uninhibited.

These definitions of id, ego, and superego give meaning to what are called *psychoanalytic mechanisms.* These are unconscious patterns of behavior which resolve conflicts between the id, ego, and superego. Thus the *repression* mechanism is the unconscious process of resolving a conflict between the superego and the ego by driving the conscious wish or need into the id. Repression serves to protect the conscious ego from unbearable pain, but it also leads to all kinds of serious maladjustments, for the repressed wishes, like prisoners, try to escape from the id.

Projection is the process whereby a person attributes to other people or to objects his own unconscious (id) drives. These drives which have been repressed are projected into the environment and are regarded consciously as belonging to the external world. (This concept of projection is similar to but not the same as the more general word "projective" as used to describe tests in Chapters XVII, XVIII, XIX, and XXIII, where projective is used to describe any behavior in which a person reveals that he believes that others have the attributes, skills, and motives which really belong to himself.)

The list of psychoanalytical mechanisms is long and complex. One should consult a special text (Freud, 1938), if interested in further definitions.

Among psychiatrists and clinical psychologists, one of the most widely accepted theories of personality development is Freud's psychosexual theory. Freud uses the words *love* and *sex* to cover a wide variety of activities of various parts of the body. Almost all types of pleasure or satisfaction are considered to give sexual or erotic satisfaction, because they seem to be closely associated, at least in early childhood. A brief outline of the usual stages or levels of development follows.

a. At birth and for a few months thereafter the infant is in the *oral erotic* stage when its chief satisfactions come from the mouth region. The mother's body is the first object to be recognized and a strong attachment for her develops. Fixation at this stage or later regression is indicated by intense satisfaction from oral stimulation.

b. The first stage normally develops into a second, called *oral sadism*. Here the infant gradually recognizes various objects and seeks to incorporate them into his own body or to destroy them. This stage is usually related to weaning or loss of the breast, and the activity is at first directed toward the mother. Fixation at this level is thought to be related to manic-depressive disorders in later life.

c. During the second and third years of life the pleasure and satisfactions involved in defecation become more prominent and normally supplant oral satisfactions to a large extent. This stage is called *anal eroticism*. It is usually accompanied by or followed by stages in which a child may seek to control his parents or environment, called *anal sadism* or *anal expulsiveness*. The child may smear himself and others or their property with feces. Or, he may develop *anal masochism* where he punishes himself by retaining feces, the expulsion of which would normally be a pleasure. Fixation at the oral masochism stage is probably related to miserliness, constipation, and obsessive compulsions.

d. In the third to seventh years the *early genital* or *phallic* phase becomes prominent. Manipulation of the external genitalia becomes a marked source of pleasure. Boys and girls realize the differences in the structure of their external organs and react by an inherited instinct, called the Oedipus complex. Boys retain the attachment to the mother while developing feelings of rivalry toward the father and consequently fear of castration by the father. Girls develop a strong attachment to the father, presumably from the disappointment of a lack of penis for which the mother is blamed. Girls have therefore a more difficult transition than boys, in that they must turn away from their mothers; on the other hand they do not suffer fears of castration.

e. From the seventh to the twelfth years there is usually a period in psychosexual development when one's chief love object is oneself. This love of self is called *narcissism.* A strong fixation at this stage is related to masturbation, wishful dreaming, withdrawal from reality, and schizophrenia. The narcissistic stage is often followed by *homosexuality,* which means that the love object is another person of the same sex. This is particularly common in groups made up of the same sex. During this period social and ethical attitudes toward sex are generally learned, as well as the nature of birth and something of the sexual act. Also, there is a rapid development of prohibitions, or taboos, as well as of constructive ideals for self and society.

f. In puberty, the Oedipus complex may have a resurgence, but normally social taboos of incest and a variety of social contacts lead to sexual adjustments with a partner of the opposite sex, called *heterosexuality.* Failure in this adjustment at this stage results in regression toward a narcissistic love-object.

The adolescent usually identifies self with the more successful rival. In this *identification* the frustrated individual *introjects,* or sets up within himself or herself the prohibitions of the parents, usually a mixture of both, but gives more heed to the rival parent. In addition to these negative or punishing prohibitions there is normally developed a positive set of ideals made up of the parents' good wishes and socially acceptable aspirations.

The normal sequence of psychosexual development may be disturbed at any level, and the person may *regress* to an earlier stage or *fixate,* that is, remain where he is by failing to progress to the next stage. The most frequent causes of such disturbances are thought to be deprivations or overindulgences by the parents, who thus tend to induce fears, anxieties, and repressions in their children. Another serious source of maladjustment may be sibling rivalry, which is due to feelings of rejection. The child may show hostility toward parents or the sibling, or he may react with feelings of anxiety and withdrawal. A third source of maladjustment may be physical illness or glandular imbalance, which make one mentally dependent and physically unable to cope with the demands of normal situations.

One of the recurrent criticisms of Freud's theory of personality takes exception to his insistence upon the influences of specific instinctive patterns and of very early experiences. Harold Orlansky (1948) reviewed 149 articles in an attempt to discover relationships between adult character and very early experiences. He discusses at some length the effects of bottle feeding versus breast feeding, the length of breast feeding, feeding on self-demand versus scheduled feeding, the duration of the weaning process, and thumb sucking. He concludes that there is no single factor or group of factors which are closely related to various sorts of personality factors in later life. More specifically, he finds that oral deprivation may or may not be related to other factors. Thus many reports are found of thumb sucking among children who had unlimited nursing on self-demand. Mothering, cuddling for warm protection, and sphincter training are likewise found to have little established relationship to later personality structure. The theory that too early bowel training leads in extreme cases to limiting all pleasant acts, becoming parsimonious, stingy, meticulous, punctual, self-restraining, and sadistic finds little evidence in many of the careful studies. Evidence is found that the attitude of parents and the cultural pressures applied in early childhood, pre-childhood, and adolescence, or even in adulthood are more important in character formation than very early experiences.

On the question of frustration at an early age, Dollard's (1939) definition of frustration is put forward, namely, that frustration occurs when a goal response suffers interruption or an insightful goal response is interfered with. According to this theory frustration does not follow from restraint but occurs only when some fairly well-established goal activity is interrupted. Furthermore, frustration is often tolerated by persons for a long period of time and may not lead to aggression or to serious dissatisfaction if other forms of satisfaction are available. Without adequate controls conflicting theories blossom. For instance, the cradle-board restrictions of Southwest Indians are said to have induced passivity, aggressiveness, sadism and cruelty, and stoicism and toleration.

Orlansky believes that rigid character structuring is impossible during the first few years of life because of the nature of an infant's organization and the rapid forgetting of experiences. He points out that characteristics are radically changed at various ages and that the continuity of personal behavior may be due largely to the continuity of an environment rather than to early conditioning. Specific patterns of restraint do not have specific psychological impact on the child. Any discipline's effect is related to many other forces—parental attitude, organic constitution, later social conditions, etc. He thinks that adult personality is not the result of an instinctive complex of drives mechanically channeled by early discipline, but that it is the continually changing product of many experiences. Orlansky, therefore, believes that the Freudians have greatly exaggerated the early effects of childhood experiences on the development of personality. He points out that one of the principal difficulties in understanding reports is due to the failure of most workers to define personality in terms which can be clearly understood.

OTHER PSYCHOLOGICAL THEORIES

There seem to be three other important psychological approaches which contribute to personality theory: the *factorial* approach is a logical and mathematical attempt to describe the parts or factors of a person, and the way they work together; the *configuration* or *topology* gestalt approach contends that a person is a complex configuration of forces operating with reference to an environment which is also a complex configuration; a third approach, called the personalistic approach, emphasizes the fact that gestalts, perceptions, factors, and skills are not things or entities, but only the ways a person acts. A complete description of these theories lies beyond the limits of this book. The factorial approach has given rise to a great deal of measurement activity which is described in considerable detail in Chapters XIV and XXII. The other two approaches are illustrated in the observational and projective techniques described in Chapters XVII, XVIII, XIX, XXIII, and XXIV.

USES OF MEASURES OF DYNAMIC PATTERNS

Measures of dynamic patterns may be used with normal groups, with clinical groups, or to test hypotheses with regard to personality growth and structure.

Normal Groups

The large majority of studies of dynamic patterns are probably made within what may be called normal groups. There studies are carried out by educators who wish to know the extent to which goals of personality development have been achieved—goals such as interest in social improvements, reasonable vocational choice, attitude toward various kinds of community institutions and minority groups, and the like. Emphasis upon the development of good personality and judgment through school programs has enormously increased due in part to the availability of these measures in elementary, high school, and college.

A similar development has taken place in industry where human motives are recognized more and more as vital to production. A high degree of willing and intelligent cooperation has been demonstrated to be one of the most effective ways of solving production problems and problems involving social attitudes. The measurement of dynamic traits is used both for the evaluation of employees of management and for its policies. Important studies are now being carried out, in which the success of authoritarian versus democratic procedures in industry is being compared. Military establishments in this country and abroad have made millions of ratings of attitudes and personality traits of soldiers and officers, and are now in the process of evaluating the reliability and usefulness of these ratings.

Another highly important use of measures of dynamic forces is in sociological studies of attitudes toward minority groups, toward community and religious groups and policies, and toward policies of various governing groups.

Lastly, there is a beginning of many important anthropological studies among normal groups. Racial differences have been of considerable concern to those who look forward to world peace. The temperament of the Japanese and of some Southern Pacific groups have been studied as well as the temperaments of many groups in the United States and Europe. Anthropological studies may prove to be an extremely important factor in successfully planning cooperative self-government on an international basis.

Clinical Groups

The use in clinical practice of standardized appraisals of ability or adjustment is still questioned. One group, which includes many psychiatrists and those who use nondirective therapy, believes that an early and elaborate testing procedure may hinder rather than help, because it may make the patient feel that the tests and the counselor will solve his problems or bring about a favorable change in his situation, whereas in reality the most important changes will only come from developing his own insight and motivation. Rogers (1946, p. 144) writes:

In conclusion it may be said that the counselor who has come to use the client's motivation for growth as the mainspring of the counseling process is not opposed to tests, but has found them unsatisfactory for promoting client growth. For one thing, counselor-administered tests interfere with the process of catharsis, insight, and positive choice which has been shown to be characteristic of growth as it takes place in therapy. It also seems to the client-centered counselor that the measurement of abilities and personality traits as though they were static loses much of its significance in the light of counseling experience. The changing and dynamic use the individual makes of his abilities, the self-initiated changes in personality characteristics which occur as a result of counseling, seem much more important than the measurement of these fluid entities in terms which give them a spurious permanence. Only when (1) the need to take tests is a significant aspect of the client's symptomatic behavior, or (2) it is impossible for the client to be responsible for a choice, or (3) research purposes require a measurement of an admittedly changing characteristic, do psychometric tests seem to have a purpose with which the nondirective counselor can agree.

A large majority of clinical workers, while subscribing to Rogers' ideals, feel that a battery of standard tests of ability, interest, and mode of adjustment is useful at an early stage in therapy, both to the client and to the therapist.

STUDY GUIDE QUESTIONS

1. What aspects of a person complicate the study of personality?
2. What is meant by continuum of activity?
3. How can patterns of behavior be accurately identified?
4. What are the distinguishing characteristics of Sheldon's extreme body types?
5. What is meant by dysplasia?
6. What was Spearman's analogy to a person?
7. What are the main Kraepelinian syndromes?
8. Describe the id, ego, and superego.
9. Describe the usual stages of sexual development according to psychoanalytic theory.
10. What aspects of personality does Orlansky stress?
11. What temperamental patterns does Sheldon outline?
12. What principal factors in personality were found by Cattell's factorial studies?
13. Of what importance are measures of dynamic patterns in education and industry today?

CHAPTER XVI

TYPES OF ESTIMATES

This chapter describes certain ways to make estimates of oneself or others. It also gives rules for the preparation of rating scales and for the raters to follow. Lastly, methods for determining the validity of ratings are discussed.

CLASSIFICATION OF ESTIMATES

Because they do not lend themselves to direct measurement such intangible traits as artistic and vocational preferences, attitudes toward war, racial groups, or institutions, and the relative effectiveness of workers in various situations, are estimated. Four types of recorded estimates are common:

a. Inventories or questionnaires usually contain multiple-choice items which are scored and tabulated in much the same way that objective-type tests are.

b. In *paired-comparisons* each person is compared with each of the others for some attribute.

c. In *rank-order* estimates each person is placed in the order of the amount of an attribute he possesses.

d. Rating scales employ adjectives, letters, or numbers to indicate on a scale the degrees or amounts of an attribute possessed.

These types of estimates are sometimes combined in various ways.

Inventories

When an *inventory* contains a series of items in the form of questions in answer to which one is asked to express a preference, attitude, or judgment of how accurately the items fit particular persons or situa-

ILLUS. 156. SAMPLES FROM THE BELL ADJUSTMENT INVENTORIES

THE ADJUSTMENT INVENTORY
STUDENT FORM
(For students of high school and college age)
By HUGH M. BELL

Yes	No	?	Are you subject to hay fever or asthma?
Yes	No	?	Do you often have much difficulty in thinking of an appropriate remark to make in group conversation?
Yes	No	?	Have you been embarrassed because of the type of work your father does in order to support the family?
Yes	No	?	Have you ever had scarlet fever or diphtheria?
Yes	No	?	Did you ever take the lead to enliven a dull party?
Yes	No	?	Does your mother tend to dominate your home?
Yes	No	?	Have you ever felt that someone was hypnotizing you and making you act against your will?
Yes	No	?	Has either of your parents frequently criticized you unjustly?
Yes	No	?	Do you feel embarrassed when you have to enter a public assembly after everyone else has been seated?
Yes	No	?	Do you often feel lonesome, even when you are with people?

(Reprinted from *Adjustment Inventory* by Hugh M. Bell with the permission of the author and of the publishers, Stanford University Press.)

tions, it is called a *questionnaire*. Since a large number of items can be used, many inventories show reliability correlations of from .80 to .90. Because inventories can be easily applied to groups, they are widely used, and more careful research has been done on them than on any other type of rating. Their one serious disadvantage is that they can be, and probably often are, answered untruthfully, sometimes unintentionally so. A great deal of work is now being done to set up means of detecting falsification on an inventory.

Self-rating inventories, which are to be marked or checked in some simple fashion, are more common than other forms. For example, the Bell Adjustment Inventory (1938) asks that *yes, no,* or *?* be indicated on one hundred sixty items (Illus. 156), and the Mooney Check List (1942) simply asks that the items that apply to oneself be underlined. Another inventory used in industry is Hoppock's Job Satisfaction Blank (1935) (Illus. 157).

Most inventories are scored by simply adding the answers that are thought to be or have been shown to be related to some trait or criterion.

The recent growth in the number of the size of inventories has been enormous. Those intended to appraise vocational interests are discussed in Chapter XX. Questionnaires on attitudes and opinions are illustrated in Chapter XXI, on emotional and social adjustment in Chapter XXII.

Paired-Comparisons Method

A scale which has equal-appearing intervals may be constructed by comparing pairs of items directly, and then arranging them in such a way that the proportion of judges placing one above the next will

ILLUS. 157. JOB SATISFACTION BLANK

You are asked to help in a scientific study by answering the questions in this blank. Neither your employer nor any of your associates will be allowed to see your answers. Your replies will be added to those of many other people, and only the group totals will be published. Do not put your name on the paper. Your answers will be worthless unless they are perfectly frank and truthful. If for any reason you prefer not to tell exactly how you feel about your job, please return the blank unmarked.

Choose the ONE of the following statements which best tells how well you like your job, place a check mark (√) in front of that statement:

1. ....I hate it.
2. ....I dislike it.
3. ....I don't like it.
4. ....I am indifferent to it.
5. ....I like it.
6. ....I am enthusiastic about it.
7. ....I love it.

Check one of the following to show HOW MUCH OF THE TIME you feel satisfied with your job:

8. ....All of the time.
9. ....Most of the time.
10. ....A good deal of the time.
11. ....About half of the time.
12. ....Occasionally.
13. ....Seldom.
14. ....Never.

Check the ONE of the following which best tells how you feel about changing your job:

15. ....I would quit this job at once if I could get anything else to do.
16. ....I would take almost any other job in which I could earn as much as I am earning now.
17. ....I would like to change both my job and my occupation.
18. ....I would like to exchange my present job for another job in the same line of work.
19. ....I am not eager to change my job, but I would do so if I could get a better job.
20. ....I cannot think of any job for which I would exchange mine.
21. ....I would not exchange my job for any other.

If you could have your choice of all the other jobs in the world, which would you choose? (Check one):

22. ....Your present job.
23. ....Another job in the same occupation.
24. ....A job in another occupation.

Check one of the following to show how you think you compare with other people:

25. ....No one likes his job better than I like mine.
26. ....I like my job much better than most people like theirs.
27. ....I like my job better than most people like theirs.
28. ....I like my job about as well as most people like theirs.
29. ....I like my job more than most people dislike theirs.
30. ....I dislike my job much more than most people dislike theirs.
31. ....No one dislikes his job more than I dislike mine.

Which gives you more satisfaction? (Check one):

32. ....Your job.
33. ....The things you do in your spare time.
34. ....Have you ever thought seriously of changing your present job?
35. ....Have you ever declined an opportunity to change your present job?
36. ....Are you feeling today a true sample of the way you usually feel about your job?

The following questions need not be answered if they would enable anyone to know that this paper is yours:

37. What is your job? (For example, Carpenter) ....
38. Age at last birthday ....
39. Sex ....
40. Date ....
41. On the line below, place five check marks to show how well satisfied you were with your last five jobs. Use a separate check mark for each job. You may place each mark anywhere on the line, either above one of the statements or between two of them. If you have had less than five jobs, use only as many check marks as you have had jobs. Draw a circle around the check mark which indicates your present job.

| Completely dissatisfied | More dissatisfied than satisfied | About half and half | More satisfied than dissatisfied | Completely satisfied |

Report Blank Used in Survey of Job Satisfaction, New Hope, Pa., 1933.

(Hoppock, 1935, p. 243. By permission of Harper and Bros.)

be the same. By this method each item is judged to be better or worse than each of the others, by some order of comparison which will not suggest the answer. If ten items are to be compared, one must make $\dfrac{n(n-1)}{2} = \dfrac{10 \times 9}{2} = 45$ judgments. These forty-five comparisons must be made by a number of persons, or by the same person a number of times. The more judges, the better will be the results, provided all the judges are equally competent, because chance errors tend to become less important as the number of judgments increases.

Fechner (1871) suggested a method for changing percentages to standard deviations of a normal curve. Witmer (1894) and Cohn (1894) used this same method to investigate aesthetic responses to form and to color. Titchener (1902) used it in studies of pitch and rhythm and discrimination. A thorough mathematical treatment for the scaling of paired comparisons was given by Thurstone (1927), who took into consideration the various assumptions which must be made in calculating scale values. These assumptions and calculations cannot be described in this book, but the simplest case assumes that (*a*) the distribution of responses by a large number of judges to any one stimulus will be in the form of a normal curve, (*b*) the judgments of differences between two stimuli will also fall into a normal distribution, and (*c*) errors made in responding to one stimulus are not correlated to errors made in judging the second stimulus.

When these assumptions can be made, and when judgments have been tabulated, the data can be arranged as shown in Illus. 158. Here the results of comparing six photographs for excellence in composition are shown by the percentages of judges who thought that one photograph was better than each of the others. It is shown that 70 per cent of the judges believed that A was superior to B, etc. The scale values for each item can be found by changing the per cents into standard scores, from Illus. 129, and then combining them. One should consult Thurstone (1928) or Guilford (1936) for examples of this technique.

ILLUS. 158. THE PAIRED-COMPARISONS METHOD

Item	Per cents preferring each item					
	A	B	C	D	E	F
A		.30	.24	.15	.10	.01
B	.70		.37	.22	.10	.15
C	.76	.63		.33	.05	.08
D	.85	.78	.67		.42	.33
E	.90	.90	.95	.58		.39
F	.99	.85	.92	.67	.61	

NOTE: 70 per cent of judgments preferred A over B; 76 per cent A over C; etc.

Illustration 158 also shows a marked tendency for the judges to be fairly consistent, but there are several discrepancies. For instance, Item F was judged superior to E when both were compared to B, but Item E was judged to be superior to F by 61 per cent of the judges. Such discrepancies are indications that the scale does not have high internal consistency. The judges probably selected different aspects of a photograph for comparisons on different occasions.

Although the paired-comparisons method is usually considered a precise way of securing judgments, it is seldom used because simpler methods seem to be adequate.

Rank-Order Method

When the number of items to be scaled is more than ten and the number of judges is large, the paired-comparisons method becomes laborious. The rank-order method overcomes this difficulty without much loss of effectiveness. It is far easier to rank thirty items than to make comparisons of 3,045 pairs. The rank-order method was used by Cattell (1903) in studying American scientists, and Wells (1908) in evaluating ten traits of leading American writers. Hollingworth (1911) and Strong (1911) applied it in studies of advertising appeal and memory value.

ILLUS. 159. RANKS ASSIGNED TO SAMPLES

Item No.	A	B	C	D	E	F	G	Md.	Centiles *
1	2	1	3	1	2	1	1	1	16
2	3	2	5	3	1	3	3	3	50
3	4	4	4	4	4	4	4	4	66
4	1	3	2	2	3	2	2	2	33
5	5	6	1	5	5	6	5	5	83
6	6	5	6	6	6	5	6	6	100

* There is an error introduced here because of the small number of items used. The centiles are all too high because they represent the upper limit of the ranks of the items. No simple way of correcting this error is available, but when 30 or more items are used the error is very small.

In computing scale values by this method, it is necessary to have the items ranked by a number of judges or by one judge a number of times. The median rank for each item is found rather than the mean, since the median is not influenced as much as the mean by extreme scores which sometimes are the result of errors. A median rank for any item is found by arranging all of its ranks in order of size, and then selecting the middle one. For instance in Illus. 159 the first item has the following ranks 1, 1, 1, 1, 2, 2, 3, and hence a median rank of 1.

There are several procedures for changing median ranks into scale values. One of these, proposed by Hull (1928), assumes that the items to be ranked have a normal frequency distribution. This assumption is probably true enough when the items are a large number of biological phenomena selected at random. If one had one hundred items to rank, each rank would be a centile, since it shows the per cent of items that fall below a particular item. When any number of items are used, the centiles of the items can be changed from those in Illus. 129 into standard scores. The lowest item may be taken as the arbitrary zero point and the other items assigned scale values from zero according to standard differences.

Two other important methods for scaling ranked items do not assume that the items are normally distributed, but that they may have any form of distribution. In one of these Guilford (1936) calculated the per cent of judgments which place an item above a *composite standard*. These per cents were changed to standard deviations or standard scores as before. In the other Thurstone (1931) calculated the proportion of judgments which place each item above or below every other item. This method converts the ranks into paired comparisons and follows the procedure for that method.

A variation of the rank-order method, called the method of equal-appearing intervals, is useful when a large number of items is to be ranked. Instead of ranking all in order, the items are placed in piles which appear to be equally spaced. Illustration 160 illustrates the

ILLUS. 160. SCALING BY THE METHOD OF EQUAL-APPEARING INTERVALS

Item	Piles					No. of Judges	Median Values	Q
	1	2	3	4	5			
A	18	4	2	—	—	24	1.16	.33
D	4	10	8	2	—	24	2.30	.52
G	2	5	9	6	2	24	3.40	.72
N			6	10	8	24	4.18	.62
T				4	20	24	4.90	.27

NOTE: Item A was placed in the first pile by 18 judges, in the second pile by 4 judges, and in the third pile by 2 judges, etc.

procedure used where there were five items arranged in five piles by twenty-four judges. More items were used but only 5 are shown since they are enough to illustrate the method. The median value of each item is preferred to the mean, for the items on the end piles will not be normally distributed. The Q of each item shows the range of the middle 50 per cent of judgments. In Illus. 160 the ranges are greater for items which appear in the middle piles most frequently. This situation is commonly found, and it is due in part to the fact that the scale does not extend far enough to give normal distribution to the highest and lowest items. The Q of some items is thus reduced by their extreme position. The Q is also an indication of the inability of judges to agree upon the relative position of an item. There may be disagreement owing to random errors in discrimination or to different standards of excellence. For example, a large Q may be an indication of chance errors or of a lack of internal consistency in the scale. In either case the items with the smaller Q's are preferred for scale construction.

Sanford (1908) described the method of equal-appearing intervals in scaling weights of envelopes. Thorndike (1910) had forty judges sort one thousand samples of penmanship into eleven piles. Hollingworth (1911) had thirty-nine jokes classified in ten degrees of humor. Hillegas (1912) had judges classify English compositions into classes. Thurstone (1928) applied this method to establish attitude scales toward a number of political or social issues such as the established church (Illus. 15). Approximately three hundred statements which voiced approval, indifference, or disapproval of the issue were sorted into nine piles. The median value and the Q were found for each item and from these an absolute-scale score was derived.

Finally, forty-five statements were chosen to represent nearly equal steps of attitude ranging from very favorable to very unfavorable. Statements with the smallest Q's were preferred, and two checks of validity, not described here, were applied. The care used by Thurstone and his students in the construction of approximately thirty different scales has made them among the most highly valued.

Remmers and his students (1934) showed that individuals made nearly the same scores when a group of items were presented either in a haphazard order or in the order of their scale values. The latter allowed a much more rapid scoring than the former. They also pointed out that a great economy in attitude-scale construction could be effected if a general scale of opinion toward a class of social phenomena were devised. They forthwith published six generalized scales of attitudes toward

1. An institution, such as war or Sunday observance
2. A race, such as the Chinese or the Negro
3. A homemaking activity, such as child care or preparation of a meal
4. A moral or social practice, such as petting or drinking
5. An occupation
6. A school subject

These generalized scales were composed by following the procedure devised by Thurstone. The correlation between the generalized Form

A (Illus. 161) and Thurstone's Scale of Attitude toward Communism was .816, and between the generalized Form A and A Scale of Sunday Observance, .83. Correlations between the generalized Form B and Thurstone's Scale of Attitudes toward the Negro was .669 and attitudes toward the Chinese, .72. These figures doubtless indicate similar attitudes in both scales, although the generalized forms usually contain a few items that are not well adapted to some of the situations in which they may be used.

ILLUS. 161. ATTITUDE TOWARD AN INSTITUTION

Scale Value	Q Value	Item No.	Item
11.1	0.8	2	It is the most admirable of institutions.
10.2	1.6	9	It is a strong influence for right living.
9.1	2.5	17	It is necessary to society as organized.
8.2	2.0	20	It does more good than harm.
7.4	3.2	21	It will not harm anybody.
6.1	2.6	23	It is necessary only until a better can be found.
4.9	1.9	26	It does not consider individual differences.
4.4	2.1	29	It represents outgrown beliefs.
3.3	1.7	32	It is too selfish to benefit society.
2.8	1.9	36	It is hopelessly out of date.
1.9	1.3	42	It will destroy civilization if it is not radically changed.
1.7	1.0	44	It benefits no one.

(Remmers et al., 1934, Samples from Form A, p. 19. By permission of the Editor, Journal of Social Psychology.)

The generalized forms have also been criticized by Stagner and Drought (1935) because they found that scale values changed considerably when the same form was used for different items.

Another method of scaling which avoids the neutral items of the scales just described, and yields a reliable score with a minimum of labor is that described by Likert (1932). He presented a group of persons with a large number of items designed to measure attitude toward a particular institution, such as attitude toward labor unions. For this purpose five categories were generally used: strongly agree, agree, undecided, disagree, and strongly disagree. Weights were assigned in accordance with the assumption of normality of the things being rated and the proportion of the total group of making each choice. For most items he found that small errors were introduced by using the weights 1, 2, 3, 4, and 5. Scores for each subject were obtained by adding the weights of his item responses. In order to select the most discriminating items, the group was divided into those with high scores and those with low scores, and the percentages of each subgroup marking each response to each item were computed. The most discriminating items were then selected for inclusion in his scale.

Rating-Scale Methods

Rating methods use scales which have been established by one of the methods just described, or use arbitrary scales.

The rater is asked to indicate on the scale the position of each person or item to be rated. This procedure is less time consuming than ranking items and is more interesting to many judges than the other procedures. It is widely used for evaluating beliefs, preferences, personal traits, and industrial efficiency.

1. *Forms of Rating Scales.* The final form in which a rating scale is cast is important because it determines to some extent the accuracy and the speed with which a rating can be made. Four common forms will be described.

a. *Classified form.* In this form the rater is asked to indicate his judgment by marking the name of a class. A common classification is: excellent, good, fair, and poor, and initials or numbers may be used to designate these headings. (See Illus. 162.)

ILLUS. 162. RATING SCALE FOR ITEMS CONCERNING THE VALUE OF MUSIC

As a first step in making this scale we want a number of persons to rate these statements by assigning them to nine different classes. We will call these classes *A, B, C, D, E, F, G, H,* and *I.* If you find a statement which you believe expresses the highest appreciation of the value of music, underline the letter *A.* For a statement which seems neutral or non-committal, underline *E* (the middle letter) while for those statements which express the strongest depreciation of music, underline *I.* Other degrees of appreciation or depreciation may be indicated by underlining one of the intermediate letters.

A B C D E F G H I 23. Music stimulates and encourages me in my life work.

A B C D E F G H I 24. To me music is of no greater or lesser importance than any other of the arts and sciences.

(From Seashore and Hevner, 1933, p. 369. By permission of the Editor, *Journal of Social Psychology.*)

Another classification uses statistical terms—above average, average, and below average. Sometimes a rater is asked to classify persons in fourths or fifths or thirds of a group.

In rating one's preferences the words like, indifferent, and dislike are often used. Sometimes one simply classifies the item using one of two choices—present or absent, yes or no, like or dislike, agree or disagree.

Classifications are often combined with other rating methods. For purposes of summary and comparison, classified ratings are usually given numerical scores.

b. Descriptive form. In this form each step in the scale is designated by a word or phrase which describes, sometimes elaborately, particular behavior patterns. (See Illus. 163.)

c. Graphic form. In this form a straight line is provided, often with numbered spaces, as in Illus. 163, and the rating is made by placing a mark on the line to designate one's judgment. The graphic form is rarely used by itself, but is usually combined with a classified or descriptive form.

ILLUS. 163. DISTRIBUTION OF RATINGS OF NURSES: UNIVERSITY OF MICHIGAN SCHOOL OF NURSING

Rating of Performance in Service

Directions: ITEM # 5 *M.D. Q*

Adjustment to situations:	Sometimes at a loss in familiar situations	Slow to adapt to new situations	Learns new arrangements fairly soon	Quick to adjust to new routine	Very quick to respond to emergencies		
			TOTAL				
1st Rater:	10	20	15	3	2	2.27	.67
2nd Rater:		9	32	9		3.01	.37

NOTE: When the medians and quartile ranges were calculated, each space was allotted one point on a scale from 1 to 5. The lowest value was assigned to the space at the left, and the highest to that at the right. When the values were interpolated, the whole points were assumed to be located in the middle of the space.

d. Man-to-Man form. This form (Illus. 164) was designed to make comparisons more definite by placing in blanks on a key sheet the names of men known to the rater to represent standard levels of ability. Each person to be rated was compared to this standard and assigned a numerical score. In 1919 this man-to-man scale was used for rating a large number of United States Army officers.

Most of the rating methods that have been described have serious shortcomings, such as the following:

a. They use general character traits or descriptive terms, such as leadership, poise, and work attitudes, which are difficult to define. It is almost impossible for all raters to give the same meaning to such a term as leadership, but it is possible for them to agree on what the ratee did with regard to planning, handling grievances, training his workers, or other activities involved in leadership.

ILLUS. 164. UNITED STATES ARMY RATING SCALE

I. PHYSICAL QUALITIES	Highest	15
Physique, bearing, neatness, voice, energy, en-	High	12
durance. Consider how he impresses his	Middle	9
command in these respects.	Low	6
	Lowest	3

II. INTELLIGENCE	Highest	15
Accuracy, ease in learning; ability to grasp	High	12
quickly the point of view of commanding officer,	Middle	9
to issue clear and intelligent orders, to estimate	Low	6
a new situation, and to arrive at a sensible de-	Lowest	3
cision in a crisis.		

III. LEADERSHIP	Highest	15
Initiative, force, self-reliance, decisiveness, tact,	High	12
ability to inspire men and to command their	Middle	9
obedience, loyalty, and co-operation.	Low	6
	Lowest	3

IV. PERSONAL QUALITIES	Highest	15
Industry, dependability, loyalty; readiness to	High	12
shoulder responsibility for his own acts; free-	Middle	9
dom from conceit and selfishness; readiness and	Low	6
ability to co-operate.	Lowest	3

V. GENERAL VALUE TO THE SERVICE	Highest	15
Professional knowledge, skill and experience;	High	12
success as administrator and instructor; ability	Middle	9
to get results.	Low	6
	Lowest	3

(Note from p. 259 of *The Personnel Manual*.) It will be noted that it is really five separate scales, one each for each of the five essential qualities of an officer, namely, physical qualities, intelligence, leadership, personal qualities, and general value to the service. Each of the spaces is to be filled with the name of an officer who is taken as a standard for the qualification and the degree of the qualification indicated by the terms, "highest," "high," "middle," "low," and "lowest."

Each of the officers is ordinarily of the same rank as the rater and hence the rank next superior to that of the officer to be rated. Each of them is well known to the rater and stands in his mind as an exemplar of the qualification. With each of them he compares the officer to be rated on a man-to-man basis to find which one he most nearly equals in that qualification. The officer to be rated is compared with officers of superior rank because the object is to discover his fitness for promotion.

The accuracy of the result depends largely upon the care with which the rating scale is constructed. When instructions are followed closely and raters do their work conscientiously the ratings show a high degree of accuracy and uniformity.

(*The Personnel Manual*, Committee on Classification of Personnel, Adjutant General's Dept. 1919, p. 260. By permission of the Govt. Print. Office, Washington, D. C.)

b. Rating methods employ adjective or point scales with such poorly defined steps that most raters can seldom distinguish between them. For example, the difference between average and above average is almost always debatable, because one rater's average does not correspond to another's.

c. Rating methods combine two difficult psychological processes in one judgment; (1) the observation and recording of performance and (2) the evaluation of performance. This combination usually results in inaccurate observation and evaluation.

d. In many military and industrial situations practically every one is rated above average, and those who are really doing excellent work are not given much more credit than mediocre workers. This leniency on the part of raters is due to a desire to have friendly relations with those supervised, and to give them as good ratings as other supervisors in the organization.

In order to avoid overgenerous rating based on fragmentary evidence and expressed in vague terms, a rating technique must (*a*) yield specific evidence of past performance, (*b*) separate the observation procedure from the evaluation, and (*c*) base the evaluation upon well-validated factors in job success.

The Forced-Choice Method

To meet these specifications the United States Army Personnel Research Section developed the forced-choice technique (Sisson, 1948). In the *forced-choice* rating the rater is furnished from twenty to thirty small groups of specific descriptive terms and required to indicate which items in each group are most typical and which least typical of the ratee. Each group of items usually contains two favorable items (*a* and *b*), two unfavorable items (*c* and *d*), and one neutral item (*e*): (*a*) commands respect by his actions, (*b*) cool-headed, (*c*) indifferent, (*d*) overbearing, and (*e*) quiet.

In order to separate the process of observation from that of evaluation, six hundred items were all pretested in such a way as to yield two indices for each item, one for discriminative value and the other for preference value. All the items were applied in experimental form to two groups of officers, which had been carefully selected to represent the most and the least competent. The discriminative value of an item was the difference between the percentages of officers described by the item in the most competent and the least competent group. The preference value was secured by having a large number of officers rate each item for apparent degree of praise or blame.

In each group of items the two favorable items have nearly equal preference values but different discriminative values, and the same is true of the two unfavorable items. In scoring these forms, only the discriminative items are counted. Since these are not known to the rater, he cannot know if he is rating the person relatively high or low, and therefore cannot play favorites. The results on large numbers of officers showed that the forced-choice ratings were not as skewed toward the desirable end of the scale as were scale ratings of the same officers, and that the scoring keys could not be guessed or detected by any means usually available to the raters. The forced-choice method is promising because it requires reporting of observations, and eliminates rater judgments concerning the over-all evaluation of performance. The combining of two pairs of items in one group is a device used to overcome rater resistance to unfavorable items. A great deal of careful research will be needed in applying this method, because the discriminative values of items will doubtless change as the criteria of success are changed or improved.

Nominating Techniques

Another rating procedure that has been used in only a few military situations but in many school situations asks the raters to nominate or name persons in the group for particular roles. Thus Wherry and Fryer (1949) found that "buddy nominations" of five out of a section of twenty men, who possessed the most desirable traits for an army officer showed much greater retest reliability over a 3-month period than ratings of ten leadership qualities on an adjective scale. These results are probably due in part to the differences in procedure. It is easier to select the five top people in a group than to rate or rank members of the whole group. Also it is easier to nominate a specific person than to rate him with regard to abstract and hard-to-define qualities.

CONSIDERATIONS IN RATINGS

Relative Intangibility of Items

Regardless of the form used for rating, some items appear to be more difficult to discriminate than others. With regard to physical judgments the finer discriminations are clearly the most difficult to discriminate. The results of differentiating between personal traits that are complex, that have been ambiguously defined, and that are rarely observed, vary greatly. This fact is clearly shown in Illus. 165, which shows the ratings for one boy on ten traits by from ten to fifteen observers. The observers were consistent with one another in rating resistance to authority, self-assertion, social responsibility, and popularity. Less uniformity is indicated by the longer lines for the

ILLUS. 165. CONSISTENCY OF RATINGS OF DIFFERENT TRAITS
BY VARIOUS OBSERVERS

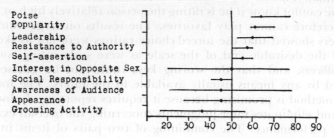

Highest and lowest ratings are indicated
by the extremes of each horizontal line.

(Drawn from data in the files of the Institute of Child Welfare,
University of California. Courtesy of H. E. Jones.)

ratings of poise and leadership. Great lack of agreement is shown in
ratings of interest in the opposite sex, awareness of audience, appearance, and grooming activity. The last two items, which one
would think could be judged uniformly, showed more variations than
such intangible items as leadership and poise. These results should
make one realize the need of a check on the inconsistencies of raters
in any situation.

Number of Desirable Steps

The number of steps in rating scales range from two to a hundred,
or more. Four or five steps are most frequently used in ratings of
attitudes and traits in fifty-two samples which have been collected
by the writer. In the self-rating of academic or vocational preferences
three or four steps or classes are most common. The most satisfactory
number of steps to use is that number which can be clearly distinguished by the judges in a reasonable time, without distorting
the results. This may be determined by trying out scales with various
numbers of steps. Symonds (1924; 1931) found from empirical evidence, that a 7-point descriptive scale was a little more reliable than
a 5-point scale when the judges were interested and definite traits, for
example, neatness, were clearly defined. When a trait, for example,
tact, was vague, or when the judges were immature or not interested,
only 4 or 5 points were clearly distinguished.

Champney and Marshall (1939) compared two procedures in scoring a 7-centimeter graphic scale of home conditions. In one procedure a 7-point scale was used, one point for each centimeter. In the
other, a 70-point scale was used, one point for each millimeter. Both

procedures were applied to two alternative forms applied within a 3-week interval. The two forms yielded retest correlations of .665 for the 7-point scale and .766 for the 70-point scale. This increase in retest reliability is more than could be expected by the usual methods of correcting for coarse scaling. It indicates that the judgments were more consistently recorded on the finer scale.

Another way of evaluating the number of steps to be used is to find out whether or not all the judges use all the steps or cluster the cases in one or two steps. Judges have been found to differ a good deal in this respect. Thus Illus. 163 shows the distribution of ratings assigned to the same fifty nurses by two supervisors. The results show that the second supervisor used only three of the steps while the first used all five. If some steps in a scale are never, or almost never used, they probably have little effect on the scores. Occasionally, however, a lowest step which is never used causes the step next to it to be used more frequently than might otherwise be the case.

Halos and Logical Errors

Ratings on a number of traits by one person are subject to two sources of error which are sometimes rather important. One source is called a *halo effect,* the other a *logical error.* A halo effect is a tendency to classify a person on the whole as good or bad, and then to rate him on all traits in keeping with this opinion. A logical error is introduced by a special interpretation of the task.

Halo effects and logical errors, of course, defeat one of the main purposes of rating scales, namely, to find out a person's relative strength and weakness. They can sometimes be avoided by rating all persons in a group on one trait at a time, instead of rating one person on all traits before considering the next person. Another device for avoiding halo effects in ratings is an irregular arrangement of the steps or classes. A common arrangement of items is to have all the most desirable characteristics placed on the right-hand side of the page, the least desirable on the left, and the average traits in the middle. This arrangement may lead to routinely placing checkmarks down the page by one who is too busy to use the rating carefully. If the most desirable traits are placed sometimes on the right and sometimes on the left, the rater is required to read the items more carefully. Mathews (1927) found that there is a considerable tendency in multiple-choice tests to check the responses printed near the left, rather than those printed near the right, when choices are printed across a page. When choices are set in columns, there is a marked tendency to check those nearer the top more frequently than those nearer the bottom of a series.

Halos are systematic errors which can be exposed by correlation techniques. An accurate rater will secure scores which correlate well with a true criterion, and he will also be able to repeat his performance with a high self-consistency. A rater who depends upon chance will usually show a low correlation with the criterion and also a low self-consistency. A rater who is markedly biased will have a low correlation with the criterion but a high self-correlation. Adams (1930) has shown that persons often differ a great deal in their ability to estimate size of circles, lengths of lines, and also personal qualities of their friends. He found that a good judge of self tends to differ from a good judge of others, by being rated by his colleagues as happier, more sympathetic, generous, and courageous.

In relationships among personal traits, halo effects introduce errors which raise or lower correlations spuriously. When correlations between two dissimilar traits are as high as .90, halo effects may be suspected. The true relationships may be approximated by pooling the ratings of several persons on the assumption that personal prejudices will tend to cancel one another. This assumption brings up the interesting question, how many persons' ratings should be pooled to eliminate halo effects? Bradshaw (1930) found that the rating of a personality trait of students in college attained a correlation of .80 between two trials when at least five ratings were averaged. A reliability coefficient of .90 would be reached theoretically when the ratings by ten such persons were averaged. He reported many variations from these usual findings which depended upon the trait, the accuracy of the descriptions, and the raters.

A *logical error* is one in which traits are rated alike because the rater has some reason for believing that they are similar or occur together. He substitutes logic for the direct observation of behavior. Newcomb (1931) found that ratings on a large number of personality traits in boys correlated on the average much higher (.493) than records of observed behavior of the same boys in the same traits (.141). He believed that the raters were not particularly prejudiced, but had adopted various stereotypes of personality which influenced their ratings.

MERITS OF VARIOUS METHODS

Each of the above methods of estimating has advantages. The self-inventory method, described more fully in Chapter XXII, is widely used in schools, clinics, and industry, when the subject is able and willing to cooperate. It seems to give fairly reliable indications of interests, of attitudes toward policies and social institutions, and of useful methods of overcoming obstacles. Inventories are easy to score with multiple-choice methods. However, they cannot be used with children or with adults who cannot or will not cooperate. They can, with few exceptions, be filled out so as to conceal the truth to a considerable extent.

The paired-comparisons method is usually tedious and time-consuming, if many items are to be compared. It does seem to yield more stable results than other methods, however, and some ingenious forms will minimize the labor involved.

The rank-order method is not so time-consuming as making paired comparisons, and it seems to avoid halo effects to some degree.

Rating scales are used both in schools and in industries more than any other type of appraisal. They are the least reliable and most subject to halo, but are much more economical of time, labor, and materials. Because in the forced-choice method the rater does not know what scores will be given to his ratings it is a distinct improvement over the other methods.

The relative effectiveness of various methods of comparison has rarely been studied, but Hevner (1930) scaled samples of handwriting by three methods: paired-comparison, ranking, and equal-appearing intervals. She found that the scale values of the first two methods were similar to each other but different from the values of the third. The third gave less precise discrimination among the better samples of handwriting. Ferguson (1939) reported, however, close agreement among scale values according to the three methods, and concluded that the equal-appearing interval method was superior in both economy and accuracy. In this method the scale value of an item was not greatly affected by the inclusion or exclusion of other items. Aesthetic judgment, according to Bullough (1908), is disturbed by paired comparisons. Conklin and Sutherland (1923) found that consistency in judging the humor of jokes was less when a ranking method was used than when a rating scale was employed.

Wherry and Fryer (1949) reported repeat-test reliability on the following three types of ratings as measured by correlations of ratings repeated after one month and again after three months for a sample of eighty-two officer candidates:

a. *Buddy nominations* were made by having each cadet nominate the five men in his section who possessed the least desirable personality traits for an Army officer and the five men who possessed the most desirable traits. The score was the times mentioned as "most desirable" minus times mentioned as "least desirable," divided by the total possible mentions, that is, an average of nominations by all the men in a section (approximately 20).

b. Buddy ratings were averages of ratings made by all students in a section, using a graphic adjective scale of ten leadership qualities.

c. Eight Junior Tactical Officers rated all the students in the class known to them, using the same scale as in (*b*). Three judges were usually available for each cadet.

Buddy nominations had correlations of .75 for the one-month interval, and .58 for the 3-month. Buddy ratings of leadership correlated .76 for the one-month interval and only .17 for the 3-month. The ratings by superior officers showed correlations of .58 for the one-month interval and .28 for the 3-month. Some fairly clear results emerge. The longer the interval between the ratings, the smaller the correlation. The buddy nominations were much more stable over the 3-month period than the buddy ratings, which means that the rating procedure using ten leadership qualities introduced more variability among the raters than the nominating procedure. Thus the cadets still considered many of the same persons to be the five best or five worst as leaders, after 3 months, while they failed markedly to rate all candidates consistently, using a group of verbally defined traits. The practical significance of this finding is great, for the nominating technique is also easier to administer, score, and interpret.

The superior tactical officers' ratings had lower repeat-test reliability than the buddy nominations for both intervals. This is probably due to the smaller number of judges, as well as the smaller degree of acquaintance of judges with candidates.

The superior tactical officers' judgments correlated with buddy nominations .36 after one month of training, .45 after 2 months, and .53 after 4 months, which means that the Tactical Officers evaluated leadership at the end of 4 months about as well as the cadets did at the end of one month.

The United States Army Personnel Research Section Report No. 672 (1945) compared the validity of five efficiency reporting methods, which included two adjective rating forms each, with about ten traits to be rated, a forced ranking form, a check list, and a forced-choice form. These were validated against the ratings of carefully selected groups of officers. The forced-choice method showed clear superiority over the other methods on several large groups of officers. Predictions could be increased slightly by combining the forced ranking and the check list with the forced choice.

CONSTRUCTION OF ITEMS

The same considerations which were presented for the construction of test items (Chapter IV) apply also for rating items, particularly self-rating inventories. These rules are designed to eliminate ambiguities and to supply important information more quickly and accurately than is possible by other means. One should use simple language and positive statements. The character-sketch items (Illus. 228) seem to yield more accuracy than many shorter items which permit a variety of interpretation, but both kinds are useful.

The Wording of Items

Benton (1935) applied the Personal Inquiry Form of Landis and Zubin to 20 normal adults and 20 psychotic patients, and then asked each to explain his answers. From 44 questions he obtained approximately one hundred interpretations. Of the forty-four questions 20 displayed qualitative differences, 17 showed quantitative differences, and 7 had no differences. In the interpretation of "Have you ever felt that life is a dream?" a qualitative difference is seen. Some thought that this meant that life is very unreal—like a dream; others that life is very easy and beautiful. A quantitative difference in interpretation involved ambiguity in the amount of a trait or quality.

The various interpretations were cast into another form of one hundred items called the Interpretation Questionnaire. Both the Personal Inquiry Form and the Interpretation Questionnaire were applied twice to 90 normal and 100 psychotic individuals at intervals of from 3 to 21 days. Answers on both were tabulated to show differences in the amounts of variation in interpretation. The differences were most apparent among items which had been changed to reduce the quantitative variations. Thus, the original item, "Do you feel mentally inferior to your friends?" was changed to, "Do you feel mentally inferior to most of your friends?" The original form is quantitatively more vague than the revised form. The original item did not differentiate between normal and psychotic groups, but the revised item brought out large differences. This study shows that the usefulness of items is greatly increased by changes which reduce the number of possible interpretations. The revised items proved to be more reliable on a retest and more discriminative of psychotic tendencies than the original items from which they were derived. Nearly every item available today can be considerably clarified.

EMOTIONAL REACTIONS TO ITEMS

When using any rating some persons will be on the defensive, and some will have the desire to show off. Many investigators have emphasized the superiority of somewhat indirect measures of motives and adjustment tendencies. Maller (1932) reported that although approximately 70 per cent of pupils felt somewhat embarrassed by direct questions about their own shortcomings, only 43 per cent were irritated by impersonal questions. He therefore preferred the character-sketch type of test in which one identified oneself with a pen portrait. Rundquist and Sletto (1936) preferred to state their items in the third person rather than in the first.

Another indication of emotional response is seen in responses to positive and negative items. Lorge (1935) reported that some people showed a tendency to check either positively or negatively any kind of question on the Bernreuter Scale. This tendency was greater in some persons than their consistency in checking one item *yes,* and its opposite *no.*

R. B. Smith (1932) found that positive and negative items which were designed to be opposites of each other did not call out opposite responses. For example, "Feels he has failed at most everything he tried" was not statistically opposite "Feels he has succeeded in most everything he tried." Smith believed that the two items called out different emotions.

Rundquist and Sletto (1936) found that their negative or gloomy statements were more discriminative of morale than their positive or happy statements. The positive statements tended to be answered more uniformly than the negative ones, and also to have smaller correlations with total scores in all except the scale for family adjustments.

These studies indicate clearly that reactions to specific items vary in ways which can be measured, and suggest the possibility of appraising emotional behavior by comparing responses to various items.

Is a rating more truthful when the raters are anonymous? is a question that is often raised. Spencer (1938) found that students in a fairly large group admitted that they would have answered some questions untruthfully had they been required to sign their names. These students were those who showed the greatest mental conflict scores; hence Spencer concludes that signing one's name materially reduces the effective selection of those who need counseling help. Olson (1936) and Moore (1937) also found that frankness increases with the degree of anonymity of the report.

According to Johnson (1934) administration should take cognizance of the mood of the subject. He reported marked differences in *dominance* scores of subjects when they felt cheerful and when they felt depressed.

Hartshorne and May (1929) found a large increase in names given for cooperative children by classmates when the raters' names were placed in the ballots, as compared with anonymous ballots, but not much change in names of noncooperative children. When raters' names were required, children centered their votes on positive votes and fewer names, and also voted less often for themselves.

A distinct departure from the conventional rating schedule in general use is the Employee Guidance Sheet developed by the Alabama State Personnel Department and reported by I. S. Smith (1944). The five descriptive phrases accompanying each of ten traits to be rated are couched in language intended to help to encourage the employee rather than to report findings in a coldly impersonal and blunt manner. The following illustrates the effort that was made to humanize the report and stimulate the employee to greater effort:

Usual Form

Quality of work:
( ) unusually high output
( ) high output
( ) normal output
( ) limited output
( ) insufficient output; unsatisfactory

Alabama State Form

Quantity of work (just a friendly suggestion):
( ) Exceptionally high output. Keep it up.
( ) Better than average. Good going.
( ) Meeting our requirements.
( ) You could do more. Try harder.
( ) You could do a lot more. Try much harder.

INTENTIONAL MISREPRESENTATION

The only way to eliminate intentional misrepresentation in rating either oneself or others is to construct the rating situation so that the rater will not know how his judgments are to be scored. The best single approach is probably the forced-choice method discussed earlier, when one of two attributes, which are equally acceptable socially, must be chosen. One attribute had been found to distinguish between the highest and the lowest third of officers, while the other did not. This technique should have wide application in both school and industry.

Several inventories now include scores which show any tendency to lie or exaggerate or to give bizarre answers (Chapter XXII).

Intentional misrepresentation can be reduced to a marked degree by eliminating fear of reprisals and by convincing the rater that his honest appraisal will be beneficial to him. In many situations this is not easy to do. For instance, when service or efficiency ratings are used by government agencies there is a marked tendency to rate nearly everyone considerably above average. While this practice avoids the unpleasant feelings and the appeals which realistic ratings might evoke, by not pointing out needs for improvement, one main purpose of the rating is defeated.

RULES FOR RATERS

The considerations just discussed suggest the following rules which should prove helpful in avoiding errors in using rating procedures:

1. Each trait should be defined as clearly as possible; vague terms should be avoided.

2. Each trait should refer to only one relatively independent pattern of behavior.

3. Raters should judge on the basis of their actual experiences, avoiding prearranged schemes which may not apply to a particular situation.

4. Complete integrity should be secured in rating either self or others. It may be an advantage to secure ratings from judges who are ignorant of the use that is to be made of them, and who do not know how the form will be scored.

5. Raters should frequently check their definitions and scales of value with the accepted criteria.

6. The combined ratings of several equally competent judges should be used rather than the ratings of one judge.

Good evaluations depend upon four complex conditions: opportunity to observe, competence, willingness to report a fair rating, and the availability of an accurate evaluation procedure.

COMBINATIONS OF RATINGS

It has been shown that the most self-consistent ratings often come from combining the work of several raters. Raters often seem to cancel out one another's idiosyncrasies. The process of combining ratings is, however, frequently complicated by the fact that different raters vary in their leniency and in the scope of their judgments. This is well demonstrated by Illus. 163. The median ranks and dispersions are different for each rater. The first nurse ranked the group nearly a whole step lower than did the second nurse. This discrepancy means that the ranks assigned by one are not comparable to those assigned by the other. Such differences as these are frequently found among raters. Training tends to reduce the differences, particularly if judges are told to use all the classes and to make their results fall in a normal curve. There are, however, some objections to this procedure. It may lead to artificiality, and the probability is that in many small samples the curve of distribution is not a normal curve.

In situations where it is desirable to have the results of all raters comparable, it is possible to change all into standard scores. Symonds (1931, p. 81) has facilitated such changes by giving a table of the per cents which may be expected from 3- to 7-point scales, applied to two groups, one of 40 and one of 185 persons. However, Conrad (1932, 1932 A) found that adjustments to a common distribution did not significantly increase the validity of combined ratings in the United States Army Man-to-Man scale (Illus. 164) nor in the rating of intelligence of nursery school children. He concluded that in these situations such time-consuming adjustments were not worth the trouble required. When large differences occur between two raters, however, an adjustment that makes their ratings comparable may be advisable.

Another and more difficult problem in combining ratings is that of securing equally good raters. In many industrial situations it is impossible to find more than one rater who has had adequate opportunity to observe the persons to be rated, and even when more than one judge is available, it is probable that they vary a great deal in their competency as raters. Often a good rating may be contaminated by several poor ratings, because the validity of the separate raters could not be determined, but no criterion was available, to which the good rater could appeal.

VALIDITY OF RATINGS

The desire to have definite information concerning the degree to which ratings reveal the true situation has led to considerable research, chiefly along two lines. One of these correlates actual measures with ratings, and is therefore limited to situations where actual measures are available. The other procedure sets up some combination of judgments as the nearest available approximation of the truth and compares other judgments with this.

The first procedure is used in the work of Marsh and Perrin (1925), who correlated ratings with various direct measures. The judges observed students performing certain tests, and then judged the performance. The correlation between estimated and measured aiming was only .36; between estimated and measured intelligence, .78; and between appraisals of card sorting, .68. Ratings of head size correlated .76 with measures of head circumference. These facts indicate considerable discrepancy and lead one to suspect that ratings of more intangible traits may be even less in keeping with the facts.

The second procedure is well illustrated by the work of Adams (1936), who also furnished formulas for showing certain qualities of a scale. In one of his experiments, on two different occasions a number of persons ranked ten printed circles in order of size. The two rankings of each person were correlated to give a *personal consistency*. These correlations were averaged to give *self-consistency* for the whole group. Another figure called *group-consistency* was secured by correlating the rank order assigned by each person with the rank orders of all other persons. Since in practice this procedure involved too many calculations, a sample thought to be representative of all person-to-person correlations was taken. In this experiment and also in a large number of other similar experiments with objects, the self-consistency was found to be the same as the group-consistency. Both group-consistency and self-consistency were high or low depending upon the difficulty of the discrimination.

In another experiment the same persons ranked ten students on personality traits, for example, courage. The results showed that self-consistency was considerably higher than group-consistency. This finding indicated that persons were more consistent with their own biases than with those of others. The group-consistency indicated the amount of random error, whereas the self-consistency was raised by systematic errors of personal sorts. Adams, therefore, proposed an index of *objectivity* found by dividing group consistency (GC) by self-consistency (SC). If GC equaled .81 and SC equaled .90, then the equation from which the index is derived will be $\dfrac{GC}{SC} = \dfrac{.81}{.90} = .90 =$ objectivity index.

When this index is 1.00, group- and self-consistency are identical, as in judging the size of circles. The judgments are considered to be completely objective even though they may not be accurate. Objectivity is therefore defined as the lack of systematic errors in judging. An objectivity index of less than 1.00 indicates systematic errors on the part of the judge. The lower the index, the lower is the objectivity. This index is a useful one which should be applied to both rating and measuring techniques.

In the experiment on judging sizes of circles there was an acceptable criterion for size, namely, the areas calculated from actual measures. When there are no widely acceptable criteria available, as in the judgment of courage, tact, or artistic ability, then there is no possibility of a conclusive check on the degree to which a rating approximates the truth. There are two procedures, however, which are designed to furnish criteria of approximate truth. In one the central tendency of a group of judges is taken as the best approximation. In the other the agreement of several similar procedures is taken as evidence that all are yielding true appraisals.

The use of a central tendency as the best approximation of a fact is, of course, open to question. If a number of judges make the same error, the opinion of a single expert will be closer to the truth. If, however, all judges have nearly equal ability, then a central tendency has been shown in many experiments to be nearer the fact than the judgment of any one of the judges. This discussion raises the very interesting question, who is the best judge? or, in the case of instruments or tests, which is the least subject to errors? In some instances the qualifications of the judges or of the persons who constructed the tests are considered. Thus an expert in chemistry would be considered a more competent judge of chemical analysis than an untrained person. In many other cases, however, no accepted qualifications are available. Although some work has been done, further intensive research is needed to show the extent to which accuracy of a particular judgment is related to personal characteristics. Hollingworth (1911), Hoffman (1923), Shen (1925), Adams (1927), Conrad (1932), and others have reported that self-ratings are usually too high on desirable traits and too low on undesirable traits, and that superior individuals often underestimate themselves and the inferior overrate themselves. Adams found that a good judge of self is likely to be more intelligent, observing, sympathetic, generous, courageous, and happier than a good judge of others. Hollingworth believed that there was a positive correlation between possession of a desirable trait and ability to estimate it in others.

The other approach to the criterion for validity is made by using four ratings, all of which are designed to appraise the same quality. First, one must show that the appraisals are free from systematic error, by methods described for securing objectivity. Next, as Adams (1936) has shown by Spearman's logic, the four appraisals may all be considered to measure the same function if together they satisfy the

formula: $\dfrac{r_{ab}}{\sqrt{r_{aa}r_{bb}}} = 1.00$. Here, if a correlation between raters a

and b is equal to the square root of the product of their reliability coefficients, the validity index is 1.00. For example, if on two occasions persons a and b ranked ten photographs for their advertising appeal, and if the following correlations were found: r_{aa}, .60; r_{bb}, .30; and r_{ab}, .42; then, by substitution of these values in the formula,

we have $\dfrac{.42}{\sqrt{.60 \times .30}} = .99$. In this case Adams would conclude that

both persons were using the same set of standards in rating the photographs, even though one rater was much more consistent than the other. If the index is much less than 1.00, the raters are not using the same standards.

Applications of these procedures for studying validity are noted in the subsequent chapters.

STUDY GUIDE QUESTIONS

1. What are the processes involved in making a numerical rating? How do they differ from those involved in securing a test score?

2. How are inventories prepared to yield unequivocal scores?

3. What is the procedure in the paired-comparisons method? What advantage has it?

4. What is the rank-order method? Does it depend upon a normal distribution of persons in the group?

5. How can a scale of attitude toward such an institution as the church be made to have equal steps, that is, equally often noticed differences between the steps?

6. How are rating scales prepared?

7. How were the forced-choice items prepared for the United States army officer rating procedure?

8. How may the relative intangibility of various items be determined?

9. How may the optimum number of steps to use in a graphic scale be determined?

10. What is the halo error in rating? How may it be avoided?

11. What can be done to reduce unwanted fear or emotional reactions to ratings?

12. How can intentional misrepresentation be reduced?

13. What advantages and what difficulties are there in combining ratings from various judges?

14. What are the principal methods of rating or estimating personality traits? What aspect of comparison does each stress? What are the advantages of each?

15. What are the advantages and disadvantages of the forced-choice method?

16. What evidence is there of emotional reactions to specific items or to questionnaires as a whole?

CHAPTER XVII

DRAWING, PAINTING, AND HANDWRITING

INTRODUCTION

Broadly defined, visual-motor behavior consists of a large variety of visual perceptions followed by expressive movements. All techniques discussed in this chapter have in common the sensory-motor patterns involved in making marks on paper. They differ from each other with regard to restrictions of content, the use of media and tools, and the administration and scoring procedures. Different degrees of encouragement are employed and some procedures employ a considerable amount of recording of verbal comments or stories. Evaluations of intellectual growth and of artistic design in drawings are discussed in Chapters VIII and X. Character or dynamic evaluations are discussed in this chapter.

VISUAL-MOTOR GESTALT

Drawing or copying tests have often been used to appraise not only the normal maturation of visual and motor functions, but also variations associated with mental defect and personal adjustment or integration. The work of Lauretta Bender (1938) is well known with regard to the latter. Over a period of 20 years Miss Bender followed and supplemented the work of Wertheimer (1923), Köhler (1929), Schilder (1934), and Koffka (1935), who emphasized the dynamic aspects of perceiving and understanding. The act of copying a pattern is a complex one in which the comprehension of directions,

473

ILLUS. 166. BENDER GESTALT FIGURES

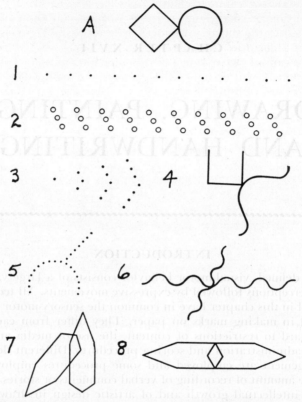

(Gestalt drawings after Wertheimer, 1923, furnished through the courtesy of Dr. Max L. Hutt. In the test situation the figures are shown one after another and without numbers.)

willingness to cooperate, sensory-motor mechanisms, and personal motives and integration all have a part. Two opposing tendencies are always thought to be present: an integrative one, which results in good coordination and complete, accurate drawings; and a disintegrative one, which results in patterns that are simplified, warped, elaborated upon, made fragmentary, or destroyed. A drawing always represents a momentary equilibrium between various forces, but it also frequently indicates fairly stable modes of adjustment.

Bender used nine of the thirty drawings developed by Wertheimer (Illus. 166) in her studies of normal and abnormal persons. The first design (marked A) is usually perceived in horizontal sequence and represents two contiguous figures, each of which is known as a "good gestalt" or complete figure. The figures marked 1, 2, and 3 consist of dots or small loops without boundaries. The patterns are determined by the shortest distances between parts. Figures 4, 5, and 6 present difficulties in organization by being partly open and requiring careful perception and drawing of points of contact between patterns which are not usually perceived as wholes. The last two figures are combinations of two closed polygons which involve conflict and various perceptual relationships.

Administration (Bender)

The designs are printed on separate cards and presented in order with informal directions, such as, "I am going to show you some cards one at a time. Each has some simple figures on it. Copy the figures as well as you can. This is not a test of artistic ability. If you have any questions feel free to ask them." Any questions concerning time allowed, size of drawings, number of sheets to use, are answered by saying, "That's up to you. There are no rules." Blank sheets of 8½- by 11-inch paper are furnished, with a soft pencil and eraser. Figures from all the cards may be copied on the same piece of paper or additional sheets may be furnished if the subject wishes. There is no time limit. Hutt (1949) asks the subject to elaborate the drawings after he has completed all of them. He also includes an inquiry period in which the subject is asked, "What could it be?" and a testing-the-limits period when the perceptual and integrative processes are investigated.

Interpretation

Behavior during the course of the test is observed, and pertinent oral responses are written down. No standard numerical scores are available, but drawings are evaluated by signs or patterns which are compared with those which have previously been made by known groups of persons.

Hutt (1949) points out that in completing the Bender-Gestalt Test or any drawing test there are usually four steps which often, though not always, follow a definite temporal sequence:

1. *Motivation.* In this step the subject is told about what is expected on the test. He agrees to cooperate, probably with some reservations, and observes the first card.

2. *Selective attention and perception.* The subject then explores the card visually and selects the aspects to be reproduced. The selection is partly controlled by one's needs.

3. *Motor response.* In this step complicated visual-motor behav-

ior produces marks on paper, and sometimes speech. The movements are usually independent of educational level, except for training in drawing. Symbols are seldom inhibited unless the subject knows their social significance.

4. *Reaction to motor response.* In this step there may be a fantasy, or a period of autocriticism, when the subject compares his drawing with the stimulus, or he may strive to complete what seems to be incomplete. During this period unconscious needs often appear because, in the drawing process, the ego is less likely to be inhibited than during speech. However, the subject may be aware of some aspects of his conflict and may show emotional behavior, such as postural and vasomotor changes.

Hutt (1949) has listed four determinants which will be briefly surveyed here to show their nature and complexity:

Organization

a. Order and sequence of placing drawings on a page range from very rigid through regular, irregular, to chaotic. Egocentric persons have been found to start in the middle of a page and to use several pages. Insecure persons often start in the upper left corner. Normal folks usually begin near the middle or left of middle at the top.

b. Normal subjects usually use a page or page and a half. Paranoid reactions to protect self from a hostile world often result in the use of a small part of one page. Neurotic tendencies are often shown in large amounts of empty space and in small figures. Compulsive trends are related to the use of margins either as a guide or for support. Compactness of figures and collisions between figures are related to dependency and poor planning.

Size

Size is related to anxiety. Marked deviations in size, especially smaller figures than the originals, or less frequently larger, indicate insecurity. Often the disturbing part of the figure is out of proportion to the rest of it. A progressive increase in size is related to release of tension or to the development of greater assertiveness during the test, and a progressive decrease to feelings of failure and defense needs. Fear of authority tends to reduce vertical dimensions and increase relative horizontal dimensions.

Changes in Form

In general poor closure and organization and specific symbols are related to anxiety and dissociation. Difficulty with drawing curves reveals several tendencies. Thus, poor social adaptability is often related to greater angularity and poor balance between impulses and controls to great irregularity. Organic brain damage is related to decreases in angularity and poor integration or simplification of pattern in overlapping figures, particularly where angles appear.

Distortions of Gestalt

The rotation or partial rotation of figures beyond approximately 10 degrees either way is found most frequently among schizophrenics. The original gestalt of the drawing is frequently lost. Those with organic lesions produce partial rotation of figures more often than full rotation or reversal. Rotation usually indicates degrees of disorientation.

Among cases of serious regression dots are converted into loops or sometimes into vertical or nearly vertical scribbles. Rows of dots become wavy lines, and perseverations from one figure to another appear. These may be due either to inaccurate perception or to an attempt to simplify the task. They may be due to damage, especially in the parietal-temporal regions of the brain.

Doodling, elaborations, perseverations, and artistic sketching are often related to various tensions and can be explained only by associative techniques. Boundary lines and symmetry often relate to arbitrary restrictions in life space.

In addition to these determinants Hutt also records type and direction of movements and methods of work. If movements are related either to great tension or to flaccidity, the reasons should be explored. They are often related to ego strivings. Movements away from the body are usually indicative of aggression or repulsion, while movements toward the body indicate passive states. Movements in vertical planes reveal something of one's reaction to authority, and in lateral direction to contacts with peers or to interpersonal relations in general. Diagonal trends on a page sometimes result from indecision or poor solution of conflicts.

Methods of work vary from extremes of precise detailing of a compulsive kind to impulsive motor responses which have little connection with the figure. A normal person usually draws without much speed, frequently stopping to look at the model in order to correct his work or to anticipate what comes next. Setting up guide lines, counting dots, and measuring distances are done in excess by compulsive and rigidly controlled individuals.

This discussion of determinants does not include fantasy and symbols which are often important in personality diagnosis. These are introduced in Chapter XVIII. No significant body of normative data is as yet available to indicate frequency of patterns and their relationship in various syndromes. This extremely important field of research is now being actively investigated.

Stages of Maturation

Bender (1938) found fairly clear age norms from four to ten years, which she presented with charts together with percentages of children at each age who succeeded. Her findings are briefly summarized here.

When children below the age of three are asked to copy drawings, they normally scribble with large arm movements which result in whirls or pendulum waves. Dots are made by heavy punching movements. The results are not meaningful pictures, but the products of motor expression.

At four years some inhibition of movement occurs which often results in smaller single or concentric loops or circles. Patterns are made by combining these loops and making them wider or higher to resemble the exposed pattern. Dotted forms are usually reproduced in the form of curved figures, and there is much motor perseveration both in number of strokes and in pattern. The first pattern produced may be given for all the rest or influence the rest. Among right-handed children there is a marked tendency to draw from left to right, and the opposite is true of the left-handed. Contiguous or overlapping objects are often seen and drawn separately.

Between four and seven years there is rapid improvement in form. At five years short vertical and horizontal lines are managed, but diagonal or slanting lines are difficult. Thus the square in Illus. 166 is drawn on its side. Dots are usually drawn as small loops. Contiguous or overlapping forms, as shown in Items A, 4, 5, 6, and 7, are drawn as separate objects. The figures are usually arranged on the page to follow large concentric circles which correspond to arm movements.

At the six-year level, a real diamond appears in the drawing (Illus. 166A) but with irregular sides, usually a little curved. In Item 1 dots are made as dots, or as very small circles. There is still a tendency to separate contiguous or overlapping figures, but most of these patterns show correct contacts.

At seven years the child still has difficulty in producing slanting angles as is shown in 2 and 3, and producing lines, as shown in 7.

The diagonal slants are all well handled by 60 per cent of the ten-year-old group, the detail forms are correct, and there is a marked tendency to count the dots. Adults make only slightly more precise drawings.

Typical Deviates

Bender points out that clinical classifications hardly ever represent pure types, but that wide variations in personality structure occur in every group. In using the Bender-Gestalt Tests she finds it is desirable to determine an age level from the gestalt drawings and also from a Binet-type test. When the level of mental development is known, then the effects of conflict or injury can be seen. Bender's (1938) findings with deviate groups, which are typical of the reports of others, are summarized here.

Mental defect. Among those with mental defects, drawings are fairly typical of their mental-age level. However, motor maturity is greater than for the normal of the same mental age, hence the drawing may be more definitely controlled. These mentally deficient also often show patterns which are typical of aphasic, schizoid, or confused states, indicating that mental retardation is often complicated with emotional disturbances.

Brain injuries. In the case of violent brain injuries or internal bleeding, as in arteriosclerosis, there is first a confused state in which perception and drawing responses are very difficult. Later, as the patient improves, the drawings may indicate which parts of the brain have suffered the most injury. Bender reported eight cases where sensory aphasia was a prominent symptom and others where various injuries had been caused by syphilitic infection, alcohol, and trauma. It is possible that lesions of basal ganglia cause reductions in the number of elements of drawings and also fragmentation at points not related to the maturation principles of gestalt theory. Injuries of the cortex are often related to the difficulties in integration of patterns. Korsakow psychoses with few organic features show many confabulations with past memories, as well as reversion to primitive responses, and disorientation, but the essential designs are maintained.

Functional difficulties. Bender found catatonic schizophrenic patients showed marked tendencies to revert toward more primitive or elementary types, but in doing so to express change in rate of movement or direction in parts of the patterns. This often causes extreme exaggeration or disregard of the inherent gestalt. In addition, there is often much perseveration, and the original stimulus may be lost in elaborations of inner impulses to establish one's own identity.

In mild manic states there are rapid attempts at careful reproduction, often with erasures, and with expressed feelings of satisfaction. Often embellishments are rapidly added, which do not destroy the original figure, but represent a flight of ideas. These frequently incorporate local present details. Quick verbal associations usually run ahead of the drawing.

In mild depressed states the same type of response is given but with less satisfaction and more slowly. Inhibitions may reduce the details of small dots and circles. Sometimes negative or shadow images are used.

Lying, malingering, and the so-called Ganzer syndrome, where the client answers simple questions with understanding but foolishly, are usually reflected in drawings which in some systematic way alter the patterns. Such alteration could be made only with perception of the true pattern. Usually the true mental level is indicated and the elaborations are trivial.

Motor Gestalt (Mira)

A pencil-drawing test which nearly eliminates the visual control by using a blindfold or a screen, has been described by Emilio Mira (1940), who wished to measure the degree to which movements were varied by imagery and posture. The subject is seated comfortably so that his body and face point directly at an $8\frac{1}{2}$- by 11-inch sheet, fastened to a drawing board. In the first part of the test the examiner first demonstrates by drawing a horizontal 5-cm line from left to right with the right hand, and two similar lines just beneath it. (The wrist is *not* allowed to touch the table at any time during the test.) The subject is then blindfolded and the examiner guides his hand to the starting point on the paper. After drawing ten lines from left to right, the subject is given a fresh space on the paper and asked to draw ten more similar lines from right to left with the right hand. Then the left hand is used to make two similar sets of lines. When this is finished the subject first makes ten lines perpendicular to the bottom of the sheet moving away from the body and ten moving toward the body with the right hand, and then similar sets with the left hand. After a short rest the experimenter demonstrates and the subject begins the second part of the test.

In Part II the subject is not blindfolded, but a screen is used to prevent visual control. He draws the following:

a. Zig-zag lines an inch in length with angles of about 10 degrees, with both hands simultaneously, beginning at the top of the page and working down to the middle, then reversing direction and working upward from the middle.

b. Chains of separate $\frac{3}{10}$-inch circles from right to left, and in reverse direction with each hand separately.

 c. A staircase with steps $\frac{1}{10}$ of an inch in height, moving diagonally up and then down with each hand separately.

 d. A pattern similar to the turret of a castle, drawing horizontally
in each direction with each hand separately:

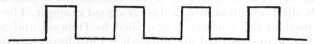

 The scoring of the results in Part I is objective, for Mira measures
the absolute and relative lengths of lines for each hand, computes
averages, variability, trends toward longer or shorter lines than those
in the model, shifts in direction, and a coefficient of coherence, which
is the average relative shifting divided by the average absolute shifting. Shifts in direction are found by measuring the distance of the
midpoint of each line to a perpendicular from the midpoint of the
first line. Positive values are assigned to shifts in the direction that
the lines are drawn. Thus if nine lines had as shift distances in millimeters 0, -1, -2, -2, $+1$, $+3$, $+3$, $+4$, $+5$, they would have an
absolute shift of 21, a relative shift of $+11$, and a coefficient of coherence of $+.523$. The score of Part II is more subjective, for the
straightness of lines, their pressure or load, and their orientation are
considered. Meticulousness, impetuousness, and failures or emotional
blockings, and other characteristics of the method of drawing are
observed.

 Mira's results, as yet tentative, show retest reliability on scores in
Part I in the neighborhood of .80 among thirty-five normal adults.
Among right-handed persons the right-hand scores are slightly less
reliable than the left-handed. There is evidence that the right-hand
behavior is more influenced by intellectual activity and the left more
by muscular and emotional constitution. Depressed persons show
more downward tendencies with the left hand than with the right.
In general, vertical shiftings are related to ascendant or withdrawing
tendencies, and vertical length to amount or strength of activity.
Mira offers no simple theory related to horizontal shiftings.

 Among the clinical groups the schizophrenics showed unusual
tendencies to lose original direction, to reverse direction, and to fall
in drawing patterns in Part II. As was expected, elation and depression were related to both length and shift. Data from other groups
are being collected. The Mira test has interesting possibilities because it stresses basic postural movements and yields some results
which can be scored objectively. It is simple to administer and score.
It should give interesting results with children and with other clinical

groups besides the schizophrenics, particularly those with organic brain damage.

Mosaic Tests

Among the tests designed to reveal methods of organization of materials, the Lowenfeld Mosaic Test is a good example. The Mosaic Test as used in this country is described by Dimond and Schmale (1944). The materials used are altogether 130 pieces—squares, diamonds, right-triangles, rectangles, and isosceles triangles. The colors black, white, red, blue, green, and yellow are so used that there are not more than ten shapes of any one color and shape. The squares are 1 inch square, and the other shapes nearly the same size, so that they can be made to fit together nicely. All blocks are $\frac{3}{16}$ of an inch thick. A wooden tray, 18 by 26 inches, is also used for the test.

The instructions state, "Make anything you like out of the pieces," but in practice it was found that nearly one third of the subjects mildly or strongly disliked the patterns they produced. Detailed notes of the subject's attitude, manner of selecting and placing the pieces, and verbalizations were used in rating the following nine items: (1) ideation or ability to think up patterns, (2) cooperation, (3) attention, (4) anxiety (specific or not to the test situation), (5) carefulness in selection, (6) carefulness in placing, (7) persistence, (8) manner of completion, and (9) approval of results. Dimond and Schmale finally distinguished five patterns of behavior—normal, mildly defective, moderately defective, severely defective, and unclassified. They found certain results to be typical of mental disease. Thus, the psychotics were usually cooperative while the psychoneurotics were often uninterested, evasive, and resistant. The schizophrenics showed disregard of color or active color rejection by using only black and white. They made literal or bizarre configurations with precise symmetry, but often showed blocking and incompletions, and severely defective gestalt. The psychoneurotics had many variations similar to normal and usually made normal or mildly defective gestalt.

This type of test covers somewhat the same areas of perception and color reaction as the Rorschach, but requires in addition constructive planning and movements toward completing the plan. A good deal of research is now going on which will allow much more important interpretations to be made with more confidence.

DRAWING OF OBJECTS

The use of freehand drawings as indications of personal dynamics is old in practice, since artists and art critics have always emphasized that art can be and usually is an expression of one's interests, satisfactions or fears, conscious or unconscious. Technical articles on children's drawings by Barnes (1893), Burk (1902), and a number of others have described in detail nearly all of the categories used at present.

Freehand drawings or paintings yield extremely complicated results and hence have, to date, defied the comprehensive analysis of factors and synthesis of findings which are typical of standard tests of number ability. Nevertheless as yet relatively little research has been done with regard to drawing when compared with number skills, and it is highly probable that many fairly definite dynamic patterns in drawing will be found. All of the analyses used in the Bender-Gestalt Test seem applicable to pencil drawings, and most of them to brush and finger painting. In addition, drawings call for original compositions, so that the subject's mental content is given opportunity for greater expression. Drawings are thought by many to be more directly expressive of deep or unconscious desires than written or spoken language, because drawings are not a common method of communication, and have more symbolic content which is not recognized by the subject and hence not censored. Space is allowed here for only two samples of analytical procedures and interpretation.

Karen Machover (1949) described a technique for securing and interpreting drawings of persons. She simply presents the subject with a white 8½- by 11-inch sheet and a medium-soft lead pencil and requests him to "Draw a person," or, in the case of young children, "Draw somebody." During the drawing careful observations are made and recorded of the subject's questions and comments, the time used, and the sequence of the parts drawn. When one drawing is complete, the subject is given another sheet and asked to draw a picture of a person of the sex not represented in the first. If there is time for only one drawing, it is preferable to have the subject draw a figure of the same sex as himself. Resistance may need to be overcome by stating, "This has nothing to do with your ability to draw. I'm interested in how you try to draw a person." If an important part is omitted, the subject may be urged to draw it. The two drawings usually require less than 20 minutes.

In order to gain insight into structural weaknesses and conflict an inquiry period of from 10 to 20 minutes is used. The subject is told, in language appropriate to his age, "Let's make up a story about the person as if he were a character in a novel or a play." Resistance may be overcome in various ways, such as by asking, "How old is the person? Is he married? What gets him angry? What is the best part of the body? The worst?" Twenty-four questions of this sort have been listed on a standard record sheet. The subject is further asked if the figure reminds him of anyone in particular, and which of his statements refers to himself as well as to the picture, and to explain unusual details in the picture.

In interpreting the results, Machover finds much evidence that the subject projects his own characteristics and some of his conflicts into the drawing. For instance (page 31), she finds:

The size of the figure, where it is placed on the sheet, the rapidity of graphic movement, the pressure, the solidarity and variability of the line used, the succession of parts drawn, the stance, the use of background and grounding effects, the extension of arms toward the body or away from it, the spontaneity or rigidity, whether the figure is drawn profile or front view are all pertinent aspects of the subject's self-presentation.

In interpretation the proportions of the body, shading, detailing, incompletions, erasures, line changes, symmetry, and mood expressed in the face or in the postural tone of the figure are all given consideration. The significance of variations in space, line, and proportions is thought to be similar to that reported for the Bender-Gestalt Test. Machover also gives 70 pages of principles of interpretation covering in detail the head, hair, features, neck, extremities, trunk, breast, shoulders, hips, clothing, movement, conflict indicators, and developmental considerations. Part of the interpretation of the head (page 36) is:

The head is the important center for the location of "self." Heads generally receive emphasis, except in drawings of neurotic, depressed, or socially withdrawn individuals. The head is essentially the center for intellectual power, social dominance, and control of body impulses. It is the only part of the body which is consistently exposed to view, thus being involved in the functions of social relationships. . . . The obsessive-compulsive will frequently give an almost ape-like presentation of physical power in the figure he draws, while underplaying the head. In this instance the head is definitely considered to be the organ responsible for his conflict concerning free expression of his impulses.

Disproportionately large heads will often be given by people suffering from organic brain disease, those who have been subjected to brain surgery, and those who have been preoccupied with headaches or other special head sensitivity. . . .

. . . The youngster whose emotional and social adjustments have been dislocated because of a severe reading or other subject disability will frequently draw a large head in his figure. . . . The mental defective will for similar reasons often give a large head. The paranoid, narcissistic, intellectually righteous, and vain individual may draw a large head as an expression

of his inflated ego. . . . The sex given the proportionately larger head is
the sex that is accorded more intellectual and social authority.

It is not altogether clear why a young child of three or four will often
draw a large head, perhaps with appendages issuing from it, as a completed representation of a person. It may be speculated that, since locomotion and manual exploration of the environment (and of the child's own
body) are important features of a child's early development, the appearance
of legs or arms before the body is functionally comprehensible. . . . It is
with the head that surrounding adults smile, approve, frown or scold. The
head of the adult is the most important organ relating to emotional maturity
of the child. Perhaps the large head that dependent male adults give to the
female figure in their drawings represents an emotional fixation on a supporting mother-image similar to that experienced by the child as a normal
phase in its development.

. . . Girls are said to draw larger heads, shorter arms, smaller hands,
shorter legs, and smaller feet than boys do. . . . While girls have only to be
pretty and decorative to command social attention, boys are expected to
make rapid strides in the development of physical and sexual power, in
proficiency in athletics, to reach out into the environment more vigorously,
and to show more tangible accomplishment. . . .

Machover gives eight illustrative case studies with clinical histories
and interpretations of drawings. The interpretations show the relations between the drawing, the associations given by the subject, and
the clinical history. No attempt has been made as yet to develop a
carefully defined set of diagnostic signs such as those used in the
Rorschach Test, but the material and the method lend themselves
to similar systematic analysis and recording. Machover considers her
monograph only the beginning of a larger and more complex project.

Paula Elkisch (1945) issued a monograph in which the scoring of
the Draw-A-Man Test is divided into four sections. These are summarized here:

1. *Rhythm* and its opposite, *rule* or rigidity, are indicated by
variations in the flexible quality of the stroke, elasticity, and spontaneity. In rigidity there are tight spasmodic movements which seem
automatic or mechanical.

2. *Complexity* and *simplexity* are expressed through tendencies
toward complete representation of individual differences. In simplexity there is a lack of differentiation indicating to Elkisch a lack of
ability to detach oneself.

3. *Expansion* and its opposite, *compression*. Expansion is seen
through the widening of the space used, in creations of spacious backgrounds, and by a well-formed presentation which uses all the space
available. Compression is revealed by the meticulous and frugal use

of the space at the drawer's disposal. Expansion stands for potential ability to make contacts.

4. *Integration* and its opposite, *disintegration,* are indicated by the degree to which the whole drawing shows relationship between its parts. Here there must be an essential center theme with other themes supplanting or contributing to it. The lack of integration is seen when objects are piecemeal, broken, or contaminated by two or more things overlapping or crowding each other, and when there is a lack of center or any central theme.

In addition to these four types of scores Elkisch evaluates the symbols from drawings according to psychoanalytical theory.

PAINTING

Painting is similar to pencil drawings in many respects, but it adds two complexities to an already complex dynamic pattern. One of these is the use of color and the other the use of a variety of tools for applying the color. Since the special techniques of palette knife and brush used in oil painting are rarely used in clinics and ordinary schools, nearly all the reports dealing with diagnostic or remedial painting describe the use of inexpensive colors that are carried well in water. Two different procedures are widely followed. One uses glossy paper and the fingers or hand to spread the paint. The other uses a rough paper and medium-sized brushes.

Finger painting is doubtless one of the oldest forms of art, but its modern form owes much to Ruth F. Shaw (1934). It has been used a great deal for therapy, since it releases tensions, elicits spontaneous fantasy material, and yields a permanent record of growth in adjustment. A good illustration of its use is that of Napoli (1946). In the procedure he uses the examiner first demonstrates the preparation of the paper, the selection of colors, getting seated comfortably, painting, and engages in a patter of comments on what he is doing while portraying a story. The story is very important in securing rapport, and later in making interpretations. Then putting the picture to dry, putting the paints away and washing one's hands in a bucket of water is demonstrated. These activities are all carefully observed, and what is said is recorded by notes or mechanically. No time or motion patterns have been presented statistically or quantitatively, but Napoli notes carefully the posture, types of movement, position of first daub of paint, the use of space, order of procedure, the parts of the hand used, the colors and amounts of colors taken, the development of a plan, span of interest, and satisfaction with the end product. Napoli has laid a good analytical foundation for the establishment of norms and the synthesis of complex patterns. For instance, the parts of the hand used are described (p. 161) roughly as follows:

1. Whole hand flat and relaxed
2. Flat palm with fingers raised
3. Lateral aspect of hand with fingers extended
4. Clenched fist with thumbs up
5. Outer side of thumb with fingers raised
6. Base of thumb with fingers raised
7. Base of palm with rest of hand raised
8. Knuckles in not too comfortable position
9. Flat part of finger or fingers relaxed
10. Finger tips
11. Finger nails
12. Whole arm including wrist relaxed
13. Fleshy part of arm with wrist raised

The frequency with which each mode is used by normal and by clinical groups, and the reasons for the use will be an extremely interesting study. Napoli has recorded some observations already. Thus picking or "teasing" the paint was related to oral erotic or masturbatory tensions. Pressure with the palm of the hand and fingers up often indicated impulsive urges. Exclusively using tips of the fingers often went with unusual fear of being soiled, and the lateral side of the hand, with feelings of inferiority.

Napoli reported typical characteristics for schizophrenic, paranoid, and unstable patients, which indicate dynamic patterns. Thus the schizophrenics invariably showed two or more strata, illogically related or disoriented, usually symbolizing aspects of conflicting areas in the person. The paranoid had a central figure with well-integrated objects on all sides for the purpose of protecting the central figure. Some form of violent attack was usually found either in the drawing or in the concurrent verbalization.

Rose Alshuler and LaBerta Weiss Hattwick (1947) published a report of drawings, daily observations, and case studies of one hundred and fifty children, ages from two to five years, covering an entire school year. They reported that in general these children expressed the same patterns in overt social behavior that they showed in creative media, but some children showed their feelings much more clearly in paintings than in overt behavior. They compared the children's preferences for brush, finger painting, crayons, clay, blocks, and dramatic play, and found that in the nursery schools studied the brush or easel painting was used more frequently as a means of self-expression than any other media and that it provided a medium for observing diverse patterns and subtle variations. Children's choice when they were alone often differed from those made when they were in a group, but the group situations where principally those reported. The authors found fairly strong evidence that

a. Children who predominantly sought easel painting were more concerned with self and internal problems than the rest. They were among the least mature in the group; they came from homes which exerted too much control; and they were preoccupied with emotional conflicts.

b. Children who preferred crayons tended as a group to be more concerned with expressing ideas than with finding emotional outlets. They showed more awareness of environment and a drive to control it. All of them came from homes where they were exposed to high adult standards and lacked opportunities to function on their own levels of readiness. They were more tense and unhappy, and the crayon activity did not seem to provide a release. Often children who sought crayons when they were new to the nursery school situation turned to easel painting as they became freer in behavior.

c. Children who preferred blocks stood out in the group for their spontaneous, outgoing, adaptive behavior. Blocks have little or no color, but require much aligning, fitting, and definite structuring. For some the manipulation of blocks provided a transition from impulsive action to discovering and interrelating the facts in the world about them. When they did paint they produced highly structured patterns, angular strokes, and enclosures.

d. Children who preferred clay, or any children working with clay, tended to talk about and to represent emotional problems related to excrements and sex rather freely. The children who worked with clay usually were grouped around a small table, with three or four other children near by.

e. The children who preferred dramatic play showed less dependence on materials and more reliance on interaction with other children, or on monologues and pantomimes with imaginative content. They all were highly developed in their social orientation and were affectionate and cooperative.

Alshuler and Hattwick developed a sheet, having twelve main divisions, upon which the following twelve characteristics of a drawing were checked: general characteristics, mass, line, form, direction, spacing, size, color, techniques or manner of working, organization, general effect, and content.

Each of the divisions contains items to be rated or checked for intensity or frequency. The second through the ninth divisions refer to fairly objective judgments; the other divisions refer to more subjective, but nonetheless important ratings. Thus the tenth division, organization (p. 254), includes: (1) unrelated lines, forms, (2) organized lines, forms, (3) focused on one object, (4) variety unrelated to object, (5) partial synthesis, (6) pure picture, (7) experiment with themes, and (8) successive pictures to develop theme.

The organizational activities noted here should be compared with those recorded for Rorschach and Thematic Apperception Test interpretations. The development of age, sex, and other norms is still a pressing need in this field.

HANDWRITING

The interpretation of personality traits from handwriting, called *graphology*, has a long history, but it has had the misfortune of being abused and exploited commercially, and up to now little careful research has been reported. There are two extreme methods of approach; one, called a *global* approach, attempts to build a picture of the whole personality by interrelating many complex estimates of aspects of handwriting without measuring them carefully; the other, called an *atomistic* approach, attempts to establish a relationship between a single sign, such as length of stroke above the middle zone, and a particular personality trait. Of course, most workers have used some combination of these approaches.

Typical of the global approach is a report by Cantril and Rand (1934), who located six individuals who showed high scores in one and only one of five parts of the Allport-Vernon Tests of Values: aesthetic, economic, theoretical, political, and religious (Chapter XXI). Each of these persons then copied the same letter on uniform paper and signed a fictitious name. When the six letters were photostated and submitted to twenty-four graphologists, seventeen of them indicated correctly the main interests of four or more of the writers, an occurrence that would theoretically happen by pure chance about once in a million times. When the six letters were submitted to twenty-six educated adults who had no knowledge of graphology, no adult succeeded in naming the main interests of as many as four students correctly.

Typical of a more atomistic approach is the work of Klages (1919), who is sometimes referred to as the "father of modern graphology." He described sixteen aspects of handwriting which have been used and elaborated upon by many other workers (Illus. 167).

Thea S. Lewinson and J. Zubin (1942) and Geral R. Pascal (1944) have well elaborated Klager variables by using precise sampling, and measuring written words with a millimeter rule. They used a magnifying glass to discover differences of as little as .2 millimeters, and made several hundred measurements of each sample.

Lewinson and Zubin (1942) define four main components (Illus. 167). Each of these writing elements is analyzed and rated on a 7-point scale, ranging from +3, extreme contraction, to —3, extreme release. For instance, element g, height of middle zone, ranges from ¾ mm. for extreme contraction to 6 mm. for extreme release, and element a, ornamentation, ranges from contraction into queer and distorted forms, through conventional, neglected, equivocal, and symbolic to decadent forms.

Lewinson and Zubin postulate that if a person's handwriting is well balanced between contraction and release his personality is also likely to be well balanced. If one exhibits much contraction in writing, he is likely to be too hemmed in by compulsions and ra-

ILLUS. 167. COMPONENTS OF HANDWRITING

I. *Form and Stroke:* related to ability to plan and integrate complex patterns.

- *a.* Ornamentation—simplification
- *b.* Contraction—amplification of contour
- *c.* Contraction—amplification of connecting form
- *d.* Width of stroke
- *e.* Border of the stroke
- *f.* Curvature of stroke

II. *Vertical Component:* related to intellectual, ego, and instinctive balance.

- *g.* Height of middle zone (expression of self-feeling)
- *h'.* Height of lower zone (expression of instinctive aspects)
- *h".* Height of upper zone (expression of intellectual aggression, physical sphere)
- *i.* Direction of the line (enterprising, balanced, gloomy moods)
- *k.* Amplitude of fluctuation of the line
- *l.* Contraction in fluctuation of line
- *m.* Space between lines

III. *Horizontal Component:* related to spontaneity and receptivity, self-confidence.

- *n.* Space between letters
- *o.* Breadth of letters
- *p.* Direction of slant
- *q.* Parallelism of downstroke
- *r.* Left-right tendency
- *s.* Distance between words
- *t'.* Width of left margin
- *t".* Width of right margin

IV. *Depth Component:* related to available energy, vitality, and its control.

- *u.* Degree of pressure
- *v.* Control of pressure
- *w.* Cursiveness of writing, degree of connection

(Reprinted from Thea Stein Lewinson and Joseph Zubin, *Handwriting Analysis.* Copyright 1942 by Columbia University Press.)

tional controls. Conversely, great release in writing, they believe, often concurs with impulsive behavior. The regions where contractions or release are most noticeable are detected by an analytical record sheet and a table of norms. The provision of 20 pages of sample scoring makes this work a definitive text.

Pascal (1944) used in his study twenty-two male college graduates who had been studied carefully by the staff of the Harvard Psychological Clinic. Thirty-six personality variables were measured by the TAT (Chapter XVIII), and thirty-nine variables were secured from samples of spontaneous handwriting, for which each man used his favorite fountain pen. The twenty-two men's scores were changed to rank-order for the group. Rho coefficients were computed and changed to Pearson correlation coefficients. The results show that ten handwriting variables bear a significant relationship to five personality variables. The following correlations are all significant at the 5-per-cent level, and the larger correlations at the one-per-cent level:

1. Play—avoid serious tension, relax;
   with mean upper projection divided by mean mid-zone height .60
   with total vertical expanse .51
   with mean distance between words .60
   with lower-zone fullness; mean lower-loop width divided by
   mean lower-projection height −.45
   multiple regression .78

2. Projectivity—tendency to project one's anxiety, evoked beliefs, mild delusions of self-reference;
   with mid-zone ratio: width divided by height .56
   with lower-zone fullness .53
   multiple regression .78

3. Dominance and defendence vs. abasement;
   with mid-zone ratio .42
   with balanced projections. Upper projections minus lower projections .59
   multiple regression .68

4. Infavoidance—to avoid failure, ridicule, or shame;
   with width of stroke of pen without pressure .46
   with angularity .42
   multiple regression .62

5. Nurturance—to aid and protect a helpless object;
   with primary width of letters m, n, and u .48
   with width of stroke of pen without pressure −.45
   multiple regression .66

Pascal concludes that for his twenty-two male subjects certain aspects of handwriting are significantly related to measured aspects of personality. Because of the small sample he refrains from specifying these variables, but an inspection of his results shows that play and relaxation go with relatively tall upper projections of letters and with distance between words, while projectivity and anxiety are related to relatively narrow letters in the mid-zone and relatively narrow loops on g, j, q, and y. Dominance was found to be higher among those having upper projections longer than lower projections, and the reverse was true for abasement. These findings are in line with those reported from the Bender-Gestalt and other drawing tests in which there is a tendency for the extent of vertical distances to be related to ascendancy and submission, and for cramped or narrow drawing to be related to anxiety.

Another study by Pascal (1943) reported the use of a kymograph to measure pressure in handwriting. He found fairly constant pressure (5.4 grams) for one subject's normal writing on ten occasions during a 2-week period, but the same subject varied from 7.8 to 2.1 when asked to use a heavy or a light touch. Pascal found it necessary to use a standard pen, for the type of instrument used influenced the pressure scores considerably. Among his results are a correlation of .69 between average pressure and range of pressure and of .30 between average pressure and speed. To indicate the significance of pressure, he secured ratings of twenty-one men by seven psychologists who had known them about a year. The five traits for which they were rated were energy, expressiveness, impulsiveness, dominance, and determination. A correlation of .54 was found between average pressure and energy, of .60 between pressure range and energy, and of .63 in a multiple correlation between energy and average pressure and pressure range combined. The correlations between pressure and determination and pressure and dominance were much lower—from .01 to .33 respectively. These results show in general that an important aspect of writing can be measured by this sort of apparatus. Considerable research is needed to devise methods for appraising pressure from ordinary samples of handwriting.

A number of studies have reported results of relatively untrained observers using rough inspection or global approaches. To the trained graphologist these results are analogous to a layman's interpretation of an electrocardiogram or of a complex mathematical formula when the interpreter does not know what the symbols stand for. However, the results are usually much better than chance, hence are worth considering. Graphologists usually insist upon knowing

the sex, age, and handedness of a subject before attempting an interpretation.

Typical of a blind analysis is the report of Castelnuovo-Tedesco
(1948), who secured two samples of handwriting from each subject;
first, a direct copy of a 73-word mimeographed newspaper report; and
second, a spontaneous sample of what each subject could remember
of this report immediately after the sample and his original copy had
been removed. For the "copy" test the subjects were fifty men and
fifty women those IQ's ranged from 68 to 132. Those with IQ's below
82 were excluded from the "spontaneous" writing, hence forty-four
men and thirty-eight women were included. The spontaneous writing
gave clues to vocabulary, grammar, length, punctuation, and style
as well as to the handwriting itself.

A group of six judges were used, three men and three women, only
one of whom had had training in graphology, two had Doctor's degrees in French, two were graduate students, and two were undergraduate students in literature or arts. All had marked aesthetic
interests and interest in the experiment. The judges rated each specimen independently on a 5-point scale based on total impression, on
the six traits shown in Illus. 168. Each trait was rated at a separate

ILLUS. 168. HANDWRITING AND PERSONALITY; CONTINGENCY
COEFFICIENTS BETWEEN MEASURES AND RATINGS OF
SIX JUDGES, AFTER TRAINING

Variable	Copy	Spontaneous
Intelligence	.64 *	.51
Originality	.60	.56
Anxiety	.41	.54
Compulsiveness	.32	.40
Masculinity	.33	.41
Physical sex	71% correct	76% correct

* All figures are significant at the 1 per cent level.

(Arranged from Tables 3 and 4, p. 207, *Genetic Psychology Monograph* No. 37,
by permission of Peter Castelnuovo-Tedesco and the editor of *Genetic Psychology
Monographs*.)

session. In order to provide criteria for these traits, scores were obtained from various tests. To provide IQ's the Verbal Wechsler-
Bellevue was used with college groups, the full W-B Scale with
prisoners, and a Stanford-Binet was given for nine patients in a
state home.

This variety of IQ testing procedure probably lowers any correlation with the results. Intelligence quotients were also taken as

the best available criterion of originality. The other traits were evaluated by multiple-choice Rorschach scores where anxiety was indicated by poor form, color dominance, and outright rejection of the card; compulsiveness by good form and small detail responses; and masculinity-femininity by responses to Cards IV, VI, and VII, which were considered to be characteristic of one sex and not of the other. From Illus. 168 it appears that these judges were able to estimate all of these traits by inspection of samples of handwriting to a substantial degree. The differences between estimates from "copy" work, and from "spontaneous" recall and writing were generally small. In this connection it should be recalled that the "spontaneous" group eliminated eighteen of the subjects with low IQ's from the "copy" group. The "spontaneous" samples yielded somewhat better coefficients for anxiety, compulsiveness, masculinity, and physical sex than the "copy" samples.

A fascinating field of research lies here which seems to offer the advantages of objective measurement of commonly available material.

STUDY GUIDE QUESTIONS

1. What is included in a visual-motor gestalt?
2. What patterns are included in the Bender-Gestalt Test? How are the results interpreted?
3. What stages of maturation did Bender describe?
4. What sorts of clinical findings does the Bender-Gestalt Test supply?
5. How is the Mira Motor Test administered and scored?
6. What patterns were found in the Mosaic Test?
7. How did Machover administer the drawing test and the inquiry period?
8. How does Elkisch determine four factors of personality from drawings?
9. What are the chief advantages of finger painting?
10. How may preference for different media be an indication of personality?
11. Make a list of characteristics of drawings and check each medium against it.
12. Make a list of character traits related to characteristics of drawings. Indicate some needs for more research.
13. What are the main variables in handwriting?
14. How may these variables be interpreted to show contraction and release?
15. Which personal traits did Pascal find were most related to handwriting characteristics?
16. What controls are necessary to develop more insight into the significance of handwriting variables?

CHAPTER XVIII

STORIES AND FANTASIES

In this chapter the appreciation and production of stories and poems are considered from two widely different points of view—the classroom and the clinic. In the classroom much emphasis is placed on style and little on symbolic meaning or methods of production, while in the clinic style is usually a minor consideration, and symbolic content and method are analyzed in great detail and interpreted according to various theories. The tests described here usually stress content and yield results somewhat like those described in Chapter XIX, but the latter stress perceptual organization more than content.

LITERARY APPRECIATION

Although literature is one of the oldest of the arts, attempts to construct standard measuring instruments in this field are among the most recent. These instruments are usually classified as tests of style, appreciation, and composition.

Literary Style

A number of language elements are basic to literary experiences but probably have little, if any, relationship to artistic appreciation. Such elements of language include recognition of spoken or written words and knowledge of the meaning of grammatical forms and punctuation. Tests of discrimination of these language elements have been described in Chapter VII.

Another group of tests, designed to measure discrimination of literary style, are illustrated by two tests from the University of Chicago, reported by Stalnaker (1935). In one of the tests, five different versions of a stanza are presented, and the students are asked to mark one as the best and each of the others as poor for one, and only one, of the following reasons: too sentimental, lack of imagery, faulty rhythm, inappropriate imagery, and poor diction. The version which was most frequently (25 per cent) chosen as best by five hundred scholarship applicants but which was considered by the judges to be poor because of inappropriate imagery and poor diction was:

> Steeped in dust sleeps a pallid lady:
> Thin and tall and blond was she;
> She'd the palest hair and the bluest eyes
> That ever were seen in this hot country
> But loveliness dies and blue eyes slumber,
> And the tomb is dark as dark can be;
> And when I decay, who will remember
> This lady of the West Country?

The selection which was chosen next most frequently (24 per cent) as the best but which the judges considered to be poor because of sentimentality was:

> Here slumbers a wonderful mother
> Bereft and sad her children three
> They sadly mourn for their wonderful mother
> Who taught them all to pray at her knee.
> But mothers, alas, are a gift to heaven
> We all must make, whoe'er we be;
> And now she lives enshrined forever
> In the heart of hearts of her children three.

The following selection which was considered best by the judges was selected by 23 per cent of the students, but 30 per cent of them felt that it lacked imagery:

> Here lies a most beautiful lady:
> Light of step and heart was she;
> I think she was the most beautiful lady
> That ever was in the West Country.
> But beauty vanishes; beauty passes;
> How rare—rare it be!

Five per cent of the students got perfect scores and 20 per cent, zero. The mean was 1.7, which is only slightly above chance success.

In another type of test described by Stalnaker (1935), the students were asked to match seven prose passages with seven short descriptions of the prose passages. Two of the descriptions are given below together with their passages:

Descriptions

Humility and acceptance of the orthodox have never been his weakness. Heterodoxy has always been a quality of the vigorous intellect, and his mind is electrically charged. Thus, when with nippiness and assurance he tells us what he thinks, what relationships he has discovered between the old and the new, we are ready to accept his precise and confident views. He writes with simplicity and clarity, with the firmness of tone that one expects from one whose spirit is firm and unyielding.

He has curiously mingled simplicity and gorgeousness all his own. His delight in expression communicates to the reader delight in what he expresses. He conceives them only by the desire to render his thought clear and concrete. No one can, like him, pile up splendor of description, exotic richness of phraseology, color, tones instinct with music, and then turn in an instant to a sober, solemn, stately simplicity, direct and appealing like the call of a herald. He makes life a procession to the grave but crowns it with garlands.

Passages

When I was a child and was told that our dog and our parrot, with whom I was on intimate terms, were not creatures like myself, but were brutal whilst I was reasonable, I not only did not believe it, but quite consciously and intellectually formed the opinion that the distinction was false; so that afterwards, when Darwin's views were first unfolded to me, I promply said that I had found out all that for myself before I was ten years old; and I am far from sure that my youthful arrogance was not justified; for this sense of the kinship of all forms of life is all that is needed to make Evolution not only a conceivable theory but an inspiring one. St. Anthony was ripe for the Evolution Theory when he preached to the fishes, and St. Francis when he called the birds his little brother. Our vanity . . . had led us to insist on God offering us special terms by placing us apart from and above all the rest of his creatures.

But as when the sun approaches towards the gates of the morning, he first opens a little eye of heaven, and sends away the spirits of darkness, and gives light to a cock, and calls up the lark to matins, and by and by gilds the fringes of a cloud, and peeps over the eastern hills, thrusting out his golden horns, like those which decked the brows of Moses when he was forced to wear a veil, because himself had seen the face of God; and still while a man tells the story the Sun gets up higher, till he shows a fair face and a full light; and then he shines one whole day, under a cloud often, and sometimes weeping great and little showers, and sets quickly; so is man's reason and his life.

Only 4 per cent of five hundred students of English who were scholarship applicants received perfect scores and 21 per cent received a score of zero. The mean score was 2.3 correctly matched out of 7.

In an attempt to substitute actual discrimination for verbal vagaries, Cannon (1937) selected two short passages of approximately one hundred and fifty words, from each of the following authors: Joseph Addison, Ernest Hemingway, Francis Bacon, Charles Lamb, R. L. Stevenson, H. L. Mencken, Samuel Pepys, John Lyly, Jonathan Swift, and Lytton Strachey. Students were presented with the twenty passages typed in random order and asked to indicate the two selections by each author. (The authors' names were not given.) Among 51 college students, 37 succeeded in matching the passages from Bacon, 28 from Pepys, 26 from Lamb, and 26 from Lyly. Only 7 students matched the two paragraphs from Stevenson, 13 from Strachey, 16 from Swift, and 16 from Mencken. Stevenson's work was more frequently matched with Hemingway's than with his own. The average number of correct matches was 4.09.

Such discrimination-of-style tests seem to have been applied principally in college and to have proved extremely difficult even there. The technique is simple enough, however, and the emphasis on first-hand discrimination is good both in testing and in training.

Literary Information

Both discrimination and appreciation of literary work are probably to a large extent based on memory of the literature which one has read. A widely read person with a good memory will almost always make finer discriminations than one with equal ability who has not enjoyed the same experience. Furthermore, although a certain literary work may not be associated with a particular individual's pleasure, still a wide knowledge of literature will certainly affect his feelings toward various masterpieces. From these considerations it follows that discrimination, appreciation, and information in the field of literature are all intimately connected. Quite a number of tests about authors, literary characters, and characteristics of literature are available. Typical of these are the Jordan and Van Wagenen (1933) Scales of Attainment in Literature for the seventh through twelfth grades, and the Cooperative Literary Acquaintance Test of Beers and Paterson (1933) for secondary schools and colleges. Both are composed mainly of 5-choice items which deal with books usually assigned in literature study courses.

The first yields a total literary-age score similar to a mental age and also separate scores for evaluating the emphasis in learning, as follows:

1. *Information about literature,* shown on such items as:

The poem *Miles Standish* is about: (1) a shipwreck, (2) an exploring party, (3) an Indian attack, (4) a courtship, (5) scattering a settlement.

2. *Information about authors:*

The Lady of the Lake was written by: (1) Shakespeare, (2) Scott, (3) Dickens, (4) Cooper, (5) Stevenson.

3. *Outcomes of situations:*

In *Snowbound*, the family spent their evening in: (1) listening to stories, (2) dancing, (3) reading books, (4) playing cards, (5) reading newspapers.

4. *General impressions and characters:*

Holmes' poem *How the Old Horse Won the Bet* is: (1) joyful, (2) inspiring, (3) sad, (4) mysterious, (5) humorous.

The Cooperative Literary Acquaintance Test yields a total score and also separate scores for: (*a*) Pre-Renaissance and Foreign, (*b*) English and American from 1500 to 1900, and (*c*) modern English and American. It consists of 12 pages which can usually be answered in about 40 minutes.

Tests of this sort are by far the most widely used in the field of literature. Research is needed to show the interrelationships of abilities to discriminate, appreciate, remember, and compose literary work.

Sounds and Poetry

In the measurement of responses to oral presentations there appear to be two somewhat independent aspects—sound and meaning. The sound stimuli include various consonant, vowel, pitch, timbre, and rhythm combinations. Memories of sound stimuli may also be important in individual silent reading. The meaning of a selection involves the recognition of simple words and literary references, and also judgments of their appropriateness in a total pattern. The following samples are representative of appreciation tests:

Sounds. The problem of determining the relative pleasantness of speech sounds was approached by Roblee and Washburn (1912), who read aloud a list of nonsense syllables which consisted of one vowel followed by one consonant. The listeners rated each syllable on a 7-point scale of pleasantness. The average ratings showed the following order of preference for vowels:

1. *a* as in *father*	6. $\begin{cases} oo \text{ as in } boot \\ i \text{ as in } hid \end{cases}$
2. *e* as in *get*	
3. *o* as in *wrote*	7. $\begin{cases} o \text{ as in } hot \\ ee \text{ as in } feet \\ aw \text{ as in } bawl \end{cases}$
4. *a* as in *fate*	
5. $\begin{cases} i \text{ as in } write \\ a \text{ as in } hat \end{cases}$	8. *oi* as in *boil*
	9. *u* as in *mud*

The differences between the best and worst were so small and the range for each vowel so large that there seemed to be no marked agreement. Consonants showed slightly greater average differences in the following order of pleasantness: l, m, n, v, th, s, z, p, d, b, zh, t, sh, k, and g. Givler (1915) found similar results from experiments in which vowels and consonants were combined in various ways, and reported that the explosive consonants and the shorter vowels were judged to be less agreeable than the others. No standard test using such judgments seems to have been made.

Downey (1927) asked college students to record their reactions to single words. In evaluating the responses she used the following classification similar to that which Bullough (1910) used with colors. (A few examples from her observers are also given.)

1. Objective responses to the sound or appearance of a word: *Murmur*—the sound is the meaning
2. Associative responses: *Drowsy*—sleepy, or *Lily*—visualization of one fall lily in a bare space
3. Physical responses within the subject: *Pendulous*—feeling of being suspended
4. Symbolic, an arbitrary association: *Melancholy*—a green and purple word
5. Personalized: The word is treated as a person: *Twilight*—word looks half asleep

Downey found no marked tendency, as Bullough had, for a person to use mainly one type of response. The three subjects who made the largest number of symbolized and personalized responses were those chiefly interested in literature and visual art, but the most "literary" person made many objective responses. No clear relation between type of response and literary ability was demonstrated, but the test needs to be refined and enlarged to give it reliability and internal consistency. This method may possibly be made to appraise important types of responses better than other methods.

Prose and Poetry. A number of tests have appeared which ask a person to indicate relative literary merit among a series of short samples. In none of these is any definition of literary merit provided; hence emotional appeal, content, clarity, and style are probably effective in unknown amounts. In view of the difficulty of analyzing these elements, however, the standard tests doubtless represent a marked advance over cruder methods of rating literary appreciation of individuals.

Three test forms were prepared by Carroll (1935), one for use in junior high school, another in senior high school, and a third in college. Each form consists of a 16-page booklet. On each page four short paragraphs of approximately one hundred words each are printed. The paragraphs on each page are all concerned with the same topic. Thus, in the college test the topics are a man, an interior, a sunset, a fire, a tryst, spring, a woman, homecoming, wind, literary criticism, twilight, remarks to a son, delirium, and sunrise. The paragraphs on each page were selected to represent four levels of literary excellence on the basis of reputation of the authors and judgments of experts (Illus. 169). No elaborate analyses of judgments were made to insure equally often-noticed steps between the levels of literary excellence, but the ranking of the four samples by judges showed marked agreement in making first and last choices, and fairly marked agreement in selecting second and third choices. The student is asked

ILLUS. 169. SAMPLES OF A PROSE APPRECIATION TEST

AN INTERIOR *

A

I went with the little maid into a gorgeously decorated bedroom, all of cream color and light blue that blended prettily. The bed was a great, wide affair of beautifully carved and ornamented wood, painted creamy white with blue and gold trimmings. There was a wonderful bureau and a dressing table to match, and in one corner of the room a mirror that went from floor to ceiling. I had to hold my breath.

B

Lollie had never seen such a pretty room, and it made her gasp to see how pretty the furniture was, as well as how pretty the rugs were, and the curtains at the windows and the pictures on the wall, but what she really liked best was that furniture, for it looked comfortable as well as pretty, and she knew it must have cost hundreds and hundreds of dollars. She wished she could live and die in that one room, it was so pretty.

C

An air of Sabbath had descended on the room. The sun shone brightly through the window, spreading a golden lustre over the white walls; only along the north wall, where the bed stood, a half shadow lingered. . . . The table had been spread with a white cover; upon it lay the open hymn book, with the page turned down. Beside the hymn book stood a bowl of water; beside that lay a piece of white cloth. . . . Kjersti was tending the stove, piling the wood in diligently. . . . Sorine sat in the corner, crooning over a tiny bundle; out of the bundle at intervals came faint, wheezy chirrups, like the sounds that rise from a nest of young birds.

D

Major Prime had the west sitting-room. It was lined with low bookcases, full of old, old books. There was a fireplace, a winged chair, a broad couch, a big desk of dark seasoned mahogany, and over the mantel a steel engraving of Robert E. Lee. The low windows at the back looked out upon the wooded green of the ascending hill; at the front was a porch which gave a view of the valley.

* KEY: First, C; second, D; third, A; fourth, B.

(Carroll, 1935, p. 3. By permission of the Educational Test Bureau, Minneapolis, Minn.)

to rank the four selections on each page in the order of his estimate of its "literary merit." The pages are arranged in order of ease of discrimination ranging from the easiest, which was correctly ranked by approximately 60 per cent of a group, to the most difficult, which was ranked correctly by only 30 per cent.

Both split-half reliability and retest reliability for groups of three hundred students were approximately .70. In scoring 2 points were allowed for each correct ranking of the best and worst selections and one point each for the second and third selections. The total score for each page was therefore 6, and for the whole test, 84. The mean scores for college freshmen were 45.9, for sophomores, 47.0, for juniors, 49.8, and for seniors, 52.8. Centiles are furnished for each class in college. Grade norms in junior and senior high schools are also provided for their respective forms.

A test designed to measure poetry appreciation was published by Rigg (1937). Forty short selections by recognized poets were paired with forty other inferior selections on the basis of similarity of central thought. The task was to choose the best selection in each pair. Two equivalent forms were found to correlate .815 among 342 college students.

A multiple-choice test of literary appreciation was described by Fox (1938). The test requires that omissions in various passages of prose and poetry by famous authors be filled in by choosing one of four alternatives. It was found that graduates in literary subjects chose the words written by the author more frequently than did graduates in nonliterary subjects. From introspections Fox concluded that the students of literature employed a "literary feeling" and the others tried to exercise "critical judgment."

STORY PRODUCTION AND WORD ASSOCIATIONS

Analyses of Fantasies

Fantasies are stories which are normally recognized by the teller as make-believe. They may express a large variety of themes, some of which are wishes of the author. Some wishes are deeply disguised, some quite obvious. Much fantasy is expressed in painting, folk lore, drama, and dancing. Clinical experience has often shown that analyses of fantasy reveal an individual's needs, his method of meeting them, and his attitudes toward himself. Fantasy analysis may show that a successful person may be making a fine record as a compensation for feelings of inferiority or a physical disability. Clinicians believe that a free expression of fantasy should generally be encouraged, since it relieves tensions and is usually less harmful than repression. Fantasies of death or anxiety often give considerable relief and reveal causes of emotional disturbances which must be removed if one is to do his best. Clinicians and psychiatrists use fantasy analyses as one of the principal means of discovering both superficial and deeper needs.

Thematic Apperception Test (TAT). This test was developed over a period of years at the Harvard Psychological Clinic by Dr. Henry A. Murray and his associates (1943). A series of twenty somewhat ambiguous pictures are presented to a person and he is encouraged to tell spontaneous stories about them. The pictures are effective in three ways: they stimulate fanciful imagination and make the subject less self-conscious, encourage the subject to react to certain common conflict situations, allow more systematic and comparable appraisals of individuals than might be made without standard pictures.

The TAT were standardized on groups of persons between fourteen and forty years of age. Of the 1943 set of thirty-one pictures, eleven are suitable for both sexes, seven are used only for boys and men, seven for girls and women, and one each for boys, girls, men, women, boys and girls, and adults. Illustration 170 is a sample from this series.

The pictures were selected from a larger series according to the amount of information that each contributed to the final diagnosis. The most revealing pictures were usually found to be those which contained a representation of a person of about the same age and sex as the subject.

Figures are included which may represent father, mother, siblings, and marital partners in various situations of acceptance or rejection. The first ten pictures are of usual situations; the last ten are vague, dramatic, or bizarre, and there is one white blank space. The first ten are to be shown during one hour on one day, and the second ten during one hour on the next day or several days later.

Congenial surroundings and a sympathetic examiner are essential in administering this test, because good results depend upon creativity. Even in good circumstances about one third of the stories will usually not contain personal elements. The subject is seated comfortably in a chair, usually with his back to the examiner, and one of two sets of instructions is read at the first session (Murray, 1943, p. 3):

Form A (suitable for adolescents and for adults of average intelligence and sophistication).

This is a test of imagination, one form of intelligence. I am going to show you some pictures, one at a time; and your task will be to make up as

ILLUS. 170. THEMATIC APPERCEPTION TEST NO. 12F

(By permission of Dr. H. A. Murray and the Harvard University Press.)

dramatic a story as you can for each. Tell what has led up to the event shown in the picture, describe what is happening at the moment, what the characters are feeling and thinking; and then give the outcome. Speak your thoughts as they come to your mind. Do you understand? Since you have 50 minutes for ten pictures, you can devote about 5 minutes to each story. Here is the first picture.

Form B (suitable for children, for adults of little education or intelligence, and for psychotics).

This is a story-telling test. I have some pictures here that I am going to show you, and for each picture I want you to make up a story. Tell what has happened before and what is happening now. Say what the people are feeling and thinking and how it will come out. You can make up any kind of story you please. Do you understand? Well, then, here is the first picture. You have 5 minutes to make up a story. See how well you can do.

After finishing the first story the subject is commended (if there is any ground for it), and then reminded of the instructions (unless he has obeyed them faithfully). For example, the examiner might say:

"That was certainly an interesting story, but you forgot to say how the boy behaved when his mother criticized him and you left the narrative hanging in the air. There was no real outcome. You spent 3½ minutes on that story. Your others can be a little longer. Now see how well you can do with the second picture."

Young children, people of other cultures, and psychotics often need a good deal of encouragement before they will speak freely. In administering the test to extremely reticent children it is permissible to offer rewards. The examiner may say, "I'll give you a present if you tell me some nice long stories today"; or, "If you do well now I'll tell *you* a very exciting story when you're through"; or, "There's a prize for the one who tells the best stories."

At the second session either Form A or Form B instructions are given as follows:

Form A. The procedure today is the same as before, only this time you can give freer rein to your imagination. Your first ten stories were excellent, but you confined yourself pretty much to the facts of everyday life. Now I would like to see what you can do when you disregard the commonplace realities and let your imagination have its way, as in a myth, fairy story, or allegory. Here is Picture No. 1.

Form B. Today I am going to show you some more pictures. It will be easier for you this time because the pictures I have here are much better, more interesting. You told me some fine stories the other day. Now I want to see whether you can make up a few more. Make them even more exciting than you did last time if you can—like a dream or fairy tale. Here is the first picture.

Blank Card. Card No. 16 is accompanied by a special instruction. The examiner says:

"See what you can see on this blank card. Imagine some picture there and describe it to me in detail." If the subject does not succeed in doing this, the examiner says, "Close your eyes and picture something." After the subject has given a full description of his imagery, the examiner says, "Now tell me a story about it."

The stories should be recorded stenographically, or by a sound recorder, or by detailed notes. A subsequent interview is held immediately after the second session or within a few days, at which the subject is urged to indicate the source of each theme or incident in each story. He is reminded of the plot of each story, if necessary.

The instructions state that the interpreter of the material

. . . should have a background of clinical experience, observing, interviewing and testing patients of all sorts; and, if he is to get much below the surface, knowledge of psychoanalysis and some practice in translating the imagery of dreams and ordinary speech into elementary psychological components. In addition he should have had months of training in the use of this specific test, *much practice in analyzing stories when it is possible to check each conclusion against the known facts of thoroughly studied personalities.*

Before starting to interpret the stories, the examiner should know the sex and age of the subject and his siblings, his vocational and marital status, whether his parents are dead or separated, and other pertinent relationships. The following three steps are in Murray's interpretation:

a. First, one determines the character with whom the subject has identified himself (hero) and records the strength of his needs or drives. The needs described by Murray (1938, pp. 211–213) are as follows:

I. Primary (viscerogenic) needs:
    1. *n* Air
       a) n Inspiration;
       b) n Expiration;
    2. *n* Water;
    3. *n* Food;
    4. *n* Sex;
    5. *n* Lactation;
    6. *n* Urination;
    7. *n* Defecation;
    8. *n* Harmavoidance (avoidance of physical pain);
    9. *n* Noxavoidance (avoidance of noxious substances);
    10. *n* Heatavoidance;
    11. *n* Coldavoidance;
    12. *n* Sentience (sensuous gratification).
II. Secondary (psychogenic) needs:
    1. Actions associated with inanimate objects:
       a) n Acquisition (acquisitive attitude);
       b) n Conservance (conserving attitude);
       c) n Order (orderly attitude);
       d) n Retention (retentive attitude);
       e) n Construction (constructive attitude);
    2. Actions expressing ambition, will-to-power, desire for accomplishment and prestige:
       a) n Superiority (ambitious attitude);
       b) n Achievement (achievant attitude);
       c) n Recognition (self-forwarding attitude);
       d) n Exhibition (exhibitionistic attitude), combined with *n* Recog-

nition in Explorations in Personality, and the opposite of n Seclusion;

3. Desires and actions which defend the status or avoid humiliation:
   a) n Inviolacy (inviolate attitude), divided into three needs:
      1) n Infavoidance (infavoidant attitude), to prevent humiliation;
      2) n Defendance (defensive attitude);
      3) n Counteraction (counteractive attitude), need to redeem the self after failure, etc.;
4. Needs having to do with human power exerted, resisted, or yielded to:
   a) n Dominance (dominative attitude);
   b) n Deference (deferent attitude);
   c) n Similance (suggestible attitude);
   d) n Autonomy (autonomous attitude);
   e) n Contrarience (contrarient attitude);
5. Sado-masochistic needs:
   a) n Aggression (aggressive attitude);
   b) n Abasement (abasive attitude);
6. n Blamavoidance (blamavoidant attitude);
7. Needs regarding affection between people;
   a) n Affiliation (affiliative attitude);
   b) n Rejection (rejective attitude);
   c) n Nurturance (nurturant attitude);
   d) n Succorance (succorant attitude);
8. n Play (playful attitude), included in list with some hesitation;
9. Need to ask and to tell:
   a) n Cognizance (inquiring attitude);
   b) n Exposition (expositive attitude);
10. Needs associated with energy:
    a) n Activity;
    b) n Passivity.[1]

The strength of each drive in each story is rated from 1 to 5, with 1 representing a slight occurrence and 5 a great *intensity, duration, frequency or importance in the plot.* After the twenty stories have been scored, the ratings for each variable are added and compared with norms for the subject's age and sex.

b. Second, one determines the "press," that is, the types and strengths of the environmental forces which press upon the "hero." Particular attention is given to imaginary situations or persons not represented in the picture, to the type of persons who exert the most press, and also to the absence of beneficial associates. The presses as listed by Murray (1938, p. 291) are as follows:

[1] From *Explorations in Personality* by H. A. Murray *et al.* Copyright 1938 by Oxford University Press.

1. *p* Family Insupport
2. *p* Danger or Misfortune
3. *p* Lack or Loss
4. *p* Retention, Withholding Objects
5. *p* Rejection, Unconcern and Scorn
6. *p* Rival, Competing Contemporary
7. *p* Birth of Sibling
8. *p* Aggression
9. *Fp* Aggression-Dominance, Punishment (fusion press)
10. *p* Dominance, Coercion and Prohibition
11. *Fp* Dominance-Nurturance
12. *p* Nurturance, Indulgence
13. *p* Succorance, Demands for Tenderness
14. *p* Deference, Praise, Recognition
15. *p* Affiliation, Friendships
16. *p* Sex
17. *p* Deception or Betrayal

Intraorganic Press:
18. *p* Illness
19. *p* Operations
20. *p* Inferiority [2]

c. Third, the interaction of the hero and the environment is summarized to show typical patterns or "themas," which are abstracts of the dynamic patterns and their outcomes. These patterns show certain facts, for example, to what extent the hero strives to make things happen or waits for things to happen, how much he helps others and they help him, whether he gets properly punished or let off, and the ratio of happy and unhappy endings (Illus. 172). These abstracts are made by taking each unusually high *need* of the hero and noting the press which supports or defeats it. An inspection of these need-press combinations may yield significant over-all thematic patterns, which are regarded by Murray as good "leads" or hypotheses to be verified by other methods.

Although Murray points out that the use of the TAT is not dependent upon any particular theory of personality, he distinguishes three layers of normal personality.

a. The inner layer is composed of repressed unconscious needs rarely known or expressed in their crude form. These are usually expressed symbolically in the second TAT session, but cannot be known without careful psychoanalytical interpretation.

b. The middle layer contains conscious needs which are known but not usually confessed. They are manifested in secret and when

[2] *Ibid.*

one is off guard. These are usually shown in either the first or the second TAT session.

c. The outer layer consists of tendencies which are publicly acknowledged and openly manifested in behavior. Stories composed in the first TAT session are usually more closely related to the outer layer of personality.

Murray points out that the TAT themas often reflect the exact opposite of one's obvious usual behavior. Strong but inhibited needs appear in the TAT findings. Thus correlations of .40 or more between TAT ratings and behavior ratings of the same traits of college men were found for traits which have cultural sanction, for example, creation, dominance, exposition, nurturance, passivity, and dejection. For other traits without cultural sanctions, for example, sex behavior, the correlations were from —.33 to —.74.

Additional TAT Studies. The TAT has stimulated a large number of researches, some of which have applied the materials to various groups and others have proposed variations in administration and scoring. Only a few samples are mentioned here.

R. N. Sanford (1943) analyzed children's stories in the extensive Harvard Growth Study of School Children and described interrelations between personality, physique, and environmental conditions. He combined those that correlated with each other in the neighborhood of .40 into syndromes and gave them names which were intended to describe common elements. Thus one syndrome called "orderly production" included creativity, endurance, and needs for order, construction, and counteraction. This syndrome correlated only .16 with mental age, but .70 with school grades when age was held fairly constant. Another syndrome called "conscientious effort" included deliberation, conjunctivity, endurance, and needs for understanding, construction, counteraction, blamavoidance, and order. The average correlation between pairs of variables in the orderly-production syndrome was .52, and in the conscientious-effort syndrome .58. He described twenty such syndromes which form an interesting basis for personality study.

One example of clear-cut results from the use of the TAT is reported by Klebanoff (1947) who compared alcoholics with normal men. The essential findings are summarized in Illus. 171, which gives the mean percentage of occurrence of all the major thematic categories. The individual records showed a striking similarity to the group means as was borne out by inspection and by the standard deviations presented in Illus. 171. The alcoholics showed much greater emotional stress and failure of the central character, and

ILLUS. 171. COMPARISON OF NORMAL AND ALCOHOLIC
MALES ON THE TAT

| | Percentage of Total Themas | | |
| | Alcoholic | | Normal |
Major Categories	Mean	SD	Mean
Physical Aggression	21	9.8	33
Nonphysical Aggression	17	7.9	20
Internal Emotional Stress	48	11.3	25
Miscellaneous Themas	14	7.0	22
	100		100

Successes and Failures:			
Failure:			
Central Character	59	15.8	35
Success:			
Central Character	10	4.1	28
Failure:			
Minor Characters	9	4.1	20
Success:			
Minor Characters	22	12.5	17
	100		100

Areas of Failure:		
Economic Failure	6	6.2
Social Failure	37	9.1
Power Failure	42	8.9
Love Failure	15	6.5
	100	

(After Klebanoff, 1947. By permission of the Editor of *Journal of Consulting Psychology*.)

much less physical aggression, and failure of minor characters than the normal group.

Illustration 171 also analyzes the failures among the alcoholics' themas of the central characters in terms of economic, social, power, and love inferiority. Failure at the power level predominates in the alcoholics and accounts for nearly half of all the failures of central characters. Of the 17 patients studied, 7 place greatest emphasis upon power failures, 6 are dominated by social failure, and the remaining 4 reveal an equality of social and power failure. Among all patients power and social failures were more numerous than economic and love failures.

L. D. Eron (1948) points out that there is a serious lack of adequate normative data for the TAT. Many investigators have published characteristics as representative of clinical groups, but only a few of them have given frequencies substantiating these diagnostic cues. The norms seem to be the result of subjective impressions left after the examination of persons who have particular diagnoses.

Eron's procedure was to follow Murray's directions in presenting all twenty cards to adult males at the Harvard University Clinic and to male patients who had been diagnosed as schizophrenics in the Ventura Veterans Hospital. A total of one thousand stories containing 1,988 themes was recorded for all subjects. The difference in the total number of themes was not significant—963 schizophrenic stories and 1,025 student voices. With rare exceptions no themes appeared in one group which were absent from the other, and in those few categories in which this did occur the frequency of the theme was no more than one or two. More than a hundred comparisons were made between the two groups, but differences that were significant at or beyond the 5-per-cent level were found in only thirteen themes. It appeared that the greatest difference is among themes of moral struggle where students exceed the schizophrenics by a significant number. However, such themes of moral struggle have been given as one of the diagnostic cues in schizophrenic patients. The other themes likewise give rise to serious questions concerning the diagnostic validity of the particular theme.

Eron has further compared the most frequent themes for college students and schizophrenics and finds that the college students give significantly more imaginary and symbolic stories, more themes of guilt, remorse, pressure from parents, and disequilibrium than do the schizophrenics. The schizophrenics give more themes of religion, retribution, pressure, illness, or death of heterosexual partner, and succorance from the parents. Eron finds, however, that the most significant results are the trait similarities between the two groups. There are no broad group differences. At least some of the schizophrenics fall into every one of the normal categories. He feels, therefore, that the responses on the TAT cards are determined more by the actual stimulus cards than by the personality deviations of the subjects.

Lastly, Eron lists, picture by picture, a tabulation of the most common themes appearing in one thousand TAT stories of 25 hospitalized schizophrenics and of 25 nonhospitalized students (Illus. 172). Both groups are comparable in education, age, sex, IQ, veteran status, and marital status. All are male veterans with an IQ of at least 100. All the themes were related by at least ten subjects. For sixteen of the twenty cards the number of themes showing disequilibrium is much greater than the number of themes showing equilibrium. There were only forty-five instances of confusion or indecision about the sex of the central character in one thousand stories, and a few more of these came from college students than from patients. In the light of these results it is felt that a particular examiner must be cautious

ILLUS. 172. PICTURE BY PICTURE TABULATION OF COMMON THEMES
IN TAT STORIES

[Included in this table are responses of 25 hospitalized schizophrenics and 25 nonhospitalized college students. Both groups are comparable in terms of age, education, sex, IQ, veteran status, marital status. All are male veterans of ages 20
to 34 years, with twelve to seventeen years' education, and an IQ of at least 100.
Twelve are married and thirty-eight are single. All themes related by at least
ten subjects for each picture are included.]

Theme	Definition	Fre-quency
Picture I		
pressure from parents	parent figures are prohibitive, compelling, censuring, punishing, quarreling with child	26
aspiration	dreaming of future, hoping for future, determination	26
vacillation	wasting time, putting off a distasteful task, procrastination, loitering	12
curiosity	wondering or inquiring about construction of object, contents of room, etc.	11
inadequacy	realization, whether justified or not, of lack of success	10
belongingness	desire expressed to be with or accepted by peers	10
Picture II		
aspiration	dreaming of future, hoping for future, determination	26
economic pressure	compelled to or prohibited from, or limited in doing something because of lack of money	21
Picture III BM *		
pressure from parents	parent figures are prohibitive, compelling, censuring, punishing, quarreling with child	13
suicide	attempted or completed, preoccupation with	12
generalized restriction	environment is generally frustrating	12
Picture IV		
pressure from partner	partner is prohibitive, compelling, censuring, punishing or quarreling, etc.	20
partner comforts	a positive relationship, sets at ease, conciliates, regales	18
Picture V		
pressure from parents	parent is prohibitive, compelling, censuring, punishing, quarreling with child	20
curiosity	wondering or inquiring about construction of object, contents of room, etc.	12
Picture VI BM		
pressure from parent	parent is prohibitive, compelling, censuring, punishing, quarreling with child	21
departure from parent	child is taking leave of parental home	18

* The initials stand for B (Boy), M (Man), F (Female).

ILLUS. 172. PICTURE BY PICTURE TABULATION OF COMMON THEMES
IN TAT STORIES *(Cont'd)*

Theme	*Definition*	*Frequency*
filial obligation	child feels it his duty to remain with, comply with, or support parents	13
disappointment to parent	child does not live up to parent's expectations	13
concern of parent	parent is worried over physical or mental well-being of child	11
aggression toward environment	robbery, accident, murder (of unspecified individual)	10
Picture VII BM		
succorance from parents	child seeks or receives aid, advice, consolation, protection from parent	31
pressure from parents	parent is prohibitive, compelling, censuring, punishing, quarreling with child	11
Picture VIII BM		
aspiration	dreaming of future, hoping for future, determination	23
aggression from impersonal source	war, accident, nature, animal, disease	10
Picture IX BM		
retirement	central character asleep, resting, etc.	41
Picture X		
partner contentment	serenity in marital life, satisfaction with partner, marital bliss, heterosexual bliss	27
Picture XI		
aggression from impersonal source	war, accident, nature, animal, disease	22
aggression towards peer	physical harm inflicted or intended for individual of same sex and approximately same age—physical violence between two animals	10
Picture XII M		
religion	prayer, seeking consolation from God, religious conflict, religious awakening	19
death or illness of son		14
Picture XIII MF		
guilt-remorse		22
death or illness of partner		18
illicit sex	extra- or pre-marital heterosexual relation, non-incestuous	18
aggression toward partner	physical harm inflicted or intended for heterosexual partner	16

ILLUS. 172. PICTURE BY PICTURE TABULATION OF COMMON THEMES
IN TAT STORIES (*Cont'd*)

Theme	Definition	Frequency
Picture XIV		
aspiration	dreaming of future, hope for future, determination	16
tranquillity	peace of mind, content with environment and own accomplishments	15
Picture XV		
death or illness of partner		17
religion	prayer, seeking consolation from God, religious conflict, religious awakening	16
Picture XVI	Since there is no individual category of sufficient frequency, only more general categories can be included.	
intrapersonal disequilibrium		17
interpersonal equilibrium		15
impersonal disequilibrium		13
intrapersonal equilibrium		12
interpersonal disequilibrium		10
Picture XVII BM		
self-esteem	egocentricity, self-confidence, self-respect, self-approbation	14
Picture XVIII BM		
drunkenness		22
succorance from peer	seek or receive aid, advice, consolation, protection from peer	17
pressure from peer	friends are prohibitive, compelling, censuring, punishing, quarreling	15
Picture XIX		
aggression from impersonal source	war, accident, nature, animal, disease	28
imaginary theme level		11
Picture XX		
vacillation	wasting time, putting off a distasteful task, procrastination, loitering	23
loneliness	central character misses someone, is an outcast, friendless, homeless	18

(From Eron (1948), page 393. By permission of Leonard D. Eron and the editors of the *Journal of Consulting Psychology*.)

in using the TAT as a diagnostic instrument, and in applying the cues reported in the literature by various investigators.

A large number of other studies on the application of the TAT have reported:

   a. Variations in scoring and interpretation

   b. Group administration with responses to a check list of prepared stories

   c. Comparisons between TAT scores and variations of age, sex, and conditions of administration

   d. Comparisons with dreams and autobiographies

   e. Norms for stutterers, neurotics, the mentally deficient, and other clinical groups

   f. Anti-Semitism and attitudes toward labor as reflected in some of the TAT results

Much more work is needed on analyzing the results of fantasy tests and to give the interpretations clearer meanings. One of the most rewarding uses of the TAT is not a metricized score or profile but a picture of the way a person is reacting to his drives and opportunities.

Symonds Picture-Story Test. Another set of twenty pictures, all drawn by Lynd Ward, were issued by Symonds (1948) to be used to study adolescents. It is not designed to yield a clinical diagnosis or indicate learning status or potentialities. It is a procedure used to study drives, conflicts, and methods of dealing with drives, and should be of value in planning psychotherapy. There is evidence that the test has some therapeutic value of its own. It contains twenty pictures separated into Set A and Set B. Set A is to be used at the first sitting and B on a later day. Set B usually gives the more significant results. The same pictures are used for both boys and girls, because Symonds found that sex differences were relatively insignificant in the interpretation of stories.

The test, which is to be administered only after good rapport has been established, is introduced as a test of creative imagination. About one hour is needed for each set of pictures. Following Set B there should be a "period of association" in which the examiner reads back the story while the subject holds the corresponding picture. After each story is read the subject is asked where it came from, and the answers are recorded. The analysis of results yields a series of hypotheses regarding underlying motives, parent-child relations, and modes of operating. The frequency of the various topics or themes used by a person is compared with a frequency table for adolescents. Symonds' *Adolescent Fantasy* (1949) gives case material and elaborates on the use of this test.

Picture-Frustration. Rosenzweig (1945) described a picture-association test which is in some respects similar to a word-association test and to a thematic-apperception test. His stimuli contain both pictures and words, and the test administration limits the responses in both length and content. Each of twenty-four cartoon-like pictures illustrates a fairly common frustrating situation for one of two persons in the picture, who is always shown on the right side of the picture (Illus. 173). On the left is the other person who is saying certain words which either describe the situation more fully or actu-

ILLUS. 173. ROSENZWEIG'S FRUSTRATION TESTS

(Situation 2 is of the superego frustration type; the other three are ego-blocking types. Copyright, 1948, by Saul Rosenzweig.)

ally intensify the frustrating situation for the person on the right. Features and facial expression are purposely omitted to facilitate the projection of feelings by the person being tested. The stimulus pictures include sixteen ego-blocking situations when the person is directly frustrated, as by being splashed with muddy water by a car. Eight other pictures are intended to involve the superego by means of accusations, charges, or incriminations. In these attacks there is an implication that the blocking of the ego has already occurred. They add insult to injury!

The subject, in order to show his reaction, is asked to write in an empty space above the picture on the right the first reply that comes into his mind. "Avoid being humorous. Work as quickly as you can." Early experiences showed that comical replies did not allow the same type of scoring as serious replies. Speed is emphasized in order to avoid studied evasions.

The examiner reads the words of the character on the left aloud, then asks the subject to think of a reply and write it down. The total for all twenty-four responses is recorded, whether in group or individual administration. If the administration is for a single individual, a subsequent period is used for having the subject read aloud the responses he has written. Tone of voice, manners, and hesitations are noted and nonleading questions are asked about very brief responses.

Each response is scored on two scales—Direction of Aggression, and Ego Situation. Aggression or blame can take three directions: (a) toward the environment, including other persons, (b) toward self, and (c) toward no one, when it is claimed that no one is to blame, that the situation is not significant, or that just waiting will correct it. The Ego Situation may also take three main forms: (a) obstacle-dominance—the "barrier" is emphasized, (b) ego-dominance—the defense of subject (ego) plays the chief role, or (c) need-persistence—the need for solving the problem or for relieving the situation is stressed.

Sample answers derived from one hundred normal individuals and fifty mental patients are given. In scoring a test the individual answers are classified and entered on a record blank which has printed on it the expected scores of twelve items. These expected scores are used as criteria of normalcy, and a Group Conformity Rating (GCR) is secured by computing the percentage of complete agreement with the criteria. Thus if half of the subject's scores on the twelve items agree with the criteria, his GCR is 50 per cent. GCR's for a group of 50 normal adult men averaged 72, for 50 normal adult women 68, and for 50 mental patients 57. Additional scores are secured to show the frequency of each type of response. Thus the median per cents for one hundred and fifty normal men and women were approximately 40 per cent extrapunitive (blame environment), 30 per cent intrapunitive (blame self), and 30 per cent impunitive (blame no one). The median percentages were approximately 20, 50, and 30 for obstacle-dominance, ego-dominance, and need-persistence respectively. Sex differences were not outstanding on these adult samples. Other scores were also computed for responses to ego-blocking and superego-blocking situations, and for trend or tendency to change from one type of response to another.

The interpretation of scores is not simple, but in general a paranoid tendency shows itself in excessive blame of others, and a depressed or guilt complex in blame of self. Constructiveness is shown by high scores in need for problem solution. Emphasis on the role of the barrier is a poor or weak adjustment. High ego-dominance scores are typical of extremely selfish or schizophrenic patterns of behavior. There are, of course, many combinations. The uses of the test are being investigated.

Insight into Human Motives Test.   Helen Sargent (1944) attacked the problem of devising a verbal paper-and-pencil test which would present somewhat ambiguous stimuli to subjects in such a way that they would reveal their own feelings and methods of perceiving and organizing material, without being aware of the purpose of the test. She chose the title, Test of Insight into Human Motives, in order to arouse interest and to mislead subjects as to the nature of the test. The test consists of items called armatures, because they are bare frameworks of conflict situations. Each item describes an individual in a conflict situation. The characteristics (except sex) of the imaginary person are not described, proper names are not used, and indications of feeling are avoided in most of the items. Thirty-six items were finally adopted, of which 24 were applicable to either men or women, 6 to men, and 6 to women. From these, two forms of fifteen armatures each were assembled for each sex. Sample items are shown in Illus. 174. Recently two forms of ten armatures each have been recommended which produce sufficient data and simplify computations. The six main areas of conflict sampled in each form are: family, opposite sex, social and friendship relations, vocation, religion or beliefs, and health.

The subjects were tested singly and in small groups with no time limits. About an hour was adequate for one form, and those who had already taken one form usually took less time on the second. Blank sheets of paper were issued with instructions to answer the two questions which follow each armature, as part of a test to analyze what

ILLUS. 174. SARGENT'S INSIGHT INTO HUMAN MOTIVES TEST

Form 1. Men

I. 1. A young man who is working or studying away from home gets a letter from his mother, after the death of his father, asking him to move back home.
   a. What did he do and why?
   b. How did he feel?

II. 2. A young man has acquired religious and political opinions away from home which are in direct conflict with his parents' ideas. He is home for a visit and religious and political subjects are discussed.
   a. What did he do and why?
   b. How did he feel?

III. 3. A young man falls in love. In order to marry he must give up his studies and make some money immediately.
   a. What did he do and why?
   b. How did he feel?

IV. 4. A young man gets a good deal of razzing because he spends his week-ends at home instead of dating.
   a. What did he do and why?
   b. How did he feel?

V. 5. A young man's father has always looked forward to having his son take over his business and has educated him for it. The son becomes interested in another vocation.
   a. What did he do and why?
   b. How did he feel?

Form 1. Women

I. 1. A girl who is working or studying away from home gets a letter from her mother, after her father's death, asking her to move back home.
   a. What did she do and why?
   b. How did she feel?

II. 2. A girl has acquired religious and political opinions away from home which are in direct conflict with her parents' ideas. She is at home for a visit, and religious and political subjects are discussed.
   a. What did she do and why?
   b. How did she feel?

III. 3. A girl gets the impression that others are discussing her. On several occasions she thinks conversation has stopped or the subject changed when she enters the room.
   a. What did she do and why?
   b. How did she feel?

IV. 4. A girl is disapproved by her friends because she spends her week-ends at home instead of dating.
   a. What did she do and why?
   b. How did she feel?

V. 5. A girl's parents have always looked forward to having her follow a particular career and have educated her for it. She becomes interested in something else.
   a. What did she do and why?
   b. How did she feel?

(By permission of Dr. Helen Sargent and the editors of *Psychological Review Monographs*.)

people do and feel under various circumstances. The subjects were asked to write for an hour, and to write first on the most interesting items since they might not have time to finish all of them. It was pointed out that there are no right and wrong answers, but that the explanations should show insight into the character. The test also may be given and answered orally.

In developing a scoring system a large number of variations were noted, such as number of questions answered, number of lines written, conflict areas, emotional words, elaborations, irrelevant statements, conflict solutions, philosophizing, and clichés. From the answers given by forty-five volunteer students from college psychology classes and twenty patients at a state hospital, scoring categories were prepared. Later when additional data were available these were revised. These categories were much influenced by Murray's analyses of "need" and "press," but Sargent felt that fewer, less-overlapping categories were preferable. She did a great deal of careful work in defining categories, checking the reliability of scoring, and determining the stimulus value of each armature.

In scoring and interpreting a record, the scorable phrases are identified and classified into categories, then raw and weighted scores are computed and changed to standard scores. Lastly standard scores and ratios are compared with norms. Three main categories (A, E, and M) are used. The twelve A categories (Illus. 175) include all affective reactions, including such feeling verbs or adjectives as "She

ILLUS. 175. SARGENT'S SCORING CATEGORIES

A. *Affective expressions regarding the central character:*
1. Frustrating: She felt trapped. His death was a shock.
2. Challenging: The job struck him as a challenge.
3. Aggressive: He wanted to get ahead in life.
4. Passive: She just had to take it.
5. Evasive: She put it out of her mind.
6. Depressive: He felt much discouraged.
7. Pleasant: So glad to see them.
8. Positive: She wanted to help all she could.
9. Negative: He didn't like her attitude.
10. Guilt or inadequacy: She felt self-conscious.
11. Conflict and confusion: He didn't know what to think.
12. Rationalization: She couldn't help it.

E. *Ego activity:*
El. Elaboration: Additions to the armature: In the end he was fired. The father had left a lot of money.
Ev. Evaluation: General evaluative statements: Children owe a duty to their parents. He should . . .
Q. Qualification: At first, but if, probably.

M. *Maladjustment indicators:*
Ir. Irrelevant feelings, inappropriate to the content.
Subj. Subjectiveness: Highly personalized: It's not God's method.
P.P. First person pronoun: I, me, my, myself.
Un. Unreal solution.
Zero. No working out of the problem.

(By permission of Dr. Helen Sargent and the editors of *Psychological Review Monographs*.)

felt miserable." These are signs of arousal of affect or emotional sensitivity. The three E categories include elaboration, evaluation, and qualification, such as "Children owe a duty to their parents." These are thought to represent ego activity and to show strength of ego. Experience has shown that the normal relationship between A and E is an approximate balance in standard scores on this test. Hence the ratio (A/E) 100 is approximately 1.00. Certain evidence shows that among well-adjusted persons the A may be considerably higher than the E, because they feel little need for caution or defense. If both A and E are very high, there is some possibility that ego controls are in danger of breaking. At very low A levels, found only in schizophrenics, the E activity is relatively high, although the E may represent only a residual of ego activity. The A/E rating is, therefore, with certain qualifications an indication of ego effort to overcome anxiety and frustration. The Insight Test supplements the Rorschach and TAT by providing a quantitative index of the amounts of affect aroused, the intellectual defense activity, and the balance between these.

The M category includes evidences of maladjustment such as irrelevant feeling, introduction of subjective or bizarre material, too little or too much use of the pronoun I, unreal or illogical solutions or no solution, and zero categories or zero armatures.

Sargent concluded that there is strong evidence of projection brought out by the use of this paper-and-pencil test, that the scoring is reasonably reliable, and that the test yields valid indicators of balance, as shown by tentative results from various clinical and normal groups.

Fables Test

Reuben Fine (1949) reported a study of one hundred children between the ages of four and fourteen years using his revision of L. Louise Despert's Fables Test. In this test twenty short unfinished stories are read to a child who is asked to make up the end of the story. About 20 minutes is usually needed. Samples of these stories are (Fine, 1949, p. 106):

1. A daddy bird and a mommy bird and their little birdie are asleep in a nest in a tree. All of a sudden a big wind blows; it shakes the tree and the nest falls to the ground. The three birds awaken all of a sudden. The daddy flies quickly to the pine tree, the mommy to another pine tree, the little bird knows how to fly. What is the little bird going to do?

The major behavior variables tested by the fables were listed by Fine as dependency, hostility, identification, sibling rivalry, reactions to parental rejection, castration fears, and the Oedipus complex. He gave several protocols which illustrated how the Fables Test was a useful supplement to the Rorschach. Thus the Rorschach scores for one nine-year-old boy showed a high degree of compulsion and suppressed spontaneity and rejection of Card VI. The Fables Test showed intense hostility toward the father; his solutions consisted of running away and of growing up quickly. By comparing the Fables Test scores of thirty asthmatic children with their thirty closest siblings. Fine discovered three marked trends which were statistically significant: (1) the asthmatic children were a little more dependent upon the mother than their siblings, (2) the asthmatic children were also much more hostile to the mother and less hostile to the father than their siblings and (3) the trends were a little more significant for boys than for girls in these small samples.

The results are similar to those derived from other studies of asthmatic children which used more elaborate approaches. The advantage of the Fables Test is that from a rapid but systematic procedure several scores showing hostility and dependence can be secured in a friendly informal situation.

Blacky Test

Blum (1949) described a test which seems to have considerable reliability in indicating psychosexual development, but which was specifically designed to yield evidence regarding several of the Freudian concepts. A series of twelve cartoons was prepared featuring a pup named Blacky, his parents, and a sibling pup named Tippy. The cartoons were presented to 119 men and 90 women college students separately. When presented to men Blacky is described as a son, and when shown to women as a daughter. Each of the cartoons is designed to portray a stage of psychosexual development or a type of object relationship as described in Illus. 177.

Each cartoon (Illus. 176) was thrown upon a large screen, and 2 minutes were allowed "for you to make up a little story about what is happening and why it is happening, and so on. Since this is a sort of test of how good your imagination can be, try to write vividly about how the characters feel. . . . It is desirable to write as much as possible within the time limits." Each cartoon was introduced orally with some nonleading comment, except Cartoon III, "Here Blacky is relieving himself (herself)," and Cartoon V, "Here Blacky is discovering sex." After the first presentation, an inquiry period allowed the answering of about seven multiple-choice questions on each cartoon and direct questions requiring one or two short sentences (Illus. 178). Upon finishing the inquiry, the subjects were

ILLUS. 176. BLACKY TEST

(By permission of Dr. G. S. Blum and the Editor of *Genetic Psychology Monographs*.)

ILLUS. 177. SUBJECT OF BLACKY CARTOONS

A. Four heads of dogs identified as Papa, Mama, Tippy, and Blacky; used for introduction (Illus. 176).

 I. Oral Eroticism. Blacky is suckling the mama dog.

 II. Oral Sadism. Blacky is biting a dog collar marked "Mama."

 III. Anal Sadism: Retention or Expulsion. Blacky has defecated near two large kennels marked "Papa" and "Mama."

 IV. Oedipal Intensity. Papa and Mama are flirting while Blacky looks on.

 V. Masturbation Guilt. Blacky is licking own genital region.

 VI. Castration Anxiety (Males), Penis Envy (Females). Tippy is about to have tail cut shorter. Blacky watches.

 VII. Positive Identification. A large dog threatens a small wooden toy dog.

 VIII. Sibling Rivalry. Papa and Mama show affection for Tippy. Blacky watches at a little distance.

 IX. Guilt Feelings. Blacky cringes; an insert of a small dog with wings points an accusing finger at him.

 X. Positive Ego Ideal (males), Love Object (females). Blacky dreaming sees a handsome large black male dog.

 XI. Positive Ego Ideal (females), Love Object (males). Blacky dreaming sees a large black female dog.

(By permission of Dr. G. S. Blum and the Editor of *Genetic Psychology Monographs*.)

asked to indicate degree of liking for each cartoon, using the letter *L* for like and *D* for dislike. Then the cartoon liked best was to be

ILLUS. 178. BLACKY TEST. INQUIRY FORM FOR CARTOON VI (MALES)

1. How does Blacky feel here?
   a. Terrified that he is going to be next.
   b. Puzzled and upset.
   c. Curious but calm.
2. What does Blacky suspect might be the reason for the scene?
   a. Tippy is being punished for having done something wrong.
   b. Tippy is the innocent victim of someone else's ideas.
   c. Tippy is being improved in some way.
3. How does Blacky feel about his own tail?
   a. He's not particularly worried.
   b. He's thinking desperately about a way to save it.
   c. He thinks he might look better with it cut off.
   d. He's so upset he wishes he never saw or heard of tails.
4. Do you suppose Blacky would prefer to have his own tail cut off right away rather than go through the suspense of wondering if it will happen to him? Why?
5. Which member of the family most likely arranged for Tippy's tail to be cut off?
6. What will other dogs in the neighborhood do when they see Tippy's short tail?
   a. Start worrying about their own tails.
   b. Make fun of Tippy.
   c. Wonder what's going on.
   d. Admire Tippy.

(By permission of Dr. G. S. Blum and the Editor of *Genetic Psychology Monographs.*)

chosen and a short statement written of the reasons for liking it best. Last, the one liked worst was to be selected and the choice explained. The test was scored by determining for each person the degree of involvement in each of the categories listed in Illus. 177. The involvement was determined to be strong (—), fairly strong (–), or weak or absent (0) on the basis of the spontaneous story, the inquiry, the cartoon preference, and related comments. Illustrations in Blum (1949) of strong involvements are:

Cartoon I. *Oral Eroticism:* Blacky has just discovered the delightful nectar that Mama can supply—it is an endless supply and she is enjoying it. She doesn't know where it comes from, but she doesn't care. Mama is pacific throughout it all, and so forth.

Cartoon III. *Anal Expulsiveness:* Blacky, still frustrated, shows his contempt of Mama by leaving a pile of defecation near her house. "There," he is probably thinking, "that will take care of her!"

Illustrations of weak involvement are:

Cartoon I. *Oral Eroticism:* Blacky, a male pup of a few weeks, is having his midday lunch. Mama is bored with the proceedings, but as a mother with her maternal instincts is letting Blacky have his lunch to Blacky's satisfaction.

Cartoon III. *Anal Expulsiveness:* Blacky was not too slow when it came to housebreaking. It took him little time to learn that he must relieve himself outdoors. Outdoors he went when the occasion demanded, unconfined and relieved.

Blum found that differences between sexes among college students generally supported psychoanalytical theory. Thus the most prominent differences between the sexes in raw scores were that women exceeded men in oral sadism, ambivalence, and aggressiveness toward the parent of the same sex, general guilt feelings, superego with motherly characteristics, blaming others, and in being narcissistic in love-object choice; and that men exceeded women in expression of oedipal intensity, identification toward parent of same sex, superego with fatherly characteristics, blaming no one, and in being more hopeful of attaining ego ideal.

The results are also treated by Blum to show intercorrelations between the categories shown in Illus. 177. Although many of the correlations are not significantly different from zero, all the significant correlations tend to support the evidence presented by many non-Freudians as well as by Freudians that disturbances at one stage delay or prevent successful completion of a subsequent stage, and may, if serious enough, cause a regression to or condensation with an earlier stage. The dominating characteristics of earlier stages nearly always persist along with the later stage to some extent.

In conclusion, all of the significant test findings show agreement with psychoanalytic theory where specific evidence is available. In addition Blum points out that there are many interesting points of comparison which have not yet been specifically reported in Freudian writings, and that such systematic comparisons may extend the knowledge of psychosexual behavior in many important ways. Blum also notes the need of much more research with other groups and on validating the technique itself.

Group Projection Sketches

Recent applications of techniques similar to the TAT to the study of small groups have been reported by Horwitz and Cartwright (1950) and by Henry and Guetzkow (1950). The way an interacting group tells a story about a picture is analyzed to provide evidence of the structure and dynamics of the group itself. This technique has an advantage over such methods of group observation as that done by teams of direct observers, transcribing recorded discussions, and the use of sociometric analysis. It is considerably less time-consuming and yields a fairly objective result of group activity which is adaptable to quantified study. It does not reveal to the group members the significance of their responses.

Henry and Guetzkow (1950) present five 18 by 21-inch sketches, one at a time, with the request that the group compose a story about each: "Tell me what is happening in the picture, what happened in the past to bring this situation about, and what is going to happen in the future." Usually a group produces a story in about 10 minutes; it is written by a member of the group or by a stenographer. The five pictures are designed to educe different group responses as follows:

Sketch 1. A group of six young men are around a large table which has some letter-size sheets of paper on it, and one man is standing with his back to the group. This picture is designed to elicit thought content and feelings about divisions of labor, roles within a group, and types of group functions.

Sketch 2. A man leans in a leisurely manner against the side of a doorway and looks out at a landscape. This picture often reveals the group's attitude to a lone individual, and toward his inactivity, and the group's concepts of his inner drives and environmental pressures (Illus. 179).

ILLUS. 179. GROUP PROJECTION SKETCH NO. 2

(From Henry and Guetzkow (1950). Used by permission.)

Sketch 3. An older man leans toward a younger man in a close face-to-face position. This picture often elicits the group's feelings about authority and its own use of authority.

Sketch 4. A middle-aged woman sits in the foreground with a puzzled or worried expression; a younger man in the background, holding an object in his hands, is looking at her. This picture is designed to reveal concepts of dependence and the breaking of established relationships and ties.

Sketch 5. Four middle-aged men, two sitting and two standing, are facing one another in a comfortable clubroom or living room. This picture usually discloses feelings toward informal groups of persons in authority, toward new developments, and toward sincerity in a group task.

The stories that were told by two groups are given here for Sketch 2, The Man in the Doorway:

Group I felt this to be a farm scene. The man in the door is pensively looking at the sunset contemplating his future. He has just returned from college where he has been graduated and has to decide whether to take graduate work, stay on the farm, or accept a job in the city. It is this problem that he is thinking about.

His decision will be to travel during the summer and then take up graduate work in the fall when school opens again. He is a thoughtful, serious individual.

Group II thought that this was a young man with time on his hands. April. Undecided as to whether he should leave or not. Waiting for something to happen which will help him to make up his mind.

To interpret these stories two procedures are suggested: one a clinical approach showing content and themes and the other a rating approach using eighteen categories. The first procedure is illustrated by the following analysis of the first story given above:

The task-orientation theme already noted in the first picture recurs (making vocational choice). The story reemphasizes the staff-function of the group (he takes school work rather than working on farm or in city). The work of the group consists in making plans which will be executed by the individual ("contemplating his future"). Again, there is evidence that the group reaches decisions (definite conclusion to story, as in Picture 1). Yet, it is not too well motivated ("pensively looking," "thinking about"—indirect statements, "It is this problem that . . ."—and the leisure evidenced in "when school opens again"). It allows itself time for enjoyment while pursuing its goal ("travel during summer"—similar to social fraternity setting in Picture 1). The relative youthfulness and inexperience of the group is again evidenced in the reference to "just returned from college" and its felt need for further training ("take graduate work"). The lack of intense conflict and emotionality indicates that the group is free from intensive internal friction or strife. (Henry and Guetzkow, 1950, p. 8)

The group which produced this story consisted of five division heads in a personnel-planning department which was still attempting to determine its role in a large corporation. The second story was made up by members of a group of branch managers in a large civil-service organization.

The second type of interpretation is made by having trained judges rate the group, after reading their stories, on a 6-point scale in the following categories. The authors recognize the exploratory nature of their schema.

1. *Sociodynamics:* the interrelations of people within groups and their concurrent emotions.

    a. Communication clarity: shown by unequivocal statements and clear outcomes.

    b. Content-procedure ratio: the relative emphasis on the content or problem, and on the time spent in discussing what procedure the group should follow in making up the story.

    c. Information providing: the amount of new information which the group provides.

    d. Goal concentration: the degree to which the plot outcome and hero or other figures are integrated in the story is taken to indicate the concentration on a unified goal.

    e. Problem source: the extent to which the group feels the problem to be one of its own, or one forced upon it by some outside agent.

    f. Value orientation: the kinds of group goals indicated by the stories are classified under six headings:

        1) *Achievement:* definite plans made for considerable period.

        2) *Learning and contemplation:* considers many implications.

        3) *Product:* quality and amount to be or actually produced.

        4) *Persuasion:* some of the group try to convince others.

        5) *Advisory:* weighs alternatives but recommends action.

        6) *Fact-finding:* interested in getting more facts.

    g. Tension level: the amount of tension or energy from sluggish to very alert and active.

    h. Tension direction: the amount of support given each other or the expenditure of energy in conflict.

    i. Pacing level: the rate at which group operated in discussing and reaching decisions.

    j. Personal interdependence: how much each individual depends upon others in the group.

    k. Personal affect: how much the group members look upon each other as friends rather than just members of a group.

2. *Group Structure:*

    a. Participation spread: the degree to which all members of the group take part.

    b. Role differentiation: the extent to which the members of the group perform different functions.

    c. In-group feeling: the degree to which the group distinguishes between those present and those outside, and the possible intrusion of out-group persons.

    d. Individuality of members: the extent to which the individual places the group's activity above his own personal goals.

  3. *Process Outcome:*
  a. *Quality of group product.*
     1) *Reality orientation:* the degree to which the group's actual situation is considered in the story.
     2) *Organization of outcome:* the extent to which the outcome is well organized and coherently presented.
     3) *Creativity:* stereotyped versus original thinking.
  b. *Group satisfaction with outcome:* satisfied or not with the story. The solution of conflicts and the quality of endings are taken as evidence.
  c. *Motivation to execute outcome:* ready and willing versus unwilling to carry out a solution or to continue to find a solution.

The categories listed above are described in more detail by Henry and Guetzkow (1950) and evidence from stories is given to illustrate each. The authors also point out that much valuable supporting evidence can be secured from observations of the group and knowledge of its composition and place in an organization. Ratings in these categories lead to quantitative descriptions of groups and form the groundwork for objective analysis and a basis for the preparation of norms. An interesting comparison can be made between these categories for group structure or functioning and the categories used in the TAT or Rorschach techniques. Both group and individual analyses deal with the strength of somewhat independent persons, their different needs or goals, their tendency to work together or to have conflicts, and the resulting patterns of behavior.

The Szondi Test

Lipot Szondi, an Hungarian psychologist, began in 1930 to develop a procedure for evaluating as test stimuli the photographs of persons known to be extremely abnormal. The procedure, as described by Susan K. Deri (1949), requires that forty-eight photographs be presented to a subject, eight at a time. From each set of eight the subject is asked to choose the two he likes the most and the two least liked. After all forty-eight pictures have been viewed, the twelve which the subject liked the most (he may not have liked any of them) are again presented, and he is asked to choose the four that he likes the most among the twelve. Similarly the twelve least liked are again presented to allow a selection of the four most disliked. The test, which takes only 5 minutes, is administered to the subject eight or ten times on different days.

Each set of eight photographs contains one of each of the following: a homosexual, a sadistic murderer, an epileptic during a quiet period, an hysteric, a catatonic, a paranoiac, a depressive, and a manic person. Of course the lay subject does not know this, and even well-trained clinicians have seldom been able to identify correctly the clinical syndromes presented in more than three or four of the pictures.

The scoring simply records the number of photographs liked or disliked in each syndrome or category. The interpretation is based on Szondi's belief that each person has eight areas of adjustment which correspond to the eight categories, and that a fairly good balance among all eight is essential to mental health. Szondi's experience with the test led him to think that an unusual number of likes for photographs in one category is usually associated with repression and tension in that area, because of inability to find normal outlets there. When none or only one picture is chosen from a category, however, Szondi interprets this to mean that the subject has little or no tension because he has developed socially acceptable outlets in this area. Szondi found that disliked photographs were often chosen from the same category as the liked photographs. He found evidence that dislikes indicated the same sorts of repressions as likes, and a large number of dislikes imply that the tension is near manifestation. Deri, a psychoanalyst, presents several fairly complete cases and an interesting discussion of the possible contributions of this test to diagnosis. She believes that the test may contribute uniquely to a revelation of a subject's personality, because it seems to tap unconscious levels of behavior, and requires neither language nor movement.

Single-Word Associations

Following the technique of Jung, Kent and Rosanoff (1910) secured the first response to one hundred common words from one thousand normal persons (Illus. 17). The subjects were simply instructed to give, after a stimulus word, the first word which came to mind. The frequency of each response to each word was secured, and an individual's score was calculated to show the proportion of unusual responses. They found that among average normal persons 7 per cent of the total responses were unusual, and that 247 mental patients gave an average of 27 per cent unusual responses. The list of Kent and Rosanoff has been widely used among groups of college students, feeble-minded persons, Negroes, and school children, so that per cents of unusual responses are available for these groups. However, the variety of explanations of unusual responses makes the interpretation of these results difficult. Rosanoff (1920) and O'Connor (1934), working with what they thought to be fairly average adult samples, believe that unusual responses are largely due to unusual modes of behavior, such as autistic thinking and a tendency toward extroversion or introversion. McClatchy (1928) and several others advanced the theory that persons with a large number of unusual responses are generally those with a large vocabulary or high intelligence. This is certainly true of college and high school groups. Wheat (1931) found that those with low intelligence also gave a larger proportion of unusual responses than the average. This was because of lack of understanding of the stimulus word or lack of ability to vary responses.

Another standardization of results of a free-association test has been described by Wyman (1925). On the basis of teachers' ratings of interest in "intellectual, social, or activities programs," three groups of children were selected. The word-association responses of each group were tabulated and compared. Three keys were then devised to allow three scores, one for similarity to those with intellectual interest, another to those with social interests, and a third to those with activity interests. A more elaborate study of a similar sort was reported by Kelley and Krey (1934). In this case both teachers' and pupils' ratings were used to select groups of children who would be characterized by "courtesy, fair play, honesty, loyalty to fellows, mastery, poise, regard for property rights, and school drive." Word-association tests were applied, and keys constructed to give scores in these eight divisions.

On subsequent applications, both Wyman's and Kelley's tests proved to have little discrimination. Other groups of children, when rated and tested, showed low correlations between ratings and test scores. Kelley applied Hotelling's technique to the analysis of tests and ratings and discovered two main components which seemed to him to correspond to general social conformity and to assertiveness.

These tests of free association have in general been disappointing, but the basic assumptions and techniques are probably worthwhile. The failure to be discriminating is probably due to the shortness or fragmentary nature of the answers. One is often left in doubt as to the nature of response when only the first word is considered. If a large number of responses were allowed for each stimulus word, as is the case in appraising the Rorschach ink blots, the classification of responses would be much more accurate.

Meltzer (1935) investigated children's associations with parents by encouraging the children to think aloud after each stimulus word. In the list of stimuli were the words father and mother. Unlimited responses to these two words were classified for pleasantness, degree of attachment, level of socialization, and other parent-child relationships. He reported 82 per cent agreement on the classification of responses by several investigators.

More recently Rapaport, Gill, and Schafer (1946) have pointed out that the first quick response to a stimulus word is a reflection of the relative strength of the id and the ego. Hence they are often more interested in the effective behavior of the individual than in the reaction word. After the test is given a standard inquiry period is used to seek reasons for the behavior noted. They have reported significant differences among 151 patients in number of

a. *Close reactions*, which indicate difficulty in the associative process; i.e., stimulus word repeated, self-reference, attributes, or naming of present objects.

b. *Distant reactions*, which indicate difficulty in the synthetic process, such as little or no connection between stimulus and reaction word.

c. *Content analyses*, unusual disturbances around words which have particular connotations, such as sex, aggression, family, and food.

d. *Disturbances* in answering, such as long reaction time, failure to react, voice, and gestures.

Sentence Completion

A type of test for appraising insight and adjustment in which one writes a few words to complete an unfinished sentence was described by Payne (1928), but it has not been developed thoroughly or used widely to date. However, it has the following advantages:

1. Is suitable for administration to groups or to individuals of twelve years of age or more,
2. Samples a wide variety of provocative situations,
3. Has no time limits,
4. Provides material that allows fairly objective scoring methods,
5. Supplies more information than a single-word association test,
6. Keeps the subject unaware of the method of scoring or the purposes of the test.

To make use of all these advantages, however, each item must be carefully constructed and evaluated in practice. In the best forms, much effort is given to avoid items which tend to yield single-word responses or stereotyped completions. The item is, therefore, usually vague or unstructured, and the subject of the sentence changes from first person to other persons. Illustration 180 shows twenty items from Rohde's (1946) test, and the answers given by a fifteen-year-old boy with an IQ of 114.

The content of most sentence-completion tests tends to embrace

ILLUS. 180. ROHDE-HILDRETH SENTENCE COMPLETION TEST

(Sample of 20 items and answers. The complete test has 64 items.
From Rohde, 1946, p. 175)

Subject A   Age: 15 yrs., 7 mos.   IQ 114

1. I want to know *if all have the same feeling for art as I do.*
2. The future *seems very bright and cheerful.*
3. My school work *has been very interesting to me.*
4. Earning my living *is a thrill.*
5. My greatest longing *is to paint.*
6. Secretly *I steal food from the pantry.*
7. If I *fail in algebra, I would practically "die."*
8. There are times *when I feel like running away and start a new life.*
9. Work is *pleasant and hard.*
10. Friends *are a help and encouragement.*
11. I become *embarrassed when I can't dance.*
12. Girls *fascinate me.*
13. Love *is grand!*
14. Other people *are quite interesting.*
15. The laws we have *are sometimes unjust.*
16. I cannot understand what makes me *so nervous and stammer.*
17. My stomach *is fine and holds a lot.*
18. At night *I study.*
19. My mother *is dead!*
20. Death *is sometimes inviting.*

(By permission of Amanda R. Rohde and the editor of the
Journal of Applied Psychology.)

many areas of activity in an attempt to discover the subject's principal drives or needs, his self-ideals, his degree of success or failure, and his attitudes toward self, others, and the world. One of the most thorough approaches is the 100-item sentence-completion test of the Office of Strategic Services (1948) which was designed to shed light on twelve areas of adjustment, which were described somewhat as follows:

1. Family; relation with parents and siblings
2. The past; childhood and early events
3. Drives; major motivating forces
4. Attitudes toward self
5. Goals; conscious objectives, self ideals
6. Cathexes; likes and interests, objects and ideas
7. Energy; productivity
8. Reaction to frustration
9. Time perspective
10. Optimism; expectation
11. Reaction to inferiors, equals, superiors
12. What he thinks others think of him

Shor (1946) reported a 50-item Self-Idea Test for military use, in which 15 per cent of the items were concerned with military life, 35 per cent with attitudes relative to situations which could be either military or civilian, and 50 per cent with general life situations. Shor developed a sequence of items which had "shock absorbers" planted between the more emotionally charged items, and a sequence intended to develop greater emotional involvement. Much more study is needed on the effects of the sequence of items.

The scoring of sentence-completion tests always involves appraising uniqueness of responses, their logical sufficiency, personal reference, and repetitions of responses. Rohde (1946) and Sanford et al (1943) analyzed and rated the number of *need, press,* and *inner states,* according to intensity on a 3-point scale of intensity. Rotter and Willerman (1947), using a 40-item test in the Army, analyzed the number and rated the degree of the following:

1. Conflict or unhealthy responses were given plus values from 1 to 3. Thus: "I can't *think straight*" was given $+3$.

2. Positive or healthy responses were given minus values from 1 to 3. Thus: "Other people *are swell*" was scored -3.

3. Neutral responses were given no score.

These authors published an illustrative set of scoring standards for each item which make possible fairly objective scoring. The standards are based on answers from 15 patients with serious psychiatric disorders, 15 with combat disturbances, and 15 with no serious psychological problems. Rohde (1946) used 670 ninth grade students of about fifteen years of age. On all of these scales a great deal more work is needed to establish reliable norms.

The reliability of sentence-completion tests is reported to be fairly high. Rohde (1946) found after 8 months a retest consistency of .82 with girls, and .76 with boys. Rotter and Willerman (1947) found a split-half correlation of .85 when corrected by the Brown-Spearman formula, and an average inter-scorer reliability of from .81 to .91 among seven scorers on a population of fifty convalescents.

Rotter and Willerman (1947) found a correlation of .61 between test scores and a judgment of "severity of disturbance" based on case studies. They also reported correlations of from .39 to .41 between test scores and psychiatric diagnoses. These findings indicate that this type of test will yield a fairly stable and meaningful score. Much work is needed to determine its best form for various groups.

Proverbs

Rabin and Boida (1948) selected forty-one proverbs from a larger number which were thought by five psychologists to have possibilities in tapping deep psychological experiences of the subject. Eight of these proverbs were:

1. It takes two to make a quarrel.
2. An idle brain is the devil's workshop.
3. A round peg in a square hole.
4. A man alone is either a saint or devil.
5. Marriages are made in heaven.
6. All truths are not to be told.
14. A bad woman is worse than a bad man.
38. A contented mind is a continual feast.

Two groups, one of hospital patients and the other of nurses, were asked to indicate the ten "best" proverbs. The patients show significantly more preference for the last three items above. Numbers 6 and 38 seem to be related to paranoid trends and anxiety, but number 14 seems to be principally a sex difference. Comparison of individual patients' choices with their situations often indicated that certain proverbs had direct or indirect reference to failures, anxieties, and preoccupations. An inquiry period following individual tests yielded evidence of the types of behavior similar to those yielded in the inquiry period of the Rorschach, for example, construction, confabulation, perseveration, and self-reference.

STUDY GUIDE QUESTIONS

1. How can appreciation of literary style be measured most accurately?
2. How can the pleasantness of speech sounds be evaluated?
3. What is the rationale for the use of proverbs in personality examining?
4. On what basis were the stimuli used in the TAT test chosen?
5. What are the advantages of using pictures, rather than inkblots or proverbs as stimuli?
6. To what extent do the directions for administration of the TAT disclose its purpose and stimulate the subject to cooperate?
7. On what basis has Murray classified needs and press?
8. What sorts of scores and summaries are used in interpreting TAT results?
9. What syndromes of needs did Sanford discover among children?
10. In what ways did alcoholics show personality traits different from normals?
11. What differences did Eron find between TAT themes of schizophrenics and of normals?
12. What are basic scoring categories for the Picture-Frustration Test, and how are they measured?
13. What scoring categories did Sargeant describe?
14. What are the basic assumptions of Blum in preparing the Blacky Test?

15. What scoring categories are proposed for group characteristics as shown by group stories about pictures?

16. What are the advantages and disadvantages of single-word stimulus and response tests?

17. What categories can be used in scoring sentence completions for personality characteristics?

18. Make a chart comparing the scoring categories of the various types of tests.

CHAPTER XIX

PLAY AND DRAMA

~~~~~~

INTRODUCTION

Three main divisions are used below in describing projective measures employing play or drama as techniques: (a) play in normal situations; (b) role playing; and (c) miniature stage settings. All three divisions seem to yield similar types of evidence regarding the use of space and materials, thought content, and emotional involvements. The subjects show by language and other expressive movements their defenses, abilities, and feelings. Several investigators have pointed out that both children and adults often make toys do what they themselves would actually like to do but dare not!

The principal problems of measurement in this field are to define accurately the phenomena being observed, to establish degree or intensity of involvement, to determine what part of the activity is symbolic of deeper individual tensions and what part is merely a reflection of cultural stereotypes, and lastly, to discover the variability that is typical of individuals and of groups.

PLAY SITUATIONS

The use of play situations for therapeutic purposes is probably as old as the human race. All ages and both sexes use play to relieve tensions and develop confidence. Play has been defined in several ways, depending upon the type of activity involved. The physical activity employed may be marked, as in playing tennis, or merely incidental, as in talking or thinking games. The social aspects of play vary from solitaire to situations requiring fine team coordination. The ideational content varies widely—from strict adherence to definite rules, as in card games, to the wildest fancies, found in various types of unstructured play. Kanner (1940) has given a number of reasons or explanations for play, namely, (*a*) recapitulation of racial experiences or instinctive patterns, (*b*) expenditure of energy, (*c*) relaxation, (*d*) self-expression, (*e*) communication, and (*f*) experimentation. The psychoanalysts have studied the dynamics of play in children intensively and find much evidence of *catharsis,* that is, an outlet for a libidinal urge accompanied by emotional satisfaction. Among clinicians play has frequently been used for diagnosis and concurrent treatment, but little is as yet available which may be called standardized observation and measurement of play.

One advantage not found in most measurement procedures is that play usually provides a natural situation in which a child or adult reveals his feelings, wishes, and fears rather freely. The great diversity of responses, however, has emphasized the uniqueness of a performance and has made its observation and standardization extremely complicated. For accurate interpretation there must be norms and well-defined experimental controls. Unless one knows with considerable accuracy the degree to which a person varies from his group norms, any reliable appraisal or diagnosis is impossible.

Among the most careful technical studies of play are those recently published by the Iowa Child Welfare Research Station, prepared under the leadership of Robert R. Sears. Bach (1945) made quantitative studies of fantasies in young children, measuring the amount and type of thematic play, the effect of environmental variables, and the degree to which play themes reflected actual experiences. Phillips (1945) reported the effects of different amounts of realism in play objects, and of different lengths of play periods on aggression and "tangentability" (i.e., turning to other activities away from the experimental situation). Pintler (1945) studied the effects of different amounts of stimulation by the observer, and Robinson (1946) compared the effects of using dolls representing the child's own family with the effects of using dolls of a standard set. These studies were summarized in part by Pintler, Phillips, and Sears (1946) in a study of sex differences. The type of behavior most frequently found among children is summarized in Illus. 181. The girls showed more stereotype themes; the boys had more nonhuman themes, more theme changes, and more nontangential aggression, and there were no reliable sex differences in exploratory or organizational activity and nonstereotyped thematic play. The authors believe that social learning in early childhood caused most of these differences. Although no standardized scales or individual profiles have come from these studies as yet, they lay the foundation for categories of behavior

ILLUS. 181. BEHAVIOR CATEGORIES IN DOLL PLAY *

Category	Girls	Boys
Exploratory	26.3	23.4
Organizational	35.1	58.4
Inappropriate Organizational	2.7	7.1 **
Stereotyped-Thematic	71.1	43.4 **
Self Thematic	4.2	4.1
Nonhuman Thematic	1.6	7.5 **
Nonstereotyped Thematic	32.3	34.0
Tangential Thematic	32.6	45.6
Tangential Play	16.8	15.5
Nontangential Aggression	18.9	30.4 **
Tangential Aggression	5.3	8.7
Total Aggression	24.2	39.1 **
Number of Theme Changes	4.5	8.9 **

* Adapted from Pintler, Phillips, and Sears (1946), *Journal of Psychology*, 21, p. 77.

** Differences significant at or below the 5 per cent level.

(By permission of the authors and the editors of the *Journal of Psychology*.)

which can be reliably observed and recorded. The original reports should be consulted for specific definitions of the terms listed in Illus. 181 and also for much more detailed information.

A great deal of thoughtful use has been made of play therapy by clinicians in dealing with anxiety. Although therapy falls outside of the scope of this book, the therapists have contributed a number of basic concepts which are important in test development. For instance Erikson (1941) noted variations in psychosexual status and maturity in the play sphere or setting, such as play with small objects (microcosmic), play with life-sized objects (macrocosmic), and play with own body, fingers, voice, and sensations (autocosmic). He also described location determinants, such as up and down, backward or forward, left or right, open or closed. He placed special emphasis on play disruption, that is, on onset of inability to play, which may be sudden or slow. Lastly, he described psychoanalytical symbols which are usually condensed and abstracted in form and sublimated. Among older children and adults, studies of spontaneous play are rare, but such studies using careful observation and techniques might be very revealing.

ROLE PLAYING

Role playing has been given considerable impetus in this country by J. L. Moreno (1946), who used it principally for training in spontaneity and, when necessary, for therapy. Incidentally it is an important method of personality diagnosis.

Moreno and his students have developed what they call *psychodrama,* a procedure for releasing emotions which uses a specially constructed stage and a director who initiates, stimulates, and guides the action of both players and audience. They point out that a psychodrama test is superior to other projective methods because it is an actual sample of behavior in a social setting with "real obstacles." It reveals cultural levels as well as personality. Their psychodrama test consists of placing a person on the stage and observing and recording his performances under as many as nine test situations. The first requires the subject to imagine a person and to give time, place, identity, and characteristics. The director may introduce a wide range of themes, such as love, death, economic problems, and self-realization. The other situations are designed to give further information concerning the subject's goals, choice of methods, perception of themes already in progress, and rapid adjustment to changing situations. As yet the observing techniques and interpretative schemes are rather vague, but they are rapidly being improved.

In industrial personnel work role playing has recently taken on significance, both in training of supervisors and in appraisal of candidates for employment (Chapter XXIV).

MINIATURE STAGE SETTINGS

During the last ten years considerable attention has been given to the development of procedures in which a miniature stage or table top is used for analysis and therapy. All of these procedures record the progress and final results of manipulating objects and also encourage oral explanations.

The World Test

Lowenfield (1939) experimented for ten years at the Institute for Child Psychology in London with a World Test, which furnished a wide variety of small objects and dolls to be constructed into a "world" on a flat space. Buhler and Kelly (1941) further developed the test and published materials and a manual for careful observations. They placed on a table top 150 pieces representing houses, people, animals, trees, fences, cars, and other common objects and asked the subject to build whatever he would like. Bolgar and Fischer (1947), using 232 pieces, have developed detailed scoring schemes and norms for 100 adults—50 men and 50 women. They divide the scoring into six categories: (1) order of choice of first and subsequent pieces, (2) amount and variety of pieces and spaces, (3) Gestalt or configurations based on such needs as: practical, logical, social, vital, or esthetic ones, (4) content (ideas and items used and rejected), (5) behavior or organizational activity, and (6) verbalization.

Michael and Buhler (1945), working with normal and abnormal adults, found indications of basic personality structure in the world structures made by individuals. Thus psychotics in general indicated the world as aggressive or threatening. Sex-problem cases and compulsive children constructed unpopulated worlds, indicating fear or hostility to people. Mentally defective adults and alcoholics used less than one third of the items, indicating lack of imagination and interest. Psychopathic and compulsive personalities revealed anxieties by building fences or protective walls and closed spaces. Hysterical persons built disorganized and confused worlds, and obsessive-compulsive persons made rows or rigid patterns indicating deep-seated inhibitions.

Erik Homberg (1938), a psychoanalyst, cooperated with Murray in the study of character formation of a group of college men. Each subject was brought into a room where a table was covered with small toys. These included toys readily identified as a father, mother, son, daughter, little girl, maid, policemen, farmers, animals, furniture, autos, blocks, and walls. The observer stated that he was interested in ideas for moving pictures and wished the subject to use the toys to construct a dramatic scene. The observer left the room 15 minutes while the subject believed he was unobserved. Actually his actions were watched and recorded through a one-way screen. Then the observer reentered the room and wrote down the subject's explanations and sketched the scene. Of 22 subjects, 5 failed to produce a dramatic scene, 13 produced auto accidents or arrangements which prevented an accident, 9 made the little girl the object of danger. In other parts of these scenes 7 females were kidnaped, or bitten, or fainted, or died. The little girl was also handled or "run over" by a car in many of the preliminary situations. No male figures were ever in danger. The dog was the victim of an accident in the scene constructed by a masculine and socially adapted person who said it was the little girl's dog and later, that women are faithful, they are dogs. The red racer had accidents in scenes by two persons who were nearest to manifest homosexuality and manifest psychosis. For a similar group of five college women the most frequent scene showed a criminal man who deserts, neglects, or murders his family, or strangles his wife, or steals, or tries to do these things but is prevented.

Homberg reported that much of the behavior was indicative of personality structure and that when asked for a dramatic production, most of the subjects produced symbolic traumatic tensions of their own. In offering little toys for a dramatic task, he provoked a return of infantile conflict, and the subjects seemed to have continued from where they left off in childhood. The main recurring themes may be partly reflections of newspaper and movie drama, but also seem to reflect convincingly the personal sexual needs among unmarried young adults. The method, as Homberg uses it, certainly brings out much material which, like the TAT or Rorschach results, may be analyzed and quantified.

Make-a-Picture Story (MAPS) Test

E. S. Shneidman (1948) described the Make-A-Picture Story Test in which the subject is allowed to place sixty-seven small cardboard figures on a table, and then make a picture and tell a story about it, using a background card. The twenty-two backgrounds (8½- by 11-inch achromatic pictures) include:

living room	doorway
street scene	cellar
medical scene	landscape
bathroom	cave
dream	raft
bridge	attic
bedroom	shanty
blank	cemetery
forest	nursery
closet	schoolroom
camp	stage

Some of these backgrounds are unstructured or ambiguous, as the blank and doorway; some are semi-structured, as the forest and cave; and 15 pictures are definitely structured. A wide enough variety of backgrounds is included to touch nearly all the problem areas found in clinical cases. The 67 figures, listed in Illus. 182, are 9 male white adults, 11 female white adults, 12 children, 10 minority-group figures, 6 legendary figures, 5 silhouette figures with blank faces. Most of these are standing and clothed, but some are partly clothed or nude. The tallest human figure is 5½ inches. The numbers in Illus. 182 are a code for rapid recording of results.

The examiner presents one background at a time, asking the subject to "select one or more of the figures, put them on the background and tell a story about who the characters are, what they are doing and thinking and how they feel, and how the whole thing turns out." The number of backgrounds used depends somewhat upon the subject. If possible the first ten in the list are presented, and then the subject is allowed to choose from among the rest.

ILLUS. 182. MAKE-A-PICTURE STORY (MAPS) TEST •

Code	Subject
	MALE ADULT
M – 1	Nude male; rear view
M – 2	Man undressing
M – 3	Soldier standing at attention
M – 4	Military figure; right hand pointing down
M – 5	Policeman
M – 6	Supine figure with blood spots
M – 8	Priestlike; in long robe
M – 9	Man with brief case; coat over arm
M – 10	Man carrying baseball bat and box
M – 11	Man with fist raised
M – 12	Man with both hands on left cheek
M – 13	Man with both hands folded in front of him, looking down
M – 14	Man with polka dot necktie; eyebrows raised
M – 15	Man with right hand in pants pocket
M – 16	Older man with mustache; dressing gown; left fist raised
M – 17	Rear view of man on haunches looking at picture
M – 18	Cripple; man on crutches
M – 19	Figure with back of right hand on hip; left arm extended; possibly effeminate
	FEMALE ADULT
F – 1	Nude female
F – 2	Female undressing
F – 3	Woman both hands on left thigh
F – 4	Rear view; dress torn at left
F – 5	Both hands to mouth
F – 6	Bending over; arms up; apron
F – 7	Eyes wide open; eyebrows raised
F – 8	Left hand up; right hand holding booklike object
F – 9	Woman; right hand to right ear
F – 10	Old lady with shawl
F – 11	Young woman in defensive position; left elbow in air
	INDETERMINATE AS TO SEX
I – 1	Supine figure in slacks or pants; left hand on belt
I – 2	Rear view of seated figure; head resting on left arm
	CHILDREN
C – 1	Sad girl; hands behind back
C – 2	Girl; hands folded on dress
C – 3	Girl with ribbon in hair
C – 4	Girl; rear view running
C – 5	Nude girl
C – 6	Nude boy
C – 7	Boy; rear view walking
C – 8	Boy with left hand to eye
C – 9	Boy with left fist raised
C – 10	Boy; both arms outstretched; bandage on left leg
C – 11	Boy; hands on chest; looking up
C – 12	Little boy; right hand extended

ILLUS. 182. MAKE-A-PICTURE STORY (MAPS) TEST * *(Cont'd)*

Code	Subject
	LEGENDARY AND FICTITIOUS
L – 1	King in 16th century costume
L – 2	Pirate
L – 3	Santa Claus
L – 4	Ghost
L – 5	"Futureman" with cape and tights
L – 6	Witch; ugly old woman with tongue out
	ANIMAL
A – 1	Cocker spaniel pup
A – 2	Snake
	MINORITY GROUPS
N – 1	Old Negro man; patched clothes
N – 2	Mammy-type Negress; headkerchief
N – 3	Negro man reading paper
N – 4	Negress in business suit
N – 5	Negro zoot-suiter; with knife
N – 6	Negress in white dress and shoes
N – 7	Pious Jew; beard and skull cap
N – 8	Merchant Jew; wearing vest
N – 9	Latin-American female; bracelets on left arm
N – 10	Oriental female; kimono
	SILHOUETTE AND BLANK FACES
S – 1	Solid black male silhouette
S – 2	Man with blank face
S – 3	Woman with blank face
S – 4	Boy with blank face
S – 5	Girl with blank face

* List of figures from Shneidman (1948), p. 169.

(By permission of the author and the editor of *Genetic Psychology Monographs*.)

The picture results are recorded on location charts and the stories are taken down as nearly verbatim as possible. The quantitative results include:

1. The number of figures used on each background and the average number of figures for all backgrounds used.
2. The number of times the same figure is used and the number of times a type of figure, such as legendary, is used.
3. The placement of the figure, such as walking, floating, prone, outside background, and on top of another figure.
4. The number of times a specific figure and a type of figure are used with a specific background.
5. Number and type of figure interaction.
6. Number of times figures are described in a particular activity, such as sightseeing, cleaning up, eating, and murdering.

7. Number of times figure represents a specific person—self, others, no one, etc.
8. Time at which a figure is brought into the action—before the story began, as story unfolds, after story is completed, etc.
9. Use of backgrounds—ignored, rejected, two used for one story, used for mood, etc.
10. Time in seconds to placement of first figure, to the beginning of story, and to the end.

In a careful analysis of the results of applying this test to fifty normal males convalescing in a veterans' hospital, and to fifty schizophrenic patients, Shneidman reported 64 "signs" that differentiated the psychotic from the normal groups. Of these signs 42 were found more frequently in the normal group and 22 in the psychotic. An individual's score was then determined by subtracting the number of psychotic signs from the number of normal signs in his record. These scores alone showed marked and reliable differences between the normal and the psychotic groups. Further analyses of the results yielded qualitative indicators of the most usual schizophrenic trends—individuality of response, self-identification, social isolation, overinclusion, inappropriateness, symbolization, desire for environmental simplification, inhibition of fantasied violence, punitive conscience, lack of identification with normal masculine role, religiosity, and debasement of women.

Shneidman also points out that the MAPS Test may be of considerable value as a tool for studying prejudice, the psychology of minority groups, improvement during treatment, readiness for treatment, as a supplement to psychodrama, and as a therapeutic device.

Three-Dimensional Apperception Test

Doris Twitchell-Allen (1946) developed an interesting variation of a miniature dramatic technique which employs twenty-eight small plastic figures (Illus. 183). The figures include simple rectangular and curved polygons to represent well-established gestalts, and one vague human figure; and the rest of the figures are purposely made vague in order to represent symbols and to elicit fantasy. The material is used in a naming test and for storytelling or dramatic action. A 6-page summary booklet allows space for the recording of both first responses and the replies given during a period of inquiry. Tentative norms are available for children, adolescents, and adults, with respect to usual and bizarre associations, modes of organization, and the use of objects in patterns. This test has some of the advantages that the Rorschach has in its use of certain relatively unstructured vague patterns into which the subject may project concepts and feelings.

ILLUS. 183. TWITCHELL-ALLEN THREE-DIMENSIONAL APPERCEPTION TEST

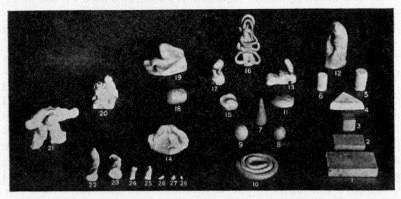

(By permission of Doris Twitchell-Allen and the Psychological Corporation.)

SUMMARY

The brief description of dramatic and play techniques given above does not do them justice, and may appear to oversimplify their administration and interpretation. At present none of the tests can be easily or quickly applied or interpreted, even by experienced examiners. Although the progress with these tests is to date considerable, controlled experimental variation with well-defined groups is badly needed. There are good observation techniques and some norms for social play among children. Studies have been made of racial attitudes, maladjusted children, social groups, and candidates for employment. Role playing is being widely used in school, in industry, and in military establishments. Miniature-drama techniques have been developed and used for diagnosis and therapy among children and adults. They are on the way toward adequate norms for interpretation.

STUDY GUIDE QUESTIONS

1. What are the theoretical advantages and disadvantages of using play situations for appraising needs and drives?

2. Compare the two main categories used to describe play with those of the TAT test.

3. What sorts of basic personality structure are shown by evidence taken from the results of the World Test?

4. What aspects of the MAPS Test make it of value in projective testing?

5. What aspects of personality are reflected most accurately by natural play and role playing, and by using miniatures in play?

6. How may significant group differences be used in determining personal characteristics?

CHAPTER XX

INTERESTS

~~~~~~

This chapter begins with a short analysis of the nature of motivation. Following this are illustrations of five types of evaluation of interest: case histories, logs, reasons for choices, special knowledge, and inventories. A discussion of some practical results is followed by a comparison of methods and a discussion of needed research.

THE NATURE OF MOTIVATION

Motivation is notoriously difficult to define, partly because of the complexity of the behavior involved and partly because of widespread unanalytical ways of thinking. Thinking in this field can often be made more accurate by the use of *operational definitions,* which always refer to particular acts in a particular situation. For example, in physics a force of one dyne is defined as the force which moves a mass of one gram a distance of one centimeter in a particular region of the earth's surface. All other forces can be measured by comparing them with one dyne. Furthermore, work is defined as the total force exerted during a given period of time. Forces also have direction, indicated by the angle between an arbitrary plane or base line and the line of trend.

In the appraisal of human behavior, a *motive* or an *interest* is similarly defined as that which moves a person or part of a person in a particular direction when he is in a given situation. In order to measure a motive one must define its direction and give quantitative values to its strength. This can be done by placing a person in a standard situation and securing indications of the amounts of work he does to reach certain goals. The work or energy expended seems to depend on two independent factors called *drive* and *incentive*. *Drive* is defined as internal tension, mental or physical, and *incentive* is the external goal, the achievement of which relieves a particular tension. For instance, a drive would be a dryness in the throat, and the incentive the glass of water, or the memory of how to get a glass of water.

The most careful workers try to evaluate separately the effects of drive and incentive, because two persons may show the same amount of goal-seeking for different reasons. One person may have been deprived of water for 48 hours and hence have an intense drive. Another may have had plenty of water a half-hour earlier, but has an intense liking for the particular fluid that is being offered.

For the most useful predictions it is better to secure scores which represent known quantities of particular patterns of behavior, rather than an unknown combination of several patterns. This can be done in a laboratory, either by holding the incentive constant and measuring the strength of the drive or by holding the drive constant and measuring the effect of the incentive.

In usual testing or classroom situations, however, it is not easy to control either drives or incentives. In most of the appraisals of interest described in this chapter, no attempt is made to distinguish between drives and incentives. The projective techniques have made some progress in the appraisal of strength of drives (Chapters XVII, XVIII, XIX, and XXIII).

In his analyses of motivation, Thorndike (1935) suggests that unlearned likes or dislikes should be distinguished from learned. He lists tentatively, without devising a scale, the sorts of unlearned drives which should be included—preferences for tastes, smells, bodily temperature, muscular activity and rest, courtship and love, motherhood, receiving favorable attention, successful competition, familiar surroundings and changes of scenery, and mental activity. Thorndike believed that an inventory of unlearned likes would probably not contribute as much to adult education as to the planning of early education. Items of this kind are included in almost all studies of interest, attitude, and adjustment reported here.

Interests of children often seem to be motivated by desires for security, for domination, for escape from arbitrary limitations of home or school, and for unrestricted freedom and adventure. Such interests often have little relation to vocational abilities and opportunities. Adolescents' interests usually undergo changes concomitant with the realization of abilities and limitations and the establishment of more mature ideals. Adults are to some degree motivated by escape, but they also have strong desires to build up and maintain health, family, and financial security. Older persons usually show strong interests in activities which provide security or escape from limitations imposed by age.

Interests Defined

There seems to be no standard or widely used definition of interest. *Interests* are concerned with enjoyment of or displeasure in past, present, or future experiences. They are acceptance reactions to all kinds of incentives both real and imagined.

Two kinds of interests are often pointed out. One, called *intrinsic* or primary interest, is shown when a person does what he likes to do. He may sing a song, dance or work with numbers or with tools for the fun of it. Here the satisfaction is immediate and the activity is an end in itself. The other kind of interest, called *extrinsic* or secondary, is shown when a person does a certain kind of work because he believes it may bring him wealth or social satisfactions most quickly. There may be little or no satisfaction in the activity itself but the reward which is expected to come later is desired. Such interests are remote, and the activity is a *means* to an end.

Uses of Measures of Interest

A survey of measures of motivation shows two important uses. First, educators and philosophers have emphasized for many centuries that one of the principal goals of human development is a strong and well-balanced set of interests. Recently the Commission on the Relation of School and College of the Progressive Education Association indicated as one of the major goals of education,

. . . that interests should be developed in each major area of living. These may be classified broadly as economic interests, civic interests, interests centering in the home, and recreational interests. (Smith and Tyler, 1942, p. 317)

In order to gauge one's progress in developing worthwhile interests, accurate evaluating tools are necessary. The same tools could be used in determining the most effective ways of developing interests.

The second use of measures of motivation is almost the reverse of the first. Here appraisals of interest are used to help in choosing a vocation, on the assumption that present interest is a fair predictor of future success. This is typically a counseling and employment approach. To date most of the studies emphasize vocational or economic interest patterns.

METHODS OF EVALUATION

Cattell, Heist, and Stewart (1950) have described twenty-five possible approaches to the measurement of interests, most of which have been used only in a few laboratory situations. A list of this type points to the need of a large amount of research, and to the possibility of the use of many more objective indicators of interests than are in use today. The list is summarized here:

1. *Money:* amounts and per cents of money spent on certain activities.
2. *Time:* per cent of time given to certain courses of action.
3. *Opinionaire:* self-appraisals of typical behavior.
4. *Preferences:* choices between courses of action, real or described.
5. *Attention time:* spontaneous attention to various stimuli.
6. *Immediate memory:* amount of material recalled soon after an experience.
7. *Reminiscence:* amounts of material recalled spontaneously after various periods of time.
8. *Distraction:* failure to perceive surrounding material when an interesting object is present. Narrowing an attention area.
9. *Retroactive inhibition:* acceleration of forgetting due to subsequent learning of more interesting material.
10. *Information:* amounts of facts related to a course of action in which one is interested.
11. *Speed of decision:* time needed to make a decision or to reject or accept a statement.
12. *Level of skill:* amounts of skilled activity in a field of interest as skill in playing the piano may indicate interest in music.
13. *Misperception:* errors in perception in the direction of an interest or failure to notice errors due to a distracting interest.
14. *False belief:* the amount of distortion of factual statements in supporting belief or interest
15. *Fantasy:* the time spent in spontaneous fantasying or the choice of fantasy reading where alternatives are presented.
16. *Projection:* two types of measures are noted: (*a*) A picture or verbal statement of an activity is presented and the subject selects the best explanation of the behavior, and (*b*) the subject chooses from a list those activities for which he prefers to explain the motive.
17. *Ego defense dynamisms:* interests connected with ego conflicts may be appraised from a defense dynamism, such as reaction-formation, identification, and rationalization.
18. *Fluency:* the relative amounts written or spoken concerning various activities.
19. *Speed of reading:* the rapidity with which material is read is thought to indicate interest or the degree to which the subject agrees with the statement. Difficulty must be controlled.
20. *Work-endurance measures:* the amounts of effort or discomfort endured to obtain a desired end.
21. *Psychogalvanic response:* changes in skin resistance for various activities.
22. *Pulse rate:* changes in pulse rate during various activities.

23. *Metabolic rate:* changes in metabolic rate during various activities.
24. *Muscle tension:* changes in general muscle tension during various activities.
25. *Writing pressure:* the amount of pressure exerted in writing answers to questions related to various activities.

In discussing these methods Cattell pointed out that the first two result from observations or free interaction over periods of considerable time. The next two are introspective self-assessments. Methods 5 through 9 are tests involving immediate attention and memory, and 10, 11, and 12 are tests of more permanent learning effects. Methods 13, through 17 detect distortions of perception and belief, and amounts of wishful thinking or fantasy, often in a frustrating situation. Methods 18, 19, and 20 relate to output of energy or endurance of discomfort, and the last five methods seek measures of physiological changes.

The five commonly used methods for evaluating interests are: (*a*) case histories or autobiographies, (*b*) reasons for vocational choices, (*c*) logs, (*d*) measures of special knowledge, and (*e*) inventories. These are illustrated in considerable detail below. Case histories are usually the best method of revealing a long-time trend and conflicting forces. Observations are most accurate for showing the relations between drives and incentives. Tests of special knowledge are thought to be closely related to interest when ability and opportunity are held constant. Vocational choices show individual practical judgments, and inventories are good for wide sampling of many interests in a way which makes comparisons of individuals meaningful.

Case Histories

The following case histories illustrate the complexity of factors which determine vocational interests (Fryer, 1931).

SUBJECT 33: male; education, two years of college; age, about fifty years

As I think back, it seems to me that I have just gone from one relationship into another relationship, each growing naturally out of the previous situation. I left college when I was preparing to be a surgeon. Because of family objections to a choice of that vocation, I went into business without any particular choice of vocation. I began at about twenty years of age and continued in business until I was about thirty-two, making one change of vocation which was that of salesman; finally, I became an expert in style patterns.

At the age of thirty-two a secretary of the YMCA was foolish enough to see some qualifications in me for the religious work of the Association and extended to me a call. The determining factor in that change was the facing up to all that would be involved in refusing it, and the consequent conviction of moral and spiritual cowardice. This was a period of real crisis, and for two months and a half, I studied the situation and wrestled with the problem. The final decision was reached on as clear a venture of faith as anything I have ever undertaken, and speaking very honestly, I feel that the experiences of the past eighteen years have shown the wisdom of that venture in faith. I know that it was a great personal good to me to change from the interest in things and selling things to the interest in men and the putting across of ideas and ideals. The mental reorganization that was necessary, compelling me to go through about five years of hard study, gave me a new mental freedom and developed within me a capacity of which I was not aware. The settling of questions on the basis of deep inner convictions has almost become a habit with me and that is why it is now difficult to think back to the period when very many choices were dictated by chance and opportunism.

Subject 33 gives an account of a life that began on a casual and opportunistic basis. The vocation of surgeon is relinquished and business accepted without any definite, powerful interests being involved. The branch of business likewise seems not to have been very important. The basis for the great change after thirty, into an occupation of social service, is not clearly given but the appeal appears to have been unusually powerful. The resulting success in the new work, following success in the business world, suggests that more of the same qualities are involved than at first sight appears to be the case. However, a very definite shift in interest is obviously required to bring the salesman's capacities into the service of the YMCA secretary.

SUBJECT 34: female; education, A.B. degree; age, about twenty-five years
High School, from age fifteen to eighteen and one-half years
Early in high school, possibly during first year, I became ambitious to become a nurse. This ambition persisted and increased in intensity of desire until I was about twenty years of age and in the second year of university. Reasons for change: (1) marked opposition to nursing profession by my parents; (2) unexpected opportunity to complete university course; (3) gave up idea of becoming public-health nurse because I flunked chemistry, a requisite course at this time.
University Life, from age nineteen to twenty-three years
Early in college my aspirations to become a nurse waned, and I aspired to higher goals. I next went through a period of intense desire to become a writer, colored partly by the fact that I had for instructor in English a poet who took a personal interest in my ambitions. This ambition I still harbor, but without any very definite ideas or plans for the future.
At about twenty-one or twenty-two years of age, I decided that I would like above all else to become a physician. This was impossible because of economic pressure so I went into sociology for the last two years of college, specializing in hygiene and medical social work. I always held very definitely to the idea of doing medical social work, and became part-time worker in

a clinic during the last year of college. At this time (twenty-three years) I was in the neuro-psychiatry department of the clinic, and became definitely interested in that particular field. This interest still persists and I still have faint hopes of studying medicine and specializing in psychiatry. It was because of this interest that I accepted my present position, so that I could be in close contact with psychiatric work.

I have always fostered a desire to become a dancer to such a degree that it has become an avocation with me. However, I feel it might have as well become a vocation, were it not for my family prejudices and objections early in my life, which prevented my ever taking dancing lessons.

Vocational interests mentioned by Subject 34 show a definite sequence from the original interest in nursing, through medicine, medical social work, to psychology. Outside of this line of development, which has led to work related to the work of a psychiatrist, are the two esthetic interests, one in writing and a stronger one in dancing. The influence of family prejudice is shown in checking the nursing and the dancing as vocations, while the positive influence of others is shown in the writing and in the psychiatric work.

SUBJECT 36: woman; age, slightly over forty years

She had to go to work when she graduated at thirteen from elementary school. Before this she had had aspirations to be a teacher or a nurse. She was a clerk for a number of years, after which she did war work. Further office work was followed by positions in a hospital in which she took histories, passed on admissions, etc. Difficulties with a superior finally led to her leaving this position, which she had held for several years. Since that time she has been unsuccessfully seeking work over a period of months. In the fall she secured a part-time selling job in a department store, and was kept on after the Christmas rush. She does not like selling but she loves keeping records. She thought she would like medical social work, anything to do with hospitals or medicine.

On the Stanford-Binet she has a mental age of 16 years. On the Stenquist she made a score less than that for the twelve-year-old median, but in spite of her lack of ability to do the problems she worked steadily without complaints and tried practically all of them. She has a quiet, appealing personality and claims to be very patient and hard-working. Her situation is such that she must undertake whatever is open to her, and the probability appears to be that she will be faithful and industrious in anything she tries.

Reasons for Choices

These cases from Fryer show that educational and vocational choices resulted from a fairly large number of *causes* which were often in conflict with one another. Goals may change rapidly with maturation of abilities, and also with the acquisition of information and with emotional conditioning. The causes for vocational choices, therefore, deserve special study. A thorough study of this field would involve all the dynamics of behavior. A number of special studies limited to academic and vocational situations are all that can be included here.

Choice of a vocation must be distinguished from interest or satisfaction. Williamson (1937) states that nearly 40 per cent of men and 46 per cent of women do not choose the occupations they prefer. Strong (1945) found that 36 per cent of Stanford seniors gave no occupational choice or were not sure what they were going to do. Some had strong negative choices and others were unwilling to admit a low-level choice.

Reasons for vocational preferences may be inferred to some extent from the preferences of various age groups. The vocational choices of 640 boys and girls from eight to seventeen years of age in Topeka, Kansas, were reported by Lehman and Witty (1927). Each person was asked to indicate which three occupations in a list of two hundred he liked best. Marked changes with age were found; thus, among girls, 5 per cent of the eight-year-olds and 32 per cent of the sixteen-year-olds chose stenography. In the same group, movie actress was named by 20 per cent of the eight-year-olds and 3 per cent of the sixteen-year-olds. Among boys the percentages increased with age for the professions and decreased for such occupations as cowboy, auto racer, and president of the United States.

Fryer (1931) reported these same tendencies in a study of 181 early adolescents. The choices tended to change from exciting, romantic, artistic, or frontier occupations to those which seemed more practical. This shift of choices is probably not a true shift of likes or enjoyment, but is due rather to a growing realization that normal existence requires a considerable amount of monotonous, if not unpleasant, work.

A number of reports which are available show marked tendencies toward impractical choices, even among late adolescents and adults. Loomis' report (1949) is typical of many others. Among about three thousand Michigan high school senior boys he found 40 per cent had aspirations for professional work, 25 per cent really expected to succeed in professional work. According to the 1940 census, however, only 16 per cent with twelfth grade or more education would be able to secure professional work. Illustration 184 compares the aspirations, expectancy, and real chances of employment for such boys in seven areas of work: unskilled, semi-skilled, skilled, farmer, clerical and sales, manager and proprietor, and professional.

Another approach to the evaluation of reasons for choices is that of direct questioning. Vernon (1938) derived from interviews with forty-seven university women students the following list of main

ILLUS. 184. VOCATIONAL ASPIRATIONS AND EXPECTATIONS

PERCENT 12th GRADE BOYS' OCCUPATIONAL ASPIRATIONS AND EXPECTATIONS, COMPARED WITH THE OCCUPATIONAL DISTRIBUTION OF THE MALE LABOR FORCE WHO HAVE COMPLETED 12 OR MORE YEARS OF SCHOOLING, NORTH CENTRAL STATES, 1940**

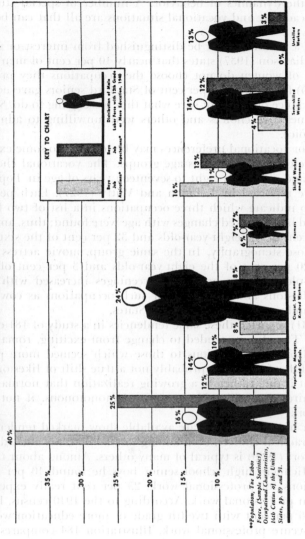

***Population, The Labor Force, (Sample Statistics) Occupational Characteristics, 16th Census of the United States, pp. 89 and 91.*

**14 percent did not indicate aspirations; 22 percent did not indicate expectations.*

More 12th grade boys hope to be professionals than can be. About one third of these do not actually expect to attain professional positions. Even the jobs they expect, not hope to have, are much higher than their chances of entering them.

The proportion of workers employed in clerical and sales, semi-skilled, and unskilled occupations is much greater than

the percentage of high school boys who hope to enter these jobs.

Only one third as large a proportion of 12th grade boys expect to enter clerical and sales work as the percentage of high school graduates who have entered these occupations in the past.

drives: social conformity, humanism, activity, independence, security, ease, inferiority, power, and social admiration. Activity and independence were named most frequently. Different drives were sometimes found to lead to the choice of similar careers, and similar drives to lead to the choice of different careers. Knowledge of the interaction of all the factors of a situation was essential for a complete understanding of the course of action.

Anderson (1934) required 673 college men to rank twenty-five occupations in order of their (a) contribution to social well-being in general, (b) contribution to one's social prestige, and (c) probable economic return. The numerical ranks for each occupation based on group medians are shown in Illus. 185. There is a marked relationship between all three values. Correlations between rankings for social contribution and social prestige made by agricultural, engineering, business, and textile students were all approximately .82; between social contribution and economic return, .72; and between

ILLUS. 185. OCCUPATIONAL VALUES

	MEDIAN RANKING		
	Social Contribution	Social Prestige	Economic Return
Clergyman	2.9	4.8	14.5
Physician	3.2	4.7	4.9
Professor	4.6	6.6	10.9
Banker	6.1	3.1	2.9
School teacher	6.4	11.6	17.3
Manufacturer	7.6	6.7	3.0
Lawyer	7.8	6.1	5.8
Farmer	8.3	14.4	13.2
Engineer	8.4	9.4	6.4
Artist	8.6	7.0	8.9
Merchant	11.0	11.7	10.5
Factory manager	11.7	11.4	8.6
Machinist	15.6	17.2	12.9
Carpenter	15.6	18.8	15.2
Bookkeeper	15.8	15.6	17.0
Insurance agent	16.3	15.4	13.9
Salesman	17.0	15.5	14.0
Factory operative	18.3	21.2	19.8
Barber	18.9	20.1	19.9
Blacksmith	19.6	21.7	20.1
Baseball player	19.8	14.2	8.9
Soldier	20.7	21.7	23.7
Chauffeur	23.0	23.1	22.5
Man of leisure	23.8	7.3	14.4
Ditch digger	24.9	25.5	24.6

(Anderson, 1934, p. 443.   By permission of the Editor, *Journal of Social Psychology*.)

prestige and economic return, .86. The rankings by various classes in college were very similar, and two classes three years apart also gave almost identical rankings. Anderson concludes that these occupational values are widely and uniformly held and play an important part in the selection of one's vocation.

A study by Greene (1938) of college sophomores showed that 81 per cent of 278 men and 64 per cent of 320 women had made fairly definite choices. The main reasons given for these choices are shown in Illus. 186. From these results it appears that men were more fre-

ILLUS. 186. REASONS FOR VOCATIONAL CHOICES OF
COLLEGE SOPHOMORES
N = 598

| | | Per Cent | |
Reason Given	Men		Women
1. Opportunity for employment	1		15
2. Opportunity for training	2		0
3. Initial income	3		6
4. Expectation of advancement	54		13
5. Desire to be of service	18		41
6. Pleasantness of the work	5		9
7. Ability as tested or demonstrated	5		10
8. Family tradition	9		4
9. Location, part of country	2		0
10. Health	1		2

(Greene, 1938.)

quently influenced by considerations of advancement than women, and that women more often than men considered opportunity for employment and service to others as sufficient reason for choice. Persons who had chosen teaching or other professions usually gave "service to others" as the main reason for their choice. The fact that most persons had not considered "ability as tested or demonstrated" or "enjoyment of the work" of major importance in choosing a career is challenging. In the long run these two factors are probably important for vocational adjustment. It points to a need for more accurate self-appraisal.

Logs

Direct observation of behavior is most effective in a laboratory where conditions are well controlled, but it is also widely applicable in industry, school, home, and recreational situations. Direct observation either results in a tabulation, or a log of actual activities, or a rating which attempts to summarize these activities.

Logs can be made by self or others. One check of interests is a Reading Record reported by Smith and Tyler (1942). More than a thousand high school students entered their unassigned or voluntary reading on a record each morning for two weeks. Later a shorter form was prepared to be made out once a week and to include a rating of how well the book or article was liked. These records yielded indication of amount, variety, special emphasis, and maturity. Similar check lists of radio and motion picture programs yielded measures of extent, character, experiences, and degree of satisfaction. Students were found to be listening to the radio about 2 hours a day—far more time than was spent in voluntary reading. Records of radio listening seem to be one of the most valid and reliable indicators of interest in music, drama, current affairs, and social problems. They bring out clearly interests that are undesirable or a waste of time. The data gathered by activity records are illustrated by the following summary.

Elizabeth read 15 books during the year. Fiction included Mary Johnston's *To Have and To Hold,* Churchill's *The Crisis, The Prince and the Pauper,* Bertita Harding's *Farewell 'Toinette,* and *Let the Hurricane Roar;* two college stories, *Iron Duke* and *College in Crinoline;* one dog story; *The Count of Monte Cristo; The Girl of the Limberlost; Anne of Green Gables.* Nonfiction included *The Boy's Life of Will Rogers, Life with Mother, Men Are Like Street Cars,* and *Daily Except Sundays.* Eight of these books were read during the summer and seven during the school year. The class of students of which Elizabeth is a member read an average of 12 books during the summer and 24 books during the school year. She did not read books of as great difficulty and maturity as did the group as a whole. The fiction she read is distributed over Levels III (e.g., *The Crisis*), II (e.g., *Jock the Scot*), and I (*Girl of the Limberlost*); whereas the median maturity level of the fiction read by the group as a whole is IV.

In October 1938, Elizabeth checked *New Yorker* as the only magazine she read regularly; in March 1939, *Life.* In October she was reading no magazine completely; in March, two—*Life* and *Look.* She was below the class median in the number of magazines read regularly and the number read completely. This evidence, together with the number of books which she read, suggests that she does not like to read to an extent comparable with other students in her group.

Elizabeth far exceeded most of the members of her class in the number of motion pictures which she attended. She recorded seeing 39 during the summer and 86 during the school year. The median number of motion pictures attended by students of her class during the school year was 27; the range, 0 to 99. Also, she saw many of these 86 different motion pictures more than once. Evidently, then, a large amount of her leisure time was spent in viewing motion pictures. During the year, Elizabeth saw two plays: *The Boys from Syracuse* and *Abe Lincoln in Illinois,* and attended a performance of *The Mikado.* The medium number of plays, operas, and concerts attended by students in her class, however, was five.

Elizabeth's five favorite radio programs in December 1938, were Benny Goodman, Bob Crosby, Kay Kyser, Make Believe Ballroom, and Tommy Dorsey. Of the 19 programs which she checked as the ones she listened to regularly, seven were dance orchestras such as the ones listed as favorites. In addition to dance music, she listened regularly to five variety programs, three question-and-answer programs, two dramatic programs—Big Town and Lux Radio Theatre—and to Walter Winchell and Jimmie Fiddler. Elizabeth was approximately at the median of her class in the number of programs she heard regularly.[1]

This account shows that Elizabeth's leisure was largely spent on motion pictures and radio of a popular sort, and that her reading was limited in amount and maturity.

Special Knowledge

A fairly large number of workers have pointed out that people often enjoy and hence are interested in what they do well. A good talker likes to talk and a good electrician likes to make fine installations and repairs. From this it follows that measures of skill or special knowledge may be good indicators of interest—better perhaps than inventories, which may reflect desire for escape rather than an intrinsic satisfaction. The relation between special knowledge and interest needs a good deal of investigation, however, because knowledge results from several factors—opportunity to learn, learning ability, good emotional balance, industry and health. Few careful analytical studies are at hand, although analytical tests of knowledge have been developed by the United States Army Air Force Testing Division and the Cooperative Test Service, and in the Michigan Vocabulary Profile. Wesley, Corey, and Stewart (1950) reported a comparison between Kuder Preference Record scores and various measures of ability, for example, The Iowa High School Content Examinations for Science and English Literature, The Stanford Arithmetic Test, The Meier Art Judgment Test, The Seashore Measures of Musical Talent, and The Minnesota Test for Clerical Workers.

Intra-individual correlations for each of 156 male college students were computed using three procedures. In one, in which the individual's deviations from group means were used, the correlations averaged .30; in another, in which his deviations from his own means were used, the correlations averaged .42; and in the third, in which a rank order correlation was used, the correlations averaged .46. The lowest correlation—between musical interest and tests of tonal memory and discrimination—was about .23. The correlation between preferences

[1] From E. R. Smith and Ralph Tyler, *Appraising and Recording Student Progress*, pp. 334–35. Harper & Bros., 1942.

and measures in the artistic, scientific, and clerical fields was about .33. A correlation of nearly .50 was found in the mechanical and computational fields, and of .68 in the literary field. These figures may mean that interests are little related to ability to perform in art and music, where appreciation rather than performance is often the chief satisfaction. Additional research is needed to determine relationships between knowledge and interest in the clerical, artistic, and musical fields.

Inventories of Preferences

In evaluating interests most authors and counselors feel that practical, ideal, and recreational activities should be included, because all are important in securing and holding some types of employment, and in achieving a well-balanced life. Furthermore, considerations of ability, financial rewards, and opportunity are usually to be avoided in appraising interests since these may not be closely related to intrinsic satisfaction in a type of work. This counseling approach has been effective in producing scales which with few exceptions have only small correlations with ability and choice of a specific occupation among the groups studied, but which seem to predict long-time trends in satisfaction in fairly wide areas.

The simplest inventories are short check lists or blanks for indicating one's preferences. The most elaborate include about 1,200 items of various kinds. In some cases blanks are to be filled in by a counselor after an interview and in others, a person is to rate himself. Both interviews and questionnaires have good and bad points. The questionnaire allows a person to check a larger number of items than could be considered in a short interview, but an interview often yields a more coherent account of developments and conflicts between goals. The questionnaire is free from whatever effect the interviewer's personality may have, but it lends itself to intentional misrepresentation which may be reduced by a careful interviewer. An inventory often shows relative strength of preference more clearly than an interview, because it allows a quantitative comparison with the ratings of large groups of persons.

Today there are at least thirty published questionnaires in the United States. The five which will be described here are by Strong (1938), Kuder (1942 and 1948), Lee and Thorpe (1943), Thurstone (1948), and Guilford-Shneidman-Zimmerman (1948). These are not necessarily the best available for a particular situation, but illustrate different approaches and are based on a good deal of careful thinking and research.

Strong Vocational Interest Blank (1938). Strong published his first edition in 1927, a revised edition for men in 1938, a large book of results and conclusions in 1945, and a revised scale for women in 1947. He used some of the items and followed closely the same methods used by Ream (1924) and Freyd (1922). The present men's and women's blanks consist of four hundred items each (of which 163 are identical items) divided into eight parts as follows:

100 names of occupations	47 peculiarities of people
36 school subjects	40 order of preference of activities
49 names of amusements	40 comparisons of two activities
48 activities	40 self-ratings of characteristics

These items were selected to give wide coverage and for their power to indicate differences in interest among a large variety of occupational groups. It was found that the average high school and college student would check the total blank in about 40 minutes. The directions ask for first impressions, and instruct the subject not to ponder long over any item. Scoring keys are now available for 38 male occupations and 24 female occupations; for 6 occupational groups; and for maturity of interest, occupational level, and masculinity-femininity.

The men's schedule was standardized in 1938 on groups of men who were considered to be successful in a particular occupation. These men, whose average age was about forty-three years, had been engaged in one occupation at least 3 years. Most of these groups included from five hundred to one thousand men, each of whom earned $2,500 a year or more.

The procedure for making a scoring key was the same for each occupational or other group. First the percentages of those who marked each item like (L), indifferent (I), or dislike (D) was found and compared with similar percentages for a large general group. The differences between the special and the general groups were found for each item. For instance, in calculating the weights to be assigned to the first item, "actor," when the interest of personnel managers was to be evaluated, the per cents of personnel managers who checked each response were compared with the per cents of the general group, thus:

	L	I	D
Personnel managers	49	38	13
All others	38	35	27
Difference	+11	+3	−14

For ease of handling, the differences were transposed into smaller figures ranging from +4 to −4, so that the final weights for this

ILLUS. 187. ENGINEERING INTEREST SCALE NORMS

Raw Score	Standard Score	Rating	Engineers	306 Stanford Freshmen	285 Stanford Freshmen
	513 ENGINEERS			PERCENTILE SCORES	
220	76	A	99		
210	74	A	99		
200	71	A	99		
190	69	A	98		
180	67	A	96	99	99
170	64	A	93	99	99
160	62	A	89	99	98
150	60	A	83	98	96
140	57	A	75	97	95
130	55	A	66	95	94
120	53	A	57	92	92
110	50	A	48	88	88
100	48	A	42	87	83
90	45	A	33	83	80
80	43	B +	24	79	76
70	41	B +	17	75	73
60	38	B	14	69	68
50	36	B	9	63	66
40	34	B −	6	59	62
30	31	B −	4	53	54
20	30	B −	2	48	44
10	27	C +	1	42	41
0	24	C +	1	37	35
− 10	22	C	1	31	27
− 20	20	C	1	25	22
− 30	17	C		20	18
− 40	15	C		14	12
− 50	12	C		10	9
− 60	10	C		7	7
− 70	8	C		5	5
− 80	5	C		2	2
− 90	3	C		1	2
− 100	1	C		1	2
− 110	− 2	C			1
− 120	− 4	C			1

(Strong, 1938, p. 10. By permission of the Stanford University Press.)

item were: L $= +2$, I $= +1$, and D $= -3$. An individual's score is the sum of his plus and minus marks on all items. If his score falls within the highest 69 per cent of the scores of personnel managers, he is given an A rating in this field. If his score falls within the next lowest 29 per cent of the scores, he is given a B rating. If it is lower than the score obtained by the lowest 2 per cent of the personnel-manager group, he is given a C rating.

The A rating indicates marked similarity of interests with those of persons successfully engaged in an occupation. The B rating shows some similarity, and the C rating, no similarity or contrary tendencies. An individual's score may also be transposed into standard scores or centiles from norms, such as those shown for engineers in Illus. 187. The blank must be scored once for each occupational scale desired. Hence, if scores are desired for thirty-eight occupations, it is necessary to score the blank thirty-eight times. The labor involved is large, whether the scoring is done by hand or machinery. A report blank (Illus. 188) gives a profile which indicates both strength and direction of interest.

Three uses for these profiles are suggested by Strong: in hiring employees, in admitting students in college, and, chiefly, in aiding a person to decide upon which occupation to enter. A low score in interest of musicians, for instance, is taken to mean that one would probably not be satisfied in this occupation. A high score presumably means that one's satisfaction will be as great as most of those in the profession. If one has several high scores, some occupation may be found which will combine these interests.

Strong (1938) reports fairly high reliabilities. The mean correlation of odd-even items was .87 for the thirty-six occupational scales based on records of 285 Stanford seniors. After an interval of one week the retest correlation averaged approximately .869. The mean retest correlation on twenty-one occupational scales over a 5-year period was .75 for a group of 285 college men. This is a high figure for retests of this kind.

The intercorrelations between scales for 273 seniors showed a number of scales to correlate higher than .60. Strong has placed these in groups which, for the most part, seem logical. (They are discussed on page 584.)

Kuder Preference Record (1942, 1948). Three scales, outdoor, mechanical, and clerical, have been added to the seven previously established in 1939, namely, computational, scientific, persuasive, artistic, musical, literary, and social service. Instead of 330 2-choice items, the 1942 form has 168 3-choice items, yielding a larger number of scores. All the items have the same form (Illus. 189).

The testee indicates his choices by pushing a large pin through a 4-sheet folder. Seven sides of these pages are printed with scoring keys. To secure scores in each area of interest, one simply counts the number of circles in the key which have pin holes. One point is allowed for each. (Another procedure uses a machine-scored answer sheet.) A V score indicates validity or adequacy in following directions on the test. If the V score is below or above the limits set by experience, the student made careless mistakes, or he is an extreme

ILLUS. 188. STRONG VOCATIONAL INTEREST TEST PROFILE

HANKES REPORT FORM FOR—
STRONG VOCATIONAL INTEREST TEST – MEN
See other side for explanation

GROUP	OCCUPATION STANDARD SCALE	C	C+	B-	B	B+	A
I	ARTIST						
	PSYCHOLOGIST						
	ARCHITECT						
	PHYSICIAN						
	OSTEOPATH						
	DENTIST						
II	MATHEMATICIAN						
	PHYSICIST						
	ENGINEER						
	CHEMIST						
III	PRODUCTION MANAGER						
IV	FARMER						
	AVIATOR						
	CARPENTER						
	PRINTER						
	MATH. PHYS. SCI. TEACHER						
	POLICEMAN						
	FOREST SERVICE MAN						
V	Y.M.C.A. PHYS. DIRECTOR						
	PERSONNEL DIRECTOR						
	PUBLIC ADMINISTRATOR						
	Y.M.C.A. SECRETARY						
	SOC. SCI. H.S. TEACHER						
	CITY SCHOOL SUPT.						
	MINISTER						
VI	MUSICIAN						
VII	C.P.A.						
VIII	ACCOUNTANT						
	OFFICE MAN						
	PURCHASING AGENT						
	BANKER						
	MORTICIAN						
IX	SALES MANAGER						
	REAL ESTATE SALESMAN						
	LIFE INSURANCE SALESMAN						
X	ADVERTISING MAN						
	LAWYER						
	AUTHOR-JOURNALIST						
XI	PRESIDENT-MFG. CONCERN						
	INTEREST MATURITY						
	OCCUPAT. LEVEL						
	MASCULINITY-FEMIN.						

NAME *Brown, John R.* AGENCY OR SCHOOL AGE *50* DATE CASE NO.

(By permission of E. K. Strong and the Stanford University Press.)

NOTE: Scores to the right of the shaded area show interests similar to those in the occupation; scores to the left show less than average interest.

ILLUS. 189. KUDER PREFERENCE RECORD, VOCATIONAL

This blank is used for obtaining a record of your preferences. It is not a test. There are no right or wrong answers. An answer is right if it is true of you.

A number of activities are listed in groups of three. Read over the three activities in each group. Decide which of the three activities you like most. There are two circles on the same line as this activity. Punch a hole with the pin through the left-hand circle following this activity. Then decide which activity you like least and punch a hole through the right-hand circle of the two circles following this activity.

In the examples below, the person answering has indicated for the first group of three activities, that he would usually like to visit a museum most, and browse in a library least. In the second group of three activities he has indicated he would ordinarily like to collect autographs most and collect butterflies least.

EXAMPLES

Put your answers to these questions in column O.

P.	Visit an art gallery	
Q.	Browse in a library	←LEAST
R.	Visit a museum	MOST→
S.	Collect autographs	MOST→
T.	Collect coins	
U.	Collect butterflies	←LEAST

(By permission of G. F. Kuder and the Science Research Associates, Inc.)

deviate. Raw scores are transferred to a profile sheet (Illus. 190), which yields centiles based on large groups of students in the last 3 years of high school.

Separate norms are furnished for men and women. Men and high school boys average higher in mechanical, computational, scientific, and persuasive interests, while the women and high school girls have higher raw scores in artistic, literary, musical, social-service, and clerical interests. The sex differences are a little smaller among high school students than among adults. The adult male sample shows significantly higher scores than the sample for high school boys in persuasive and social-service interests and slightly lower scores in musical and scientific interests. Adult women and high school girls have similar means and standard deviations.

To aid in interpreting the scores, Kuder has provided a table of occupations listed according to major interests. If your preference profile shows only one high score, the occupations listed in that area should be given special consideration. If the profile shows two high scores a list of occupations which combines these two areas is provided. If there are more than two high scores, pairs of high scores should be considered in turn. If there are no high scores, that is,

ILLUS. 190. KUDER INTEREST TEST PROFILE

NAME Brown John R AGE 24 SEX M GROUP_____ DATE OF TEST 2-2-52
Print Last First Initial M or F

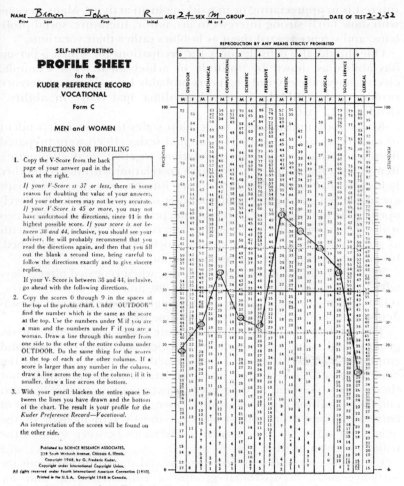

(By permission of G. Frederic Kuder and the Science Research Associates.)

none above the 75th centile, then lower scores are considered with reservations. If all scores are near the medians—a very rare occurrence—the person's preferences may be evenly balanced, or he may have no well-developed interests, or his interests may fall in the areas of personal service or manual labor, which are not scored on this form.

Very low scores are considered by Kuder to be indicators of areas to be avoided. The counselor should also ascertain whether a person's interest is in appreciating or in working in an activity. Many persons who show fairly strong interests in art, music, literature, social problems, and science regard them as hobbies rather than vocations.

One should also consider only the occupations for which a person has ability as shown by aptitude or achievement. "For example, electricians and electrical engineers probably have similar preference profiles, but would be expected to differ materially in ability." (Kuder, 1942, p. 6.)

Kuder took unusual care to develop scales that are independent of each other and reliable. His original scales (1939) were prepared by placing items with high correlations together, and eliminating items which had more than one high correlation with items in other fields. His first scale, that for literary interest, was developed with great internal consistency, and the other scales were gradually developed to include pure measures of independent areas. The last two scales, mechanical and clerical interests, could not be prepared with as great independence as the others which were already established, because independent items were not found.

The reliabilities for the separate scales, when repeated after 3 days with graduate students, were all above .90, and other reliability correlations for groups of grade school, high school, and college students, and employed adults averaged close to .90.

The intercorrelations between separate scales were found for six groups: high school girls and boys, college men and women, and employed men and women. These showed a slight tendency for the male groups to have higher intercorrelations than the female, but there were no significant differences between age groups or between employed and unemployed groups. Disregarding signs, the range of correlations was from .00 to .56 with the over-all median in the neighborhood of .20. The median correlations between some of the scales are given in Illus. 191.

Kuder also presents scale-score means and standard deviations for forty-five small occupational groups of employed men, and for twenty-three groups of employed women. Graphic profiles of the same groups are also given in order to facilitate a comparison between an individual's profile and that of a group in which he may be interested.

A masculinity-femininity score has been developed by weighting each raw score by a multiplier and adding the weighted scores. The multipliers were determined by comparing the function of each scale in discriminating between the sexes. Thus, the mechanical scale has a weight of plus 73, the computational, plus 101, while the

ILLUS. 191. CORRELATIONS BETWEEN KUDER INTEREST SCORES
FROM THE MANUAL, KUDER VOCATIONAL
PREFERENCE RECORD, 1942

Correlation	Men	Women
Positive		
Mechanical-Scientific	.42	.34
Clerical-Computational	.49	.43
Negative		
Mechanical-Literary	—.44	—.31
Mechanical-Social-Service	—.20	—.22
Mechanical-Clerical	—.30	—.14
Scientific-Persuasive	—.38	—.38
Scientific-Musical	—.29	—.29
Scientific-Clerical	—.24	—.20
Artistic-Persuasive	—.20	—.15
Artistic-Literary	—.20	—.15
Artistic-Social-Service	—.25	—.30
Artistic-Computational	—.26	—.24
Clerical-Artistic	—.25	—.29
Clerical-Social-Service	—.20	—.23

(By permission of G. F. Kuder and the Science Research Associates, Inc.)

artistic scale has a minus 74. A high plus score indicates masculinity.

A score for a specific occupational group, accountants and auditors, has been derived by a similar procedure, that is, by weighting each raw score according to the degree that it distinguished between people in general and the persons in this group. Whether or not these weighted scores will be of more value than the profile is still to be demonstrated.

Occupation Interest Inventory, Lee and Thorpe (1943). The authors state that "the major purpose of this inventory is to aid in discovering basic occupational interests possessed by an individual in order that he may become or remain an interested, well-adjusted, and effective person, as well as a profitable employee." They believe that interests are associated primarily with certain types of activities, not with occupations as such, hence the form consists of items which usually require a choice between two or more activities. The form yields scores for six fields of interest, three types of interests, and a level of vocational aspiration. The classification of items according to fields, types, and levels, is "based upon the obvious nature of the items themselves."

The six fields of interest are each indicated by 40 items; 10 items representing a low skill level; 20, a medium level; and 10, a high level. In preparing the items, a low skill in one field was paired with a low skill in another field, a medium with a medium, and a high skill with another high skill. Eight choices in each field were matched with

eight choices in each of the other fields. Thus, the deciding factor is
the field of activity rather than the level of complexity. The six fields
of interest are:

1. *Personal-Social:* personal service, social service, teaching, law enforce-
   ment, health, and medical service.
2. *Natural:* farming, forestry, and lumbering activities.
3. *Mechanical:* machine operation, repairing, construction work, and
   designing activities.
4. *Business:* clerical, bookkeeping, accounting, sales, supervision, and
   management.
5. *Arts:* painting, drawing, decorating, landscaping, drama, literary, and
   musical activities.
6. *Sciences:* laboratory, engineering, chemistry, biological research, and
   physics.

The three types of interest scores, which are secured from the same
items, are verbal, manipulative, or computational. The verbal include oral, reading, and writing activities in sales, business, teaching,
and the arts. The manipulative involve gross and fine dexterity, such
as in shipping, crafts, typing, and surgery. The computational include use of numbers in business and science.

The level-of-interest scores are derived from thirty additional items
in which three levels are contrasted in the same field of interest.

The form is scored by simply adding items which are coded similarly on the face of the form, and then changing the raw score to a percentile and placing it on a profile sheet (Illus. 192). This hand-scoring
operation takes about 15 minutes per person. The percentile norms
are furnished for male and female separately. The females average
significantly higher in personal-social, business, arts, verbal, and computational, while the males seem more interested in natural, mechanical, sciences, and their level of interest scores are higher. The sexes
show nearly the same results on manipulative scores.

The authors report retest reliabilities after 4 weeks, using the
same form on one hundred twelfth-grade students, as at or above
.88, median about .90.

Thurstone Interest Schedule (1948). This form consists of a single
11- by 17-inch sheet divided into one hundred rectangles (ten columns
of ten each). In each rectangle two titles of professional or semi-pro-
fessional occupations are printed. The subject is asked to circle the
preferred title and to cross out the disliked title, or if he prefers, both
titles may be circled or crossed out. Thus, there are four hundred
different answer combinations.

Ten vocational fields were selected, including Spranger's six life
interests as well as other categories which factorial analyses have

ILLUS. 192. SAMPLE PROFILE, OCCUPATIONAL INTEREST INVENTORY

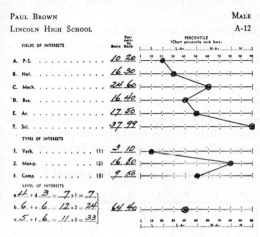

This illustration presents the Inventory data for a twelfth-grade boy and shows that his major interest is in the field of the Sciences. His second highest interest is Mechanical and the two lowest are in the Personal-Social and Natural fields. In types of interests his choices are high in the Manipulative and he appears to avoid choices requiring Verbal activity. His level of interests indicates a preference for activities of moderate difficulty.

We should expect that he would be more interested and successful in aspects of the science field which are associated with construction and mechanical pursuits and that he should probably avoid those in which talking or writing and dealing with people is a primary requirement.

An adequate interpretation in this, as in all instances, requires that Occupational Interest Inventory data be supplemented by information regarding mental maturity, physical condition, personality, special aptitudes and abilities, and educational background.

(Lee and Thorpe, 1943, p. 7. By permission of the authors and the California Test Bureau.)

shown to be independent and which seem vocationally significant. They are:

P.S.	physical science	P	persuasive
B.S.	biological science	L	linguistic
C	computational	H	humanitarian
B	business	A	artistic
E	executive	M	musical

This is a short check list designed to be used when an honest expression of choices can be expected. Its purpose is not disguised. It requires less than 10 minutes of the subject's time. It gives a profile of ten scores and the scoring, which can be finished in about 2 minutes, requires no stencils or other equipment. The interpretation is made immediately from a profile sheet, printed on the last page of the form.

A separate mechanical category is not included, since it is thought to be well represented in physical sciences. The computational occupations include those which use the results of computations, for example, tax specialist, rather than actual computational work, such as bookkeeper. The linguistic category represents skill in communication rather than in literature.

The reliabilities for each scale, as shown by two split-half methods using two hundred cases, were all at or above .90. Also, each item was correlated with the scale to which it contributes. The item validities ranged from .30 to .95 and averaged about .78, which is high for this type of scale.

The intercorrelations between the ten scales for a group of two hundred men, all high school graduates, ranged from .37 to .68. The highest of these, as might be expected, were: Business–Computation .57, Business–Executive .64, Executive–Persuasive .68, Persuasive–Linguistic .51, and Artistic–Musical .49.

To find a score for a category one simply counts the circled items in the proper row and column. The unmarked or crossed-out items are ignored. The profile sheet (Illus. 193) is made by simply marking these raw scores in the columns for each occupational field.

ILLUS. 193. THURSTONE INTEREST SCHEDULE PROFILE

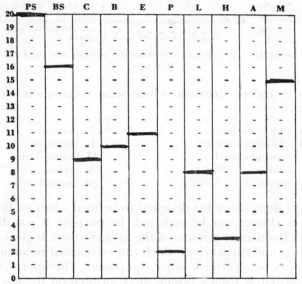

(By permission of L. L. Thurstone and The Psychological Corporation.)

In the interpretation of an individual profile, Thurstone states that since the raw scores are directly comparable, a person's relative strength of interests can be seen without comparison with group norms. The ten scores are arranged in a chart with the most analytical occupations on the left and the more social and artistic categories on the right. The general slope of the profile, therefore, gives a rough indication of these broad types of interests.

The Guilford-Shneidman-Zimmerman (G-S-Z) Interest Survey (1948). This form differs from those already described in that it secures separate scores for hobbies and for vocational interests by having one indicate, for each of 360 items, whether it represents a hobby, a vocational interest, both, or neither. The items are scored to yield centiles in nine main divisions and eighteen subdivisions, as shown in Illus. 194.

The items are all short phrases, for example, "Judge entries in a photo contest" and "Direct an orchestra or a band."

Each item is scored for only one trait, and twenty items are used for each interest area. The present Form A is the result of an internal-consistency item analysis on 540 items, using three hundred college men. The twenty items in each field which showed the highest consistency were retained.

The G-S-Z Interest Survey may be administered either to individuals or to groups and should be completed in about 45 minutes, but there is no time limit. The examinee is instructed and required to keep the answers he has given covered while working on each new column so that he can locate the proper spaces on the answer sheet and also prevent earlier answers from influencing later ones. A novel scoring method using location on the answer sheet makes it possible to score the whole sheet and prepare the profile in about 3 minutes.

Norms are furnished for high school and college students, each sex separately. Split-half reliability coefficients for two hundred high school students ranged from .60 to .95, median .87. Intercorrelations between the nine categories (not given) are expected to be small, and between hobbies and vocational interests large. It is interesting to note from Illus. 194 that most of the students check many more items as hobbies than as vocational interests.

PRACTICAL RESULTS

During the past few years the application of scales, such as those just described, to many thousands of persons, most of them students, has probably had far-reaching results. Just the act of filling out a questionnaire may make a person more interested in analyzing himself and in learning about occupations. The discussion of interest scores, whether admitting their limitations or exaggerating their values, has doubtless led to more thorough vocational planning, and more satisfactory adjustments among many persons. For the number of questionnaires administered, surprisingly little in the way of results is yet reported. Aside from the measurement of groups to estab-

ILLUS. 194. PROFILE: GUILFORD-SHNEIDMAN-ZIMMERMAN INTEREST SURVEY

THE G-S-Z INTEREST SURVEY - PROFILE SHEET - HIGH SCHOOL NORMS

		Girls											Boys											C-score
		0	1	2	3	4	5	6	7	8	9	10	0	1	2	3	4	5	6	7	8	9	10	C-score
		2	7	16	30	50	70	84	93	98	99		2	7	16	30	50	70	84	93	98	99		Centile
ARTISTIC Appreciative	H		1	3	6	9	13	16	18	19	20				1	4	8	12	14	17	18			
	V			2	4	8	12	16	19							1	3	5	8	11				
Expressive	H		1	3	5	8	11	14	17	19	20			1	2	4	8	11	14	18	19			
	V			1	3	7	11	14	16	18						3	6	9	12	16				
LINGUISTIC Appreciative	H			1	3	5	10	14	17	19	20			1	3	6	11	15	17	19				
	V				2	4	7	13	17							1	2	6	12					
Expressive	H			2	4	8	12	16	18	20					2	5	9	13	18	19				
	V			1	4	9	13	17	19							2	7	11	16	19				
SCIENTIFIC Investigatory	H			2	4	8	12	16	19					1	3	12	15	18	19					
	V				2	6	14	17	19						1	3	7	11	16	19				
Theoretical	H			1	2	7	13	16	19					1	3	7	11	16	18	19				
	V				3	9	17	19							1	5	11	14	18					
MECHANICAL Manipulative	H			1	4	8	11	14	18				1	3	6	11	15	18	19	20				
	V				1	5	9	15						3	9	15	17	19						
Designing	H				1	3	10	16	19					1	4	8	13	17	19	20				
	V				1	3	8	15						8	14	18	19	20						
OUTDOOR Natural	H		2	3	5	8	11	14	17	18	19			1	3	7	10	13	16	18	19			
	V			1	2	5	8	14	18						3	7	11	18						
Athletic	H	1	3	5	7	9	12	15	17	19	20		1	4	8	12	15	18	19	20				
	V			1	4	8	14	17						1	3	6	9	15	20					
BUSINESS-POLITICAL Mercantile	H			1	2	3	5	9	12	17				1	2	4	8	12	14	16				
	V			1	2	4	7	12	18						1	4	8	13	17	19				
Leadership	H			1	2	4	6	9	14	17					3	4	8	10	14	16				
	V			1	3	6	10	15							3	6	9	14	19					
SOCIAL ACTIVITY Persuasive	H			1	3	5	8	12	15	17					2	4	7	10	15	19				
	V			1	3	6	9	13							1	5	9	12	17					
Gregarious	H	1	3	6	9	12	15	17	18	19	20			1	4	8	12	15	18	19	20			
	V			1	3	7	10	13	16						1	3	5	9	12					
PERSONAL ASSISTANCE Personal service	H	1	2	4	6	8	10	13	16	18	19			1	2	4	6	8	11	15	18			
	V			1	3	6	9	11	12	14						1	2	4	7	9				
Social welfare	H			1	3	6	8	12	16	18	19			1	2	5	8	11	14	17				
	V			1	5	9	13	16	18	19						1	3	6	10	16				
OFFICE WORK Clerical	H			1	3	7	12	17	18					1	3	6	10	15	17					
	V			2	7	12	16	18	20						2	11	17	20						
Numerical	H					3	7	11	16						1	2	5	11	16	18				
	V				1	5	11	16	18							2	10	19	20					
		25	30	35	40	45	50	55	60	65	70	75	25	30	35	40	45	50	55	60	65	70	75	T-score

Right margin (handwritten): Name — Brown, last; John, first; E, middle; Sex M; Age 24; Date 2-2-52

(By permission of the authors and the Sheridan Supply Company. Copyright 1948.)

lish norms, most studies have been based on samples of less than one hundred persons, often less than fifty. The results of applying interest questionnaires will be discussed under four headings: age and sex differences, predicting success in school, predicting vocational success, and correlations with personality measures.

Age and Sex Differences

Probably the most careful studies are those reported by Strong (1945), who found that likes for a particular item remained much the same over wide age ranges, but differed considerably between sexes. When educational and occupational levels were held fairly constant, he found that about two fifths of the items of the Strong Blank for Men showed straight-line increases or decreases in percentages of likes from fifteen to fifty-five years. Some of these items, for example, aviator, decreased considerably (from 60 per cent to 20 per cent). Others, for example, raising flowers and vegetables, increased from 25 per cent to 60 per cent. The majority of items showed less variation. Another two fifths of the items showed curvilinear patterns, either rising from fifteen to twenty-five years and then declining, as was the case with playing tennis, or decreasing from fifteen to twenty-five years and then rising, as with fishing. The other one fifth of the items showed different age curves for different groups of men.

In spite of these changes, the rank-order correlation of item position was .82 between fifteen and twenty-five years, .88 between twenty-five and fifty-five years, and .73 between fifteen and fifty-five years, which means that items that were well liked by fifteen-year-olds were also well liked by twenty-five- and fifty-five-year-olds.

Strong also reported a tendency for total likes to increase from fifteen to twenty-five years, and to decrease slightly thereafter. The increases were principally in those activities which are least familiar to fifteen-year-olds: linguistic activities and occupations, self-rating of present abilities, school subjects, influencing others as in teaching, supervision, sales, and cultural amusements. Little difference was found between fifteen and twenty-five years in likes for physical skill and daring, working conditions, working with things, mechanical pursuits, noncultural amusements, and unfortunate people. The slight decreases in likes between twenty-five and fifty-five years were in physical skill and daring, writing activities and occupations, and interference with established habits.

Similarities of sexes, as shown by rank-order correlations of average likes of each sex for various items, are given in Illus. 195. These figures, which are based on reactions of fifteen-, twenty-five-, and fifty-five-year-olds of both sexes, show that the averages of the two sexes are most alike in their self-ratings of Present Abilities and their likes for Kinds of People and for Comparisons between Items. They are least alike in preferences for School Subjects, Occupations, Activities.

Nearly all authors of scales report that when the same scale is used, men and boys show higher average scores in scientific, mechanical,

ILLUS. 195. COMPARISON OF INTERESTS, MALE AND FEMALE, FROM STRONG, 1945

| | | Correlations; Male vs Female | |
		Likes	Attitudes *
100	Occupations	.28	.36
36	School Subjects	.26	.27
49	Amusements	.66	.69
48	Activities	.27	.28
47	Kinds of People	.96	.96
40	Order of Preference of Activities	.50	.49
40	Comparisons between Items	.82	.87
40	Present Abilities	.95	.95
400	Entire Blank	.69	.71

* Attitudes is the average like-minus-dislike Score.

(Reprinted from *Vocational Interests of Men and Women* by Edward K. Strong with the permission of the author and of the publishers, Stanford University Press.)

and computational interests, while women and girls average higher in musical arts and social service interests. Persuasive and manipulative interests seem to be more equally distributed between the two sexes, depending somewhat on the particular groups under consideration. Thus, Strong (1945, p. 229) reports that purchasing agent and vacuum cleaner salesman correlate positively with male interests, while life insurance salesman, advertising man, and lawyer correlate significantly with female interests. Girls are thought to be slightly more mature in their academic and vocational choices than boys.

Predicting Success in School

Thorndike (1912, 1917, 1921) reported correlations between students' self-ratings of interests in seven educational subjects and their self-ratings of abilities in these same subjects. He found correlations by a rank-order method of approximately .89, and concluded that interests were highly predictive of abilities. King and Adelstein (1917) reported that on two different occasions they found correlations of approximately .73 between self-ratings for interest and for ability. Fryer (1927) made a similar study of college students and reported correlations of approximately .60 when the number of academic subjects was not limited. These correlations are probably spuriously high because they are all based on self-ratings.

Terman (1925) compared self-ratings of interest in school subjects with teachers' estimates of ability in the same subjects, among 527 normal children and 643 gifted children with IQ's of 140 or higher. The separate correlations for boys and girls in each group averaged approximately .417.

Garretson (1930) found only insignificant correlations between academic interests measured by his blank and academic grades in high school and scores on Terman's Group Test of Mental Ability. Between commercial interest and grades in commercial subjects the correlation was also zero. Between technical interest and grades in technical subjects the correlation was .29.

Strong (1945, p. 524) reports that among 141 freshman dental students who completed the blank there were no differences in scholarship found between those rating A, B+, B, or B— on the dentist scale, but students rating C had inferior grades. Of those rating A or B+, however, 92 per cent graduated; of those rating B or B—, 67 per cent; and of those rating C, only 25 per cent graduated. Moreover, the fifty students who rated A on the dental scale usually had high interest in the occupations which correlate over .50 with dentistry— physician, chemist, engineer; while the opposite was true of those with C interest ratings.

Super (1947) summarized seven reports by others of relations between the Kuder Scores and school grades. The results show correlations among small groups of from nearly .00 to .60, median about .30, when course grades are compared to interest scores in a similar area. Correlations are slightly higher for boys than for girls and for scientific than for nonscientific subjects. In some instances the range of interest scores is so small for a group that the correlations are not indicative of the true relationship.

Bolanovich and Goodman (1944) found that although interest scores yielded low correlations with grades of women trainees in electrical engineering, those who continued training showed higher Kuder scientific and computational interest, and lower persuasive interest than those who dropped the course for various reasons.

Attempts to predict interest areas from intelligence-test scores, or vice versa, have usually resulted in insignificant correlations. When the vocational choices are arranged in order of complexity or amount of training needed, however, students in large populations have a tendency to choose occupations at or a little above their ability levels. Such choices do not necessarily reflect primary interests, for they are also influenced by practical considerations.

It seems that interest scores do not predict scholastic achievement well, since this is determined to a large degree by ability, industry, and previous preparation. In the long run, however, interest does seem to have a marked effect on completing a course of study.

Predictions of Vocational Success

A widely accepted belief is that enjoyment of a type of activity plays a dominating role both in the selection of an occupation and in continuous and successful employment in it. This belief is neither widely confirmed nor denied by the present results. Many persons doubtless succeed in a vocation in spite of early or continued dislikes. Reasons for occupational choices often include financial and moral considerations. One would not expect, therefore, that a statement of probable enjoyment of a type of work, which a person may never have tried, would clearly predict success in it in later years. In order to evaluate the part played by interest in vocational success, one would have to study a large group of persons over a period of years, and note in what ways and to what extent interests influence vocational choices and success.

Data of this sort are meager. One study by Strong (1945) reports a 10-year follow-up of college seniors. Of 400 men who were requested to complete the form, 287 complied in 1927. Of these, 223 returned another blank in 1932, and 197 in 1937. Of the 197, 39 could not be followed, because they entered occupations for which Strong had prepared no scales. Of the total, 99, or 50.3 per cent, were sure of their choices in 1927 and made no occupational changes, while 41, or 20.8 per cent, were sure in 1927 but nevertheless had changed occupations by 1937. There were 17, or 8.6 per cent, who were not sure of their choices in 1927, but made no change, while 40, or 20.3 per cent, were not sure but by ten years later had changed. Many of the changes were normal types of vocational development, however, as from engineer to physicist, production manager, teacher of mathematics-science, or sales manager. Also, the interest of the occupation to which he changed was in many instances nearly as high as that of the occupation left, for there was a mean difference of only 3.4 points in the Standard Score Scales. College students usually have three or four fairly high scores on the Strong Blank, and the occupations on which these scores are made may have much in common. Hence, it is clear that this study indicates more continuity of interest than is indicated by the percentage who changed occupations. Moreover, the original choice was usually not the occupation on which the highest score was made, but the occupation chosen had a median rank of 2.2 for those who continued in that occupation 10 years, and of 2.9 for those who changed from it. The "changed-to" occupation ranked 4.2—one of the five highest scores. The prediction among seniors is good, therefore, that their score which is one of the highest five on the Strong Blank will indicate the occupation 10 years later. These predictions would doubtless have been more accurate, if the study had reported the scores for rather broad classes of occupations.

Another study by Strong (1945) reported a follow-up study of 174 college freshmen over a period of 9 years. The results were similar to those of the study cited above, but about 50 per cent of the freshmen changed their occupational choices during the 9 years.

Hahn and Williams (1945) found that among Marine Corps women reservists the typists, stenographers, and general clerks who were satisfied with their work made significantly higher Kuder clerical interest scores than those who were dissatisfied.

An interesting application of an interest questionnaire to an industrial situation is that reported by Bolanovich (1948) for groups of inexperienced women in factory jobs. In order to establish a scale, 271 items were applied to 666 women. Seven months later each item was studied to determine how well it differentiated women who quit within 3 months from those who stayed on the job more than 6 months. Weights were then assigned to each of 114 items of plus or minus one or two points. From these weighted scores a fairly accurate prediction of tendency to stay on the job was made. It was estimated that turnover could be reduced 55 per cent during the first 3 months. The interest blank applied at another plant in a different state was found to work equally well there, that is, turnover during the first 2 months of employment, which was very extensive, could be cut in half by selecting only those applicants who received scores among the highest 60 per cent on the interest scale. Contrary to expectation, the workers who stayed on the job did not say they liked activities and conditions similar to those in the factory, but rather that they liked very simple activities that were free from any responsibility for thought or application.

Correlations with Personality Measures

Since almost all interest questionnaires include items regarding personal adjustment, and since a satisfactory job is often a large factor in satisfactory emotional balance, and since particular types of adjustment may reduce or change alleged interests a good deal, the question, how closely are interests and adjustments related? is extremely interesting. As yet there are few reports. One which shows a good research pattern is discussed here.

Lewis (1947) compared the Kuder Preference Record scores with the Minnesota Multiphasic Personality Inventory scores (MMPI) for fifty white male insurance agents, mean age 44.7 years, who had sold insurance three or more years, and for fifty white female social workers, mean age 37.7, who had a median of about 8.8 years of experience. The insurance men showed a median centile of 93.2 on persuasive interest, 64.0 in musical, 55.9 in social service. All the rest were lower than 50. The social workers showed a median centile of 92.0 in social service interest, 72 in literary, 55.0 in persuasive. All the rest were lower than 51.

In an attempt to discover relationships between interest and personality characteristics, Lewis compared the MMPI scores of the highest and lowest quarters of salesman, as shown by the Kuder Persuasive Scale. On nearly every scale the highest quarter showed slightly more normal scores than the lowest, and the differences were most noticeable for depression and psychasthenia. A similar comparison of the highest and lowest quarters of social workers showed smaller differences, but in the same direction. Lewis concludes that there is a slight tendency for those who are less interested in their work area to be less well adjusted personally. The MMPI profiles for salesmen and social workers are both close to normal and fairly similar. Lewis thinks the differences are likely to be due to more psychological sophistication among the social workers.

Correlations among Inventories

From an inspection of the forms and their bases of construction, high agreements are not expected, and actually have not been found. Super (1947) reviewed five studies of the relation between Kuder and Strong scores on small samples. All the correlations range from low but significant (Literary-Author .28) up to moderately high (Scientific-Chemist .73) with most of them falling at approximately .40 (Computational-Accountant .49). Thus, the Kuder Persuasive Interest emphasizes a great variety of promotional activities and personal contacts, while the Strong salesman must somehow close a deal to stay in business.

Thurstone (1948) reported the correlations between scores on the Kuder (1942) Preference Record and the Thurstone Interest Schedule shown in Illus. 196.

ILLUS. 196. COMPARISON OF KUDER AND THURSTONE
INTEREST SCORES

Kuder	*Thurstone*	*Correlation*
Scientific	Physical Science	.62
Mechanical	Physical Science	.63
Scientific	Biological Science	.39
Computational	Computational	.63
Literary	Linguistic	.66
Persuasive	Persuasive	.66
Social Service	Humanitarian	.69
Musical	Musical	.72
Artistic	Artistic	.48

(By permission of L. L. Thurstone and The Psychological Corporation.)

The conclusion must be reached that most of the scales are made up or scored differently enough to be sampling different patterns, even though the names given to the scores are similar. At this stage of development research is probably more desirable than high conformity with preceding work.

NEEDED RESEARCH

In order to secure cooperation and accurate scores, an interest inventory should have the following characteristics:

a. Lack of ambiguity: evidence that the item scores represent a person accurately is needed
b. Good coverage: all important vocational areas should be represented by separate scores
c. Factorial analysis: evidence of the relative independence of items and of scores
d. A good rationale of scores
e. Reliability high enough for individual prediction
f. Freedom from intentional misrepresentation
g. Free expression of choice
h. Optimum number of items
i. Validity

Although the previous parts of this chapter bear witness that a good deal of progress has been made in evaluating interests, still any one of the present questionnaires can be improved in one or more of the following respects.

Ambiguity

Questioning a little those who have filled out a questionnaire will usually reveal that different interpretations are often given to the same item. It seems probable that some of the age, group, and individual differences that now appear may be largely due to differences in the interpretation of items and not to differences in satisfaction. Thus, two persons may have the same experience and satisfaction in "Spending the summer as a camp counselor," but one marks the item "dislike," thinking chiefly of how much time would be spent in getting the children to take care of their clothes and obey the rules, while the other marks it "like," remembering the hiking, outdoor cooking, and singing around the campfire. Or two other persons may mark the item "like," but also for different reasons. One likes to work with children, but dislikes rough-and-ready camp life, while the other dislikes caring for children, but enjoys outdoor life. A good deal of research and revision is needed to develop items which will have the same or nearly the same meaning for all those whose interests are being evaluated. No accurate comparison of persons can result when items are interpreted differently.

Coverage

A comparison of five schedules (Illus. 197) shows that each author has usually tried to measure areas which are given somewhat the same names, with the exception of Strong. Strong's method of scoring does not yield areas directly, but occupational scores, which in some instances are easily grouped into areas by factorial analysis or other logic. Guilford carries the logical division to nine areas, each of which is subdivided into two subareas which seem to him to be fairly independent. Thus, Lee and Thorpe combine clerical and persuasive with business, while Thurstone and Guilford subdivide business into executive or leadership and into mercantile or managing a business. Lee and Thorpe, and Guilford combine art and music, while the others keep them separate. Thurstone finds good evidence for separating biological from physical science interests, while Guilford finds significant differences between scientific investigative and scientific theoretical interests.

Strong's groups, based solely on correlations above .60 between his scales in a group of college seniors, are shown in Illus. 188. Strong prefers *not* to identify them as scientific, sales, etc., because he feels that at present such generalization is not well justified. For instance, he reports types of salesmen who do not belong in Group IX, but in Group V or VIII. For purposes of a rough comparison, however, Strong's groups are included in Illus. 197 to show that he has covered these areas to a marked degree, perhaps better than some of the other authors. None of the inventories yield scores for important semiskilled and skilled groups of workers.

Factor Analysis of Interests

Inspection of the various questionnaires reveals a preponderance of three sorts of subject matter: familiar activities, names of occupations, and personal adjustments.

The familiar-activity items include recreations, hobbies, travel and social activities, and work and work situations. It is claimed that they have two outstanding advantages. First, because of their limited scope and familiar content, they can be answered more quickly and surely than less familiar names of occupations or complicated processes. Second, it is assumed that the person who fills out the form does not know how the items are to be scored and hence he cannot, even if he wishes, intentionally misrepresent himself in order to get

ILLUS. 197. COMPARISON OF INTEREST INVENTORIES

Area	Lee & Thorpe	Kuder	Guilford	Strong	Thurstone
1. Arts	Artistic	Artistic	Artistic Appreciate Express	Group I Artist Architect	Artistic
2. Music	*	Musical	*	Group VI Musician	Musical
3. Language	Language	Literary	Linguistic Appreciate Express	Group X Author Journalist	Linguistic
4. Clerical	†	Clerical	Office Work Clerical	Office Worker	
5. Number	Computational	Computational	Office Work Number	Groups VII, VIII Accountant CPA	Computational
6. Business	Business		Business Political Mercantile Leadership	Production Manager Banker President Mfg. Co.	Business Executive
7. Persuasive	†	Persuasive	Social Acts Persuasive Gregarious	Groups IX, X Salesman Lawyer	Persuasive
8. Humanitarian	Personal-Social	Social Service	Personal Assistance Personal Service Social Welfare	Group V Social Worker Minister Personnel	Humanitarian
9. Outdoor	Natural	Outdoor	Outdoor Natural Athletic	Group IV Farmer Forest Service	
10. Mechanical	Manipulative	Mechanical	Mechanical Manipulative Designing	Group IV Carpenter Printer	†
11. Scientific	Science	Scientific	Scientific Investigative Theoretical	Groups I, II Physicist Chemist Physician	Physical Science Biological Science

* Included in Art.
† Included in Business.
‡ Included in Physical Science.

a job or to seem more socially acceptable. Research is needed to show to what extent these supposed advantages are real, because there is good evidence that other types of subject matter are about as valid, and that persons in high school can intentionally "warp" their scores significantly.

Names of occupations usually include most of the professions and managerial positions, technical work, and skilled trades. Thurstone's Interest Schedule consists entirely of such items and in other questionnaires usually from 25 to 33 per cent of all the items are occupational titles or similar items. They are thought to have two advantages: First, they call attention to a whole job so that one reacts to a complicated set of memories combined into a pattern. This reaction may be different and more significant vocationally than reactions to the separate tasks. Second, one may be inclined to regard names of occupations as possible vocational choices rather than as recreations or as hobbies. If this reaction leads to a more serious consideration of interests, it will be an advantage. But if it means that practical aspects, such as wages and opportunity, are considered rather than intrinsic interest, it will be a disadvantage. Another possible disadvantage is that the titles may represent occupations about which the student knows little.

Personal adjustments include being annoyed, worrying, assertion and submission, nervous habits, day dreaming, and health. This subject matter is also typical of personality questionnaires (Chapter XXII). A good deal of research is needed to determine what the basic personality factors are, and how important each is for a particular occupation or vocational area. A few factorial analyses are reported below, all of which, however, have failed to show patterns of activities or adjustments needed for an occupation, because they are all based on scores which combine a great variety of items.

Thurstone (1931) applied a multiple-factor analysis to the results of Strong's Vocational Interest Blank for Men. From the eighteen scores secured for each of 237 persons, four main factors appeared. These seem to correspond fairly well to interests in science, language, business, and people. He pointed out that the variance of the scores was not fully accounted for by these four factors, and conducted another study based on the Thurstone Interest Schedule, which consists of eighty-nine names of occupations which are to be checked to show a person's like, indifference, or dislike toward the occupation named. A factorial analysis of these eighty-nine items yielded seven independent factors, which were tentatively identified as: *descriptive* (of persons and social situations), *commercial, physical science, biological science, legal, athletic,* and *academic or literary.* He also suggested an eighth factor, interest in art, which was not clearly indicated in his study because only a few items referred to artistic activities. Illustration 192 shows an individual profile based on factors from the Thurstone Interest Schedule.

In 1934 Strong made a factorial analysis of his own blank, using both men and women. The results yielded five general factors, tentatively called an interest in people, business, intellectual activities, science, and language. Interest in people also corresponded to feminine interests to a marked degree. On the basis of similar factor patterns, Strong grouped the occupations into eleven categories (Illus. 188).

The Strong Blank was applied to 133 boys in high school by Carter, Pyles, and Bretnall (1935). The boys ranged from twelve to nineteen years of age, with a median of approximately sixteen. Using Strong's scales, twenty-three scores were obtained for each boy. These were correlated with one another and with age. The correlations with age ranged from —.11 for journalist to .33 for purchasing agent, median .06. The intercorrelations of interest scores proved to be similar to those found for college men, with the exception of four scales—those for minister, YMCA secretary, schoolman, and personnel manager. Previously, Strong had found these four scales to be more highly correlated with maturity of interests than the other scales. Factorial analysis of the correlation matrix by Thurstone's method yielded three factors which seem to correspond fairly well to those found by the other investigators, namely, interests in persons, in science, and in language. A fourth factor, not so clearly isolated, seems to correspond to interest in business. The authors point out that the sum of the squares of the loadings had a mean value of .83 for seventeen scales. These same scales had previously been reported to have a mean reliability of .88. The small difference between these figures indicates that specific factors are small in the different scales.

In spite of the similarity of factors shown in these studies, the factor loadings for the various professional scales are not very similar. The specificity of items shown by factorial analyses is greater for groups of men than of boys. These results doubtless are due to the different experiences of the groups tested. The interpretations of items by boys are probably more vague and also more romantic and adventuresome than the interpretations by men.

Dwyer (1938) found that nineteen of the Strong occupational scores could be calculated from only four scores. If the scores of a person were known in the field of physicist, minister, life insurance salesman, and journalist, then all the other scores with the exception of those for certified public accountant and farmer could be calculated with remarkable accuracy.

Crissey and Daniel (1939) have reported a factorial analysis of eighteen scores on Strong's Vocational Interest Blank for Women. By using Thurstone's centroid procedure, four factors were found which accounted quite well for their correlation matrix. They tentatively named these factors:

1. *Male association:* housewife, nurse, secretary or stenographer, and general office worker
2. *Interest in people:* Y.W.C.A. secretary, lawyer, and teacher of social science
3. *Interest in language:* teacher of English, teacher in general, librarian, and author
4. *Interest in science:* physician, dentist, teacher of mathematics, and teacher of physical science

One must conclude from these factorial studies that the most valuable analyses will come from work which appraises separately each item in a battery. When a number of items are added together, as in the scales described above, the total score will usually not represent a single variable but a number of variables in unknown proportions. Factorial analysis of these data, then, is dependent to a large degree upon the particular grouping of items made by the author, and only indirectly upon the true relationship of the items, as shown by their coexistence in the same person. Factorial analysis of preference scores will usually give different results in different groups, since the groups have varying characteristics. Part of the difficulty is due to the failure of questionnaires to give adequate descriptions of activities or vocations. A check list of vocational names, such as banker or engineer, will be variably interpreted by persons according to their own experiences. Methods of factorial analysis, when used on unambiguous items, will show, perhaps more clearly than other methods, the unique patterns of interest that exist in a given group.

An analytical approach is needed which will separate work-activity interests from other factors, such as personality characteristics and adjustments. Satisfactions which are closely related to basic drives might profitably be separated from those which seem primarily related to local or temporary incentives. The present scores of Kuder, Strong, and others, which combine several unknown factors into one score, give rough interest scores, but fail to analyze the independent personal traits which are needed for accurate counseling and employment.

Rationale of Scoring

Two systems of scoring are common. One, used by Strong, yields a single score to show one's position in an occupational group. The score is computed from a key which weights all the items in the blank in accordance with significant differences between men-in-general and the group under consideration. This system assumes that most persons in an occupation have some direct satisfaction in the activities or conditions of work. This assumption needs to be explored.

Hoppock (1935) has shown a tremendous range of job satisfactions, from a maximum in certain professions to a minimum in unskilled hard labor. Almost any occupation involves four or five different activities, some of which may be distasteful. An actor spends nine tenths of his time in rigorous drill. Also, any occupational group will usually include persons who do quite different tasks although they are given the same occupational title. Any single score fails to show these differences in interest patterns between occupations and persons.

Furthermore, Strong (1945, p. 567) points out that the selection of the group of men-in-general is a matter of much importance. For instance, he found that to distinguish well between the various professions, the men-in-general group must have a preponderance of men in high-level occupations. And similarly the crafts and trades can only be well distinguished when the men-in-general group is composed of those in lower-level occupations. When the levels are mixed, the distinctions between all occupations is usually much less clear. Thus, he finds that for 285 college seniors, the correlation was —.42 between lawyers and accountants when the men-in-general group was of high level and +.61 when it was of low level—a difference of more than 100 points. In 66 such comparisons he found a median difference of about 40 points, but one third of them were differences of more than 60 points. These facts give limitations to the use of single scores computed in this fashion, and again indicate the need for a better qualitative analysis to show just what the differences between groups are.

The other scoring system is used by almost all other authors of interest blanks. It yields a profile of from eight to ten scores, one for each field of interest. The score for each field is secured by adding the likes and sometimes subtracting the dislikes for items which are considered to be pertinent to that field. The items are chosen to give a wide sampling, and are grouped into fields either by correlation techniques or by the judgments of persons who are thought to be well acquainted with the various areas. In the best scales those items that cannot be agreed upon are usually omitted, and no item is used to indicate interest in two different fields. This method at least attempts an analysis of relatively independent kinds of interests, and should be greatly extended.

An ideal scale of interests will also yield separate scores for (*a*) aspiration level, (*b*) degree of interest, and (*c*) the type of drive behind the interest.

The aspiration level can be secured by having a scale of complexity of tasks or occupations, which is based on required skill, intelligence, or some other indication of difficulty. Several ratings of occupations have resulted in scales of this type, and Lee and Thorpe (1943) added aspiration scores to their interest scores by means of thirty items of a forced-choice variety.

The degree of interest is assumed by most authors to correspond to the number of items checked in a field. This assumption can be shown to be psychologically inaccurate, for a person may be deeply interested in a particular occupation, say watchmaker, but have little or no interest in many of the activities listed in the mechanical field. A separate score is needed to allow this pattern of interest to be well indicated.

The kind of drive that is behind an interest is very important in employment or counseling work. Four drives are common; (*a*) intrinsic satisfaction in the activity, (*b*) social satisfaction in activities which one's friends are doing or which they approve of; (*c*) vocational satisfaction in an activity which brings in money, and (*d*) escape from disagreeable surroundings or activities. Guilford, Shneidman, and Zimmerman (1948) included separate scores for hobbies and for vocational interests, which is a step in the right direction.

Reliability of Scales and of Single Items

Most of the reliability coefficients of scale scores are of the test-retest type, because of the lack of alternate forms and of the labor involved in making odd-even reliability studies. With groups of two hundred or more persons who have a wide variety of interests, the reliabilities of scores for groups of items are usually in the neighborhood of .85, with slightly lower figures for high school groups. These reliabilities are considered to be high enough for practical use, and are only slightly below the reliability correlations for tests of knowledge and reasoning skills.

Reliabilities for single items are indicated by the tendency for persons to change their answers to the item on subsequent occasions. Strong (1945) reported that 65 per cent of his items were answered identically by college freshmen after one year, 60 per cent by seniors after 5 years, and 58 per cent by the same seniors after 10 years. Preferences for school subjects, peculiarities of people, and amusements showed the least change, and activities and occupations came next. The most changeable were comparisons of occupations or activities and self-ratings of present abilities. There was a slight tendency toward greater stability for familiar items expressed in few words, and also for "like" responses. Strong found that these usual shifts did not change occupational scores significantly in most cases, because some shifts increased the score, others decreased it, and some had no effect.

Research is needed here to determine to what extent shifts or stability of responses to items are due to complexity of form, to ambiguities in interpretation, or to real changes in interests.

Intentional Misrepresentation

How much can an unsophisticated person intentionally misrepresent his real interests on a standard interest questionnaire? Typical of several studies is that of Cross (1948) who administered the Kuder Preference Record to about six hundred high school seniors. The highest scoring students, 181 boys and 183 girls, in each of the nine scales, were not told their scores but were later asked to fill out the record again and to simulate a low interest in the field in which they had scored highest, and a high interest in the field in which they had scored lowest. Both sexes changed their scores significantly in every one of the scales. The conclusion is that the record should be used only when there is no reason to misrepresent oneself. Studies like this have discouraged the use of interest scales in employment for specific jobs, both civilian and military. Several studies of the Strong Blank show that, when asked to do so, students and adults can change their scores intentionally by great amounts.

A similar question arises: how much unintentional misrepresentation is likely in a questionnaire of this kind? It seems highly probable that likes which are thought to be socially unacceptable are sometimes denied when they were included in a questionnaire. The difficulty of accurately gauging one's own feelings is so great and the human mind so complex, that it is likely that we rate ourselves too high or too low at many points. Several ways of detecting misrepresentation in personality measures are discussed in Chapter XXII, but these seem to have been applied only to the Kuder Preference Record.

Free Expression of Choice

Two forms of items are commonly found. In one the subject is asked to respond to a single activity or occupational title, while in the other a choice must be made between two or more activities. Although both forms seem to yield similar reliability coefficients, each has apparent advantages and disadvantages.

The choice items are assumed to yield more accurate results because it is alleged that a person can usually choose between activities with more confidence and consistency than he can rate himself on each one separately. More research is necessary to show in what situations this assumption is true. The choice items are also a little more economical of space, particularly when three or more items are compared and six or more scoring combinations are obtained.

Choice items, however, often seem to force a decision between items for which one has the same degree of preference. A score may thus be the sum of many inconsequential choices which were forced by the form of the test, and not be a good indication of important preferences. Choice items also impose arbitrary relationships among scores since by choosing one item, two other items are discarded. Such relationships are not imposed by the separate-response items. Thus, Kuder's scores, all based on choices between three activities, show approximately 70 per cent of the correlations between scales to be negative, while Thurstone's and Strong's scores, in which choices are not important, show about 35 per cent negative correlations. For instance, Kuder's correlation between musical and artistic interests is —.20, while Thurstone's correlation for his scale of musical and artistic interests is .47, and Strong's .57. This means that on Kuder's Record a person with high artistic interests will usually have below average musical interests, and vice versa. On Strong's or Thurstone's Schedules the opposite is true. Choice items thus influence the *shape* of the individual's profile. The choice item is probably not as accurate as the single-response item. Considerable research is needed to determine the significance of the number and type of combinations presented. Thurstone's method of presenting pairs of items, with instructions to indicate (*a*) a preference for one or (*b*) a preference for both or (*c*) a preference for neither, seems to have an advantage over either the choice item or the single-response item.

Number of Items

The schedule with the smallest number of items seems to be Thurstone's (1948) Interest Schedule, where only twenty paired comparisons are used to establish each scale. Each answer is scored only once so that scales do not overlap with respect to basic items. Strong's scales, however, use several hundred answers for each scale, but no scale has exclusive use of an item. For instance, the scale for policeman has 670 weighted answers out of a possible 1,200 for the whole booklet. By scoring only the like responses about 61 per cent would be omitted, but the resulting scores correlated between .75 and .95, mean .85, with scores on the Standard scales, and the differentiation between occupations was slightly reduced in three fourths of the comparisons. Strong believes that the slight decrease in scoring time does not justify this loss of reliability and validity. Other shortcuts in sampling or scoring were all reported as unsatisfactory by Strong.

A comparison of the Strong and Thurstone schedules shows, however, about equal reliabilities, with Thurstone using only one sixth the number of items. Reliability is achieved by lack of ambiguity among items, and lack of variation among the subjects. A good deal of research is needed to show which items are least ambiguous and which show differences between groups most consistently. A maximum of forty satisfactory, well-scaled items will yield reliabilities at or above .90 on populations with a reasonable spread of scores, as has been demonstrated many times.

Validity

The validity of a scale is always a relative matter—it is valid or invalid for predicting a particular situation or group of situations. Strong believes his test has great validity because of three sorts of evidence. First, it distinguishes quite clearly those who are successfully engaged in one occupation from men in general. Illustration 187 shows a large difference between scores of successful engineers and scores of Stanford students. Only 15 per cent of 933 nonengineering men rated A in engineering interest, and of this 15 per cent many were in occupations which applied physical and mathematical concepts. Second, validity is indicated by the degree to which interest scores correspond to success in occupations. Among 181 life insurance agents it was found that 67 per cent of those with A ratings wrote at least $150,000 worth of policies a year, and less than 6 per cent of men with C ratings achieved this result. A third evidence of validity comes from records showing that men who continue in an occupation obtain high interest scores in it.

Estes and Horn (1938) questioned the validity when they found remarkable differences in engineering interest scores among groups of engineering students in five curricula. The students who were studying the mechanical-engineering curriculum had a median score which was approximately the 99th centile in Strong's engineering group, while the students in civil engineering and in chemical engineering had scores similar to those of the lowest three or four per cent of Strong's Engineers.

In order to evaluate the interests of these five groups, five new scales were constructed following Strong's technique. Then it was found that when students in one curriculum were scored on the scale of another curriculum 61 per cent were rated either B— or C.

The authors also calculated the correlations between the Estes-Horn Scales and the Strong Engineering Scale. The scales for electrical and mechanical curricula groups correlated approximately .70 with Strong's Engineering Scale. The correlation with the chemical-engineering interest scale was —.27; with the industrial, —.63; and with the civil, —.09. Since chemical and industrial engineers had not been included in Strong's criterion group, there is some justification for the negative correlations. Strong did, however, include civil engineers in his group, hence the zero correlation is difficult to explain. These results probably indicate that interest patterns vary so much among engineering students that a single scale will not suffice to measure their interests accurately. Only the electrical- and mechanical-engineering students showed patterns of interest similar to Strong's sample of engineers of approximately forty-three years of age.

Kuder also feels that his interest scores are valid indicators of the relative strength of broad interest areas, as shown by the profiles of occupational groups, the profiles of women in training for specific occupations, and the significant differences between clerical workers who were satisfied and those who were dissatisfied with their work.

In order to maintain and improve these predictions continual research is needed along two lines. One is the refinement of the scales discussed above, and the other is the comparison of interest scores with later vocational success among carefully selected groups.

The building of better norms also depends upon a more analytical approach to the criteria of job satisfaction. Many persons like some aspects of their work, tolerate others, and dislike still others. Holding a job for a few years or even achieving a marked degree of success on a job does not indicate intrinsic satisfaction with the work activities. Questionnaires which show reliably the aspects of the work that give one greatest satisfaction would probably yield better criteria of vocational interest than those now generally used. To be most useful, such job-satisfaction questionnaires would have to have divisions comparable to the independent areas evaluated by the interest questionnaire.

STUDY GUIDE QUESTIONS

1. Distinguish between motive, drive, and incentive.
2. How may primary and secondary interests be defined and measured?
3. How can the development of interests in an individual be traced? What light do such studies throw on the nature of interests?
4. What value are logs or diaries in the determination of the strength and direction of interests?

5. Why do most of the interest inventories try to eliminate the considerations of ability or interest?

6. How was the Strong Vocational Interest Blank put together? What principal topics does it cover?

7. Compare the scoring methods of Strong, Kuder, and Thurstone.

8. Compare the types of items used by Strong, Kuder, and Thurstone.

9. What use are level-of-interest scores? How can they best be obtained?

10. To what extent do interest questionnaires lend themselves to intentional misrepresentation? What methods might yield less error of this kind?

11. What typical age and sex differences have been found?

12. What correspondence between interests and academic success has been found?

13. What evidence is there of interest as an important factor in occupational success?

14. How may ambiguity of items be reduced?

15. What are the advantages and disadvantages of using names of occupations as items in an interest questionnaire?

16. How well do the various interest questionnaires correlate with each other? What reasons can be given to explain the results?

17. What effect may the forced-choice form of item have on the final scores?

CHAPTER XXI

APPRAISALS OF
ATTITUDES

~~~~~~

INTRODUCTION

There does not appear to be a clear-cut distinction between likes and
dislikes, discussed in the previous chapter, and attitudes, discussed
here, but a rough practical discrimination can be made on the basis
of subject matter and ethics. The subject matter of a preference inventory is limited to personal activities, whereas attitudes usually
involve broader questions of policy or values for a group. In indicating his personal preferences, one is usually asked to state his
satisfactions regardless of their moral significance. A person may like
an activity which he believes is immoral. In attitude scales, however,
a person is often required to voice his approval or disapproval of institutions, activities, races, or principles. His personal activities are
not emphasized as much as his opinion concerning what should be
done for the good of all.

A simple type of unscaled appraisal of attitude is a single vote or
judgment for or against a given act. Voting activities range from
selecting a beauty queen to approving a far-reaching government reform. Voting is often considered to be a superficial method of evaluating attitudes, since many persons cast votes without understanding
a proposal. Often those who are least informed vote with most assurance; then, a few minutes later, after a dramatic appeal, they are
ready to change their votes. When persons are adequately informed
and uninhibited, however, voting is an excellent means of attitude
appraisal. Practically, voting is designed to decide a present issue,

594

and rating scales are designed to evaluate usual goals or preferences. However, there seem to be no important psychological differences between voting and the rating scales discussed below. The scales represent attempts to refine voting.

McNemar (1946) in a thorough review of opinion-attitude methodology indicated that many opinion gaugers were content with low degrees of reliability and that verbal expression of an attitude should be carefully checked for validity with other aspects of behavior. Gallup (1944), Cantril (1944), and Link (1943) have published substantial reports on polling methods and results; and Blankenship (1943) has published reports on consumer opinion.

A great deal of activity is now going on in public-opinion research, because samples of public opinion have been found to be of great value for sales organizations, managers of political parties, government agencies, social scientists, and policy makers in general. Public-opinion polls have become a big business and will probably play an important role in national and international affairs for some time. They usually employ short series of unscaled items which are made up for a particular group and time. However, some opinion research begins with a "depth" interview.

Link (1943) and several other workers, using projective techniques, have experimented with photographs or pictures. Cantril (1944) points out that opinion has four important "dimensions": direction, intensity, breadth, and depth. Nearly all polls report only the direction, but the intensity of emotional involvement, the breadth or inclusion of many related details, and the depth or foundations of tradition and personality are important determiners of the course of opinion and action.

Cantril (1944) has reported in detail on the problem of devising questions which will give the most accurate results in public-opinion polls. He found that general questions concerning the acceptance of or deviation from well-established policies or ideals were less likely to show true individual opinion than questions which presented specific issues having a personal context.

With regard to form, Cantril preferred a leading statement with three or four choices which do not irritate or becloud the alternatives. The 2-choice question has simplicity which makes it most useful when it will not force answers into a poor representation. Free responses were recommended on small samples, in order to discover what people think are the issues and to secure meaningful alternatives.

TYPICAL SCALES

Among the typical scales in this field are Watson's (1925) Test of Public Opinion, Thurstone and Chave's (1929) Scales of Attitudes, Allport and Vernon's (1931) Study of Values, and Murphy and Likert's (1938) Study of Public Opinion. Two scales which illustrate interesting techniques are Horowitz's (1936) measurement of attitude toward the Negro, and Brandt's (1937) analysis of replies to questions of personal ethics. These scales will first be described, and then typical results will be quoted.

Watson's Test of Public Opinion

Watson's Test of Public Opinion consists of six parts of approximately 50 items each. Each part uses a different method of eliciting opinions. The first part is a cross-out test of 51 items in which one is instructed to cross out every word which is more disagreeable or annoying than agreeable or attractive. The second part is called a degree-of-truth test. In this a person is asked to rate 53 items on a 5-step scale, from utterly true to utterly false. The first five items are shown in Illus. 198. The third part is called an inference test. Here a paragraph is followed by seven or eight short statements. The student is asked to consider whether the conclusions follow from the paragraph, as shown in Illus. 199. Prejudice is supposed to be indicated when persons check items which do not logically follow from the paragraph. The fourth part, called a moral-judgment test, asks a student to indicate approval or disapproval of instances which are described in short paragraphs (Illus. 200). The fifth part is called an arguments test. Here one is asked to distinguish between strong and weak arguments in support of a particular question. The last part is a *generalization* test which is similar to the second part. Watson also secured information concerning one's approximate wealth, schooling, vocational and religious experience, and membership in political parties and clubs. The method of scoring is to obtain the sum of all points of credit allotted for statements favoring one point of view. A general picture of a person's prejudice may be had from a gross score, and the separate scale scores give a profile showing the strength of opinion along the twelve lines of economic, religious, and moral values shown in Illus. 201.

The scoring standards were secured by submitting the items to small groups of judges including teachers, industrial leaders, and psychologists. No items were retained in a preliminary form which were not agreed upon by at least 75 per cent of the judges. In the final form, items were excluded unless they showed some plausibility

ILLUS. 198. DEGREE OF TRUTH TEST

Directions: No one knows just what the American people are thinking. There is need to find out just what convictions are most firmly held on some disputed issues.

Indicate your opinion about each of the statements on the following pages by drawing a circle around the one of the numbers in the margin which expresses your judgment. The meaning of each number is as follows:

Mark:

(+2) +1 0 −1 −2 If you feel the statement is utterly and un-qualifiedly true, so that *no one who had a fairly good understanding of the subject could sincerely and honestly believe it false.*

+2 (+1) 0 −1 −2 If you feel that it is *probably true* or true in large degree.

+2 +1 (0) −1 −2 If you feel that it is quite undecided, an open question or one upon which you are not ready to express an opinion.

+2 +1 0 (−1) −2 If you feel that it is *probably false* or false in large degree.

+2 +1 0 −1 (−2) If you feel that the statement is utterly and unqualifiedly false, so that *no one who had a fairly good understanding of the subject could sincerely and honestly believe it true.*

Work rapidly, but do not fail to circle one figure in each line.

1. +2 +1 0 −1 −2 The churches are more sympathetic with capital than with labor.

2. +2 +1 0 −1 −2 Dancing is harmful to the morals of young people.

3. +2 +1 0 −1 −2 Jesus was more interested in individual salvation than in social reconstruction.

4. +2 +1 0 −1 −2 To have experienced business men, who have made a financial success in private enterprise, hold the public offices of the country would be better than the present personnel.

5. +2 +1 0 −1 −2 The modern laxness in the observation of Sunday is, on the whole, harmful to the best interests of the people.

6. +2 +1 0 −1 −2 Foreigners who work in our mines or factories should be paid on the basis of the same standard of living which we would set for American homes.

(Watson, 1925. By permission of the Bureau of Publications, Teachers College, Columbia University.)

by being chosen by several persons among a sample of two hundred. The odd-even reliability was approximately .96 for total scores. The separate parts showed a median odd-even reliability of .80, and a median correlation with the total scores of .63. Part II, Degree of Truth, showed the highest correlation, .94, with the total, and also with total scores of the remaining parts, .42. The first part, Cross-Out Test, showed low correlations with the other parts, .11. Watson con-

ILLUS. 199. INFERENCE TEST

Directions: Mere facts may mean different things to different people. It is often important to know just what people think certain facts mean. In the following pages you will find several statements of fact and, after each, some conclusions which some people would draw from them.

Put a check ($\sqrt{}$) in front of each conclusion that you believe is fairly based upon the fact as given here. *Do not assume anything else than the evidence given in the statement here,* with all its terms understood. You are not to consider whether the conclusions are right or true in themselves, but only whether they are rightly inferred from the facts given in the statement. You may check as many as you believe to be perfectly sure and certain. Do not check any merely probable inferences.

Example: 6,500 students recently attended a conference in which the questions of race relations and of possible attitudes toward war were discussed, these being the problems the students felt to be most vital today.

___ The students were all pacifists.

___ The students were all militarists.

___ The students came from all sections of the country.

___ Some students are interested in the treatment of Negroes and Japanese in this country.

___ Some students felt war was wrong.

$\sqrt{}$ The question of attitudes toward war is considered by many students to be important enough to be discussed.

I. Statistics show that, in the United States, of 100 men starting out at an age of 25, at the end of 40 years one will be wealthy and 54 will be dependent upon relatives or charity for support.

___ 1. The present social order cheats the many for the benefit of the few.

___ 2. The average young man, under present conditions, cannot count on being wealthy at the age of 65.

___ 3. Most men are shiftless, lazy, or extravagant; otherwise they would not need to be dependent.

___ 4. The one man is living upon luxuries ground out of the bones of the mass of common people.

___ 5. Some day the workers will rise in revolt.

___ 6. None of these conclusions can fairly be drawn.

(Watson, 1925. By permission of the Bureau of Publications, Teachers College, Columbia University.)

---

cluded that each part of the test was reliable enough to use in attitude measurement and valuable because of its special contribution.

Correlations of intelligence and reading test scores with total prejudice were nearly zero. Part III, Inference, and Part IV, Moral Judgment, also show zero correlations with two group intelligence tests. Watson believed that the incorrect inferences were usually made not from failure to reason correctly among these college students, but from strong convictions which overcame intellectual conclusions.

Illustration 201 shows the results of applying the Test of Public

ILLUS. 200. MORAL JUDGMENT TEST

Directions: Most actual judgments of right and wrong have to be made in concrete instances. Mere general principles are not enough.

In the following pages you will find several instances upon which the moral judgment of individuals would differ. Read each carefully. You may assume each fact as stated. Then look at the alternatives suggested below it. Place a check ($\sqrt{}$) in front of the one with which you most fully agree. If you do not fully agree with any, check the one which comes nearest to expressing your opinion about the incident.

Example: A man stumbled into his house, drunk with bootleg whiskey. He smashed up some of the furniture and beat his wife and children. Then he stole some money from his small son's bank in order to buy more whiskey.

___ His action is worthy of approval.

___ The people who tolerated the sale of bootleg whiskey were in some degree responsible.

___ The occurrence is worthy neither of approval nor of disapproval. It is quite indifferent.

$\sqrt{}$ It would be desirable to prevent such a thing happening again, if possible, by establishing a better type of character in the man himself.

I. In 1793 the government of the United States recognized the young French republic, and President Washington received Genêt, the French ambassador. At the time Paris ran red with blood, the jails were full of the nobles who had been driven from power, and the government was in the control of a few high-handed dictators.

___ 1. Washington was right in recognizing this government.

___ 2. It made no difference whether recognition was extended or not.

___ 3. Washington was unwise. The government should not have been recognized under such circumstances.

___ 4. If it was a government which the majority of the French people really wanted, then it should have been recognized.

(Watson, 1925. By permission of the Bureau of Publications Teachers College, Columbia University.)

Opinion to two groups of normal school students, one in New Jersey and the other in Wisconsin. In general the scores are similar, although the New Jersey students show consistently more preference for economic conservatism, and strict moral standards than the midwestern group. In other reports marked differences have also been found among groups of persons who would be expected to show marked religious or economic preferences. Watson's Test of Public Opinion has in the past been used to appraise the effects of courses of instruction, but some of its items are now out of date.

Thurstone and Chave's Attitudes Scales

Another type of attitude scale was constructed by Thurstone and Chave (1929), who designed a single scale for attitudes toward an in-

ILLUS. 201. A TEST OF PUBLIC OPINION

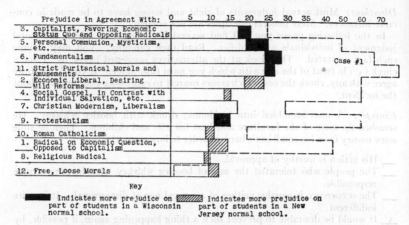

Key

Indicates more prejudice on part of students in a Wisconsin normal school.

Indicates more prejudice on part of students in a New Jersey normal school.

(Watson, 1925. By permission of the Bureau of Publications, Teachers College, Columbia University.)

stitution, such as the church. They first procured approximately three hundred statements which showed a wide range of approval or disapproval of the institution in question. The method of selecting and scaling the items is discussed in Chapter XVI. Illustration 17 shows the odd-numbered half of the items in their scale for measuring attitudes toward the church. Similar scales have been made up for evaluating attitudes toward a fairly large number of institutions and racial groups. The advantages of this type of scale are: (a) it insures a wide range of opinion among items, (b) the items have been selected to nearly equivalent steps in a scale, and (c) items which are irrelevant or ambiguous have been excluded. A person's score is simply the median scale value of the items which he checks.

Murphy and Likert's Study of Public Opinion

The work of these investigators was carried on over a period of five years among college students in several universities. They sought to determine what attitudes were held by these groups and what experiences had determined these attitudes. They used three sorts of appraisals of attitudes: self-rating inventories, reactions to pictures and paragraphs, and autobiographies. They also secured measures of amount of specific information about controversial issues and records of scholastic success.

The self-rating inventories called attitude scales were constructed to evaluate opinions on:

1. *Internationalism:* war and peace
2. *Imperialism:* the use of force by great powers to maintain or extend their empires
3. *Negro activities:* social, economic, political, and educational

Some items for these scales were selected from questionnaires which had been extensively used; others were designed to sample opinions in the three fields listed above. In the selection of items the following five criteria were to be applied:

1. All statements were to be an expression of desired achievements, not merely statements of fact, since persons with opposing attitudes often agree on questions of fact.

2. Clear statements involving only one issue were to be used.

3. Each statement was to be worded so that the modal reaction to it would be near the middle of possible responses.

4. Approval of about one half the statements and disapproval of the other half would express the same attitude.

5. All the items in one scale were to measure the same attitude. This was to be achieved in part by requiring each item to show a high correlation with the total score, median .60.

Total scores were the sums of values assigned to various degrees of approval or disapproval of each statement. The retest reliabilities of the three scales when applied twice, after a 3-week interval, were found to be approximately .85, using small samples of college students.

The median correlations between the scales were: internationalism with imperialism, .63; internationalism with Negro activities, .40; and imperialism with Negro activities, .34. A fourth scale on economic liberalism, which was not so widely used, dealt with organized labor and the distribution of wealth. Scores on this scale correlated .40 with internationalism, .39 with imperialism, and .30 with attitudes toward the activities of Negroes. The authors believe that their scales demonstrate "high generality rather than specificity in social attitudes." They also feel compelled to admit the presence of a general radicalism-conservatism factor as an explanation of the intercorrelations among these scales and data from autobiographies.

Films, photographs, and paragraphs depicting scenes of violence or force were also extensively used. Illustration 202 gives the questions that were asked after a picture of the wrecked automobile of a worker who refused to go out on strike had been shown. In addition to similar pictures, three short motion picture films were used and a number of paragraphs. The results indicated that attitudes toward specific events could be measured reliably, but low correlations were found between items. This fact led to the conclusion that specific fac-

ILLUS. 202. APPRAISAL OF ATTITUDES BY PHOTOGRAPH

(Questions asked after viewing photograph No. 14, showing a wrecked automobile of a workman named Langlois who refused to go out on strike)

1. Describe briefly in outline form your reaction to this photograph.
2. Indicate, by checking, how this picture affects you. Double check those which are especially intense.

Excites	Angers (irritates or enrages)
Depresses	Amuses
Thrills	Disgusts
Bores	Others . . . .
Interests	. . . .

3. In this situation, with whom do you sympathize?
4. What do you *like* or *dislike* in this photograph?
5. Why? (Answer briefly.)

(Total response to this photograph scored 2.)

(Murphy and Likert, 1938. By permission of Harper and Bros.)

tors in each situation were large as compared with a general factor. Similar results were found for single items in the attitude scales.

The Bogardus (1925) Test of Social Distance, shown in Illus. 203, was also applied by Murphy and Likert. It yielded specific scores of attitudes toward particular races and a general tolerance score whose odd-even reliability was found to be .88 among small groups of college students. This high coefficient was taken to indicate a high degree of generalization of attitudes toward persons in national and racial groups who are regarded as outsiders. The total tolerance score correlated approximately .68 with the separate scores from the questionnaires on internationalism, attitudes toward the Negro, and economic liberalism.

All of these opinion scores show only zero relationships with measures of specific information in the same fields or with intelligence test scores. However, a positive relationship between grades in college and radicalism scores on the opinion scales was discovered. Scholarship was more highly related to a radical stand for peace than to the other attitude scores. The authors believe that high scholarship usually involves much reading of recent literature, which happens to be largely radical in nature. The only other factor which corresponded with attitude scores was attitudes of parents. The authors conclude that the appraisals of attitudes dealing with public issues can best be studied from biographical material supplemented by systematic inventories.

Attitude toward the Negro

Horowitz (1936) investigated attitude toward Negroes by using three kinds of tests which were administered to boys from the kinder-

ILLUS. 203. BOGARDUS' TEST OF SOCIAL DISTANCE, REVISED

	To close kinship by marriage	To my club as personal chums	To my street as neighbors	To employment in my occupation in my country	To citizenship in my country	As visitors only to my country	Would exclude from my country
Canadians	1	2	3	4	5	6	7
Chinese	1	2	3	4	5	6	7
English	1	2	3	4	5	6	7
French	1	2	3	4	5	6	7
Germans	1	2	3	4	5	6	7
Hindus	1	2	3	4	5	6	7
Indians (Amer.)	1	2	3	4	5	6	7
Irish	1	2	3	4	5	6	7
Italians	1	2	3	4	5	6	7
Japanese	1	2	3	4	5	6	7
Jews — German	1	2	3	4	5	6	7
Jews — Russian	1	2	3	4	5	6	7
Mexicans	1	2	3	4	5	6	7
Mulattoes	1	2	3	4	5	6	7
Negroes	1	2	3	4	5	6	7
Norwegians	1	2	3	4	5	6	7
Portuguese	1	2	3	4	5	6	7
Filipinos	1	2	3	4	5	6	7
Russians	1	2	3	4	5	6	7
Scotch	1	2	3	4	5	6	7
South Americans	1	2	3	4	5	6	7
Spanish	1	2	3	4	5	6	7
Turks	1	2	3	4	5	6	7
Roman Catholics	1	2	3	4	5	6	7
Fundamentalists	1	2	3	4	5	6	7
Liberal (Modernist) Protestants	1	2	3	4	5	6	7
Agnostics	1	2	3	4	5	6	7
Atheists	1	2	3	4	5	6	7
Trade Union Members	1	2	3	4	5	6	7
Socialists	1	2	3	4	5	6	7
Communists	1	2	3	4	5	6	7

Name.................................

Date.................................

(Murphy and Likert, 1938, p. 133. By permission of Harper and Bros.)

garten through the eighth grade in various communities in or near New York City and in Georgia and Tennessee. Two of the tests used a page of 12 pictures of boys' faces, 4 of white and 8 of Negro; all judged to be pleasant by a group of adults (Illus. 204). On one test,

ILLUS. 204. PHOTOGRAPHS OF WHITE AND NEGRO BOYS

(Courtesy of Horowitz, 1936. By permission of the *Archives of Psychology*.)

called "Ranks," the instructions were to "Pick out the one you like best, next best, next best, and so on, until all are ranked." The score was the sum of the ranks assigned to the white boys' pictures; the smaller the score, the greater the preference for whites. On another test called "Show Me," the instructions were:

1. Show me all those that you want to sit next to you on a street car.
2. Show me all those that you want to be in your class at school.
3. Show me all those that you would play ball with.
4. Show me all those that you want to come to your party.
5. Show me all those that you want to be in your gang.

6. Show me all those that you want to go home with you for lunch.
7. Show me all those that you want to sit next to in the movies.
8. Show me all those that you would go swimming with.
9. Show me all those that you'd like to have for a cousin.
10. Show me all those that you want to be captain of the ball team.
11. Show me all those that you want to live next door to you.
12. Show me all those that you like.

The score was the per cent of total selection which were white boys. The higher the per cent, the greater was the preference for whites.

A third test consisted of thirty-nine photographs showing activities of playing marbles, choosing sides for baseball, hand wrestling, sitting outdoors, playing a piano, listening to a radio, playing checkers, eating in an ice cream parlor, eating dinner in a home, and common situations in lavatory, workshop, museum, library, and schoolroom. Each situation was posed twice, once by four white boys and again with a Negro boy substituted for one of the whites. Each picture was observed in turn and the examiner asked, "Do you want to join in with them and do what they're doing along with them?" The scores were the difference between the number of times all-white groups and groups with one colored boy were chosen. The results of each test proved to be fairly reliable when checked for retest consistency. The general trends for New York City whites are shown in Illus. 205. Here the ranking test showed the most prejudice, and this was true for all grades. The Show Me Test indicated little prejudice at the fifth year, but a rapid increase until approximately the eighth year. The Social Situations Test showed little prejudice at the fifth year, and a slow increase to the fourteenth year. Intercorrelations between these tests increased with age. The New York City group showed responses similar to those of the Southern groups. The degree of prejudice,

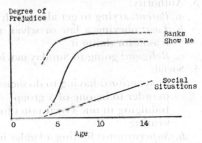

ILLUS. 205. GROWTH OF ATTITUDES TOWARD THE NEGRO

(Horowitz, 1936, p. 25. By permission of the Editor, *Archives of Psychology*.)

as shown by a tendency to exceed chance scores, was greater in the less specific test situations. Horowitz concludes that prejudice is a socially developed response which is derived from various sources. The most important source, at first, is probably the attitudes of friends and relatives. Later, the attitude may be the result of specific experiences.

Reasons for Acts

Direct approaches are inadequate when the subjects do not wish to reveal their true attitudes. Brandt (1937) made an approach to the analysis of replies to questions of ethical significance which is interesting because it is somewhat indirect. In a group test situation the following instructions were read:

> In each of the situations given below, a person would have to make a choice between two possible actions. For each situation write down *all* of the points he should consider before he decides which to do. Remember we are not in the least bit interested in which decision you think is the right one, or which one you would make. You are to concern yourself with writing down *only the things that are to be considered* in making the decision.

At this point the experimenter gave orally an example (losing one's fountain pen—to buy a new one or not). He then discussed with the group the particular things involved in a consideration of the situation presented. Samples of the situations used are:

1. Property:
   - *a. Stealing:* finding an unlocked car on the street; to drive it around awhile and return it or leave it alone
   - *b. Destruction:* finding some things one wants in a magazine in the public library; to tear out some pages or not
2. Persons:
   - *a. Friends:* finding out about someone who has been doing serious injury to other people; to report him or not
   - *b. Group loyalty:* under what circumstances would one join a club?
3. Authority:
   - *a. Parent:* trying to get along with the family or leaving home
   - *b. Law:* obeying a law or school ruling even though you don't see the reason for doing it
   - *c. Religion:* going to Sunday movies or not
4. Social:
   - *a. Conventions:* having to do something that injures your physical health in order to be one of a group

     Indulging in one's own tastes for clothes regardless of what others are wearing
   - *b. Superstitions:* finding a ladder in one's path; to go under it or avoid it

The answers were classified into six groups on the basis of type of goal. These are illustrated in Illus. 206 for the item, "Indulging in one's own tastes for clothes regardless of what others are wearing." The boundaries of these classes are doubtless somewhat vague, but it seems probable that in a more extended and refined study a high degree of uniformity would be found among judges in classifying the answers.

ILLUS. 206. BASES OF JUDGMENTS

For the item "To indulge in one's tastes for clothes regardless of what others are wearing":

1. Self-regard (17 per cent)
   Will I be looked down upon?
   Will people laugh at you?
2. Parental approval (8 per cent)
   Do my parents think them O.K.?
3. Friends' approval (7 per cent)
   What do my friends think?
4. General welfare (8 per cent)
   Wear the best you can.
   Clothes do not make the man.
5. Objective or practical considerations (39 per cent)
   Does the clothing fit? Is it appropriate for the weather? Where are you living? What is the comparative cost and durability?
6. Social institutions (21 per cent)
   Who are the people you associate with? Have I social ambitions? Do you like to dress like other people?

(After Brandt, 1937. By permission of the University of Iowa, *Studies in Child Welfare*.)

The per cents in the parentheses in Illus. 206 are the distribution of all answers given by all persons to all the items. Brandt found that individuals varied a great deal from this average distribution of answers. Some subjects emphasized their self-regard, others parental approval, and others social orientation. This is a valuable diagnostic technique which should be more widely used. It is interesting to note that moral or religious considerations were nearly lacking in this group. The answers would doubtless vary if the study were conducted in a Sunday school.

Responses to particular questions showed that there was a good deal of hedging or evasion or making of particular exceptions for unethical acts. Thus, most of the group were willing to take an unlocked car for a spin on such considerations as: "Is there sufficient gas in the tank? Can they drive? Can they get away with it? What are the chances of wrecking the car? Is there an urgent need? Who is the owner? Will he care?" Considerations of this sort were most frequent on items which seemed to be or to have been of immediate concern to the subjects.

Allport and Vernon's Study of Values

The Study of Values Questionnaire is interesting in that it attempts to appraise attitudes in the six fields which were described by Spranger (1928). The test includes 120 items, distributed equally between the six fields. An inspection of the test shows the following sorts of items classified as

1. *Theoretical:* discovery of natural laws, mathematical relations, and scientific facts
2. *Economic:* activity in real estate, finance, industrial development, and vocational training, and practical applications in general
3. *Aesthetic:* indulging in artistic appreciation or composition in poetry, literature, music, dancing, architecture, and scenery
4. *Social:* responding to others' needs with unselfishness and sympathy as shown by charity, freeing of slaves, hospital and social service work, and general friendliness and co-operation
5. *Political:* managing governmental and legal affairs, curtailing charity, aggression in war, debating, playing on athletic teams, organizing, holding a seat in Congress, exploration of little known parts of the world, and acquiring professional and social prestige
6. *Religious:* abolishing war, laying up treasures in heaven, being reverent in a church, believing in God, comparing religious faiths, and evaluating life as a whole

The test has two parts. All the items in Part I require that a preference be expressed between two fields of activity (Illus. 207). These items combine judgments of *Yes* or *No* with ratings from 0 to 3, to show amounts of preference. The first item demands a judgment between discovery of scientific laws and applications of scientific laws; the second item, between aesthetic creation and social compatibility. The items in Part II require that four choices be rated in order of their appeal (Illus. 207). In item I the first choice emphasizes social values; the second, economic; the third, religious; and the fourth, political. Parts I and II are combined into a final score for each field, which may be expressed in profiles, such as those in Illus. 208. Here the mean scores of a group of sixty-one engineering students show that their greatest interests lay in theoretical and economic activities, and their least in the aesthetic and religious. The highest interests for a group of eighty-one missionaries of both sexes are shown by this figure to be in religious activities, the next highest in social, and the lowest in political and economic activities. A fairly large number of studies using this questionnaire have reported differences of the same kind between various professional and social groups.

A statistical evaluation of this form has been reported by Cantril and Allport (1933), who reviewed fourteen published studies of this questionnaire. The original means were found to be correct for an additional group of 2,755 subjects. The range of scores varies from a standard deviation of 5.5 in social values to 9.7 in economic. The

ILLUS. 207. A STUDY OF VALUES

PART I

Directions: A number of controversial statements or questions with two alternative answers are given below. Indicate your personal preferences by writing the appropriate figures in the right-hand columns, as indicated :

	(*a*)	(*b*)
If you agree with alternative (*a*) and disagree with (*b*), write 3 in the first column and 0 in the second column, thus	3	0
If you agree with (*b*); disagree with (*a*), write	0	3
If you have a slight preference for (*a*) over (*b*), write	2	1
If you have a slight preference for (*b*) over (*a*), write	1	2

Do not write any other combination of figures after any question except one of these four.

There is no time limit, but do not linger long over any one question or statement, and do not leave out any of the questions, unless you find it really impossible to make a decision.

	(*a*)	(*b*)
1. The main object of scientific research should be the discovery of pure truth rather than its practical applications. (*a*) Yes; (*b*) No.		
2. Do you think that it is justifiable for the greatest artists, such as Beethoven, Wagner, Byron, etc., to be selfish and negligent of the feelings of others? (*a*) Yes; (*b*) No.		

PART II

Directions: Each of the following situations or questions is followed by four possible attitudes or answers. Arrange these answers in the order of your personal preference from first to fourth by writing, in the left-hand margin,

1   beside the answer that appeals to you most,

2   beside the answer which is next most important to you,

3   beside the next, and

4   beside the answer that least represents your interest or preference.

You may think of answers which would be preferable from your point of view to any of those listed. It is necessary, however, that you make your selection from the alternatives presented, and arrange all four in order of their desirability, guessing when your preferences are not distinct. If you find it really impossible to guess your preference, you may omit the question.

1. Do you think that a good government should aim chiefly at —

   a. More aid for the poor, sick, and old

   b. The development of manufacturing and trade

   c. Introducing more ethical principles into its Policies and diplomacy

   d. Establishing a position of prestige and respect among nations

(Allport and Vernon, 1931. By permission of Houghton Mifflin Co.)

ILLUS. 208. PROFILE OF VALUES

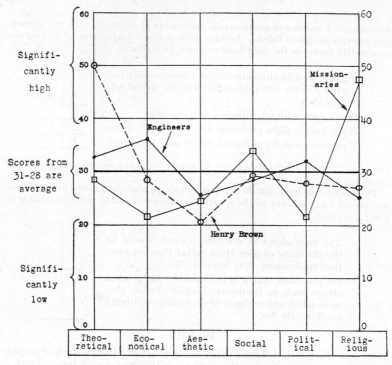

Profile of Values

Mean Scores of 64 Engineering Students and 80 Missionaries

(Arranged from Allport and Vernon, 1931. By permission of the *Journal of Abnormal and Social Psychology*.)

repeat reliability is reported for eighty-four students over one hundred days as follows:

Religious	.87	Political	.76
Aesthetic	.86	Theoretical	.68
Economic	.79	Social	.50

The authors point out that these figures show that the test of social values is less discriminating and less consistent than the other tests. The unsatisfactory results from the social-values test are attributed to confusion in defining the term *social,* which led to the inclusion of several independent traits under this heading, and also to ambiguities in interpretation of certain items. The authors question the existence of Spranger's "social type" and conclude (p. 272):

On the theoretical side the evidence from recent applications of the Study of Values must be interpreted as establishing the Values, with the exception of social, as self-consistent, pervasive, enduring, and above all, generalized traits of personality. Several experiments demonstrate a clear relationship between values and conduct. They show that a person's activity is not determined exclusively by the stimulus of the moment, nor by a merely transient interest, nor by a specific attitude peculiar to each situation which he encounters. The experiments prove on the contrary that *general evaluative attitudes* enter into various common activities of everyday life, and in so doing help to account for the consistencies of personality.

According to Allport and Vernon, proof for the existence of these generalized attitudes lies in a number of findings, set forth as follows:

1. The internal consistencies of the various subtests. Items were selected which showed the highest relationships between item score and total subtest score.

2. The diversity of items in a subtest. The authors tried to select items which would test as many different applications of a generalized interest as possible.

3. Correlations between the Study of Values scores and activities, such as reading a newspaper, showing interest in clothes, securing high grades in college studies, attending church, speaking, handwriting, and artistic activities. Such correlations range from approximately $+.25$ to $+.66$ on small groups of students.

From an examination of these findings, however, the existence of these five general attitudes does not seem to the writer to be well established. The internal consistencies, which are generally low, would in any case merely show a coincidence of pattern among the persons tested. Such coincidences may occur from a number of factors rather than one of the five general attitudes selected. The moderate correlations between scores on the Study of Values Test and various activities might also be explained as resulting from a larger or smaller number of factors. Moreover, the test items for a single field appear to many to be quite independent. Thus, in the field of economics, there seems to be little if any connection among interests in financial transactions, in vocational training programs, and in problems of practical engineering. In the field of politics, which is more accurately described as interest in power, there seem to be small similarities among such varied activities as debating, playing on athletic teams, curtailing charity, aggression in war, and exploring strange lands.

Furthermore, an inspection of test items reveals an overlapping of fields of interest, a fact which makes their identification difficult. For instance, the writer has found that many persons cannot distinguish between a search for truth in the theoretical field, an attempt to evaluate life in the religious field, and appreciation of true art in the aesthetic field. There is also a marked similarity between unselfishness in the social field and ethics in the religious.

Indirect Approaches

All of the studies reported above, except that of Watson, attempt to appraise attitudes by direct approaches, such as by asking a person to what extent he agrees with a statement. A direct approach allows a person to falsify purposely his answers. There seem to be many situations where a person prefers to conceal his real feelings, because he believes their disclosure would get him into trouble or cause him to lose a friend. The studies reported below are noteworthy in that the methods used attempt to disguise the purpose of the test.

Hammond (1948) approached attitude measurement by using an information test in which one was asked to choose between two answers. In one group of items (Hammond, 1948, p. 39) both answers were placed about equally distant from the right answer, as:

The average weekly wage of war workers in 1945 was
(1) $37　　　(2) $57

In another group of items the two choices indicated extremes but the truth was indeterminate, as:

Russia's removal of heavy industry from Austria was
(1) legal　　　(2) illegal

Hammond called both of these types of items nonfactual, because the true answer did not appear. Two tests were prepared, one concerning labor-management attitudes, and the other attitudes toward Russia. Hammond applied these tests to a businessmen's luncheon club and to a group of clerical and semiprofessional employees of a large labor union. The critical ratio of the difference between the means was about 12 for each test. An item analysis revealed that only five of the forty items used on the two tests failed to show a significant difference between the two groups. The split-half reliability coefficients were approximately .80.

Hammond also experimented to see if the same tests would work equally well as attitude questionnaires, with instructions which explained that the nonfactual items had no correct answers. For a large group of college students the test concerning labor-management facts gave almost the same results when used as an attitude questionnaire. In the case of the test concerning Russia, however, there was considerable variation between the information test and the attitude questionnaire results. Moreover the attitude-questionnaire results yielded much lower split-half reliabilities than the information-test results. Hammond believed that the information type of test gave a better indication of attitudes because the purpose of the test was somewhat disguised.

Another indirect approach to the appraisal of attitudes toward another person is that reported by Stogdill (1949), who used data from four naval organizations. In his procedure each officer was asked to name those with whom he spent the most time—his assistants, his associates and superiors, or those in other departments. Lastly, each officer was asked to consider lists of names of officers and to rank them in order according to the time spent. In making these estimates each officer was asked to make the results typical of a usual working month.

The data were plotted and analyzed to show working relations among the members of each organization. Considerable variation was found among organizations and among persons in similar positions. Deviations from formal lines of communication were most marked in organizations where the commanding officer had expressed an active interest in "cutting red tape." Deviations among individuals seemed to indicate personal likes or dislikes, but the total amounts of time spent had little significance as indicators of preferences.

Factorial Analyses of Attitudes

The application of multiple-factor analyses to data of this sort may be of value in discovering underlying patterns. Such an analysis was made by Lurie (1937), using a 141-item test similar to the Study of Values Test in content and construction. The test sheets were given to six hundred students, but only 203 (128 men and 75 women) returned them complete enough to be used. A 7-step rating scale, ranging from complete rejection to complete acceptance, was used for each item. Twenty-four scores were secured for each person by subdividing each of the six main divisions into four smaller ones on the basis of (*a*) present interests, (*b*) ideals or standards, (*c*) preferences for associates or famous persons, and (*d*) beliefs or opinions. An analysis of these 24 scores by Thurstone's method resulted in the seven independent factors tentatively named:

1. *Social* or *altruistic:* friendly, tolerant
2. *Philistine:* aggressive, utilitarian, anti-cultural
3. *Theoretical:* interest in science, criticalness
4. *Religious:* ethical doctrine and practice (not mystical)
5. *Open-minded:* liberal vs. conservative
6. *Practical:* pressure to do something
7. *Aesthetic:* superficial lip service to culture, negatively related to aesthetic ideals

Lurie states that the first four of these factors may be taken as stable categories which cover all six of Spranger's types. The philistine factor is found to be large in both the economic and the political fields and also large, but in a negative way, in the aesthetic ideals. Reports by other investigators support these findings about the intercorrelations among scores on the Study of Values Tests. Lurie believes that the last three factors are temperament traits or adjustments which cut across fields of interests, and which were not controlled in setting up the test. Lurie's findings also include some low correlations among scores which were supposed to measure similar interests.

The fact that Lurie found evidence for a basic unitary social or altruistic interest, whereas Allport and Vernon did not find it, needs an explanation. The evidence is not at hand for a complete explanation, but the different findings must have resulted from a different sampling, either of interests or of persons. It may be that in Lurie's form a larger number of items clearly differentiate between altruistic and nonaltruistic activities than in the Study of Values Test. Or it may be that Lurie's subjects were actually more variable in altruistic tendencies than those of Allport and Vernon, and hence showed distinct individual differences in this field. A combination of both explanations may be nearer the truth. The results nicely illustrate the point that the statistical factors are always related to the particular items used and the particular population tested.

Whisler (1934) designed a set of questions which were intended to evaluate "generalized attitudes." He avoided the use of specific-situation items such as are found in nearly all the other inventories discussed, believing that a few questions, such as those in Illus. 209, would yield as adequate a sample of attitude as a larger number of specific items. A factor analysis of thirty-one items was made, using 126 undergraduates. Six factors were reported and identified from the items which had the largest loadings: (*a*) acceptance of conventional ethical principles, (*b*) enjoyment of momentary pleasure, (*c*) interest in conflicts and controversies, (*d*) desire to be an effective agent, (*e*) participation in casual social relations, and (*f*) criticalness and interest in the truth.

The identification of these factors is not conclusive, owing to the different interpretations which may be placed on an item. Thus, Item 16, "having a standard of goodness by which plays are judged," may be interpreted as (*a*) having a moral standard of goodness, or (*b*) the possession of any standard, or (*c*) referring to particular types of plays, or (*d*) referring to the rendition of a play rather than to its construction. Various interpretations of other items are probable. Less ambiguous statements would allow more accurate interpretations of the results. Yet Whisler's approach is an interesting one which has given results different from those of other workers.

ILLUS. 209. QUESTIONS ON PERSONAL ATTITUDES

Instructions: Take the words used as roughly indicating a three-fold scale into which responses to the question may be put. The scale refers to your judgment of yourself, not to what you think other people's judgment may be. Consider each question carefully, but if in doubt as to the proper checking, guess.

Abbreviations used: M, much or frequently; S, considerable or sometimes; L, little or rarely.

1. How much would your liking for an acquaintance of the same sex be affected by whether that person had a genuine liking for and interest in children, or was indifferent?

   M _____ S _____ L _____

2. How much enjoyment do you get out of doing or saying things which are quite shocking to most of the people who see or hear you?

   M _____ S _____ L _____

3. How much change has there been in the last two years in the type of people you prefer and seek to associate with?

   M _____ S _____ L _____

4. How much enjoyment do you get out of working with materials or making things with your hands?

   M _____ S _____ L _____

5. To what extent, in general, is your evaluation, judgment, and opinion of an acquaintance of the opposite sex based on speculation and thought as to how satisfactory the person might be as husband or wife?

   M _____ S _____ L _____

6. To what extent are you interested in politics? (That is, — local, provincial, national, or international politics)

   M _____ S _____ L _____

(*25 more items*)

(Whisler, 1934, p. 285. By permission of the Editor, *Journal of Educational Psychology.*)

Carlson (1934) reported the results of applying five of Thurstone's attitude scales to 215 seniors at the University of Chicago. The correlations between measures of intelligence by a group test and attitude scores were:

Prohibition	.036	Communism	.330
God	−.191	Birth Control	.211
Pacifism	.402		

These results lead to the conclusion that the more intelligent students are likely to be more liberal in attitudes toward these issues. Carlson also found that a multiple-factor analysis of these five attitude scales and intelligence test scores yielded three factors. These were tentatively named intelligence, radicalism, and religiousness by an inspection of the various loadings.

The question of the existence of basic general attitudes, such as those named in the three studies just examined, will lead to useless controversies unless careful definition and unbiased procedures are used. Apparently, if one is allowed to select some observations and ignore others, overwhelming evidence can be secured supporting almost any hypothesis about the nature of attitudes. Furthermore, test items are carefully chosen to represent a certain general attitude and if a random selection of persons is tested, that general attitude will usually seem to be supported by an analysis of the test results. In order to secure a complete picture of basic opinions and their relationships, items must be included which clearly represent all possible attitudes. The results of applying such a test to large normal populations will make possible a more adequate analysis of attitudes. Those factors described thus far may be found to be unique, or they may be combined with other patterns or subdivided in more essential traits.

PRACTICAL RESULTS

The strength of various attitudes among students, employees, or voters is a major concern of educators, employers, advertisers, and statesmen. A large share of their time and effort is spent in trying to develop particular attitudes in their communities. Measuring instruments which may give accurate pictures of changes in attitudes are therefore in great demand and the field is rapidly developing. Some studies of nation-wide scope have been of little value because they neglected to secure measures of a representative group of people. Carefully controlled studies which measure the same persons twice are usually limited to a few highly selected students; hence their results are also of limited significance. The sampling of attitudes of large populations requires a great deal of careful planning and hard work. Sampling techniques are discussed in Chapter III.

Modification of Attitudes

The effects of propaganda have been studied in a fragmentary fashion by a number of investigators. Generally, propaganda techniques include dissemination of reading matter, oral arguments, pictures, and films of actual scenes. Although many efforts at propaganda combine several of these techniques, several studies have tried to evaluate them separately. A few studies will be reported to illustrate the chief results and some of the difficulties which have been encountered in attempting to measure changes in attitudes.

Modifications Due to Actions or Arguments. Modifications of attitudes in line with the attitudes of instructors have been reported by Manske (1936) and Kroll (1934). Manske, using Hinkley's scale of attitudes toward the Negro, reported that among thirty-two classes of high school students, eight showed slight changes opposed to teachers' attitudes during ten "non-indoctrinating" lessons taught by one of sixteen teachers. This study seems to indicate that teachers are able to be impartial in presenting material of this sort. Kroll measured the result of one semester's instruction in English history. He found that when the teacher held a radical point of view, scores on Harper's scales of social attitudes changed toward radicalism among 183 high school boys, but that when the teacher took a conservative position, the boys showed no reliable changes toward conservatism.

A number of studies report changes in attitudes due to purposeful instruction. Results from grade school and college groups have been reported on attitudes toward racial groups, propaganda, treatment of criminals, patriotism, prohibition, war, and other topics. Murphy *et al.* (1937) wrote a thorough discussion of such studies, which may be summarized as follows:

1. High school groups are usually more susceptible to changes in attitude than college or adult groups but the changes may be less permanent.
2. Changes, generally in the direction of liberalism, usually accompany both high school and college instruction in social, economic, and political studies.
3. The attitudes of the instructor may be as important as the information which is discussed.
4. A violent argument or episode tends to make people take sides, for a neutral position becomes untenable. The negative response to the appeal may be as great or greater than the positive. The distribution of scores tends to become flattened or bimodal.

Biddle (1932) reported that among 350 high school and college students susceptibility to propaganda was greatly reduced by reading pamphlets on the techniques of propaganda. Among ten thousand college students Knower (1935) found that there was little difference between the effects of "emotional" and "rational" appeals concerning prohibition, and that significant changes were larger among all groups when students read the appeal than when they heard it delivered orally. Other reports by Cherrington and Miller (1933) and Wilke (1934) indicate that speeches given in person or over the radio are at least as effective as printed presentations of the same material.

Changes in attitude which follow the viewing of a motion picture have been reported by Thurstone (1931) and his collaborators. For instance, a film which showed Chinese people as able and artistic caused a mean change toward more favorable scores on the scale of attitude toward Chinese equal to ten times the standard error of the change. Another film in which some Chinese were pictured in a more unfavorable light resulted in a mean change to a less favorable attitude equal to 2.2 PE. Another film which showed bootlegging as a vice resulted in no significant change in attitude toward bootlegging, which was already unfavorable. In other studies attitudes toward war, crime, and racial groups have, in general, showed that changes in scores occurred after the subjects viewed films, and these changes were retained for periods of as long as 19 months, with a gradual return toward the original position.

Murphy and Likert (1938) reported a study of the effects of written propaganda. Fourteen test items were selected which appraised attitudes toward war, imperialism, and Negro activities. These were administered to two small groups of college students. A week later one group read propaganda material which argued for radical changes and the other group read material supporting conservative points of view. The material consisted of seven short excerpts from speeches by army officers, college professors, and persons well known in public life. These selections could be read in about 30 minutes.

A week after the propaganda material had been read, the test was repeated. Then each group was given material to read which supported the point of view opposed to that which had been previously presented. Four weeks later the attitude tests were repeated. These three tests showed how much each student was affected by this amount of conservative and radical propaganda. Although there was some shifting of opinion among students, there was no marked tendency for those with radical inclinations to vary more or less than other students. In one of the two groups there was a slight tendency for the more radical students to show greater susceptibility to propaganda. The lack of positive results may be due to several factors—the combining in one score of attitudes toward several different issues, the use of several short excerpts from speeches rather than one long concentrated speech on one topic, the delay of from one to four weeks between reading the propaganda material and repeating the tests, and the sophistication of the students.

Cantril (1944) noted that public-opinion surveys showed that opinion was highly sensitive to important events, and that events were much more important than words or propaganda. Opinion in this country seldom anticipated emergencies and reacted to emergencies only when self-interest was involved. Thus the German invasion of Czechoslovakia and Poland aroused few Americans, but the German invasion of the Low Countries and Norway made people realize that a German victory would affect them personally. Cantril believed that if people in America were given ready access to information, public opinion would reveal a hard-headed common sense and would tend to agree with the opinions of experts.

Remmers (1950) reported a practical way of measuring empathy or its opposite, the projection of one's own attitudes. He applied the method specifically to measuring the "gap" between management's and labor's attitudes. The questionnaire "How Supervise" was filled out by a group of industrial managers and also by a group of labor leaders. The labor leaders were later asked to fill out the same questionnaire the way they thought businessmen would answer it. The difference between the mean scores of labor leaders on the two occasions showed their estimate of the gap between themselves and businessmen. The difference between mean scores of labor leaders and businessmen showed degree of empathy—the ability of the labor leader to put himself in the other person's place. The results furnished important information on points of agreement and disagreement, both real and imaginary, and marked individual differences were found.

Modifications Due to Prestige. Marple (1933) reported that high school seniors, college seniors, and adults, in that order, were susceptible to the influence of majority opinion, although the differences between groups were not great. The opinions of these persons were secured on two occasions, the second a month later than the first. They were asked to mark seventy-five controversial statements about government, war, races, schools, and morals to show agreement, uncertainty, or disagreement. On the second occasion the group was supplied with a record of the answers which had actually been given on the first occasion. Changes between two trials in the direction of group opinion were: for high school students 64 per cent, for college students 55 per cent, and for adults 40 per cent. A similar experiment showed that the influence of opinions given by a group of 40 experts was not quite so great as the influence of the opinions of one's own group, although both were marked.

A study by Moore (1921) reported that conservative students accepted majority opinion more regularly than radical students, but Murphy and Likert (1938) reported no relationship between radical attitudes and changes in attitudes due to knowledge of majority opinion. They found that announcing the majority opinion orally after reading a statement on a second test did cause students to vary somewhat from the first test. The correlations between scores on the internationalism scale and shifts toward majority opinion were, however, nearly all zero.

Modification Concurring with Age. The work of Horowitz (1936) described above gives an excellent illustration of age-group differences in attitudes among grade school pupils. Two other illustrations are given below which are typical of the many reports available.

Murphy and Likert (1938) reported that approximately 5 years after the first survey in 1929, a retest using three attitude scales was made of 129 individuals who had been graduated from college. The odd-even reliability of attitude scores was nearly the same as that reported for the first trial. The mean scores shifted slightly toward more liberal and radical attitudes. The most significant differences were found on the scales for imperialism and economic practices. The reasons for these shifts were discussed at length without any clear-cut conclusions. Data on personal incomes indicated that the shifts were probably not due to personal want. The authors believe that the change during 5 years probably reflected awareness of the seriousness of the causes of the widespread world depression.

The reasons for attending church were recorded by Kingsbury (1937) for a group of Protestant churchgoers in Chicago. The percentages of persons who checked eight reasons were found for the four age groups: fifteen to twenty-five, twenty-six to thirty-five, thirty-six to fifty, and over fifty. Nearly 80 per cent of the youngest group checked "to formulate a philosophy of life," "to hear music and literature," and "to gain new friends," but only about 20 per cent of the oldest group checked these items. Thirty per cent or less of the youngest group reported that they attend church "to keep alive the spirit of Christ," "to encourage family attendance," or "from habit," whereas nearly 80 per cent of the oldest group checked these reasons. "To solve personal problems" was checked by approximately 50 per cent of all ages. "Just some place to go" dropped from 30 per cent to 7 per cent with thirty years of growth. "For reassurance of immortality" dropped from 30 per cent to nearly zero between the twenty- and thirty-year-old groups. This reason became increasingly important with advance in age, 30 per cent of the fifty-year-olds having checked it.

The Relation of Information to Attitudes

The question whether accurate knowledge about a situation accompanies a liberal attitude is one which can be answered by comparing information test scores with attitude scale scores.

A remarkably widespread study by Watson (1929) reported the application of a questionnaire on Far Eastern relations among three thousand adults in church groups, prisons, business clubs, and schools. The questionnaire contains both information items and attitude items. The scores of information on Japanese issues correlated .82 with favorable attitudes toward the Japanese, and information on Chinese issues correlated .70 with favor toward Chinese nationalism. Another study by Manry (1927) found among college students a correlation of .69 between knowledge of international affairs and a favorable attitude toward world citizenship. Wrightstone (1934) found that historical knowledge correlated .58 with economic liberalism among four hundred pupils in the ninth grade to the twelfth grade.

Reckless and Bringen (1933) found that among college students information about Negroes and their problems had a mean correlation of .64 with favorable attitudes toward the Negroes.

In contrast to these results are those of Murphy and Likert (1938), who found a zero correlation between rough measures of information and liberalism in a study of internationalism and attitudes toward the Negroes. Biddle (1931) reported correlations between zero and .26 between knowledge and unfavorable attitudes toward Filipinos, Japanese, and Chinese. Bolton (1935) found zero correlations between information and attitude toward Negroes for seven hundred college students. The low relationships reported are probably due in part to sampling of narrow groups, to mixing of issues, and to the fragmentary nature of the tests.

The general conclusion is that well-informed persons usually take a fairly liberal or experimental view on controversial issues. Poorly informed persons are more likely to approve extreme radical or reactionary policies.

Cantril (1944) reported several public-opinion polls which showed that one effect of greater information is to make the well-informed more sensitive to the implications of points of view. Persons well informed in one area, for example, European affairs, tended to be well informed also in another area, such as Far Eastern affairs. Where personal wishes or identification was strong, however, greater information about a topic did not carry much weight in opinion polls.

In a study of students in Bennington College and the Catholic University of America, Newcomb (1946) found that the "attitude climate" of a group was related to the information of the group. Newcomb secured an indication of attitude climate by a questionnaire on attitudes toward the Spanish Civil War parties in 1937. Instructions were given to make one of the following answers to each item: strongly agree, agree, uncertain, disagree, or strongly disagree. Typical statements (Newcomb, 1946, p. 301) were:

I hope the Loyalists win the war.
The real issue in this war is nationalism versus communism.

The conflict in Spain may be fairly accurately described as a German-Italian attack on the Spanish Government.

The answers were weighted so that the higher scores showed greater Pro-Nationalist sympathy and the lower scores greater Pro-Loyalist sympathy. From this questionnaire a critical ratio of 16.5 was found between the mean scores of the two colleges.

Newcomb then measured information by three 20-item true-false tests. One test (p. 301) contained items thought to be neutral, for example:

The present seat of the Loyalist Government is in Madrid.

The government in power when the civil war broke out represented a coalition of left and liberal parties.

Another test (p. 301) consisted of Pro-Loyalist items such as:

The Loyalist planes have in no instance been guilty of shelling noncombatants.

General Franco's government has been recognized as the legitimate power in Spain only by governments which are overly fascist or near fascist.

The third test (p. 301) consisted of items which were Pro-Nationalist, as:

Indisputable evidence has been adduced showing that some clergy have been executed and many persecuted by Loyalist sympathizers.

The scores on these tests were correlated with the scores on the attitude scales with the following rather striking results:

Type of Information	Bennington	Catholic University
Neutral	—.45	.38
Pro-Loyalist	—.57	—.08
Pro-Nationalist	—.04	.51

These results show that the persons at Bennington with most Pro-Loyalist sympathy had the most neutral information, while the persons at Catholic University with the most Pro-Nationalist sympathy had greater neutral information. Also the Pro-Loyalist information was correlated about .50 with Pro-Loyalist feeling at Bennington, and Pro-Nationalist information about .50 with Pro-Nationalist feeling at Catholic University. Newcomb (p. 292) believed that the following hypotheses were supported by these figures:

1. That individual information relevant to a social issue is determined by degree of *concern*, opportunity for becoming familiar with the evidence, and *usefulness* of information in supporting existing attitudes.

2. That the manner in which these factors serve to determine information is a function of attitude climate defined in terms of uniformity, direction, and intensity of the attitude in question, in a given community.

The figures seem to indicate that degree of concern increased the amounts of neutral and favorable information learned. Opportunity or accessibility of information could not be well appraised in this experiment. The usefulness of information in supporting an attitude is shown by the significant correlations between attitudes and favorable information and the near zero correlations between attitudes and unfavorable information. Newcomb points out that generalizations about attitude-information relationships can never be safely made without a careful analysis of the attitude climate.

Comparison of Various Techniques

Biographies, Inventories, and Rating Scales. The question, which techniques are most valuable in the study of attitudes, can only be answered in terms of their accuracy and their uses. The three most common techniques employ biographies, inventories, and ratings of general attitudes. Nearly all writers who have used case histories or autobiographies report that these yield the most complete accounts. A good deal of emphasis is therefore being placed upon securing accurate and complete histories. Comparisons of thorough case histories with measurement techniques have been made by several persons. Stouffer (1930) compared a scale of attitudes toward prohibition with a written account of activities, and with a graphic rating of attitude toward prohibition. Two hundred and thirty-eight college students first completed the scale, and then wrote accounts, using approximately one thousand words, of their experiences with the prohibition law and drinking liquor. Four judges rated these accounts on a graphic scale of indulgence. The agreement of judges found by correlating the rating of each judge with the ratings of the others ranged from .83 to .89, mean .87. These figures show a high degree of consistency. The correlation between scores on the attitude scale and the composite rating by four judges was .81.

The same students also rated themselves on two occasions with a graphic rating scale for attitudes toward prohibition. When the two self-ratings were combined, it was found that the combined self-ratings correlated .80 with Smith's scale and .80 with judges' ratings of accounts. These correlations are all high enough to suggest that the three methods were appraising the same aspects of persons with about the same accuracy. It is probable that each of the three methods introduces unique aspects which may be of importance in particular evaluations.

Another study by Watson (1925) compared scores on his test of public opinion with short descriptions written by friends. The following account is a description of the person whose profile is shown in Illus. 201. Both the profile and the account show extremely marked preference for fundamental Protestant beliefs and strict morals, and a less marked preference for mild economic reforms.

This man is a farmer in a small Wyoming town. He is the leading pillar in the Methodist church. When I visited one Sunday he was drilling the children in the Sunday School on the names of the persons and the significant details of each of the Old Testament miracles. His neighbors consider him, next to ——————, the most stubborn man they have known. He is a rank-and-file member of the Farm Bureau, so should share some of their progressive economic ideas. (From Watson, 1925, p. 46.)

A much more elaborate study by Murphy and Likert (1938) also showed close correspondence between scores on their test and autobiographies written by students. Several cases were found, however, where apparent inconsistencies were cleared up only by a careful rereading of the autobiographies.

Thurstone and Chave (1929) compared scores on the Attitude-to-ward-the-Church Scale with students' self-ratings made at the same time. A graphic rating scale was used which consisted of a horizontal line and the words "strongly favorable to the church" printed at one end, "neutral" in the middle, and at the other end, "strongly against the church." The correlation between scores and ratings was .67, a fairly high figure. The same students also indicated whether or not they attended church frequently and were active members in a church. The frequent churchgoers were ten times as numerous among those whose scores were favorable to the church as among those whose scores were unfavorable.

Median Scale Value vs. Total Score. Likert (1932), using two scoring techniques, applied several of Thurstone's scales. First, he used Thurstone's method of having a person simply check the statements with which he agreed, a procedure which yields a median scale-value score. This score implies that a person agrees with all the statements which are less extreme than his own median statement. In practice this may not be the case. Likert also used a total score method which required a person to rate the same items on a 5-step scale, using the words: (5) strongly approve, (4) approve, (3) undecided, (2) disapprove, (1) strongly disapprove. A person's score was secured by adding the points checked on all the items. A comparison of the results of these two techniques showed that the retest reliability for the median scale values was .76, whereas that for total scores was .85. The scale values correlated with total scores .88. Thus it appears that while both methods of scoring yield similar results, the total-score method shows considerably more self-consistency. The reasons advanced for this superiority of total scores are: (1) each item bears a share of the score directly, and (2) persons can probably express themselves more accurately with a 5-step scale than with only two choices, as when given the choice of either agreeing or disagreeing. The total scoring technique can be applied without the elaborate scale construction which is preliminary to the median scale-value scores. Thurstone's scale construction has the advantage, however, of guaranteeing the inclusion of items which represent a wide range of attitudes and an equal number of items at each level.

These comparisons of various techniques lead to five tentative conclusions:

1. A scored biography and a questionnaire yield, under fairly well-controlled conditions, about equal retest consistencies, ranging from .60 to .80, depending upon the range of scores in the group, and the ambiguity of the items. Scores which depend upon the summation of a large number of items show greater retest or odd-even reliability than scores which depend upon a few judgments, or on a median value.

2. Self-ratings and self-inventories of activities seem to have about the same validity, as shown by agreement with various criteria. The selection of satisfactory criteria is particularly difficult.

3. The graphic rating of single general attitudes, as toward prohibition, is likely to yield retest reliabilities in the neighborhood of .70 among college groups, using the optimum number of steps.

4. Convenience and economy in appraisal lie with the verbal inventories and graphic scales.

5. All of the direct appraisals of attitudes are subject to intentional misrepresentations which are hard to detect. No indirect or observational methods have been widely used.

Group Norms

A fairly large number of studies have been reported of differences in attitudes found in age and occupation, sex, race, locality, and educational and economic groups. Such differences have often been cited as indications of the validity of the scales. Most of these reports require a great deal of study because the interpretation of results involves the simultaneous evaluation of all factors which might contribute to attitudes. Thus a small difference between attitudes of men and women toward war may be due to differences in age, training, and occupations, rather than to the difference in sex. No studies have come to hand where all these factors have been held constant, although some studies have produced significant results. In view of the complexity of the material the reader is referred to the able discussions by Murphy et al. (1937), Rundquist and Sletto (1936), Allport (1937), and Cantril (1944).

NEEDED RESEARCH

Research in this field is considerably behind research in the field of interests, discussed in Chapter XX. Additional research is much needed outside of the classroom. Comprehensive studies of attitudes evaluating age, race, experience, and other factors will be of great significance. Reduction of misrepresentation is a pressing problem, the solution of which may come from indirect self-ratings, or observations made by others. The construction of less ambiguous test items is feasible. With such items thorough factorial analyses may indicate more clearly the basic patterns of attitudes of a group of persons.

STUDY GUIDE QUESTIONS

1. How are attitudes defined? How are they formed in an individual?
2. Describe a method used to develop an attitude scale in which items are scaled in equally often-noticed units.
3. What are the six fields of activity described by Spranger?
4. What results have thus far been secured in measures of knowledge about an issue and the attitudes toward the issue?
5. What are the relations between attitude categories and interest categories (Chapter XX)?
6. What methods seem to yield the best results in studying attitudes?

CHAPTER XXII

PERSONALITY
INVENTORIES

This chapter describes general and analytical questionnaires which are designed to appraise strength and types of impulses and typical adjustive activity. Certain uses of such questionnaires are indicated. Lastly, the content and scoring are discussed together with indications of need for research.

CHARACTERISTICS OF INVENTORIES

One of the most natural developments of the interviewing technique is to take questions which a good interviewer would ask and present them in written form to a subject. Many lists of such questions have been prepared. The earlier lists included a large variety of miscellaneous items designed to yield a general index of maladjustment. Later, by the use of factorial and logical analyses, inventories were developed which yielded analytical scores corresponding to profiles of clinical syndromes or to psychological traits or sometimes to both.

General Questionnaires

One of the earliest of these is the Personal Data Sheet, prepared by Woodworth (1917) during World War I, which asks the subject to check one hundred and sixteen items which were derived from psychiatrists' descriptions of neurotic or of prepsychotic patients. Mathews (1923) adapted this form for use with children by changing some of the situations and language. Thurstone (1930) published an inventory of 223 items, some of which were from Woodworth and other sources. McFarland and Seitz (1938) published a 92-item inventory, half of which related to somatic symptoms and the other half to mental situations or beliefs.

During World War II, two short general inventories had considerable application: the Cornell Index and the Personal Inventory.

The Cornell Index. This index (Weider, 1945) was issued in 1948 by the Psychological Corporation, revised as Form N2 for civilian use. It is designed to be a rough screening device for personal and psychosomatic disturbances. It consists of one hundred short questions about behavior or symptoms, such as: Do you frequently feel faint? The person being tested is asked to answer all the questions *Yes* or *No,* and if he is not sure to guess. The items are designed to represent the types of symptoms shown in Illus. 210.

ILLUS. 210. CONTENT OF CORNELL INDEX

	Question No.
Defects in adjustment expressed as feelings of fear and inadequacy	2–19
Pathological mood reactions, especially depression	20–26
Nervousness and anxiety	27–33
Neurocirculatory psychosomatic symptoms	34–38
Pathological startle reactions	39–46
Other psychosomatic symptoms	47–61
Hypochondriasis and asthenia	62–68
Gastrointestinal psychosomatic symptoms	69–79
Excessive sensitivity and suspiciousness	80–85
Troublesome psychopathy	86–101

(By permission of Arthur Weider and The Psychological Corporation.)

The Index is administered to groups and without time limits. College students usually finish in 5 minutes, and those who have not finished grammar school take from 10 to 15 minutes. The reliability is calculated by the Kuder-Richardson technique because the distributions are usually very skewed. Among a thousand subjects tested the reliability was .95.

Norms are available only for male adults at this time, and they are given in form of cut-off score centiles (Illus. 211). This shows, for instance, that if a cut-off score of seven had been used, 86 per cent of those rejected for military service would have been detected, and 14 per cent not detected. At the same time 28 per cent of the normals would have been tentatively classified as disturbed. In military selection the Index was a practical tool, because a large proportion of persons in trouble could thus be selected and sent for psychiatric interviews immediately and only about a quarter, 28 per cent, of the normals were so selected. The relatively small number of disturbed

ILLUS. 211. PER CENT OF REJECTS * IDENTIFIED AT VARIOUS
CUTOFF LEVELS, CORNELL INDEX

Cut-off Level	Per Cent of Psychiatric Rejects (400)	Per Cent of Normal Rejects
0	100%	100%
1	99	82
2	97	67
3	94	54
4	93	46
5	92	39
6	90	32
7	86	28
8	85	24
9	83	20
10	81	18
11	78	16
12	76	15
13	74	13
14	72	12
15	68	10
16	66	9
17	62	8
18	61	7
19	60	7
20	57	6
21	55	5
22	53	4
23	50	4
24	48	4
25	45	3
26	42	3
27	41	3
28	40	2
29	39	1
30	35	1
31	34	1
32	32	1

* In terms of opinion at psychiatric interviews at five induction stations.

(By permission of Arthur Weider and The Psychological Corporation.)

persons not detected by the Index were later discovered during the first few weeks of service.

"Stop" items refer to crucial symptoms, such as, "Have you ever had a fit or convulsion?", or, "Were you ever a patient in a mental hospital?" These items are scored separately when desired.

The Cornell Index was not found to be effective in indicating obsessive states, and does not screen hysterical palsies or prepsychotic and early psychotic states thoroughly. It is more effective in indicating anxiety, hypochondriasis, asocial trends, convulsive disorders, migraine, asthma, peptic ulcers, and borderline psychosomatic disorders. The Index is not designed to analyze difficulties but to give a composite score. Although responses can be falsified, the authors believe that the follow-up results show that gross falsification is uncommon.

The Personal Inventory. This inventory, by Shipley, Gray and Newbert (1946), is a questionnaire prepared originally for the United States Navy, but used by other branches of the military establishment for the purpose of screening large numbers of recruits or selectees. A long form contains 145 items, and a short form 20 items which were selected from the long form because of their capacity to distinguish between normal navy personnel and psychiatric discharges. The items are cast into a forced-choice form, and one is required to check the alternative which better describes himself. One alternative is always more characteristic of the normal as revealed by a large-scale case-history and analysis. The other characterizes the psychiatrically undesirable. An attempt was made to pair choices which are apparently equal in social desirability.

Upon analysis sixty items of the long form were found to have critical ratios of 2.7 or more between 1,004 normals and 84 psychiatric discharges. These sixty items were assigned a weight of one point each for purposes of scoring, and the other eighty-five items were retained as a filler and for experimental purposes.

The odd-even reliabilities of the short and long forms proved to be almost identical—.66 for naval recruits and .91 among psychiatric discharges. The validity as shown by critical ratios between normal and psychiatric discharges was 18.5 for the long, and 20.9 for the short form.

The correlations between the General Classification Test and the two forms were both—.28 among normal recruits. The short form therefore seemed to be as good a testing instrument as the long form.

Psychiatric Classifications

The most carefully prepared and validated work in this field is the *Minnesota Multiphasic Personality Inventory (MMPI), Hathaway and McKinley* (1942, 1947). This inventory was designed to aid in two basic aspects of clinical diagnosis: the quality of the disorder and the intensity or the amount of disturbance. In order to develop a scale for qualitative analysis, types of abnormalities were first defined, then groups of persons who clearly represented these types were secured, then the tests were applied to these groups and to normal persons. Items which show differences between various groups were then selected, and arranged in a battery of tests. The psychiatric syndromes described by Kraepelin or his successors were used. Krae-pelin emphasized that these syndromes were complex patterns of behavior which appeared fairly frequently but were apparently not organic nor rigidly structured nor independent of each other.

Hathaway and McKinley, working in a large mental hospital, se-cured samples of approximately eight hundred carefully studied clinical cases. To these and to a group of normal adults they applied a battery of 550 items on separate cards. Each person was asked to respond by indicating whether or not the situation in the item was typical of his own situation. The three choices were: *true* or *mostly true, not usually* or *entirely true, cannot say*. The 550 questions were classified into twenty-six groups, as shown in Illus. 212.

ILLUS. 212. CONTENT OF MINNESOTA MULTIPHASIC PERSONALITY INVENTORY (MMPI)

1. General health (9 items)
2. General neurologic (19 items)
3. Cranial nerves (11 items)
4. Motility and coordination (6 items)
5. Sensibility (5 items)
6. Vasomotor, trophic, speech, secretory (10 items)
7. Cardio-respiratory system (5 items)
8. Gastro-intestinal system (11 items)
9. Genito-urinary system (5 items)
10. Habits (19 items)
11. Family and marital (26 items)
12. Occupational (18 items)
13. Educational (12 items)
14. Sexual attitudes (16 items)
15. Religious attitudes (19 items)
16. Political attitudes—law and order (46 items)
17. Social attitudes (72 items)
18. Affect, depressive (32 items)
19. Affect, manic (24 items)
20. Obsessive and compulsive states (15 items).
21. Delusions, hallucinations, illusions, ideas of reference (31 items)
22. Phobias (29 items)
23. Sadistic, masochistic trends (7 items)
24. Morale (33 items)
25. Items primarily related to masculinity-femininity (55 items)
26. Items to indicate whether the individual is trying to place himself in an ac-ceptable light (15 items)

(By permission of Hathaway and McKinley and the University of Minnesota Press.)

From these items scoring scales were derived by selecting items which showed the largest differences between normal and other groups, and between the various clinical groups. From 40 to 60 items are scored for each scale. The same item is often found in more than one scale. Nine scales of personality characteristics, as they are called, are now available for scoring. These are described by Hathaway and McKinley somewhat as follows:

a. Hypochondriasis. This scale includes worry about bodily functions. Usually the patient has a long history of exaggeration of physical complaints and of seeking sympathy.

b. Hysteria. This scale measures conversion-type symptoms, such as paralyses, contractures, gastric or intestinal complaints, or cardiac symptoms. They have attacks of weakness, fainting, or even epileptiform convulsions. Hysterical cases are more immature psychologically than any other group. Although their symptoms can often be miraculously cured by a strong emotional experience, there is great likelihood that other symptoms will appear if stress continues or recurs.

c. Depression. This scale measures the depths of discouragement or lack of self-confidence, which may be suicidal.

d. Hypomania. This scale measures overproductivity in thought and action. The patient has usually got himself into trouble because he has undertaken too many things. He is overenthusiastic and overactive, and his activities may interfere with other people through his attempts to reform social practice, or his stirring up of projects in which he soon loses interest, or his disregard of social conventions.

e. Psychopathic deviate. This scale measures a group of persons whose main difficulty lies in a usual absence of deep emotional responses. Nothing really matters. They are commonly likeable and intelligent, but they frequently digress by lying, stealing, alcohol and drug addiction, and sexual immorality. They may have short periods of disorientation and excitement or depression following a discovery of their antisocial acts. They differ from some criminals in that they seem to commit crimes with little thought of possible gain to themselves or of avoiding discovery.

f. Paranoia. This scale shows persons characterized by suspiciousness, oversensitivity, and delusions of persecution. Patients with paranoid suspicions are common in many situations, and paranoiacs usually appear normal when on guard. They are usually quick to take vengeance against anyone who tries to control them. Persons with high scores on this scale must be handled with special appreciation of this possibility.

g. Psychasthenia. This scale shows persons with phobias or compulsive behavior, expressed in hand-washing, vacillation, or other ineffectual activities. The patient has queer thoughts or obsessive ideas from which he cannot escape when awake or asleep, and which serve him as a symbolic protection. Many persons, however, have phobias, such as minor fears of snakes or spiders or locked doors, without being greatly incapacitated. As long as they can avoid these things they operate on a fairly even keel.

h. Schizophrenia. This scale measures responses which are bizarre and unusual, caused by a splitting of the subjective life of the person from reality. He reacts almost exclusively to his own thoughts, wishes, and fears. Advanced cases seldom consciously respond to the environment for long periods.

i. Masculinity-femininity. This scale contains items which were selected to distinguish between the two sexes in the normal group. Some items were inspired by the work of Terman and Miles (1936).

Finally, there are three scales the scores of which are not indicative of clinical syndromes but show personality traits. One of these, called the K score, is the number of answers which are omitted because the client cannot say or will not choose. A large number of omitted questions shows a tendency to withdraw or vacillate. Another score, called the lie score, is composed of answers to fifteen items which indicate rather gross exaggerations, such as "I always tell the truth." Another score, called the validity score, is made up of answers to sixty-four items which have seldom been answered in the scored direction by normal persons. These scores show either highly independent persons or those who are neurotic or psychotic. The latter usually reveal themselves by high scores in other scales as well.

The present scales do not measure all qualities of personality, and the authors promise that other scales will be developed as time goes on, showing groups of primary or closely associated traits. Although it is thought that the personality characteristics named above are independent in the sense that they can occur in a person independently from any other trait, yet in practice they are often found together. In fact, it is seldom that a single characteristic is found by itself.

Two administrative procedures are now available. In one procedure each item is on a separate card and the client sorts the cards into two piles—*right* and *wrong*. The other is called the group procedure and in it the items are printed in a booklet. The subject marks an answer sheet to show one of two choices—*true* or *false*. This form may also be scored for only the first 367 items, thus reducing the time needed for administration and scoring.

The scores for all scales are changed to standard scores for a large adult group where the mean is 50 and the standard deviation is 10. On a profile chart (Illus. 213) the heavy lines show values at 30 and 70, representing two standard deviations below and above the mean. The highest scores always represent the deviations toward abnormality. Scores above 70 indicate either a borderline condition or a need

ILLUS. 213. PROFILE OF MINNESOTA MULTIPHASIC PERSONALITY INVENTORY (MMPI)

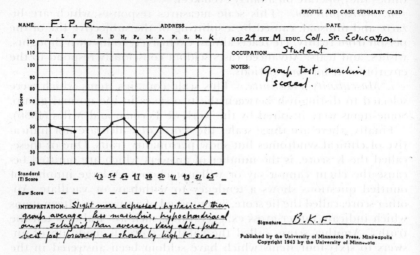

PROFILE AND CASE SUMMARY CARD

NAME __F. P. R.__ ADDRESS_____ DATE_____

AGE __24__ SEX __M__ EDUC. __Coll. Sr. Education__

OCCUPATION __Student__

NOTES: *Group Test machine scored.*

INTERPRETATION: *Slight more depressed, hysterical than group average, less masculine, hypochondriacal and schizoid than average, very able, puts best foot forward as shown by high K score*

Signature __B. K. F.__

Published by the University of Minnesota Press, Minneapolis
Copyright 1943 by the University of Minnesota

for careful examination of the clinical evidence. In some instances scores below 70 are also indicative of serious trouble. In looking at a profile, the two or three highest points must be considered together. Slight differences between several high points may be due to ineffective scaling. The authors reported test-retest reliabilities ranging from .71 to .83 for the various scales.

The immediate diagnosis may not always agree with the highest point on the chart, for a person may show a violent symptom which is of less importance than another symptom of abnormal condition. For instance, a client may show a great amount of depression with feelings of guilt, while at the same time he is progressively withdrawing from reality to a degree that may completely disorient him (schizophrenia).

Psychological Classifications

Other scales are based on psychological theories of personality, and are designed to include estimates of such traits as introversion-extroversion, ascendance-submission, sufficiency-dependence, and despondency-elation. Nearly thirty scales of this sort have been edited by various investigators. They are illustrated by the work of Bernreuter (1931), Guilford-Zimmerman (1949), Adams (1945), Thorpe, Clark, and Tiegs (1946), Kuder (1948), and others.

The Bernreuter Personality Inventory. This test consists of 125 items, similar to those in Illus. 149, describing both adjustments and interests. Each item is to be answered with *yes, no,* or *unable to answer with yes or no.* Four scores are obtained for each person from keys which were prepared on the basis of results from four previous tests: Thurstone's (1930) Personality Schedule of Neurotic Tendencies, Laird's (1925) Inventory of Extroversion-Introversion, Allport's (1928) Ascendance-Submission Scale, and Bernreuter's Test of Self-Sufficiency. These four tests and the Personality Inventory were administered to adults selected in part to represent extreme groups. Each item in the inventory was correlated with total scores on each of the four tests. The answers to each item were assigned points on the basis of these correlations, the higher the correlation, the greater number of points allotted. For instance, the answers to the item, "Do you daydream frequently?" were given plus and minus values as follows:

TEST

Answer	Neurotic	Introversion	Dominance	Self-Sufficiency
Yes	5	3	—1	1
No	—4	—4	1	—1
Doubtful	—2	0	2	—2

Total scale scores were secured by adding the figures in each column. These totals were found to correlate highly with the corresponding previous tests. Thus, Bernreuter's score for neurotic tendencies correlated .94 with Thurstone's schedule. Laird's and Bernreuter's introversion scores correlated .79. Allport's measure of ascendancy and Bernreuter's dominance correlated .81, and the two measures of self-sufficiency, .89.

The Bernreuter scores show high split-half reliability, median .90. Their intercorrelations are interesting. Neurotic tendencies correlated .95 with introversion. This shows either that the same persons have both sorts of adjustments, or that the two scales are measuring approximately the same patterns of behavior. Neurotic tendencies correlated with ascendancy .81, and with self-sufficiency .35. The self-sufficiency scores showed a low correlation with the others since self-sufficiency cuts across both ascendancy and introversion.

These high intercorrelations led Flanagan (1935) to make a factorial analysis of Bernreuter's scores from 305 eleventh-grade boys. He used Hotelling's method of principal components. Two factors appeared to account for the intercorrelation of the four Bernreuter scores. The first, a large factor in the test, is a combination of neurotic, introversion, submission, and low self-sufficiency items. Flanagan named this *lack of self-confidence.* The second factor, a much smaller one, was called *sociability*. Flanagan constructed two new scoring keys to aid in appraising these modes of behavior.

The stability of responses on the Bernreuter scale was studied by Farnsworth (1938). Retests after 1, 2, and 3 years showed no significant shifts in individual centile ranks, and there were high retest correlations. For the average person 71 per cent of single items were answered in identical fashion after an interval of 1 year, 65 per cent after 2 years, and 65 per cent after 3 years.

The Guilford-Zimmerman Temperament Survey, 1949. The work of many years of Guilford and his associates in the appraisal of personality by elaborate inventories has resulted in a 300-item questionnaire, called the Guilford-Zimmerman Temperament Survey. Thirty items are provided for each of ten traits, and no item is used for appraising more than one trait. Seven of the traits are the same as those described for the Guilford-Martin Inventories (1940, 1945), and three of the traits are combinations of six previously described traits. All of Guilford's work is characterized by great care in the preparation and the analysis of items. The traits have been defined by several factorial analyses on various populations, and the wording of items has been studied to increase their uniqueness for one trait. The traits are described as follows:

G *General activity:* hurrying, liking for speed, liveliness, vitality, production, efficiency, and their opposites.

R *Restraint:* serious, deliberate, persistent versus carefree, impulsive, excitement-loving.

A *Ascendance:* self-defense, leadership, bluffing, speaking in public versus submissiveness and hesitation.

S *Sociability:* many friends, seeking friends and social activities, seeking limelight versus few friends and shyness.

E *Emotional stability:* evenness of moods, optimistic, composure versus fluctuation of moods, pessimism, day-dreaming, excitability, feelings of guilt, worry, loneliness, and ill health.

O *Objectivity:* thick skinned, accurate observing versus hypersensitive, self-centered, suspicious, having ideas of reference.

F *Friendliness:* tact, acceptance of domination, respect for others versus hostility, resentment, desire to dominate, and contempt for others.

T *Thoughtfulness:* reflective, observing of self and others, mental poise versus interest in overt activity and mental disconcertedness.

P *Personal relations:* tolerance of people, faith in social institutions versus fault-finding, uncooperative, suspicious, self-pitying.

M *Masculinity:* interest in masculine activities, not easily disgusted, hard-boiled, inhibits emotional expression, little interest in clothes and styles versus easily disgusted, fearful, romantic, emotionally expressive, and dislike of vermin.

The items are all in the form of statements, usually affirmative, and often using the second person pronoun, for example:

You like to play practical jokes on others.
Most people are out to get more than they give.

The affirmative form is preferred because it is usually a little simpler than a question, and according to Guilford and Zimmerman, may allay resistance and increase the number of projective answers.

The answers are all to be placed on an IBM answer sheet by marking *yes, ?,* or *no* for each item. The use of these three categories was determined by polling the attitudes of several hundred students toward different kinds of responses. About 60 per cent stated that they could not do without the question mark very well, and the preferences were about equal for 3, 4, and 5 choices.

In scoring the test one point is allowed for each item answered in the direction of the trait. The question mark and the other possible response are not counted. The average proportion of persons scoring on each item was about .60, and the range from .10 to .90. The means of total scores for any trait center around 18, and the standard deviations are a little more than 5 points. The reliability coefficients for the various traits ranged from .75 to .87, and the standard error of an obtained score was approximately 2.5. The intercorrelations of trait scores for 266 college men show that traits S and A correlated .61; traits O and E correlated .69; all the rest were considerably lower, showing a desirable uniqueness.

Separate norms are furnished for 523 college men and 389 college women. There are small differences between the mean scores of men and women. The men had slightly higher scores for traits R, A, E, and O, and much higher scores for trait M. The women had higher means for traits S, F, and P, and the means were the same for traits G and T. In all except trait M the overlapping of scores between the two groups was large. Profile charts giving separate male and female norms are provided (Illus. 214). Scores can be read from this in centiles, C scores, or T scores. No age differences have yet been found for an application of the form to high school students and their parents yielded similar distributions for the two groups.

The interpretation of scores for both industrial and clinical use is indicated by Guilford and Zimmerman. Thus they have accumulated some evidence that supervisory and administrative personnel should have C scores between 5 and 9 for all except trait P, where the most favorable C scores are from 6 to 10. The least favorable scores are usually from 0 to 3 or 4. The authors point out that, while in general a high degree of a trait is good, clinically it must be considered along

ILLUS. 214. TEMPERAMENT PROFILE

PROFILE CHART FOR THE GUILFORD-ZIMMERMAN TEMPERAMENT SURVEY

SCALED SCORES FOR MEN

Date 2-28-52
Name John Bacon

C SCORE	G General Activity Energy	R Restraint Seriousness	A Ascendance Social Boldness	S Social Interest Sociability	E Emotional Stability	O Objectivity	F Friendliness Agreeableness	T Thoughtfulness Reflectiveness	P Personal Relations Cooperativeness	M Masculinity (of emotions and interests)	CENTILE RANK	NEAREST T SCORE
10	30 / 29	30 / 29 / 28 / 27	30 / 29	30	30 / 29	30 / 29	29 / 28 / 27 / 26	30 / 29 / 28	30 / 29 / 28	30 / 29 / 28	99	75
9	28 / 27	26 / 25	28 / 27 / 26	29 / 28	28 / 27	28 / 27	25 / 24 / 23	27 / 26	27 / 26	27		70
8	26 / 25	24 / 23	25 / 24 / 23	27 / 26	26 / 25	26 / 25	22 / 21	25 / 24	25 / 24 / 23	26 / 25	95 / 90	65
7	24 / 23 / 22	22 / 21	22 / 21	25 / 24	24 / 23 / 22	24 / 23	20 / 19 / 18	23 / 22	22 / 21	24	80	60
6	21 / 20 / 19	20 / 19 / 18	20 / 19 / 18	23 / 22 / 21	21 / 20 / 19	22 / 21 / 20	17 / 16	21 / 20	20 / 19 / 18	23 / 22	70 / —60—	55
5	18 / 17 / 16	17 / 16	17 / 16 / 15	20 / 19 / 18	18 / 17 / 16	19 / 18 / 17	15 / 14 / 13	19 / 18	17 / 16	21 / 20	50 / —40—	50
4	15 / 14 / 13	15 / 14	14 / 13 / 12	17 / 16 / 15 / 14	15 / 14 / 13 / 12	16 / 15 / 14	12 / 11 / 10	17 / 16 / 15	15 / 14	19 / 18	30	45
3	12 / 11 / 10	13 / 12 / 11	11 / 10 / 9	13 / 12 / 11 / 10	11 / 10 / 9	13 / 12 / 11	9 / 8	14 / 13 / 12	13 / 12 / 11	17 / 16 / 15	20	40
2	9 / 8 / 7	10 / 9	8 / 7 / 6	9 / 8 / 7 / 6	8 / 7 / 6	10 / 9 / 8	7 / 6 / 5	11 / 10 / 9 / 8	10 / 9	14 / 13	10 / 5	35
1	6 / 5	8 / 7 / 6	5 / 4	5 / 4 / 3	5 / 4	7 / 6 / 5	4 / 3	7 / 6 / 5	8 / 7 / 6	12 / 11 / 10		30
0	4 / 3 / 2 / 1	5 / 4 / 3 / 2	3 / 2 / 1 / 0	2 / 1 / 0	3 / 2 / 1 / 0	4 / 3 / 2 / 1	2 / 1 / 0	4 / 3 / 2 / 1	5 / 4 / 3 / 2	9 / 7 / 5 / 3	1	25
	Inactivity Slowness	Impulsiveness Rhathymia	Submissiveness	Shyness Seclusiveness	Emotional Instability Depression	Subjectivity Hypersensitiveness	Hostility Belligerence	Thoughtlessness Extraversion	Criticalness Intolerance	Femininity (of emotions and interests)		

(Guilford-Zimmerman, 1949. By permission of J. P. Guilford and The Sheridan Supply Company.)

with other qualities. Thus a high general activity score is good if combined with reflectiveness, and bad if combined with emotional instability or contempt for others. The authors have not yet furnished any indicators of faking, or the dependability of the score, but they suggest that the number of question marks used as answers should not be more than three for any trait, because the standard deviation for a trait is approximately 6. Furthermore any person whose scores are all very high or very low should be interviewed to ascertain the behavior pattern involved.

Attitude-Interest Analysis Test. Terman and Miles (1936) reported a 7-year investigation designed to give a more factual basis to concepts of masculinity and femininity. They devised two equivalent paper-and-pencil forms with contents as follows:

Exercise 1. Word Association: 60 items. (.62)*
Exercise 2. Ink Blot Association: 18 items, a rough silhouette is followed by four words. (.34)
Exercise 3. Information: 70 items. (.68)
Exercise 4. Emotional and Ethical Responses: 105 items. (.90)
Exercise 5. Interest: 119 items. (.80)
Exercise 6. Personalities and Opinions consist of 41 items. (.64)
Exercise 7. Introvért Responses consist of 42 items. (.32)

* The figures in parentheses are average split-half reliabilities for both sexes combined, for ten narrow groups of about one hundred persons each.

Each exercise was prepared by trying out many more items on groups of from one hundred to two hundred of each sex in the eighth grade, high school, and college, then retaining only those items which showed reliable sex differences. A scoring key, which assigned weights from $+15$ to -15, was devised for each response to each item. It was based on the degree to which the response distinguished between groups of different sexes. Later trials on new groups showed conclusively that unweighted scores showed as much reliability and as much difference between the sexes as the weighted scores.

Each exercise was given a different weight depending upon its own reliability, its discrimination between sexes, its independence from the other variables, and its standard deviation. The split-half reliabilities of subtests ranged from about .34 for Exercises 2 and 7, to .90 for Exercise 4. Thus Exercise 4, Emotional and Ethical Responses, is reliable enough to locate a person with reasonable accuracy by the use of one form of the test. If both forms are used all except exercises 2 and 7 are reliable enough to compare small populations. Profiles of individuals are therefore not recommended from these tests.

The split-half reliabilities of total scores on small populations of one sex only averaged .78, and for both sexes together .92, when only one form was used. When both forms were combined the reliabilities rose to .88 for one sex and .96 for both sexes. The standard error of a score on one form was approximately 15 points. The total scores on

one form range from —200 to +200. The general-population average
for males was +52 and for females —70.

Terman reported that college sophomores easily faked masculine
or feminine scores to an extreme extent, when they knew the purpose of the test and were asked to see how much they could change
their scores. The test is called an Attitude-Interest Analysis, however,
and only a few naive subjects suspect its purpose.

Terman and Miles (1936) furnished a number of interesting comparisons of total scores of racial, age, and sex-delinquent groups, all
of which show wide average differences between male and female
groups, but some variations. Thus the average differences between
sexes are smaller for persons over seventy years of age, for English
private school children, for college-of-music students, and for Japanese adolescents in Hawaii, than for somewhat random high school
or college groups. Male average scores rose from about 45 for fourteen-year-olds to 72 for sixteen-year-olds, and then decreased to 67
for twenty-year-old college sophomores, to 58 for adults from twenty
to thirty years, to 39 for forty to fifty years, and to 10 or less for those
over sixty years. Female average scores rose from —95 at fourteen
years to —60 at twenty years, and then decreased slowly with age to
—89 for those sixty or older.

Physical measures showed no marked relationship with M-F scores
of either men or women, but more research is needed. Slight relationships were found between masculinity and height of males, and between femininity and length of trunk in relation to height in females. The relation of M-F scores to occupations was studied by
comparing the means of small groups of persons in different occupations. Journalists, clergymen, and artists averaged about 16; police
and firemen 28; farmers and building trades 33; clerks and mer-
chants 42; mechanics, teachers, physicians, surgeons, dentists 46; lawyers, salesmen, bankers 58; engineers and architects 81; and college
athletes 93. Among women those in domestic occupations had the
lowest average scores, about —100; stenographers, dressmakers, and
hairdressers averaged —90; musicians and artists —80; clerks and
business women —78; teachers —70; nurses —65; and physical-educa-
tion teachers —36. Among both men and women the relationship between masculinity or lack of femininity and an education-intelligence
factor was significant. The more educated showed higher scores. The
differences were more marked among men than among women.

The relation of M-F scores with alleged interests, as shown by a
self-rating on twelve fields of activity, was studied for 212 male adults
and 533 female adults with high school educations. The men with
"very much interest" in science, mechanics, sports, and travel had

average M-F scores of from 51 to 59, while those with "very much interest" in art averaged 16, in domestic arts 28, in religion 31, and in music 38. The M-F score of those with high interest in literature, politics, pets, and social life ranged from 42 to 46. Among the women similar trends appeared. Those with "very much interest" in mechanics, sports, politics, and pets had average M-F scores of from —77 to —66, while the scores of those with high interest in religion, art, domestic art, music, and social life ranged from —93 to —86.

Finally, a detailed analysis and classification of items showed males to be more interested in adventure, outdoor strenuous occupations, machinery and tools, science, and business, while females were more interested in domestic, artistic, humanitarian, and social affairs. Emotionally the males manifested greater self-assertion and aggressiveness, fearlessness, and roughness of manners and language, while the females showed more timidity, sympathy, fastidiousness, and weakness in emotional control. Neither sex showed any superiority over the other in unselfishness or moral principles or reasoning. No evidence was presented as to the relation between sex differences and innate factors. It was pointed out that additional studies where either environment or inheritance are closely controlled are necessary to throw light on the relation of sex differences and culture.

Sheldon's Scale for Temperament. One theory of the dynamics of personality is based on the idea that physical or physiological characteristics largely determine dynamic patterns of behavior.

Sheldon (1942) developed a Temperament Scale (Illus. 215) using a preliminary list of 50 traits and a 5-point scale with a group of thirty-three male college graduates. He found three clusters of traits which correlated highly with one another and much less with traits in the other two clusters. Several similar experiments carried on during a period of 4 years resulted in three clusters of twenty traits each. The first group of traits, which he called *viscerotonia*, typify a person who is overrelaxed, gluttonous, oversocialized, too dependent upon people, and overcomplacent, and who looks backward toward childhood. The second group, called *somatotonia*, includes characteristics of those who are extremely aggressive, energetic, dominating, fond of risk, combative, ruthless, loud, active, and adjusted to the present. The third group, called *cerebrotonia*, includes traits of the person who is unusually tense, restrained, sensitive, secretive, inhibited, intent, and emotionally involved, and looks toward the future. Sheldon believed that ideally the scale should be made up of sets of 3-way traits, such as is shown in Illus. 215, Item 1, where relaxation has two opposites, one in assertiveness, and the other in restraint or tightness.

The three temperament types are determined by rating each trait on a 7-point scale thus:

4%	1.	Extreme antithesis is shown to the trait.
15%	2.	Trait is weak, although there are traces.
29%	3.	Trait is present, but falls a little below average.
29%	4.	About half-way between extremes.
15%	5.	Trait is strong, but not outstanding.
6%	6.	Trait is very strong and conspicuous.
2%	7.	Extreme manifestation.

ILLUS. 215. SHELDON'S SCALE FOR TEMPERAMENT

Name .... Date .... Photo No. .... Scored by ....

I. VISCEROTONIA	II. SOMATOTONIA	III. CEREBROTONIA
( ) * 1. Relaxation in posture and movement	( ) * 1. Assertiveness of posture and movement	( ) * 1. Restraint in posture and movement, tightness
( ) 2. Love of physical comfort	( ) 2. Love of physical adventure	.... 2. Physiological overresponse
( ) 3. Slow reaction	( ) 3. The energetic characteristic	( ) 3. Overly fast reactions
.... 4. Love of eating	( ) 4. Need and enjoyment of exercise	( ) 4. Love of privacy
.... 5. Socialization of eating	.... 5. Love of dominating, lust for power	( ) 5. Mental overintensity, hyperattentionality, apprehensiveness
.... 6. Pleasure in digestion	( ) 6. Love of risk and chance	( ) 6. Secretiveness of feeling, emotional restraint
( ) 7. Love of polite ceremony	( ) 7. Bold directness of manner	( ) 7. Self-conscious motility of the eyes and face
( ) 8. Sociophilia	( ) 8. Physical courage for combat	( ) 8. Sociophobia
.... 9. Indiscriminate amiability	( ) 9. Competitive aggressiveness	( ) 9. Inhibited social address
.... 10. Greed for affection and approval	.... 10. Psychological callousness	.... 10. Resistance to habit, and poor routinizing
.... 11. Orientation to people	.... 11. Claustrophobia	.... 11. Agoraphobia
( ) 12. Evenness of emotional flow	.... 12. Ruthlessness, freedom from squeamishness	.... 12. Unpredictability of attitude
( ) 13. Tolerance	( ) 13. The unrestrained voice	( ) 13. Vocal restraint, and general restraint of noise
( ) 14. Complacency	.... 14. Spartan indifference to pain	.... 14. Hypersensitivity to pain

ILLUS. 215. SHELDON'S SCALE FOR TEMPERAMENT *(Cont'd)*

I. VISCEROTONIA	II. SOMATOTONIA	III. CEREBROTONIA
.... 15. Deep sleep	.... 15. General noisiness	.... 15. Poor sleep habits, chronic fatigue
( ) 16. The untempered characteristic	( ) 16. Overmaturity of appearance	( ) 16. Youthful intentness of manner and appearance
( ) 17. Smooth, easy communication of feeling, extraversion of viscerotonia	.... 17. Horizontal mental cleavage, extraversion of somatotonia	.... 17. Vertical mental cleavage, introversion
.... 18. Relaxation and sociophilia under alcohol	.... 18. Assertiveness and aggression under alcohol	.... 18. Resistance to alcohol, and to other depressant drugs
.... 19. Need of people when troubled	.... 19. Need of action when troubled	.... 19. Need of solitude when troubled
.... 20. Orientation toward childhood and family relationships	.... 20. Orientation toward goals and activities of youth	.... 20. Orientation toward the later periods of life

* The thirty traits with parentheses before them constitute collectively the short form of the scale.

(By permission of W. H. Sheldon and Harper & Bros.)

There are more cases at the lower extreme because the antithesis of a trait may take two forms, while there can be only one extreme manifestation. Rating 1 is therefore about twice as common as rating 7. A mean for each type is secured and written as IT, *Index of Temperament,* thus an IT 243 indicates a mean rating of 2 for viscerotonia, 4 for somatotonia, and 3 for cerebrotonia. For 200 thoroughly studied cases the split-half reliabilities for these ratings were approximately .90. The correlations between temperament types and body types were found to be approximately .80, and in rare cases where temperament varied by 2 or more points from the corresponding morphological predominance, difficult adjustments or maladjustments were the rule.

Sheldon also gives evidence that poor emotional adjustment and unsatisfactory achievement are related to differences or conflict between ideals or habits and body types. For instance, a man with a 263 morphological index would have a bad time trying to live a life of a theoretical scientist, but would adjust well as an athlete, or playground director.

Sheldon has analyzed two hundred male adults and grouped them according to degree of good adaptation:

14%	Group 1.	Superior adaptation
64%	Group 2.	Well adapted:
		2a. Naturally adapted
		2b. Overcame difficulties
17%	Group 3.	Socially unadaptable:
		3a. Overendowed, ectomorphic
		3b. Overcompensated, mesomorphic
		3c. Reversals of dominance
		3d. Sex-environment clash
5%	Group 4.	Constitutional inferiors:
		4a. Underendowed.

He found a wide variety of types in each of the first two groups, but Group 1 contained 26 per cent of those who were predominantly cerebrotonics, and only 1 per cent of visceretonics, 6 per cent of somatotonics, and 8 per cent of balanced types. In general, Group 2 contained most of the dominant visceretonics (75 per cent), and smaller proportions of the other types. Group 3 had practically no visceretonics, but Group 4 had 14 per cent of them.

Sheldon has defined a number of other indices for total dysplasia, gynandromorphy, gynandrophrenia, textural components, health, central strength, physical intelligence (how effectively one uses his muscles), aesthetic intelligence (sensitive appreciation of one's environment), and manifest sexuality, which are to be rated independently of the morphological and temperamental traits. The gynandromorphy index is interesting because two persons can be nearly the same in total bodily pattern but differ considerably in sexual components.

Child and Sheldon (1941) made a study among Harvard undergraduates of correlations between somatotypes and ability and personality test scores. None of the correlations were significant, but the results cannot be considered to be conclusive, because of narrow sampling and vague analysis of the traits measured. Sheldon points out that an enormous amount of careful research is needed to determine the significance of physique and related physiological reactions in personality patterns, and to secure more adequate norms for various age groups, for women, and for racial groups.

Cattell's Personal Characteristics. One of the most thorough attempts to include all possible personality characteristics in an analysis is that of R. B. Cattell (1947) who collected more than 1,800 trait names from psychiatric, psychological, and literary sources and reduced them to 171 names that seem important and somewhat independent. Ratings were obtained on one hundred adults for 171 traits, and the intercorrelations of all 171 traits were analyzed. Traits which correlated at least .45 with one another were grouped together. This resulted in thirty-five clusters of traits (Illus. 216). Each of these clusters was phrased as a single trait and was used in rating another group of 208 male adults. From a factorial analysis of these ratings, eleven factors emerge which Cattell considers basic or primary.

ILLUS. 216. CATTELL'S THIRTY-FIVE CLUSTERS OF TRAITS

DEFINITIONS

1. Readiness to cooperate   *vs*   Obstructiveness
Generally tends to say yes when invited to cooperate. Outgoing. Ready to meet people at least halfway. Finds way of cooperating despite difficulties.   Inclined to raise objections to a project, cynical or realistic. "Cannot be done." Uninterested or unfavorable attitude to joining in. Inclined to be "difficult."

2. Emotionally stable   *vs*   Changeable
Can be depended upon to look at questions objectively, without emotional prejudice, and in the same constant light from day to day. Above emotion in his judgments. Dependable and realistic.   Sees things in terms of the emotion of the moment. Emotional bias changes from day to day and place to place. Does not remain the same person from day to day. Undependable.

3. Attention-getting   *vs*   Self-sufficient
Shows off in company. Not happy unless in center of the stage. Talks about self, accomplishments, important friends, etc. Likely to show some "affected" behavior.   Not under compulsion to impress or to get sympathy or attention.

4. Assertive, self-assured   *vs*   Submissive
Assumes he can impose his (or her) will on others. Tends to lead or influence his associates. Tends to dominate. Tends to be boastful and assertive. Not held back by doubts. Invulnerable self-esteem.   Tends to let other people have their way. Tends to back down in a conflict. Humble, quiet, retiring. Not sure he is right. "Embarrassable."

5. Depressed, solemn   *vs*   Cheerful
Earnest and solemn most of the time. Not easily moved to laughter. Seeming slow and depressed rather frequently.   Generally bubbling over with good cheer. Optimistic. Enthusiastic. Prone to cheerful witty remarks. "Laughterful."

6. Frivolous   *vs*   Responsible

7. Attentive to people   *vs*   Cool, aloof

8. Easily upset   *vs*   Unshakable poise, tough

9. Languid, slow   *vs*   Energetic, alert

10. Boorish   *vs*   Intellectual, cultured

11. Suspicious   *vs*   Trustful

ILLUS. 216. CATTELL'S THIRTY-FIVE CLUSTERS OF TRAITS (Cont'd)

DEFINITIONS

12. Good-natured, easygoing	vs	Spiteful, grasping, critical
13. Calm, phlegmatic	vs	Emotional
14. Hypochondriacal	vs	Not so
15. Mild, self-effacing	vs	Self-willed, egotistic
16. Silent, introspective	vs	Talkative
17. Persevering, determined	vs	Quitting, fickle
18. Cautious, retiring, timid	vs	Adventurous, bold
19. Hard, stern	vs	Kindly, soft-hearted
20. Insistently orderly	vs	Relaxed, indolent
21. Polished	vs	Clumsy, awkward
22. Prone to jealousy	vs	Not prone to jealousy
23. Rigid	vs	Adaptable
24. Demanding, impatient	vs	Emotionally mature
25. Unconventional, eccentric	vs	Conventional
26. Placid	vs	Worrying, anxious
27. Conscientious	vs	Somewhat unscrupulous
28. Composed	vs	Shy, bashful
29. Sensitively imaginative	vs	Practical, logical
30. Neurotic fatigue	vs	Absence of neurotic fatigue
31. Esthetically fastidious	vs	Lacking artistic feeling
32. Marked interest in opposite sex	vs	Slight interest in opposite sex
33. Frank, expressive	vs	Secretive, reserved
34. Gregarious, sociable	vs	Self-contained
35. Dependent, immature	vs	Independent-minded

(By permission of R. B. Cattell, 1947, and the editor of *Psychometrika.*)

The reliability of these ratings was determined by correlating the mean of a group of eight raters with the mean of a second group of eight raters. Correlations ranged from .51 to .60 for a group of men, which is about 20 points lower than similar correlations for a group of college women. This finding is typical of the care with which college women rated one another and the lack of care by the men. The thirty-five traits were then correlated with one another and the matrix was analyzed by factorial analysis, using the centroid method. The first five traits below appear to be clearly determined and the last six have smaller loadings. The letters assigned to these factors were de--

rived from a previous study. The present order indicates the size of factorial loadings. The factors are named (Cattell, 1947, p. 211) as follows:

E *Dominance versus submissiveness:* The traits which contribute to this factor are variables 4, 33, 35, 19, 26, and 5. (Illus. ~~198~~) 216

G *Positive integration versus immaturity:* Strong, silent, hard, thoughtful, stable versus weak, slipshod, quitting and changeable, social person. The traits contributing most highly to this factor are 7, 2, 6, 24, and 17.

H *Charitable, adventurous, cyclothymia versus withdrawn:* The traits contributing to this factor are 34, 32, 27, 28, and 6. This is supposed to be the constitutional factor lacking in schizophrenic tendency. It brings in good character qualities, sex interest, and conscientiousness.

F *Surgency versus desurgency.* Its representative traits are 9, 5, 13, 18. The person is energetic, cheerful, talkative, with some show of emotion.

A *Cyclothymia versus schizothymia:* This is represented by traits 1, 24, 12, 15, 7, 26, and 23. These show a factor which it is not easy to distinguish from Factor H, the main difference being that Factor H emphasizes withdrawal, shyness, bashfulness, and cautiousness, while Factor A stresses obstruction, spitefulness, worrying, anxiety, and a rigid behavior. This is probably a marked contribution to our knowledge of personality structure, for two independent traits appear here as in previous studies by Cattell and others.

K *Trained, socialized, cultured mind versus boorishness:* 10, 28, 21, 29, 8, 27.

B *Intelligence versus mental defect:* 20, 27, 17, 10.

I *Sensitive, imaginative, emotionality versus rigid, mature, poise:* 24, 35, 31, 6, 3, 36, 29.

J *Thoughtful, neurasthenic versus vigorous, simple character:* 1, 13, 4, 8, 10, 30.

M *Spiessburger concernedness versus Bohemian intellectualism:* 25, 29, 26, 23, 10.

L *Paranoic schizothymia versus sensitive, trustful acceptability:* This factor again brings in schizophrenia but with an emphasis this time on suspicion and jealousy: 22, 26, 36, 28, 11.

A previous study was made of men averaging thirty-five years of age, and it was thought to be a more significant one for adults than the study reported here upon college students. The same factors appeared, however, in nearly the same order. Cattell has shown that this evidence has been supported from many sources, and he believes that these eleven traits are basic personality factors which remain fairly constant in different populations.

In order to provide an instrument to measure the personality factors isolated by his careful research, Cattell and his associates have published the Sixteen Factor Personality Questionnaire (1950). It is unique in that each item has a known saturation with all factors, but it is scored only for the one factor which it best represents. By including the factors listed on page 645 the authors believe that no important aspect of personality has been omitted. Each factor is appraised by from 20 to 26 items when Forms A and B are used. Each form can usually be completed in 30 minutes or less time.

There are three types of items. One type asks an opinion about oneself to be answered with *yes, in between,* or *no.* An example of the questions is, "Are you well described as a happy, nonchalant person?" Another type of item is designed to measure intellect through knowledge of word relations, such as, "Which word does not belong with the other two? *North, East, Down."* A third type of item asks one to choose between two occupations, activities, or values. For example, "Would you rather work as an engineer or a social science teacher?"

For most of the items there is a score of 0, 1, or 2, to be recorded according to a key. The raw score totals for each factor are changed to standard scores and placed on a profile. In general a high score indicates a strong development of the positive aspect of the factor, and a low score the negative aspect of the factor. This schema is similar to that used by Guilford and Martin (1945), but differs from that of Sheldon (1942) who proposed factors having three poles.

Cattell and Luborsky (1942), stimulated by Freud's hypothesis that wit is an expression of needs which are repressed in everyday life, experimented with the possibility or measuring personality characteristics by one's reaction to various kinds of jokes. One of the results is the C-L Humor Test (1949). Form A of this test consists of ninety-one pairs of jokes. One of each pair is to be marked as "more amusing" than the other, not "more witty, or tasteful, or intellectual." An example is:

a) Shall I clip the ends of your hair, sir?
No thanks. One end will be sufficient.

b) Chatty assistant; Shall I go over it again, sir?
No. I heard every word you said.

Form B of the C-L Humor Test consists of 112 jokes. The person being tested is to indicate opposite each joke whether he thinks it is funny or dull. Both forms were selected from a much larger sample of jokes as the result of three successive researches which brought to light eleven correlation clusters. Each cluster is now represented in each form by from seven to fourteen items. The raw scores, which are the number of items preferred in each cluster, are changed to standard scores of adults and placed on a profile. The interpretation of this profile should be made in the light of a number of other variables, but in general it is believed that a high score indicates both a strong drive and a high degree of inhibition against the drive. The eleven clusters are described as follows:

1. *Debonair sexuality versus guilt, inhibition.* These are correlated with sociable, happy-go-lucky versus shy, anxious reactions to jokes.
2. *Derision versus pathos and calm acceptance.* These jokes on the one hand deride stupidity, laziness, gullibility and innocence, and on the other show a wry acceptance of human fate.
3. *Self-composure versus nervous insecurity.* These jokes show enjoyment of shocking events or some reassurance in the face of a nervous doubt.
4. *Disregard of conventions versus light badinage.* Positive jokes indicate pleasure in violating conventions.
5. *Negativism versus secure robust enjoyment.* These jokes ridicule persons who customarily receive some deference, such as the parson or the father, or at the opposite pole there is robust enjoyment without spitefulness.
6. *Resigned masculinity versus pleasure in active discomfiture.* The positive jokes involve a blunt aggression against men and the negative tilt at the foibles of women.
7. *Ironic dominance versus masochism.* The positive jokes play without spite on weaknesses of people, while the negative stress self-punishment and also attacks on others.
8. *Good-natured play versus smart wit.* The positive are slapstick jokes and the negative indicate sophisticated criticism with a slight tone of disgust.
9. *Wanton aggressiveness versus whimsy.* The positive jokes show unprovoked aggression which brings surprise and discomfort to well-meaning people. The negative show cheerful acceptance of the blows of fortune.
10. *Sociable good humor versus dry comment.* The positive jokes have a hale-fellow-well-met mood, while the negative show dry or even bitter aggression.
11. *Cynicism versus intellectual play.* The positive jokes are critical of a wide range of moral values: deceit pays, culture is hypocrisy, etc. The negative tend to be a play on words.

An inspection of these clusters seems to indicate considerable overlapping among them, but Cattell points out that with these, as in other personality appraisals, valid tests cannot be based on inspection, but rather on a goodly number of empirical checks. This type of test has the advantage of being interesting for most adults, hard to fake, and even in its present form fairly reliable.

Other Scales. a. The Kuder Preference Record Personal (1948) is a questionnaire which is the result of several years of research. It involves approximately forty-two thousand correlations between various scales and items in experimental samples. In his search for independent variables, Kuder found five and these are represented in this questionnaire. They are called preferences for

Sociable activities: taking the lead and being the center of a group.
Practical activities: dealing with external needs and getting things done.
Theoretical activities: thinking, speculating.
Agreeable activities: those which make for smooth, pleasant personal relations.
Dominant activities: use of authority and power.

The questionnaire consists of 168 items, each of which lists three activities. One is asked to indicate the most liked and the least liked of the three. He is also asked to choose as if he were equally familiar with all the activities, and to put down his first reaction. There are no time limits. In addition to the five trait scores, a verification score is computed to identify those who have answered carelessly or not followed directions. It is also pointed out that the obtained scores may not indicate usual behavior, but rather, wishful thinking. Indeed the directions in this and other preference questionnaires seem to encourage such answers. Norms and prediction studies are now being developed.

b. The Mental Health Analysis of Thorpe, Clark, and Tiegs (1946) comes in four levels: elementary (grades 4 to 8), intermediate (grades 7 to 10), secondary (grades 9 to college), and adult. At each level the same traits are evaluated by two hundred items. Some of the items are repeated in the various levels. Each item is a short statement to be answered by *yes* or *no*. The authors have tried to disguise questions which might conflict with one's tendency to protect himself. Thus, instead of asking, Are you immature? the question is, Are you quick enough to get the best seats at a program? And instead of, Do you offend people? they ask, Have you found that many people's feelings are easily hurt? The Lewerenz Vocabulary Grade Placement Formula was followed to keep the language difficulties considerably below the grade levels of those to be tested.

The traits, which are each evaluated by twenty items, are divided into two main groups, liabilities and assets, but since each trait is considered a continuum and all high scores are assets, there is a total over-all score which gives a general index of mental health. The traits are called:

I-A. *Behavioral Immaturity.* The behaviorally immature individual reacts on the basis of childhood (infantile) ideas and desires. He has not learned to assume responsibility for, or to accept the consequences of, his own acts. He attempts to solve his problems by such childish methods as sulking, crying, pouting, hitting others, or pretending to be ill. He has failed to develop emotional control and thinks primarily in terms of himself and his own comfort.

I-B. *Emotional Instability.* The individual who is emotionally unstable is characteristically sensitive, tense, and given to excessive self-concern. He may substitute the joys of a fantasy world for actual successes in real life. He may develop one or more physical symptoms designed to provide him with an escape from responsibilities and thus to diminish his distress. He is quick to make excuses for failure and to take advantage of those who will serve him.

I-C. *Feelings of Inadequacy.* The inadequate individual feels inferior and incompetent. This feeling may be related not only to particular skills or abilities but may be general in nature. Such a person feels that he is not well regarded by others, that people have little faith in his future possibilities, and that he is unsuccessful socially. He feels that he is left out of things because he is unattractive and because he lacks ability.

I-D. *Physical Defects.* The individual who possesses one or more physical defects is likely to respond with feelings of inferiority because of unfavorable comparisons or of handicaps in competition with other persons. It is usually not the physical defect *per se* that brings unhappiness but the restrictions and social disapprovals which come in its wake. Thus the extremely short, the homely, or the crippled individual may feel that his handicap is insurmountable.

I-E. *Nervous Manifestations.* The individual who is suffering from nervous symptoms manifests one or more of a variety of what appear to be physical disorders such as eye strain, loss of appetite, inability to sleep, chronic weariness, or dizzy spells. Persons of this kind may be exhibiting physical (functional) expressions of emotional conflicts. Stuttering, tics, and other spasmodic or restless movements are also symptomatic of this type of mental ill-health.

II-A. *Close Personal Relationships.* The individual who possesses this asset to mental health counts among his acquaintances some in whom he can confide, who show genuine respect for him as a person, and who welcome friendship of a warm and substantial nature. Such an individual enjoys sense of security and well-being because of having status with those who mean something to his welfare.

II-B. *Inter-Personal Skills.* The socially skillful individual gets along well with other people. He understands their motives and is solicitous of their welfare. He goes out of his way to be of assistance to both friends and strangers and is tactful in his dealings with them. The socially skillful person subordinates his egoistic tendencies in favor of the needs and activities of his associates.

II-C. *Social Participation.* The socially adjusted individual participates in a number of group activities in which cooperation and mutuality are in evidence. In contrast to the isolate who prefers his own company, the mentally healthy individual enjoys the companionship of others. His willingness to contribute to the success of group endeavors provides him with the feeling of belongingness and of having status which his nature requires.

II-D. *Satisfying Work and Recreation.* The well-adjusted individual experiences success and satisfaction in his work, whether it be the seeking of an education or occupational relationships in the world of professions, industry, or business. He also participates in a variety of hobbies and recreational activities which provide release from tension. He will have chosen tasks that challenge him and that satisfy his need for approval and a sense of achievement.

II-E. *Outlook and Goals.* The mentally healthy individual has a satisfying philosophy of life that guides his behavior in harmony with socially acceptable, ethical, and moral principles. He also understands his environment and the forces and cause and effect relationships which shape his destiny as a member of a social group. He establishes approved personal goals and makes reasonable progress toward their attainment.

The Kuder-Richardson reliabilities based on 1,225 cases were .967 for total score, .935 for liabilities, and .931 for assets. The desirable response for liability items is *no,* and for the asset items is *yes.* Each item is marked with a tiny letter to show the trait which it evaluates. Scores are the totals of desirable responses for each trait. The authors recommend that the test be used in industry for selecting employees, up-grading employees, increasing employee efficiency, and improving employee-management relations. Clinical uses are also listed, and the usual causes of disturbances and methods of treatment are outlined. The centile norms for each level of maturity group are given on one chart, for it was found that sex and age differences were insignificant within the groups.

c. The California Test of Personality, Tiegs, Clark, and Thorpe (1934, 1943) has five different levels, ranging from the first grade to adulthood. On each level 144 items are divided equally into twelve sections. Each section is designed to evaluate a component of personality. The first six components are related to self-adjustment in that they show how a person feels about himself. The called: self-reliance, sense of personal worth, sense of personal free dom, feeling of belonging, withdrawing tendencies, and nervous symptoms. The second group is related to social adjustment, and these items indicate how one feels toward others or gets along with others. They are called: social standing, social skill, freedom from anti-social tendencies, family relations, school relations, and community relations. Percentile ranks are furnished for each level, both sexes together. The authors have found small differences, but have thought that these were not large enough to require separate norms for boys and girls. A number of studies have been made surveying mental-health problems among school children and adults. In general, the maladjustment corresponds to poor parental and home relations, speech defects, and neurotic traits. One study compared the scores of 303 ninth-grade pupils with the multiple-choice Ink Blot scores. It showed that those who seemed to be maladjusted according to the Rorschach Test made a higher number of undesirable responses on the California Test of Personality than those who were apparently adjusted according to the Rorschach Test. Bi-serial correlations of approximately .30 were found between the Rorschach scores and the total social-adjustment and self-adjustment scores. Another study reported the applications on students from grade four to eight of the California Test of Personality and a sociometric study using three questions: "Who is your best friend?" "Who do you like to work with?" and "Who among your companions would you like to be like?" This study showed that superior adjustment, as indicated on the personality test, is not widely recognized by children as a criterion for acceptance. Acceptance or aspiration was more closely associated with above average accomplishment and aggressiveness.

d. Forer (1948) published a Diagnostic Interest Blank designed to give data on psychodynamics, such as frustrated overt needs, psychological defenses, basic needs of which the individual may not be aware. The blank consists of lists of 88 hobbies and sports, 70 personal characteristics, 22 reading interests, 74 occupational interests, and 25 secret hopes and ambitions. The items are all single words or short phrases, such as "play baseball, optimistic, tall, insists on his rights, mechanic magazines, teach others, and become invisible at will." The directions ask the testee to circle *yes, U.* or *no* to indicate whether the item is characteristic, unimportant, or not characteristic of his ideal person or the person he would like to be. Forer believed that the use of the ideal person leads to freer expression of needs and impulses, than the use of self. Six scoring categories are suggested:

1. *Social orientation:* personal or interpersonal emphasis on cooperation, competition, autism, narcissism.
2. *Group identification:* conformity, moral values.
3. *Major role:* dominant or dependent, diffuse or rigid, occupational orientation and consistency.
4. *Means of achieving goals:* acceptance of responsibility, attitude toward discipline.
5. *Realism:* practical interest, fantasy, occultism, over-extension versus reasonable selection.
6. *Sexual adjustment:* acceptance of opposite sex, conditions of acceptance, compensatory factors.

No quantitative scales have as yet been set for this blank, but qualitative interpretations of results are described. The results from this blank must be interpreted in part by comparing them with a case history showing usual social, recreational, and occupational behavior. The discrepancies between the actual and the ideal will show areas of frustration, which may be further explored for content and basic conflicts by a clinician.

Sociological Classifications

Several inventories have been issued which indicate the adequacy of adjustments in what may be called sociological areas. Widely used examples of these are the Minnesota Scale for the Survey of Opinions (1936), the Bell Adjustment Inventory (1934, 1938), and the Mooney Problem Check List (1943).

The Minnesota Scale for the Survey of Opinions. In constructing scales to be used for measuring the effects of the depression on personality and family life of young people, Rundquist and Sletto (1936) drew most of the preliminary items from their own logical considerations. Care was exercised to secure informal language and clarity of statement. The personal pronoun was avoided since they believed that impersonal statements of majority opinion might be more frank. Positive and negative statements were made in equal numbers, the positive usually expressing optimistic or socially acceptable views. The items were submitted to groups of students for criticism. Statements containing the words *all, always, none,* and *never* were considered to be unsatisfactory, for students sometimes disagreed with this type of statement although agreeing with the main conclusion of the item.

The statistical selection of items included two considerations: reliability and discriminative ability. The reliability of each item was secured by giving the scales twice within a week. Items which showed wide fluctuations were discarded. The discrimination of an item was measured by noting differences in answers to it by the highest and lowest quarter of a group. The items finally selected usually showed the largest differences. More negative than positive statements were found to be discriminative.

The final inventory of 132 items contains scales for measuring six aspects of adjustment:

1. *Morale:* feelings of inability to cope with one's problems
2. *Social inferiority:* feelings of inability to succeed in association with others
3. *Family:* ideas about pleasantness and intimacy of family life
4. *Law:* attitudes toward legal institutions
5. *Economics:* conservatism and radicalism
6. *Education:* belief about the values of education

Each scale consists of 22 items, and each item is to be marked on a 1 to 5 scale, using the words strongly agree, agree, undecided, disagree,

ILLUS. 217. MINNESOTA SCALE FOR THE SURVEY OF OPINIONS

Directions: READ EACH ITEM CAREFULLY AND UNDERLINE QUICKLY THE PHRASE WHICH BEST EXPRESSES YOUR FEELING ABOUT THE STATEMENT. Wherever possible, let your own personal experience determine your answer. Do not spend much time on any item. If in doubt, underline the phrase which seems most nearly to express your present feeling about the statement. WORK RAPIDLY. Be sure to answer every item.

1. THE FUTURE IS TOO UNCERTAIN FOR A PERSON TO PLAN ON MARRY—ING.
    Strongly agree ^{5} Agree ^{4} Undecided ^{3} Disagree ^{2} Strongly disagree ^{1}
2. AFTER BEING CAUGHT IN A MISTAKE, IT IS HARD TO DO GOOD WORK FOR A WHILE.
    Strongly agree ^{5} Agree ^{4} Undecided ^{3} Disagree ^{2} Strongly disagree ^{1}
3. HOME IS THE MOST PLEASANT PLACE IN THE WORLD.
    Strongly agree ^{1} Agree ^{2} Undecided ^{3} Disagree ^{4} Strongly disagree ^{5}
4. THE LAW PROTECTS PROPERTY RIGHTS AT THE EXPENSE OF HUMAN RIGHTS.
    Strongly agree ^{5} Agree ^{4} Undecided ^{3} Disagree ^{2} Strongly disagree ^{1}
5. THE GOVERNMENT SHOULD TAKE OVER ALL LARGE INDUSTRIES.
    Strongly agree ^{5} Agree ^{4} Undecided ^{3} Disagree ^{2} Strongly disagree ^{1}
6. A MAN CAN LEARN MORE BY WORKING FOUR YEARS THAN BY GOING TO HIGH SCHOOL.
    Strongly agree ^{5} Agree ^{4} Undecided ^{3} Disagree ^{2} Strongly disagree ^{1}
7. IT IS DIFFICULT TO THINK CLEARLY THESE DAYS.
    Strongly agree ^{5} Agree ^{4} Undecided ^{3} Disagree ^{2} Strongly disagree ^{1}
8. IT IS EASY TO EXPRESS ONE'S IDEAS.
    Strongly agree ^{1} Agree ^{2} Undecided ^{3} Disagree ^{4} Strongly disagree ^{5}
9. PARENTS EXPECT TOO MUCH FROM THEIR CHILDREN.
    Strongly agree ^{5} Agree ^{4} Undecided ^{3} Disagree ^{2} Strongly disagree ^{1}
10. A PERSON SHOULD OBEY ONLY THOSE LAWS WHICH SEEM REASON—ABLE.
    Strongly agree ^{5} Agree ^{4} Undecided ^{3} Disagree ^{2} Strongly disagree ^{1}
11. LABOR SHOULD HAVE MUCH MORE VOICE IN DECIDING GOVERNMENT POLICIES.
    Strongly agree ^{5} Agree ^{4} Undecided ^{3} Disagree ^{2} Strongly disagree ^{1}
12. THE MORE EDUCATION A MAN HAS THE BETTER HE IS ABLE TO ENJOY LIFE.
    Strongly agree ^{1} Agree ^{2} Undecided ^{3} Disagree ^{4} Strongly disagree ^{5}
13. THE FUTURE LOOKS VERY BLACK.
    Strongly agree ^{5} Agree ^{4} Undecided ^{3} Disagree ^{2} Strongly disagree ^{1}
14. IT IS DIFFICULT TO SAY THE RIGHT THING AT THE RIGHT TIME.
    Strongly agree ^{5} Agree ^{4} Undecided ^{3} Disagree ^{2} Strongly disagree ^{1}
15. ONE OUGHT TO DISCUSS IMPORTANT PLANS WITH MEMBERS OF HIS FAMILY.
    Strongly agree ^{1} Agree ^{2} Undecided ^{3} Disagree ^{4} Strongly disagree ^{5}
16. IT IS ALL RIGHT TO EVADE THE LAW IF YOU DO NOT ACTUALLY VIOLATE IT.
    Strongly agree ^{5} Agree ^{4} Undecided ^{3} Disagree ^{2} Strongly disagree ^{1}
17. LEGISLATURES ARE TOO READY TO PASS LAWS TO CURB BUSINESS FREEDOM.
    Strongly agree ^{1} Agree ^{2} Undecided ^{3} Disagree ^{4} Strongly disagree ^{5}
18. EDUCATION HELPS A PERSON TO USE HIS LEISURE TIME TO BETTER ADVANTAGE.
    Strongly agree ^{1} Agree ^{2} Undecided ^{3} Disagree ^{4} Strongly disagree ^{5}

(Rundquist and Sletto, 1936. By permission of the University of Minnesota Press.)

and strongly disagree. Illustration 217 shows the first eighteen items of which 1, 7, and 13 are scored for morale, 2, 8, and 14 for social inferiority, etc.

Norms are available for 1,000 young persons—400 from college, 200 from regular high schools, and 400 from continuation high school classes. No significant differences between high school and college students were found. Individual profiles can be made to show one's position in this sample of persons. The scores on the separate scales had reliability coefficients of approximately .85. The intercorrelations between these six scales for a sample of five hundred young adults were:

		2	3	4	5	6
1.	Morale	.511	.420	.518	.235	.534
2.	Inferiority		.248	.262	.205	.234
3.	Family			.388	.081	.303
4.	Law				.191	.396
5.	Economic Conservatism					.087
6.	Education					

Morale scores were found to be most highly correlated with the other scores, and economic conservatism the least highly correlated.

In a small group of high school students correlations between these adjustment scores and mental ability were low with two exceptions. Morale correlated with honor points .506 for boys but not for girls, and attitude toward education correlated —.40 with IQ for girls but not for boys. The correlations of IQ's and honor points were .47 for boys and .56 for girls. The authors' original work should be consulted for a clearer analysis of their results from applying this scale to many parent-child, age, and social groups.

The Bell Adjustment Inventory (1934, 1938). This inventory consists of 160 items divided equally among five areas of adjustments: home, health, other persons, emotional disturbances, and occupations (Illus. 156). The items were selected from a preliminary set on the basis of their discrimination between the upper and lower 15 per cent of individuals when ranked for total adjustment scores. Each item is to be checked *yes, no,* or *?.* Separate scores are available for each field as well as the total. The odd-even correlations ranged from .81 to .91 for the separate sections, and to .94 for the total scores. The intercorrelations of the separate sections ranged from —.06 to .51, median .24, which is an indication of a marked degree of independence among these self-ratings. Two forms of this inventory are now available, one for adults, the other for students in high school and college. This is a widely used inventory, the value of which has been reported in more than fifty technical articles.

Mooney Problem Check Lists. Three check lists for the study of student problems have been devised by Mooney (1943), one for college, one for high school, and one for junior high school. In each list the student is asked to "Read the list slowly and as you come to a problem which is troubling you, draw a line under it. For example, if you are often bothered by headaches, you would draw a line under the first item, like this. '1. Often have headaches.' " On the last page the student is asked to answer such questions as:

1. Which of the problems you have marked are troubling you most? Write about two or three of these if you care to.
2. Have you enjoyed using this check list of problems?
3. Would you like to spend more time in school trying to do something about some of your problems?
4. Would you like to talk to someone about your problems?

The college and high school check lists each have 330 short items which are classified into eleven areas. (Sample items are given in parentheses.)

1. Health and physical development. (Often get sick)
2. Finances, living conditions, and employment. (Too crowded at home)
3. Social and recreational activities. (Slow in getting acquainted with people)
4. Courtship, sex, and marriage. (Boy friend) (Too few dates)
5. Social-psychological relations. (Unpopular) (Being snubbed)
6. Personal psychological relations. (Too easily discouraged)
7. Morals and religion. (Drinking) (Dislike church service)
8. Home and family. (Family quarrels) (Want to leave home)
9. The future, vocational and educational. (Need to decide upon a vocation)
10. Adjustment to school work. (Getting low grades)
11. Curriculum and teaching procedures. (Tests unfair)

The junior high school list includes 210 items grouped in seven areas, which are similar to numbers 1, 4, 6, 7, 8, 9, and 10 above. The average number of problems marked by about 1,000 college students was 30, by 1,025 high school students 27, and by 684 junior high school students 23. The range was from 16 to more than 100 problems. Over 90 per cent of college and high school students indicated that they enjoyed filling out the check list. More than 60 per cent in college and 70 per cent in high school requested a chance to talk over their problems with someone. The manuals for administering these check lists give samples of individual counseling uses and research applications. The relations of problems to age, sex, and locality have been tentatively found. More research is in progress.

COMPARISON OF SCALES, NEEDS FOR RESEARCH

Correlational Analyses

In view of the fact that nearly all of the appraisals of modes of behavior thus far discussed secure total scores by adding together items which are somewhat ambiguous, factorial analysis of scores cannot be expected to give clear results. Such analyses, however, are of value in showing whether the items which have been grouped together on the basis of logical or empirical considerations are found to depend upon one or upon several factors. The statistical approach may, if carefully interpreted, furnish an answer to the question, What are the main independent modes of behavior in a particular group of persons? The methods of Thurstone and of Spearman are most frequently used. Since they employ somewhat different procedures, both will be illustrated.

Results from Thurstone's Method. Vernon (1938) applied Thurstone's technique to the results of the elaborate Boyd Personality Questionnaire given to fifty men and fifty women student teachers. The 175 correlations among nineteen separate scores averaged .366 ± .06 when corrected for attenuation. Only four independent factors were needed to account for the correlation matrix. Vernon identified them tentatively as:

1. *Self-depreciation:* This was prominent in items which emphasize depression, instability, anxiety, shrinking from responsibility, and lack of self-sufficiency. This was the largest factor. It accounted for 41 per cent of the total variance. The next 3 factors together accounted for only 35 per cent.
2. *Carefreeness:* This was prominent in items representing suggestibility, freedom from worries, dissociation, inability to concentrate, lack of definite interests, and freedom from tenseness.
3. *Scrupulousness:* This is found in obsessional carefulness, strong self-control of feelings, freedom from emotional thinking, strong concentration, and acting readily without pressure.
4. *A factor which differentiated men from women:* Women showed stronger dislikes and fears, and more instability and dependency. Men showed more scrupulousness, inability to concentrate, and introspectiveness.

A careful study by Layman (1937) obtained twelve factors from correlations between sixty-seven items which had been answered by 276 students. The twelve factors were tentatively named:

Gregariousness   Inferiority, or lack of confidence
Social inadequacy   Impulsiveness
Social initiative   Moodiness
Social aggressiveness   Sensitivity
Changeability of interests   Emotional introversion
Self-sufficiency, or independence   Inability to face reality

The first four factors in this list are modes of social adjustment. They indicate four independent modes of behavior, not a single elemental sociability. Although these four modes are not easy to distinguish, they seem to be reasonable subdivisions of social activity. Thus, a person may be gregarious, that is, desire the company of others, because he feels socially inadequate, because he is aggressive, or because he desires to initiate some cooperative venture. There may be other independent aspects of social contact which will appear in other investigations. The last eight factors listed by Layman seem to be emotional adjustments. It is difficult to secure an accurate verbal description of emotional modes of behavior from this material, but the factor names are fairly descriptive and they confirm the work of others.

Carter, Conrad, and Jones (1935) used Thurstone's method to analyze an inventory of children's annoyances and their relationship with a measure of intelligence. They found three independent factors called (1) general annoyability, (2) annoyance at untidiness, and (3) personal annoyance from interest in self-esteem. Intelligence showed a negative relationship with the tendency to be annoyed.

A factorial analysis by Burt (1938) is of unusual interest because he arrived at essentially the same results, using correlations among traits and among persons. His sample included 124 persons chosen from a larger group because they all had similar average ratings on eleven emotional tendencies. Analyses following the methods of Spearman, Thurstone, and Kelley produced factors of general emotionality, of aggressive-inhibitive emotions, and of pleasurable-unpleasurable emotions.

Thorndike (1936) applied Thurstone's (1935) method to social-intelligence and mental-alertness tests. He found that the social intelligence tests measure primarily the ability to understand and to work with words, which is such a large factor in verbal-intelligence tests.

A factorial analysis was made by Brogden (1940) of intelligence and character tests applied to one hundred sixth grade children. He used the Otis Group Intelligence Test and thirty performance tests which included 4 designed to measure honesty; 3, perseveration; 3, persistence; 2, slang usage; and 1 to indicate each of the following: inhibition, suggestibility, conscientiousness, deportment, and grades in school subjects. By using Thurstone's (1935) method seven factors were delineated.

1. *Resistance to suggestion,* similar to Spearman's *W*
2. *Honesty,* as shown by unwillingness to cheat
3. *Persistence,* as shown by continuing work in spite of fatigue, boredom, or distraction
4. *Verbal facility,* as shown by the Otis Test, similar to Thurstone's *V*
5. *A factor probably related to reasoning,* not clearly identified
6. *Self control,* or *dutifulness*
7. *Acceptance of a moral code*

Spearman's Method. During Spearman's research on cognitive experience, he found evidences of traits which corresponded to variations in energy. These were called Perseveration, Oscillation, and Will.

1) *Perseveration (P) and Its Opposite, Fluency (F).* The idea that persons differ in their ability to shift rapidly from one activity to another has been investigated by many since Wiersma (1906) reported tests of speed of sensory adaptation. A survey of elaborate studies by Lankes (1914) and Cattell (1934) shows that five kinds of tests have been used:

Persistence of sensory after-effect, as shown by
1. Speed at which different colored sectors of a color-disk fuse, called flicker limen
2. Time needed for light and dark visual adaptation
3. Time needed for recovery of hearing after a loud noise
4. Time needed for recovery of touch after a severe electric shock

Spontaneous recurrence of an experience
1. In free association the tendency to give the same reaction to the same or to different stimulus words
2. Direct questions about tunes, poetry, phrases, problems, and dreams coming to mind again and again

Hindrance of new mental activity by similar past activity
1. Comparison of writing S's continuously with writing them as they appear in a mirror. This reversal technique is also applied to various letters, numbers, and drawings.
2. Comparison of immediate recall of a drawing with recall which has been delayed by the exposure of a second drawing. This technique was also applied to short narratives.
3. Direct questions on effects of being interrupted in various tasks, homesickness, seasickness, desire for change, and tendency to finish a task, although a reason no longer exists for completing it.

Usual rates of activity
1. Natural rate of tapping. The subject was told to tap with his finger just as he feels inclined at the time.

2. Speed of free association

Emotional patterns
1. Aroused with difficulty but long in duration
2. Pessimism and lethargy
3. Few likes
4. Either unusually submissive or else negativistic
5. Inability to make small decisions quickly
6. Either untruthful or punctiliously truthful
7. Gives up easily

The results of applications of such tests, usually to small numbers of students, have been summarized by Spearman (1938). From correlation analyses he concludes that there exists in various amounts in each person a tendency for mental processes to lag. It is measured by inertia or slowness in shifting energy from one arrangement to another.

Line and Griffin (1935) applied a factorial analysis to tests of word association, reaction time, oscillation, perseveration, and Bernreuter scores, in an attempt to find the factors underlying mental health. A major factor emerged, which was called objectivity, and thought to be related to Spearman's fluency (F), which is the reverse of perseveration or inertia (P).

A factorial research by Kleemeier and Dudek (1950) investigated the possible existence of an independent factor which they defined as flexibility. A battery of thirteen tests was composed and applied to 205 college students. The battery contained nine tests where no flexibility was required, and four where some flexibility was required. The no-flexibility tests required one to add single or 2-digit numbers in one test, or in another test to subtract similar numbers. The flexibility test required one to shift from addition to subtraction, and vice versa in random order. Other no-flexibility tests required the addition of a final letter to make a word and the addition of an initial letter to make a word. In a flexibility test these requirements were varied in a random fashion without any instructions to indicate whether the answer was an initial or a final letter. Still other no-flexibility tests consisted of printed rows of M's among which were a few N's. One was asked to count the N's. A similar test required one to count all the W's in rows of M's. The flexibility test here was composed of rows of M's some of which contained N's and some W's. All of these tests were prepared in two equivalent forms and administered in a rotated order to avoid practice effects. The centroid analysis did not reveal any common elements in the flexibility tests although four well-defined factors appeared corresponding to perceptual speed, verbal ability, single-digit, and double-digit computation, which accounted very well for the variances of the scores on all the tests. This study points to the conclusion that an independent factor of flexibility is not necessary to explain the results of these tests. It may be that in much more complex situations a flexibility factor will appear.

2) *Oscillation (O)*.   Another energy adjustment which Spearman finds unique is fluctuation or oscillation. It is supposed to be shown by:

a. The duration of attention shown in the waxing and waning of faint sensory stimuli, such as a light or small weight
b. The fluctuations in stereoscopic vision between the patterns which will not fuse, and also in monocular vision, the fluctuations in reversible perspective drawings
c. Changes in rate of continuous work in aiming or cancellation test, or crossing out circles

Measures of this factor are not related to perseveration. Although both measure rapidity of change of some central mechanism, oscillation is dependent upon recuperation from fatigue, while perseveration is not due to fatigue but to difficulties in changing direction of energy. By analogy, oscillation would correspond to variations of the steam pressure in a power plant; perseveration to the time required for the steam to be turned off for one machine and turned on for another; and *g*, or intellectual power, to the average steam pressure maintained in the plant.

3) *Will (W)*.   On the basis of quantitative results, Aveling (1926) concluded that conation in the sense of striving for a goal was quite different from volition in the sense of resolving or selecting a goal. If we accept the former as a rough definition of will, it is possible to assemble three types of appraisals which have been used by many investigators:

1. Tests involving variations in effort, shown by test of
   a. Quality of handwriting, Courtis (1925)
   b. General mental tests
   c. Rate tests
   d. Tests of persistence in the face of distractions (see Hartshorne and May, 1930)
2. Ratings of behavior, such as those by Webb (1915) and Bernreuter (1931)
3. Observations of effort and persistence, such as time-sampling and log records

Results from variations of incentives indicate that the amount of effort which is effective usually increases with the complexity of the task or the speed with which the task must be performed. Great effort, however, such as produced by a much desired prize, tends to increase speed at the expense of accuracy, even when aimed at producing more accuracy. Effort when effective in unspeeded tests of complex sorts seems to direct one toward relevant processes and continued action. In group measures variations in effort seldom produce any significant changes in intercorrelations.

Maller (1934) reported an analysis of correlations of measures of four aspects of character: honesty, cooperation, inhibition, and persistence. To measure and estimate such behavior he applied an elaborate schedule of tests used by Hartshorne and May. A total of 708 pupils in three schools which served persons in upper, middle, and lower economic levels, were tested. The correlation between the scores taken to represent the four phases of character were low but positive, mean .29. The tetrad differences resulting from the analysis of separate tables of correlations for each school group were extremely small and in no instance more than three times their respective PE's. According to Spearman's logic, all the correlations may, therefore, be attributable to the presence of one common factor. When two measures of mental ability were introduced into the correlation matrices, the tetrad differences were large, hence the factor common to the behavior tests cannot be identified with g. Maller believed that the common factor was a readiness to forego an immediate goal for the sake of a remote but more valuable goal. Behavior of this kind was demanded in all of the tests, and was typical of the will (W) factor described by Spearman. Tests of honesty and cooperation doubtless involve in addition to a factor of will, other independent factors determined by moral ideals. In some cases it may take more effort to be dishonest than honest. The intercorrelations among tests of honesty were usually low.

These analyses use the words *will, effort, steadfastness, determination,* and *persistence* somewhat interchangeably, and leave one with a vague impression of the meaning of the mathematical factor (W). Spearman (1938) also fails to be specific on this point. Apparently will, defined as effort, refers to a general discharge of energy in many activities including both cognitive and muscular processes. If the discharge is too feeble or too violent, it reduces g, the mental process which demands complex comparison. Will may also refer to persistence in the face of distractions implying a channelizing of energy to increase success in a particular situation which may or may not require much of the g factor. As used by Webb and by Hartshorne and May, will is identified with kindness, trustworthiness, and cooperation, which are social goals rather than effort or distribution of energy. More careful definition and research are needed to clarify this factor. It will probably be resolved into two or more subdivisions with further scrutiny.

It is too early to write an adequate summary of primary traits. The field is being actively investigated. The following general conclusions, however, are in order:

1. The results of factorial analysis depend upon the variety of items, the ambiguity of the items, and the variety of the persons who respond to the items. When few persons (less than 300), and few items (less than 40) are used, the investigation suffers from a paucity of facts. The best results will doubtless come from factorial analyses of unambiguous items, rather than from analyses of total scores from several divisions of a test. Total scores invite ambiguity through the arbitrary selection by the author of items which seem to indicate a particular trait. When items which are really independent of one another are added together, no quantitative analysis is feasible.

2. An inspection of the illustrations above shows rather startling similarities between results of measures on different populations. Spearman's g factor, and its variations, inertia (P) and oscillation (O), are found in all other investigations where comparison and

ILLUS. 218. COMPARISON OF PERSONAL INVENTORIES

Trait	Guilford-Zimmerman		MMPI	
A. *Amount of dominance*	G	General activity—slow, tired		
	A	Ascendance—submission		
	*M	Masculinity—femininity	*Mf	Masculine-feminine
B. *Control of impulses:*				
Rigid or lax	R	Restraint—carefree		
Variable control	*E	Emotional stability—fluctuation, guilt	Ma	Hypomania
C. *Self-defense or offense:*				
Rationalize or somatic symptoms	O	Objective—oversensitive	Hy	Hysteria
			Hs	Hypochondriasis
			Pt	Psychasthenia
Blame others	*P	Personal relations—uncooperative	Pa	Paranoia
	F	Friendliness—sadistic	Pd	Psychopathic deviate
Blame self	*E	Emotional stability—fluctuation, guilt	D	Depression
Withdraw	S	Sociability—shyness	Sc	Schizophrenia
	T	Thoughtfulness—overactivity		

* These traits are more general in nature than the rest.

energy factors are evaluated. Until the similarities have been pointed out, these factors are usually given other names by other investigators.

A group of factors underlying particular modes and mental disorganization is well described by Mosier's work. (See Chapter XIV.) One of his factors is quite like Spearman's g, but the other seven are patterns of ineffective modes of adjustments which seem to be dependent upon social experiences, health, and physique rather than upon intellectual activities.

Content of Various Scales

In order to indicate roughly the extent to which current methods evaluate the same or similar types of behavior Illus. 218 has been prepared. This compares two batteries according to three broad aspects of a person: amount of energy, control of impulses, and methods of self-defense. These three aspects are only partly independent of each other. Their subdivisions are not unique traits, but are rather broad groupings of modes of behavior. With few exceptions each of the inventories yields indications of each mode, but the methods of evaluation are sufficiently different to make a different contribution to the analysis. The authors do not feel that their evaluations are complete.

The difficulty of observing or self-rating intangible traits is so great that much more care is needed to define modes of adjustment operationally, and then to set up and validate measures of the more important patterns. For instance, dominance is usually a function of strength, energy, ideals, impulses, and experiences. Thus, a young man may dominate a basketball court and be very retiring in an economics class or at a social dance. His reasons for dominating in basket ball may be fine health and physique, or a desire to gain the admiration of a particular person, or a compensation for failures elsewhere. Also one must define the methods of dominating. Loud and continual talking, issuing public writings, and getting elected to offices are usually taken as evidence, but often the action of a group is swayed by a few well-chosen words quietly spoken by one whose judgment is respected.

SUMMARY

Although there has been much activity in the sampling of behavior patterns by self-ratings, the careful worker must use these inventories with caution. They may have no value or do harm, if they substitute inaccurate analyses for a clear picture of the true situation or if they give a person a false feeling of security or insecurity. They may, however, indicate clearly and quickly areas for further investigation and the type of remedial action that is needed. More care is needed in defining the patterns to be measured and the ways of measuring them. The description and measurement of personality have been dealt with in considerable detail by Ellis (1946), who reviewed 360 articles dealing with the validity of personality questionnaires. He concluded that group-administered inventories resulted in valid discrimination between adjusted and maladjusted groups in only about one half of the reports. There was little indication that such questionnaires can be used for individual diagnosis, because one or more of the following criticisms are applicable:

1. *The questions* are often ambiguous, in that they may be interpreted differently by different individuals. The manner of response, for example, *yes, no,* or *?,* has a wide range of interpretations. Vocabulary range is often too difficult. Moreover, the questions are often so artificial as to have little to do with real actions. Forced-choice items may not give reasonable alternatives.

2. *The administration* may influence the validity, namely, the situation, the directions, and the personality of the examiner. For instance, a test given two days before Christmas vacation had no relation to similar measures given later.

3. *The insight* which a respondent has with regard to his own intangible qualities is often not clear, and is often biased by his wishes or protective reactions. Some persons nearly always have incentives to overrate or underrate themselves.

4. *The content* of most questionnaires is so miscellaneous that total scores have very different meanings for different persons. Many items which are used to measure a unique trait have no correlation with each other.

5. *The cultural factors* of one group may vary so much from those of another that valid indicators in the first group will not hold for the second.

On the positive side Ellis points out that personality inventories usually have some useful potentialities, such as:

1. As research tools they allow a high degree of systematic analysis and sampling, which if carried on will eventually yield positive results, and greater internal consistency.

2. The truthfulness with which an inventory is filled out may be detected by special lie scores and other devices, and may be increased by paired comparisons when the two alternatives are about equal in social acceptance.

3. There is marked uniformity among both normal and abnormal

subjects in interpreting both questions and directions. This can be improved by intensive study.

4. At present, unfavorable scores are nearly always indicative of maladjustment, although favorable scores do not necessarily indicate good adjustment.

STUDY GUIDE QUESTIONS

1. Upon what theories were the items selected for the Cornell Index, the MMPI, the Guilford-Martin Inventories, and the Bell Adjustment Inventory?

2. What effectiveness did the Cornell Index show when the cut-off score was 10? 15? 20?

3. Why was the reliability of the Naval Personal Inventory so much higher among psychiatric discharges than among normal recruits?

4. How did Hathaway and McKinley select items for their nine scales of personality characteristics?

5. How did Hathaway and McKinley secure a validity score?

6. Compare the scoring categories of the MMPI, the Guilford-Martin Inventories, the Adams Personal Audit, and Cattell's Personal Characteristics.

7. Summarize the strong and weak aspects of personality inventories.

CHAPTER XXIII

RORSCHACH TECHNIQUES

This chapter concerns techniques which present ink blots of various colors, and request the subject to tell what they could represent. The results are analyzed principally in terms of mental activities which lead to perceptual integration and concept formation. The patterns of these activities and the symbolism or content of the responses are used to infer underlying personality structure and function.

INTRODUCTION

In 1921 a report by Hermann Rorschach, a Swiss psychiatrist, was published which described an elaborate technique for determining modes of behavior from a person's verbal responses to ten ink blots. Five of the ink blots consist of various shades of gray, two of the blots are gray with one shade of red, and three are entirely in color. Various shades of red, yellow, green, orange, and blue are used. Today there are several hundred technical reports on the use and interpretation of these ink blots, and a research exchange for publications concerning this technique has been established.

In 1937 Beck issued a book giving the first fairly comprehensive set of directions and interpretations in English, and in 1944 and 1945 issued a 2-volume work giving basic considerations and a large number of cases. Klopfer and Kelly (1942) issued a definitive text on Rorschach techniques. Rappaport, Gill, and Schafer (1946) issued an extensive review with representative case histories. Efficient methods of recording responses have been developed so that the exact portion of an ink blot which served as stimulus can be identified, and the types of responses codified quickly. Frequency tables for various age, sex, clinical and other groups have been published by Beck (1944), Hertz (1946), Rappaport, Gill, and Merton (1946), and Klopfer and Davidson (1946).

TEST ADMINISTRATION

The technical manuals of Klopfer and Kelly (1942) and Beck (1944) for individual test administration and scoring are the most widely used. The administration usually consists of three parts, although the third may be omitted if the first two have resulted in sufficient information. In the first part, *spontaneous reactions* to all the cards are secured if possible. In the second part, called the *inquiry*, nonleading questions are asked to determine specifically which parts of the cards called out each reaction and some of the mental processes which resulted in the concept formation. In the second part additional spontaneous responses are also elicited. The third part is the *testing-the-limits* phase. Here the examiner exerts systematic pressure by asking leading questions to ascertain the patterns of behavior not made clear in the first two parts and the degrees of rejection of common responses. The three parts will be briefly described.

Spontaneous Reaction

In this part of the test Klopfer and Beck usually prefer to seat the subject somewhat in front of the examiner so that both can see the same card and the subject does not face the examiner. Rorschach advised this position in order to keep the personality of the examiner in the background. Other examiners prefer to face the subject so as to observe his facial expressions and to give him more security if it is needed. Then, the subject is handed the first card and informally told something like this: "People see all sorts of things in these blot pictures; now tell me what you see. What might it be for you? What does it make you think of?" Hertz provides a subject with a trial blot, so that he will have become oriented to the test and the examiner before the actual test begins. The Trial Blot (Illus. 219) is not one of Rorschach's, and is reproduced here simply to show typical aspects of outline, shading, and white spaces.

Since the past experience of the subject may lead him to make a limited interpretation of the instructions, the examiner will correct and encourage him as needed. Thus some subjects who indulge in free association without much regard for the ink blot in hand are asked to limit their responses to what the card might be. Others who only describe the blots on the card are asked to tell what the card

ILLUS. 219. HERTZ TRIAL INK BLOT

(Designed by Marguerite Hertz and published with her permission.)

makes them think of. Subjects are not instructed to make up a story, and few stories appear.

Many subjects ask questions such as, "Am I to look at the whole card or to pick out parts of it, or am I to imagine things?" The examiner makes a noncommittal answer such as: "It doesn't matter; just tell me whatever the card brings to mind." When the examiner is asked whether the card may be turned, the answer is, "It's okay to turn the card." Subjects are not instructed to turn the card.

When a subject has given two or more fairly complete associations with a card, he may be allowed to relinquish it since the material necessary for a significant score has probably been obtained. If he rejects the card without any responses, or with only a single fragmentary response, as in some shock or depressed cases, Beck encourages more responses by saying, "Take a little more time, most people see more than one thing." Sometimes subjects will continue to make associations with a card almost indefinitely, so that the examiner must give him another card after a period which has been adequate for sampling the subject's responses. Beck suggests 10 minutes, but Hertz recommends 2 minutes for most subjects.

Although no time limits are definitely set, the examiner is to keep a record of three periods for each card: first, the reaction time between taking the card and giving the first content responses to it; second, the time between taking the card and finishing the last content response; third, fairly long intervals between responses. The examiner should note the reasons for these intervals. By adding the response times the total time is secured.

Since spontaneous reactions are believed to have a significance somewhat different from that of nonspontaneous reactions, a nearly verbatim record must be taken of what is said by both the subject and the examiner, and any unusual behavior is recorded. Several standard record cards are now available with detailed summaries or ratings of responses (Illus. 220).

The Inquiry

The inquiry must determine the where and how of the responses. A general question such as, "Where is the _____?" will usually draw out an answer to show whether the subject used the whole or virtually the whole card or selected only a part of it. Sometimes the subject may be asked to outline with a wooden pointer the figure he has seen on the card, or to draw it with a pencil on a special location chart. Each Rorschach card has now been charted and coded with numbered areas. For instance, Klopfer and Kelly (1942) show six large details and six small details commonly found on Card I.

During this period any spontaneous additions to the original replies must be reported carefully. A good deal of importance is also attached to the omission of parts of cards. These omissions throw light on the ability of the subject to organize and on his rejection of certain details.

In determining how the concept was formed, the examiner must, without the use of leading questions, get clear information with regard to color, motion, form, shading, and other aspects. Usually the question, "What is it in this card which makes you think of a _____ ?" is sufficient. In other instances the examiner must ask additional nonsuggestive questions to get the subject to give a complete picture.

Testing-the-Limits

If the two previous parts of the test are well done, some examiners feel that testing-the-limits is unnecessary and that it may prevent adequate retests later. However, experience accumulated in the last few years has given more importance to this phase, because it has often been found that subjects, particularly psychopathic subjects, will not give clear and complete accounts of concept formation without a systematic series of direct questions. The examiner must find out why a subject has failed to respond to obvious features, whether his failure was due to embarrassment or oversight, and specifically what prompted the subject's responses when he made only fragmentary answers. For instance, when the subject always uses parts of a card and never the complete card, he may be asked to respond to

ILLUS. 220. RORSCHACH SYMBOLS AND PART OF RECORD BLANK

EXPLANATION OF SYMBOLS USED

LOCATION

W   *Whole Blot Used for Interpretation*
W   no part of blot omitted except white space
W⁺ intended use of whole blot but part or parts omitted or cut off
WS whole blot and white space used
(tabulate as main W and additional S)
DW a detail interpreted, with meaning assigned to the whole blot without justification (contabulation)

D   *Large Detail Used for Interpretation*
(tabulate as main F and additional m)
D   large detail (first grade normal)
D(W) detail interpreted and remainder of blot used as background
(tabulate as main D and additional W)
DS white space used in addition to D
(tabulate as main D and additional S)

d   *Small Detail Used for Interpretation*
(second grade normal)

Dd *Rare or Very Small Detail Used for Interpretation*
dd tiny detail
de edge detail (only contour used)
di inside detail
dr normal or small detail combined with rare adjacent parts

S   *White Space Used for Interpretation*
only white space used
SD a detail used in addition to S
(tabulate as main S and additional D)

CONTENT

H* Human Figures
Hd Parts of Human Figures, not Anatomical
A* Animal Figures
Ad Parts of Living Animals
A At Animal Anatomy
Aobj Fur, Skins, Skulls, and the like
At Human Anatomy (dissected parts, x-rays, anatomical charts)
Obj All Kinds of Man-Made Objects
N   Nature (landscapes, mountains, sunsets, rivers, and other scenery)
Geo Topographical and Outline Maps and Geographical Concepts like Islands, Gulfs, Channels, not seen in vista
*Caricatures and mythological figures indicated by parentheses as (H) or (Hd)
Note: Other symbols like Arch (architecture) Pl (plant) are self-explanatory.
O   Original Responses Found Not More Than Once in 100 Random Records
P   Popular Responses Found in At Least 20 Out of 100 Random Records

DETERMINANTS

M   *Figures in Human-Like Action*
(human, superhuman, or animal)
FM *Animals in Animal-Like Action*
Inanimate Movement or Expression
m   inanimate movement, form disregarded
mF inanimate movement, form secondary
Fm expressions of human or animal (tabulate as main F and additional m)
k   *Three Dimensional Expanse Projected on a Two-Dimensional Plane (x-ray, topographical map)*
k   form disregarded
kF form secondary
Fk fusion of form and k
K   *Shading Used as Diffusion (smoke, clouds)*
K   form disregarded
KF form secondary
FK *Shading Used as Three Dimensional Expanse in Vista or Perspective*
F   *Form Only Used for Interpretation*
F+ form on level of popular response
F+ form more accurate than popular
F− form less accurate than popular
Shading Used as Surface Texture of a Clearly Seen Form
Fc *Shading Used as Texture (fur, velvet)*
c   form disregarded
cF form secondary
C' *Black, White, or Gray Used as Color*
FC' fusion of F and C'
C'F form secondary
C' form disregarded
FC *Fusion of Form and Bright Color,*
Both Determinants Indispensable
F/C combination of F and C where form is definite and the color arbitrary (a colored chandelier)
Bright Color Determines Response,
Form Secondary
CF combination of C and F where the color is arbitrary and the form indefinite (anatomical chart, political map)
C/F combination of C and F where the color is arbitrary and the form indefinite (anatomical chart, political map)
Color Only Determinant
C   concrete association to bright color, form and context disregarded (blue sky or water, red fire or blood)
Cdes color description
Cn color naming
Csym color symbolism—abstract association to the bright color (Spring, Fall, Gayety)

DISTRIBUTION OF DETERMINANTS

(To be filled in by Examiner)

Number of Responses

	M	FM	m	k	K	FK	F	Fc	c	C'	FC	CF	C
M and Tendency to M						Form	Chiaroscuro	Texture, White Gray and Black				Bright Color	

RELATIONSHIPS BETWEEN FACTORS

Total Responses (R) =

Total Time (T) =

Average time per response $\left(\dfrac{T}{R}\right)$ =

Average time up to 1st response to Cards I, IV, V, VI, VIIₐ

Average time up to 1st response to Cards II, III, VIII, IX, X=

$F\% \left(\dfrac{\text{Total F}}{R}\right)$ =

$A\% \left(\dfrac{A + Ad}{R}\right)$ =

$P\% \left(\dfrac{P}{R}\right)$ =

$O\% \left(\dfrac{O}{R}\right)$ =

$(H+A) : (Hd+Ad) =$

sum $C = (.5x...FC) + (1.0x...CF) + (1.5x...C) =$

$M : sum C =$

$(FM+m) : (Fc+c+C') =$

Number of responses to Cards VIII, IX, X =

$W : M =$

Succession

Manner of Approach: W   D   Dd   d   S

Indicate proportion of each category as follows:

W	D	d	Dd+S
<10% (W)	<30% (D)	<10%	<10% Dd+S
10-20 (W)	30-45 (D)	10-20 d	10-15 Dd+S
20-30 W	45-55 D	20-30 d	15-20 Dd+S
30-45 W	55-65 D	30-40 d	20-25 Dd+S
45-60 W	65-80 D	40-50 d	>25 Dd+S
>60 W	>80 D	>50 d	

Estimate of Intellectual Level

Very superior — Dull normal
Superior — Feebleminded
Average
High
Low

Note that this estimate is based on the following:
number and quality of W
number and quality of D
number of P (on popular level (P),
number of F more accurate than popular (F+)
number of F less accurate than popular (F−)
variety of content
succession

Succession   Rigid
Orderly
Loose
Confused

(By permission of Bruno Klopfer and the World Book Company.)

the whole card. Or, where no color has been mentioned he may be specifically asked to respond to color. Where no human figures have been seen in action, instructions may be given to try to find such figures. Sample concepts may even be given to get the subject started along fairly obvious lines.

Hutt and Shor (1946) use twenty common responses listed by Beck (1944) to suggest those not already reported by the subject. Three levels of suggestion are used. On the first level the examiner says, "Some people see _____ in this card. Can you make it out?" If the subject fails, then the examiner says, "Well, this is where they see it," indicating the area. If the subject still fails, the examiner says, "You see, here are the _____," and indicates some of the details. Hutt and Shor also tell the subject, "Divide the cards into those you like to look at, those you don't like, and those about which you don't care one way or the other." Reasons for these preferences are sought.

Group Rorschach Techniques

In order to reduce the time and labor of administering and scoring a test, several workers have developed procedures for giving modified Rorschach tests to groups. Probably the best known is that of Harrower-Erickson and Steiner (1945) who give three sets of instructions (p. 33) as follows:

INSTRUCTIONS FOR SPONTANEOUS ANSWERS

The test which you are about to take is rather an interesting one and I think you will enjoy it. All you have to do is to look at some slides which will be projected on the screen and write down what you see. Now the point about these slides is that they are nothing more or less than reproductions of ink blots. Probably all of you at one time or another have shaken your pen on a piece of paper, caused a blot of ink, and on folding the paper produced a weird splotch which may or may not have resembled something that you recognized. Now these slides are nothing more than reproductions of inkblots formed in this way. Your task is simply to write down what the splotches remind you of, resemble, or might be. You will see each of these slides or blots 3 minutes, and you may write your answers at your own time. Is that understood? It may help you later in the test if you make a point of numbering your answers to each slide as you write them down.

INSTRUCTIONS FOR THE LOCATING OF RESPONSES

Well, this is the first part of the experiment. Now we shall go on to the second. I'm sure you will have seen a lot of amusing and different things in the various ink blots, but one of the most important aspects of this test is the fact that I must know as accurately as possible just what it is you have seen and where it is you have seen it. In order that you can do this, you will find on each page a little diagram representing the slide.

At this point the slide of Card I is thrown on the screen and the examiner continues:

Now perhaps some of you saw on this particular slide a butterfly, and then perhaps you also saw the legs of some person in the center here, and perhaps a boxing glove in this little protuberance here or a dog's head here on the side. [While speaking of these objects the examiner points to the areas referred to which are encircled by a dark line on the slide.] Your next task, therefore, is to number your own answers, if you forgot to do so before, and then with your pencil to draw a line around the area where you saw that particular object and attach to that area the number of the answer you are describing. For example, let us suppose you have seen just those four things which I mentioned. You would put a number 1 by "a butterfly," draw a line all the way around the miniature ink blot and put a number 1 beside this line. If "somebody's legs" was your second answer, you would number that 2, draw a careful pencil line around the area on the diagram and attach a number 2 to it. In other words you will do for all your own answers what has been done for these hypothetical answers on the screen.

INSTRUCTIONS FOR OBTAINING ADDED INFORMATION

After the instructions concerning the recording of the location of responses have been given, the slide of Card VIII may be thrown on the screen and added information concerning the responses may be asked for. Instructions at this point are:

Before you begin to mark off your answers, there is something else you have to do for me. You have to help me reconstruct as accurately as possible the kind of experiences you have been having or some of the characteristics of the things you saw. You might, for instance, have seen two bears or two animals here on the side. You might have seen two flags here in the center, or you might have called these same parts two cushions. This part here (pink and orange) might have reminded you of some kind of flower.

Some of you may have said, for example, that the bears looked as if they were climbing up, but it is also very possible that you did not put in that last bit of information. Now is your chance to do so if you want to. If you want to explain to me that the animals you saw looked as if they were stepping from one rock to another, you may add that information now. But perhaps you did *not* see them as if they were stepping. Fine! That is just as important. Perhaps they looked to you as if they were some kind of animal on a heraldic design and you may have already said so. In that case you will not need to give any more information.

Let us suppose that you not only saw cushions here but saw *blue satin* cushions. In this case you would again amplify your answer because it is important for me to know whether you got the impression of the satiny or silky feel of the cushion, and whether you were impressed by its blueness.

Again this area may have reminded you of a flower because it was the color of the sweet peas in your backyard. If it was the color that attracted your attention and made you think of those sweet peas, then add this information by writing in the word *color.*

After the instructions have been given and after any pertinent questions have been answered, the slides may be projected again in the usual order. Each is shown approximately 2 minutes.

Self-recording techniques such as this have not as yet given as significant results as the clinical testing approach, but those who have used them believe that they deserve further exploration. These directions yielded booklets which were in some cases complete protocols. However, if the results are to be complete and accurate the subject must be able and willing to cooperate fully.

In another set of directions, the subject is asked to check multiple-choice items from Harrower-Erickson and Steiner (1945, p. 253) as shown in Illus. 221.

ILLUS. 221. MULTIPLE-CHOICE RORSCHACH ITEMS

You are going to see ten ink-blot pictures one after another.

Begin by taking a good look at Ink Blot I and see if it, or any part of it, reminds you of anything or resembles something you have seen.

Then read through each of the three groups of answers for Ink Blot I (A, B, C).

Now underline the one answer in Group A, the one answer in Group B, and the one answer in Group C, which you think is the best description of that ink blot or any of its parts. You, therefore, underline three answers for Ink Blot I.

When you have done this, if you wish, you may put a check beside any other answer in any of the three groups which you also feel is a good description of the ink blot or any of its parts.

Then do exactly the same thing for each of the other ink blots.

INK BLOT I

A	B	C
An army or navy emblem	A headless figure	A Halloween mask
Crumbling cliffs	Vertebra	Storm clouds
A bat	Tiny boxing gloves	A moth
Nothing at all	Spilt ink	Two people
Two people	Someone's insides	A bell in the center
A pelvis	Nothing at all	An X ray picture of the spine
An X ray picture	A butterfly flying	Animal heads on the sides
Pincers of a crab	Lava	The stomach
A dirty mess	A coat of arms	Nothing at all
Part of my body	An X ray picture of the chest	Eyes glaring at me

(By permission of Mary R. Harrower-Erickson and the Charles C. Thomas Co.)

In the simplest scoring procedure the total number and per cent of poor first choices are found. In a comparison of 329 normal adults,

225 prisoners, 53 students referred to a psychiatrist, and 143 mental-hospital patients, it was found that only 3 per cent of normal adults had 40 per cent or more poor answers, while 15 per cent of prisoners, 30 per cent of students referred to a psychiatrist, and about 65 per cent of mental-hospital patients had 40 per cent or more poor answers.

In a more detailed scoring procedure the first and the second choices are both considered and the significance of each scoring category is weighed. The Multiple-Choice Rorschach is still being developed. The selection of items and their significance for various behavior patterns will be studied a great deal in the next few years. If the instructions are varied by asking the subject to list in order of preference *all* the answers which he finds acceptable, then a profile and detailed interpretation can be made, using the symbols for interpreting individual Rorschach tests which are discussed below.

SCORING

There are two procedures for scoring: first, an analysis of quality or pattern of responses; and second, a standardized rating of quality and amount of responses, using codes. Not all responses are scored. Some are merely repetitions, with slight changes, of responses already given. Others are extraneous material in the way of elaborations, accessories or exclamations, which influence the scoring of other responses. However, these accessories or afterthoughts are noted as additional to the main concepts. The differences between main and additional scores are believed to be of considerable significance in many situations. The main scores may indicate ready-to-function elements of the personality while the additional scores may indicate potentialities. The determination of which responses are scorable requires considerable experience.

About ninety Rorschach codes are defined and indicated by a letter symbol followed sometimes by plus or minus. Letter combinations are often used with the first letter indicating dominant responses and the second subsidiary responses. The codes from Klopfer and Kelly (Illus. 220) are fairly well established. Three general categories are recognized in scoring, namely, location, determinants, and content.

Location

The letter symbols used in this category indicate the location of the parts of the card that are reacted to or ignored. Location symbols yield scores which indicate degree and order of organizing processes.

These processes are believed to be related to intellectual and reasoning abilities, but are also molded by emotional adjustment patterns.

Determinants

The dominant percepts which guide the subject's interpretation are called *determinants,* which are thought to indicate strength of impulses and degree of control.

Content

Specific objects, when related to the subject, seem to provide indications of the nature of a conflict and various mechanisms used to resolve conflicts. The scoring symbols are numerous. In Klopfer's procedure the proportions of popular responses (P) are scored by using frequency tables.

Indices

A large number of ratios or indices are now used to indicate balance and emphases (Illus. 220). They must be learned from the texts on this subject, but three of them—approach, sequence, and experience balance—are given as illustrations:

An *approach index* is concerned with location or organizing ability. It shows to what extent an individual distributes his attention between W, D, and Dd. Rorschach found averages of 7 W, 20 D, and 3 Dd among normal individuals who gave thirty responses. According to Beck (1944) the expectancy based on normal adults has the following percentages: W, 24 per cent; D, 66 per cent; and Dd, 10 per cent. Klopfer believed that an individual has not over- or under-emphasized any location if he shows from 20 to 30 per cent W, from 45 to 55 per cent D, from 5 to 15 per cent d, and up to 10 per cent Dd and S. Marked variations from this distribution, together with other findings, are often found to have clinical significance.

In addition to approach, an *index of sequence* is sometimes used. This refers to the order in which the location categories are used on each card. If a subject gives only one response to a card, there can be no indication of sequence. However, if on the first card his responses are W, D, d, Dd, S, and if he follows this same order on all the other cards, it would be noted that he has a rigid sequence pattern. Other sequence patterns are designated as orderly, loose, or confused.

The *experience balance index* was described by Rorschach, who followed Jung's extroversion—introversion hypothesis but developed somewhat more dynamic concepts. The introverted person is more original and productive in mental life, more stabilized and organized inwardly, more intensive in his relation to others, and more clumsy or awkward. Such persons usually give few or no movement or color responses, or their movement responses are considerably more numerous than their color responses. The extroverted persons are more stereotyped mentally, more in touch with reality, more excitable and unstable emotionally, and more dextrous. Such persons usually give considerably more color than movement responses.

A General Rorschach Score

A number of persons have combined Rorschach signs into general indices of integration of adjustment. One by Munroe (1945) is discussed on page 687. Another is the systematic work of Drs. Charlotte Buhler, Karl Buhler, and D. W. Lefever (1948). Using individual examinations and the Klopfer-Kelly Scoring System, they compared statistically each of ninety-nine diagnostic signs among five groups: 30 well-adjusted normals; 70 psychoneurotics; 39 hysterics; 13 anxiety neurotics; 11 mixed psychoneurotics; 7 obsessive-compulsive and 8 depressed cases; 50 psychopaths; 30 organic cases; and 27 schizophrenic cases. From these comparisons a single summarizing score was developed (Illus. 222). Later the research included 518 cases and 16 clinical groups.

The results for these groups were often different. Weights of from —5 to +5 were assigned to each Rorschach sign in accordance with the differences in the per cents of persons in two of the groups who showed the sign. For instance, 93 per cent of normals and 46 per cent of psychoneurotics gave sign 94: *Three or more M's and Sum C equal to 3 or more.* This sign was then given a weight of +2 in accordance with a table of weights of degrees of significance. Since each group was compared with the other four groups, ten comparisons were made and ten sets of weights computed. The ten sets of weights gave similar results, but the weights from the comparison of normals versus schizophrenic patients produced the greatest ratio for the variance between groups to the variance within groups. These weights were, after some slight modifications to give more significance to rare but important signs, called basic Rorschach weights.

To secure a score, an individual record is analyzed and recorded on a score sheet which shows the positive or negative weight for each item. The algebraic sum of the weights is the basic Rorschach score. The means and standard deviations for clinical groups given in Illus. 223 shows a fairly constant trend on a scale from normal to badly disintegrated. The ranges of scores are larger for minus than for plus groups, but this may be due to sampling and to the fact that the scale contains more negative than positive items. Even for these

ILLUS. 222. MEAN PROFILE FOR VARIOUS GROUPS

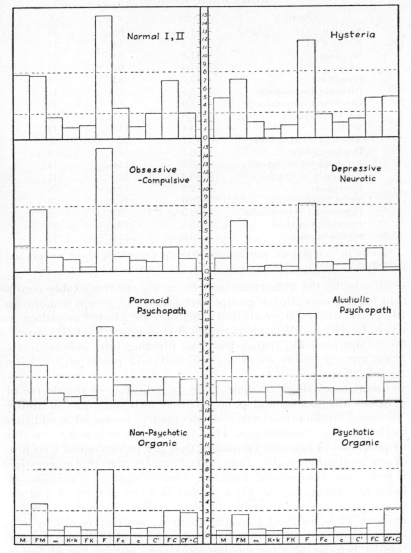

(Buhler, Buhler, and Lefever, 1948, pp. 20, 21. By permission of the authors and publishers.)

ILLUS. 223. NORMS FOR CLINICAL GROUPS ON BASIC
RORSCHACH SCORES *

Group	Mean	σ	N
Normals I, II	21.4	6	30
Normals III	14.4	4.6	16
Neuroses	11.8	8.8	53
Anxiety	11.6	6.5	13
Hysterias	10.7	8.2	45
Paranoid Psychopaths	5.5	7.4	15
Obsessive-Compulsive	4.0	7.9	10
Sex Psychopaths	—2.0	15.0	22
Maniacs	—3.8	11.9	18
Alcoholic Psychopaths	—5.7	12.4	30
Depressed Cases	—6.3	8.5	8
Paranoid Schizophrenics	—8.5	11.5	14
Nonpsychotic Organics	—10.3	13.7	17
Epileptics	—12.4	12.8	26
Social Psychopaths	—13.0	11.7	20
Introverted Melancholia	—13.2	9.2	9
Psychotic Organics	—16.5	12.4	26
Schizophrenics	—19.2	11.9	35

* (From Buhler, Buhler, and Lefever, 1948. By permission of the authors and publishers.)

small samples the differences between means are remarkably significant for different clinical groups. Overlapping of groups is shown in Illus. 224, where larger clinical categories are plotted according to levels. Level I is called adequacy; level II, conflict; level III, impairment; and level IV, reality loss. The dividing lines between these levels are tentatively set at +15, 0, and —15 points on the basic Rorschach score.

The authors think of these scores as indicators of the degree of personal integration, and point out that such indicators of ability "to master conflict situations and meet reality" are useful in addition to the clinical classifications. They believe that such scores are aids to prognosis. They also emphasize that the psychological structure of one level differs widely from that of another, and that integration is *not* a one-dimensional function. Two prominent dimensions or fields of conflict appear: (1) a conflict between immediate and deferred goals, and (2) a conflict between reality awareness and imagination. Thus, in level I tendencies to act are determined by adequate aspiration and awareness of reality. In level II there is a severe conflict because of unreasonable aspiration, but no loss of reality awareness. In level III there is little control of impulses and considerable loss of reality awareness; and in level IV there may again be control of impulsive activity, but contact with reality is almost entirely lost.

ILLUS. 224. DISTRIBUTIONS OF GENERAL RORSCHACH SCORES FOR VARIOUS GROUPS

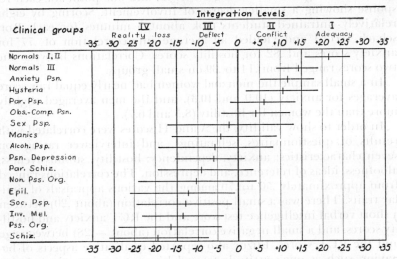

(Buhler, Buhler, and Lefever, 1948, p. 14. By permission of the authors and publishers.)

Additional monographs are proposed which will define these and other dimensions of personality, and explore the differences between clinical groups more thoroughly.

Anxiety and Hostility Scores

Elizur (1949) reported a method of analyzing and scoring Rorschach protocols so as to yield two indices—one for anxiety, another for hostility. He used only the content of responses and called the results a Rorschach Content Test (RCT) score. Anxiety is shown (Elizur, 1949, p. 259) by such responses as:

A.[1] A frightening giant, a weeping child, a dangerous crevice, darkness and gloom, a girl escaping, a rabbit running away, snakes, monsters, witches, skeletons, blood, clouds, fire, smoke, twister.

a.[1] An unpleasant animal, an unbalanced figure, an impression of coldness, spiders, mosquitoes, church priest.

Hostility is judged to be shown by such responses as:

H. A type of man I hate; ugly figure, a stupid animal, an angry face, two animals fighting, a killed animal, arrow, gun.

h. Gossiping women, a primitive war mark, pliers, knife, and teeth.

[1] The capital letters indicate strong involvement and the lower-case letters, less involvement.

The scores are sums of responses allowing 2 points for each response showing clear or strong evidence, and one point for each response showing a smaller degree of involvement. Scoring by eight relatively untrained students took about 5 minutes for each Rorschach record and yielded an average intercorrelation of .77 for anxiety scores and .82 for hostility scores. Correlations between the two scores ranged from .14 to .39 on small groups.

In a small sample the men and women had nearly equal raw score averages for anxiety (10.9 and 10.3), and the men averaged slightly more than the women for hostility (8.5 and 6.7).

In order to show validity, the A and H scores were correlated with results of questionnaires, self-ratings, and interviewer ratings on seven characteristics: anxiety, dependency, hostility, submissiveness, aloofness, ideas of reference, and depression. The correlations ranged from approximately .50 to .70 among the various appraisals of similar traits. There was a small positive correlation (about .20) between a short verbal intelligence test score and the RCT anxiety and hostility scores, and a small negative correlation (about —.28) between age and the RCT scores. Elizur also reported qualitative aspects of behavior, such as one's attitude toward his own anxiety, the relative amounts of tensions as shown by the proportion of strong and weak responses, the sequence, emergence, and recovery from anxiety, and sex responses. Lastly he computed RCT scores for published Rorschach records of neurotics and normals. The neurotics averaged 16.5 (average of A and H) and the normals 8.8.

Elizur points out that the RCT scores are fairly reliable and objective, do not require familiarity with usual Rorschach procedures, and also yield quantitative and qualitative results. He also indicated the need for much more research on larger samples.

INTERPRETATION

Authorities agree that at least two years of careful study are needed to develop adequate skill in interpreting Rorschach scores. A few broad interpretations are given here to show the types of inferences that are supported by many studies.

Location scores indicate the individual's manner of approaching life situations. Rorschach described persons who gave only complex and ingenious W responses as superior in intelligence and drive. Whole responses indicate capacity for abstraction *if* there is originality and form accuracy. Many whole responses of a vague sort point to superficiality and to drive without capacity. An absence of W responses may mean lack of ability to generalize, but may also indicate that the detail approach is more typical of the subject's mode of meeting new situations. An excess of Dd, that is, tiny, or unusual details, is frequently related to anxiety, overcritical activities, and feelings of inferiority. Unusual attention to edge details may be related to need to avoid the inner aspects of self, and predominance of details inside the blot may be related to preoccupation with one's inner life. Attention to white spaces often reveals opposition either toward self or toward others. Fragmentary responses, such as where one sees only part of a butterfly when most people see the whole, are typical of the feeble-minded, the depressed, and those who have severe difficulty with perceptual synthesis.

In interpreting determinants Rorschach and nearly all of the subsequent writers in this field assume that persons have basic impulses or drives from within which are controlled consciously or unconsciously to varying degrees and by different mechanisms. Some persons exercise rigid or stifling control of these impulses; other persons let them explode. Normal persons show fairly strong impulses, which are accepted as natural and directed into harmless or useful activities. The Rorschach test attempts to indicate both the strength of the inner impulses and the degree and manner of controlling them. The normal use of controls is indicated by a good balance between normal drives as shown by M, human movement, and adjustment to the environment, as shown by F, form and content. One type of repressive control is indicated by an unusual proportion of F responses. A preoccupation with form is an indication of a rigid and unreasonable or obsessional attempt to control impulses. Any percentages of F+ above 80 are usually found to indicate pathological conditions among adults. Unusually good form responses to complicated patterns indicate high intellectual efficiency. Poor form accuracy is typical of organic pathology, feeble-mindedness and schizophrenia, and other conditions where details are synthesized into concepts with great difficulty.

Usual movement responses indicate a fairly normal attitude toward instinctive drives, acceptance of them as something positive and constructive rather than as uncontrollable forces which constantly interfere with one's success. Many more than average movement responses are associated with inventiveness or fantasies and rare or no movement responses with depression and conflict or feeble-mindedness, or with young children.

Color responses indicate emotional involvement or intensity of emotional relationships to objects and people. Some neurotic subjects respond to color either with exhilaration or with shock. The normal response for many cards is FC, that is, form with a supporting color determinant. CF, that is, color with a supporting form determinant, indicates excitability, and sometimes suggestibility, or infantile emotional control. An unusual number of color responses is often associated with egocentricity and intense impulsiveness. A dominant or excessive color reaction is usually indicative of marked inability to control inner impulses, and a tendency to substitute imaginary situations for real situations.

Responses to shading (K) imply indefiniteness or attention to small differences in lighting, which is often associated with anxiety, repression, and caution, sometimes vague and sometimes specific. Texture and touch-feeling reactions are indicative of sensitivity both in intellectual and in emotional fields. A normal number of texture responses are essential for well-balanced behavior.

The interpretation of specific-association content must take into account the background of the examinee. Thus, an unusually large number of references to human anatomy might be normal for a surgeon, but it might be indicative of a morbid tendency in a baker or a stenographer. Frequently repeated responses may indicate stereotypy, as in feeble-mindedness, or a special interest, or a recurring fear. The number of uncommon responses is indicative of either originality or of unusual usage of usual words. Breadth of interests is roughly indicated by the number of different fields represented in the reports.

A good many authors have now published profiles of Rorschach scores, of which those shown in Illus. 220 and 224 are typical. Both of these use Klopfer's system of scoring. It appears that the normal group averages more total responses than any of the others and establishes a set of ratios which are important indicators of balanced modes of behavior. Thus the average M, FM, and FC responses are all about the same (nearly 8) while the F are almost twice as great (15). Then there are important symbols of sensitivity and caution—K, Fc, C′, CF, and C—with between 3 and 4 responses each. For the hysterical group the FM is about the same as for the normal—the M, FC, and F are considerably reduced, while the CF and C are increased significantly. For the obsessive-compulsive group the FM and F remain about normal, but the M and FC are much reduced. For the depressive-neurotic group the FM remains nearly normal, but all the rest are only about one half normal expectancy. For the paranoid psychopath marked reductions occur in about the same proportion in all factors. For the alcoholic psychopath there is a relatively greater reduction in the M and FC factors than in the rest. For two groups with organic (brain) injuries, the profiles show great reduction of all types of responses, but the greatest in M. The FC is a particularly difficult response for the psychotic-organic group.

This rough inspection of profiles shows that a great deal may be learned by close attention to small differences, once these differences are determined to be significant. At present the individual variations from such profiles are sometimes large and always important, so that *no* individual diagnosis is justified on the basis of profiles alone.

All Rorschach workers emphasize the great importance of interpreting the responses of a person in terms of his whole personality picture. No rigid interpretation of one determinant is possible; each determinant must be accurately appraised and related to all the rest. Complete records of persons who are fairly typical of classes of behavior, such as healthy adults, the feeble-minded, the depressed, hypomanics, schizophrenics, neurotics, adults with conduct disorders, problem children, and mental hygiene cases are now available from many sources.

RELIABILITY

Reliability has been indicated by three main approaches. In one the variations among examiners in procuring and scoring protocols is noted. In another the results from repeated applications of a test to the same individuals are shown. In still another the ability of examiners to agree upon interpretations is indicated.

Cerf (1946) reported significant differences among nine examiners in the number of responses obtained from Air Corps cadets. The highest averaged 24.3 responses and the lowest 14.6, median 20.5. These differences are far too large to be explained by chance and probably indicate differences in the attitude, training, or skill of the examiners.

The scoring of a Rorschach protocol is still far from simple. It depends partly on the examiner's own knowledge and bias, and partly on the completeness of the protocol. Among experienced examiners trained in the same method, the correspondence in scoring usually is high and the differences are thought to be insignificant. The use of scoring charts and more detailed definitions will doubtless raise these reliabilities.

The test-retest reliability is fairly high for signs which have the higher frequencies, but for rare signs the consistency between trials is, of course, lower. The Basic Rorschach Score, which is made up of about one hundred signs or indices, has a high split-half reliability and will doubtless show satisfactory retest reliabilities, although none have come to hand as yet. Ford (1946), using 123 young children, found test-retest correlations of from .38 to .86 for various patterns. Fosberg (1943) reported that attempts to fake results by test-wise subjects were not successful in altering any fundamental patterns and that attempts to misrepresent oneself were not successful among naive subjects. There is considerable need for more research along these lines, and also need to determine the effects of the subject's mood at the time he takes the test. Kimble (1945) found that subjects tended to be more extroverted when examined in public.

The ability of examiners to agree upon interpretations was investigated by Munroe (1945), who compared eleven examiners. They used the "inspection technique" to classify independently eleven women college students' records. These records had been procured by the group-administration method when the students were asked to write their impressions in booklets. The examiners simply ranked them in four groups in order of degree of disturbance. Under these rather adverse conditions about 43 per cent of the judgments agreed perfectly, 30 per cent differed by one rank, 12 per cent by two ranks, and 15 per cent by more than two ranks. With this amount of agreement from such data it can be seen that if the first four steps of the Munroe scale (Illus. 225) were used with more adequate instruction, the agreement between judges should regularly be more than 90 per cent.

USEFULNESS

The evidences of validity are to be found in comparisons of Rorschach results with other criteria of adjustment, such as degree of school and occupational success, delinquency, and psychoneurotic manifestations. In all of these fields the evidence still leaves much to be desired, but available reports are significant enough to make Rorschach results of considerable use. A few reports will be discussed.

School Groups

Davidson (1943) found that children, nine through twelve years of age, with high intelligence ratings showed a wide variety of personality patterns. They tended to be well balanced but more often in an introverted than in an extroverted way. There seemed to be no relationship between socio-economic status and Rorschach patterns, but degrees of good adjustment were reflected reliably by a group of signs.

Hertzman and Margulies (1943) found significant differences between junior high school boys and college men in line with usual developmental changes toward more control of impulses.

ILLUS. 225. MUNROE'S RORSCHACH GROUPS

A. Unusually sound integration of the personality. Emotional problems either very mild or very well handled:

Case 1. A girl with fair intelligence, conventional, practical, a little too conscientious, with some restraint of imagination and spontaneity. Emotional responsiveness is basically sound and of adequate range. (Rorschach items which deviated somewhat from the normal range: low W; many good D; form accuracy good; 3M, 1 popular, 2 with constrained action; 3 common FM; 5 FC and 2 vague CF; succession rather rigid.)

B. Emotional problems observable, too slight to affect behavior markedly or cause serious inner discomfort.

Case 4. Immature, expansive girl. Unsystematic, rather careless, probably socially oriented and not much interested in studies. Moderate intelligence. Warm, lively, but rather superficial. (Rorschach items: 1 popular M; 3 lively FM; 3 FC and 14 CF; succession loose; Hd and Ad overemphasized; but a fair number of H and A are given; 50 per cent W, popular or rather vague; form accuracy adequate but inexact.)

C. Emotional difficulties rather marked, very likely to affect attitudes, interests and performances, but not to an extreme degree.

Case 6. A girl whose adequate intelligence is poorly used because of great timidity and self-doubt. Passive, submissive attitudes. Tries hard but is vulnerable to criticism and easily discouraged. Strong hostility which is largely unconscious and a source of anxiety, preventing free mobilization of energies, but not serious enough to cause overt symptoms. (Rorschach items: predominantly flexor or passive movement with occasional vigorous responses of disguised hostile content followed by evasive F or K; mild color shock, CF, FC, usually vague or pretty but "fire" in II; overemphasis on W, often insubstantial; several S; form accuracy not bad but often vague or restricted; F per cent moderately high.)

D. Serious difficulty in meeting reality demands adequately, or marked inner distress or both.

Case 7. Very intelligent, creative girl with serious emotional problems which must markedly affect her work and relations with people. Extremely self-absorbed. Thinking original, lively, resourceful, but too often inaccurate or at least highly selective in choice of facts because of a tendency to project her own ideas or emotions into the data. Erratic in work habits; resistant to authority; brusque or aloof in social relations. (Rorschach items; almost every response contains some sort of movement, many originals, some verging on the bizarre with clear symbolic connotations; lack of Fc or FK; definite color shock; few color responses; explosive CF.

E. Severe psychopathology. Not discussed in Munroe's report.

(By permission of Ruth Munroe and the editors of *Applied Psychology Monographs*.)

Munroe (1945), working with college-freshman women, secured a Rorschach Adjustment Rating by inspecting about twenty-five signs indicating unbalance or mental difficulties and grouping the results qualitatively into five ratings. Samples of the first four ratings are shown in Illus. 225. She found that 74 per cent of the academic grade averages at the end of the freshman year were well predicted by these adjustment ratings, and that students who failed or had difficulty because of emotional conflicts were detected almost 100 per cent. The adjustment ratings did not predict very closely the academic success of the highest third of the group, but these were well predicted, as might be expected, by the ACE Psychological Examination. It was shown that poorly adjusted girls who achieved better than average grades all stood well above average in the ACE Psychological Examination. With few exceptions the well-adjusted girls who did poorly academically stood in the lowest test quarter of the ACE Psychological Examination. Thus the adjustment ratings and the test scores supplemented each other and together gave accurate predictions of success.

Occupational Groups

Piotrowski and others (1944) compared outstanding young male mechanical workers with average workers and found significant differences in several Rorschach signs. Kurtz (1948) reported a carefully controlled application of the Rorschach test to life-insurance sales managers. Two competent Rorschach experts used the results of individual tests of forty-two satisfactory and thirty-eight unsatisfactory sales managers to develop a scoring system. About thirty-two signs or combinations of signs occurred more frequently in one group than in the other. Seventy-nine of the eighty managers were correctly classified by this system. Later, when the same process was tried on another sample of managers, twenty good and twenty-one poor, the Rorschach results gave only a chance indication of success. At the same time a short Experience Record Form which has been frequently used in this field, correlated with success .48.

Kurtz also quotes from six other studies using group Rorschach results with adults in the military forces or in civilian occupations. All of these studies show that success in one or a number of occupations was not significantly predicted by the test scores used.

Cerf (1946) reported the application of both individual and group Rorschach tests to candidates for pilot training. Predictions of success or failure to complete the course were not usually significant either from single signs or from various combinations based on examiners' judgments of what might be most significant. The highest biserial corrected correlation was .26 among 281 pilots, 92 per cent of whom graduated. For such a highly selected group this is fairly significant.

In spite of these usually meager results, the value of the Rorschach is being actively explored in industry, and it is highly probable that many important uses will be found.

Clinical Groups

Most of the technical Rorschach reports deal with maladjusted persons. The important uses which have been demonstrated include:

a. *Diagnosis:*

To determine the degree of impairment of mental ability

To indicate the depth of illness or psychotic malignancy

To aid in differential diagnosis

To detect organic cerebral damage

To show by retest a tendency toward improvement

b. *Treatment:*

To aid in determining the best course of treatment, and the probable success of treatment

As a therapeutic agent, since the test may give the patient some emotional release

c. *Evaluation:*

To aid in evaluating therapeutic programs

SUMMARY

From the foregoing it seems clear that the Rorschach is not a technique to yield a clear and adequate measure of specific knowledge, skills, interests, or attitudes. It does not give a sharp profile of types of impulses. However, it is probably the best single test to show the ways one perceives and imagines in accordance with his experiences and personality. It is a sensitive and complex technique, so that unusual training is essential for its administration and interpretation. It has already yielded valuable practical assistance to clinical practice, but its full contribution in analyzing personality is yet to be made. The close association of many Rorschach workers with Kraepelin's clinical syndromes and with Freud's theories has resulted in diagnostic uses of the Rorschach principally along these lines. There is need for systematic analyses of the results of Rorschach examinations to detect independent aspects of behavior and to determine the usual relationships of functional patterns. Such analyses may well result in more original contributions concerning the nature of personality.

STUDY GUIDE QUESTIONS

1. What basic assumptions are made in administering and interpreting the Rorschach Test?

2. What types of information are usually secured in the three periods of administration?

3. What aspects of behavior are related to location, determinants, and content?

4. Why are indices or ratios often more significant than raw scores?

5. How was the Basic Rorschach scoring system developed?

6. To what extent does the Basic Rorschach Score distinguish clinical groups?

7. What interpretation of the Basic Rorschach Score do the authors give?

8. What limitations are given to Rorschach results by group administration? By multiple-choice questions?

9. What results did Munroe find in predicting success in college from Rorschach scores?

10. What evidences of reliability are there for various types of Rorschach administration and interpretation?

11. How can the validity of Rorschach results be evaluated?

CHAPTER XXIV

OBSERVATIONS OF BEHAVIOR

~~~~~~

The last two chapters have described ways of evaluating personality patterns by means of inventories and other test situations most of which appraise a restricted sample of behavior. In this chapter various methods of rating or analyzing behavior from direct observation and the application of these methods to various situations are discussed.

METHODS OF OBSERVATION

There appears to be only one basic method of observation, namely, to have one or more observers pay close attention to a situation and to record, as soon as possible, what they think happened. In a laboratory this method is supplemented by objective records made by apparatus. There are many varieties of observation of which time sampling, record analysis, and sociometry are the most frequently used.

Time Sampling

Time-sampling methods have been found to be particularly well adapted to the study of modes of adjustment. A large number of studies in this field are reviewed periodically in the Review of Educational Research.

A good illustration is the work of Goodenough (1930), who reported twenty-five 1-minute observations on thirty-three nursery school children. The scores for each child were the sums of the amounts of time spent in each activity. The odd-even reliability of observed time in laughter, sociability, leadership, and physical activity was approximately .80. Reliabilities of observed time in compliance and talkativeness were approximately .50 and .60. The correlations between sociability, leadership, and talkativeness were generally above .60. Leadership also showed small positive relationships with height, weight, chronological age, and mental age, but zero relationships with sex, physiological tests, and size or status of family.

Another good example of the time-sampling method of observation is reported by Anderson, Brewer, and Reed (1946), who studied the behavior of children and teachers in the first, second, and third grades. They devised a check sheet to be used in 5-minute observations of a single child. The sheet contained fifty-one code numbers, each of which referred to a carefully defined situation. For instance (p. 23):

DC   *domination by the teacher* with evidence of conflict. The child has given some expression of his goals or desires and the teacher behaves in a manner to stop that behavior between them . . . eight types are differentiated.

DC 1 *determines a detail* of activity in conflict.

DC 3 *relocates* child because of some disturbance.

DC 4 *direct refusal or contradiction; evasion* of child's protest or complaint; postponement without expressed reason or consideration.

DC 5 *disapproval, blame,* or *shame* directed toward child as a person. Includes rejective behavior.

DC 6 *warnings, threats, reminders, conditional promises, obstruction,* or *interruption.*

DC 7 *calls to attention,* because of slow, indifferent or negativistic behavior.

DC 11 *punishment,* sending out of room, attack, or depriving child of material or activity.[1]

In similar fashion, DN, domination with no evidence of conflict; DT, domination in working together; IN, integration with no evidence of working together; and IT, integration with evidence of working together are defined along with a large number of other situations such as the child's activity in problem solving, in social contacts, and in conforming to the teacher's demands.

By taking twenty-four observational records of each child for 5-minute periods over various parts of several days, it was possible to record a large number of episodes and to establish high reliabilities for teacher behavior, group behavior, and individual pupil behavior.

[1] *Applied Psychology Monographs,* No. 11, 1946, p. 23.

It was found that the teacher who used more integrative direction had children with much more spontaneous initiative and social contributions to others, and with much less whispering, playing, and nonconforming than the teacher who used more dominating direction.

Record Analysis

The facts recorded in a carefully prepared biography are seldom as accurate as the direct observations which are made in time sampling, but the analysis used in biographical studies and case studies may include a systematic personality study. A good illustration is the report of Friend and Haggard (1948) who carefully analyzed extensive counseling and follow-up records of eighty men who sought vocational counseling from the Family Society of Greater Boston. Each worker's record was studied intensively and rated on the basis of the judgments of at least two carefully chosen and well-trained raters. The difficulties of making unambiguous ratings were studied and numerous revisions of items were made which increased the probability of securing only one meaning for each item. Each worker was rated on a schedule of 173 items distributed among seven general sections.

		Number of Items
I.	Early life	29
II.	Mature or current family life	16
III.	Early or beginning jobs	7
IV.	Response to counseling	20
V.	Personality patterns and general work reactions	40
VI.	Reactions to specific work conditions	34
VII.	General work capacities, adjustment, and improvement	27
	Total	173

Sections V and VI, items which are related to work interest, are reproduced in Illus. 226.

Correlational and other analyses led to important conclusions such as:

a. People who deviate in mental health tended to recreate their early family patterns in their own current families, and to have ambivalent or fluctuating feelings in many fields.

b. Moderate rivalry with brothers or sisters paralleled a favorable attitude toward usual job competition, whereas intense rivalry was linked with a shunning of competition. The boss was often identified with the qualities of a parent.

ILLUS. 226. RATING SCHEDULE FOR REACTIONS TO WORK

V. PERSONALITY PATTERNS AND GENERAL WORK REACTIONS

73. Strength of goal orientation and ability to make realistic, long-range plans: * (1) practically none; (2) some; (3) considerable

74. Amount of interest in learning: (1) practically none; (2) some; (3) considerable

75. Amount of interest or energy devoted to leisure-time activities: (1) practically none; (2) some; (3) considerable

76. Amount of thought about jobs: (1) practically none; (2) some; (3) considerable

77. Rigidity, or unwillingness to change set ideas: (1) strong; (2) some; (3) practically none

78. Balance between give and take: (1) poor; (2) some; (3) good

79. Amount of self-disparagement directly expressed: (1) considerable; (2) some; (3) practically none

80. Amount of self-disparagement more unconsciously or indirectly expressed: (1) strong; (2) some; (3) practically none

81. Fear of failure directly expressed: (1) strong; (2) some; (3) practically none

82. Fear of failure indirectly or unconsciously displayed: (1) considerable; (2) some; (3) practically none

83. Willingness to risk disappointment or turndown: (1) practically none; (2) some; (3) considerable

84. Amount of tolerance for frustration: (1) practically none; (2) some; (3) considerable

85. Types of reaction to difficulty: (1) blames self; (2) frenzied or disorganized activity; (3) blames particular persons or groups; (4) devil-may-care attitude

86. Further type of reaction to difficulty: (1) blames general conditions or bad luck; (2) gets sick; (3) wants to get even, as by "chiseling"; (4) runs away or drinks

87. Further type of reaction to difficulty: (1) hopeless, "limp" attitude; (2) feels "kicked around"; (3) continuing on in same direction; (4) renewed striving in new direction

88. Counteraction or the ability to persistently fight or struggle—an additional reaction to difficulty: (1) practically none; (2) some; (3) considerable

89. Insistence on getting along solely by his own efforts and making his own decisions: (1) considerable; (2) some; (3) practically none

90. Reliance on "pull" or favoritism in job-getting: (1) considerable; (2) some; (3) practically none

91. Reliance on counseling, courses, etc., as magical means for job-getting or getting ahead: (1) considerable; (2) some; (3) practically none

92. Reaction to work where "fitting" with the boss is chief means of getting ahead: (1) very unfavorable; (2) unfavorable; (3) indifferent; (3?) † ambivalent; (4) favorable; (5) very favorable

93. Reaction to work where hard work or industry are the chief means of getting ahead: (for scoring, see item 92)

* A realistically oriented positive stick-to-itiveness in the sense that the goal was within the occupational level on which the client could operate.

A compulsive quality is suggested in the use of the word *rigidity*.

† On the IBM cards, the scale 1, 2, 3, 3?, 4, 5, was represented respectively, by punches of 1 and 4; 1; 2; 2 and 4; 3; 3 and 4, because we had only four numbers to punch and needed six categories.

ILLUS. 226. RATING SCHEDULE FOR REACTIONS TO WORK (*Cont'd*)

94. Reaction to work where brains, skill, or long-time training are the chief means of getting ahead: (for scoring, see item 92)
95. Reaction to work where aggressiveness or initiative are the chief means of getting ahead: (for scoring, see item 92)
96. Reaction to work where loyalty to the company is the chief means of getting ahead: (for scoring, see item 92)
97. Reversal or tendency to follow patterns in work opposite to early family situation: (1) considerable; (2) some; (3) practically none
98. Repetition or compulsive tendency to re-enact in work earlier family situations: (1) considerable; (2) some; (3) practically none
99. Job-change rating: changed to job requiring less skill; (1) approximately same amount of skill; (2) somewhat more skill; (3) a great deal more skill
100. Changed categories of work: (1) considerable; (2) somewhat; (3) practically none
101. Degrees of skill involved in chief occupation: (1) practically none; (2) some; (3) considerable
102. Tendency of client to spoil own job chances: (1) strong or repeated; (2) some; (3) practically none
103. Ambivalence about jobs or vocations or earning a living: (1) considerable; (2) some; (3) practically none
104. Mental health or emotional stability: (1) psychotic; (2) neurotic; (3) some neurotic tendencies or symptoms; (4) normal ‡
105. Physical-mental (emotional) rating of change: (no score indicates worse); (1) the same; (2) somewhat better; (3) much better
106. Generalized or free-floating fear: (1) considerable; (2) some; (3) practically none
107. Physical health: (1) poor or handicapped; (2) fair; (3) good
108. Accident-proneness: (1) considerable; (2) some; (3) practically none
109. Amount of delinquency: (1) considerable; (2) some; (3) practically none
110. Over-all relation of job difficulties to personal difficulties: (1) very close relation; (2) some; (3) practically none
111. Impact of depression: too young; (1) continued unemployment; (2) employed off and on; (3) poorly paid work; (4) impact not severe
112. Relief history: (1) considerable; (2) some; (3) practically none

VI. REACTIONS TO SPECIFIC WORK CONDITIONS

Ratings for this section: (____) no information; (1) very unfavorable; (2) unfavorable; (3) indifferent; (3?) ambivalent; (4) favorable; (5) very favorable

113. Reaction to work involving sharp competition
114. Reaction to work involving little or no competition
115. Reaction to usual competition
116. Reaction to work where there are good possibilities of advancement
117. Reaction to work where client can receive a good deal of special recognition on the job, when his work objectively merits some
118. Reaction to familiar work and/or familiar surroundings
119. Reaction to opportunities to gain new experience
120. Reaction to work where he is "left alone," not closely supervised

‡ For purposes of correlation, this item was arranged in a continuum as follows: deviation in mental health— (1) considerable, (2) some, (3) practically none.

ILLUS. 226. RATING SCHEDULE FOR REACTIONS TO WORK (Cont'd)

121. Reaction to work where good pay is the major reward
122. Reaction to work where he is sure of future security
123. Reaction to work where he can be his "own boss"
124. Reaction to work where the boss takes a special friendly interest
125. Reaction to work where the boss is domineering
126. Reaction to work where there is an atmosphere of favoritism
127. Reaction to work where there is an objective atmosphere
128. Reaction to work where the company treats him as an individual, not a number
129. Reaction to presence of congenial fellow-workers
130. Reaction to work which does not involve contact with others
131. Reaction to work which involves contact with strangers
132. Reaction to responsibility for the performance of his work
133. Reaction to responsibility for supervising or leading others
134. Reaction to work which involves the acquisition and use of considerable skill
135. Reaction to work of a virile sort
136. Reaction to work commanding relatively high social prestige
137. Reaction to presence of good physical working conditions
138. Reaction to work geared to his abilities
139. Reaction to work which appears to him as constructive or useful
140. Reaction to unions
141. Reaction to civil service jobs
142. Reaction to having a sense of group "belongingness" on the job
143. Reaction to feeling that perhaps through a union he has a certain grasp (at least understanding, if not control) over the forces which affect him in the job situation
144. Reaction to the necessity for a strenuous or exciting exertion
145. Reaction to possibility of accidents
146. Reaction to work where he can move around and be outside

(Adapted from Friend and Haggard, 1948, p. 24. By permission of the authors and the editor of *Applied Psychology Monographs*.)

c. Strong interest in learning went with actually taking courses of specialized training.

d. Family disruption, through death, separation, or placement in foster homes, was linked with sensitivity to turndowns or to rejection, but not to good work adjustment.

e. Tendency to sabotage himself by spoiling his job chances was a device by which an individual avoided possible job failure, or settled a grudge against a parent, or showed self-hatred. It was closely related to several items, such as rejection by an antagonism toward father or family, rigidity and unrealistic thinking about jobs, and reliance on pull.

About twenty other findings were reported which were summarized under two general topics:

1. A feeling of good *interrelatedness with others* and a history of

strongly knit family life were found among those who make good work adjustments, and vice versa.

2. Strong job satisfactions were often those which compensated for early deprivations. Among well-adjusted workers these drives led to accomplishment, but at the other extreme early deprivations were used as excuses for failure to make reasonable efforts.

The significance of such findings needs a good deal of study. It also points to the need for more systematic evaluations by interview or inventory of the satisfactions of deprivations of early and later home and school life.

Sociometry

Sociometry is a name given to a procedure for sampling the attitudes or behavior of members of a group toward each other. This procedure usually consists of short questionnaires or interviews. For small children the questions include such as these: "Who would you like to play with? Who do you like to work with? Who do you like to have sit near you?" Among adults the questions might deal with activities in business, recreation, civic enterprises, or the home. The results are then put in graph form to show the relative acceptance of members of the group, or degree of activity in various social or economic contacts for various members of the group. A good sociometric chart can be the basis of careful planning for a balance of activities within a group.

Since no standardized procedures or accepted norms have yet come to hand, no attempt is made here to give specific illustrations or to review the voluminous literature on this topic. But the sociometric approach is an important one, because it deals with interpersonal relations in a more direct and comprehensive manner than most of the other methods. *Sociometry,* a monthly magazine, and a series of monographs is now published under the editorship of Jacob L. Moreno, who has long been the advocate of this technique in this country.

USUAL SITUATIONS

Usual situations are those in which there is little attempt to control the environment for the purposes of making an observation. Such situations are thought to be the most valid indicators of a person's real adjustment because he is presumably not trying to influence an observer, but is acting naturally. Situations where conduct is directly measured will be discussed first, then observations of conduct, and lastly interview situations.

Conduct Measures

Among the most elaborate quantitative reports of adjustment behavior from the point of view of ethics are those of Hartshorne and May (1928–30), which describe a 6-year project made for the Institute of Social and Religious Research. These workers and their assistants summarized existing methods of appraising deceit, self-control, suggestibility, moral knowledge, reputation, and integration. With great ingenuity they improved old tests, devised new ones, and applied them to many different groups of school children to discover typical performances in various environments. The work of these men has inspired many others to continued research and test refinement. Although their schedules included many types of appraisal, conduct measures were prominent. Outlines of their work are given below to show the thoroughness of their investigations and to allow an evaluation of the various methods of procedure.

Conduct measures were secured by placing persons in natural situations, and then recording the number of times a pupil used unethical conduct to attain a goal. The test situations discussed immediately below were used to appraise deception.

Measures of Deception, Hartshorne and May (1928). 1) *Copying technique.* This appraisal was conducted by having the pupils sit together in pairs. Each pair was then given two forms of multiple-choice tests that looked alike. Both forms contained the same words, but the choices were arranged in different orders, so that if one pupil copied from the other this might be detected by comparing their answers. This method was found ineffective because of the difficulty of distinguishing chance from copied errors, and also because it did not furnish equal opportunities to all who might have a desire to copy.

2) *Self-scoring technique.* In order to make an appraisal of deception in self-scoring, ordinary mental or achievement tests were given, collected, and scored without marking the test sheets. They were then returned to the pupils, who were asked to score their own tests from keys which were provided. Deception can be measured by the amount of difference between scores secured in these two ways. Tests of this kind, unless they have a wide range of difficulty, tend to present different motives for cheating among those with different abilities. This method proved to be fairly effective, but rather expensive.

3) *Improbable achievement.* In this situation tests were used twice: once under supervision, in order that the pupil's actual achievement could be determined; and once without observation,

in order that he could raise his score by cheating. A wide variety of these tests were used, such as:

1. Puzzle solution in which the rules of the game may be broken
2. Weight discrimination in which seven pill boxes have the weights printed on the bottom
3. Peeking tests in which mazes or other figures are to be traced with the eyes closed, and in parlor games, such as "pinning the tail on the donkey"
4. Two equivalent forms of mental tests in which the answer sheet is furnished with only one form
5. Two vocabulary tests, one taken home
6. Athletic tests. (Self-recorded measures of strength of grip, lung capacity, chinning, and broad jump are used, one test in public, one test in private.)
7. Potato race. (Cheating is measured by the number of times a child broke the rules by picking up two potatoes.)
8. Three trial-of-speed tests, such as cancellation of A's, digit symbol substitution, and making dots in small squares.

4) *Stealing.*   This group of tests included two types of appraisal: (1) tests in which coins are used in puzzles or problems (the score indicates the number of coins not returned to the experimenter) and (2) situations in which a storekeeper returns too much change, or in which a purse with money is found.

5) *Lying.*   In order to measure lying to escape disapproval, the pupils were asked to answer questions concerning their cheating activities on the tests just described. Lying to win approval was evaluated by a questionnaire on socially approved activities (Illus. 227).

Deception was inferred by a comparison of the actual (or probable) and the self-reported achievements. If the self-report was considerably beyond the limits of probable achievement, the pupil was discredited.

Measures of Cooperation, Hartshorne and May (1929, Chap. III).
1) *Self-or-class test.*   In this situation pupils were required to choose between working for the class or for themselves. Cash prizes in spelling were announced for both class and individual honors, but a child was not allowed to participate in both contests.

2) *Allotment of prize money.*   Pupils were asked to vote whether the money should be distributed to members of the class, or given to the school or some hospital child.

3) *Sharing of equipment.*   Each pupil was given a box containing ten articles: a drinking cup, pencil sharpener, ruler, eraser, pen, penholder, double pencil, and three other pencils. He was then allowed

ILLUS. 227. LYING TO WIN APPROVAL

This method consists of a series of rather personal questions. There are many specific acts of conduct which on the whole have rather widespread social approval, but which at the same time are rarely done. The questions revolve around situations of this sort.

The test is in two forms. Each form contains 36 questions.

CEI ATTITUDES SA

Form One

Name _____ Date _____

School _____ Grade _____

Answer the following questions by underlining YES or NO. If your answer is YES, draw a line under <u>YES</u>. If your answer is NO, draw a line under <u>NO</u>. Please answer every question.

1. Did you ever accept the credit or honor for anything when you knew the credit or honor belonged to someone else? . YES <u>NO</u> 1.
2. Did you ever act greedily by taking more than your share of anything? . . . . YES <u>NO</u> 2.
3. Did you ever blame another for something you had done when you knew all the time it was your fault? . . . . . YES <u>NO</u> 3.
4. Do you usually report the number of a car you see speeding? . . . . <u>YES</u> NO 4.
5. Do you always preserve order when the teacher is out of the room? . . . . YES NO 5.
6. Do you report other pupils when you see cheating? . . . <u>YES</u> NO 6.
7. Did you ever pretend to understand a thing when you really did not understand it? . . . . YES <u>NO</u> 7.
8. Have you ever disobeyed any law of your country or rule of your school? . . . . YES <u>NO</u> 8.
9. Do you speak to all the people you are acquainted with, even the ones you do not like? . . . . <u>YES</u> NO 9.
10. Do you usually call the attention of people to the fact that you have on new shoes or a new suit or dress? . . . . YES <u>NO</u> 10.

(And 26 more questions.)

(Hartshorne and May, 1928, p. 98. By permission of The Macmillan Co.)

to give whatever he wished to make up boxes for children who had no useful or pretty things.

4) *Providing material for hospital children.* Each child was given a set of four envelopes and asked either to make or to find jokes, puzzles, pictures, and stories for sick children. He was also asked whether he would do this later, or whether he would like to help, but would not be able to do so.

5) *Records of service.* Teachers made records from December to

June on the actual activities of each pupil in the cooperation and service projects just described.

6) *Verbal description.* This test was suggested by the ancient but vivid word sketches of the Greek writer Theophrastus. In order to get up-to-date materials, items representing cooperative or helpful acts were listed and arranged in rank order. The situations were then cast into short sketches of boy and girl behavior, ranked from most to least helpful, and given values from 9 to 0. Illustration 228 shows some of these sketches. Teachers were asked to match each pupil with the approximate portrait. A variety of this test is the Guess Who Test of Maller (1932), which includes a wider variety of characteristics.

7) *Check list of traits.* Two forms of eighty words, each describing cooperative acts, were applied to each child by at least two teachers. They also used 5-point descriptive rating scales of cooperation and selfishness.

Measures of Persistence and Inhibition. 1) *Story Completion.* In this test situation an exciting story was read to a class as far as the climax. The ending of the story was supplied in forms difficult to read, such as (1) with capital letters run together, (2) with small letters and capitals run together, and (3) with spaces between capital letters in the wrong places. As the child was instructed to draw vertical lines between words in order to facilitate reading, a score was readily determined by the number of words correctly marked off.

2) *Puzzles.* Both mechanical and verbal puzzles were used. The scores were the time spent working.

3) *Letter counting.* Pupils were asked to count the letters in a page of pied type, and the time worked was recorded.

4) *Distraction tests.* In these tests, lines of digits were to be added. The digits were printed among curious sets of pictures and lines. The results were compared with normal addition scores.

5) *Inhibition tests.* These included situations where each child was given a small box of candy and asked not to touch it until after a series of tests. On another occasion a small combination safe was placed on each desk with instructions not to work at it until after a series of six tests. Scores on these tests were the number of times a child failed to comply by eating candy or manipulating the intriguing little safe before the set time.

6) *Ratings by Teachers.* Check lists of words describing self-control were used together with 5-point descriptive scales of eight items: control of temper, control of attention, control of laughter, talking too much, telling secrets, impatience, overindulgence in candy, and control of body movements.

ILLUS. 228. VERBAL CHARACTER SKETCHES

The final set, in order of helpfulness and with the score values based on the distribution of the pictures by the judges, is presented here:

9 — T.   T is sincerely interested in promoting the happiness and welfare of everyone.   His warm spirit of friendliness extends to all, no matter where they are or what their race, class, or creed may be.   Even the slightest need stirs him to some friendly act.   So strong is this purpose that he would endure the scorn of his fellows in order to help a struggling cause or to help persons in trouble, even though they might not seem to deserve help of any kind.

7 — F.   F is quite sincere in wanting to be of help.   To him it is not so much a matter of high purpose as of plain decency.   When the cause seems to be a worthy one, he is very generous and would give a cherished possession or deny himself long-anticipated pleasures even for such seemingly remote interests as scholarship funds for older students in other lands or for hospitals for adults.   He would persist in his helpful acts even though people thought he was very foolish to do so.   He is prompt to offer his services to anyone obviously in trouble.

5 — N.   N does not think much about being helpful as a general thing, but he has a kindly nature and his sympathies are easily aroused.   When his emotions are appealed to, he is ready to help almost anyone or any cause, but would probably draw the line at helping people he disliked or who seemed foreign or undeserving.   He always lends a hand when the occasion is obvious and, if the appeal is strong enough, would give away his own things or money he had saved for himself in order to help even such objects as a college for an underprivileged section of the country or a hospital for poor people.   The disapproval of his parents or teachers would not dissuade him.

1 — L.   L is not likely to help anyone at all unless he finds that others are doing so, especially his best friends.   He'd chip in a little for flowers for a classmate or help his elder brother take care of his small sister if it did not take too much time from his play or if he didn't have to do too much work or spend more than a few cents.   But for the most part he doesn't want to help, nor does he care whether he is regarded by others as helpful.

0 — P.   Here is your thoroughly hard-boiled youngster.   The person or cause needing help makes no difference at all to P; but if someone would call for it, he would let him take away some object he wanted to get rid of provided he would get some thanks or reward or prestige.   Or he would leave something he didn't want to do anyway in order to engage in some helpful activity if it were very interesting on other grounds and if people would applaud him for doing so.   But he does not care two cents about the object or about helpfulness as a duty or as the proper thing or as a way of winning favor or grace.

(Hartshorne and May, 1929, p. 82.   By permission of The Macmillan Co.)

Measures of Integration. The correlation of tests of honesty, co-operation, persistence, inhibition, moral knowledge, attitudes, and intellect tended to be so nearly zero that children in the fifth to eighth grades appeared to be loosely organized in these respects. It was possible, however, to calculate for each child the consistency of his scores. Illustration 229 shows two profiles, one characterized by remarkable consistency and the other by great variation. Both have

ILLUS. 229. PROFILE OF HONESTY SCORES IN
TWENTY-ONE SITUATIONS

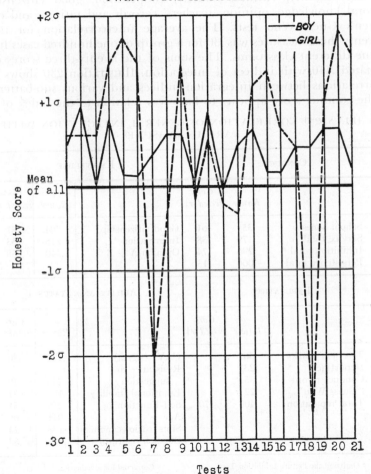

(Hartshorne and May, 1930, p. 290. By permission of the Macmillan Co.)

the same average SD scores on twenty-one measures of deception. The index of integration chosen was the standard deviation of the SD scores. The boy in Illustration 229 was found to have an index of .296, and the girl an index of 1.114. The reliability of such indices was found to be in the neighborhood of .411 for tests of deception. The correlation between indices and total honesty scores was .522, or .882 when corrected for attenuation.

Similar indices of integration were calculated on the basis of twenty-three measures of various sorts, including intellect, emotional stability, culture, honesty, cooperation, good citizenship, moral knowledge, opinion, teachers' records and ratings, and children's Guess Who tests. The average intercorrelation for these twenty-three measures was .30 for a group of one hundred cases from nine different classrooms. The sums of the twenty-three scores correlated .440 with indices of integration. Illustration 230 shows the correlations between integration indices and various sub-batteries. The conduct score appears to have less relation to the index of in-

ILLUS. 230. CORRELATION OF GENERAL INTEGRATION WITH VARIOUS MEASURES

Conduct			Knowledge		
	Raw r	Cor- rected r†		Raw r	Cor- rected r†
School honesty	.354	.61	Good citizenship	.504	.87
Service total	.179	.38	Information	.315	.53
Inhibition total *	.296	.74	Opinion A + B	.340	.58
Persistence total	−.066	−.13			

Reputation			Ability and Status		
	Raw r	Cor- rected r†		Raw r	Cor- rected r†
Teachers' marks	.361		CAVI (sigma)	.120	.20
Deportment	.232		Resistance to		
Conduct record	.352		suggestion	.246	.49
"Guess Who"	.223		Emotional stability	.194	.37
Total reputation	.400	.70	Self-Functioning	.289	.51
			Age	−.041	−.06
			Sims (socio-economic)	.138	.24
			Burdick (culture)	.184	.33

* Omitting the Picture Inhibition Test.   † Corrected for attenuation.

(Hartshorne and May, 1930, p. 351. By permission of the Macmillan Co.)

tegration than measures of knowledge, opinion, and reputation. Intellect, as shown by the CAVI tests, cultural status, and emotional stability, show a correlation below .20 with integrity, and age correlates nearly zero. There is a marked tendency for those who are more aggressive in deception to have lower indices of integrity than do those who are more aggressive in service and persistence.

The interpretation of this material is difficult, since all one has to be guided by is a pupil's relative position in his class on twenty-three tests and ratings. It was shown that a pupil might have a low integration index and still be rated as well adjusted by a teacher. The index of integrity is thus not an indication of consistent individual behavior, but rather of consistency of measures of abilities and adjustment among a group of persons. The authors conclude that motives, interests, and attitudes are dependent upon a variety of environmental and natural forces, some of which tend to make persons alike and some different from one another. Opinions and behavior scores of parents and associates were found to correlate fairly well with scores of pupils.

Records of Observation

Records of direct observation of persons are among the most valuable indicators of adjustments. Three procedures are commonly used. In one a continuous record is kept of all important episodes and their stimuli 24 hours a day. This sort of record can only be made in a hospital, or camp, or home situation where trained observers are available. The second procedure is called time sampling. Many scattered periods, usually from 5 seconds to 5 minutes, are used for observing a particular person. The third procedure records observation in a single interview or test period. All three of these procedures will be described.

One of the most thorough studies of a 24-hour record of a family situation was reported by Buhler (1939), who sent trained workers into private homes. The work of Newcomb (1929) is an outstanding example of analysis of detailed daily records made by counselors at a summer camp. In order to check the value of the general type concept of extroversion-introversion, he selected thirty items usually found in extroversion scales. Each item was printed with a 4 point scale of specific behavior, as shown in Illustration 231. The specific behavior consistency of each boy on each situation was fairly high from day to day, mean r equaled .78, but considerable variation took place over longer periods.

From the same items he determined "trait" consistency by grouping together those specific behavior situations which seemed to in-

ILLUS. 231. DAILY BEHAVIOR RECORD

Numbers indicate how many times a day the behavior was observed.

Date _____   Counselor _____

Name of Boy:	John	Henry	Pete	Ed	Frank
Did he show confidence in his own abilities?					
boasted loudly of greater abilities than he had	2				
spoke confidently of ability he really had	1		4	2	
expressed lack of confidence in own abilities		6		1	1
hesitated even to try his ability		3		1	
Did he take the initiative in organizing games?					
insisted on doing the organization himself	4				
gave constant advice to the leader	6	3			2
helped to plan, but loyal to the leader		1		1	
let others do all the planning — follower			4	4	
Did he submit to criticism or discipline from counselors?					
resisted violently, or fought back					1
retorted angrily, sarcastically, with threats	2				2
showed resentment by mumbling or sullenness	6	0	0		
accepted it quietly and in good spirit				0	

A new record sheet was used each day to avoid the possibility that the counselor might be influenced by previous records.

(After Newcomb, 1929, p. 21. By permission of the Bureau of Publications, Teachers College, Columbia University.)

volve similar activities or goals. Thus, under *volubility* were clustered instances of loud threats, loquacity, chattering, boasting, and announcing intention. An average intercorrelation of .26 was found among specific situations which were thus grouped together. This was not considered to be evidence of the existence of a central factor. Similarly, ten traits were distinguished and scored: energy output, ascendancy toward authority, ascendancy toward other boys, volubility, seeking limelight, interest in environment, impetuousness, social forwardness, ease of distraction, and preference for the group. The mean intercorrelation of total trait scores was only .37, a fact which led Newcomb to conclude that there was no evidence here for an extroversion-introversion type of person.

Ratings of behavior, based on several months of observation, have come to hold an important place in surveys of school populations. Two types of schedules are illustrated in the widely used form prepared by Haggerty, Olson, and Wickman (1930). Schedule A asked the rater to indicate the frequency of occurrence on a 4-point scale of fifteen types of behavior problems, such as cheating, lying, temper outbursts, speech difficulties, imaginative lying, sex offenses, and truancy. In total scores the more serious problems, as shown from clinical records, were given three times as much weight as the less serious. Schedule B has thirty-five items in four divisions. Items in the first division referred to intellectual aspects of behavior, in the second to physical, in the third to social, and in the fourth to emotional aspects. Each of these items, examples of which are shown in Illus. 232, is in the form of a 5-point rating scale. The points were assigned by finding the average scores on Schedule A for pupils who received a particular rating on an item in Schedule B. Illustration 232 shows that the subdivisions of the item, How intelligent is he? were assigned points on the basis of lack of intelligence. The reason for doing this is that the groups having the lowest intelligence rating also had the greatest number of behavior problems. In Item 2, Is he abstracted or wide awake? the points do not correspond directly to amounts of this trait, for it was found that the most alert had more behavior difficulties than two less alert groups.

Schedule B was found to correlate .60 with total scores on Schedule A, and a composite score using both schedules correlated .76 with the frequency with which children were sent to the elementary school principal by teachers or monitors. The self-consistency of teachers when rating twice within a short period was found to be .86 using Schedule B, and the split-half reliability of single rating was .92. Ratings of two elementary school teachers commonly correlated .60 with each other when rating small groups of children.

An unusually thorough schedule designed to appraise causes as well as symptoms is the Detroit Scale for the Diagnosis of Behavior Problems by Baker and Traphagen (1935). It requires ratings by a trained investigator on sixty-six items. Each item is rated on a 5-point scale: 1 very poor, 2 poor, 3 fair or average, 4 good, and 5 very good. The ratings are to be based on direct observations, medical and school records, and questioning of both parents and children. The ratings are described in detail for each item. Thus for Item 25, Later Recreational Facilities, the pupil is asked, "How do you amuse yourself after school, or during vacation? What do you have to play with?" and the parents are asked, "What does he have to play with and how does he spend his time?" Six additional questions for parents (p. 65) are also suggested:

What things does he have to play with? With what does he amuse himself?

ILLUS. 232. BEHAVIOR RATING SCALE

Directions for Using

SCHEDULE B

1. Do not consult anyone in making your judgments.
2. In rating a person on a particular trait, disregard every other trait but that one. Many ratings are rendered valueless because the rater allows himself to be influenced by a general favorable or unfavorable impression that he has formed of the person.
3. When you have satisfied yourself as to the standing of this person in the trait on which you are rating him, indicate your rating by placing a cross (X) immediately above the most appropriate descriptive phrase.
4. If you are rating a child, try to make your ratings by comparing him with children of his own age.
5. The masculine pronoun (he) has been used throughout for convenience. It applies whether the person whom you are rating is male or female.
6. In making your ratings, disregard the numbers which appear below the descriptive phrases. They are for use in scoring.

Division I

1. How intelligent is he?

Feeble-minded	Dull	Equal of average child on street	Bright	Brilliant
(5)	(4)	(3)	(2)	(1)

2. Is he abstracted or wide-awake?

Continually absorbed in himself	Frequently becomes abstracted	Usually present-minded	Wide-awake	Keenly alive and alert
(5)	(4)	(2)	(1)	(3)

3. Is his attention sustained?

Distracted: jumps rapidly from one thing to another	Difficult to keep at task until completed	Attends adequately	Is absorbed in what he does	Able to hold attention for long periods
(5)	(4)	(3)	(1)	(2)

Division II

8. Is he slovenly or neat in personal appearance?

Unkempt, very slovenly	Rather negligent	Inconspicuous	Is concerned about dress	Fastidious, foppish
(5)	(4)	(2)	(1)	(3)

9. How does he impress people with his physique and bearing?

Repulsive	Makes an unfavorable impression	Generally unnoticed physique and bearing	Makes a favorable impression	Excites admiration
(5)	(4)	(3)	(2)	(1)

(Haggerty, Olson, and Wickman, 1930. By permission of the World Book Co.)

Is there a purpose in his play or is it spasmodic and of no educational value?

Does he play at having shows or at make-believe school? Does he play ball, skate, or build model houses?

Does he have a pet and does he care for it well?

Does he get any companionship with his parents through sharing play and recreation with them?

Does he complain that time hangs heavy on his hands?

Finally, for rating this factor, the following scale (p. 66) is given:

Points	*Factors*
5	Has a few well-organized things to do and desirable companions in doing them.
4	Has good attitude but little opportunity to play or express himself constructively with companions.
3	Except for one or two things or for short periods, does not know what to do.
2	Has little to play with; is alone most of time; has no particular purpose or drive to activities.
1	No purpose in play activities; no place to play; playthings in poor shape; plays mostly away from home; no interest on parents' part.

The sixty-six items are classified under five headings: (1) health and physical factors, (2) personal habits and recreational factors, (3) personality and social factors, (4) parental and physical factors of the home, and (5) home atmosphere and school factors. A summary sheet shows the rating assigned to each item, the number of items which were given each rating, and also a total score obtained by simply adding all the credits together. The total score is then transmuted into a letter grade according to a table, which gives the letters nearly the same significance as that found in the usual class in elementary school or in the United States Army Alpha tests. The following summary of a case (from pp. 336–38) will illustrate the procedure:

CASE 5. Behavior Rating C—

D. M., considered as a behavior case, was a fifteen-year-old boy, with a score of 218. The distribution of his items is as follows:

SUMMARY OF FACTORS

Category	Number	Weighted Score
very poor	5	5
poor	13	26
fair	22	66
good	9	36
very good	17	85
	66	218

He was considered as an extreme behavior case in his locality, which was somewhat above the average. The five very poor items were as follows: early health, Item 1, seems to have had a considerable influence on his problem, as his father particularly was very indulgent to him on account of his health. Item 29, on anger and rage, shows that he was inclined to yield to fits of anger easily and was frequently picked on by other children. Item 36, vocational interests, seems to be very negative on account of his health, poor scholastic record, and too much parental indulgence. Item 48 shows that the father is an unskilled laborer, doing truck driving and janitorial jobs, with some possible feelings of inferiority about it. As to Item 65, D. M's record was consistently poor, with D's and E's, which reflect in part his poor vocational interests.

The items rated poor are as follows: degree of vision defect, Item 7— he always had very poor vision in one eye, but the other eye was approximately normal. His father was rather opposed to making any adjustments to improve his vision. Item 5, accidents—he was hit by an automobile, with minor injuries, and two years before he had broken his nose in a bicycle accident. Item 15—he was very unattractive in appearance because of his crossed eyes. Items 16 and 17—his early care and present care were poor. Items 19 and 20—he ate meals at irregular times, hurried his eating, and was rather fussy and disagreeable about what he ate. Item 33 showed an IQ of 76 on the Stanford-Binet Test, which explains some of his difficulty in making adjustments to regular grade standards. Item 35, initiative and ambition, showed him not very ambitious. Items 40 and 41, education of both parents, showed that they had completed only two or three grades and in European countries. Item 61—his discipline was inconsistent and modified by pity on account of his physical health. Item 66, his attitude toward the school—in this respect he was poor because the regular school work was too difficult for him. The parents refused to place him in any type of special class.

It seems that in D. M's case, in the next two or three years of school, vocational and social adjustments would be critical factors in determining whether he would make a successful final adjustment or whether this combination of factors would tend to carry him downhill.

Baker and Traphagen reported correlations between total scores and each item on two groups: 189 behavior cases, 180 nonbehavior cases. The total scores on the first group correlated most highly with family recreation, .699; ideals of the home, .657; conditions of eating, .562; time of sleeping, .555; father's age at birth of child, .551; economic status, .526; child's intelligence, .525; mother's personality, .495; and similar items. Among the nonbehavior cases, the total scores correlated most highly with scholarship, .663; later recreational facilities, .616; personal hygiene, .583; initiative and ambition, .569; discipline, .558; mother's intelligence, .542; conditions of eating, .526; father's intelligence, .512; mother's personality, .500; and early self-care, .507.

The following items had low correlations with total scores among the behavior-problem children: children's diseases, .03; size for age, .11; speech defects, .13; infectious diseases, .182; early self-care, .175; mother's health, .200; and broken home, .254. Among the well-adjusted group the total scores showed low correlations with general home atmosphere, .117; children's diseases, .05; defects of vision, .154; size for age, .230; economic status, .220; and child's intelligence, .275.

These figures illustrate very well the results of correlation analyses of different groups of pupils. The differences among poorly adjusted pupils seemed to be largely dependent upon the interplay of living conditions and the personality of parents and associates. Among the well-adjusted group, total scores corresponded to differences in scholarship, recreations, and personal hygiene. When both groups of pupils were combined, a correlation of .91 was found between total scores and a combination of the five items: discipline, child's attitude toward the home, parents' attitude toward child, general behavior, and scholarship.

Interviews

Employment officers have long relied upon their judgments of an applicant's modes of adjustment. Doubtless, capable interviewers can size up fairly well a person's moods and mannerisms during an interview, but the brevity of the interview and the bias of the interviewer may result in fragmentary or erroneous records. In order to help interviewers and oral examiners make accurate and systematic appraisals, the rating form shown in Illustration 233 was prepared. This form is also typical of many that are used in ratings of employees who have been in service for a long time. It consists of nine general aspects, each of which is described by a brief paragraph and followed by a graphic and descriptive rating scale. This particular form, which has been made so that it can be scored by a machine, gives a profile for each individual.

Another worthwhile approach, reported by Brody and Powell (1947), is called group performance or group interviewing. Here a group of from four to six candidates are seated around a table and asked to discuss informally a topic of some interest and complexity. Three or more observers record for each candidate the main activities under the following six headings (Brody and Powell 1947, p. 287 and following):

1. *Appearance and Manner:* poise, physical alertness, nervousness, attentiveness, mannerisms
2. *Speech:* power of expression, vocabulary, diction, modulation
3. *Attitude towards Group:* tact, cooperation, ability to mix, flexibility

ILLUS. 233. RATING FORM FOR USE OF INTERVIEWERS AND
ORAL EXAMINERS — 2 — 1938

INSTRUCTIONS: Ask yourself how this applicant compares with those who are doing work of this kind. Consider whether his voice, appearance, etc., would be a liability or an asset in such a position. Rate him by making a check (✓) at that point on each scale where, in your judgment, the applicant stands. Rate the following traits:

1. **VOICE AND SPEECH.** Is the applicant's voice irritating, or pleasant? Can you easily hear what he says? Does he mumble, or talk with an accent which offends or baffles the listener? Or is his speech clear and distinct, his voice so rich, resonant and well-modulated that it would be a valuable asset in this position?

2. **APPEARANCE.** What sort of first impression does he make? Does he look like a well-set-up, healthy, energetic person? Has he bodily or facial characteristics which might seriously hamper him? Is he well-groomed or slovenly? Erect or slouchy? Attractive or unattractive in appearance?

3. **ALERTNESS.** How readily does he grasp the meaning of a question? Is he slow to apprehend even the more obvious points, or does he understand quickly, even though the idea is new, involved or difficult?

4. **ABILITY TO PRESENT IDEAS.** Does he speak logically and convincingly? Or does he tend to be vague, confused or illogical?

5. **JUDGMENT.** Does he impress you as a person whose judgment would be dependable even under stress? Or is he hasty, erratic, biased, swayed by his feelings?

6. **EMOTIONAL STABILITY.** How well poised is he emotionally? Is he touchy, sensitive to criticism, easily upset? Is he irritated or impatient when things go wrong? Or does he keep an even keel?

7. **SELF-CONFIDENCE.** Does he seem to be uncertain of himself, hesitant, lacking in assurance, easily bluffed? Or is he wholesomely self-confident and assured?

8. **FRIENDLINESS.** Is he a likeable person? Will his fellow-workers and subordinates be drawn to him, or kept at a distance? Does he command personal loyalty and devotion?

9. **PERSONAL FITNESS FOR THE POSITION.** In the light of all the evidence regarding this person's characteristics (whether mentioned above or not) how do you rate his personal suitability for work such as he is considering? Recalling that it is not in his best interest to recommend him for such a position if he is better suited for something else, would you urge him to undertake this work? Do you endorse his application?

Fuller instructions and space for comments on applicant's behavior will be found on the back of this sheet.

ILLUS. 233. RATING FORM FOR USE OF INTERVIEWERS AND
ORAL EXAMINERS — 2 — 1938 *(Cont'd)*

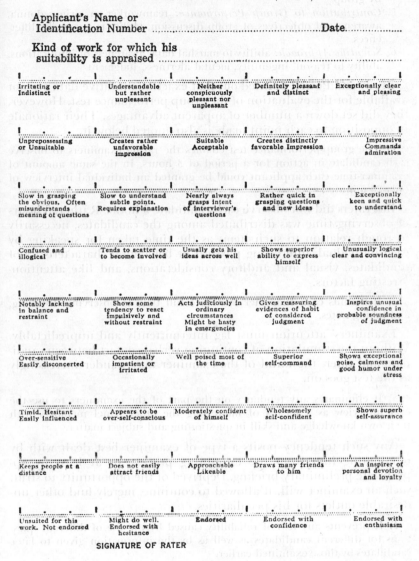

**Applicant's Name or
Identification Number** ....**Date**...................

**Kind of work for which his
suitability is appraised** ....

Irritating or Indistinct	Understandable but rather unpleasant	Neither conspicuously pleasant nor unpleasant	Definitely pleasant and distinct	Exceptionally clear and pleasing
Unprepossessing or Unsuitable	Creates rather unfavorable impression	Suitable Acceptable	Creates distinctly favorable Impression	Impressive Commands admiration
Slow in grasping the obvious. Often misunderstands meaning of questions	Slow to understand subtle points. Requires explanation	Nearly always grasps intent of interviewer's questions	Rather quick in grasping questions and new ideas	Exceptionally keen and quick to understand
Confused and illogical	Tends to scatter or to become involved	Usually gets his ideas across well	Shows superior ability to express himself	Unusually logical clear and convincing
Notably lacking in balance and restraint	Shows some tendency to react impulsively and without restraint	Acts judiciously in ordinary circumstances Might be hasty in emergencies	Gives reassuring evidences of habit of considered judgment	Inspires unusual confidence in probable soundness of judgment
Over-sensitive Easily disconcerted	Occasionally impatient or irritated	Well poised most of the time	Superior self-command	Shows exceptional poise, calmness and good humor under stress
Timid. Hesitant Easily influenced	Appears to be over-self-conscious	Moderately confident of himself	Wholesomely self-confident	Shows superb self-assurance
Keeps people at a distance	Does not easily attract friends	Approachable Likeable	Draws many friends to him	An inspirer of personal devotion and loyalty
Unsuited for this work. Not endorsed	Might do well. Endorsed with hesitance	Endorsed	Endorsed with confidence	Endorsed with enthusiasm

SIGNATURE OF RATER

This rating form prepared from suggestions furnished by W. V. Bingham.
(By permission of W. V. Bingham and the International Business
Machines Corporation.)

4. *Leadership:* ability to assume lead without giving offense, acceptance by group
5. *Contribution to Group Performance:* teamworker or prima donna, awareness of objectives of group discussion, ability to reconcile differences
6. *Scientific Approach:* ability to marshal data, awareness of implications, ability to reason, ingenuity, mental alertness, judgment

Brody and Powell pointed out that exact quantitative data are not available for the evaluation of the group-performance test. However, they did set down a number of apparent advantages. Their rationale in opposition to each point made is also quoted below it.

1) The group-performance test enables the rating examiners to observe each candidate in action for a period of 3 hours. In the same amount of examiner-time each applicant could be granted an individual interview of only 20 minutes.

But raters did not observe each candidate 3 hours. Rather, 3 hours of observing time was distributed among the candidates, necessarily in rough relation to such items as the time taken for speaking by each individual, interesting physical or behavioral characteristics of candidates, visual and auditory considerations, and like attention-arresting factors.

2) It permits each examiner to devote full time to observing, listening, and taking notes.

Examiners' attention must lag intermittently and unpredictably. Without the stimulation of continuing verbal contact between candidate and rater, the mind of the examiner may wander increasingly as the test goes on.

3) It eliminates any tendency on the part of the examiners to use the oral interview as a means of impressing the other panel members with their own knowledge and skill in questioning and subject matter.

Any such tendency posits a type of examiner best dealt with by eliminating him from the examining process, or at least by appropriate preliminary briefing. Deprived of the opportunity to strut, such an examiner will, if allowed to continue, merely find other undesirable outlets for his peculiarities.

4) It prevents any loss of reliability caused by the use of different questions for different candidates as well as by the information given to later candidates by those examined earlier.

This assumes that the candidates are so few in number as to be expeditiously handled in one group session. Furthermore, in the ordinary oral test, it is quite possible to arrange to use the same questions, if desired, for different candidates. In the group oral-performance test itself, standardization of detail tends to be at a minimum, inasmuch as the candidates may roam almost as they will.

5) It minimizes the effect of the inevitable lack of continuous concentration on the part of the examiners.

But it tends to maximize the probability that the examiners' concentration will not be continuous. The fact that the examiner is, in a sense, himself under observation in the usual oral test keeps him, at least seemingly, wide awake.

6) It provides a more natural situation than the usual question-and-answer contact between a candidate and his examiners.

It is certainly unnatural for adults to be required to discuss a particular matter under the silent and somewhat remote inspection of examiners. The usual question-and-answer contact possesses the virtue of being usual; candidates are accustomed to such a situation and are more likely to regard it as natural.

7) It eliminates the suspicion on the part of any candidate that other candidates may be received more kindly and may be given easier questions. It may even convince him that some other candidates are better qualified than he is.

This is errant assertion, not evidence. Suspicious candidates could in any case imagine partisanship or other bias on the part of the examiners.

8) It eliminates the following dangers in the conventional oral-interview situation:
a) There exists a tendency for panel members to slant their attention to the candidate's response to their own questions.
b) It has been found that the rating given to any candidate tends to carry over positively to the following candidate. The consequence is a kind of halo effect.

a) In the conventional interview we can be quite sure that the rater listens to the answers to his own questions, if nothing else. A similar near-guarantee is absent in the group situation.

b) Perhaps kindred biases occur in the group test. Where individual candidates sit is determined by chance, but where they sit may be correlated with their rating.

9) It provides very valuable information concerning the attitude of each candidate toward the other members of the group, as well as of his reaction to their attitudes. This is particularly important in testing for positions where group discussions and conferences are essential.

But the situation may be regarded as so unreal as to yield perverted findings. In the real conference situation, each member generally has a defined status. Very importantly, conferees probably have prior acquaintance with one another and the good conferee will use to advantage the information which he possesses about the personalities of his colleagues in reaching a predefined objective.

10) It presents specific evidence concerning the ability of each candidate to be a leader in a group.

More accurately, the group test provides specific evidence of the candidate's ability to lead the particular group in whose deliberations he participates on a specified subject under the conditions set in the test. It remains possible that varying elements of the situation may result in varying the performance of candidates.

11) Those who participate (examiners as well as candidates) find it more interesting than the individual interview.

Interest is not to be confused with validity and public-relations values. The latter are the significant aspects of a test.

12) It requires no skill in asking questions on the part of examiners.

Here in fact, is one of the greatest weaknesses of the group examination. Opportunity is denied to the examiner to explore the candidates' statements, to follow up leads in order to verify the apparent competence or incompetence of the applicant.

Obviously, there is much to be said for and against the group oral-performance test. The test is promising in many ways; it has decided weaknesses. Perhaps the best argument which can be advanced at the present time in support of the group test is a negative one—it is unlikely to be as bad as the orthodox oral-interview test.

Certainly additional experimentation by public personnel agencies with the group examination is most desirable. To be sure, this is a feeble conclusion and bears resemblance to the traditional position of the liberal whose feet are firmly planted in mid-air. Yet the fact appears to be that all that can confidently be said about the group oral-performance test is that its possible utility is worth exploring.

In connection with their study of sexual behavior in the human male, Kinsey, Pomeroy, and Martin (1948) have listed a number of important rules for interviewing. This study required the cooperation of persons largely unknown to the interviewers in obtaining data on from 300 to 500 items in one interview which could not last much more than 2 hours. To be most effective they found it was necessary to be introduced to the subject by someone the subject trusted, usually someone who had already been interviewed. Next it was necessary to put the subject at ease, to insure absolute privacy, and to show interest by face-to-face talking without any evasion. Another important aspect of the interviewing was the sequence of topics. Interviews should progress from easier to harder types of information, from the least disturbing to the more intimate or possibly disturbing. Variations in the order and in the actual form of questions, however, did not permit any variations in the kinds of question, and were not allowed to interfere with a systematic completion of the interview. The authors pointed out that it is necessary to recognize the mental capacity of the informant. Persons of various degrees of mental ability required different rates of speed and different types of questions. They found that fast, accurate coding of the material during the interview was by far the best method of recording. It resulted in much more accurate records, and also made the subjects feel that the interview was important and was being properly recorded. They stressed the importance of asking matter-of-fact questions to determine overt behavior as well as questions which elicited attitudes or opinions or feelings.

Carl R. Rogers and his students have contributed notably to the appraisals of therapeutic interviews by making electrical recordings and subjecting these to detailed analysis. They have thus been able to determine what kinds of statements tend to lead to acceptance, spontaneity, and insight by the subject. They have used these analyses to train therapists and to predict the outcome of therapy. A good example of a check list is that reported by Porter (1943) (Illus. 234), which includes twenty-four categories under four main headings: (1) defining the interview situation, (2) bringing out and developing the problem situation, (3) developing the client's insight and understanding, (4) sponsoring client's activity/fostering decision making. The various categories were used, after some training, by thirteen judges in appraising eighteen recorded interviews. The agreement between judges was perfect in 31.6 per cent of all codings, and the correlation between pairs of judges in total number of identifications was approximately .95 for both typewritten transcripts and sound recordings. The ratio of words spoken by the counselor to those spoken by the client was also reported. Counselors were found to have fairly consistent ratios, and the most talkative counselor had a ratio twenty-seven times as large as that of the least talkative. Differences in points of view on counseling were reflected in the patterns of the counselor interviews, and the effects of training in nondirective counseling were quite clear in these quantitative codings. The directive counselors used many more direct questions and sug-

ILLUS. 234. CATEGORIES IN THERAPEUTIC COUNSELING

Code No.   *Judge*   *Date*

DEFINING THE INTERVIEW SITUATION

1*a*   Defines in terms of diagnostic/remedial purposes, procedures, etc.
1*b*   Defines in terms of client responsibility for directing the interview/reaching decisions, etc.

1*u* (Unclassifiable)

BRINGING OUT AND DEVELOPING THE PROBLEM SITUATION

Uses lead which
2*a*   Forces choosing and developing of topic upon client.
2*b*   Indicates topic but leaves development to client.
2*c*   Indicates topic and delimits development to confirmation, negation, or the supplying of specific items of information.

2*u* (Unclassifiable)

DEVELOPING THE CLIENT'S INSIGHT AND UNDERSTANDING

Responds in such a way as to indicate
3*a*   Recognition of subject content or implied subject content.
3*b*   Recognition of expression of feeling or attitude in immediately preceding verbal response(s).
3*c*   Interpretation or recognition of feeling or attitude not expressed in immediately preceding verbal response(s).
3*d*   Identifies a problem, source of difficulty, condition needing correction, etc., through test interpretation, evaluative remarks, etc.
3*e*   Interprets test results *but not* as indicating a problem, source of difficulty, etc.
3*f*   Expresses approval, disapproval, shock, or other personal reaction in regard to the client (but not to identify a problem).

3*u* (Unclassifiable)

4   Explains, discusses, or gives information related to the problem or treatment.

SPONSORING CLIENT ACTIVITY/FOSTERING DECISION MAKING

Proposes client activity
5*a*   Directly or through questioning technique.
5*b*   In response to question of what to do.
Influences the making of a decision by
5*c*   Marshaling and evaluating evidence, expressing personal opinion, persuading pro or con.
5*d*   Indicates decision is up to client.
5*e*   Indicates acceptance or approval of decision.
5*f*   Reassures

5*u* (Unclassifiable)

I   Irrelevant
OU   Otherwise unclassifiable   Total number of checks _____
      Nondirective—1 2 3 4 5 6 7 8 9 10 11—Directive

(By permission of E. H. Porter and the editor of *Educational and Psychological Measurements*.)

gestions (Illus. 234, categories *2a, 2b, 2c, 3d,* 4, and *5a*). The non-directive counselors did much less talking than the clients and they used categories *3a, 3b,* and *3c* almost exclusively.

An interesting approach to the appraisal of an interview, reported by Chapple (1949), makes use of an elaborate recording machine called an Interaction Chronograph. This machine, which was developed from several earlier models over a period of 15 years, consists of a series of 10 printing counters and a signal counter, each activated by a different key. The operator observes the interview and records variations in the activities of both the applicant and interviewer by pressing the various keys. From the record (See Chapple, 1949, p. 298) one obtains measures of:

1. *Tempo:* how often a person starts to act.
2. *Activity or energy:* how much longer he talks or responds than he is silent.
3. *Adjustment of applicant to interviewer:* length of his interruptions of the interviewer minus length of his failures to respond to the interviewer.
4. *Initiative:* the frequency with which one person takes the initiative from the other.
5. *Dominance:* the frequency with which one person out-talks or out-acts the other when there has been an interruption.
6. *Synchronization.* the frequency with which a person fails to synchronize with the other either by interrupting or by failing to respond.
7. *Number of Exchanges:* the total number of responses to the other person.

From these records several derived scores were obtained, such as the rate per exchange of a variable, ability to listen, and flexibility. No clear definition of these terms has yet come to hand, nor indications of the relationships among the measure of results. Chapple indicated that reliability correlations were satisfactory, and stated that the observer must be thoroughly trained in basic concepts. The criteria were objective in that a key was moved only when there was a visible contraction or relaxation of facial muscles.

In order to secure easily comparable results among interviewers, controls of content and behavior of the interviewer were rigidly defined. The interviewer used three patterns of behavior during different periods. In one the interviewer introduced a topic then endeavored to adjust to the subject by a nondirective type of behavior, using such phrases as "That's interesting" or "Could you tell me more about that?" After 10 minutes the interviewer changed the topic and then ten consecutive times waited at least 15 seconds after the applicant had stopped talking. If the applicant did not start talking again within 15 seconds, the interviewer rephrased the question. In the third procedure the interviewer interrupted and tried to talk down the applicant after ten consecutive starts. Flexibility is indicated by a person's tendency to react differently to these situations. Studies of certain types of mental hospital patients showed much greater rigidity or inflexibility than was found in normal people.

Chapple compared the scores of sixty-six industrial line supervisors with the scores of several hundred nonsupervisory workers. He found that the supervisors were more active, quicker in tempo, and showed more initial dominance at the beginning of the interview than the nonsupervisory workers. They were also able to operate at a slower pace (flexibility) when the second interviewing procedure was used. Chapple noted differences in scores among maintenance foremen, machine-shop foremen, foundry foremen, and superintendents. He was also able to construct a single interaction index which correlated well with general ratings of efficiency.

In another study various employees of a large department store were compared. The activity variable alone discriminated well between good and poor salesmen, and also between sales and clerical workers. Ability to listen was important in selling jobs where one had to find out a complicated customer specification, but it was a handicap in a rapid over-the-counter transaction. More initiative was needed in selling of high-priced articles. Personnel officers and supervisors showed more flexibility and less dominance or aggression than buyers, but both had high activity levels. Chapple stressed the need of developing more accurate job profiles using Interaction Chronograph scores for purposes of transfers and promotions and for more research in defining and refining the behavior variables used.

STRESS SITUATIONS

In stress situations the subject is aware that he is to some extent "on the spot," and in some cases the limits of his endurance are tested. These situations are described under painful stimuli, reactions to tests, hand pressures, and lie detectors.

Painful Stimuli

A laboratory approach to the measurement of persistence was reported by Howell (1933), who tried to get at an element of personality which seemed independent of strength or skill. He used tasks which involved constantly increasing distress from one of several sources, such as fatigue from gripping a hand dynamometer, forcing a needle or blunt peg into the flesh, heat from an electric grill, and electric shock. The procedure was to apply the stimulus gradually until the student gave the signal to stop, indicating that he had reached his limit of endurance. Individual tests were made with 102 subjects who were told that they were competing for rank and that their names and ranks would be posted. Twenty-four of these students had been previously threatened with dismissal from college for academic failures.

The results of the tests involving strength and pressure were found to correlate .44 with one's weight; hence a corrected score on these tests was made to equalize weight. The reliability of the battery, estimated by correlating the odd-even tests, ranged from .19 to .85 for small samples. The intercorrelations of the test ranged from .18 to .72, median approximately .47. The willingness to endure the needle and the willingness to endure heat had low correlation with each other and with the painful-pressure situations. The total scores on these persistence tests were found to correlate .81 with the volitional-perseverance section of the Downey Will-Temperament Profile, and .44 with the Allport (1928) Ascendance-Submission Test. Persistence scores correlated .18 with "being a male," when the influence of weight was held constant. The correlation between Ohio State University Intelligence Test scores and persistence scores was .10, but the latter correlated with grades in college, 44. The prediction of grades from intelligence tests was .51. This was raised to .64 when persistence scores were combined with intelligence by a multiple correlation.

James C. Coleman (1949) reported a careful study of the judgment of emotions from a facial expression by 379 psychology students. The photographs were made of persons who were subjected to the following situations.

1. *Natural:* sitting quietly.
2. *Effort:* squeezing a hand dynamometer as hard as possible with both hands.
3. *Startle:* sudden blast of horn.
4. *Shock:* severe electric shock received in cervical region.
5. *Threat:* told that shock would be repeated.
6. *Disgust for horror:* crushing a live snail with bare fingers.
7. *Fear horror:* seeing live snake suddenly set free in front of subject.
8. *Humor:* listening to a joke.

The judges were given printed tests of these situations, and asked to indicate which photograph was made during each situation. Four groups of subjects viewed the whole face, the mouth only, and the eyes only—rotating the order of presentation. The results showed that the identification of the photograph was more accurate from the whole face than from its parts, but for situations 2 and 8 the judgment from the mouth alone was nearly as accurate as those from the whole face, and for situations 6 and 7, the judgments from the eyes alone were nearly as accurate as from the whole face. Situation 8 was the only one where the accuracy reached approximately 90 per cent of judgments. The average percentage correct for all situations was approximately 50. Situations 3, 4, 5, and 6 showed the lowest accuracy of judgments—about 40 per cent correct. Coleman also varied the procedure by having the subject photographed while acting out the responses considered appropriate for each situation. The natural and acted series of photographs had considerable resemblance, but the acted series showed in most cases exaggerations of the natural reactions. Coleman also secured introspective reports from his subjects. These showed a considerable variety of feelings toward the experimental situations. He concluded that the judgment of emotions from photographs of facial expression under these circumstances was in need of much more thorough control and study.

Reactions to Tests

Elaborate reports of individual adjustments during test situations have been prepared by a number of authors. Illustration 235 shows a rating scale by Vernon (1938) which lists a large number of items. Such lists will have to be supported by careful definitions and much training before they will give consistent and significant results.

Hand Pressures

An interesting laboratory technique, developed by Luria (1932), has been widely applied in Russia and more recently in America. He made two records of hand movements in conjunction with free-association responses to words. The dominant hand was required to press a bulb to which a pressure recorder was attached. The other hand, about which nothing was said, was allowed to rest on a movable plate to which a movement recorder was attached. For each verbal response, his results showed the intensity of two kinds of motor responses, voluntary and involuntary. From his results, measures on a scale of integration were available. At one extreme of the scale was complete coordination of speech and motor responses, and at the other extreme involuntary motor responses of considerable violence which often preceded or followed the voluntary hand and speech reactions. Luria believed that the degree of integration depends upon the cortical mechanism. In persons best integrated all conflicts were settled in the cortical centers before motor responses

ILLUS. 235. GENERAL RATING SCALE

Name............................Date.................Examiner.................

ACTIVITY

Excited, restless, unable to keep still
Quick and vivacious
Calm and deliberate
Inert and listless

Impulsive
Stable
Cautious
Inhibited

Poses, motor attitudes...

Tics.................Nail-biting.................Twitchings.................

Fiddling with
material.............clothes.............hands.............feet.............

Peculiar
expressions.........................
excessive
wrinklings.........................

MOVEMENT

Fluent and graceful
Accurate and well controlled
Angular and awkward
Clumsy

Quick stride and movements
Slow stride and movements

PHYSIQUE AND BEARING

Impressive in bearing
Satisfactory impression
Unimpressive
Forceful, efficient, energetic, upright posture and gait
Slouching gait
Weak, inefficient movements and bearing
Plump (pyknic) proportions
Well and symmetrically proportioned
Thin (asthenic)

Healthy looking, well developed, and nourished
Unhealthy, feeble physique

Florid

Pale

PERSONAL APPEARANCE AND EXPRESSION

Attractive and good-looking (positive reaction)
Pleasant
Uninteresting, indifferent attractiveness
Ugly and repulsive (negative reaction)
Strong expressiveness of face and gestures
Expressionless
Quick and strong sense of humour
Slow but sure
Unable to see humour
Mature, serious, philosophical
Immature, childish

Sensual.................

Effeminate.................
Frank
Secretive
Cheerful, optimistic
Depressed, melancholy
Excitable, irritable
Even-tempered
Calm, phlegmatic

SPECIAL CHARACTERISTICS...
....
....

SPEECH

Voice resonant, pleasing, well modulated
Hard, harsh, pinched
Expresses meaning directly, grammatically, with facility
Unable to express himself, ungrammatical
Garrulous, overtalkative
Rather voluble
Seldom speaks of own accord
Reticent, taciturn

Clear, fluent, distinct
Stutters, stammers

Accent.................
Brilliant in talking, wide vocabulary
Dull and stolid, narrow vocabulary

PERSONAL CARE

Fastidious in dress, overmanicured
Good taste, neat and clean
Passable and inconspicuous
Careless in dress and cleanliness
Slovenly and unkempt

ILLUS. 235. GENERAL RATING SCALE (*Cont'd*)

SELF-ASSERTION

Pompous and overbearing   Decisive
Complacent
Self-confident and possessed   Wavering
Self-critical and deprecatory
Embarrassed, bashful, self-conscious   Contrasuggestible
Anxious, apprehensive
Submissive, retiring   Suggestible

CO-OPERATIVENESS

Willing to co-operate in every respect; enters into spirit
Reserved and formal
Constrained and suspicious, outside the situation
Surly and hostile
Scrupulous, punctual and regular in attendance, application
Industrious
Easy-going, indifferent
Lazy and irregular

ALERTNESS AND CONCENTRATION

Intelligently attentive, wide-awake
Concentrated
Absent-minded
Easily distracted, inattentive

TEST REACTIONS: PLANNING

Analytical
Serious but unsystematic
Trial and error   Profits by past experience
Haphazard   Repeats same mistakes

EMOTION

Wild and unrestrained emotional behavior and remarks
Wilful and childish reactions, capricious
Some loss of self-control, and overt emotion
Humorous and unconcerned
Serious, philosophical
Repressed and inhibited

(Vernon, 1938, p. 56. By permission of the *British Journal of Educational Psychology*.)

were made. The opposite was true in the most disorganized persons, where motor responses in many patterns were typical of conflict situations. The difficulty of the task could be varied experimentally. Marked tendencies toward disorganization were found in small children, feeble-minded persons, and hysterical patients.

Huston, Shakow, and Erickson (1924) repeated one of Luria's experiments with hypnotized subjects, and found that under hypnosis the subjects tended to exhibit few motor disturbances when they gave verbal responses related to the conflict. When normally awake, the same subjects gave fewer verbal responses, but more motor reactions. Consequently, the investigators suggested the hypothesis that there are various levels of discharge of nervous impulses. If the excitation created by a stimulus is not discharged verbally, it tends to spread to voluntary motor responses, and if not discharged there, to involuntary motor responses.

Olson and Jones (1931) and Sharp (1938) applied the Luria technique to find out what kinds of stimulus words cause the greatest responses among various types of subjects. Stimulus-word lists containing fifteen words each were prepared by Sharp to sample responses to given regions of activity: family, social, religion, health, and intellect. These words were distributed among 125 neutral words, and administered to college and high school groups, scholastic failures, and stutterers. The following directions were used (p. 114):

Rest your arms comfortably on the table. Place the first and second fingers of each hand on [the rubber which is stretched across the] cups in front of you. Now, I shall read a list of words to you. As soon as you hear my words respond at once with the first word that comes to your mind. At the same time press your right hand. Your left hand is to remain quietly in the same position throughout the experiment.

Each response was scored to show the reaction time and the amount of voluntary and involuntary motor disturbance as shown by the right and the left hands respectively. The test was repeated on a later day and the correlations were found to be fairly high between corresponding scores, as recorded in Illus. 236. This table indicates

ILLUS. 236. CORRELATIONS BETWEEN FIRST AND SECOND
TRIALS OF AN ASSOCIATION-MOTOR TEST

Test	Reaction Time	Somatic Disturbances
Total	.94 ± .01	.87 ± .02
Family	.95 ± .01	.84 ± .03
Social	.96 ± .01	.87 ± .02
Religious	.93 ± .01	.88 ± .02
Health	.90 ± .02	.67 ± .05
Intellect	.92 ± .01	.85 ± .03
Neutral	.75 ± .04	.68 ± .05

(Sharp, 1938, p. 118.   By permission of the University of Iowa, *Studies in Child Welfare*.)

a greater consistency between trials for the verbal reaction times than for the motor disturbances, and also for the supposedly affectively toned words than for the neutral words. All reliabilities are so high that chance variations are fairly well ruled out.

The differences among group averages are also interesting, as shown in Illus. 237. Here it appears that average freshman girls in the university had shorter reaction times than either the scholastic failures or the high school girls. Words related to social situations caused the longest reaction times and also the greatest somatic disturbances among the average college freshmen, whereas words related to intellectual situations produced these effects among the

ILLUS. 237. GROUP MEANS OF REACTION TIME AND
SOMATIC DISTURBANCES

Category	Reaction Time (Sec.)			Somatic Disturbances		
	GROUP: 1	2	3	GROUP: 1	2	3
Family	1.79	1.99	2.10	2.56	1.69	2.73
Social	2.14	2.14	2.55	6.58	4.17	4.23
Religious	1.60	2.25	2.43	2.78	3.25	2.73
Health	1.54	2.07	2.39	1.78	2.42	3.97
Intellect	1.88	2.12	3.00	3.62	2.90	13.73
Neutral	1.57	1.95	2.05	1.06	1.55	1.00

NOTE: Group 1. College Freshman Women
Group 2. High School Girls
Group 3. College Women Scholastic Failures and Stutterers

(After Sharp, 1938, p. 121. By permission of the University of Iowa, *Studies in Child Welfare*.)

scholastic failures. The high school girls showed more verbal and nonverbal blocking from words concerned with religion and social activities. Individual profiles indicated quite clearly the existence of particular regions of stress which were in some cases not previously diagnosed.

Lie Detectors

The use of laboratory methods for the detection of lying has become fairly common in police groups. Early work by Larson and Marsden has grown today into fairly well-established practices which often result in confessions, thus avoiding expensive court trials. The usual procedure secures records of physiological responses during a period of interrogation. If peculiar responses are noted, deception is suspected. The responses most often measured are breathing, pulse, blood pressure, and electrical skin resistance, sometimes called the psychogalvanic reflex. Changes in these responses are recorded mechanically after each stimulus question or situation. A good appraisal of this technique is given by Larson and Haney (1932) and by Marsden (1948). Inhau (1946) gave a critical discussion of lie detectors and estimated that the best methods and technicians probably gave accurate results in only 75 per cent of the cases. Bitterman and Marcus (1947) made respiratory and cardiac tracings with a Keeler Polygraph on eighty-one men in a college dormitory where one hundred dollars had been stolen. They reported that the respiratory tracings did not yield a differential classification. From the cardiovascular data three general classes of persons appeared: (*a*) negligible to all questions, (*b*) significant to all questions, or (*c*) different reactions to relevant and irrelevant questions.

Reliability and Validity

The reliabilities reported in various ways are well illustrated by Illus. 238. This shows that two similar forms of measures of deception gave high correlations in all the tests of cheating by scoring one's own paper. Peeping when the eyes should be shut, faking a solution to a puzzle, and getting help from a dictionary were more variable activities. Hartshorne and May (1930) reported that separate meas-

ILLUS. 238. RELIABILITIES OF TECHNIQUES USED FOR MEASURING DECEPTION

Types of Conduct	1*	2†
1. Copying from a key or answer sheet (3 tests)	.871	.863
2. Copying from a key or answer sheet (duplicating technique)(7 tests)	.825	
3. Adding on more scores (6 speed tests)	.825	.887
4. Peeping when eyes should be shut (3 co-ordination tests)	.721	.750
5. Faking a solution to a puzzle (3 tests)	.750	
(2 tests: Pegs and Fifteen Puzzle)	.620	
6. Faking a score in a physical ability test (4 tests)	.772	
7. Lying to win approval	.836	
8. Getting help from a dictionary or from some person on one test done at home		.240

* The correlations in this column are based on intercorrelations between similar forms, and predicted by the Spearman-Brown formula.
† The correlations in this column are based on retests.

(Hartshorne and May, 1928, p. 136. By permission of the Macmillan Co.)

ures of Service showed retest reliabilities near .90, but that the combined measures showed odd-even correlations between six sub-batteries of only .78. The Moral Knowledge Tests showed a high correlation between two vocabulary forms, .94, but the Opinion tests showed less consistency because, in part, of smaller numbers of items and shorter times. When items and time were held constant all of these tests had high and similar reliability. Opinion Battery A showed considerably less consistency than Battery B, probably owing to the length of the tests.

These results emphasize the fact that consistent behavior is more evident in large samples of items than in small, because of the elimination of errors of measurement and of individual variations. Under the best conditions self-ratings, conduct measures, and ratings by teachers of other pupils are nearly as reliable as are measures of skills, and all have high reliabilities when enough items are combined.

Definite answers can be given to questions of validity only when some true criterion of truth is available. Since there are no very reliable and accepted criteria for most of the traits under consideration, one can only compare various appraisals to see how well they agree. A few comparisons are given below.

Maslow (1937) found from extensive studies of dominance that feelings of dominance as shown by self-ratings and observed dominant behavior were not closely related. Jarvie and Johns (1938) compared ratings on Bernreuter traits for students intimately known by the raters with the actual Bernreuter scores. From the low correlations reported, they concluded that the scores had little value in the solution of adjustment difficulties.

A comparison by three questionnaires of normal adults and mental hospital cases who had been matched for age, schooling, occupations, and mental ability was made by Landis et al. (1935). The results showed that all three questionnaires, the Bernreuter Personality Inventory, the Page Questionnaire of Schizophrenic Traits, and the Woodworth Psychoneurotic Inventory, were not valuable for distinguishing normal from insane persons, although the various types of psychosis showed small differences in scores.

Burnham and Crawford (1935) marked the items on the Bernreuter test 10 times according to a pair of dice. They found that chance marks secured in this fashion yielded fairly high neurotic and introverted scores.

Ratings on the Hagerty-Olson-Wickman Scale by teachers were compared with the results of simply asking teachers to name the boys and girls causing the most trouble in school. Of the lowest 10 per cent of the most poorly adjusted pupils as shown by H–O–W scores, only about half were named by the teachers.

In a boys' camp Newstetter (1937) made a check on the validity of a preferred-associate ballot by actual observation of free time spent with various boys. He found a mean correlation of .73 between the two measures, and also reported that the best-liked boys were not necessarily those who were cordial, but those who had some skill.

A valuable comparison of three types of appraisal was made by Hanks (1936). He secured six judges who read fifty autobiographies of about one thousand words which had been written as part of the requirements of a college freshman English class. Each judge wrote a short analysis of each case showing the main types of responses, and also estimated the scores which had been made on three tests: (1) the Wilke Attitude Scale, (2) the Clark revision of Thurstone's Personality Schedule, and (3) the Deutsch Conformity Tests. The correlations between actual scores and estimates were all low, but slightly higher for the second test than for the other two. In most cases the SD of estimated scores was smaller than the SD of actual scores. In a further investigation Hanks instructed six judges to rate students after reading their autobiographies, using 28 items which concerned family relationships, adjustments in social, religious and economic spheres, and interests. These ratings were compared to self-ratings on the same items. The results showed an average of only 40 per cent correspondence which was raised to 46 per cent when the same judges were instructed in Adler's classification of types according to variations in cooperation and activity. This instruction did not lead to the use of Adler's types by all judges, but it did lead to a more logical and thorough approach to the task.

Hartshorne and May (1930) found that classmates' judgments, shown by a guess-who test of reputation for desirable traits correlated .48 with teachers' judgments as represented by a weighted sum of grades in deportment, a conduct record, and a check list of traits. The teachers' check lists showed a correlation of .84 with the pupils' conduct records, and .49 with their deportment grades.

An inspection of these reports does not result in definite conclusions about the value of the several methods. We find much evidence that two methods designed to measure the same traits usually show positive correlations. These become higher as the appraisals become more similar in procedure and more complete in sampling, and as the groups of persons become larger and more similar in environment. The actual correlations between self-ratings on questionnaires and behavior records are usually low. The correlations between ratings by teachers, counselors, and interviewers and behavior records are often low. The correlations between conduct tests and time-sampling methods are usually moderate. Since all of these appraisals have been shown to have high self-consistency, one must conclude that they are evaluating different aspects of the rater, the ratee, or both. A more analytical approach is needed to discover basic patterns of behavior.

SUMMARY

This chapter has presented a great variety of both content and procedures, and it should be admitted that the techniques are far from being well developed. The variety of possible acts is such as to make observation and recording an extremely complicated affair. This usually results in oversimplifying the observation and the scoring by means of a simple rating scale or check list. These are often found to have serious limitations which are undesirable in the long run, although they may give immediate results of value. An enormous amount of research is needed in order to determine more adequately what independent variables are best observed in particular situations.

STUDY GUIDE QUESTIONS

1. What are the chief advantages and disadvantages of measures based on observation of behavior when the subjects do not know they are being observed?

2. Why were verbal character sketches found to yield more reliable results than studies based on ratings of single items?

3. What are some of the advantages and disadvantages of sociometry?

4. What are the advantages and disadvantages of group interviewing techniques?

5. What are the main assumptions made in using a lie detector?

6. How have laboratory controls been used in studying emotional behavior?

7. Summarize Porter's categories relating to a therapeutic interview.

APPENDIX I

PUBLISHERS OF TESTS AND INVENTORIES

Code numbers used in Appendix II are shown in parentheses after some of the addresses in this bibliography.

Acorn Publishing Co., Inc., Rockville Centre, N.Y.   (13)
American Council on Education, 744 Jackson Place, Washington 6, D.C.
American Foundation for the Blind, Inc., 15 West 16 St., New York 11, N.Y.
American Hearing Society (formerly American Society for the Hard of Hearing), 817 Fourteenth St., N.W., Washington 5, D.C.
American Psychological Association, Inc., 1515 Massachusetts Ave., N.W., Washington 5, D.C.
California Test Bureau, 5916 Hollywood Blvd., Los Angeles 28, Calif.   (1)
Center for Psychological Service, George Washington University, Washington 6, D.C.
College Book Co., 1836 North High St., Columbus, Ohio.
College Entrance Examination Board, Box 592, Princeton, N.J.
Columbia University, Teachers College, Bureau of Publications, New York 27, N.Y.   (11)
Committee on Diagnostic Reading Tests, Kingscote Apt. 39, 419 West 119 St., New York 27, N.Y.   (21)
Cooperative Test Service. Now the Cooperative Test Division, Educational Testing Service, Princeton, N.J.
Educational Records Bureau, 21 Audubon Ave., New York, N.Y.
Educational Test Bureau: Educational Publishers, Inc., 720 Washington Ave., S.E., Minneapolis 14, Minn.   (3)
Educational Testing Service, Princeton, N.J.   (2)
George Washington University, Washington, D.C.   (14)
Graybar Electric Co., 420 Lexington Ave., New York 17, N.Y.

Gregory, C. A., Company   (4)

Hale, E. M. and Company, Eau Claire, Wis.   (15)

Houghton Mifflin Co., 2 Park St., Boston 7, Mass.; 432 Fourth Ave., New York 16, N.Y.   (5)

Institute for Personality and Ability Testing, 313 West Avondale St., Champaign, Ill.

Institute of Living, 200 Retreat Ave., Hartford 2, Conn.

Kansas State Teachers College, Emporia, Kansas.   (16)

Kentucky Cooperative Testing Service, University of Kentucky, Lexington 29, Ky.

McGraw-Hill Book Co., Inc., 333 West 42 St., New York 18, N.Y.

McKnight and McKnight, 109–11 West Market St., Bloomington, Ill.

The Macmillan Co., 60 Fifth Ave., New York 11, N.Y.

Management Service Co., 3136 North 24 St., Philadelphia, Pa.

Marietta Apparatus Co., Marietta, Ohio.

National Office Management Association, 2118 Lincoln-Liberty Bldg., Philadelphia 7, Pa.   (22)

New York State Department of Education, Albany, N.Y. (Regents Examinations)

Ohio Scholarship Tests, Ohio State Department of Education, Columbus 15, Ohio.

Ohio State University, Bureau of Publications, Columbus, Ohio.   (18)

Psychological Corporation, 522 Fifth Ave., New York 18, N.Y.   (7)

Public School Publishing Co., 509–13 North East St., Bloomington, Ill.   (8)

Purdue University, Lafayette, Indiana, Bureau of Publications.   (19)

Science Research Associates, Inc., 228 South Wabash Ave., Chicago 4, Ill.   (9)

Sheridan Supply Co., P.O. Box 387, Beverly Hills, Calif.   (20)

Society for Research on Child Development, National Research Council, 2101 Constitution Ave., Washington 25, D.C.

Stanford University Press, Stanford, Calif.   (10)

State High School Testing Service for Indiana, Division of Educational Reference, Purdue University, Lafayette, Ind.

Steck Company, Austin, Texas.

Stoelting, C. H., Company, 424 North Homan Ave., Chicago 20, Ill.

University of California Press, Berkeley, Calif.

University of Iowa, Iowa City, Iowa, Bureau of Educational Research.   (6)

University of Minnesota Press, Minneapolis 14, Minn.   (17)

Western Reserve University Press, Cleveland, Ohio

World Book Co., 313 Park Hill Ave., Yonkers 5, N.Y.   (12)

Publishers arranged by code numbers:
   (1) California Test Bureau
   (2) Educational Testing Service
   (3) Educational Test Bureau
   (4) C. A. Gregory Company
   (5) Houghton Mifflin Company
   (6) University of Iowa

(7) Psychological Corporation
(8) Public School Publishing Company
(9) Science Research Associates
(10) Stanford University Press
(11) Bureau of Publications, Teachers College, Columbia University
(12) World Book Company
(13) Acorn Publishing Company
(14) George Washington University
(15) E. M. Hale and Company
(16) Kansas State Teachers College
(17) University of Minnesota
(18) Ohio State University
(19) Purdue University
(20) Sheridan Supply Company
(21) Committee on Diagnostic Reading Tests
(22) National Office Management Association

APPENDIX II

CLASSIFIED LIST OF TESTS AND INVENTORIES *

~~~~~~

Each test title is followed by:
   a. A Roman numeral which indicates the general type of test.
   b. An Arabic number which shows the subject matter or method.
   c. A number or numbers in parentheses which show the grade or age levels covered by the test.
   d. Numbers which represent the publishers listed in Appendix I.
   e. Numbers in italics (where given) which indicate pages in this text.
The following lists give the classification structure in detail:
   A. *Main Types*
       I. Achievement
       II. Aptitude
       III. Intelligence
       IV. Interest
       V. Adjustment and Attitude
   B. *Subject Matter for Achievement and Aptitude Tests*
       1. Applied Science
       2. Arithmetic
       3. Art
       4. Batteries of Tests
       5. Business
       6. English
       7. French
       8. German

* Adapted from Test Service Notebook No. 6, "Organization of a Test Library in a School of Education," by W. N. Durost and M. E. Allen, by permission of Dr. Durost and the World Book Co.

9. Handwriting
10. Health
11. Home Economics
12. Italian
13. Language
14. Latin
15. Library Skills
16. Mathematics
17. Music and Sound
18. Natural Science
19. Reading
20. Social Studies
21. Spanish
22. Spelling
23. Teaching Skills
24. Vocational Skills
25. Miscellaneous
Types of Tests for Intelligence
1. Group
2. Individual
Types of Tests for Adjustment and Attitude
1. Inventories
2. Projective Techniques
C. *Grade or Age*
1. Below Grade 1; 1–5 years
2. Grades 1, 2, 3; 6–9 years
3. Grades 4, 5, 6; 10–12 years
4. Grades 7, 8, 9; 13–15 years
5. Grades 10, 11, 12; 16–18 years
6. College or more; 19 or more years
D. For index of publishers see Appendix I. In the list below only the largest publishers are represented by numbers, others are identified by name.

For example, a test title followed by II-5 (4, 5, 6) 12, is an aptitude test in the field of business for persons more than twelve years old published by the World Book Co. The title gives additional information on test content, e.g., Turse Shorthand Aptitude Test. The list of tests follows:

I. ACHIEVEMENT

Applied Science

Cooperative Pre-Flight Aeronautics Tests
1. Aerodynamics and Aircraft Structures   I-1(5,6)2
2. Aircraft Engines   I-1(5,6)2
3. Meteorology (*see Natural Science*)
4. Navigation   I-1(5,6)2
5. Radio and Communications   I-1(5,6)2

Applied Science Cont'd

Arithmetic

Batteries of Tests Cont'd

Form C, Division 2   I-4(3)3
Form C, Division 3   I-4(4)3
Minimum Essential Battery, Form A, Division 1   I-4(3)3
Minimum Essential Battery, Form A, Division 2   I-4(3)3
Minimum Essential Battery, Form A, Division 3   I-4(4)3
Minimum Essential Battery, Form B, Division 2   I-4(3)3
Minimum Essential Battery, Form B, Division 3   I-4(4)3
Minimum Essential Battery, Form C, Division 1   I-4(3)3
Minimum Essential Battery, Form C, Division 2   I-4(3)3
Minimum Essential Battery, Form C, Division 3   I-4(4)3
Primary Division, Form A, Grade 1, first half   I-4(2)3
Primary Division, Form A, Grade 1, last half   I-4(1)3
Primary Division, Form A, Grade 2, first half   I-4(2)3
Primary Division, Form A, Grade 3   I-4(2)3
Primary Division, Form B, Grade 1, first half   I-4(1)3
Primary Division, Form B, Grade 2, last half   I-4(2)3
Primary Division, Form B, Grade 3   I-4(2)3
Primary Division, Form C, Grade 1, first half   I-4(1)3
Primary Division, Form C, Grade 1, last half   I-4(1)3
Primary Division, Form C, Grade 2, last half   I-4(2)3
Primary Division, Form C, Grade 3   I-4(2)3

Business

Blackstone Stenographic Proficiency Tests, Stenography   I-5(6)12
  Typewriting   I-5(6)12
Bookkeeping Test (Indiana High School Tests)   I-5(5)19
Breidenbaugh Bookkeeping Tests, Test 1   I-5(5)8
Breidenbaugh Bookkeeping Tests, Test 2   I-5(5)8
Breidenbaugh Bookkeeping Tests, Test 3   I-5(5)8
Breidenbaugh Bookkeeping Tests, Test 4   I-5(5)8
Clerical Perception Test   I-5(4,5)3
Elwell-Fowlkes Bookkeeping Test   I-5(5)12
General Test of Business Information   I-5(4,5,6)16
Hiett Stenography Test (Gregg), Test I   I-5(5)16
Hiett Stenography Test (Gregg), Test II   I-5(5)16
Kauzer Typewriting Tests, Test I   I-5(5)16
Kauzer Typewriting Tests, Test II   I-5(5)12
Kimberly-Clark Typing Ability Analysis   I-5(5)9
NOMA Bookkeeping Test   I-5(5)22
NOMA Business Fundamentals and General Information   I-5(4,5)22
NOMA Filing Test   I-5(4,5)22
NOMA Machine Calculation Test   I-5(5)22
Parke Commercial Law Test   I-5(5,6)16
Parke Commercial Law Test   I-5(5)6
Shemwell-Whitcraft Bookkeeping Test—I   I-5(5)16

Latin Cont'd

Godsey Latin Composition Test   I-14(4,5)12
Holtz Vergil Test   I-14(5)16
Hutchinson Latin Grammar Scale   I-14(5)8
Kansas First-Year and Second-Year Latin Tests   I-14(5)16
Power's Diagnostic Latin Test   I-14(4,5)8
Ullman-Kirby Latin Comprehension Test, I   I-14(5,6)1
Ullman-Kirby Latin Comprehension Test, II   I-14(5,6)11
White Latin Test   I-14(5,6)12

Library Skills

Library Test for Junior High Schools   I-15(4)1
Peabody Library Information Test, College   I-14(6)3
Peabody Library Information Test, Elementary   I-15(3,4)3
Peabody Library Information Test, High School   I-15(5)3

Mathematics (General)

Cooperative College Mathematics Test   I-16(6)2
Cooperative General Mathematics Test   I-16(5)2
Cooperative Mathematics Pre-Test for College Students   I-16(6)2
Cooperative Mathematics Test   I-16(4)2
Cooperative Test in Secondary School Mathematics   I-16(5)2
Foust-Schorling Test of Functional Thinking   I-16(5,6)12
Junior High School Mathematics Test:
    Acorn Achievement Tests   I-16(4,5)13
Progressive Mathematics Test, Advanced   I-16(5,6)1   *177, 178*
Progressive Mathematics Test, Advanced, machine scoring   I-16(5,6)1
Purdue Industrial Mathematics Test   I-16(5)19
Rasmussen General Mathematics Test   I-16(5,6)16
Rogers Achievement Test in Mathematics   I-16(5)7
USAFI Tests of General Educational Development
    Test 5:General Mathematical Ability   I-16(5)2

Mathematics (Algebra)

Breslich Algebra Survey Test:First Semester   I-16(5)8
Breslich Algebra Survey Test:Second Semester   I-16(5)8
Columbia Research Bureau Algebra Test, 1   I-16(5,6)12   *191*
Columbia Research Bureau Algebra Test, 2   I-16(5)12
Colvin-Schrammel Algebra Test, Tests I and II   I-16(5)16
Cooperative Algebra Test—Elementary Algebra through Quadratics
    I-16(4,5)2
Cooperative Intermediate Algebra Test   I-16(5)2
Garman-Schrammel Third Semester Algebra Test   I-16(5)16
Survey Test in Elementary Algebra, Douglas   I-16(5)3
USAFI Elementary Algebra   I-16(5)2
USAFI Second-Year Algebra   I-16(5)2

Mathematics (Calculus)

USAFI Calculus II—Integral Calculus   I-16(6)2
USAFI Differential Calculus   I-16(6)2

Mathematics (Geometry)

American Council Solid Geometry Test, Form A   I-16(5,6)12   *193*
American Council Solid Geometry Test, Form B   I-16(5,6)12
Becker-Schrammel Plane Geometry Test   I-16(5)16
Columbia Research Bureau Plane Geometry Test   I-16(5,6)12
Cooperative Plane Geometry Test   I-16(5)2
Cooperative Solid Geometry Test   I-16(5)2   *193*
Lane-Greene Unit Tests in Plane Geometry   I-16(5)6
Orleans Plane Geometry Achievement Test, 1   I-16(5,6)12
Orleans Plane Geometry Achievement Test, 2   I-16(5,6)12
Survey Test in Plane Geometry   I-16(5)3
USAFI Analytic Geometry   I-16(6)2
USAFI Plane Geometry   I 16(5)2

Mathematics (Trigonometry)

American Council Trigonometry Test   I-16(5,6)12   *193*
Cooperative Trigonometry Test   I-16(5)2
USAFI Plane Trigonometry   I-16(5,6)2

Music and Sound

Beach Music Test   I-17(3,4,5,6)16
Drake Musical Memory Test:Test of Musical Talent, A   I-17(2,3,4)8
Drake Musical Memory Test:Test of Musical Talent, B   I-17(2,3,4)8
Knuth Achievement Tests in Music, Form A, 1   I-17(2,3)3
Knuth Achievement Tests in Music, Form A, 2   I-17(3)3
Knuth Achievement Tests in Music, Form A, 3   I-17(4,5)3
Knuth Achievement Tests in Music, Form B, 1   I-17(2,3)3
Kwalwasser Test of Music Information and Appreciation   I-17(4,5,6)6   *302*
Kwalwasser-Dykema Music Tests   I-17(4,5,6)   *301*
Kwalwasser-Ruch Test of Musical Accomplishment   I-17(3,4,5)6   *303*
Musical Achievement Test   I-17(3,4)11
Providence Inventory Test in Music   I-17(3,4)12
Seashore Measures of Musical Talents, Revised Edition   I 17(3,4,5,6)   *301, 305, 307*
Strouse Music Test   I-17(3,4,5,6)16
Western Electric Audiometer, Graybar Electric Co.   I-17(2,3,4,5,6)   *299*

Natural Science (General)

Analytical Scales of Attainment, Division 3   I-18(4)3
Analytical Scales of Attainment, Elementary Science   I-18(4)3
Calvert Science Information Test, Elementary   I-18(3)1

Natural Science (Geology)

Cooperative Geology Test:Historical Geology   I-18(6)2
Cooperative Geology Test:Physical Geology   I-18(6)2

Natural Science (Meteorology)

Cooperative Pre-Flight Aeronautics Tests·
    Test 3:Meteorology   I-18(5,6)2
USAFI Meteorology   I-18(5)2

Natural Science (Physics)

Columbia Research Bureau Physics Test   I-18(5,6)12
Cooperative Physics Test for College Students   I-18(6)2   *194*
Cooperative Physics Test, High School   I-18(5)2
Fulton-Schrammel Physics Test, I   I-18(5)16
Fulton-Schrammel Physics Test, II   I-18(5)16
Iowa Achievement Examination in College Physics   I-18(6)6
USAFI Physics, College, Sections I, II   I-18(6)2
USAFI Physics, College, Section III   I-18(6)2
USAFI Physics, High School   I-18(5)2

Reading

Chapman-Cook Speed of Reading Test, Forms A and B   I-19(3,4)3   *184*
Chicago Reading Tests, Test A   I-19(2)15
Chicago Reading Tests, Test B   I-19(2,3)15
Chicago Reading Tests, Test C   I-19(3)15
Chicago Reading Tests, Test D   I-19(3,4)15
Cooperative Vocabulary Test   I-19(4,5,6)2
Detroit Reading Test, Test I   I-19(2)12
Detroit Word Recognition Test   I-19(2)12d
Devault Primary Reading Test   I-19(2)1
Diagnostic Examination of Silent Reading Ability, Intermediate
    I-19(3)3
Diagnostic Examination of Silent Reading Ability, Junior   I-19(3,4)3
Diagnostic Examination of Silent Reading Ability, Senior   I-19(5)3
Diagnostic Reading Tests:Diagnostic Battery, Vocabulary   I-19(4,5,6)21
Diagnostic Reading Tests:Diagnostic Battery, Comprehension
    I-19(4,5,6)21
Diagnostic Reading Tests:Diagnostic Battery, Rates of Reading
    I-19(4,5,6)21
Diagnostic Reading Tests:Diagnostic Battery, Word Attention
    I-19(4,5,6)21
Diagnostic Reading Tests:Survey Test   I-19(4,5,6)21
Durrell Analysis of Reading Difficulty   I-19(2,3)12
Durrell-Sullivan Reading Achievement, Intermediate   I-19(2,3)12
Durrell-Sullivan Reading Capacity and Achievement, Primary
    I-19(2,3)12

Social Studies (General) Cont'd.

Cooperative Test of Social Studies Ability   I-20(5)2
Progressive Tests in Related Sciences, Elementary   I-20(3,4)1
Stanford Achievement Test:Social Studies   I-20(3,4)12
USAFI General Educational Development
  Test 2:Interpretation of Reading Materials in Social Studies College
    Level, Form B   I-20(6)2
  High School Level, Form B   I-20(5)2

Social Studies (Civics)

Brown-Woody Civics Test   I-20(4,5)12
Burton Civics Test   I-20(3,4)12
Cooperative American Government Test   I-30(5)2
Cooperative Community Affairs Test   I-20(5)2
Mordy-Schrammel Civics Test   I-20(4)16
Mordy-Schrammel Constitution Test   I-20(5,6)16
USAFI Civics   I-20(5)2
USAFI Problems of Democracy   I-20(5)2

Social Studies (Economics)

Cooperative Economics Test   I-20(5,6)2

Social Studies (History)

American History Tests:National Achievement Tests   I-20(4)13
Cooperative American History Test   I-20(5,6)2   *197*
Cooperative Ancient History Test   I-20(5)2
Junior American History Test   I-20(4)12
Kansas American History Tests I and II   I-20(5)16
Kansas Modern European History Tests I and II   I-20(5)16
Kniss World History Test   I-20(5)12
Public School Achievement Tests:History   I-20(3,4)8
Reading Scales in History, Forms A and B   I-20(4,5)3
Taylor-Schrammel World History Test   I-20(5,6)16
USAFI American History   I-20(5,6)2
USAFI Modern European   I-20(5,6)2
USAFI World History   I-20(5)2

Spanish

Columbia Research Bureau Spanish Test   I-21(5,6)12
Cooperative Spanish Test, Advanced   I-21(5,6)2
Cooperative Spanish Test, Elementary   I-21(5,6)2
Cooperative Spanish Test, Higher Level   I-21(5,6)2
Cooperative Spanish Test, Lower Level   I-21(5,6)2
USAFI Spanish Grammar   I-21(5)2
USAFI Spanish Reading Comprehension   I-21(5)2
USAFI Spanish Vocabulary   I-21(5)2

Business

Clerical Aptitude Tests   II-5(4,5,6)13
Detroit Clerical Aptitudes Examination   II-5(5)8
ERC Stenographic Aptitude Test   II-5(5,6)9
Minnesota Clerical Test   II-5(4,5,6)7   *23, 376*
Psychological Corporation General Clerical Test   II-5(4,5)7   *158, 203*
SRA Clerical Aptitude   II-5(5,6)9   *203*
SRA Dictation Skills   II-5(4,5)9   *203*
SRA Language Skills, Stenographers   II-5(4,5)9   *203*
Stenographic Aptitude Test   II-5(4,5,6)7   *203*
Turse Shorthand Aptitude Test   II-5(4,5)12

Latin

Orleans-Solomon Latin Prognosis Test   II-14(5,6)12

Mathematics

California Algebra Aptitude Test, Keys   II-16(4,5)3
Iowa Algebra Aptitude Test   II-16(4,5)6
Iowa Plane Geometry Aptitude Test   II-16(4,5)6
Lee Test of Algebraic Ability   II-16(4)8
Lee Test of Geometric Aptitude   II-16(5,6)1
Orleans Algebra Prognosis Test   II-16(4,5)12
Orleans Geometry Prognosis Test   II-16(5,6)12

Reading Readiness

Betts Ready-to-Read Tests, Keystone View Co., Meadville, Pa.   II-19(1,2)
     102
Gates Reading Readiness Tests   II-19(1,2)11
Lee-Clark Reading Readiness Test   II-19(1,2)1
Metropolitan Readiness Tests   II-19(1,2)12   *99*
Monroe Reading Aptitude Test   II-19(2)5   *100*
Murphy-Durrell Diagnostic Reading Readiness Test   II-19(1,2)12
Stevens Reading Readiness Test   II-19(1,2)12
Van Wagenen Reading Readiness Test   II-19(1)3

Teaching Skills

Coxe-Orleans Prognosis Test of Teaching Ability   II-23(5,6)12
Stanford Educational Aptitude Test   II-23(6)10

Vocational Skills

Acorn Mechanical Aptitude Tests   II-24(4,5,6)13
Bennett Hand-Tool Dexterity Test   II-24(4,5,6)7
Detroit Mechanical Aptitude Examination   II-24(4,5,6)8   *30*
Detroit Retail Selling Inventory   II-24(5,6)8
Dynamometer, Stoelting   II-24(4,5,6)   *21*
Eames Eye Test   II-24(3,4,5,6)12   *298*

III. INTELLIGENCE

1. Group

1. *Group Cont'd*

Henmon-Nelson Mental Ability, College, A   III-1(6)5
Henmon Nelson Mental Ability, College, B   III-1(6)5
Henmon-Nelson Mental Ability, Elementary   III-1(2,3,4)5
Henmon-Nelson Mental Ability, High School   III-1(4,5)5
Inductive Reasoning Test   III-1(5,6)3
Junior Scholastic Aptitude Test, Educational Records Bureau   III-1(4)
Kent Series of Emergency Scales   III-1(1,2,3,4)7
Kuhlmann-Anderson Tests, Grade 1–1   III-1(2)3   *323*
Kuhlmann-Anderson Tests, Grade 1–2   III-1(2)3
Kuhlmann-Anderson Tests, Grade 2   III-1(2)3
Kuhlmann-Anderson Tests, Grade 3   III-1(2)3
Kuhlmann-Anderson Tests, Grade 4   III-1(3)3
Kuhlmann-Anderson Tests, Grade 5   III-1(3)3
Kuhlmann-Anderson Tests, Grade 6   III-1(3)3
Kuhlmann-Anderson Tests, Grades 7–8   III-1(4)3
Kuhlmann Anderson Tests, Grades 9 and up   III-1(4,5,6)3
Langmuir Oral Directions Test   III-1(4,5,6)7   *226*
Miller Mental Ability Test, Form A   III-1(4,5,6)12
Modified Alpha Examination, Form 9   III-1(4,5,6)7
Multi-Mental Scale   III-1(2,3,4,5,6)11
National Intelligence Tests, Scale A, Form 1   III-1(2,3,4)12
New California Short-Form Test of Mental Maturity
    Advanced   III-1(4,5,6)1
    Advanced, machine scoring   III-1(4,5,6)1
    Elementary   III-1(3,4)1
    Intermediate   III-1(4,5,6)1
    Intermediate, machine scoring   III-1(4,5,6)1
    Pre-Primary   III-1(4,5,6)1
    Primary   III-1(2)1
Non-Language Multi-Mental Test, Form A   III-1(3,4,5,6)11
Non-Language Multi-Mental Test, Form B   III-1(3,4,5,6)11
O'Rourke General Classification Test   III-1(5,6)   *227*
Ohio State University Psychological Test   III-1(5,6)18
Otis Classification Test (Revised)   III-1(3,4)12   *226*
Otis Classification Test for Industrial and Office Personnel, Western
    Reserve University Press   III-1(4,5,6)
Otis Employment Tests, Tests 1 and 2   III 1(6)12
Otis Group Intelligence Scale, Advanced   III-1(3,4,5,6)12
Otis Quick-Scoring Mental Ability Test
    Alpha, Form A   III-1(2,3)12
    Beta, Form A   III-1(3,4)12
    Beta, Form Cm   III-1(3,4)12
    Beta, Form Dm   III-1(3,4)12
    Gamma, Form Am   III-1(5,6)12
    Gamma, Form C   III-1(5,6)12

2. *Individual Cont'd*

IV. INTEREST

2. *Projective Techniques Cont'd*

Hurlock Spontaneous Drawings of Adolescents. *Journal of Genetic Psychology,* 69, 97–120 (1941)   V-2(3,4,5)

Kent-Rosanoff Free Association Test, Wiley   V-2(3,4,5)   *34*

Machover Draw-a-Person Test, C. C. Thomas, Springfield, Ill.
V-2(1,2,3,4,5,6)   *483, 485*

Mira Motor Gestalt (MYOKINETIC)   V-2(3,4,5,6)   *480, 481*

Napoli Finger Painting, *Genetic Phychology Monographs,* 34, 129–231
V-2(1,2,3,4,5,6)   *486, 487*

Apperception

Lowenfield Mosaic Test   V-2(1,2,3,4,5,6)7   *482*

Rorschach Test, Hans Huber, Bern   V-2(1,2,3,4,5,6)   *669–689*

Rorschach Group Test, Harrower and author   V-2(4,5,6)   *673–677*

Stern Cloud Pictures, Character and Personality, 6, 132–46 (1938)
V-2(1,2,3,4,5,6)

Szondi Test, Deri, Hans Huber, Bern   V-2(3,4,5,6)7   *529*

Twitchell Three-Dimension Apperception Test   V-2(1,2,3,4,5,6)7   *545*

Stories, Themes

Blacky Test, Blum   V-2(2,3,4,5,6)7   *522, 524*

Buhler and Kelly World Test   V-2(1,2,3,4,5)7   *540*

Cattell-Luborsky Humor Personality Test Instructions for Personality
and Ability Testing   V-2(4,5,6)   *648, 649*

Despert Fables Test, *Psychology Quarterly,* 10 (1936)   V-2(1,2,3,4,5,6)
521

Group Projection Sketches, Henry and Guetzkow, Chicago University
Book Store   V-2(4,5,6)   *525–529*

Haggarc Comic Strip Characters, Character and Personality, 10, 289–
295   V-2(1,2,3,4,5,6)

Make-a-Picture Story Test MAPS, Shneidman, *Genetic Psychology Monographs,* 32, No. 2   V-2(2,3,4,5)7   *542–545*

Murray Thematic Apperception Test, Harvard University Press
V-2(4,5,6)   *503–515*

Proverbs Test, Rabin and Boida, *Journal of Consulting Psychology,* 12,
246–250   V-2(3,4,5,6)   *534*

Rosenzweig Picture Frustration Test, author   V-2(3,4,5)   *576*

Sargent Insight into Human Motives Test, *Psychological Monographs,*
57, No. 5 (1944)   V-2(4,5,6)   *518–520*

Sentence Completion, Rohde-Hildreth, *Journal of Applied Psychology,*
175 (1946)   V-2(2,3,4,5,6)   *533*

Sentence Completion, Rotter and Willerman, *Journal of Consulting
Psychology,* 11, 43–48, and author   V-2(3,4,5,6)   *534*

Sentence Completion, Shor, *Journal of Clinical Psychology,* 2, 279–82
V-2(4,5,6)   *534*

Symonds Picture Story Test   V-2(3,4)11   *515*

INDEX OF AUTHORS

~~~~~~

The author of this book acknowledges his indebtedness to the authors and publishers of the following works. Wherever substantial quotations have been used, page references appear in the appropriate places.

Page numbers for this text are printed in italics at the end of each reference. These numbers refer only to the beginnings of the discussions, although in some cases the discussion covers several pages.

List of Abbreviations

Abn.	Abnormal	Elem.	Elementary
Acad.	Academy	Empl.	Employment
Acoust.	Acoustical	Engl.	English
Am.	American *or* America	Examin.	Examination
Anthro.	Anthropological	Exch.	Exchange
Appl.	Applied	Exp.	Experimental
Arch.	Archives	Fact.	Factory
Assn.	Association	Found.	Foundation
Bull.	Bulletin	Gen.	General
Brit.	British	Genet.	Genetics
Bur.	Bureau	Govt.	Government
Cath.	Catholic	Hered.	Heredity
Char.	Character	Inst.	Institute
Clin.	Clinic *or* Clinical	J.	Journal
Col.	College	Juv.	Juvenile
Comp.	Comparative	Mainten.	Maintenance
Consult.	Consulting	Mgmt.	Management
Contrib.	Contribution	Math.	Mathematics
Corp.	Corporation	Meas.	Measurement
Delinq.	Delinquency	Med.	Medical
Dept.	Department	Ment.	Mental
Devel.	Development	Minn.	Minnesota
Dis.	Diseases	Mo.	Monthly
Ed.	Education	Monog.	Monograph

Mus.	Music	Pub.	Publication *or* Publishing
Musicol.	Musicological	Q.	Quarterly
Nat.	National	Rec.	Record
Nerv.	Nervous	Rep.	Report
Neur.	Neurology	Res.	Research
No.	Number	Rev.	Review
Off.	Office	Roy.	Royal
Ophthal.	Ophthalmology	Sch.	School
Ped.	Pedagogical	Sci.	Science
Pediat.	Pediatrics	Sem.	Seminary
Pers.	Personnel *or* Personality	Soc.	Society
Philos.	Philosophy	Sociol.	Sociology
Physiol.	Physiological	Stud.	Studies
Pop.	Popular	Suppl.	Supplement
Print.	Printing	Surg.	Surgery *or* Surgical
Proc.	Proceedings	Teach.	Teachers
Psychiat.	Psychiatry	Univ.	University
Psychol.	Psychology *or* Psychological	Yr.	Year

ADAMS, C.R., AND LEPLEY, W. M. (1941–46) Personal audit. Science Research Associates. Form and Manual. *634*

ADAMS, H. F. (1927) The good judge of personality. J. Abn. and Social Psychol., 1, 122–135. *471*

——. (1936) Validity, reliability, and objectivity. Psychol. Monog., 47, 329–350. *470, 471*

ADKINS, D. C. (1940) The relation of primary mental abilities to vocational choice. Am. Council on Ed. Studies, Psychol. Examin. 1939 Series 5, IV, No. 2, 39–53. Am. Council on Ed., Washington, D.C. *253*

ALLPORT, G. W. (1928) A test for ascendance-submission. J. Abn. and Social Psychol., 23, 118–136. *635*

——. (1937) Personality: a psychological interpretation. Henry Holt, N.Y. Pp. 588. *426*

ALLPORT, G. W., AND VERNON, P. E. (1931) A test for personal values. J. Abn. and Social Psychol., 26, 231–248. *607, 609, 610*

ALSCHULER, R. H., AND HATTWICK, L. B. W. (1947) Painting and personality. Univ. of Chicago Press. *487*

ANASTASI, A., AND FOLEY, J. P. (1936) Analysis of spontaneous drawings by children of different cultures. J. Appl. Psychol., 20, 689–726. *317*

ANDERSON, H. H., BREWER, J. E., AND REED, M. F. (1946) Studies of teachers' classroom personalities, III. Appl. Psychol. Monog. No. 11. Pp. 156. *692*

ANDERSON, H. R., AND LINDQUIST, E. F. (1949) Selected test items in American history. Second Edition. Nat. Council for Social Studies, Bull. No. 6 revised. Nat. Ed. Assn., Washington, D.C. Pp. 113. *198*

ANDERSON, J. E. (1935) The effect of item analysis upon the discriminative power of an examination. J. Appl. Psychol., 19, 237–244. *59*

ANDERSON, W. A. (1934) Occupational attitudes of college men. J. Social Psychol., 5, 435–465. *557*

ANDREW, D. M., AND BIRD C. (1938) A comparison of two new type questions, recall and recognition. J. Ed. Psychol., 29, 175–193. *73*

ANDREW, D. M., PATERSON, D. G., AND LONGSTAFF, H. P. (1933) Minnesota vocational test for clerical workers. The Psychol. Corp., N.Y. *23*

ARTHUR, GRACE. (1930) A point scale of performance tests. Commonwealth Fund. Pp. 82. *144*

ASCH, S. E. (1936) A study of change in mental organization. Arch. Psychol., No. 195. Pp. 30. *214*

BIDDLE, W. W. (1931) The relationship between knowledge and a measure of autistic thinking on certain international problems. J. Social Psychol., 2, 493–496. *621*

——. (1932) Propaganda and education. Contrib. to Ed., Teach. Col., Columbia Univ. Press, No. 531. *617*

BILLS, A. G. (1937) Fatigue in mental work. Physiol. Rev., 17, 436–453, *281*

BINET, A. (1898) La mésure en psychologie individuelle. Revue Philosophique, 46, 2d Sem., 113–123. *113*

——. (1900) Attention et adaptation. L'Année Psychologique, 6, 248–404. *113*

BINGHAM, W. V. (1937) Aptitudes and aptitude testing. Harper, N.Y. Pp. 390. *38, 712*

BIRD, M. H. (1932) A study in aesthetics. Harvard Univ. Press, Cambridge, Mass. Pp. 117. *311, 322*

BIRKHOFF, G. D. (1933) Aesthetic measure. Harvard Univ. Press, Cambridge, Mass. Pp. 226. *303*

BISBEE, E. U. (1933) Commercial education survey tests: Junior and senior shorthand. Public Sch. Pub. Co., Bloomington, Ill. *202*

BITTERMAN, M. E., AND MARCUSE, F. L. (1947) Cardio-vascular responses of innocent persons to criminal investigation. Am. J. Psychol., 60, 407–412. *726*

BLACKSTONE, E. G. (1923) Blackstone stenographic proficiency tests: Typewriting test. World Book Co., Yonkers, N.Y. *201*

BLACKSTONE, E. G., AND McLAUGHLIN, M. W. (1932) Blackstone stenographic proficiency tests: Stenography test. World Book Co., Yonkers, N.Y. *203*

BLUM, G. S. (1949) A study of psychoanalytic theory of psychosexual development. Genetic Psychol. Monog., 39, 3–102. *522, 524*

BOBERTAG, O. (1912) Über Intelligenzprufungen nach der Methode von Binet und Simon. Zeitschrift fur angewandte Psychologie, 5, 495–538. *115*

BOLANOVICH, D. J. (1948) Interest tests reduce factory turnover. Pers. Psychol., 1, 81–93. *579*

BOLANOVICH, D. J., AND GOODMAN, C. H. (1944) A study of the Kuder preference records. Ed. and Psychol. Meas., 4, 315–325. *577*

BOLGAR, H., AND FISCHER, L. K. (1947) Personality projection in the world test. Am. J. Orthopsychiatry, 17, 117–128. *540*

BOLTON, E. B. (1935) Effect of knowledge upon attitudes toward the negro. J. Social Psychol., 6, 68–90. *621*

BOVARD, J. F., AND COZENS, F. W. (1938) Tests and measurements in physical education. Saunders. Pp. 427. *276*

BRANDT, H. F. (1937) A logical decision test: an indirect approach to the study of the emotional orientation of the adolescent. University of Iowa Study in Child Welfare Studies in Emotional Adjustment, 13, No. 4, 9–24. *606*

BRAY, C. W. (1948) Psychology and military proficiency. Princeton Univ. Press. Pp. 243. *328*

BREIDENBAUGH, U. E. (1940) Breidenbaugh bookkeeping tests. Public Sch. Pub. Co., Bloomington, Ill. *204*

BRENNAN, F. M. (1926) The relation between musical capacity and performance. Psychol. Monog., 36, No. 167, 190–248. *301*

BRODY, W., AND POWELL, N. J. (1947) A new approach to oral testing. Ed. and Psychol. Meas., 7, 289–298. *711, 714, 716*

BROGDEN, H. E. (1940) A factor analysis of forty character tests. Psychol. Monog., 52, No. 3, 39–56. *659*

BROWN, WM., AND THOMSON, G. H. (1925) The essentials of mental measurement. Univ. Press, Cambridge, England. Pp. 216. *56*

BROWNELL, W. A. (1946) The measurement of understanding. Nat. Soc. Study of Ed., 45th Yearbook. Univ. of Chicago Press. Pp. 338. *156*

BUCKINGHAM, B. R. (1927) Extension

of the Ayres spelling scale. Public Sch. Pub. Co., Bloomington, Ill. *179*

BUCKINGHAM, G. E., AND DOLCH, E. W. (1936) Combined word list. Ginn, Boston. Pp. 185. *165*

BUCKINGHAM, G. E., AND LEE, R. E. (1936) A technique for testing unified concepts in science. J. Ed. Res., 30, 20–27. *194*

BUHLER, C., BUHLER, K., AND LEFEVER, D. W. (1948) Rorschach standardization studies, No. 1. Published by the authors. *678, 679, 680, 681*

BUHLER, C., AND KELLEY, G. (1941) The world test; a measurement of emotional disturbance. Psychol. Corp., N.Y. Manual and materials. *540*

BUHLER, C., *et al.* (1939) The child and his family. Harper, N.Y. Pp. viii + 187. *705*

BULLOUGH, E. (1910) The perceptive problem in the aesthetic appreciation of simple color combinations. Brit. J. Psychol., III, 406–447. *314*

BURK, F. (1902) The genetic versus the logical order in drawing. Ped. Sem., 9, 296–323. *483*

BURNHAM, P. S., AND CRAWFORD, A. B. (1935) The vocational interests and personality test scores of a pair of dice. J. Ed. Psychol., 26, 508–512. *728*

BUROS, O. K. The 1948 mental measurements yearbook, 1, 200. Rutgers Univ. Press, New Brunswick, N.J. *7*

BURT, C. (1947) Factor analysis and physical types. Psychometrika, 12, 171–188. *435*

——. (1909) Experimental tests of general intelligence. Brit. J. Psychol. 3, 94–177. *222*

——. (1922) Mental and scholastic tests. P. S. King and Son, Ltd., London. Pp. 432. *124, 126, 131*

——. (1938) Analysis of temperament. Brit. J. Med. Psychol., 17, 158–188. *405, 659*

BUSWELL, G. T., AND JOHN, L. (1925) Diagnostic chart for individual difficulties fundamental processes in arithmetic. Public Sch. Pub. Co., Bloomington, Ill. *190*

BUXTON, C. (1938) The application of multiple factorial methods to the study of motor abilities. Psychometrika, 3, 85–93. *288*

CANNON, A. (1937) Testing the appreciation of style. Engl. J., 26, 648–654. *498*

CANTRILL, H. (1944) Gauging public opinion. Princeton Univ. Press. Pp. 317. *595, 618, 621, 626*

CANTRIL, H., AND RAND, H. G. (1934) An additional study of the determination of personal interests by psychological and graphological methods. Char. and Pers., 3, 72–78. *489*

CARLSON, H. B. (1934) Attitudes of undergraduate students. J. Social Psychol., 5, 202–213. *615*

CARROLL, H. A. (1935) Prose appreciation test. Test Bureau, Minneapolis. *500, 501*

CARROLL, H. A., AND EURICH, A. C. (1932) Intelligence and art appreciation. J. Ed. Psychol., 23, 214–221. *308, 325*

CARTER, H. D., CONRAD, H. S., AND JONES, M. C. (1935) A multiple factor analysis of children's annoyances. J. Genet. Psychol., 47, 282–298. *585, 659*

CARTER, H. D., PYLES, M. K., AND BRETNALL, E. P. (1935) A comparative study of factors in vocational interest scores of high school boys. J. Ed. Psychol., 26, 81–98. *585*

CASTELNUOVO-TEDESCO, P. (1948) A study of the relationship between handwriting and personality variables. Genet. Psychol. Monog., 37, 167–220. *493*

CATTELL, J. McK. (1903) A statistical study of eminent men. Pop. Sci. Monthly, 62, 359–377. *451*

CATTELL, J. McK., AND BRYANT, SOPHIE. (1899) Mental association investigated by experiment. Mind, 14, 230–250. *222*

CATTELL, P. (1931) Constant changes in the Stanford-Binet I.Q. J. Ed. Psychol., 22, 544–550. *136, 137*

——. (1940) Measuring intelligence of

multiple-response test. J. Ed. Res., 18, 211–219. *63*

DALE, E., AND CHALL, J. S. (1948) A formula for predicting readability. Ed. Res. Bull., Coll. of Ed., Ohio State Univ., 27, 11–20. *186*

DANIELS, P. C. (1933) Discrimination of compositional balance at the preschool level. Psychol. Monog., 1. *318*

DAVIDSON, H. H. (1943) Personality and economic background: a study of highly intelligent children. King's Crown Press, N.Y. *686*

DAVIS, A. (1948) Social-class influence upon learning. Harvard Univ. Press, Cambridge, Mass. Pp. 100. *152*

DAVIS, C. JANE (1946) Correlation between scores on orthorater tests and clinical tests. J. Appl. Psychol., 30, 596–603. *297*

DAVIS, F. B. (1947) The A.A.F. qualifying examination. Report No. 6. U.S. Govt. Print. Office. Pp. 266. *337*

DAWSON, H. L. (1936) Technics for measuring infants. J. Pediatrics, 9, 187–202. *86*

DE SANCTIS, SANTE. (1906) Types et degrés d'insuffisance mentale. L'Année Psychologique, 12, 70–83. *115*

DEARBORN, W. F., ANDERSON, J. E., AND CHRISTIANSEN, A. O. (1916) Construction tests of mental ability. J. Ed. Psychol., 7, 445–458. *140*

DEARBORN, W. F., AND ANDERSON, J. H. (1938) Controlled reading by means of a motion picture technique. Psychol. Rec., II, 219–227. *186*

DESCOEUDRES, A. (1911) Les Tests de Binet and Simon et leur valeur scolaire. Archives de Psychologie, II, 331–350. *115*

DIAMOND, B. L., AND SCHMALE, H. T. (1944) The mosaic test. I. An evaluation of its clinical application. Am. J. Orthospychiatry, 14, 237–250. *482*

DOLLARD, J., et al. (1939) Frustration and aggression. Yale Univ. Press, New Haven. *443*

DOWNEY, JUNE E. (1927) Individual differences in reaction to the word-in-itself. Am. J. Psychol., 39, 323–342. *500*

DREPS, H. F. (1933) The psychological capacities and abilities of college art students of high and low standing. Psychol. Monog., 45, 1, 134–146. *324*

DU BOIS, P. H. (1947) The classification program. A.A.F. aviation psychological program. Research Report No. 2. U.S. Govt. Print. Office. Pp. 394. *339*

DUNLAP, J. W. (1938) Relationship between type of question and scoring errors. J. Exp. Ed., 6, 376–379. *61*

DVORAK, BEATRICE J. (1935) Differential occupational ability patterns. B. Empl. Stabilization Res. Inst., Vol. 3, No. 8, Univ. of Minn. Press. Pp. 47. *254, 376*

——. (1947) The new USES general aptitude test battery. J. Appl. Psychol., 31, No. 4, 372–376. *243*

DWYER, P. S. (1938) An analysis of 19 occupational scores of the Strong vocational interest test given to 418 students entering the University of Michigan medical school during the years 1928, 1929, 1930. J. Appl. Psychol., 22, 8–16. *585*

DYER, H. S. (1948) Some observations on the College Board language tests. Educ. and Psychol. Meas., 6, 261–264. *215*

EBBINGHAUS, H. (1885) Über die Gedachtniss. Trans. 1913 by H. A. Ruger. Teach. Col., Columbia Univ., New York. *222*

——. (1897) Über eine neue methude zur prüfung geistigen fahigkeiten und ihre anwendungbei schulkindern. Zeitschrift für angewandte Psychologie, 13, 401–459. *222*

EBERT, E., AND MEUMANN, E. (1905) Ueber einige Grundfragen der Psych. der Uebungsphanomene im Bereiche des Gedachtnisses. Arch. f. Gesante Psychologie, 4, 232. *222*

ELIZUR, A. (1949) Content analysis of the Rorschach, anxiety and hostility. Rorschach Res. Exch., 13, 247–284. *681, 682*

HOPPOCK, R. (1935) Job satisfaction. Harper, N. Y. Pp. xxi + 303. *448, 449, 587*

HORN, C. A., AND SMITH, L. F. (1945) The Horn art aptitude inventory. J. Appl. Psychol., 29, 350–355. *321*

HORN, E. (1926) A basic writing vocabulary; 10,000 words most commonly used in writing. State Univ. of Iowa Monog. in Ed. Series, No. 4. *165*

HOROWITZ, E. L. (1936) Development of attitude toward the negro. Arch. Psychol., No. 194. Pp. 47. *602, 604, 605*

HORROCKS, J. E., AND TROYER, M. E. (1946) Case study tests of ability to use knowledge of human growth and development. Ed. and Psychol. Meas., 7, 23–36. *198*

HOTELLING, H. (1933) Analysis of a complex of statistical variables into principal components. J. Ed. Psychol., 24, 417–441. *405*

HOWELL, T. H. (1933) An experimental study of persistence. J. Abn. and Social Psychol., 28, 14–29. *720*

HULL, C. L. (1928) Aptitude testing, World Book Co., Yonkers, N.Y. Pp. 535. *452*

HUSTON, P. E., SHAKOW, D., AND ERICKSON, J. H. (1924) A study of hypnotically induced complexes by means of the Luria technique. J. Gen. Psychol., 11, 65–97. *724*

HUTT, MAX L. (1949) From unpublished notes. *474, 475, 476*

HUTT, M. L., AND SHOR, J. (1946) Rationale for routine Rorschach "testing the limits." Rorschach Res. Exch., 10, 70–76. *673*

INHAU, F. E. (1946) The lie detector. J. Clin. Psychol., 8, 151–158. *726*

JACOBS, J. (1887) Experiments on prehension. Mind, 12, 75–79. *222*

JARVIE, L. L., AND JOHNS, A. A. (1938) Does the Bernreuter personality inventory contribute to counseling? Ed. Res. Bull., 17, 7–9. *728*

JASTROW, J. (1891–1892) Some anthropological and psychologic tests on college students—a preliminary survey. Am. J. Psychol., 4, 420–427. *222*

JENKINS, W. M. (1950) A single chart for tetrachoric r. Ed. and Psychol. Meas., 10, 142–145. *388*

JERSILD, A. T., AND BIENSTOCK, S. F. (1935) Development of rhythm in young children. Child Devel. Monog., No. 22. Pp. 97. *281*

JERSILD, A. T., AND MEIGS, M. F. (1939) Observation as a research method. Rev. Ed. Res., 9, 472–482. *35*

JOHNSON, K. L. (1911) M. Binet's method for the measurement of intelligence: some results. J. Exp. Ped., 1, 24–31. *115*

JOHNSON, W. (1934) The effect of mood on personality traits as measured by Bernreuter. J. Soc. Psychol., 5, 515–522. *466*

JONES, H. E., AND SEASHORE, R. H. (1944) The development of fine motor and mechanical abilities. Adolescence, chapter 7, 123–145, Univ. of Chicago, Dept. of Ed. *276, 290*

JORDAN, A. M., AND VAN WAGENEN (1933) Analytical scales of attainment in literature. Ed. Test Bur., Minneapolis. *498*

JORGENSEN, A. N., AND GREENE, H. A. (1927) Iowa high school silent reading tests. Bur. Ed. Res. and Service, Univ. of Iowa. *185*

JURGENSEN, C. E. (1943) Extension of the Minnesota rate of manipulation test. J. Appl. Psychol., 27, 164–169. *292*

KANNER, L. (1935) Child psychiatry. Thomas, Springfield, Ill. Pp. 527. *77, 106*

——. (1940) Play investigation and play treatment of children's behavior disorders. J. Pediat., 17, 533–546. *538*

KELLEY, T. L. (1916) A constructive ability test. J. Ed. Psychol., 7, 1–17. *140*

——. (1924) Statistical Method. Macmillan, N.Y. *396*

KROLL, A. (*cont'd*)
boys in the twelfth grade. J. Ed. Psychol., 25, 274–280. *617*

KUDER, G. F. (1939) Preference record. Univ. of Chicago Press. *564, 568*

——. (1942, 1948) Preference record, vocational. Science Research Associates, Chicago. Manual and Forms. *564, 567, 569*

——. (1948) Preference record, personal. Science Research Associates, Chicago. Manual and Forms. *567, 634, 649*

KUDER, G. F., AND RICHARDSON, M. W. (1937) Theory of estimation of test reliabilities. Psychometrika, 2, 151–161. *388*

KUHLMANN, F. (1911) Binet and Simon's system for measuring the intelligence of children. J. Psychoasthenics, 15, 76–92. *115*

——. (1912) A revision of the Binet-Simon system for measuring the intelligence of children. J. Psychoasthenics, Monog. Suppl. *116*

——. (1939) Tests of mental development. Ed. Test Bureau, Minneapolis. Pp. 314. *119, 125, 134*

KURTZ, A. K. (1948) A research test of the Rorschach test. Pers. Psychol., 1, 41–52. *688*

KWALWASSER, J. (1927) Tests and measurements on music. Birchard and Co. Pp. 145. *302*

——. (1930) Kwalwasser-Dykema music tests. Carl Fisher, N.Y. *301*

KWALWASSER, J., AND RUCH, G. M. (1924) K-R tests of musical accomplishment. Extension Div., State Univ. of Iowa. *301*

LAIRD, D. A. (1925) Detecting abnormal behavior. J. Abn. and Soc. Psychol., 20, 128–141. *635*

LANDIS, C. *et al.* (1935) Empirical evaluation of three personality adjustment inventories. J. Ed. Psychol., 26, 321–330. *728*

LANKES, W. (1914) Natural rate of tapping. Brit. J. Psychol., 7, 390–391. *660*

LARK-HOROVITZ, BETTY. (1936) Inter-linkage of sensory memories in relationship to training in drawing. J. Genet. Psychol., 49, 69–89. *317*

LARSON, W. S. (1938) Practical experience with music tests. Music Educators, 24, No. 5, 31, 68–74. *306*

LARSON, J. A., AND HANEY, G. W. (1932) Cardio-respiratory variations in personality studies. Am. J. Psychiat., 11, 1035–81. *726*

LAWSHE, C. H. (1948) Principles of personnel testing. McGraw-Hill, N.Y. Pp. 227. *291*

LAYMAN, E. McC. (1937) An item analysis of the adjustment questionnaire. Psychol. Bull., 34, 782. *658*

LEHMAN, H. C., AND WITTY, P. A. (1927) The psychology of play activities. A. S. Barnes, N.Y. Pp. 242. *555*

LEWERENZ, A. S. (1927) Test in fundamental abilities of visual arts. S. Calif. School Book Depository, Hollywood, Calif. *323*

LEWINSON, T. S., AND ZUBIN, J. (1942) Handwriting analysis. King's Crown Press, N.Y. Pp. 147. *489*

LEWIS, J. A. (1947) Kuder preference record and MMPI scores for two occupational groups. J. Consult. Psychol., 11, 194–201. *579*

LEWIS, M. M. (1936) Infant speech: a study of the beginnings of language. Harcourt, Brace, N.Y. Pp. 335. *105*

LIEBOLD, R. (1936) Kind und Metronom. Z. Pedag. Psychol., 37, 317–322. *281*

LIKERT, R. (1932) A technique for the measurement of attitudes. Arch. Psychol., No. 140, 1–55. Columbia Univ., *454, 624*

LIKERT, R., AND QUASHA, W. H. (1934) Revised Minnesota paper form board. Published by the authors, New York University. *268*

LINE, W., AND GRIFFIN, J. D. M. (1935) Some results obtained with the Rorschach test, objectively scored. Am. J. Psychol., 92, 109–114. *661*

LINFERT, H. E., AND HIERHOLZER, H. M. (1928) A scale for measuring the mental development of infants during the first year of life. Cath. Univ. Am., Stud. in Psychol. and Psychiat., 1, No. 4. Pp. 33. *108*

LINK, H. C. (1919) Employment psychology. Macmillan, N.Y. Pp. 440. *366*

———. (1943) An experiment in depth interviewing on the issue of internationalism-isolationism. J. Appl. Psychol., 30, 1–9. *595*

LOEVINGER, JANE (1948) The technique of homogeneous tests compared with some aspects of scale analysis and factor analysis. Psychol. Bull., 45, 507–529. *420*

LOOMIS, CHARLES P. (1949) Youth and the world of work. Social Research Service, Michigan State College, East Lansing, Mich. *555*

LORGE, I. (1935) Personality traits by Fiat. II. The consistency of the Bernreuter personality inventory by the Bernreuter and by the Flanagan keys. J. Ed. Psychol., 26, 6, 427–434. *466*

———. (1944) Predicting readability. Teach. Col. Record, 40, 404–419. *186*

———. (1945) Methods of research and appraisal in education. Rev. of Ed. Res., 15, 333–468. *156*

LOWENFIELD, M. (1939) The world pictures of children. Brit. J. Med. Psychol., 18, 65–101. *540*

LURIE, W. A. (1937) A study of Spranger's value-types by the method of factor analysis. J. Soc. Psychol., 8, 17–37. *613*

McADORY, MARGARET. (1929) art test. The construction and validation of an art test. Contrib. to Ed., Teach. Col., Columbia Univ., No. 11. *33, 307, 308*

McCARTY, S. A. (1924) Children's drawings. Williams and Wilkins, Baltimore. *318*

McCASKILL, C. L., AND WELLMAN, B. L. (1938) A study of common motor achievements at the pre-school ages. Child Devel., 9, 141–149. *273*

McCLATCHY, V. R. (1928) A theoreti-cal and statistical study of the personality trait originality as herein defined. J. Abn. and Social Psychol., 23, 379. *531*

McCLOY, W. (1939) Creative imagination in children and adults. Psychol. Monog., 51, No. 5, 88–102. *319*

McCLUSKY, H. Y. (1934) An experimental comparison of two methods of correcting the outcome of an examination. Sch. and Soc., 40, 566–568. *63*

McNEMAR, Q. (1942) Revision of the Stanford-Binet scale. Houghton Mifflin, Boston. Pp. 189. *124, 134*

———. (1946) Opinion-attitude methodology. Psychol. Bull., 43, 289–374. *595*

———. (1949) Psychological statistics. Wiley, N.Y. Pp. 364. *376*

MACFARLANE, J. W. (1938) Methodology of data collection and organization. Monog. Soc. Res. Child Devel., 3, No. 6, 253. *92, 109, 628*

MACHOVER, K. (1949) Personality projection. C. C. Thomas, Springfield, Ill. Pp. 181. *483*

MAGARET, A., AND SIMPSON, M. M. (1948) A comparison of two measures of deterioration in psychotic patients. J. Consult. Psychol., 12, 265–269. *151*

MAIZLISH, I. L. (1936) New possibilities in intelligence testing: interview form. J. Appl. Psychol., 20, 599–608. *226*

MALLER, J. B. (1932) Character and personality tests. Teach. Col., Columbia Univ., N.Y. Pp. 53. *465*

———. (1934) General and specific factors in character. J. Soc. Psychol., 5, 97–102. *663*

MANSKE, A. J. (1936) The reflection of teachers' attitudes in the attitudes of their pupils. Contrib. to Ed., Teach. Col., Columbia Univ., No. 702. Pp. 67. *617*

MANUEL, H. T., AND HUGHES, L. S. (1932) The intelligence and drawing ability of young Mexican children. J. Appl. Psychol., 16, 382–387. *322*

MARPLE, C. H. (1933) The compara-

Appl. Psychol. Monog., No. 7. Stanford Univ. Press. *678, 686, 687, 688*

MURPHY, G. (1947) Personality. Harper, N.Y. Pp. 999. *426*

MURPHY, G., AND LIKERT, R. (1938) Public opinion and the individual. A psychological study of student attitudes on public questions, with a retest five years later. Harper, N.Y. Pp. 316. *600, 602, 618, 620*

MURPHY, G., MURPHY, L. B., AND NEWCOMB, T. M. (1937) Experimental social psychology. Harper, N.Y. Pp. 1119. *617*

MURRAY, H. A. (1938) Explorations in personality. Oxford Univ. Press, N.Y. *506, 507*

——. (1943) Manual for the thematic apperception test. Harvard Univ. Press, Cambridge, Mass. *503*

MUSICO, B. (1922) Motor capacity with special reference to vocational guidance. Brit. J. Psychol., 13, 157–184. *277*

NAHM, HELEN (1948) An evaluation of selected schools of nursing Appl. Psychol. Monog., 17. Stanford Univ. Press. *199*

NAPOLI, P. J. (1946) Finger-painting and personality diagnosis. Genet. Psychol. Monog., 34, 129–231. *486*

NETZER, R. L. (1938) Stimuli for oral language. Elem. Engl. Rev., 15, 91–94. *164*

NEWCOMB, T. M. (1929) The consistency of certain extrovert-introvert behavior patterns in 51 problem boys. Contrib. to Ed., Teach. Col., Columbia Univ., No. 382. *705, 706*

——. (1931) An experiment designed to test the validity of a rating technique. J. Educ. Psychol., 22, 270–289. *462*

——. (1946) The influence of attitude climate upon some determinants of information. J. Abn. and Soc. Psychol., 41, 291–302. *621*

NEWSTETTER, W. I. (1937) An experiment in the defining and measuring of group adjustment. Amer. Sociol. Rev, 2, 230–236. *728*

NYSTROM, G. (1930) Minneapolis self-corrective handwriting charts. St. Paul Book and Stationery Co., St. Paul, Minn. *160*

O'CONNOR, J. (1928) Born that way. Williams and Wilkins, Baltimore, Md. Pp. 323. *277, 283*

——. (1934) Psychometrics. Harvard Univ. Press. Pp. 64. *531*

OEHRN, A. (1895) Experimentelle Studien zur Individualpsychologie. Psychologischen Arbeiten, 1, 92–152. *222*

OFFICE OF STRATEGIC SERVICES, ASSESSMENT STAFF. (1948) Assessment of men. Rinehart, N.Y. Pp. 541. *346, 533*

OLSON, D. M., AND JONES, VERNON. (1931) An objective measure of emotionally toned attitudes. Ped. Sem. and J. Genet. Psychol., 39, 174–196. *725*

OLSON, W. C. (1936) The waiver of signature in personal reports. J. Appl. Psychol., 20, 442–450. *466*

ORLANSKY, HAROLD. (1948) Destiny in the nursery: child rearing techniques and adult personality. Commentary, 5, 563–569. *442*

ORLEANS, J. B., AND ORLEANS, J. S. (1934) A study of prognosis in high school algebra. Math. Teach., No. 22, 23–30. *216*

O'ROURKE, L. J. (1934) Rebuilding the English usage curriculum. Psychol. Inst., Washington, D.C. Pp. 98. *174, 227*

ORTMANN, O. (1929) The physiological mechanics of piano technique. Dutton, N.Y. *301*

PASCAL, G. R. (1942) Handwriting pressure, its measurement and significance. Char. and Pers., 11, 235–254. *489*

——. (1944) Analysis of handwriting: a test of significance. Char. and Pers., 12, 123–144. *491*

PATERSON, D. G., AND DARLEY, J. G. (1936) Men, women, and jobs. Univ. of Minn. Press. Pp. 145. *38*

PATERSON, D. G., ELLIOTT, R. M., ANDERSON, L. D., TOOPS, H. A., AND HEIDBREDER, EDNA. (1930) Minnesota mechanical ability tests. Univ. of Minn. Press. Pp. 586. *29, 264, 265, 277, 278, 280, 284, 287,*

PATRICK, C. (1937) Creative thought in artists. J. Psychol., 4, 35–73. *317*

PAYNE, A. F. (1928) Sentence completions. N.Y. Guidance Clinic. *532*

PEARSON, K. (1904) On the laws of inheritance in man. Biometrika, 3, 131–190. *384*

——. (1914) Tables for statisticians and biometricians. Cambridge Univ. Press, England. Pp. 143. *371*

PERSONNEL MANUAL. (1919) Committee on Classification of Personnel. Adjutant General's Dept., Washington, D.C., C.C.P. 400. Pp. 342. *223, 225*

PERSONNEL RESEARCH SECTION, A.G.O. (1943) Personnel research in the army. II. The classification system and the place of testing. Psychol. Bull., 40, 3, 205–211. *328, 329*

——. (1945) The army general classification test. Psychol. Bull., 42, 10, 760–768. *330, 331, 333*

——. (1945) Achievement tests for the army specialized training program. Psychol. Bull., 42, 8, 553–560. *329*

——. (1944) The new army individual test of general ability. Psychol. Bull., 41, 532–538. *335*

PETRAN, L. A. (1937) An analysis of the Ortmann tests in tonal discrimination and memory. Bull. Amer. Musicol. Soc., No. 2, 25. *304, 306*

PHILLIPS, R. (1945) Doll play as a function of the realism of materials and the length of the experimental session. Child Devel., 16, 123–143. *538*

PIAGET, JEAN. (1926) The language and thought of the child. Trans. by Marjorie Warden. Harcourt, Brace, N.Y. Pp. xxiii + 246. *106*

——. (1929) The child's conception of the world. Harcourt, Brace, N.Y. Pp. ix + 397. *106*

——. (1930) The child's conception of physical causality. Trans. by Marjorie Gabain. Harcourt, Brace, N.Y. Pp. 309. *106*

PINTLER, M. H. (1945) Doll play as a function of experimenter-child interaction and initial organization of materials. Child Devel., 16, 145–166. *538*

PINTLER, M. H., PHILLIPS, R., AND SEARS, R. R. (1946) Sex differences in the projective doll play of preschool children. J. Psychol., 21, 73–80. *538*

PINTNER, R. (1918 a) Aesthetic appreciation of pictures by children. Ped. Sem., 25, 216–220. *311*

——. (1931) Intelligence testing, methods and results. Henry Holt, N.Y. Pp. 555. *134, 148*

PINTNER, R., AND PATERSON, D. G. (1915) The Binet scale and the deaf child. J. Ed. Psychol., 6, 591–600. *140*

——. (1917) A scale of performance tests. Appleton-Century-Crofts, N.Y. *140, 144*

PIOTROWSKI, ZYGMUNT A., et al. (1944) Rorschach signs in the selection of outstanding young male mechanical workers. J. Psychol., 18, 131–150. *688*

POFFENBERGER, A. T., AND BARROWS, B. E. (1924) The feeling value of lines. J. Appl. Psychol., 1, 187. *312*

PORTER, E. H. (1943) Development and evaluation of a measure of counseling interview procedures. Ed. and Psychol. Meas., 3, 215–238. *717, 718*

PORTEUS, S. D. (1924) Guide to Porteus maze test. Vineland Train. School Bull., No. 25. (Original scale published in 1915). *144*

PRATT, C. C. (1931) The meaning of music. McGraw-Hill, N.Y. Pp. 253. *306*

PRESSEY, L. C. (1924) An investigation of the technical vocabularies of the school subjects. Ed. Res. Bull., Ohio State Univ., 3, 182–185. *166*

——. (1934) Tests and measurements in the social sciences, Chapter III. Scribners, N.Y. Pp. 155. *166, 168, 169, 197*

PRESSEY, S. L. (1933) Psychology and

the new education. Harper, N.Y. Pp. 594. *212*

PRESSEY, S. L., AND L. M. (1918) Pressey's group point scale for measuring general intelligence. J. Appl. Psychol., 2, 250–259. *226*

PYLE, W. H. (1913) The examination of school children. Macmillan Co., N.Y. Pp. 70. *223*

RABIN, A. I. (1945) Use of the Wechsler-Bellevue scales with normal and abnormal persons. Psychol. Bull., 42, 410–422. *151*

RABIN, A. I. AND BOIDA, D. (1948) Projection via proverbs. J. Consult. Psychol., 12, 246–250. *534*

RAND, G. (1925) A discussion of the quotient method of specifying test results. J. Ed. Psychol., 16, 599–618. *214*

RAPPAPORT, D., GILL, M., AND SCHAFER, R. (1946) Diagnostic psychol. testing. Vols. I and II. Yearbook Publishers, Chicago. *146, 151, 532, 668, 669*

RATHS, L. E. (1938) Appraising certain aspects of student achievement. Nat. Soc. Stud. Ed. Yr. Book, Chap. 3, 89–117. *37*

REAM, M. J. (1924) Ability to sell: its relation to certain aspects of personality and experience. Williams and Wilkins, Baltimore. Pp. 64. *562*

RECKLESS, W. C., AND BRINGEN, H. L. (1933) Racial attitudes and information about the Negro. J. Negro Ed., 2, 128–138. *621*

REMMERS, H. H., AND SILANCE, E. F. (1934) Generalized attitude scales. J. Social Psychol., 5, 298–312. *453, 454*

REMMERS, L. J., AND REMMERS, H. H. (1949, 1950) Studies in industrial empathy. Pers. Psychol., 3, 33–40. *619*

RICHARDSON, M. W., AND STALNAKER, J. M. (1935) Comments on achievement examinations. J. Ed. Res., 28, 25–32. *216*

RIEGEL, E. J. (1949) Evolution of mathematics tests. College Board Rev., 1, 95–98. *216*

RIGG, M. (1937) Rigg poetry test, forms

C and D. Sch. of Ed., Stillwater, Okla. *502*

ROBLEE, L., AND WASHBURN, M. F. (1912) The affective value of articulate sounds. Am. J. Psychol., 23, 579–583. *499*

ROGERS, C. R. (1946) Psychometric tests and client-centered counseling. Ed. and Psychol. Meas., 4, 139–144. *445*

ROHDE, A. R. (1946) Explorations in personality by the sentence completion method. J. Appl. Psychol., 30, 169–181. *532*

RORSCHACH, H. (1921) Psychodiagnostik: Methodik und Ergebnisse eines wahrehmungs-diagnostischen Experiments. Pp. 174. (1932) Second Edition, Huber, Bern, Switzerland. Pp. 227. *668*

ROSANOFF, A. J. (1920) Manual of psychiatry. Wiley, N.Y. Pp. 684. *34, 531*

ROSENZWEIG, S. (1945) The picture-association method and its application in a study of reactions to frustration. J. Pers., 14, 3–23. *515*

ROTTER, J. B., AND WILLERMAN, B. (1947) The incomplete sentences test. J. Consult. Psychol., 11, 43–48. *534*

ROUSSEAU, J. J. (1762) Emile, or education. Dutton, N.Y. Pp. 444. *77*

RUCH, G. M., CLEETON, G. U., AND STODDARD, G. D. (1925) Iowa high school content examination. Copyright by G. M. Ruch. *195*

RUCH, G. M., KNIGHT, F. B., GREENE, H. A., AND STUDEBAKER, J. W. (1925) The compass diagnostic tests in arithmetic. Scott, Foresman, Chicago, *189*

RUCH, G. M., AND STODDARD, G. D. (1925) Comparative reliabilities of five types of objective examinations. J. Ed. Psychol., 16, 89–103. *72*

——. (1927) Tests and measurements in high school instruction. World Book Co., Yonkers, N.Y. Pp. 381. *64, 73, 74*

RUNDQUIST, E. A., AND SLETTO, R. F. (1936) Minnesota scale for the survey of opinion. Univ. of Minn. Press. *466*

RUNDQUIST, E. A., AND SLETTO, R. F. (1936) Personality in the depression. Univ. of Minn. Press. Pp. 398. *626, 654, 655*

SALISBURY, F. S., AND SMITH, H. B. (1929) Prognosis of sight singing ability. J. Appl. Psychol., 13, 425–439. *303*

SANFORD, E. C. (1908) A course in experimental psychology. Heath, Boston. Pp. 449. *452*

SANFORD, R. N., *et al.* (1943) Physique, personality and scholarship. Monog. Soc. Res. Child Devel., 8, No. 1. *509, 534*

SARGENT, H. (1944) An experimental application of projective principles to a paper and pencil personality test. Psychol. Monog., 57, No. 5. *518, 520*

SAUNDERS, A. W. (1936) The stability of artistic aptitude at the childhood level. Psychol. Monog., 48, 126–154. *318*

SCHILDER, PAUL. (1934) Psychic disturbances after head traumas. Am. J. Psych., 91, 155 (July). *473*

SCHILLER, B. (1934) Verbal, numerical, and spatial abilities of young children. Arch. Psychol., No. 161, 1–69. *214*

SCHNECK, M. M. R. (1929) The measurement of verbal and numerical abilities. Arch. Psychol., No. 107. Pp. 49. *214*

SCHORLING, R., AND SANFORD, V. (1926) Achievement test in plane geometry. Bur. of Publications, Teach. Col., Columbia Univ., N.Y. *192*

SCHRAMM, W. L. (1935) Approaches to a science of English verse. Univ. of Iowa. Stud. Service, Aims, and Progress Res., No. 46. Pp. 82. *303*

SEASHORE, C. E. (1919) Psychology of musical talent. Silver Burdett, N.Y. Pp. 288. *22, 280, 299, 301*

——. (1927) Phonophotography in the measurement of expression of emotion in music and speech. Sci. Mo., 24, 463–471. *302*

——. (1938) Psychology of music. McGraw-Hill, N.Y. Pp. 408. *303*

SEASHORE, R. H. (1926) Studies in motor rhythm. Iowa Stud. Psychol., 9, 142–199. *301*

——. (1928) Stamford motor skills unit. Psychol. Monog., 39, 51–66. *280, 282*

——. (1930) Individual differences in motor skills. J. Gen. Psychol., 3, 38–66. *287*

SEASHORE, R. H., AND ADAMS, R. D. (1933) Measurements of steadiness, a new apparatus, and results on marksmanship. Sci. 78, 285–287. *280*

SEASHORE, R. H., AND HEVNER, K. (1933) A time-saving device for the construction of attitude scales. J. Soc. Psychol., 4, 366–372. *455*

SEGUIN, E. (1846) (1906) Traitement moral, hygiene et education des idiots. Alcan, Paris. Pp. 20. *139*

SHAFFER, L. F. (1936) Psychology of adjustment. Houghton Mifflin. Pp. 600. *426*

SHARP, D. L. (1938) Group and individual profiles in the association-motor test. Univ. Ia. Stud. Child Welfare, 15, No. 1, 97, 171. *725, 726*

SHAW, R. F. (1934) Finger painting. Little, Brown, Boston. *486*

SHELDON, W. H. (1940) The varieties of human physique. Harper, N.Y. Pp. 347. *19, 430, 433, 434, 436*

——. (1942) Varieties of temperament. Harper, N.Y. Pp. 529. *641, 642, 643, 648*

SHEN, E. (1925) The reliability coefficient of personal ratings. J. Ed. Psychol., 17, 232–236. *471*

SHEPARD, J. F. (1913) Keyboard puzzle box and apparatus for experimental phonetics. Psychol. Bull., 10, 66–67. *302*

SHIPLEY, WALTER C. (1946) A self-administering scale for measuring intellectual impairment and deterioration. J. Psychol., 9, 371–377. *231*

SHIPLEY, W. C., GRAY, F. E., AND NEWBERT, N. (1946) The personal inventory. J. Clin. Psychol., 2, 318–322. *630*

——. (1935) Adult interests. Macmillan, N.Y. Pp. 265. *426, 549*

——. (1935 a) Thorndike-Century junior dictionary. Scott, Foresman, Chicago. Pp. 970. *165*

THORNDIKE, E. L., COBB, M. V., ORLEANS, J. S., SYMONDS, P. M., WALD, E., AND WOODYARD, E. (1923) The psychology of algebra. Macmillan, N.Y. Pp. 483. *190*

THORNDIKE, E. L., *et al.* (1934) Prediction of vocational success. Commonwealth Fund, N.Y. Pp. 284. *218*

THORNDIKE, R. L. (1936) Factor analysis of social and abstract intelligence. J. Ed. Psychol., 27, 231–233. *659*

——. (1947) Logical dilemmas in the estimation of reliability. Am. Council Ed. Stud., 1, 11, 28, pp. 21–30. *56*

——. (1947a) Prediction of intelligence at college entrance from earlier test. J. Ed. Psychol., 38, 129–147. *149, 255*

——. (1948) An evaluation of the adult intellectual status of Terman's gifted children. Ped. Sem. and J. Genet. Psychol., 72, 17–27. *138*

——. (1948) Growth of intelligence during adolescence. J. Genet. Psychol., 72, 11–15. *138*

THORPE, L. P., CLARK, W. W., AND TIEGS, E. W. (1946) Mental health analysis. California Test Bureau. Forms and Manuals. *634, 650*

THURSTONE, L. L. (1919) (1940) American Council on Education. Psychological examination for college freshmen. Published annually. Am. Council on Ed., Washington, D.C. *226*

——, (1921) Business information Form A. Bureau of Personnel Research, Carnegie Inst. of Tech., Pittsburgh. *205*

——. (1922) Examination in clerical work: Form A, Thurstone employment tests. World Book Co., Yonkers, N.Y. *201, 204*

——. (1925) A method of scaling psychological and educational tests. J. Ed. Psychol., 16, 433–451. *56, 274*

——. (1927) The method of paired comparisons for social values. J. Abn. and Soc. Psychol., 21, 384–400. *450*

——. (1928a) The measurement of opinion. J. Abn. and Soc. Psychol., 22, 415–430. *452*

——. (1931) The measurement of change in social attitudes. J. Soc. Psychol., 2, 230–235; Influence of motion pictures on children's attitudes. J. Soc. Psychol., 2, 291–305. *617, 452*

——. (1931 b) A multiple factor study of vocational interests. Pers. J., 10, 198–205. *584*

——. (1938) Primary mental abilities. Psychometrika Monog. Pp. 121. *266, 325*

——. (1946) Factor analysis of body types. Psychometrika, 11, 15–21. *434*

——. (1948) Interest schedule. Psychol. Corp. Forms and Manual. *570, 580*

——. (1946) Multiple factor analysis. Chicago Univ. Press. Pp. 537. *405*

THURSTONE, L. L., AND CHAVE, E. J. (1929) The measurement of attitude, a psychophysical method. Univ. of Chicago Press. Pp. 96. *32, 624*

TIEBOUT, C. (1933) The psychophysical functions differentiating artistically superior from artistically inferior children. Psychol. Monog., 45, 108–133. *319*

TIEBOUT, C., AND MEIER, N. C. (1936) Artistic ability and general intelligence. Psychol. Monog., 48, 95–125. *309, 319, 320, 323*

TIEGS, E. W., AND CLARK, W. W. (1934) Progressive achievement tests—advanced Battery Form A. Southern California School Book Depository. Los Angeles. *177, 178*

TIFFIN, J. (1947) Industrial psychology. Prentice Hall, N.Y. Pp. 354. *296*

TIFFIN, J. AND LAWSHE, C. H., Jr. (1944) How tests can strengthen the training program, Fact. Mgmt. Mainten., 102, 3, 119–121. *292*

TITCHENER, E. B. (1902) Ein Versuch die Methode der paarweisen Vergleichung auf die verschiedenen Gefühlsrichtungen anzuwenden. Phil. Stud., 20, 382–406. *450*

TOMLINSON, R. R. (1934) Picture making in children. Studio Pub. Co., N.Y. Pp. 120. *317*

SUBJECT INDEX

Ability, general, 225; and intelligence, 255; comparison of batteries, 256

Abstraction (see also Perception, Apperception), 146

Academic (see also Scholastic), predictions from tests, 249

Accomplishment quotient (AQ), 214

Achievement test, 37; correlational analysis, 214

Adaptive behavior, 86

Age level, 117, 127, 130; for instruction, 216

Age norms, 126

Age score, 118

Agencies using tests, 9

Aggressiveness, 642

Agility tests, 273

Alcohol, 510

Algebra tests, 189

Altitude test (same as Power test), 39

Ambiguity, 69

Analogies test, 225; spatial, 414; verbal, 118

Apperception, thematic, 503; three dimensional, 545

Appraisal, of a test, 56; varieties of, 18

Aptitude test, 38, 238, 244, 246; results, 247

Arithmetic tests, 178, 187; diagnostic, 189

Art, and intelligence, 322; analytical studies, 323; appreciation, 307; composition, 310, 317; drawing ability,

317; nature of, 36; preferences for pictures, 307; responses to color, 313; responses to lines, 312

Ascendance, 365 f

Association test, words, 530; pictures, 503

Attenuation, 396

Attitude, comparison of techniques of appraisal, 623; definitions, 594; factorial analysis, 613; group norms, 625; modification of, 616; needed research, 626; reasons for, 606; relation to information, 620; toward church, 321; typical scales, 486, 607; public opinion, 596; social distance, 603; study of values, 607

Audiometer, 299

Auditory, 298

Auditory span, 22

Average, 363

Axes, 409; rotation, 410

Bar chart, 380

Batteries, achievement, 156, 158; aptitude, 233; mechanical, 269; military, 327; motor, 281

Behavior rating, 708

Bias, 597

Bi-modal, 366

Binet-type test, 112

Biographies, 552, 693

Block counting, 225, 330; design, 145

Borderline, 133

786